CASES AND MATERIALS ON

EQUITY AND TRUSTS

Paul Todd, MA, BCL

BLACKSTONE
PRESS LIMITED

First published in Great Britain 1994 by Blackstone Press Limited,
9–15 Aldine Street, London W12 8AW. Telephone 081-740 1173

ISBN: 1 85431 319 3

British Library Cataloguing in Publication Data
A CIP catalogue record for this book is available from the British Library

Typeset by Style Photosetting Ltd, Mayfield, East Sussex
Printed by Ashford Colour Press, Gosport, Hampshire

Contents

Preface

There is, in my opinion, a place for textbooks in the scheme of legal scholarship. There is a school of thought which states that any moderately intelligent student, given a syllabus and adequate library facilities, can obtain a good law degree without any need for a textbook. That may well be so, but work at the initial stages will be very slow. An introductory textbook can save a lot of time here by providing a structure upon which to build. So textbooks have their uses.

Textbooks are not the be-all-and-end-all of the subject, however. For the law is made not by writers of textbooks, but by cases and statutes. These are the primary sources, and you cannot hope to progress far without consulting them. Indeed, if you cannot find a primary source, then you cannot make a legal statement. Again, of course, some would argue that there is no substitute for looking at the cases and statutes themselves, and that books like this, which direct your study to some extent, are positively detrimental. Given a world where students have infinite time, I would agree with these sentiments, but casebooks can be very useful when the library is closed, especially in the face of stringent essay or other deadlines, or during vacations when there may not be a convenient library available. But in any case, this book is more than just a casebook, for there are notes and questions: suggestions of ideas and lines of reasoning that you may otherwise not have thought of.

More than many other areas of law, trusts is primarily a case-based subject, and that is reflected in the coverage here. The main statutory material is also included, and since this is a cases and materials book, rather than just a casebook, there is also a selection of other published works of interest.

There are those who say that it is easier to write a cases and materials book than it is to write a textbook. I have written both, not only in this area of law but also in international trade, and I do not agree. Of course, with a cases and materials book one does not suffer from the writer's blank page syndrome, since there is no need to produce a quarter of a million words, or whatever, oneself. The problem is rather the opposite. While extracts from cases and other material can be expanded almost indefinitely, it is much more difficult to compress them. You cannot re-write somebody else's judgment or article as you can your own text, to make it fit into the finite space available (and it may not have been written with space constraints in mind). The main problem with cases and materials books is selection, and I have had to make hard choices in this book. If I explain the principles upon which those choices were based then I will have gone a long way towards explaining the nature of the book.

The first and foremost consideration is that this book is intended to be useful to students of the law of trusts. I have therefore been fairly ruthless in excluding material which is not central to most trusts courses (but for the same reason have included areas that are usually covered, such as secret trusts and mutual wills, although some would argue that they have no modern day relevance). I have also deliberately adopted a structured style for the book, and forced the materials into the structure, even though in some cases this has meant a fair amount of work with of the scissors and paste, or to be more accurate, their electronic equivalent. Of course, cases do not always fit neatly into pre-defined categories, but students rightly prefer structured to unstructured books, and it is surely the role of a law teacher to provide a basic structure upon which to build.

I am also of the opinion that a cases and materials book, or indeed any student textbook, is not a place to go on a crusade, since there is no reason why any student should be interested in my (or anyone else's) crusades. I may strongly believe that women are unfairly treated by the apportionment of beneficial interests in matrimonial property, that the equitable fraud jurisdiction in chapter 11 should be extended, that it is outrageous that crazy religions should, as charities, continue to enjoy rates and taxation advantages, that secret trusts should not be taught on trusts courses. I may believe the opposite, or I may have no views at all on any of these matters. You will not find out by reading this book. Of course, where others have debated whether the law should be changed, as with Law Commission reports, government papers and the like, I have felt free to refer to those debates.

A related point is that most trusts courses examine what the law is, by no means as trite and simple a task as some would suggest. My two degrees are both in law: I am not qualified to give opinions on social science, sociology, politics or economics, and this is therefore essentially an analytical law book. There is a number of very good books which attempt to place some or all of the law of trusts into its social context. I have made no attempt here to compete with those books. Of course, where I have discovered background information that may interest you, or help you remember something, I have felt free to include it, but there is no systematic treatment of anything that does not eventually bear on determination of what the law is, or at any rate what a court would be most likely to decide it is if it were to become an issue.

Case law development is an iterative process, with the law being continually modified and developed. A principle which previously enjoyed only a narrow application may be extended to new fields, or one which previously had been widely stated may be held not to apply as widely as had previously been thought. There may be a clash of conflicting principles, or lines of reasoning that had previously been accepted be held to be wrong. A point which had been deliberately been left open may be decided. You could be forgiven for thinking, particularly if you read textbooks of the old-fashioned style where the law is stated in rules in bold black-letter headings (the origin, I believe, of the phrase, 'black-letter law'), that cases (which are frequently relegated to the footnotes) do no more than illustrate some bold principle which is self-evident and virtually set in concrete. But why would anyone risk thousands of pounds fighting a case merely to illustrate a black-letter rule? The fact is, of course, that the cases are the basis for the so-called rule: they make the law and in the absence of the cases there would be no rule. Cases are only fought on issues of law if *both sides believe* that they have a reasonable chance of winning. Nobody can predict the outcome at the time. It is only afterwards that it appears that the losing side never had a chance.

In this book, where case law development has been relatively self-contained, I have attempted to re-create the iterative process by developing the cases in their chronological order. Examples of this can be found in chapters 4, 9 and 11, where the competing ideas can clearly be seen unfolding.

As a teacher I advise students who are short of time (are there any who are not?) as a general principle to read cases in reverse chronological order. Discussion of earlier authorities will often be found in the newer cases, saving time when it comes to reading the earlier cases themselves, whereas as a matter of logic the reverse cannot apply. If I had been really short of space I would have concentrated almost entirely on new cases for that reason, but that would have been regrettable, since then I would have been unable to present development of the law as an iterative process. It is still probably true to say, however, that new cases receive a higher proportion of coverage than old. Thus, where a lengthy 'classic' authority, from which it would be difficult to extract concise quotes, has been applied (or distinguished) in a later and more concise case, the newer case is used in preference to the 'classic' authority. For example, the *Chase Manhattan* case is covered in preference to *Re Diplock* (from the 100 or so pages of which it is *impossible* to find any concise quotes). Other examples are the use of *Bartlett* v *Barclays Bank* in preference to *Speight* v *Gaunt* and *Re Lucking* in preference to *Re Vickery*. The *Pemsel* case is not covered in detail. Nevertheless, many of the classic authorities are also covered in detail in this book. For example, the *Baden* and *Vandervell* sagas, *McCormick* v *Grogan*, *Blackwell* v *Blackwell*, *Oppenheim* v *IRC*, are all set out at length, as are the matrimonial home cases of *Pettitt* v *Pettitt* and *Gissing* v *Gissing*.

This book is intended to be useful to students of Equity and Trusts, in their 2nd, 3rd or 4th year of study at degree or equivalent level, or those studying for professional examinations. The material in this book complements *Textbook on Trusts*, but coverage is not identical, since those parts of the textbook which are largely expository cannot readily be included in a cases and materials book, whereas other areas are developed in considerably more detail in this book than in the textbook.

Paul Todd
University of Wales, Cardiff
July 1994

Acknowledgements

The authors and publishers would like to thank the following for permission
to reproduce copyright material:

Autocar & Motor: 1 November 1989, p. 9.

Bamsey, I., extracts from *Vanwall, A Technical Appraisal,* Haynes (1990).

Blackwell Publishers: extracts from the *Modern Law Review.*

Butterworth & Co. (Publishers) Ltd: extracts from the All England Law
Reports and Butterworths Company Law Cases.

The Right Honourable The Lord Browne-Wilkinson: 'Constructive Trusts
and Unjust Enrichment', Holdsworth Club Address (1991).

Chesterman, M., extracts from *Charities, Trusts and Social Welfare,* Weiden-
feld & Nicholson Law in Context Series (1979).

Gardner, S., 'Rethinking Family Property' (1993) 109 LQR 263.

Goddard, D., 'Equity, Volunteers and Ducks' [1988] Conv. 19.

Green, B., '*Grey, Oughtred* and *Vandervell* — A Contextual Reappraisal'
(1984) 47 MLR 385.

The Incorporated Council for Law Reporting for England and Wales:
extracts from the Law Reports, Weekly Law Reports and Industrial Cases
Reports.

Jordan Publishing Ltd: extracts from the Family Law Reports.

Lloyd's of London Press Ltd: extracts from the Lloyd's Law Reports.

Martin, Professor J., [1991] Conv. 364.

His Honour, Mr Justice Millett, 'The *Quistclose* Trust: Who can enforce it?'
(1985) 101 LQR 269.

New Scientist: 'Computers that Listen', NS, 4 December 1993.

Pettit, Professor P. H., 'Farewell Section 40' [1989] Conv. 431.

Sweet & Maxwell Ltd: extracts from the Property Planning and Compensation Reports, the *Conveyancer* and *Law Quarterly Review.*

Table of Cases

Table of Statutes

1 NATURE OF EQUITABLE OWNERSHIP

SECTION 1: THE EQUITABLE MAXIMS

In its early days equitable jurisdiction was exercised on an *ad hoc* basis, and its transformation into a modern system did not come until after around 1700, by which time Chancellors tended to be lawyers rather than ecclesiasts and a system of precedent was beginning to develop.

As equity shook off its *ad hoc* origins, certain principles developed which became embodied in the form of equitable maxims. These are not rules to be construed like statutes, but rather as a general basis around which much of the law of equity has formed. They frequently appear as part of the reasoning in judgments, and all have relevance to the law of trusts:

1. Equity will not suffer a wrong without a remedy.
2. Equity follows the law.
3. Where there is equal equity, the law shall prevail.
4. Where the equities are equal, the first in time shall prevail.
5. He who seeks equity must do equity.
6. He who comes into equity must come with clean hands.
7. Delay defeats equities.
8. Equality is equity.
9. Equity looks to the intent rather than the form.
10. Equity looks on that as done which ought to be done.
11. Equity imputes an intention to fulfil an obligation.
12. Equity acts *in personam*.

SECTION 2:   COMPARING LEGAL AND EQUITABLE TITLE

A: Equity Acts *In Personam*

One feature of equitable jurisdiction has always been that it is exercised against specific persons – equity acts *in personam*. This is also an important maxim of equity. In the case of the use the remedy was personal against the feoffee to uses, who held the legal estate in the land. Also in a modern trust the action is against the owner of the legal estate in land, or the legal owner of money or goods. Consequently it does not matter, for example, if the land, money or goods are themselves situated abroad, so long as the legal owner or trustee can be found.

Nevertheless, as equity developed it acted not only against the original legal owner of the property, but also against subsequent owners in certain circumstances. The exact nature of this development is considered below. As a result of this it is reasonable to describe certain equitable rights as property rights, and to talk about equitable title to land, and equitable ownership of goods. It is also the case that various statutory provisions, and in particular the 1925 property legislation (see below) and some taxation legislation treat equitable interests as property interests. So although it is still accurate to say that equity acts *in personam*, some equitable rights also have the characteristics of rights *in rem*.

Nevertheless, there are some respects in which the personal nature of equitable jurisdiction remains.

(a)   Land situated abroad

Richard West and Partners (Inverness) Ltd v *Dick*
[1969] 2 Ch 424
Court of Appeal

Decision: The English courts had jurisdiction to grant a decree of specific performance of a contract for the sale of land abroad (in Scotland).

MEGARRY J (whose decision was approved by the Court of Appeal): By the writ in this action, issued on August 9, 1967, the plaintiffs, who are the vendors under a contract for the sale of land, claim specific performance of the contract against the defendant, the purchaser. . . .

The main point in the case turns on the fact that the land in question is situate in Scotland. . . .

Mr Godfrey [for the purchaser] . . . challenged much of the alleged jurisdiction to decree specific performance of contracts relating to foreign land. Such a jurisdiction, he said, might be appropriate in cases where the land was subject to no civilised jurisdiction, or where it was subject to a jurisdiction similar to or derived from the English jurisdiction. But where, as in Scotland, the land was subject to an entirely different system, this made it inappropriate to grant a remedy which might involve grave difficulties in working out the decree. Scottish land law is probably no less obscure to the English lawyer than English land law is to the Scot.

I trust that I shall not be thought lacking in a due sense of awe at the prospect of a Chancery Master being enveloped in the coils of Scottish conveyancing. I certainly do not say that in some cases there may not be very real difficulties. But I hope that practical difficulties in applying sound principles will never too easily be permitted to distort those principles. Furthermore, in this case I do not think that there is a real prospect of there being any such difficulties. For it is not questioned that before the dispute arose the purchaser had approved the draft documents necessary to carry out the transaction, and the vendors had executed them in escrow: and no question of title has been raised.

Mr Godfrey also relied on two passages in *Dicey & Morris on The Conflict of Laws*, 8th ed. (1967) pp. 152, 153. Each may be summarised by its first sentence. The first passage, on p. 152, is: 'The jurisdiction cannot be exercised if the *lex situs* would prohibit the enforcement of the decree.' The second passage, on p. 153, is: 'The jurisdiction cannot be exercised if the court cannot effectively supervise the execution of its decree.' As regards the first head, there is nothing in this case to suggest any prohibition by Scots law against the enforcement of the decree: and as Dicey & Morris comments on p. 152, it is 'difficult to determine what constitutes a prohibition by the *lex situs* sufficiently stringent to prevent the English court from granting a decree.' On the footing that Scots law is a question of fact, I hope that it is not wrong of me to refer to the well-known comparison of the English law of specific performance with the Scots law of specific implement that was made in the House of Lords in *Stewart* v *Kennedy (No. 1)* (1890) 15 App Cas 75. I am, I think, at least entitled to inform my mind as to the English law of specific performance by reference to the comments that, being a remedy which was extraordinary and discretionary, it contrasted with specific implement, which was an ordinary remedy: see pp. 95, 102, 105. At all events, without cogent evidence to establish it (and there is none) I refuse to assume that the Scottish courts will stand aghast at the spectacle of a purchaser living within the English jurisdiction being ordered by an English court to carry out his agreement to purchase land in Scotland.

The existence of the jurisdiction to decree specific performance of a contract for the sale of foreign land against a defendant within the jurisdiction has been laid down by high authority for over two centuries. An odd feature, however, is that [counsel for the vendors] has been able to refer me to no reported case in which such a decree has actually been made. The leading authority is, of course, *Penn* v *Lord Baltimore* (1750) 1 Ves Sen 444, where Lord Hardwicke LC decreed specific performance of an English agreement relating to the boundaries between Pennsylvania and Maryland, despite the inability of the court to enforce its decree *in rem*. Lord Hardwicke said at p. 447:

The conscience of the party was bound by this agreement; and being within the jurisdiction of this court . . ., which acts *in personam*, the court may properly decree it as an agreement, if a foundation for it.

Of the many subsequent pronouncements on the subject, I will select two, merely mentioning *Fry on Specific Performance of Contracts*, 6th ed. (1921), pp. 56–59. In *Ewing* v *Orr Ewing* (1883) 9 App Cas 34, 40, the Earl of Selborne LC said:

The jurisdiction of the English court is established upon elementary principles. The courts of equity in England are, and always have been, courts of conscience, operating *in personam* and not *in rem*; and in the exercise of this personal jurisdiction they have always been accustomed to compel the performance of contracts and trusts as to subjects which were not either locally or *ratione domicilii* within their jurisdiction. They have done so as to land, in Scotland, in Ireland, in the Colonies, in foreign countries.

He then cited *Penn* v *Lord Baltimore* (1750) 1 Ves Sen 444, and the notes to it in 2 LC Eq, 4th ed., pp. 939, 940, 941. In the judgment of Byrne J in *Duder* v *Amsterdamsch Trustees Kantoor* [1902] 2 Ch 132 at 140, 141, there is conveniently set out an extensive quotation from the judgment of Lord Cottenham LC in [*Re Courtney*], *ex parte Pollard* (1840) Mont & Ch 239 at 251. The quotation includes this passage:

> Bills for specific performance of contracts for the sale of lands, or respecting mortgages of estates, in the colonies and elsewhere out of the jurisdiction of this Court, are of familiar occurrence. Why then, consistently with these principles and these authorities, should the fact, that by the law of Scotland no lien or equitable mortgage was created by the deposit and memorandum in this case, prevent the Courts of this country from giving such effect to the transactions between the parties as it would have given if the land had been in England? If the contract had been to sell the lands a specific performance would have been decreed; and why is all relief to be refused because the contract is to sell, subject to a condition for redemption? The substance of the agreement is to charge the debt upon the estates, and to do and perfect all such acts as may be necessary for the purpose; and if the Court would decree specific performance of this contract, and the completion of the security according to the forms of law in Scotland, it will give effect to this equity by paying out of the proceeds of the estate (which being part of the bankrupt's estate must be sold) what is found to be the amount of the debt so agreed to be charged upon it, which is what the creditor asks.

It is, of course, curious that neither of these cases nor any other case that has been cited to me relates to an actual decree of specific performance of a contract for the sale of foreign land; but when it has been asserted on such high authority that the grant of such decrees is of familiar occurrence and of long standing, and Scotland is in terms mentioned, I do not think it is for me to question the doctrine, even if (as is not the case) I had any inclination to do so. It may be that one reason why there is no report of any such decree is that no such case has been thought reportable. Certainly I do not think that I can treat the absence of such a report as throwing doubt on the principle that equity, acting *in personam*, may decree specific performance against a defendant within the jurisdiction whose conscience is bound by some trust or contract. Any inability of the court to enforce the decree *in rem* is no reason for refusing the plaintiff such rights and means of enforcement as equity can afford him. In the present case, of course, the vendors stand ready and willing to convey the land; and the fact that it is in Scotland provides no reason why the purchaser should not pay the money that he contracted to pay.

I accept that what Lord Selborne and Lord Cottenham said must be ranked as *dicta*. But there are *dicta* and *dicta*. Some authorities distinguish between *obiter dicta* and judicial *dicta*. The former are mere passing remarks of the judge, whereas the latter consist of considered enunciations of the judge's opinion of the law on some point which does not arise for decision on the facts of the case before him, and so is not part of the *ratio decidendi*. But there is, I think, a third type of *dictum*, so far innominate. If instead of merely stating his own view of the point in question the judge supports it by stating what has been done in other cases, not reported, then his statement is one which rests not only on his own unsupported view of the law but also on the decisions of those other judges whose authority he has invoked. He is, as it were, a reporter *pro tanto*. Such a statement of the settled law or accustomed practice carries with it the authority not merely of the judge who makes it but also of an unseen cloud of his judicial brethren. A *dictum* of this type offers, as it seems to me, the highest authority that any *dictum* can bear; and I think that a judge would have to be very sure of himself before he refused to follow it. What Lord Cottenham said plainly seems to fall within this category; and although Lord Selborne may have rested at least in part on the authorities to which he referred, it may be that he too relied on his experience in the same sense. Be that as it may, both on authority and on principle I reject Mr Godfrey's submission on this branch of the case.

Mr Godfrey took two other points. [Megarry J went on to discuss peripheral points relating to fire precautions and planning consent.]

HARMAN LJ: . . . There remains the point on which Megarry J, learned man that he is, exhibited a very interesting and powerful judgment, whereby he expressed the view that there is no objection to a grant of specific performance of a contract for foreign land by an English court. As far as I am concerned I am content to adopt the elaborate reasoning by which he reached that conclusion. I have always thought, and I still think, that the Court of Chancery, acting as it does *in personam*, is well able to grant specific performance of a contract to buy or sell foreign land, provided the defendant is domiciled within its jurisdiction. I say nothing about a case where the defendant is domiciled outside; but the purchaser here lives at Enfield: the vendors have their registered office in England (if that be relevant; I do not think it is): and I see nothing difficult about a vendors' decree of specific performance in the circumstances. There might be difficulties raised by matters of Scottish title; but here the title was accepted. The decree contains the usual recital that the purchaser has accepted the vendors' title to the property, about which I gather there is no doubt. . . .

Note
See also *Ewing* v *Orr-Ewing* (1883) 9 App Cas 34.

(b) Action by beneficiary against trustee, not third party

It is also often the trustee, not the beneficiary, who takes action against a third party in respect of the trust property. For example, where property is leased it is the trustee who sues for rent: *Shalit* v *Joseph Nadler Ltd.* [1933] 2 KB 79. Of course, the trustee is accountable to the beneficiary, and can be required by the beneficiary to sue.

Another example can be found in the law of tort. Generally speaking, only the owner of property at the time that it is damaged can sue in negligence. It is probable that an equitable owner does not count for these purposes, and that only the legal owner can sue. Again, of course, the equitable owner can require the legal owner to sue.

Leigh & Sillivan Ltd v *Aliakmon Shipping Co. Ltd, The Aliakmon*
[1986] AC 785
House of Lords

Facts: The buyers agreed to buy a quantity of steel coils to be shipped from Korea, c. and f. Immingham. A clean bill of lading was issued by the shipowners, although the steel was badly stowed aboard *The Aliakmon*, and because of this it was further damaged during the voyage to the United Kingdom.

When the sellers tendered the bill of lading the buyers were unable to pay, so after renegotiation the contract was varied, so that although the bill of lading would be delivered to the buyers to enable them to take delivery of the steel, payment would not become due until 180 days after sight. The buyers discovered the damage to the goods on unloading and brought actions against the shipowners in contract and tort.

Had the contract been performed as originally agreed the buyers would have obtained property in the steel on indorsement. One effect of the variation was that the sellers reserved a right of disposal against payment, so that property did not pass to the buyers, then or at any later time, due to s. 19(1) of the Sale of Goods Act.

Held: The buyers could not bring an action in negligence against the carriers, because (by virtue of the variation) they had no property in the goods at the time they were damaged.

LORD BRANDON (on the question of equitable ownership): . . . My Lords, under this head Mr Clarke [for the buyers] put forward two propositions of law. The first proposition was that a person who has the equitable ownership of goods is entitled to sue in tort for negligence anyone who by want of care causes them to be lost or damaged without joining the legal owner as a party to the action. The second proposition was that a buyer who agrees to buy goods in circumstances where, although ascertained goods have been appropriated to the contract, their legal ownership remains in the seller, acquires upon such appropriation the equitable ownership of the goods. Applying those two propositions to the facts of the present case, Mr Clarke submitted that the goods the subject-matter of the c. and f. contract had been appropriated to the contract on or before shipment at Inchon, and that from then on, while the legal ownership of the goods remained in the sellers, the buyers became the equitable owners of them, and could therefore sue the shipowners in tort for negligence for the damage done to them without joining the sellers.

In my view, the first proposition cannot be supported. There may be cases where a person who is the equitable owner of certain goods has already a possessory title to them. In such a case he is entitled, by virtue of his possessory title rather than his equitable ownership, to sue in tort for negligence anyone whose want of care has caused loss of or damage to the goods without joining the legal owner as a party to the action: see for instance *Healey* v *Healey* [1915] 1 KB 938. If, however, the person is the equitable owner of the goods and no more, then he must join the legal owner as a party to the action, either as co-plaintiff if he is willing or as co-defendant if he is not. This had always been the law in the field of equitable ownership of land and I see no reason why it should not also be so in the field of equitable ownership of goods.

With regard to the second proposition, I do not doubt that it is possible, in accordance with established equitable principles, for equitable interests in goods to be created and to exist. It seems to me, however, extremely doubtful whether equitable interests in goods can be created or exist within the confines of an ordinary contract of sale. The Sale of Goods Act 1893 [replaced in 1979], which must be taken to apply to the c. and f. contract of sale in the present case, is a complete code of law in respect of contracts for the sale of goods. The passing of the property in goods the subject-matter of such a contract is fully dealt with in ss. 16 to 19 of the Act. Those sections draw no distinction between the legal and the equitable property in goods, but appear to have been framed on the basis that the expression 'property', as used in them, is intended to comprise both the legal and the equitable title. In this connection I consider that there is much force in the observations of Atkin LJ in *Re Wait* [1927] 1 Ch 606, 635–636, from which I quote only this short passage:

> It would have been futile in a code intended for commercial men to have created an elaborate structure of rules dealing with rights at law, if at the same time it was intended to leave, subsisting with the legal rights, equitable rights inconsistent with, more extensive, and coming into existence earlier than the rights so carefully set out in the various sections of the Code.

These observations of Atkin LJ were not necessary to the decision of the case before him and represented a minority view not shared by the other two members of the Court of Appeal. Moreover, Atkin LJ expressly stated that he was not deciding the point. If my view on the first proposition of law is correct, it is again unnecessary to decide the point in this appeal. I shall, therefore, say no more than that my provisional view accords with that expressed by Atkin LJ in *Re Wait* . . . .

Notes
1.   The buyers had no equitable ownership, so that the remarks at the beginning of this passage are technically *obiter dicta*.
2.   This case should be contrasted with *White* v *Jones* [1993] 3 All ER 481, upholding *Ross* v *Caunters* [1980] Ch 297. Here, an intended beneficiary under a will successfully sued the solicitors for drawing up a will in such a way as to exclude him, although obviously he did not (because of the solicitor's negligence) obtain even equitable title to the disputed property; but these are exceptional cases, in that there was nobody apart from the intended beneficiary who was in any position to bring an action.
3.   The position is different for other tort actions, where possession rather than ownership is protected. *Healey* v *Healey* [1915] 1 KB 938, referred to in *The Aliakmon*, was a detinue action brought by a wife against her husband (who was not trustee). She had only to show that she was entitled to possession under the trust. *International Factors Ltd* v *Rodriguez* [1979] QB 351 reasons similarly in conversion. Nuisance actions also do not require proof of title.

B: Equitable Rights as Real Rights

Equitable rights are also sometimes treated as rights *in rem*, as in (e.g.) *Baker* v *Archer-Shee* [1927] AC 844, where an equitable owner was considered the owner of dividends for tax purposes.

It is also true that equitable interests in property are capable of binding third parties, although unlike legal interests they do not bind the bona fide purchaser for value of the legal estate without notice. This is an application of maxim 3, above: where there is equal equity, the law shall prevail. By contrast, a subsequent purchaser of an equitable estate is bound: by maxim 4, where the equities are equal, the first in time shall prevail.

Cave v Cave
(1880) 15 ChD 639
Chancery Division

Facts: The plaintiffs were beneficiaries under Mr and Mrs Frederick
Cave's marriage settlement. Charles Cave was the sole trustee, and was
also the family solicitor. He and Frederick Cave embarked on a series of
transactions whose purpose was to defraud the plaintiffs of the trust fund
to which they were entitled.

First, the moneys were used in breach of trust to purchase the freehold
of a piece of land at Wandsworth. Charles acted as the solicitor, and the
property was conveyed into the sole name of Frederick Cave. As a result
of this transaction, the moneys in the trust fund were converted into land,
so that the beneficiaries of the fund became beneficiaries of the land.

Next, Frederick Cave, posing as unencumbered freeholder to the land in
Wandsworth, and using the land as security, raised £4,500 by way of legal
mortgage. This transaction took place before the enactment of the 1925
property legislation, at a time when a legal mortgage took effect by way of
a conveyance of the entire freehold estate to the mortgagee, with a covenant
to re-convey the property to the mortgagor if the money loaned, plus
interest and administration charges, was repaid to the mortgagee on a fixed
date. Equity enforced this covenant and also allowed the mortgagor to
demand a later re-conveyance, subject to repayment of the capital loaned,
plus interest and administration charges. Thus, the mortgagee (M1 or first
mortgagee) obtained legal title. He also provided value, in the form of the
money advanced. He was a bona fide purchaser of the legal estate for value
without notice of the beneficiaries' equitable interests.

The value of the Wandsworth property presumably being greater than
the £4,500 advanced on the first mortgage, Frederick Cave was able later
to obtain various further advances, including in particular a second mortgage of £1,800. The second mortgagee, like the first, had no notice of the
beneficiaries' interests. However, the second mortgagee (M2) could not
obtain a legal estate, since that had already been conveyed to the first
mortgagee (M1). His mortgage took effect as a mortgage in equity only.
Even though he had acted bona fide, therefore, had given value and had
no notice of the prior equitable interests of the beneficiaries, he was not a
bona fide purchaser of the *legal* estate for value without notice.

Frederick Cave eventually went bankrupt, and the plaintiffs claimed
priority over M1 and M2.

Held: Fry J held that M1, as bona fide purchaser of the legal estate for
value without notice, took free of the plaintiffs' rights. On the sale of the
property, therefore, he was entitled to be repaid first, the plaintiffs being
entitled only to the balance of the proceeds of sale. M2, however, having
only an equitable interest in the property, took subject to the plaintiffs'
prior equitable interest.

FRY J: As between persons having only equitable interests, if their equities are in all other respects equal, priority of time gives the better equity, or, '*Qui prior est tempore potior est jure*'.

Notes
1.   It can be seen that this is merely a restatement, in slightly different language, of equitable maxim 4 (see above).
2.   Had the transaction taken place today, since the 1925 property legislation, M1 would have obtained a legal lease on the property, rather than the freehold estate.

C: Equitable Maxim 2: Equity Follows the Law

Maxim 2 means that all interests which are recognised at common law are also recognised at equity. This explains the development of other equitable interests, such as the equitable easement, and the equitable lease. Often, as in these cases, equity allows less formal creation.

In fact, there are now interests which are only recognised in equity, and not at common law. There are two reasons for this:

(a)   Equity also recognised other interests, not previously recognised by the common law, e.g., restrictive covenants. About 25 years ago, the development of contractual licences looked poised to develop similarly, but this development has almost certainly been curtailed.

(b)   The number of estates and interests in land which can exist at common law has been curtailed by legislation, in particular by the Law of Property Act 1925, s. 1 (see below).

D: Remedies

Originally equity developed its own remedies, which were not available to the common law. Nor did equity administer common law remedies. This position was to some extent altered by the Common Law Procedure Act 1854, which gave the common law courts some jurisdiction to give equitable remedies, and the Chancery Amendment Act 1858, which allowed the Court of Chancery to award the common law-derived remedy of damages, but only in addition to, or in substitution for an equitable remedy.

In 1873–5 the courts were fused, but the principles governing the grant of equitable remedies were not changed by that legislation, and are still applicable to actions to protect equitable interests or estates, and other rights having an equitable origin. Thus, it is still necessary to consider the equitable remedies separately from the common law remedies.

The main equitable remedies are the injunction, specific performance, and remedy of account. For breach of fiduciary duty (see chapter 15) there is also the remedy of account, and sometimes equity imposes a constructive trust (see chapter 11). Damages could not originally be awarded, and can be now only on the basis of the 1858 Act. In any event the quantum of equitable damages may differ from that appropriate in a common law action.

Equitable remedies are available for breaches of equitable obligations, such as those considered in chapters 11 and 15, but in addition injunctions can be used to prevent the commissions of torts. For some torts, such as negligence claims arising out of road accident cases, the remedy is obviously inappropriate, but it can be useful for continuing torts, such as trespass or nuisance. As will be seen in chapter 15, it can be used to prevent abuses of confidential information.

A major difference between the two systems is that whereas common law remedies are available as of right, equitable remedies retain the discretionary nature of early equitable jurisdiction. Although for the creation of wholly new equitable rights and principles the onset over the last two centuries or so of defined systems of precedent and law reporting have curtailed the early discretion somewhat, the remedies are nevertheless still discretionary, even though that discretion is now exercised in accord with fairly clear and even rigid principles. The discretionary nature of the remedies can lead to dire consequences. If an equitable estate or interest depends on the award of an equitable remedy, the refusal to grant the remedy destroys the interest.

A common ground for refusal of a remedy is the behaviour of the party claiming the equitable remedy: 'he who comes into equity must come with clean hands'. For example in *Coatsworth* v *Johnson* (1886) 54 LT 520 (CA) the plaintiff was in possession of land under a contract for a lease, where no lease that would be recognised at common law had been executed. The landlord in fact turned the plaintiff out, and the plaintiff sued for trespass. He would have won the action had he been regarded as a lessee, either at common law or in equity. As we saw above, equity in principle enforces contracts for leases, and would normally regard the plaintiff as being an equitable lessee. In the particular case he was in breach of various covenants under the agreement, however. In these circumstances, the Court of Appeal held, the equitable remedy would have been refused, and the plaintiff *therefore lost his interest*. Thus he was thrown back on his common law rights, and of course he had no lease at common law. So he lost. Not only is this case a good example of the discretionary nature of equitable remedies, but it also emphasises the need to treat common law and equitable rights and remedies separately and additionally. Also, the entire interest was lost because the remedy was refused.

The behaviour of the party claiming the remedy is not the only factor. Innocent plaintiffs can also lose their remedies. For example, a remedy might also be refused if to grant it would put the other party in breach of a contract with a third party: *Warmington* v *Miller* [1973] QB 877. Other grounds for refusing the remedy are that severe hardship might be caused to the defendant, or in a contract action where the contract has been forced upon the defendant through unfair pressure (even in the absence of undue influence or duress, on which see chapter 11).

Warmington v *Miller*
[1973] QB 877, [1973] 2 WLR 654, [1973] 2 All ER 372
Court of Appeal

Decision: The court would not grant specific performance of an oral contract for an underlease where to do so would result in the landlord of the underlease breaking a term of the head-lease (the head-lease contained a prohibition on assigning, underletting, or parting with possession of part only of the premises). The plaintiffs were therefore left to their common law remedy of damages.

STAMP LJ: . . . I turn to consider the alternative submission advanced on behalf of the defendant that the judge ought not to have ordered specific performance. Counsel for the defendant submits that the judge ought not to have ordered specific performance requiring the defendant to do that which he cannot do under the terms of the lease under which he holds the premises and which, if he did, would expose him to proceedings for forfeiture. In my judgment that submission is well founded. I can see nothing in this case to take it outside the practice of the court, in determining whether to exercise its discretionary power to grant the equitable remedy of specific performance, not to do so where the result would necessitate a breach by the defendant of a contract with a third party or would compel the defendant to do that which he is not lawfully competent to do: see *Fry's Specific Performance*, 6th ed. (1921), p. 194 and *Willmott* v *Barber* (1880) 15 ChD 96 per Fry J at p. 107. Here the landlord is under an unqualified covenant in his lease not to underlet or part with possession of part only of the premises demised to him. To order him specifically to perform the contract by granting an underlease and so allowing the plaintiffs to retain possession would be to order him to do something he cannot do or, if he did it, would expose him to a forfeiture. As Lord Redesdale LC remarked in a passage in *Harnett* v *Yielding* (1805) 2 Sch & Lef 549, 554, quoted in *Fry's Specific Performance*, at p. 194:

> [The plaintiff] must also show that, in seeking the performance, he does not call upon the other party to do an act which he is not lawfully competent to do; for, if he does, a consequence is produced that quite passes by the object of the court in exercising the jurisdiction, which is to do more complete justice.

During the course of the argument I suggested to counsel that the position of the [plaintiffs] might be sufficiently and properly protected by a declaration that [the plaintiffs] were in possession of the workshop under the terms of the agreement of August 3, 1971. That suggestion was supported by [counsel for the plaintiffs] with enthusiasm and I must deal with it. I have, for the following reasons, come to the clear conclusion that the suggestion was misconceived, and I regret having made it.

It is not and never has been the contention of the [plaintiffs] that they are lessees at law under the agreement; and [counsel for the defendant] submitted, as I think correctly, that the *Walsh* v *Lonsdale* situation, where the intended lessee is treated as having the same rights as if a lease had in fact been granted to him, applies only if the lessee is entitled to specific performance: see the judgment of Sir George Jessel MR in *Walsh* v *Lonsdale* (1882) 21 ChD 9, 14. The equitable interests which the intended lessee has under an agreement for a lease do not exist *in vacuo* but arise because the intended lessee has an equitable right to specific performance of the agreement. In such a situation that which is agreed to be and ought to be done is treated as having been done and carrying with it in equity the attendant rights. But the intended lessee's equitable rights do not in general arise when that which is agreed to be done would not be ordered to be done. The suggested declaration would thus not be justified.

There is, I think, another objection to the making of such a declaration as I am discussing – or perhaps it is putting the same point in another way. The equitable right to be in possession under the agreement could be protected only by an injunction, and, if after the making of such a declaration, the [plaintiffs] sought the equitable remedy of an injunction to protect their right to remain in possession it would be an invitation to the court to grant part specific performance of the agreement. Such an injunction, like the order for specific performance itself, would in its effect compel the [defendant] to continue to break the covenant not to part with possession of part only of the premises demised to him and be open to the same objection as an order for specific performance. The suggested declaration would be a misleading nuisance.

For these reasons, the [plaintiffs] ought, in my judgment, to be left with their remedy at law, namely, damages for the repudiation by the [defendant] of his agreement to grant the [plaintiffs] a lease.

Note

In *Mountford* v *Scott* [1975] Ch 258, an argument was advanced that equity ought not to enforce an option, granted for £1, to purchase a house for £10,000. The argument was based on the undoubted rule that equity will not specifically enforce a promise at the instance of a volunteer, although the promise, if under seal, may found an action for damages at common law (see further chapter 3). It was argued by the defendant that this rule should be extended to this situation, where the consideration for the grant of the option was a token payment, and that the plaintiffs should therefore have been left to their remedy in damages. Brightman J summed up the issue thus:

As the plaintiffs had made no more than a token payment for the defendant's promise, are the plaintiffs, so far as the equitable remedy of specific performance is concerned, in the position of volunteers who ought to be left to their remedy in damages?

The argument was rejected by Brightman J, whose decision was upheld in the Court of Appeal, Russell LJ observing:

The final contention for the appellant was that that contract should not be specifically enforced, but that the purchaser should have only been awarded damages. I see no justification for that contention. If the owner of a house contracts with his eyes open, as the judge held that the defendant did, it cannot in my view be right to deny specific performance to the purchaser because the vendor then finds it difficult to find a house to buy that suits him and his family on the basis of the amount of money in the proceeds of sale. It is to be observed, as to this particular case, that to the knowledge of the defendant, the purchasers were and are planning development on one site embracing his house together with the three other houses. It is right to say that, after this final point had been the subject-matter of a certain amount of debate in this court, counsel for the defendant found himself unable to pursue the point – unable, let me say, not because he was unable to get a word in edgeways, but because he thought in the end, after debate, that the point was not a good one. Accordingly, I reject the contention that the judge could not or should not have ordered specific performance.

But I wish to add a comment on the learned judge's approach to that point. As I have said, a valid option to purchase constitutes an irrevocable offer to sell during the period stated, and a purported withdrawal of the offer is ineffective. When, therefore, the offer is accepted by the exercise of the option, a contract for sale and purchase is thereupon constituted, just as if there were then constituted a perfectly ordinary contract for sale and purchase without a prior option agreement. The court is asked to order specific performance of that contract of sale and purchase, not to order specific performance of a contract not to withdraw the offer; provided that the option be valid and for valuable consideration and duly exercised, it appears to me to be irrelevant to the question of remedy under the contract for sale and purchase that the valuable consideration can be described as a token payment; and so also if the option agreement be under seal with no payment, which is what I take the learned judge to be referring to when he refers to a gratuitous option in his judgment. While I therefore agree that a valid option to purchase constitutes an interest in the land, I do not consider, as the learned judge appears to have thought, that that fact is necessary to his conclusion and my conclusion on what is the appropriate remedy.

SECTION 3: THE 1925 PROPERTY LEGISLATION

The 1925 property legislation comprised the Law of Property Act, Settled Land Act, Land Charges Act and Land Registration Act, the last two being amended and re-enacted in 1972. Probably the main purpose of the 1925 property legislation was to make it easier for people to sell or otherwise alienate land.

The effect on equity and trusts of this legislation was threefold. In the first place, many estates in land can now exist only in equity. Secondly, the bona fide purchaser doctrine was severely curtailed. Thirdly, the trust for sale, which was used as a conveyancing device before 1925, was substantially enhanced in importance.

A: Reduction in Number of Legal Estates

Many estates in land can now exist only in equity (i.e., as beneficial interests under a trust), because of the reduction in 1925 (in order to aid conveyancing) of the number of possible legal estates. Before 1925 purchasers might have a great number of legal titles to investigate, in addition to equitable estates and interests. For example, if land was settled in order to keep it in a family, the present tenant's life estate and the future tenant's entailed estate could both be legal estates.

Even greater complexity could arise where there were concurrent interests in the same land (i.e., where land was shared, but not divided, as for example, where a matrimonial home was held jointly by husband and wife). In this situation each party to the arrangement often had a separate legal estate. Furthermore, each of these estates could be further split, and frequently would be where land was held by large partnerships, or settled equally among sons and grandsons over several generations. Thus, a prospective purchaser would have to investigate, and buy, large numbers of legal estates, before investigation of equitable title had even begun. Effectively, this could render shared land unsaleable.

The Law of Property Act 1925, s. 1, reduced the number of possible legal estates in land to two, those that are now commonly known as freehold (fee simple absolute in possession), which must take immediate effect, and leasehold (term of years absolute). Future freehold interests and life interests, as are commonly found in settlements, can only exist in equity, and concurrent interests in land only take effect behind a trust for sale (i.e., in equity).

Law of Property Act 1925

1. Legal estates and equitable interests

(1)   The only estates in land which are capable of subsisting or of being conveyed or created at law are —

(a)   an estate in fee simple absolute in possession;

(b)   a term of years absolute.

(2)   The only interests or charges in or over land which are capable of subsisting or of being conveyed or created at law are —

(a)   an easement, right, or privilege in or over land for an interest equivalent to an estate in fee simple absolute in possession or a term of years absolute;

(b)   a rentcharge in possession issuing out of or charged on land being either perpetual or for a term of years absolute;

(c)   a charge by way of legal mortgage;

(d)   . . . and any other similar charge on land which is not created by an instrument;

(e)   rights of entry exercisable over or in respect of a legal term of years absolute, or annexed, for any purpose, to a legal rentcharge.

(3)   All other estates, interests, and charges in or over land take effect as equitable interests.

(4)   The estates, interests, and charges which under this section are authorised to subsist or to be conveyed or created at law are (when subsisting or conveyed or created at law) in this Act referred to as 'legal estates', and have the same incidents as legal estates subsisting at the commencement of this Act; and the owner of a legal estate is referred to as 'an estate owner' and his legal estate is referred to as his estate.

(5)   A legal estate may subsist concurrently with or subject to any other legal estate in the same land in like manner as it could have done before the commencement of this Act.

(6)   A legal estate is not capable of subsisting or of being created in an undivided share in land or of being held by an infant.

(7)   Every power of appointment over, or power to convey or charge land or any interest therein, whether created by a statute or other instrument or implied by law,

and whether created before or after the commencement of this Act (not being a power vested in a legal mortgagee or an estate owner in right of his estate and exercisable by him or by another person in his name and on his behalf), operates only in equity.

(8) Estates, interests, and charges in or over land which are not legal estates are in this Act referred to as 'equitable interests', and powers which by this Act are to operate in equity only are in this Act referred to as 'equitable powers'.

(9) The provisions in any statute or other instrument requiring land to be conveyed to uses shall take effect as directions that the land shall (subject to creating or reserving thereout any legal estate authorised by this Act which may be required) be conveyed to a person of full age upon the requisite trusts.

(10) The repeal of the Statute of Uses (as amended) does not affect the operation thereof in regard to dealings taking effect before the commencement of this Act.

4. Creation and disposition of equitable property

(1) Interests in land validly created or arising after the commencement of this Act, which are not capable of subsisting as legal estates, shall take effect as equitable interests, and, save as otherwise expressly provided by statute, interests in land which under the Statute of Uses or otherwise could before the commencement of this Act have been created as legal interests, shall be capable of being created as equitable interests:

Provided that, after the commencement of this Act (and save as hereinafter expressly enacted), any equitable interest in land shall only be capable of being validly created in any case in which an equivalent interest in property real or personal could have been validly created before such commencement.

Note

The words omitted in s. 1(2) were repealed by the Finance Act 1963, s. 73(8)(b), Sch. 14, Part IV, and the Tithe Act 1936, s. 48(3), Sch. 9.

B: Bona Fide Purchaser Doctrine

So far as the equitable estates and interests were concerned, the bona fide purchaser doctrine was not altogether satisfactory. Innocent owners of equitable interests could lose them to a bona fide purchaser for value without notice through no fault of their own; there was no way of being sure that they would be brought to his notice, and if they were not he might take free (i.e., without being bound by those interests). Purchasers, on the other hand, were put to great expense to discover the existence of all possible equitable interests, in case they should find themselves bound.

Broadly speaking, the 1925 legislation distinguishes between equitable estates in land (i.e., akin to full ownership) and interests less than ownership. Rights akin to ownership are overreached (see further below). For other equitable interests, the 1925 legislation was intended to replace the bona fide purchaser doctrine with registration provisions; such interests today can be and have to be registered for protection against purchasers. The idea is that if the interest is registered the purchaser has notice; if it is not registered, the purchaser is not bound whether or not he has notice, and whether or not he even acts in good faith (see, e.g., *Midland Bank Trust Co.* v *Green* [1981] AC 513, below, where a purchaser in bad faith took free from a prior equitable

interest, under certain provisions of the Land Charges Act). The Land
Charges Act 1925, which was replaced in 1972, is a transitional provision,
and eventually all land will come under the regime of the Land Registration
Act.

(a)   The regime of the Land Charges Act

Land Charges Act 1972

4.   Effect of land charges and protection of purchasers
(6)   An estate contract and a land charge of Class D created or entered into on or
after 1st January 1926 shall be void against a purchaser for money or money's worth
... of a legal estate in the land charged with it, unless the land is registered in the
appropriate register before the completion of the purchase.

17.   Interpretation
(1)   In this Act, unless the context otherwise requires —
. . . 'purchaser' means any person (including a mortgagee or lessee) who, for
valuable consideration, takes any interest in land or in a charge on land, and
'purchase' has a corresponding meaning;
. . .

Law of Property Act 1925

198.   Registration under the Land Charges Act 1925 to be notice
(1)   The registration of any instrument or matter [in any register kept under the
Land Charges Act 1972 or any local land charges register] shall be deemed to
constitute actual notice of such instrument or matter, and of the fact of such
registration, to all persons and for all purposes connected with the land affected, as
from the date of registration or other prescribed date and so long as the registration
continues in force.
(2)   This section operates without prejudice to the provisions of this Act respecting
the making of further advances by a mortgagee, and applies only to instruments and
matters required or authorised to be registered [in any such register].

199.   Restrictions on constructive notice
(1)   A purchaser shall not be prejudicially affected by notice of —
(i)   any instrument or matter capable of registration under the provisions of the
Land Charges Act 1925, or any enactment which it replaces, which is void or not
enforceable as against him under that Act or enactment, by reason of the non-
registration thereof;
(ii)   any other instrument or matter or any fact or thing unless —
(a)   it is within his own knowledge, or would have come to his knowledge if
such inquiries and inspections had been made as ought reasonably to have been made
by him; or
(b)   in the same transaction with respect to which a question of notice to the
purchaser arises, it has come to the knowledge of his counsel, as such, or of his
solicitor or other agent, as such, or would have come to the knowledge of his solicitor
or other agent, as such, if such inquiries and inspections had been made as ought
reasonably to have been made by the solicitor or other agent.

(2)   Paragraph (ii) of the last subsection shall not exempt a purchaser from any liability under, or any obligation to perform or observe, any covenant, condition, provision, or restriction contained in any instrument under which his title is derived, mediately or immediately; and such liability or obligation may be enforced in the same manner and to the same extent as if that paragraph had not been enacted.

(3)   A purchaser shall not by reason of anything in this section be affected by notice in any case where he would not have been so affected if this section had not been enacted.

(4)   This section applies to purchases made either before or after the commencement of this Act.

Note
The words in square brackets in s. 198 were substituted by the Local Land Charges Act 1975, s. 17(2), and Sch. 1.

Midland Bank Trust Co. v *Green*
[1981] AC 513
House of Lords

Facts: In 1961, a father granted to his son, for the consideration of £1, a 10-year option to purchase his 300-acre farm for £75 per acre (i.e., £22,500). Through the default of the son's solicitors the option was not registered as a Class C(iv) estate contract. Following a family dispute the father later wished to deprive his son of the option and in order to do this conveyed the farm in 1967 to his wife for £500. At this time the farm was actually worth about £40,000, and its value later rose significantly due to inflation.

Decision: The son lost out to his mother. On a literal interpretation of the Land Charges Act, the mother was a purchaser within s. 4(6).

LORD WILBERFORCE: . . . [The] case appears to be a plain one. The 'estate contract', which by definition . . . includes an option of purchase, was entered into after January 1, 1926; Evelyne took an interest (in fee simple) in the land 'for valuable consideration' so was a 'purchaser': she was a purchaser for money – namely £500: the option was not registered before the completion of the purchase. It is therefore void as against her.

In my opinion this appearance is also the reality. The case is plain: the Act is clear and definite. Intended as it was to provide a simple and understandable system for the protection of title to land, it should not be read down or glossed; to do so would destroy the usefulness of the Act. Any temptation to remould the Act to meet the facts of the present case, on the supposition that it is a hard one and that justice requires it, is, for me at least, removed by the consideration that the Act itself provides a simple and effective protection for persons in Geoffrey's position – *viz* – by registration.

The respondents submitted two arguments as to the interpretation of s. 13(2) [now s. 4(6) of the 1972 Act]: the one sought to introduce into it a requirement that the purchaser should be 'in good faith'; the other related to the words 'in money or money's worth'.

The argument as to good faith fell into three parts: first, that 'good faith' was something required of a 'purchaser' before 1926; secondly, that this requirement was preserved by the 1925 legislation and in particular by s. 13(2) of the Land Charges Act 1925 [now s. 4(6) of the 1972 Act]. If these points could be made good, it would then have to be decided whether the purchaser (Evelyne) was in 'good faith' on the facts of the case.

My Lords, the character in the law known as the bona fide (good faith) purchaser for value without notice was the creation of equity. In order to affect a purchaser for value of a legal estate with some equity or equitable interest, equity fastened on his conscience and the composite expression was used to epitomise the circumstances in which equity would or rather would not do so. I think that it would generally be true to say that the words 'in good faith' related to the existence of notice. Equity, in other words, required not only absence of notice, but genuine and honest absence of notice. As the law developed, this requirement became crystallised in the doctrine of constructive notice which assumed a statutory form in the Conveyancing Act 1882, s. 3. But, and so far I would be willing to accompany the respondents, it would be a mistake to suppose that the requirement of good faith extended only to the matter of notice, or that when notice came to be regulated by statute, the requirement of good faith became obsolete. Equity still retained its interest in and power over the purchaser's conscience. The classic judgment of James LJ in *Pilcher* v *Rawlins* (1872) LR 7 Ch App 259, 269 is clear authority that it did: good faith there is stated as a separate test which may have to be passed even though absence of notice is proved. And there are references in cases subsequent to 1882 which confirm the proposition that honesty or bona fides remained something which might be inquired into (see *Berwick & Co.* v *Price* [1905] 1 Ch 632, 639; *Taylor* v *London and County Banking Co.* [1901] 2 Ch 231, 256; *Oliver* v *Hinton* [1899] 2 Ch 264, 273).

But did this requirement, or test, pass into the property legislation of 1925?

My Lords, I do not think it safe to seek the answer to this question by means of a general assertion that the property legislation of 1922–1925 was not intended to alter the law, or not intended to alter it in a particular field, such as that relating to purchases of legal estates. All the 1925 Acts, and their precursors, were drafted with the utmost care, and their wording, certainly where this is apparently clear, has to be accorded firm respect. As was pointed out in *Grey* v *IRC* [1960] AC 1 [see chapter 6], the Acts of 1922–4 effected massive changes in the law affecting property and the House, in consequence, was persuaded to give to a plain word ('disposition') its plain meaning, and not to narrow it by reference to its antecedents. Certainly that case should firmly discourage us from muddying clear waters. I accept that there is merit in looking at the corpus as a whole in order to produce if possible a consistent scheme. But there are limits to the possibilities of this process: for example it cannot eliminate the difference between registered and unregistered land, or the respective charges on them.

As to the requirement of 'good faith' we are faced with a situation of some perplexity. [Lord Wilberforce considered the requirement of good faith elsewhere in the 1925 legislation and continued: . . .] So far as concerns the Land Charges Act 1925, the definition of 'purchaser' quoted above does not mention 'good faith' at all. 'Good faith' did not appear in the original Act of 1888 nor in the extension made to that Act by the 1922 Act, Sch. 7, nor in the 1924 Act, Sch. 6. It should be a secure assumption that the definition of 'purchaser for value' which is found in s. 4 of the Act of 1888 (. . . 'person who for valuable consideration takes any interest in land') together with the limitation which is now the proviso to s. 13(2) of the 1925 Act, introduced in 1922, was intended to be carried forward into the Act of 1925. The expression 'good faith' appears nowhere in the antecedents. To write the words in, from the examples of contemporaneous Acts, would be bold. It becomes impossible

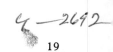

when it is seen that the words appear in s. 3(1) and in s. 7(1) [of the Law of Property Act 1925], in each case in a proviso very similar, in structure, to the relevant proviso in s. 13(2). If canons of constructions have any validity at all, they must lead to the conclusion that the omission in s. 13(2) was deliberate.

My Lords, I recognise that the inquiring mind may put the question: why should there be an omission of the requirement of good faith in this particular context? I do not think there should be much doubt about the answer. Addition of a requirement that the purchaser should be in good faith would bring with it the necessity of inquiring into the purchaser's motives and state of mind. The present case is a good example of the difficulties which would exist. If the position was simply that the purchaser had notice of the option, and decided nevertheless to buy the land, relying on the absence of notification, nobody could contend that she would be lacking in good faith. She would merely be taking advantage of a situation, which the law has provided, and the addition of a profit motive could not create an absence of good faith. But suppose, and this is the respondents' argument, the purchaser's motive is to defeat the option, does this make any difference? Any advantage to oneself seems necessarily to involve a disadvantage for another; to make the validity of the purchase depend on which aspect of the transaction was prevalent in the purchaser's mind seems to create distinctions equally difficult to analyse in law as to establish in fact: avarice and malice may be distinct sins, but in human conduct they are liable to be intertwined. The problem becomes even more acute if one supposes a mixture of motives. Suppose – and this may not be far from the truth – that the purchaser's motives were in part to take the farm from Geoffrey and in part to distribute it between Geoffrey and his brothers and sisters, but not at all to obtain any benefit for herself, is this acting in 'good faith' or not? Should family feeling be denied a protection afforded to simple greed? To eliminate the necessity for inquiries of this kind may well have been part of the legislative intention. Certainly there is here no argument for departing – violently – from the wording of the Act.

. . .

My Lords, I can deal more shortly with the respondents' second argument. It relates to the consideration for the purchase. The argument is that the protection of s. 13(2) of the Land Charges Act 1925 does not extend to a purchaser who has provided only a nominal consideration and that £500 is nominal. A variation of this was the argument accepted by the Court of Appeal that the consideration must be 'adequate' – an expression of transparent difficulty. The answer to both contentions lies in the language of the subsection. The word 'purchaser', by definition (s. 20(8) [now s. 17(1) of the 1972 Act]), means one who provides valuable consideration – a term of art which precludes any inquiry as to adequacy. This definition is, of course, subject to the context. Section 13(2), proviso, requires money or money's worth to be provided: the purpose of this being to exclude the consideration of marriage. There is nothing here which suggests, or admits of, the introduction of a further requirement that the money must not be nominal.

The argument for this requirement is based on the Law of Property Act 1925 which, in s. 205(1)(xxi) defining 'purchaser' provides that 'valuable consideration' includes marriage but does not include a 'nominal consideration in money'. The Land Charges Act 1925 contains no definition of 'valuable consideration', so it is said to be necessary to have resort to the Law of Property Act definition: thus 'nominal consideration in money' is excluded. An indication that this is intended is said to be provided by s. 199(1)(i). I cannot accept this. The fallacy lies in supposing that the Acts – either of them – set out to define 'valuable consideration'; they do not: they define 'purchaser', and they define the word differently (see the first part of the argument).

'Valuable consideration' requires no definition: it is an expression denoting an advantage conferred or detriment suffered. What each Act does is, for its own purposes, to exclude some things from this general expression: the Law of Property Act includes marriage but not a nominal sum in money; the Land Charges Act excludes marriage but allows 'money or money's worth'. There is no coincidence between these two; no link by reference or necessary logic between them. Section 199(1)(i), by referring to the Land Charges Act 1925, necessarily incorporates – for the purposes of this provision – the definition of 'purchaser' in the latter Act, for it is only against such a 'purchaser' that an instrument is void under that Act. It cannot be read as incorporating the Law of Property Act definition into the Land Charges Act. As I have pointed out the land charges legislation has contained its own definition since 1888, carried through, with the addition of the reference to 'money or money's worth' into 1925. To exclude a nominal sum of money from s. 13(2) of the Land Charges Act would be to rewrite the section.

This conclusion makes it unnecessary to determine whether £500 is a nominal sum of money or not. But I must say that for my part I should have great difficulty in so holding. 'Nominal consideration' and a 'nominal sum' in the law appear to me, as terms of art, to refer to a sum or consideration which can be mentioned as consideration but is not necessarily paid. To equate 'nominal' with 'inadequate' or even 'grossly inadequate' would embark the law upon inquiries which I cannot think were contemplated by Parliament.

I would allow the appeal.

Notes

1.   There is no good faith requirement in ss. 4(6) and 17(1) of the Land Charges Act.

2.   Later the son sued his father and mother in tort for conspiracy (see [1982] 1 Ch 529 and [1981] Conv 262). He also took proceedings against his solicitor, which were settled.

3.   Perhaps not surprisingly, the courts have been unhappy with the logic of the Land Charges Act. It applies only to a specified list of interests in land, now set out in s. 2 of the 1972 Act, and although the legislature probably considered this list to be exhaustive of all interests except those that were overreachable (see below), the courts have interpreted the list narrowly. For those interests that are omitted from s. 2 the old notice rules apply, and the courts have been unenthusiastic about extending the legislation to cover all interests by implication (see, e.g. *E. R. Ives Investments* v *High* [1967] 2 QB 379; *Shiloh Spinners Ltd* v *Harding* [1973] AC 691).

E. R. Ives Investment Ltd v *High*
[1967] 2 QB 379
Court of Appeal

Facts: In 1949 Westgate built a block of flats on land which had been bombed during World War II, in such a way that his foundations encroached on his neighbour's (High's) land by about a foot. Westgate and High made an oral agreement that the foundations could stay but that High could have access over Westgate's back garden. No deed was executed. No land charge was registered. High built a garage in reliance on the agreement, and contributed to the cost of resurfacing the yard.

Westgate sold the land to the Wrights, and in 1962 E.R. Ives bought from the Wrights with notice of High's right of way, and subject to it. They then sued High for trespass, claiming that the right of way was unenforceable against them as an unregistered equitable easement.

Held: The Court of Appeal held that an estoppel easement was not an estate contract because it was not a contract for estate. Therefore it did not need to be registered under Class C (iv). It was also not an equitable easement requiring registration under Class D (iii).

LORD DENNING MR: . . . Now here is the point. The right of way was never registered as a land charge. The purchasers, the plaintiffs, say that it should have been egistered under Class C (iv) as an estate contract, or under Class D (iii) as an equitable easement: and that, as it was not registered, it is void against them, the purchasers. Even though they had the most explicit notice of it, nevertheless they say that it is void against them. They claim to be entitled to prevent [the defendant] having any access to his garage across their yard: and thus render it useless to him. They have brought an action for an injunction to stop him crossing the yard at all.

One thing is quite clear. Apart from this point about the Land Charges Act, 1925, [the defendant] would have in equity a good right of way across the yard. This right arises in two ways:

1. *Mutual benefit and burden*
The right arises out of the agreement of November 2, 1949, and the subsequent action taken on it: on the principle that 'he who takes the benefit must accept the burden'. When adjoining owners of land make an agreement to secure continuing rights and benefits for each of them in or over the land of the other, neither of them can take the benefit of the agreement and throw over the burden of it. This applies not only to the original parties, but also to their successors. The successor who takes the continuing benefit must take it subject to the continuing burden. This principle has been applied to neighbours who send their water into a common drainage system: see *Hopgood* v *Brown* [1955] 1 WLR 213; and to purchasers of houses on a building estate who had the benefit of using the roads and were subject to the burden of contributing to the upkeep: see *Halsall* v *Brizell* [1957] Ch 169. The principle clearly applies in the present case. The owners of the block of flats have the benefit of having their foundations in [the defendant's] land. So long as they take that benefit, they must shoulder the burden. They must observe the condition on which the benefit was granted, namely, they must allow [the defendant] and his successors to have access over their yard: cf. *May* v *Belleville* [1905] 2 Ch 605. Conversely, so long as [the defendant] takes the benefit of the access, he must permit the block of flats to keep their foundations in his land.

2. *Equity arising out of acquiescence*
The right arises out of the expense incurred by [the defendant] in building his garage, as it is now, with access only over the yard: and the Wrights standing by and acquiescing in it, knowing that he believed he had a right of way over the yard. By so doing the Wrights created in [the defendant's] mind a reasonable expectation that his access over the yard would not be disturbed. That gives rise to an 'equity arising out of acquiescence'. It is available not only against the Wrights but also their successors

in title. The court will not allow that expectation to be defeated when it would be inequitable so to do. It is for the court in each case to decide in what way the equity can be satisfied: see *Inwards* v *Baker* [1965] 2 QB 29; *Ward* v *Kirkland* [1966] 1 WLR 601 and the cases cited therein. In this case it could only be satisfied by allowing [the defendant] and his successors to have access over the yard so long as the block of flats has its foundations in his land.

The next question is this: was that right a land charge such as to need registration under the Land Charges Act 1925? For if it was a land charge, it was never registered and would be void as against any purchaser: see s. 13 of the Act [of 1925]. It would, therefore, be void against the plaintiffs, even though they took with the most express knowledge and notice of the right.

It was suggested that the agreement of November 2, 1949, was 'an estate contract' within Class C (iv). I do not think so. There was no contract by Mr Westgate to convey a legal estate of any kind.

It was next suggested that the right was an 'equitable easement' within Class D (iii). This class is defined as 'any easement right or privilege over or affecting land created or arising after the commencement of this Act, and being merely an equitable interest.' Those words are almost identical with s. 2(3)(iii) of the Law of Property Act 1925, and should be given the same meaning. They must be read in conjunction with s. 1(2)(a), s. 1(3) and s. 4(1) of the Law of Property Act, 1925. It then appears that an 'equitable easement' is a proprietary interest in land such as would before 1926 have been recognised as capable of being conveyed or created *at law*, but which since 1926 only takes effect as an equitable interest. An instance of such a proprietary interest is a profit à prendre for life. It does not include a right to possession by a requisitioning authority: see *Lewisham Borough Council* v *Maloney* [1948] 1 KB 50. Nor does it include a right, liberty or privilege arising in equity by reason of 'mutual benefit and burden', or arising out of 'acquiescence', or by reason of a contractual licence: because none of those before 1926 were proprietary interests such as were capable of being conveyed or created *at law*. They only subsisted *in equity*. They do not need to be registered as land charges, so as to bind successors, but take effect in equity without registration: see an article by Mr C.V. Davidge on 'Equitable Easements' in (1937) 53 LQR 259, and by Professor H.W.R. Wade in [1956] *Cambridge Law Journal*, pp. 225–226).

The right of [the defendant] to cross this yard was not a right such as could ever have been created or conveyed at law. It subsisted only in equity. It therefore still subsists in equity without being registered. Any other view would enable the owners of the flats to perpetrate the grossest injustice. They could block up [the defendant's] access to the garage, whilst keeping their foundations in his land. That cannot be right.

I am confirmed in this construction of the statute when I remember that there are many houses adjoining one another which have drainage systems in common, with mutual benefits and burdens. The statute cannot have required all these to be registered as land charges.

I know that this greatly restricts the scope of Class D (iii) but this is not disturbing. A special committee has already suggested that Class D (iii) should be abolished altogether: see the report of the Committee on Land Charges ((1956) Cmnd. 9825, para. 16). . . .

DANCKWERTS LJ:. . . It is necessary, in connection with Mr High's case, to consider the effect of the Land Charges Act 1925, and s. 199 of the Law of Property Act 1925. The effect of the provisions of the Land Charges Act 1925 . . . is to make [the defendant's] right of way, so far as it ought to have been registered as an estate contract or an equitable easement, either void or unenforceable, and s. 199 of the Law of Property Act, 1925, prevents express notice of [the defendant's] rights being effective in any way, though the plaintiffs bought subject to the right of way and had the most positive notice of it.

But that is not the end of the matter. There is another equitable ground on which [the defendant's] rights may be protected, which has nothing whatever to do with the Land Charges Act. It is discussed in Snell's Equity, 26th ed. (1966), pp. 629–633, under the name 'proprietary estoppel', and the comment is made (p. 633) that 'the doctrine thus displays equity at its most flexible'. There are two aspects in which this equitable principle applies in the present case. First, in the present case [the defendant], in reliance on the arrangement made with Mr Westgate, allowed the encroaching foundations to remain on his land and built his house without proper access except over the yard, and finally built his garage in such a way that it was useless unless access to it and from it could be had over the yard. Mr Westgate acquiesced in the use of the yard for access, and the Wrights stood by and, indeed, encouraged [the defendant] to build his garage in these conditions and for these purposes. Could anything be more monstrous and inequitable afterwards to deprive [the defendant] of the benefit of what he has done?

Secondly, the Wrights had continued to enjoy the benefit of the encroaching foundations on [the defendant's] land. It would no doubt be quite an expensive job to remove the encroaching foundations and provide other support for the building. Equity does not allow a person who takes advantage of such a situation to deny to the other party the corresponding benefits which were the consideration for allowing the foundations to remain.

The plaintiffs bought the property subject to [the defendant's] equitable rights and the property was so conveyed to them. They had full knowledge of the situation, yet they continue to enjoy the benefits of the situation and wish to deny to [the defendant] the benefit of what he was induced to do in reliance on the mutual arrangement. As long as the plaintiffs continue to enjoy the foundations, they must accept the terms of that enjoyment.

This is not a registrable charge, and s. 199 of the Law of Property Act, 1925, has no application.

Notes

1. There was a second ground for the decision, based on the mutual benefit and burden doctrine expounded in *Halsall* v *Brizell* [1957] Ch 169.

2. The very narrow interpretation of Class D (iii) taken by Lord Denning MR was not adopted by the other two judges, although all agreed that this did not come within Class D (iii).

3. The decision was approved by the House of Lords in *Shiloh Spinners* v *Harding* [1973] AC 691. Responding to an argument that a right of entry must be included somewhere within the Land Charges Act, Lord Wilberforce said (at pp. 720–721):

This, in my opinion, only becomes compelling if one first accepts the conclusion that all equitable claims relating to land are either registrable under the Land Charges Act, or capable of being overreached under s. 2 of the Law of Property Act, i.e., are capable by use of the appropriate mechanism of being transferred to the proceeds of sale of the land they affect. If this dilemma could be made good, then there could be an argument for forcing, within the limits of the possible, an equitable right of entry into one of the registrable classes, since it is obviously not suitable for overreaching. But the dilemma cannot be made good. . . . I am impressed by the decision in *E. R. Ives Investments* v *High* [1967] 2 QB 379 in which the Court of Appeal held that a right by estoppel – producing an effect similar to an easement – was not registrable under Class D (iii). Lord Denning MR referred to the right as subsisting only in equity. Danckwerts LJ thought it was an equity created by estoppel or a proprietary estoppel: plainly this was not an equitable interest capable of being overreached, yet no member of the court considered that the right – so like an easement – could be brought within Class D (iii). The conclusion followed, and the court accepted it, that whether it was binding on a purchaser depended on notice. All this seems to show that there may well be rights, of an equitable character, outside the provisions as to registration and which are incapable of being overreached.

(b)   The regime of the Land Registration Act

The Land Registration Act avoids the pitfalls of listing the interests within it, and so is not open to an interpretation similar to that in the above cases. However, there are authorities importing a good faith requirement into the statute. This may lead to a return to a doctrine similar to that of the bona fide purchaser: see, e.g., *Peffer* v *Rigg* [1977] 1 WLR 285 (below); *Lyus* v *Prowsa Developments* [1982] 1 WLR 1044 (chapter 11). If so, then the net effect of the registration provisions will be greatly reduced where, though an interest has not been entered on the appropriate register, the purchaser nevertheless knows about it.

Peffer v *Rigg*
[1977] 1 WLR 285
Chancery Division

Facts: A house was purchased in the defendant's name but held on trust for plaintiff and defendant as tenants in common in equal shares. But the defendant transferred the house to his wife as part of a divorce agreement. The wife claimed to take free of P's interest, although she knew of it, because it was unregistered under the Land Registration Act 1925. She claimed to be a transferee for valuable consideration under s. 20(1) of that Act, which makes no reference either to any good faith requirement, or to notice.

Held: Graham J held that the wife was only protected under s. 20 if she was a purchaser as defined in s. 3. A purchaser is defined in s. 3(xxi) as being purchaser for good faith. In Graham J's view, this means a purchaser without notice.

GRAHAM J (after considering an argument that there was only nominal consideration for the transfer): . . . If, however, the proper view is that there was valuable consideration for the transfer, then it is argued as follows. . . . Section 20(1) protects any 'transferee' for valuable consideration. . . . It is to be noted, however, that s. 20, though it mentions valuable consideration, does not mention 'good faith' as being necessary on the part of the transferee, nor does it mention notice. It can be argued therefore that s. 20 seems to be saying that a transferee whether he has good faith or not and whether he has notice or not, takes free of all interests (other than overriding interests) provided he has given valuable consideration.

This at first sight seems a remarkable proposition and though undoubtedly the property legislation of 1925 was intended to simplify such matters of title as far as possible, I find it difficult to think that s. 20 of the Land Registration Act 1925 can have been intended to be as broad in scope as this. . . . By definition, however (see s. 3(xxi)), ' "Purchaser" means a purchaser in good faith for valuable consideration . . .' It seems clear therefore that as a matter of construction a purchaser who is not in fact one 'in good faith' will be concerned with matters not protected by a caution or other entry on the register, at any rate, as I hold, if he has notice thereof. . . . [The] transferee spoken of in s. 20 is in fact a 'purchaser' he will only be protected if he had given valuable consideration and is in good faith. He cannot in my judgment be in good faith if he has in fact notice of something which affects his title as in the present case. Of course if he and, *a fortiori*, if a purchaser from him has given valuable consideration and in fact has no notice he is under no obligation to go behind the register, and will in such a case be fully protected. . . .

C: Trusts for Sale; Overreaching

Full equitable estates in land are treated differently by the 1925 legislation. In the case of land held concurrently (i.e., shared), the Law of Property Act 1925 requires that it be held on a statutory trust for sale, and the interests of the co-owners thus become beneficial interests under a trust for sale. A detailed consideration of trusts for sale is beyond the scope of this book, but it should be noted that their purpose in this context is simply as a conveyancing device; in other words, the theoretical intention to sell is for all practical purposes merely a legal fiction.

The main effect is that on sale the interests of those with concurrent interests cease to be interests in land and become interests in the purchase money only. Indeed, for some purposes their interests become interests in the money only even before the sale takes place. A purchaser is thus enabled to 'overreach' them. This means that he is relieved from having to inquire of them so long as he pays the purchase money to at least two trustees (and obtains a receipt from them), because they take effect as interests in the purchase money only, rather than in the land itself. Thus the beneficiaries are protected by being able to take a share of the purchase money, and the purchaser is not concerned with their interests. A large proportion of matrimonial and co-habited property is now held in this manner, and it goes without saying, of course, that the bona fide purchaser doctrine is no longer relevant to this situation.

D: Settled Land

The purpose of the settled land legislation, which culminated in the Settled Land Act 1925, was to ensure that land was freely alienable. Commonly, land used to be settled for generations in families, which prevented it from being freely alienable, and as we shall see caused other difficulties.

The policy of the legislation was by no means new in 1925, but originated in the earlier Settled Land Acts 1882–90. Indeed, the main purpose of the 1925 legislation was merely to facilitate conveyancing.

The essence of the problem was that large, rural aristocratic estates were tied up, by means of the strict settlement, in such a way that nobody could sell them or develop them. There was some sense in this up to the Reform Act 1832, because the political power of a family depended partly upon its continued ownership of such estates. During the last century, however, the practice of settling estates in this way became a nuisance. It became more profitable in many cases to develop the land industrially, whereas on the other hand, agricultural prices became depressed. The families themselves suffered, as did workers and their families living on their land, because estates that could be neither sold nor developed became impoverished, and were allowed to decay. The general community also suffered while land continued to be inextricably tied to outdated purposes.

The strict settlement consisted in its barest essentials of a life interest followed by an entail (let us say to A for life then B in tail male). This is not the obvious way of settling land, but was the best that could be devised given the law as it then was. A succession of life interests, stretching indefinitely into the future (e.g., to A for life, then B for life, then B's as yet unborn eldest son for life, then his eldest son for life), would have infringed the rule against perpetuities, so the settlement typically ended in an entailed interest for the last living generation. Entails can be barred, however, so in order that the settlement was not defeated it was important to ensure that nobody with an entailed interest ever came into possession of the land. This is because a tenant in tail not in possession can create only a base fee (which is worthless), whereas a tenant in tail in possession can create a fee simple, enabling him to sell the land and defeat the settlement. The same applies even to a tenant in tail not in possession so long as the tenant in possession consents.

In the ordinary course of events, however, B would come into possession at A's death, so it was necessary to ensure that he no longer had an entailed interest at that time. This was achieved by a re-settlement when B came of age, before A died. For a financial inducement (usually an immediate income, secured by rentcharge on the land), B would be persuaded to bar the entail with A's consent, creating a fee simple, but A's consent would be conditional on B re-settling the land for a further generation. So B would now have only a life interest, and his eldest son would become tenant in tail. This would continue every generation, ensuring the land remained tied up in perpetuity.

Not only was the land thereby rendered unsaleable, but the tenant in possession was always a life tenant, and it was for this reason that it became impossible even to develop the land, with the undesirable consequences referred to above. The powers of life tenants are severely limited, and in the worst cases the doctrine of waste would prevent the cutting down of trees, mining, building or other commercial activity. Further, life tenants cannot normally mortgage or lease the land. Hence as agricultural prices depressed, life tenants could not (unless given express powers by the settlement) develop the land to take advantage of the increasing profitably of industrial user.

The 1882–90 legislation therefore gave extensive powers, including sale, to the tenant for life in possession, whatever the provisions of the settlement. In other words, since 1882 it has been impossible to tie up land indefinitely by means of the strict settlement. If the land was sold, all interests in it (i.e., future interests, and the life interest of the tenant for life himself) were overreached by purchasers, in much the same way as with concurrent interests described below, so long as the purchase money was paid to trustees of the settlement. One method by which the purchase money might be split would be to allow the life tenant to take the interest on it for his life, the capital sum being retained to compensate for the sale of the future interests.

The 1925 legislation continues the policy of that of 1882–90, but also gives the legal estate in fee simple to the life tenant in possession. This is a device to simplify conveyancing. It also ensures that somebody has the legal estate, because in most pre–1925 settlements nobody had the fee simple absolute in possession: usually there was a life interest followed by an entail. In accord with the policy of the 1925 legislation, these estates can now exist only in equity; so somebody had to be given the fee simple absolute in possession, otherwise nobody could have a legal estate in the land at all!

The following sections of the Settled Land Act 1925 will be relevant to the discussion in chapter 11.

Settled Land Act 1925

1. What constitutes a settlement

(1) Any deed, will, agreement for a settlement or other agreement, Act of Parliament, or other instrument, or any number of instruments, whether made or passed before or after, or partly before and partly after, the commencement of this Act, under or by virtue of which instrument or instruments any land, after the commencement of this Act, stands for the time being —

    (i)   limited in trust for any persons by way of succession; or

    (ii) limited in trust for any person in possession —

    (a) for an entailed interest whether or not capable of being barred or defeated;

    (b) for an estate in fee simple or for a term of years absolute subject to an executory limitation, gift, or disposition over on failure of his issue or in any other event;

    (c) for a base or determinable fee or any corresponding interest in leasehold land;

    (d) being an infant, for an estate in fee simple or for a term of years absolute; or

    (iii) limited in trust for any person for an estate in fee simple or for a term of years absolute contingently on the happening of any event; or

(iv)   . . .

(v)   charged, whether voluntarily or in consideration of marriage or by way of family arrangement, and whether immediately or after an interval, with the payment of any rentcharge for the life of any person, or any less period, or of any capital, annual, or periodical sums for the portions, advancement, maintenance, or otherwise for the benefit of any persons, with or without any term of years for securing or raising the same; creates or is for the purposes of this Act a settlement and is in this Act referred to as a settlement, or as the settlement, as the case requires;

Provided that, where land is the subject of a compound settlement, references in this Act to the settlement shall be construed as meaning such compound settlement, unless the context otherwise requires.

(2)   Where an infant is beneficially entitled to land for an estate in fee simple or for a term of years absolute and by reason of an intestacy or otherwise there is no instrument under which the interest of the infant arises or is acquired, a settlement shall be deemed to have been made by the intestate, or by the person whose interest the infant has acquired.

(3)   An infant shall be deemed to be entitled in possession notwithstanding any subsisting right of dower (not assigned by metes and bounds) affecting the land, and such a right of dower shall be deemed to be an interest comprised in the subject of the settlement and coming to the dowress under or by virtue of the settlement.

Where dower has been assigned by metes and bounds, the letters of administration or probate granted in respect of the estate of the husband of the dowress shall be deemed a settlement made by the husband.

(4)   An estate or interest not disposed of by a settlement and remaining in or reverting to the settlor, or any person deriving title under him, is for the purposes of this Act an estate or interest comprised in the subject of the settlement and coming to the settlor or such person under or by virtue of the settlement.

(5)   Where —

(a)   a settlement creates an entailed interest which is incapable of being barred or defeated, or a base or determinable fee, whether or not the reversion or right of reverter is in the Crown, or any corresponding interest in leasehold land; or

(b)   the subject of a settlement is an entailed interest, or a base or determinable fee, whether or not the reversion or right of reverter is in the Crown, or any corresponding interest in leasehold land;

the reversion or right of reverter upon the cesser of the interest so created or settled shall be deemed to be an interest comprised in the subject of the settlement, and limited by the settlement.

(6)   Subsection (4) and (5) of this section bind the Crown.

(7)   This section does not apply to land held upon trust for sale.

Note

Section (1)(1)(iv) was repealed by the Married Women (Restraint upon Anticipation) Act 1949, s. 1(4), and Sch. 2.

Settled Land Act 1925

18.   Restrictions on dispositions of settled land where trustees have not been discharged

(1)   Where land is the subject of a vesting instrument and the trustees of the settlement have not been discharged under this Act, then —

(a)   any disposition by the tenant for life or statutory owner of the land, other than a disposition authorised by this Act or any other statute, or made in pursuance of any additional or larger powers mentioned in the vesting instrument, shall be void, except for the purpose of conveying or creating such equitable interests as he has power, in right of his equitable interests and powers under the trust instrument, to convey or create; and

(b)   if any capital money is payable in respect of a transaction, a conveyance to a purchaser of the land shall only take effect under this Act if the capital money is paid to or by the direction of the trustees of the settlement or into court; and

(c)   notwithstanding anything to the contrary in the vesting instrument, or the trust instrument, capital money shall not, except where the trustee is a trust corporation, be paid to or by the direction of fewer persons than two as trustees of the settlement.

(2)   The restrictions imposed by this section do not affect —

(a)   the right of a personal representative in whom the settled land may be vested to convey or deal with the land for the purposes of administration;

(b)   the right of a person of full age who has become absolutely entitled (whether beneficially or as trustee for sale or personal representative or otherwise) to the settled land, free from all limitations, powers, and charges taking effect under the trust instrument, to require the land to be conveyed to him;

(c)   the power of the tenant for life, statutory owner, or personal representative in whom the settled land is vested to transfer or create such legal estates, to take effect in priority to the settlement, as may be required for giving effect to any obligations imposed on him by statute, but where any capital money is raised or received in respect of the transaction the money shall be paid to or by the direction of the trustees of the settlement or in accordance with an order of the court.

Law of Property Act 1925

130.   Creation of entailed interests in real and personal property

(1)   An interest in tail male or in tail female or in tail special (in this Act referred to as 'an entailed interest') may be created by way of trust in any property, real or personal, but only by the like expressions as those by which before the commencement of this Act a similar estate tail could have been created by deed (not being an executory instrument) in freehold land, and with the like results, including the right to bar the entail either absolutely or so as to create an interest equivalent to a base fee, and accordingly all statutory provisions relating to estates tail in real property shall apply to entailed interests in personal property.

Personal estate so entailed (not being chattels settled as heirlooms) may be invested, applied, and otherwise dealt with as if the same were capital money or securities representing capital money arising under the Settled Land Act 1925, from land settled on the like trusts.

E: Overview of the 1925 Legislation

Professor R.H. Maudsley, 'Bona Fide Purchasers of Registered Land' (1973) 36 MLR 25

There are few who fail to admire the overall success of the 1925 property legislation. However, some problems have recently arisen which, if not fully appreciated and dealt with, may cause great confusion in the present system of registered conveyancing.

. . .

The context is that of the competition between a bona fide purchaser of a legal estate for value without notice and the owner of an equitable interest. This competition is as old as trusts themselves. Unaided by statute, equity's answer was clear and simple; though difficult in application, of course, in practice. An equitable interest was valid against all the world, except for the bona fide purchaser of a legal estate for value without notice actual, constructive or imputed. The onus was on the purchaser to establish himself as such; and it was a heavy burden to discharge [Professor Maudsley notes the decision of *Pilcher* v *Rawlins* (1872) 7 Ch App 259].
. . .

Many of the defects of the old system of conveyancing were due to the fact that if there were equitable interests affecting the land a purchaser was bound by them; both beneficial interests under settlements and also by legal and certain equitable incumbrances. The task was to develop a system which was fair to a purchaser in the sense that he was able to purchase a fee simple free from any beneficial interests which affected it, and that he knew about any interests or incumbrances subject to which he would take; and fair to the beneficiary in that his interest was not at risk of destruction on a sale to a purchaser. The system which developed through the Settled Land Acts 1882–1925 and the Land Charges Act 1925 [now Land Charges Act 1972] is that, generally speaking, those interest or incumbrances which prejudicially affect a purchaser are overreachable or registrable. Beneficial interests are, by and large, overreachable. The purchaser, following the procedure of the Settled Land Act 1925, takes free of them whether or not he has notice of them. To do this, he must pay all the moneys upon the same trusts as the land was held. This is fair to the purchaser in that he takes free of the beneficiaries' interests; and fair to the beneficiaries in that each one has exactly the same interest in exactly the same amount as he had before. It is merely the nature of the investment that has changed. Equitable interests which were not overreachable were to be registered under the Land Charges Act 1925. [Professor Maudsley then described *Shiloh Spinners Ltd* v *Harding* in the Court of Appeal [1972] Ch 326, where Russell LJ, in accordance with the principle set out, was unwilling to find that an equitable interest was neither overreachable nor registrable. The decision was, however, later reversed by the House of Lords, see above.]

However, it is an over-simplification to present the situation as if all interests and incumbrances were either overreachable or registrable. Some, for various reasons, do not fit into either category. The question whether a purchaser is bound by such an incumbrance is determined, in the case of unregistered land, by the old rules of constructive notice, including the rule in *Hunt* v *Luck* [1902] 1 Ch 428, which lays down that a purchaser is bound by the interest of a person in actual occupation of the land. . . . In considering whether or not a purchaser *ought* to be bound in such circumstances, it is essential to appreciate that, in order to make a system of conveyancing work, a purchaser must be allowed to say that, having made all the inquiries required of him by the system, he may take a good title. The system cannot work if he is to be tripped up by a number of interests and incumbrances which he could by no means discover. The 1925 legislation and, one would have thought, *a fortiori* the Land Registration Act 1925[13], were intended to protect the interests of a purchaser who observes the system laid down. The legislation should be construed with this principle in mind.

Notes

1. At this point footnote 13 reads: 'The Law Commission however says (Working Paper No. 37, para. 4) that "it was never contemplated, under the

registration system as we know it, that all interests in land would be recorded on the register . . . the register was intended as a substitute for title deeds and nothing more." '

2.   The article then goes on to consider cases where the principle enunciated by Professor Maudsley breaks down. The first such case was *Weston v Henshaw* [1950] Ch 510, where a mortgagee of settled land, believing that the mortgagor was an unencumbered fee simple owner, did not pay the capital sum to trustees of the settlement, and Danckwerts J held that the mortgages, not being dispositions authorised by the Settled Land Act 1925, were void under s. 18(1)(a) of that Act. Professor Maudsley then referred to *Caunce v Caunce* [1969] 1 WLR 286, where a house intended as a matrimonial home was conveyed to the husband in fee simple. The mortgagee did not therefore know that it was held on statutory trust for sale, and did not obtain a receipt from two trustees, which would have been required to overreach the wife's interest. The old equitable notice rules were applied, but although in the case the mortgagee was held not to have had notice, this will not be the normal result: see *Kingsnorth Finance Co. Ltd v Tizard* [1986] 1 WLR 783, where *Caunce v Caunce* was not followed.

3.   The main theme of Maudsley's article is however the then recent Court of Appeal decision in *Hodgson v Marks* [1971] Ch 892 (see chapters 9 and 11), where a purchaser without notice was bound by virtue of s. 70(1)(g) of the Land Registration Act 1925. Since Maudsley's article, *Hodgson v Marks* has been approved by the House of Lords in *Williams & Glyn's Bank Ltd v Boland* [1981] AC 487, where *Caunce v Caunce* was also criticised: see also Meryl Thomas, *Casebook on Land Law* (Blackstone Press, 1992), at p. 11.

4.   It is clear, therefore, that the principle enunciated by Professor Maudsley (surely an eminently sensible principle from the conveyancer's viewpoint) has not been wholly achieved by the 1925 property legislation.

2 TRUSTS DISTINGUISHED FROM SIMILAR COMMON LAW CONCEPTS

SECTION 1: TRUST AND BAILMENT

The division of ownership, and the nature of the enforcement, serve to distinguish the trust from other concepts with which trusts share common factors. For example, possession of personal property is often separated from ownership of the property, as in common law bailment, for example hiring or hire purchase, but both legal and equitable ownership remain in the bailor or hirer; so the relationship of the bailee to the property is quite different from that of a trustee, who is the legal owner.

To some extent this is manifested in differences in the duties of bailees and trustees – those of bailees are beyond the scope of this book, while those of trustees are considered in chapters 15 to 18. Additionally, the position of third parties is different. If a bailee sells the goods, where this is unauthorised by the terms of the bailment, then unless the buyer can benefit from the provisions of the Factors Act 1889, ss. 2, 8 and 9, or the Sale of Goods Act 1979, ss. 21–26, he gets no title, even if he acts in good faith and has no notice of the existence of the bailment. This is because a bailee has no title, legal or equitable, to sell, so a purchaser from him gets neither legal nor equitable title.

If on the other hand a trustee sells goods in breach of trust, the buyer obtains legal title from the trustee, and is bound by any equitable title and interests only if he is unable to show that he is a bona fide purchaser for value without the knowledge requirement discussed in chapter 1. If he is a bona fide purchaser, etc., he obtains legal title unencumbered by equitable interests.

A: Statutory Exceptions to the Principle that Legal Title Binds the Whole World

Factors Act 1889

2. Powers of mercantile agent with respect to disposition of goods

(1) Where a mercantile agent is, with the consent of the owner, in possession of goods or of the documents of title to goods, any sale, pledge, or other disposition of the goods, made by him when acting in the ordinary course of business of a mercantile agent, shall, subject to the provisions of this Act, be as valid as if he were expressly authorised by the owner of the goods to make the same; provided that the person taking under the disposition acts in good faith, and has not at the time of the disposition notice that the person making the disposition has not authority to make the same.

(2) Where a mercantile agent has, with the consent of the owner, been in possession of goods or of the documents of title to goods, any sale, pledge, or other disposition, which would have been valid if the consent had continued, shall be valid notwithstanding the determination of the consent: provided that the person taking under the disposition has not at the time thereof notice that the consent has been determined.

(3) Where a mercantile agent has obtained possession of any documents of title to goods by reason of his being or having been, with the consent of the owner, in possession of the goods represented thereby, or of any other documents of title to the goods, his possession of the first-mentioned documents shall, for the purposes of this Act, be deemed to be with the consent of the owner.

(4) For the purposes of this Act the consent of the owner shall be presumed in the absence of evidence to the contrary.

8. Disposition by seller remaining in possession

Where a person, having sold goods, continues, or is, in possession of the goods or of the documents of title to the goods, the delivery or transfer by that person, or by a mercantile agent acting for him, of the goods or documents of title under any sale, pledge or other disposition thereof, or under any agreement for sale, pledge or other disposition thereof, to any person receiving the same in good faith and without notice of the previous sale, shall have the same effect as if the person making the delivery or transfer were expressly authorized by the owner of the goods to make the same.

9. Disposition by buyer remaining in possession

Where a person, having bought or agreed to buy goods, obtains with the consent of the seller possession of the goods or the documents of title to the goods, the delivery or transfer, by that person or by a mercantile agent acting for him, of the goods or the documents of title under any sale, pledge or other disposition thereof, or under any agreement for sale, pledge or other disposition thereof, to any person receiving the same in good faith and without notice of any lien or other right of the original seller in respect of the goods, shall have the same effect as if the person making the delivery or transfer were a mercantile agent in possession of the goods or documents of title with the consent of the owner.

For the purposes of this section —

(i) the buyer under a conditional sale agreement shall be deemed not to be a person who has bought or agreed to buy goods, and

(ii) 'conditional sale agreement' means an agreement for the sale of goods which is a consumer credit agreement within the meaning of the Consumer Credit Act 1974 under which the purchase price or part of it is payable by instalments, and the property in the goods is to remain in the seller (notwithstanding that the buyer is to be in possession of the goods) until such conditions as to the payment of instalments or otherwise as may be specified in the agreement are fulfilled.

Sale of Goods Act 1979

21. Sale by person not the owner

(1)   Subject to this Act, where goods are sold by a person who is not their owner, and who does not sell them under the authority or with the consent of the owner, the buyer acquires no better title to the goods than the seller had, unless the owner of the goods is by his conduct precluded from denying the seller's authority to sell.

(2)   Nothing in this Act affects —

(a)   The provisions of the Factors Acts, or any enactment enabling the apparent owner of the goods to dispose of them as if he were their true owner.

(b)   The validity of any contract of sale under any special common law or statutory power of sale, or under the order of a court of competent jurisdiction.

22. Market overt

(1)   Where goods are sold in market overt, according to the usage of the market, the buyer acquires a good title to the goods, provided he buys them in good faith and without notice of any defect or want of title on the part of the seller.

(2)   This section does not apply to Scotland.

(3)   Paragraph 8 of Schedule 1 below applies in relation to a contract under which goods were sold before 1 January 1968 or (in the application of this Act to Northern Ireland) 29 August 1967.

23. Sale under voidable title

Where the seller of goods has a voidable title to them, but his title has not been avoided at the time of the sale, the buyer acquires a good title to the goods, provided he buys them in good faith and without notice of the seller's defect of title.

24. Seller in possession after sale

Where a person, having sold goods, continues, or is, in possession of the goods or of the documents of title to the goods, the delivery or transfer by that person, or by a mercantile agent acting for him, of the goods or documents of title under any sale, pledge or other disposition thereof, to any person receiving the same in good faith and without notice of the previous sale, shall have the same effect as if the person making the delivery or transfer were expressly authorized by the owner of the goods to make the same.

25. Buyer in possession after sale

(1)   Where a person, having bought or agreed to buy goods, obtains with the consent of the seller possession of the goods or the documents of title to the goods, the delivery or transfer, by that person or by a mercantile agent acting for him, of the goods or the documents of title under any sale, pledge or other disposition thereof, to any person receiving the same in good faith and without notice of any lien or other right of the original seller in respect of the goods, shall have the same effect as if the person making the delivery or transfer were a mercantile agent in possession of the goods or documents of title with the consent of the owner.

(2)   For the purposes of subsection (1) above —

(a)   the buyer under a conditional sale agreement shall be deemed not to be a person who has bought or agreed to buy goods, and

(b) 'conditional sale agreement' means an agreement for the sale of goods which is a consumer credit agreement within the meaning of the Consumer Credit Act 1974 under which the purchase price or part of it is payable by instalments, and the property in the goods is to remain in the seller (notwithstanding that the buyer is to be in possession of the goods) until such conditions as to the payment of instalments or otherwise as may be specified in the agreement are fulfilled.

(3) Paragraph 9 of Schedule 1 below applies in relation to a contract under which a person buys or agrees to buy goods and which is made before the appointed day.

(4) In subsection (3) above and paragraph 9 of Schedule 1 below references to the appointed day are to the day appointed for the purposes of these provisions by an order of the Secretary of State made by statutory instrument.

26. Supplementary to sections 24 and 25
In sections 24 and 25 above 'mercantile agent' means a mercantile agent having in the customary course of his business as such agent authority either —

    (a)   to sell goods, or
    (b)   to consign goods for the purpose of sale, or
    (c)   to buy goods, or
    (d)   to raise money on the security of goods.

B: Co-existence of Trust and Bailment

Lloyds Bank v Bank of America National Trust and Savings Association
[1938] 2 KB 147
Court of Appeal

Facts: Lloyds Bank, who had advanced money on the security of shipping documents, released the shipping documents to the pledgor 'in order to enable the company to sell the merchandise as trustees for the plaintiffs'. The purpose was to enable the pledgor to sell the goods, in order to reimburse the bank. The pledgor thus became trustee of the goods for the bank, and was also in possession of the goods as mercantile agent for the bank. Note that the pledgor had general legal title to the goods, to which the bank had equitable title because of the terms of release of the shipping documents, but the bank also had special legal property as pledgees.

The pledgor did not sell the goods, but fraudulently transferred the bills of lading to the Bank of America, thereby raising further money on the goods. He then absconded with this money, without reimbursing Lloyds Bank.

Held: The pledgor was able to pass good title to the Bank of America, Lloyds Bank losing its special legal title, because of the application of the Factors Act 1889, s. 2(1). Lloyds Bank was regarded as owner for these purposes, and the pledgor was therefore a mercantile agent within the meaning of the section (even though he also had a property interest in the goods). Lloyds Bank was also unable to assert equitable title in the goods because the Bank of America were *bona fide* purchasers for value without notice of that title.

Note
Lloyds Bank probably retained equitable title in the sum raised on the second loan, but of course this was not traceable.

SECTION 2: TRUST AND CONTRACT

If A transfers to B property to hold on trust for X, only X and not A can enforce the trust against B, because A, as settlor, retains no interest in the property. This is so whether or not X has given any consideration, because he is in effect the recipient of a gift. So it is only the third party to the arrangement who can enforce it, and a gift once made cannot be revoked.

While a third party (X) can benefit from a contract, on the other hand, he or she generally cannot enforce it, by virtue of the privity of contract doctrine. Nor is the arrangement irrevocable. A and B can consensually vary the contract to deny X his or her benefit. Suppose, for example, A contracts with B, that in consideration of a payment by A to B of a sum of money, B pays X a sum of money, for example an annuity for his (X's) life, but no trust is constituted. Assume also that X does not provide consideration for this benefit, and is not party to the arrangement. X is therefore unable to enforce the contract in his own right. If B breaks the contract only A can enforce it, but there may be remedies problems.

A: Specific Performance by A

Beswick v *Beswick*
[1968] AC 58
House of Lords

A coal merchant (Peter Beswick), who was over 70 years old, transferred his business to his nephew who in return agreed, among other things, that he would, after his uncle's death, pay £5 a week to his uncle's widow. Peter Beswick died about 18 months later and his widow became his administratrix. She sued to enforce the contract.

Held: She was unable to sue in her own right, but could sue as administratrix of estate (i.e., stepping into the shoes of her dead husband, and suing on his contract). She was also able to obtain specific performance.

LORD REID: . . . For clarity I think it best to begin by considering a simple case where, in consideration of a sale by A to B, B agrees to pay the price of £1,000 to a third party X. . . .

. . . It was not argued that the law of England regards B's obligation as a nullity, and I have not observed in any of the authorities any suggestion that it would be a nullity. . . . So this obligation of B must be enforceable either by X or by A. . . .

Lord Denning's view, expressed in this case not for the first time, is that X could enforce this obligation. But the view more commonly held in recent times has been that such a contract confers no right on X and that X could not sue for the £1,000. . . . [For] the purposes of this case I shall proceed on the footing that the commonly accepted view is right.

What then is A's position? I assume that A has not made himself a trustee for X, because it was not argued in this appeal that any trust had been created. So, if X has no right, A can at any time grant a discharge to B or make some new contract with B. If there were a trust the position would be different. X would have an equitable right and A would be entitled and, indeed, bound to recover the money and account for it to X. And A would have no right to grant a discharge to B. . . .

The argument for the appellant is that A's only remedy is to sue B for damages for B's breach of contract in failing to pay the £1,000 to X. Then the appellant says that A can only recover nominal damages of 40s. because the fact that X has not received the money will generally cause no loss to A: he admits that there may be cases where A would suffer damage if X did not receive the money but says that the present is not such a case.

. . . I shall assume that he is right in maintaining that the administratrix could then only recover nominal damages because his breach of contract has caused no loss to the estate of her deceased husband.

If that were the only remedy available the result would be grossly unjust. It would mean that the appellant keeps the business which he bought and for which he has only paid a small part of the price which he agreed to pay. He would avoid paying the rest of the price, the annuity to the respondent, by paying a mere 40s. damages. . . .

LORD PEARCE: . . . It is argued that the estate can only recover nominal damages and that no other remedy is open, either to the estate or to the personal plaintiff. Such a result would be wholly repugnant to justice and commonsense. And if the argument were right it would show a very serious defect in the law.

In the first place, I do not accept the view that damages must be nominal. Lush LJ in *Lloyd's* v *Harper* (1880) 16 ChD 290, 321 (CA) [see further below] said:

> Then the next question which, no doubt, is a very important and substantial one, is, that Lloyd's, having sustained no damages themselves, could not recover for the losses sustained by third parties by reason of the default of Robert Henry Harper as an underwriter. That, to my mind, is a startling and alarming doctrine, and a novelty, because I consider it to be an established rule of law that where a contract is made with A for the benefit of B, A can sue on the contract for the benefit of B, and recover all that B could have recovered if the contract had been made with B himself.

(See also *Drimmie* v *Davies* [1899] 1 Ir R 176.) I agree with the comment of Windeyer J in the case of *Coulls* v *Bagot's Executor and Trustee Co. Ltd* (1967) 40 ALJR 471, 486 that the words of Lush LJ cannot be accepted without qualification and regardless of context and also with his statement:

> I can see no reason why in such cases the damages which A would suffer upon B's breach of his contract to pay C $500 would be merely nominal: I think that in accordance with the ordinary rules for the assessment of damages for breach of contract they would be substantial. They would not necessarily be $500; they could I think be less or more.

In the present case I think that damages, if assessed, must be substantial. It is not necessary, however, to consider the amount of damages more closely since this is a case in which, as the Court of Appeal rightly decided, the more appropriate remedy is that of specific performance.

The administratrix is entitled, if she so prefers, to enforce the agreement rather than accept its repudiation, and specific performance is more convenient than an action for arrears of payment followed by separate actions as each sum falls due. Moreover, damages for breach would be a less appropriate remedy since the parties to the agreement were intending an annuity for a widow; and a lump sum of damages does not accord with this. And if (contrary to my view) the argument that a derisory sum of damages is all that can be obtained be right, the remedy of damages in this case is manifestly useless.

The present case presents all the features which led the equity courts to apply their remedy of specific performance. The contract was for the sale of a business. The defendant could on his part clearly have obtained specific performance of it if Beswick senior or his administratrix had defaulted. Mutuality is a ground in favour of specific performance.

Moreover, the defendant on his side has received the whole benefit of the contract and it is a matter of conscience for the court to see that he now performs his part of it. . . .

LORD UPJOHN: . . . On [the damages] question we were referred to the well-known dictum of Lush LJ in *Lloyd's* v *Harper* [Lord Upjohn referred to the passage quoted above and continued: . . .] While in the circumstances it is not necessary to express any concluded opinion thereon, if the learned Lord Justice was expressing a view on the purely common law remedy of damages, I have some difficulty in going all the way with him. If A sues for damages for breach of contract by reason of the failure to pay B he must prove his loss; that may be great or nominal according to circumstances.

I do not see how A can, in conformity with clearly settled principle in assessing damages for breach of contract, rely at common law on B's loss. I agree with the observations of Windeyer J in the as yet unreported case of *Coulls* v *Bagot's Executor and Trustee Co. Ltd* (1967) 40 ALJR 471 in the High Court of Australia. But I note, however, that in *Lloyd's* v *Harper* James and Cotton LJJ treated A as trustee for B and I doubt whether Lush LJ thought otherwise.

However, I incline to the view that on the facts of this case damages are nominal for it appears that A died without any assets save and except the agreement which he hoped would keep him and his widow for their lives. At all events let me assume that damages are nominal. So it is said nominal damages are adequate and the remedy of specific performance ought not to be granted. That is, with respect, wholly to misunderstand that principle. Equity will grant specific performance when damages are inadequate to meet the justice of the case.

But in any event the quantum of damages seldom affects the right to specific performance. If X contracts with Y to buy Blackacre or a rare chattel for a fancy price because the property or chattel has caught his fancy he is entitled to enforce his bargain and it matters not that he could not prove any damage.

In this case the court ought to grant a specific performance order all the more because damages *are* nominal. C has received all the property; justice demands that he pay the price and this can only be done in the circumstances by equitable relief. It is a fallacy to suppose that B is obtaining any additional rights; A1 is entitled to compel C to carry out the terms of the agreement. . . .

Notes

1. The House of Lords restated the privity of contract doctrine. Their Lordships do not adopt a consistent lettering policy, so let us assume that A makes a contract with B under which B agrees to pay a sum of money to X. In general, assuming no trust, X will be without remedy. This is consistent with the privity of contract doctrine and with the principle expressed in the next chapter: 'Equity will not assist a volunteer'.

2. In the particular case Peter Beswick (as A) could have enforced the contract had he been alive.

3. Mrs Beswick's claim (as A) depended on her taking out letters of administration to the estate. If A dies, in general A's personal representatives will be able to enforce the contract on A's behalf. But a third party, X, cannot force them to do so, or sue B directly. Had Mrs Beswick not herself been personal representative, therefore, she could not have forced anyone else to sue on her behalf.

4. It was essential that Mrs Beswick could obtain specific performance, in her capacity as A, to ensure that (in her capacity as X) she obtained the benefit that has been bargained for. But this is not the general position. It probably depended upon:

(a)   the fact that B had actually received all the consideration (the transfer of the goodwill in A's business);

(b)   the mutuality requirement being satisfied, that is to say that the same contract would also have been specifically enforceable by B. This was the case in *Beswick*, because A had promised to transfer the goodwill of a business, but would not be, for example, where the consideration moving from A is money alone.

The nature of the payment (annuity) may also be relevant, but probably not decisive.

It should be noted, however, that Lord Upjohn thought that the mere fact that damages would be nominal would be an additional ground for awarding specific performance. That may well always apply in cases of this type (i.e., third-party contract cases). However, some contracts are never enforceable by an order of specific performance, for example if B had agreed to perform a personal service for X.

5. If A cannot obtain specific performance, if B does not perform the bargain at all, then A can get the property back on the ground of a total failure of consideration. This may be of no benefit to X, of course, unless A now makes another similar arrangement. No good for Mrs Beswick, of course.

6. If B has partially performed the bargain, A cannot obtain specific performance, he is forced to rely on contractual damages. But personally he has suffered no loss, so what are the damages? In *Beswick* v *Beswick* only Lord Pearce thought that damages would be substantial. Apart from the above passages, Lord Hodson (at 81E) also appears to accept that only nominal damages could be recovered, and Lord Guest (at 83F) agreed with Lord Reid. It is now reasonably clear that Lord Pearce's views are wrong.

B: Damages Claim by A

Lloyd's v *Harper*
(1880) 16 ChD 290
Court of Appeal

Facts: A father agreed with Lloyd's (prior to their incorporation) to act as guarantor for his son, who was an underwriting member of Lloyd's (underwriting marine insurance policies). A guarantee was required before the son could be accepted as an underwriter, in accordance with Lloyd's practice. On the son's later bankruptcy, Lloyd's attempted to enforce the guarantee on behalf of the insured property owners.

Held: The Court of Appeal took the view that the father's guarantee contract with Lloyd's was made by Lloyd's acting as trustees of the benefit of the guarantee for the property owners. On the son's bankruptcy, the father's estate was liable on the guarantee, which could be enforced by Lloyd's on behalf of those who were insured under the marine insurance policies.

Notes
1. The insured property owners were not party to the guarantee contract. Hence they were in the position of X above. Lloyd's were in the position of A and the father was in the position of B.
2. The point of interest for present purposes is that Lloyd's as contracting parties were able to obtain substantial damages, but this depended on them having contracted as trustees. Note that although the views of Lush LJ quoted in *Beswick* v *Beswick* have been disapproved (see below), the case has been accepted as authority where A contracts as trustee. Note also that the trust is of the contract not the property itself. The arrangement was not that Lloyd's would become trustees of any tangible property, and it was never envisaged that any property should be transferred to Lloyd's for them to hold on trust for others.
3. In *Lloyd's* v *Harper*, Lloyd's contracted as trustees from the start, and all parties were at all times aware of the nature of the arrangement. It must be assumed (although it has never been clearly held) that the authority is limited to this situation. Otherwise A who had originally contracted otherwise than as trustee could by the later unilateral act of declaring himself trustee of the promise affect B's damages liability. As long as A was not trustee of the promise B's liability would be limited to nominal damages, whereas once A had declared himself trustee of the promise B would become liable to substantial damages. This cannot possibly be correct.
4. Similar reasoning can be found in *The Flore* [1919] AC 801, where time charterers sued the owners for brokers' commission due under the charterparty. The brokers were not themselves party to the charterparty, but the charterers sued as trustees for them and recovered substantial damages on their behalf.

Woodar Investment Developments Ltd v *Wimpey Construction (UK) Ltd*
[1980] 1 WLR 277, [1980] 1 All ER 571
House of Lords

Decision (Lord Salmon and Lord Russell of Killowen dissenting on the repudiation issue): A condition of a contract for the sale of land required the purchasers to pay £150,000 to a third party. On the main issue, which was whether the purchasers had validly repudiated the contract, a majority of the House held that they had not. The vendors were therefore not entitled to sue the purchasers for wrongful repudiation. On the secondary issue of damages, which therefore did not arise for decision, all their Lordships agreed that damages for breach of this term would be nominal.

LORD WILBERFORCE: . . . The second issue in this appeal is one of damages. Both courts below have allowed Woodar to recover substantial damages in respect of condition I under which £150,000 was payable by Wimpey to Transworld Trade Ltd on completion. On the view which I take of the repudiation issue, this question does not require decision, but in view of the unsatisfactory state in which the law would be if the Court of Appeal's decision were to stand I must add three observations.

1. The majority of the Court of Appeal followed, in the case of Goff LJ with expressed reluctance, its previous decision in *Jackson* v *Horizon Holidays Ltd* [1975] 3 All ER 92, [1975] 1 WLR 1468. I am not prepared to dissent from the actual decision in that case. It may be supported either as a broad decision on the measure of damages (per James LJ) or possibly as an example of a type of contract, examples of which are persons contracting for family holidays, ordering meals in restaurants for a party, hiring a taxi for a group, calling for special treatment. As I suggested in *New Zealand Shipping Co. Ltd* v *A. M. Satterthwaite & Co. Ltd* [1974] 1 All ER 1015 at 1020, [1975] AC 154 at 167, there are many situations of daily life which do not fit neatly into conceptual analysis, but which require some flexibility in the law of contract. Jackson's case [1975] 3 All ER 92, [1975] 1 WLR 1468 may well be one.

I cannot agree with the basis on which Lord Denning MR put his decision in that case. The extract on which he relied from the judgment of Lush LJ in *Lloyd's* v *Harper* (1880) 16 ChD 290 at 321 was part of a passage in which Lush LJ was stating as an 'established rule of law' that an agent (sc an insurance broker) may sue on a contract made by him on behalf of the principal (sc the assured) if the contract gives him such a right, and is no authority for the proposition required in *Jackson's case* [1975] 3 All ER 92, [1975] 1 WLR 1468, still less for the proposition, required here, that, if Woodar made a contract for a sum of money to be paid to Transworld, Woodar can, without showing that it has itself suffered loss or that Woodar was agent or trustee for Transworld, sue for damages for non-payment of that sum. That would certainly not be an established rule of law, nor was it quoted as such authority by Lord Pearce in *Beswick* v *Beswick* [1967] 2 All ER 1197, [1968] AC 58.

2. Assuming that *Jackson's* case was correctly decided (as above), it does not carry the present case, where the factual situation is quite different. I respectfully think therefore that the Court of Appeal need not, and should not have followed it.

3. Whether in a situation such as the present, *viz* where it is not shown that Woodar was agent or trustee for Transworld, or that Woodar itself sustained any loss, Woodar can recover any damages at all, or any but nominal damages, against Wimpey, and on what principle, is, in my opinion, a question of great doubt and difficulty, no doubt open in this House, but one on which I prefer to reserve my opinion. . . .

LORD SALMON: . . . The Court of Appeal by a majority affirmed Fox J's decision on liability but reduced the damages to £272,943.

My Lords, for the reasons I have stated, I would dismiss the appeal on the issue of liability. Since, as I understand, the majority of your Lordships are for allowing the appeal on liability, the interesting question in relation to damages in respect of the claim for £150,000 does not now arise. I do, however, agree with what my noble and learned friend Lord Wilberforce has said about the finding of the majority of the Court of Appeal (Goff LJ with reluctance) on this topic. I would add that, in my opinion, the law as it stands at present in relation to damages of this kind is most unsatisfactory; and I can only hope that your Lordships' House will soon have an opportunity of reconsidering it unless in the meantime it is altered by statute.

LORD RUSSELL OF KILLOWEN: . . . There is no question on this appeal as to quantum of damage save under the heading of damages for breach of special condition I, under which Wimpey agreed on completion of the sale to pay £150,000 to Transworld, a Hong Kong company. Transworld was in some way connected with Mr Cornwell, who died before action. No evidence connects Transworld with Woodar, the party to the contract. No evidence suggests that Woodar could suffer any damage from a failure by Wimpey to pay £150,000 to Transworld. It is clear on the authority of *Beswick* v *Beswick* [1967] 2 All ER 1197, [1968] AC 58 that Woodar on completion could have secured an order for specific performance of the agreement to pay £150,000 to Transworld, which the latter could have enforced. That would not have been an order for payment to Woodar, nor (contrary to the form of order below) to Woodar for the use and benefit of Transworld. There was no suggestion of trust or agency of Woodar for Transworld. If it were necessary to decide the point, which in the light of the views of the majority of your Lordships on the first point it is not, I would have concluded that no more than nominal damages had been established by Woodar as a consequence of the refusal by Wimpey to pay Transworld in the light of the law of England as it now stands. I would not have thought that the reasoning of Oliver J in *Radford* v *De Froberville* [1978] 1 All ER 33, [1977] 1 WLR 1262 supported Woodar's case for substantial damages. Nor do I think that on this point the Court of Appeal was correct in thinking it was constrained by *Jackson* v *Horizon Holidays Ltd* [1975] 3 All ER 92, [1975] 1 WLR 1468 to award substantial damages. I do not criticize the outcome of that case: the plaintiff had bought and paid for a high class family holiday; he did not get it, and therefore he was entitled to substantial damages for the failure to supply him with one. It is to be observed that the order of the Court of Appeal as drawn up did not suggest that any part of the damages awarded to him were 'for the use and benefit of' any member of his family. It was a special case quite different from the instant case on the Transworld point.

I would not, my Lords, wish to leave the *Jackson* case without adverting with respectful disapproval to the reliance there placed by Lord Denning MR, not for the first time, on an extract taken from the judgment of Lush LJ in *Lloyd's* v *Harper* (1860) 16 ChD 290. That case was plainly a case in which a trustee or agent was enforcing the rights of a beneficiary or principal, there being therefore a fiduciary relationship. Lord Denning MR in *Jackson's* case said this:

> The case comes within the principle stated by Lush LJ in *Lloyd's* v *Harper*: '. . . I consider it to be an established rule of law that where a contract is made with A for the benefit of B, A can sue on the contract for the benefit of B and recover all that B could have recovered if the contract had been made with B himself'. [Lord Denning continued:] It has been suggested that Lush LJ was thinking of a contract in which A was trustee for B. But I do not think so. He was a common lawyer speaking of the common law.

I have already indicated that in all the other judgments the matter proceeded on a fiduciary relationship between A and B; and Lush LJ in the same passage made it plain that he did also, for he said [16 ChD 290 at 321]:

> It is true that the person [B] who employed him [the broker A] has a right, if he pleases, to take action himself and sue upon the contract made by the broker for him, for he [B] *is a principal party to the contract*. (Emphasis mine.)

To ignore that passage is to divorce the passage quoted by Lord Denning MR from the fiduciary context in which it was uttered, the context of principal and agent, a field with which it may be assumed Lush LJ was familiar. I venture to suggest that the brief quotation should not be used again as support for a proposition which Lush LJ cannot have intended to advance.

In summary therefore, in disagreement with the majority of your Lordships, I would have dismissed this appeal on repudiation. Had I been correct I would, as at present advised, have allowed the appeal on the Transworld point, and awarded only nominal damages on that point to Woodar, and not substantial damages to be paid to Woodar 'for the use and benefit of' Transworld, a form of order which I cannot see was justified.

LORD KEITH OF KINKEL: . . . In the circumstances the issue regarding Woodar's right to damages in respect of alleged breach of Wimpey's obligation under the contract to pay £150,000 to Transworld does not arise for decision. It is desirable, however, that I should express my agreement with my noble and learned friend Lord Wilberforce that the decision in favour of Woodar on this issue, arrived at by the majority of the Court of Appeal, was not capable of being supported by *Jackson* v *Horizon Holidays Ltd* [1975] 3 All ER 92, [1975] 1 WLR 1468. That case is capable of being regarded as rightly decided on a reasonable view of the measure of damages due to the plaintiff as the original contracting party, and not as laying down any rule of law regarding the recovery of damages for the benefit of third parties. There may be a certain class of cases where third parties stand to gain indirectly by virtue of a contract, and where their deprivation of that gain can properly be regarded as no more than a consequence of the loss suffered by one of the contracting parties. In that situation there may be no question of the third parties having any claim to damages in their own right, but yet it may be proper to take into account in assessing the damages recoverable by the contracting party an element in respect of expense incurred by him in replacing by other means benefits of which the third parties have been deprived or in mitigating the consequences of that deprivation. The decision in *Jackson* v *Horizon Holidays Ltd* is not, however, in my opinion, capable of being supported on the basis of the true *ratio decidendi* in *Lloyd's* v *Harper* (1880) 16 ChD 290, which rested entirely on the principles of agency.

I would also associate myself with the observations of my noble and learned friend Lord Scarman as to the desirability of this House having an opportunity of reviewing, in some appropriate future case, the general attitude of English law towards the topic of *jus quaesitum tertio*.

My Lords, I would allow the appeal.

LORD SCARMAN: . . . It being the view of the majority of the House that there was no repudiation, the appeal must be allowed, with the result that there is no need to consider the other issues raised. But, because of its importance, I propose to say a few words on the question of damages.

Woodar agreed to sell the land to Wimpey for £85,000. They also required Wimpey to pay £150,000 to a third party. The covenant for this payment was in the following terms: 'I. Upon completion of the purchase of the whole or any part of the land the purchaser shall pay to Transworld Trade Limited of 25 Jermyn Street, London, SW1 a sum of £150,000.' No relationship of trust or agency was proved to exist between Woodar and Transworld. No doubt, it suited Mr Cornwell to split up the moneys payable under the contract between the two companies; but it is not known, let alone established by evidence (though an intelligent guess is possible) why he did so, or why

Woodar desired this money to be paid to Transworld. It is simply a case of B agreeing with A to pay a sum of money to C.

B, in breach of his contract with A, has failed to pay C. C, it is said, has no remedy, because the English law of contract recognises no '*jus quaesitum tertio*': see *Tweddle* v *Atkinson* (1861) 1 B & S 393, [1861–73] All ER Rep 369. No doubt, it was for this reason that Transworld was not a party to the suit. A, it is acknowledged, could in certain circumstances obtain specific performance of the promise to pay C: see *Beswick* v *Beswick* [1967] 2 All ER 1197, [1968] AC 58. But, since the contract in the present case is admitted (for reasons which do not fall to be considered by the House) to be no longer in existence, specific performance is not available. A's remedy lies only in an award of damages to himself. It is submitted that, in the absence of any evidence that A has suffered loss by reason of B's failure to pay C, A is only entitled to nominal damages.

I wish to add nothing to what your Lordships have already said about the authorities which the Court of Appeal cited as leading to the conclusion that Woodar is entitled to substantial damages for Wimpey's failure to pay Transworld. I agree that they do not support the conclusion. But I regret that this House has not yet found the opportunity to reconsider the two rules which effectually prevent A or C recovering that which B, for value, has agreed to provide.

First, the jus quaesitum tertio. I respectfully agree with Lord Reid that the denial by English law of a jus quaesitum tertio calls for reconsideration. In *Beswick* v *Beswick*, Lord Reid, after referring to the Law Revision Committee's recommendation (Sixth Interim Report (1937) Cmd 5449, p. 31) that the third party should be able to enforce a contractual promise taken by another for his benefit, observed: 'If one had to contemplate a further long period of Parliamentary procrastination, this House might find it necessary to deal with this matter.' The committee reported in 1937; *Beswick* v *Beswick* was decided in 1967. It is now 1979; but nothing has been done. If the opportunity arises, I hope the House will reconsider *Tweddle* v *Atkinson* and the other cases which stand guard over this unjust rule.

Likewise, I believe it open to the House to declare that, in the absence of evidence to show that he has suffered no loss, A, who has contracted for a payment to be made to C, may rely on the fact that he required the payment to be made as *prima facie* evidence that the promise for which he contracted was a benefit to him and that the measure of his loss in the event of non-payment is the benefit which he intended for C but which has not been received. Whatever the reason, he must have desired the payment to be made to C and he must have been relying on B to make it. If B fails to make the payment, A must find the money from other funds if he is to confer the benefit which he sought by his contract to confer on C. Without expressing a final opinion on a question which is clearly difficult, I think the point is one which does require consideration by your Lordships' House.

Certainly the crude proposition for which Wimpey contends, namely that the state of English law is such that neither C for whom the benefit was intended nor A who contracted for it can recover it if the contract is terminated by B's refusal to perform, calls for review, and now, not 40 years on.

Notes

1. This case makes it clear that where A contracts with B that A will confer a benefit on X, B can only obtain nominal damages in the event of A's breach.
2. *Lloyd's* v *Harper* was clearly limited to trust or agency situations. Lush LJ's wider view (if it was a wider view) is wrong. So is the view of Lord

Denning MR (but not the decision) in *Jackson* v *Horizon Holidays Ltd* [1975] 1 WLR 1468.

3. Some judicial dissatisfaction was expressed with law, in particular by Lords Salmon, Keith and Scarman.

C: A Contracting as Trustee

It is clear from the above discussion that whether A contracts as trustee of the promise is an issue of some importance. This will not lightly be inferred. The evidential requirement is high, and it seems that a clear intention to create an irrevocable trust benefiting the third party must be shown.

Re Schebsman
[1944] Ch 83
Court of Appeal

Facts: Schebsman had entered into an agreement with his ex-employers whereby they agreed (by way of compensation for Schebsman's loss of employment) to pay money to Schebsman's wife and daughter. Schebsman was adjudicated bankrupt just under two years later, and died soon after.

The trustee in bankruptcy claimed all the sums which remained payable to Schebsman's wife and daughter as part of Schebsman's estate. He argued that either he was entitled to intercept them, or alternatively that the provision for them constituted a voluntary settlement, which could be avoided under the Bankruptcy Act 1914, s. 42(1), because his bankruptcy fell within two years of his making it.

Schebsman's wife and daughter argued that they were beneficiaries under a trust (of Schebsman's chose in action).

Held: The Court of Appeal held that Schebsman had not contracted as trustee. In spite of there being no trust in their favour, however, the wife and daughter still prevailed over the trustee in bankruptcy. The rights of the trustee in bankruptcy were no greater than those of Schebsman himself (had he still been alive). Although Schebsman could no doubt by fresh agreement with his ex-employer deprive his wife and daughter of their benefits under the arrangement, he could not do so unilaterally without being in breach of contract. The same restriction applied also to the trustee in bankruptcy.

LORD GREENE MR: . . . The first question which arises is whether or not the debtor was a trustee for his wife and daughter of the benefit of the undertaking given by the English company in their favour. An examination of the decided cases does, it is true, show that the courts have on occasions adopted what may be called a liberal view on questions of this character, but in the present case I cannot find in the contract anything to justify the conclusion that a trust was intended. It is not legitimate to import into the contract the idea of a trust when the parties have given no indication that such was their intention. To interpret this contract as creating a trust would, in my judgment, be to disregard the dividing line between the case of a trust and the simple case of a contract made between two persons for the benefit of a third. That dividing line exists, although it may not always be easy to determine where it is to be drawn. In the present case I find no difficulty. . . .

DU PARCQ LJ: . . . It now remains to consider the question whether, and if so to what extent, the principles of equity affect the position of the parties. It was argued by Mr Denning that one effect of the agreement . . . was that a trust was thereby created, and that the debtor constituted himself trustee for Mrs Schebsman of the benefit of the covenant under which payments were to be made to her. Uthwatt J rejected this contention, and the argument has not satisfied me that he was wrong. It is true that, by the use possibly of unguarded language, a person may create a trust, as Monsieur Jourdain talked prose, without knowing it, but unless an intention to create a trust is clearly to be collected from the language used and the circumstances of the case, I think that the court ought not to be astute to discover indications of such an intention. I have little doubt that in the present case both parties (and certainly the debtor) intended to keep alive their common law right to vary consensually the terms of the obligation undertaken by the company, and if circumstances had changed in the debtor's lifetime injustice might have been done by holding that a trust had been created and that those terms were accordingly unalterable. . . .

Notes
1. It is clear from the above passage that Du Parcq LJ thought the crucial consideration to be that no *irrevocable* arrangement had been agreed. The point has already been made that contracts are revocable by consensual agreement between the contracting parties, whereas a trust is in principle irrevocable. One should not lightly infer an intention irrevocably to be bound.
2. This case was approved in *Beswick* v *Beswick* (above).

Questions
1. Whose intention should be relevant? A's, B's, X's, or a combination of two or more of these?
2. Would it be correct to say that, in *Lloyd's* v *Harper*, the trust was being used as a device to avoid the privity of contract doctrine?
3. Would *Lloyd's* v *Harper* be decided the same way today?

SECTION 3: TRUSTS AND LOANS

When you lend money to a friend or business partner, or deposit money in a bank account, your friend, business partner or bank becomes a debtor, not a trustee, and you become a creditor, not a beneficiary. It should be clear from the above that a debtor will be in a very different position from a trustee. A debtor's liability to repay a loan is contractual, and therefore strict, subject to the terms of the loan. In other words, it does not require proof of negligence or bad faith. It is not avoided, for example, by the theft by a third person either of the money loaned, or of any property purchased with the money, however innocent the debtor may be. On the other hand the property the creditor has loaned passes to the debtor, so if the debtor goes bankrupt, the creditor takes his place as one among many unsecured creditors, and is unlikely to see the return of any or all his money.

A trustee's duties are less strict (see chapters 14–16), but in the event of a trustee's bankruptcy a beneficiary is in the position of a secured creditor, because he has retained equitable property which will be protected from the claims of the general creditors. In effect, the property never becomes part of the debtor's estate.

Both legal and equitable obligations can co-exist, however, so that a loan can also constitute a trust. Thus, a creditor can also be a beneficiary, and this protects him in the event of the debtor's bankruptcy.

A: *Quistclose* Trusts – The General Principle

Barclays Bank Ltd v *Quistclose Investments Ltd*
[1970] AC 567
House of Lords

Facts: Rolls Razor Ltd were in serious financial difficulties, and had an overdraft with Barclays Bank of some £484,000 against a permitted limit of £250,000. If Rolls Razor were to stay in business, it was essential for them to obtain a loan of around £210,000 in order to pay dividends which they had declared on their ordinary shares, and which in the absence of such a loan they were unable to pay. They succeeded in obtaining the loan from Quistclose Investments Ltd (who were planning to loan Rolls Razor £1 million if they remained in business), who agreed to make the loan on the condition 'that it is used to pay the forthcoming dividend due on July 24, next'. The sum was paid into a special account with Barclays Bank, on the condition (agreed with the bank) that the account would 'only be used to meet the dividend due on July 24, 1964'.

Rolls Razor went into voluntary liquidation on 27 August, without having paid the dividend. Barclays wanted to count the money in the special account against Rolls Razor's overdraft.

Held: The House of Lords (upholding the decision of the Court of Appeal) held that Barclays held the money on trust for Quistclose, so that Quistclose was able to claim back the entire sum.

HARMAN LJ (in the Court of Appeal [1968] 1 Ch 540): . . . The money was deposited with the respondent bank, and accepted on the footing that it should only be used for payment of the dividend. That purpose was, however, frustrated by the liquidation of Rolls Razor on the following August 27 before the dividend had been paid, thus making its payment illegal.

LORD WILBERFORCE: . . . The mutual intention of the respondents [Quistclose] and of Rolls Razor Ltd, and the essence of the bargain, was that the sum advanced should not become part of the assets of Rolls Razor Ltd, but should be used exclusively for payment of a particular class of creditors, namely, those entitled to the dividend. A necessary consequence of this, simply by process of interpretation, must be that, if for any reason, the dividend could not be paid, the money was to be returned to the respondents: the word 'only' or 'exclusively' can have no other meaning or effect.

That arrangements of this character for the payment of a person's creditors by a third person, give rise to a relationship of a fiduciary character or trust, in favour, as a primary trust, of the creditors, and secondarily, if the primary trust fails, of the third person, has been recognised in a series of cases over some 150 years.

. . .

The second, and main, argument for the appellant was of a more sophisticated character. The transaction, it was said, between the respondents and Rolls Razor Ltd was one of loan, giving rise to a legal action of debt. This necessarily excluded the implication of any trust, enforceable in equity, in the respondent's favour: a transaction may attract one action or the other, it could not admit of both.

My Lords, I must say that I find this argument unattractive. Let us see what it involves. It means that the law does not permit an arrangement by which one person agrees to advance money to another, on terms that the money is to be used exclusively to pay the debts of the latter, and if, and so far as not so used, rather than becoming a general asset of the latter available to his creditors at large, is to be returned to the lender. The lender is obliged, in such a case, because he is a lender, to accept, whatever the mutual wishes of lender and borrower may be, that the money he was willing to make available for one purpose only shall be freely available for others of the borrower's creditors for whom he has not the slightest desire to provide.

I should be surprised if an argument of this kind – so conceptualist in character – had ever been accepted. In truth it has plainly been rejected by the eminent judges who from 1819 onwards have permitted arrangements of this type to be enforced, and have approved them as being for the benefit of creditors and all concerned. There is surely no difficulty in recognising the co-existence in one transaction of legal and equitable rights and remedies: when the money is advanced, the lender acquires an equitable right to see that it is applied for the primary designated purpose . . . if the primary purpose cannot be carried out, the question arises if a secondary purpose (i.e., repayment to the lender) has been agreed, expressly or by implication: if it has, the remedies of equity may be invoked to give effect to it, if it has not (and the money is intended to fall within the general fund of the debtor's assets) then there is the appropriate remedy for recovery of a loan. I can appreciate no reason why the flexible interplay of law and equity cannot let in these practical arrangements, and other variations if desired: it would be to the discredit of both systems if they could not. In the present case the intention to create a secondary trust for the benefit of the lender, to arise if the primary trust, to pay the dividend, could not be carried out, is clear and I can find no reason why the law should not give effect to it.

Note

Lord Wilberforce went on to hold that the bank was bound by the trust because it had notice of it.

B: Money Must be for Specific Purpose

In *Quistclose*, the money was to be used for a specific purpose, that purpose was known to the recipient, and the money was paid into a special account, which could be used for no other purpose. The last requirement, for a special account, may not be absolutely rigid, but at the very least the money must be earmarked for the particular purpose *and no other*, in order to negative the inference that the payments are to be included in the general assets of the company. The passage above makes it clear that payments are made on the basis that they are to be included in the company's assets.

The setting up of a special fund negates the inference that the payments are to be included in the company's assets, but so long as that inference is negated, it may be that a special fund is not absolutely necessary. See, for example, *Re EVTR* (below), where there was no special fund. The reality is, however, that *Quistclose* trusts are used when the trustee is in liquidation. Merely to have a personal action against the trustee is therefore useless; it is essential for the lender to be able to point to a fund of money held by the trustee and say 'that money is my property'. To be able to do this it is necessary to be able to identify the money, and this is clearly easiest where the money has been paid into a special account. It is not essential, however, so long as the money can be traced on the principles discussed in chapter 17. In *Re Kayford Ltd* [1975] 1 WLR 279 (see chapter 3), where it was held that a trust fund had been set up for customers of an insolvent company, Megarry J did not think it fatal that the money had been mixed with small amounts of other money. The case was not decided on *Quistclose* principles, but it was essential to be able to establish that the money belonged in equity to the customers; a personal action against the company would have availed them nothing. The money in *Kayford* was clearly traceable, however, so there was no problem even though there were other small sums in the account.

C: Enforcement of *Quistclose* Trusts

The reasoning in the above passage, that there is a primary trust in favour of the creditors and, if the primary trust fails, a secondary trust in favour of the provider of the funds, suggests that the creditors can enforce the primary trust as beneficiaries, and that the provider of the funds can enforce the secondary trust, as in *Quistclose* itself. The position may not be quite as simple as this, however. In the passage below, we are asked to consider the following question:

A lends a sum of money to B for the specific purpose of enabling him to pay his (B's) creditors or a particular class of them, and for no other purpose. Can the creditors or any of them (C) compel B to apply the money in payment of debts owing to them? Or can A change his mind, release B from the obligation to apply the money only for the specified purpose, and either demand repayment or allow B to spend the money as he chooses for his own purposes? And where, pending its application by B, is the beneficial interest in the money?

P. J. Millett, QC, 'The Quistclose Trust: Who can enforce it?' (1985) 101 LQR 269, at 275–6

It was assumed without argument in the *Quistclose* case that the primary trust for the payment of the dividend to B's shareholders failed when B went into creditors' voluntary liquidation, but . . . it is far from clear why this should be so. The declaration of a dividend by resolution of the shareholders creates an immediate debt in their favour [Millett notes as authority *Re Severn and Wye and Severn Bridge Railway Co.* [1896] 1 Ch 559]. If the loan by A created a trust, and not a mere power, to discharge this debt, then it vested in the shareholders an immediate right in equity to the money in the dividend account, and there is no good reason why their right to the money should be affected by the subsequent liquidation of B. [Millett notes: 'They were not even joined as parties. If they were indeed the beneficiaries under the primary trust, it is extraordinary that they should have been given no opportunity to argue that the trust in their favour had not failed.'] In the *Northern Developments* case, Megarry V-C attempted an explanation: once the winding-up had commenced, he said, section 212(1)(g) of the Companies Act 1948, prevented the payment of the dividend in competition with other creditors, and so in the circumstances no trust for the payment of the dividend could be carried out. With respect, this is a *non sequitur*. Section 212 . . . prevents the liquidator from applying the assets of the company in payment of a debt due to a member, in his character of a member, until the debts due to other creditors have been paid in full; but it does no more than this. It does not prevent a trustee from paying trust money, which *ex hypothesi* does not belong to the company, to the persons beneficially entitled thereto. . . .

Questions
1. Is the analysis of Harman LJ as to why the primary trust had failed correct? Note that it was not adopted by the other judges in the Court of Appeal, nor by Lord Wilberforce in the House of Lords.
2. If (as suggested by Millett) it was not illegal to pay the dividends in *Quistclose*, is there any other way of reaching the conclusion that the primary trust in *Quistclose* had failed?
3. If the primary trust in *Quistclose* had failed, consider the following situation:

> A is an eccentric millionaire who delights in the name Mondeo, and is very pleased, now that Ford have produced a car by that name, that the streets are going to be full of cars called Mondeo. Suppose also that in a few years time, A believes (rightly or wrongly) that Ford is in financial difficulty, and that if they do not pay their dividends due on 1 July, their backers will pull out and there will be no more Mondeos. He therefore pays Ford £5 million for the specific purpose of paying the dividends due on 1 July. On 30 June, Ford (which is actually in a position to, and fully intends to pay the dividends) drops the Mondeo from its range of cars.

Has the primary trust failed?

Carreras Rothmans v *Freeman Mathews Treasure Ltd (in liq.)*
[1985] Ch 207, [1985] 1 All ER 155
Chancery Division

Facts: The plaintiff (cigarette manufacturer) engaged the defendant advertising agency. The defendant got into financial difficulties, but needed funds to pay its production agencies and advertising media, if it was to carry on acting for the plaintiff. The plaintiff accordingly paid a monthly sum into a special account at the defendant's bank, the money to be used for the sole purpose of paying off the agency and media creditors. The defendant later went into liquidation.

Held: The money in the special account was held for the plaintiff on a resulting trust, since it had been paid for a specific purpose. Accordingly, since the plaintiff was beneficial owner of the money in the account, the money was not part of the defendant's assets, to be distributed among the general body of creditors. The reasoning in *Barclays Bank Ltd* v *Quistclose Investments Ltd* [1970] AC 567 was adopted, and was stated to apply generally where property was transferred for a specific purpose only, and not for the recipient's own purposes. If the purpose was not carried out, equity fastened on the conscience of the recipient, and did not allow the recipient to treat the property as his own, or to use it for any other purpose.

PETER GIBSON J: There is of course ample authority that moneys paid by A to B for a specific purpose which has been made known to B are clothed with a trust. In the *Quistclose* case [1970] AC 567 at 580, Lord Wilberforce referred to the recognition, in a series of cases over some 150 years, that arrangements for the payment of a person's creditors by a third person gives rise to 'a relationship of a fiduciary character or trust, in favour, as a primary trust, of the creditors. and secondarily, if the primary trust fails, of the third person'. Lord Wilberforce in describing the facts of the *Quistclose* case said a little earlier that the mutual intention of the provider of the moneys and of the recipient of the moneys, and the essence of the bargain, was that the moneys should not become part of the assets of the recipient but should be used exclusively for payment of a particular class of its creditors. That description seems to me to be apt in relation to the facts of the present case too.

Counsel for FMT and the liquidator sought to distinguish the *Quistclose* case in this way. He submitted that for any trust one needed (i) a settlor conveying property to a trustee or declaring a trust of property in his own hands, (ii) trust property and (iii) a beneficiary. He said that in the *Quistclose* case the settlor was the provider of the moneys, who did so by way of loan. In the present case, he submitted, the settlor was not CR but FMT, to which CR owed a debt to reimburse FMT for the June debts owed to the third parties and he pointed out that CR made no claim that there was a trust of the book debt. In the *Quistclose* case [1970] AC 567 at 581, Lord Wilberforce, in rejecting an argument that the lender only had contractual rights in a transaction of loan, said:

> There is surely no difficulty in recognising the co-existence in one transaction of legal and equitable rights and remedies: when the money is advanced, the lender acquires an equitable right to see that it is applied for the primary designated purpose.

Counsel for FMT and the liquidator submitted that there was no recognition in the *Quistclose* case that anyone else had an enforceable right and that in particular a person in the position of CR discharging a debt had no right to enforce any trust.

It is of course true that there are factual differences between the *Quistclose* case and the present case. The transaction there was one of loan with no contractual obligations on the part of the lender to make payment prior to the agreement for the loan. In the present case there is no loan but there is an antecedent debt owed by CR. I doubt if it is helpful to analyse the *Quistclose* type of case in terms of the constituent parts of a conventional settlement, though it may of course be crucial to ascertain in whose favour the secondary trust operates (as in the *Quistclose* case itself) and who has an enforceable right. In my judgment the principle in all these cases is that equity fastens on the conscience of the person who receives from another property transferred for a specific purpose only and not therefore for the recipient's own purposes, so that such person will not be permitted to treat the property as his own or to use it for other than the stated purpose. Most of the cases in this line are cases where there has been an agreement for consideration, so that in one sense each party has contributed to providing the property. But, if the common intention is that property is transferred for a specific purpose and not so as to become the property of the transferee, the transferee cannot keep the property if for any reason that purpose cannot be fulfilled. I am left in no doubt that the provider of the moneys in the present case was CR. True it is that its own witnesses said that if FMT had not agreed to the terms of the contract letter CR would not have broken its contract but would have paid its debt to FMT, but the fact remains that CR made its payment on the terms of that letter and FMT received the moneys only for the stipulated purpose. That purpose was expressed to relate only to the moneys in the account. In my judgment therefore CR can be equated with the lender in the *Quistclose* case as having an enforceable right to compel the carrying out of the primary trust.

Counsel for FMT and the liquidator also submitted that the third party creditors had no enforceable right and that where the beneficiaries under the primary trust have no enforceable right no trust is created. Counsel for CR also submitted that the third party creditors had no enforceable rights. . . . In none of the many reported cases in the *Quistclose* line of cases, so far as I am aware, had any consideration been given to the question of whether the person intended to benefit from the carrying out of the specific purpose which created the trust has enforceable rights. Thus the existence of enforceable rights in such persons has not been treated as crucial to the existence of a trust. Further, in the one case which so far as I am aware the question who, in addition to the provider of the property, had enforceable rights was determined by the court, it was held that the persons intended to benefit from the carrying out of the primary trust did have enforceable rights. That case is the unreported decision on 6 October 1978 of Sir Robert Megarry V-C in *Re Northern Developments (Holdings) Ltd*. In that case the eponymous company (Northern) was the parent company of a group of companies including one (Kelly) which was in financial straits. Seventeen banks agreed to put up a fund in excess of half a million pounds in an attempt to rescue Kelly. The banks already had other companies in the group as customers. They paid the moneys into an account in Northern's name for the express purpose of providing moneys for Kelly's unsecured creditors and for no other purpose, the amounts advanced being treated as advances to the banks' other customers in the group. The fund was used to sustain Kelly for a time, but then Kelly was put into receivership at a time when a little over half the fund remained unexpended. One of the questions for the court was who was entitled to that balance. The Vice-Chancellor held that there was a *Quistclose* type of trust attaching to the fund, that trust was a purpose trust but enforceable by identifiable individuals, namely the banks as lenders, Kelly, for whose immediate benefit the fund was established, and Kelly's creditors. The reason given by the Vice-Chancellor for holding that Kelly's creditors had enforceable rights were the words of Lord Wilberforce in the *Quistclose* case [at [1970] AC at 580, [1968] 3 All ER at 654] which I have already cited, describing the *Quistclose* type of trust as giving rise to a relationship of a fiduciary character or trust in favour of the creditors. However, the Vice-Chancellor went on to describe the interests of the creditors in this way:

> The fund was established not with the object of vesting the beneficial interest in them but in order to confer a benefit on Kelly (and so consequentially on the rest of the group and the bankers) by ensuring that Kelly's creditors would be paid in an orderly manner. There is perhaps some parallel in the position of a beneficiary entitled to a share of residue under a will. What he has is not a beneficial interest in any asset forming part of residue, but a right to compel the executor to administer the assets of the deceased properly. It seems to me that it is that sort of right which the creditors of Kelly had.

The interest of the banks was held to be under the secondary trust if the primary trust failed. In the light of that authority I cannot accept the joint submission that the third party creditors for the payment of whose debts CR had paid the moneys into the special account had no enforceable rights. In any event I do not comprehend how a trust which on no footing could CR revoke unilaterally and which was expressed as a trust to pay third parties and was still capable of performance could nevertheless leave the beneficial interest in CR which had parted with the moneys. On the Vice-Chancellor's analysis the beneficial interest is in suspense until the payment is made.

Note
Peter Gibson J went on, however, to say that in his view the third party creditors must have had enforceable rights, since that inevitably followed from the conclusion that Carreras Rothmans had created a fully constituted trust to pay them.

Questions
1. Were CR enforcing the primary or secondary trust?
2. The result in *Carreras Rothmans* was that CR obtained an order to pay the third party creditors. If the creditors were indeed beneficiaries under a trust, why could CR enforce that trust? Is the answer that they had taken assignments of the third party debts against FMT? What is the value of a debt against a company in liquidation?
3. Why did not CR simply sue for the return of the money, arguing that the primary trust had failed, and pay it to the third party media advertisers themselves?

P. J. Millett, QC, 'The Quistclose Trust: Who can enforce it?' (1985) 101 LQR 269, at 290–91

. . . The answer to the question raised at the beginning of this article depends on A's intention, to be collected from the language used, the conduct of the parties, and the circumstances of the case. The following, it is suggested, may be regarded as suitable guidelines by which A's intention may be ascertained:

1. If A's intention was to benefit C, or his object would be frustrated if he were to retain a power of revocation, the transaction will create an irrevocable trust in favour of C, enforceable by C, but not by A. The beneficial interest in the trust property will be in C.

2.   If A's intention was to benefit B (though without vesting a beneficial interest in him), or to benefit himself by furthering some private or commercial interest of his own, and not (except incidentally) to benefit C, then the transaction will create a trust in favour of A alone, and B will hold the trust property in trust to comply with A's directions. The trust will be enforceable by A but not by C. The beneficial interest will remain in A.

3.   Where A's object was to save B from bankruptcy by enabling him to pay his creditors, the prima facie inference is that set out in paragraph 2 above. Wherever that it the correct inference:

(i)   Where A has an interest of his own, separate and distinct from any interest of B, in seeing that the money is applied for the stated purpose, B will be under a positive obligation, enforceable by A, to apply it for that purpose. Where A has no such interest, B will be regarded as having a power, but no duty, to apply it for the stated purpose, and A's remedy will be confined to preventing the misapplication of the money.

(ii)   Prima facie, A's directions will be regarded as revocable by him, but he may contract with B not to revoke them without B's consent.

(iii)   Communication to C of the arrangements prior to A's revocation will effect an assignment of A's equitable interest to C, and convert A's revocable mandate into an irrevocable trust for C.

D: Money Partially Spent

Re EVTR
[1987] BCLC 646
Court of Appeal

Facts: The appellant, Barber, who had just won £240,000 on premium bonds, agreed to assist a company for whom he had worked in purchasing new equipment. He accordingly deposited £60,000 with the solicitors to the company, and authorised them to release it 'for the sole purpose of buying new equipment'. The money was not paid into a special fund, but was paid out by the company in pursuit of the purpose. Before the new equipment was delivered EVTR went into receivership.

Held: The Court of Appeal held that Barber was entitled to recover his money (or at any rate, the balance of £48,536, after agreed deductions) on *Quistclose* principles.

DILLON LJ: In the forefront of the appellant's case counsel for the appellant (Mr Jackson) refers to the decision of the House of Lords in *Barclays Bank Ltd* v *Quistclose Investments Ltd* [1970] AC 567. There, Quistclose had lent money to a company (Rolls Razor Ltd) on an agreed condition that the money be used only for the purpose of paying a particular dividend which the company had declared. In the event the company went into liquidation, after receiving Quistclose's money, but without having paid the dividend. It was held that Quistclose could claim the whole of the money back, as on a resulting trust, the specific purpose having failed, and Quistclose was not limited to proving as an unsecured creditor in the liquidation of the company.

In the present case the £60,000 was released by Knapp-Fishers to the company on the appellant's instructions for a specific purpose only, namely the sole purpose of buying new equipment. Accordingly, I have no doubt, in the light of *Quistclose*, that, if the company had gone into liquidation, or the receivers had been appointed, and the scheme had become abortive before the £60,000 had been disbursed by the company, the appellant would have been entitled to recover his full £60,000, as between himself and the company, on the footing that it was impliedly held by the company on a resulting trust for him as the particular purpose of the loan had failed.

At the other end of the spectrum, if after the £60,000 had been expended by the company as it was, the Encore System had been duly delivered to, and accepted by, the company, there could be no doubt that the appellant's only right would have been as an unsecured creditor of the company for the £60,000. There would have been no question of the Encore System, or any interest in it, being held on any sort of trust for the appellant, and if, after it had been delivered and installed, the company had sold the system, the appellant could have had no claim whatsoever to the proceeds of sale as trust moneys held in trust for him.

The present case lies on its facts between those two extremes of the spectrum. . . .

On *Quistclose* principles, a resulting trust in favour of the provider of the money arises when money is provided for a particular purpose only, and that purpose fails. In the present case, the purpose for which the £60,000 was provided by the appellant to the company was, as appears from the authority to Knapp-Fishers, the purpose of (the company) buying new equipment. But in any realistic sense of the words that purpose has failed in that the company has never acquired any new equipment, whether the Encore System which was then in mind or anything else. True it is that the £60,000 was paid out by the company with a view to the acquisition of new equipment, but that was only at half-time, and I do not see why the final whistle should be blown at half-time. The proposed acquisition proved abortive and a large part of the £60,000 has therefore been repaid by the payees. The repayments were made because of, or on account of, the payments which made up the £60,000 and those were payments of trust moneys. It is a long-established principle of equity that, if a person who is a trustee receives money or property because of, or in respect of, trust property, he will hold what he receives as a constructive trustee on the trusts of the original trust property. An early application of this principle is the well-known case of *Keech* v *Sandford* (1726) Sel Cas Ch 61, but the instances in the books are legion. See also *Chelsea Estates Investment Trust Co. Ltd* v *Marche* [1955] Ch 328 where somewhat similar reasoning applied to a mortgagee. It follows, in my judgment, that the repayments made to the receivers are subject to the same trusts as the original £60,000 in the hands of the company. There is now, of course, no question of the £48,536 being applied in the purchase of new equipment for the company, and accordingly, in my judgment, it is now held on a resulting trust for the appellant.

It is irrelevant in my judgment that, if the Encore System for which the £60,000 was paid had been delivered and accepted by the company, the company's interest in that equipment would have been a general asset of the company held by the company free of any proprietary or equitable interest of the appellant by way of trust or otherwise. If that had happened, the purpose of the appellant, and any trust attaching to the money because of that purpose, would indeed have been satisfied, but it did not happen.

The company did of course have the benefit for some months of the loan of the temporary equipment. Therefore, at any rate as between the company and Quantel, there was not a total failure of consideration so far as the company was concerned. But, even assuming (contrary to submissions made by counsel for the appellant) that the appellant was at the material times aware of the loan of the temporary equipment, the loan of the temporary equipment was merely ancillary to the purchase of the

Encore System to cover the gap until the Encore System was available to be delivered to the company. On the way matters developed, it was the Encore System, and not the temporary system, that the company was to purchase, and the company never got the Encore System.

In summary there are the two factors which to my mind lead to the same conclusion in this case. Firstly, the purpose of the appellant from which any trust is to be implied was, realistically, the purpose of the company acquiring new equipment, and not the purpose of the company entering into an abortive contract for the lease/purchase of new equipment. Secondly, on the repayments being made of the £48,536 by the payees of the £60,000, the same trusts must on general principle have attached to the £48,536 as attached to the original £60,000 which were trust moneys.

Questions

1. When did the *Quistclose* trust first take effect? Was the money in a separate account at that time? What, if anything, is the relevance of what happened subsequently?

2. It is not clear from *Quistclose* itself whether the trust is express, implied, resulting or constructive. Here it is described as a resulting trust. In *Carreras* it is described as constructive. Can you conceive any situation where these distinctions might be material?

3 CONSTITUTION OF TRUSTS AND COVENANTS TO SETTLE

SECTION 1: CONSTITUTION OF TRUSTS

In general, the legal title to trust property must be vested in trustees for a valid trust to be constituted. The trustees must have control of the property. The settlor may declare himself trustee or transfer the property to trustees. If formalities are required for this transfer, for example in the case of land or shares, then they must be complied with. In the case of land in an area of compulsory registration of title, the relevant register of title must be carried out.

A: Equity Will Not Perfect an Imperfect Gift

Milroy v Lord
(1862) 4 De GF & J 264
Court of Appeal in Chancery

Facts: The settlor executed a deed poll, purporting voluntarily to transfer shares to the defendant Samuel Lord on trust for the plaintiffs. The deed poll was not the correct method of transferring legal title from one person to another, however, since that could only be achieved by registering the name of the transferee in the books of the bank.

Held: No trust had been constituted. Samuel Lord never became trustee of the shares.

TURNER LJ; . . . I take the law of this court to be well settled, that, in order to render a voluntary settlement valid and effectual, the settlor must have done everything which, according to the nature of the property comprised in the settlement, was necessary to be done in order to transfer the property and render the settlement binding upon him. He may, of course, do this by actually transferring the property to the persons for whom he intends to provide, and the provision will then be effectual and it will be equally effectual if he transfers the property to a trustee for the purposes of the settlement, or declares that he himself holds it on trust for those purposes; and, if the property be personal, the trust may, as I apprehend, be declared either in writing or by parol; but, in order to render the settlement binding, one or other of these modes must . . . be resorted to, for there is no equity in this Court to perfect an imperfect gift. The cases I think go further to this extent, that if the settlement is intended to be effectuated by one of the modes to which I have referred, the Court will not give effect to it by applying another of those modes. If it is intended to take effect by transfer, the Court will not hold the intended transfer to operate as a declaration of trust, for then every imperfect instrument would be made effectual by being converted into a perfect trust. . . .

The . . . question is, whether the defendant Samuel Lord did not become a trustee of those shares? Upon this question I have felt considerable doubt; but in the result, I have come to the conclusion that no perfect trust was ever created in him. The shares, it is clear, were never legally vested in him; and the only ground on which he can be held to have become a trustee of them is, that he held a power of attorney under which he might have transferred them into his own name; but he held that power of attorney as the agent of the settlor; and if he had been sued by the plaintiffs as trustee of the settlement for an account under the trust, and to compel him to transfer the shares into his own name as trustee, I think he might well have said – These shares are not vested in me; I have no power over them except as the agent of the settlor, and without his express directions I cannot be justified in making the proposed transfer, in converting an intended into an actual settlement. A court of equity could not, I think, decree the agent of the settlor to make the transfer, unless it could decree the settlor himself to do so, and it is plain that no such decree could have been made against the settlor. In my opinion, therefore, this decree cannot be maintained as to the 50 Louisiana Bank shares.

Notes

1.   Turner LJ recognises the two methods of creation: declaration of self as trustee, and transfer to trustees.

2.   An intention to declare oneself trustee is quite different from an intention to make a gift, since one retains no obligations regarding the property in the case of a gift, whereas onerous obligations are retained in the former case. Therefore, a perfect trust will not be construed from an imperfect gift.

3.   In the second case, of transfer to trustees, Turner LJ requires only that the settlor must have done everything which was necessary to be done in order to transfer the property. It is possible, therefore, for a trust to be constituted where the settlor has done all that is within his power to constitute the trust by transferring the property to a trustee, but has been thwarted by formalities which are outside his control. Equity regards the trust as constituted by the last act of the settlor.

4.   However, the settlor will not have done everything in his power to transfer the property where he has used the wrong form of transfer, as in *Milroy* v *Lord*. Even if the settlor uses the correct form of transfer, as in the

next case, there will be no transfer of legal title where anything remains, or may remain, to be done by the settlor.

Re Fry, Chase National Executors and Trustees Corp. v Fry
[1946] Ch 312
Chancery Division

Facts: Fry executed transfers of shares in an English company in favour of his son. Under the Defence (Finance) Regulations 1939, the transfer could not be registered until Treasury consent was obtained. Fry had filled in the necessary forms, but died before Treasury consent was obtained.

Held: The transfer was ineffective.

ROMER J: . . . Now I should have thought it was difficult to say that the testator had done everything that was required to be done by him at the time of his death, for it was necessary for him to obtain permission from the Treasury for the assignment and he had not obtained it. Moreover, the Treasury might in any case have required further information of the kind referred to in the questionnaire which was submitted to him, or answers supplemental to those which he had given in reply to it; and, if so approached, he might have refused to concern himself with the matter further, in which case I do not know how anyone else could have compelled him to do so. . . .

Note

This case was distinguished in the following cases, where the correct method of transfer was used, and the settlor had done everything necessary to effect it.

Re Rose, Midland Bank Executor and Trustee Co. v Rose
[1949] Ch 78
Chancery Division

Facts: The testator died in January 1946. In August 1944, he had executed a transfer of his shares in a company, but the transfer was not registered until March 1946.

Held: On a question on the construction of the will whether he had transferred the shares before he died, Jenkins J held that he had done so.

JENKINS J: It is argued on behalf of the residuary legatee that the testator's transfer of the 5,000 preference shares to Mr Hook, owing to the fact that the transfer was not registered in the testator's lifetime was at the time of the testator's death in the state of being an incomplete or inchoate gift. I was referred on that to the well known case of *Milroy* v *Lord*, and also to the recent case of *Re Fry* [1946] Ch 312. Those cases, as I understand them, turn on the fact that the deceased donor had not done all in his power, according to the nature of the property given, to vest the legal interest in the property in the donee. In such circumstances it is, of course, well settled that there is no equity to complete the imperfect gift. If any act remains to be done by the donor to complete the gift at the date of the donor's death the court will not compel his personal representatives to do that act and the gift remains incomplete and fails.

In *Milroy* v *Lord* the imperfection was due to the fact that the wrong form of transfer was used for the purpose of transferring certain bank shares. The document was not the appropriate document to pass any interest in the property at all. . . . In this case, as I understand it, the testator had done everything in his power to divest himself of the shares in question to Mr Hook. He had executed a transfer. It is not suggested that the transfer was not in accordance with the company's regulations. He had handed that transfer together with the certificates to Mr Hook. There was nothing else the testator could do. It is true that Mr Hook's legal title would not be perfected until the directors passed the transfer for registration, but that was not an act which the testator had to do; it was an act which depended on the discretion of the directors. Therefore, it seems to me that the present case is not in *pari materia* with the two cases to which I have been referred. . . .

Re Rose, Rose v *IRC*
[1952] Ch 499
Court of Appeal

Facts: Rose executed transfers in shares in the required form in March 1943, but they could not take effect (at any rate at common law) until the directors of the company had registered them. They did this in June 1943. Rose died more than five years after executing the transfers, but less than five years after they were registered. If the effective date of the transfer was June 1943 then estate duty was payable, whereas if the transfer took effect in March it was not.

Held: In equity the transfer was complete when Rose had done all he could, rather than when the directors consented to and registered the transfer. Equity regarded the property as transferred by Rose's last act. Rose had done all that he could to transfer the property, but was thwarted by legal formalities which were outside his control.

EVERSHED MR: For the reasons I have stated, I do not think that *Milroy* v *Lord* covers the case . . . . If, as I have said, the phrase 'transfer the shares' is taken to be and to mean a transfer of all rights and interests in them, then I can see nothing contrary to the law in a man saying that so long as, pending registration, the legal estate remains in the donor, he was, by the necessary effect of his own deed, a trustee of that legal estate. Nor do I think that that is an unjustifiable addition to or gloss on the words used in the transfer. Indeed, for my part, I find it a less difficult matter in the way of interpretation than to say that this was, upon its terms, merely a conditional gift, merely a transfer as a gift to Mrs Rose of a particular right, namely the right to get herself registered and thenceforward, but not before, to enjoy the benefits which the donor previously had in these shares. That is nothing like what the deed sets out to do. I have said that I reject the proposition that the distinction between a case such as this and a case such as *Milroy* v *Lord* is, as [counsel for the Crown] urged, indefensible. I think it is sensible and real; and for these reasons I would dismiss the appeals.

JENKINS LJ: . . . If that was the effect of the transfers, what was the position between the delivery of the transfers and the actual registration of the transferees as the holders of the shares? [Counsel for the Crown] has referred us to the well-known case of *Milroy* v *Lord*, which has been his sheet-anchor. He says that on this authority we must be forced to the conclusion that, pending registration, the transfers had no effect at all, and he arrives at that conclusion in this way: He says that these transfers, while purporting to be transfers of the property in the shares and not declarations of trust, did not transfer the property in the shares, because registration was necessary in order to get in the legal title. He says, further, that being transfers purporting to be transfers of the property in the shares and failing of their effect as such for want of registration, they could, pending registration, have no operation at all because in the case of *Milroy* v *Lord* it was held that a defective voluntary disposition purporting to operate as a transfer or assignment of the property in question would not be given effect to in equity as a declaration of trust. I agree with my Lord that *Milroy* v *Lord* by no means covers the question with which we have to deal in the present case. If the deceased had in truth transferred the whole of his interest in these shares so far as he could transfer the same, including such right as he could pass to his transferee to be placed on the register in respect of the shares, the question arises, what beneficial interest had he then left? The answer can only be, in my view, that he had no beneficial interest left whatever: his only remaining interest consisted in the fact that his name still stood on the register as holder of the shares; but, having parted in fact with the whole of his beneficial interest, he could not, in my view, assert any beneficial title by virtue of his position as registered holder. In other words, in my view the effect of these transactions, having regard to the form and the operation of the transfers, the nature of the property transferred, and the necessity for registration in order to perfect the legal title, coupled with the discretionary power on the part of the directors to withhold registration, must be that, pending registration, the deceased was in the position of a trustee of the legal title in the shares for the transferees. Thus in the hypothetical case put by the Crown of a dividend being declared and paid (as it would have been paid in accordance with the company's articles) to the deceased as registered holder, he would have been accountable for that dividend to the transferees, on the ground that by virtue of the transfers as between himself and the transferees the owners of the shares were the transferees, to the exclusion of himself.

Questions
1. Who was trustee between March and June 1943?
2. Was the trust between March and June 1943 an express or a constructive trust?

Note
Re Rose was applied to registered land in *Mascall* v *Mascall* (1984) 50 P & CR 119. The transferor of registered land had executed a transfer and sent it to the Inland Revenue, and also handed to the transferee the land certificate. At this stage, before the transfer and land certificate had been sent to the Land Registry for registration of the transferee as proprietor, the transferor changed his mind, after a quarrel with the transferee. The Court of Appeal, after considering the cases referred to above, held the transfer effective, since it was for the transferee to apply to the Land Registry for registration as proprietor, and the transferor had done everything he had to do to complete the transfer.

B: Declaration of Self as Trustee

It is not necessary for settlors, trustees and beneficiaries to be different people. A settlor can validly constitute a trust by declaring *himself* trustee of his own property, on behalf of one or more beneficiaries. The intention must be irrevocable, because trusts are of their nature irrevocable, and it must be an intention to create a trust, rather than some other transaction (e.g., an outright gift). It is more difficult to infer an intention to constitute oneself trustee than to infer an intention to make a gift, and an intention to constitute oneself trustee will not generally be inferred from a failed gift.

Richards v Delbridge
(1874) LR Eq 11
Court of Chancery

Facts: Delbridge wished to give his infant grandson, Richards, the lease he had on his place of business as a bone manure merchant. He indorsed on the lease, 'This deed and all thereto belonging I give to Edward Benetto Richards from this time forth, with all the stock-in-trade'. He gave the lease to Richards' mother to hold for Richards, but died before the lease was actually delivered to Richards himself.

Held: There had been no transfer of the lease to Richards, nor a declaration of trust in his favour.

SIR GEORGE JESSEL MR: The principle is a very simple one. A man may transfer his property, without valuable consideration, in one of two ways: he may either do such acts as amount in law to a conveyance or assignment of the property, and thus completely divest himself of the legal ownership, in which case the person who by those acts acquires the property takes it beneficially, or on trust, as the case may be; or the legal owner of the property may, by one or other of the modes recognised as amounting to a valid declaration of trust, constitute himself a trustee, and, without an actual transfer of the legal title, may so deal with the property as to deprive himself of its beneficial ownership, and declare that he will hold it from that time forward on trust for the other person. It is true that he need not use the words, 'I declare myself a trustee,' but he must do something which is equivalent to it, and use expressions which have that meaning; for, however anxious the Court may be to carry out a man's intention, it is not at liberty to construe words otherwise than according to their proper meaning.
. . .
The true distinction appears to me to be plain, and beyond dispute: for a man to make himself trustee there must be an expression of intention to become a trustee, whereas words of present gift shew an intention to give over property to another, and not retain it in the donor's own hands for any purpose, fiduciary or otherwise.

Note
In *Jones* v *Lock* (1865) LR 1 Ch App 25, the father of a baby boy handed a cheque to his nine-month-old son, uttering words which made it clear that he meant the child to have the sum represented by the cheque, although he immediately removed the cheque from the baby for safe-keeping. He died some days later, without having endorsed the cheque, which would have been necessary to pass title in it to the child. The court refused to construe his

actions as amounting to a declaration of trust, with himself as trustee, in favour of the child. Lord Cranworth LC did not think that an irrevocable intention to part with the property had been manifested. There was an intention to make an outright gift, but no gift had actually been made. It was not therefore a declaration of trust.

Question
Jessel MR observed in *Richards* v *Delbridge* that the settlor need not use the words, 'I declare myself a trustee,' but he must do something which is equivalent to it. What do you think is meant by 'something which is equivalent to it'? Is the next case a good example of this?

Paul v *Constance*
[1977] 1 WLR 54, [1977] 1 All ER 195
Court of Appeal

Facts: Constance was injured at work, and obtained £950 in damages, which he put into his bank account in his name alone. It appeared, however, that the money was intended for himself and Mrs Paul, with whom he was living but not married. For this reason (according to the evidence) no joint account was opened, in order to save Mrs Paul from embarrassment.

Subsequent additions were made to the account, in particular from bingo winnings which Constance and Paul played as a joint venture. One withdrawal of £150 was also made, which was divided equally between them.

On Constance's death, Mrs Constance claimed entitlement to the £950.

Held: Constance held the money on trust for Mrs Paul, and therefore Mrs Constance was not entitled to it. The word 'trust', was not used, but regard was had to the unsophisticated character of Constance, and his relationship with Mrs Paul. Had the decision been otherwise, the money would have been regarded as Constance's, and his wife would have been entitled to succeed to it as part of her husband's estate.

SCARMAN LJ: There is no suggestion of a gift by transfer in this case. The facts of [*Jones* v *Lock* and *Richards* v *Delbridge*] do not, therefore, very much help the submission of counsel for the defendant, but he was able to extract from them this principle: that there must be a clear declaration of trust, and that means there must be clear evidence from what is said or done of an intention to create a trust or, as counsel for the defendant put it, 'an intention to dispose of a property or a fund so that somebody else to the exclusion of the disponent acquires the beneficial interest in it'. He submitted that there was no such evidence.

When one looks to the detailed evidence to see whether it goes as far as that – and I think that the evidence does have to go as far as that – one finds that from the time that Mr Constance received his damages right up to his death he was saying, on occasions, that the money was as much the plaintiff's as his. When they discussed the damages, how to invest them or what to do with them, when they discussed the bank account, he would say to her: 'The money is as much yours as mine.' The judge, rightly treating the basic problem in the case as a question of fact, reached this conclusion. He said:

> I have read through my notes, and I am quite satisfied that it was the intention of [the plaintiff] and Mr Constance to create a trust in which both of them were interested.

In this court the issue becomes: was there sufficient evidence to justify the judge reaching that conclusion of fact? In submitting that there was, counsel for the plaintiff draws attention first and foremost to the words used. When one bears in mind the unsophisticated character of Mr Constance and his relationship with the plaintiff during the last few years of his life, counsel for the plaintiff submits that the words that he did use on more than one occasion namely 'This money is as much yours as mine', convey clearly a present declaration that the existing fund was as much the plaintiff's as his own. The judge accepted that conclusion. I think he was well justified in doing so and, indeed, I think he was right to do so. There are, as counsel for the plaintiff reminded us, other features in the history of the relationship between the plaintiff and Mr Constance which support the interpretation of those words as an express declaration of trust. I have already described the interview with the bank manager when the account was opened. I have mentioned also the putting of the 'bingo' winnings into the account, and the one withdrawal for the benefit of both of them.

It might, however, be thought that this was a borderline case, since it is not easy to pin-point a specific moment of declaration, and one must exclude from one's mind any case built on the existence of an implied or constructive trust; for this case was put forward at the trial and is now argued by the plaintiff as one of express declaration of trust. It was so pleaded, and it is only as such that it may be considered in this court. The question, therefore, is whether in all the circumstances the use of those words on numerous occasions as between Mr Constance and the plaintiff constituted an express declaration of trust. The judge found that they did. For myself, I think he was right so to find. I therefore would dismiss the appeal.

Note
This is clearly a borderline case, from which wide-ranging conclusions should not too readily be drawn.

Re Kayford Ltd (in liquidation)
[1975] 1 All ER 604
Chancery Division

Facts: A mail order company was in financial difficulties. In order to protect customers in the event of insolvency, the company considered setting up separate bank account, called the 'Customers' Trust Deposit Account', to hold customers' deposits and payments until their goods were delivered, the intention of the company being that the money should be kept separate from the company's general funds. But the company took the advice of the bank, and instead of opening a new account, used a dormant account (with a small credit balance) in the company's name.

Held: On the winding-up of the company, Megarry J held that the money in the account (apart from the small credit balance) was held on trust for the customers. He observed that a trust can be created without using the words 'trust' or 'confidence', so long as a sufficient intention to create a trust has been manifested, and he did not consider it fatal that the money had not been put into a separate account, but mixed with other moneys.

MEGARRY J: Now there are clearly some loose ends in the case. . . . Nevertheless, despite the loose ends, when I take as a whole the [evidence] I feel no doubt that the intention was that there should be a trust. There are no formal difficulties. The property concerned is pure personalty, and so writing, though desirable, is not an essential. There is no doubt about the so-called 'three certainties' of a trust. The subject-matter to be held on trust is clear, and so are the beneficial interests therein, as well as the beneficiaries. As for the requisite certainty of words, it is well settled that a trust can be created without using the words 'trust' or 'confidence' or the like: the question is whether in substance a sufficient intention to create a trust has been manifested.

In *Re Nanwa Gold Mines Ltd* [1955] 3 All ER 219, [1955] 1 WLR 1080 the money was sent on the faith of a promise to keep it in a separate account, but there is nothing in that case or in any other authority that I know of to suggest that this is essential. I feel no doubt that here a trust was created. From the outset the advice (which was accepted) was to establish a trust account at the bank. The whole purpose of what was done was to ensure that the moneys remained in the beneficial ownership of those who sent them, and a trust is the obvious means of achieving this. No doubt the general rule is that if you send money to a company for goods which are not delivered, you are merely a creditor of the company unless a trust has been created. The sender may create a trust by using appropriate words when he sends the money (though I wonder how many do this, even if they are equity lawyers), or the company may do it by taking suitable steps on or before receiving the money. If either is done, the obligations in respect of the money are transformed from contract to property, from debt to trust. Payment into a separate bank account is a useful (though by no means conclusive) indication of an intention to create a trust, but of course there is nothing to prevent the company from binding itself by a trust even if there are no effective banking arrangements.

. . . I should, however, add one thing. Different considerations may perhaps arise in relation to trade creditors; but here I am concerned only with members of the public, some of whom can ill afford to exchange their money for a claim to a dividend in the liquidation, and all of whom are likely to be anxious to avoid this. In cases concerning the public, it seems to me that where money in advance is being paid to a company in return for the future supply of goods or services, it is an entirely proper and honourable thing for a company to do what this company did, on skilled advice, namely, to start to pay the money into a trust account as soon as there begin to be doubts as to the company's ability to fulfil its obligations to deliver the goods or provide the services. I wish that, sitting in this court, I had heard of this occurring more frequently; and I can only hope that I shall hear more of it in the future.

Questions

1. Given that *Re Nanawa Gold Mines Ltd* was an early *Quistclose*-type trust, where it is absolutely necessary to infer that the trust moneys are kept

separate from the company funds, does the case have any relevance at all to the present situation?

2.   Suppose that the company had by express words declared itself trustee of the customers' deposits and payments, but had not placed them into a separate account. Would the decision have been the same?

3.   In Megarry J's view, the question is whether a sufficient intention to create a trust has been manifested. If words of trust are not used, what exactly does this mean?

4.   Why should trade creditors be treated differently from members of the public?

5.   Does the decision in any way depend on the fact that the small credit balance which was in the account initially remained there at all times thereafter? You may care to consider the equitable tracing rules discussed in chapter 17.

6.   Should placing money in a separate account always lead to the inference of a declaration of trusteeship?

Re Chelsea Cloisters Ltd (in liquidation)
(1980) 41 P & CR 98
Court of Appeal

Decision: The decision in *Kayford* was applied where a 'tenants' deposit account' was set up to hold deposits against damage and breakages. The company managing the flats (Chelsea Cloisters Ltd) had gone into voluntary liquidation.

BRIDGE LJ: We are fortunate in that we do not have to speculate about Mr Iredale's intentions [who was in effective control of Chelsea Cloisters] because he has clearly disclosed them in an affidavit. It is common ground that his statements in evidence of what his intentions were at the time when the separate bank account was opened are admissible against the liquidator if they tend to support the landlords' contention that an intention to create a trust was in fact manifested. I divide up the two critical paragraphs in Mr Iredale's affidavit . . . into three distinct statements. It may be that each considered in isolation is insufficient to manifest the intention to create a trust; but the three considered in conjunction in my judgment, are clearly sufficient. However, it is worth examining them first in isolation to see exactly what he said. The first was: 'This' – that is to say, the opening of a separate bank account – 'was a practical step, designed to ensure that the deposits would not be spent as part of the company's general cash flow.' That is entirely consistent with an intention to keep these funds from the general funds of the company in order that they should not be swallowed up by the general funds of the company. The second critical statement was this: 'I was also concerned that I and my firm could be open to criticism if deposits were spent in this way' – that is to say, if they were absorbed in the general funds of the company and spent as if they were available to be treated as part of the general funds of the company. Why was Mr Iredale apprehensive of criticism of himself and his firm? It surely can only have been that he at that time regarded the company, whose affairs he was managing, as being either under a moral or perhaps a legal duty to treat the tenants' deposits as impressed with some sort of beneficial interest in favour of the tenants and to ensure that sufficient funds were available to meet the tenants' claims to recover the deposits as and when those claims were made.

. . . Finally, there is the statement . . . : 'I regarded the tenants' deposit account as available only for repaying the deposit of any tenant who had paid a deposit on or after June 18, 1974.' That comes nearest of any of the separate statements in Mr Iredale's affidavit to amounting to a positive declaration of his intention to create a trust at the material time. When considered in conjunction with the other statements, and when considered against the background of the extremely parlous situation financially in which the company found itself, I find it possible only to construe those expressions as indicating an intention to create a trust.

OLIVER LJ: The matter is, I think, one very much of impression – what is to be deduced from the evidence as to Mr Iredale's intention. Mr Iredale himself did not expressly have in mind the creation of an express trust because it may be assumed, if he had, that he would have said so in his affidavit. He had, however, told the court what his intention was and by implication what he was trying to achieve; and the question is, as a result of that, was a trust created? Were the deposits taken out of the general assets of the company effectively and set aside for use to confirm, in the case of those sums received prior to the opening of the account, or to preserve, in the case of deposits received subsequently, the interest of the tenants who paid them. The case is, in my judgment, much less clear than *Re Kayford Ltd (in liquidation)* [1975] 1 WLR 279 because the intention of the company's directors there was unequivocally demonstrated in the advice which they had received. It is less clear . . . but, albeit with more hesitation than Lord Denning MR and Bridge LJ, I have been persuaded . . . that the nature of the transaction here does demonstrate the intention to segregate the deposits from the general assets of the company for the benefit of the tenants who had paid them; and, rather than rehearsing it again, I agree that the salient features of the case are those which have been outlined by Bridge LJ.

Question
Is it possible from this case to deduce any clear principles as to when a trust will be inferred in this type of case?

Re Multi Guarantee Co. Ltd
[1987] BCLC 257
Court of Appeal

Decision: The Court of Appeal distinguished the two previous cases where an account was set up to hold insurance premiums prior to insurance cover being effected. The case clearly turns on the fact that it had not been finally decided what to do with the money in the account, so an irrevocable intention was not established.

Notes
1. The argument in *Multi-Guarantee* apparently failed because no *permanent* decision had been made as to the disposition of the money, because of uncertainty of what Multi's position would be. Creating a trust is irrevocable, and permanence is an essential feature of a trust.
2. In general on these cases, see Bridge (1992) 12 OJLS 333, at pp. 355–7.

SECTION 2:   COVENANTS TO SETTLE

A: Cannot Make Immediate Settlement of Future Property

Most cases involve marriage settlements where the parties agree to settle property to which they have not yet become entitled. *Re Ellenborough* (below) suggests that future property, or expectancies, cannot form the subject matter of a trust.

Re Ellenborough, Towry Law v *Byrne*
[1903] 1 Ch 697
Chancery Division

Facts: Emily Julia Towry Law executed a voluntary settlement by deed of expectancies under the wills of her brother and sister. She later became entitled to the property and settled the property to which she had become entitled from her sister. She sought a summons to decide whether she could refuse to transfer the property from her brother to the trustees.

Held:
(a)   The deed could not constitute a trust of expectancies under the wills of her brother and sister.

(b)   Miss Towry Law could not be compelled to transfer the property when inherited to the trustees, because a court of equity would not enforce a voluntary covenant (i.e., a covenant unsupported by consideration) by compelling her to do what she had not yet done.

BUCKLEY J: . . . She had only a *spes successionis*, and that is not a title to property by English law: *In re Parsons* (1890) 45 ChD 51 In that state of facts the applicant . . . . executed a voluntary settlement by deed by which she granted to the trustees, who are the respondents on this summons, the real estate, and assigned the personal estate to which the applicant, in the event of the death of her brother and sister respectively in her life-time, might become entitled under their respective wills or intestacies. That deed could not operate by way of grant, but could in a Court of Equity operate as an agreement on the part of the applicant to grant and assign that which in fact could not by the deed be granted or assigned. The brother and sister are now dead, intestate, and the applicant has become entitled by devolution. The property coming to the applicant from her sister has been handed over to the trustees, and the applicant does not say that she can get it back. The property of the brother has not so been handed over, and the applicant does not desire to hand it over unless she is compelled to do so. The question to be determined upon this summons is whether she can be called upon by the trustees to assign and hand over to them that which has come to her by devolution from the late Lord Ellenborough, or whether she can refuse to do anything further to perfect that which was a mere voluntary deed. In order to raise the question in proper form a writ has been, or will be, issued by the trustees against the applicant seeking to recover the funds, and the order will be drawn up on this summons and in that action. The deed was purely voluntary. The question is whether a volunteer can enforce a contract made by deed to dispose of an expectancy. It cannot be and is not disputed that if the deed had been for value the trustees could have enforced it. If value be given, it is immaterial what is the form of assurance by which the disposition is made, or whether the subject of the disposition is capable of being thereby disposed of or not. An assignment for value binds the conscience of the assignor. A Court of Equity as against him will compel him to do that which ex hypothesi he has not yet effectually done. Future property, possibilities, and expectancies are all assignable in equity for value: *Tailby* v *Official Receiver* (1888) 13 App Cas 523, 543. But when the assurance is not for value, a Court of Equity will not assist a volunteer. . . .

Notes

1. In respect of the property already settled the settlement was permanent. Miss Towry Law could not take it back (she did not in any case wish to do so).

2. The case was followed in *Re Brooks* [1939] Ch 933. *Re Brooks* concerned the property of a mother and her son, and in particular a voluntary settlement of after-acquired property by the son. Lloyds Bank were the trustees under this voluntary settlement. Later, because of the exercise by his mother of a power of appointment in his favour, the son acquired property, which should have been caught by the voluntary settlement. The power of appointment had been granted to his mother under her marriage settlement. But Lloyds Bank were also trustees under the marriage settlement, and hence already had legal title to this property. The issue was whether Lloyds Bank held the property for the son, or on the trusts in the son's voluntary settlement. It was held that they held the property for the son. The main issue was whether this property was existing or after-acquired property at the time the son's voluntary settlement was made. It was held that it was after-acquired property until the appointment was actually made in his favour. It could therefore not form the subject matter of a trust. *Re Ellenborough* was followed.

There is, however, a problem with *Re Brooks*, of a different nature. Lloyds Bank's position was exactly analogous with that of the plaintiff in *Re Ralli's WT* (see below); they had acquired the property which was subject to the son's voluntary settlement otherwise than in their capacity as trustees under that settlement. Yet the opposite decision was reached to that in *Re Ralli's WT*. *Re Brooks* is also difficult to reconcile in this regard with *Re Bowden* (see below).

3. Because it is not possible to constitute an immediate trust of future property, the best that can be done is to make a covenant (contract) to settle the property when the settlor becomes entitled to it. There is no reason why the covenant cannot be enforceable whether or not the property is capable of immediate settlement. Buckley J suggests that such a contract, if for value, is enforceable at equity.

4. If the covenant is not made for value it will not be enforceable in equity, as *Re Ellenborough* decides. The case decides only that equity will not compel a party to a voluntary covenant to perform his or agreed obligations, say by an action for specific performance, and that equity will not assist a volunteer. The case is however silent on the attitude taken by the common law to voluntary deeds of covenant. The question never arose whether Miss Towry Law could have been sued for damages by the trustees.

Question
Can this case be reconciled with the floating (constructive) trust cases in
chapter 10?

B: Action by Beneficiary Against Settlor

The traditional marriage settlement included future property which on the
basis of *Re Ellenborough* cannot form the subject matter of an immediate trust.
The settlement will have been made by deed of covenant, however, to which
the trustees will be party, and consideration may move from one or more
parties. Actions by trustees on the covenant are considered below.

The beneficiaries are usually the issue of the marriage, and in default of
issue (typically) the next of kin of the wife. It is therefore unlikely that the
intended *beneficiaries* will be party to the covenant, since at the time of
the covenant they will not have been born. However, if they are within the
marriage consideration, specific performance can be obtained to force the
settlor to constitute the trust, or damages in lieu thereof under the Chancery
Amendment Act 1858.

Pullan v Koe
[1913] 1 Ch 9
Chancery Division

Facts: A covenant was made in consideration of marriage that the husband and wife would settle the wife's after-acquired property of the value
of £100 or upwards. The wife in breach of the covenant had not settled
property which she had later received (the sum of £285), part of which had
been used to purchase bonds. The breach took place in 1879, when the
wife failed to settle the property. On the wife's death, in 1909, the
beneficiaries under the covenant (who as issue of the marriage were within
the marriage consideration) claimed a property interest in the bonds.

Held:
  (a)   The beneficiaries being within the marriage consideration could obtain
specific performance of the covenant, to bring the bonds within the settlement.
  (b)   Since where specific performance is available, equity regards as
done that which ought to be done, the money was bound by the trusts of
the settlement as soon as it was received by the wife. Hence the beneficial
interests were created at that time, and the issue could avoid any limitation
problems that would otherwise have arisen from the fact that action was
not commenced until 30 years after the breach.

SWINFEN EADY J: It was contended that the bonds never in fact became trust
property . . . In my opinion as soon as the £285 was paid to the wife it became in
equity bound by and subject to the trusts of the settlement. The trustees could have
claimed that particular sum . . . and, if it had been invested and the investment could
be traced, could have followed the money, and claimed the investment.

This point was dealt with by Jessel MR in *Smith* v *Lucas* (1881) 18 ChD 531, 543, where he said: 'What is the effect of such a convenant in equity? It has been said that the effect in equity of the covenant of the wife, as far as she is concerned, is that it does not affect her personally, but that it binds the property: that is to say, it binds the property under the doctrine of equity that that is to be considered as done which ought to be done. That is in the nature of specific performance of the contract no doubt. If, therefore, this is a convenant to settle the future-acquired property of the wife, and nothing more is done by her, the convenant will bind the property.'

. . .

The property being thus bound, these bonds became trust property, and can be followed by the trustees and claimed from a volunteer.

Questions
1.   Who was the trustee from 1879 to 1909? (Note that the wife never constituted the trust as she was required to do by the settlement.)
2.   What were the terms of the trust from 1879 to 1909?
3.   What was the nature of the beneficiaries' interest from 1879 to 1909? (See *Oughtred* v *IRC*, considered in chapter 6.)

Notes
1.   The beneficiaries succeeded only because equity recognises marriage consideration (which is probably best regarded as an exception to the privity of contract doctrine), and therefore the remedy of specific performance was available to sue on the covenant. Because equity regards as done that which ought to be done, the beneficiaries should be regarded as having equitable interests from the moment the wife received the property (akin to the purchaser's interest under an estate contract): see *Oughtred* v *IRC*, considered in chapter 6.
2.   The beneficiaries as issue were within the marriage consideration. More remote kin, however, not being within the consideration, would be volunteers in the eyes of equity unless they had provided other consideration of value.
3.   The marriage must constitute consideration. Therefore the marriage consideration doctrine only covers covenants for future marriages.
4.   The effect of the doctrine is that not only parties to the contract, but also the issue *of that marriage* can sue, although otherwise volunteers.
5.   The doctrine is commonly regarded as a narrow and nowadays anomalous exception to rule that equity will not assist a volunteer. It probably developed originally to impose upon the conscience of the husband (forcing him to settle) at a time (prior to the Married Women's Property Act 1882 – see chapter 9) when the wife had no economic independence, since otherwise nobody would have been able to ensure that the issue of the marriage would benefit from the settlement. Lee observed (85 LQR, at p. 227):

The doctrine of marriage consideration survives as a fossil of the long era of the wife's economic subjugation to her husband. The Married Women's Property Act and the Inheritance (Family Provision) Act sounded the death knell of that era; and so the reasons of public policy which accounted for the courts' ambivalent attitude to the covenant to settle after-acquired property belong to a closed chapter of legal history.

6.   It is unclear whether the doctrine allows enforcement only against one of the spouses, or any potential settlor where there is marriage consideration.

Re Cook's ST
[1965] Ch 902
Chancery Division

Facts: Sir Francis Cook covenanted, for valuable consideration, with his father, Sir Herbert Cook, and the trustees of another settlement, that if Sir Francis sold any of the valuable pictures specified in a schedule to the agreement, during his lifetime, the proceeds would be held on the terms of the settlement. The beneficiaries under this (existing) settlement were various members of Sir Francis's family (but Sir Herbert was not himself one of the beneficiaries). Sir Francis married several times, and gave (or purported to give) one of the pictures to one of his subsequent wives. The subsequent wife wanted to sell it, and the trustees of the settlement sought directions from the court.

Held: The beneficiaries could not require the trustees of the settlement to enforce the covenant against Sir Francis. Buckley J rejected the argument that the beneficiaries were within the marriage consideration.

BUCKLEY J (on the issue of marriage consideration): It is an elementary general rule of law that a contract affects only the parties to it and their successors in title and that no one but a party or the successor in title to a party can sue or be sued upon it. There are, however, exceptions to this rule, some legal, some equitable and some statutory. If there is any such exception as Mr Brightman contends, it must be equitable.

It has long since been recognised that if marriage articles or a marriage settlement contain an executory agreement to settle property, equity will assist an intended beneficiary who is issue of the marriage to enforce the agreement. Such a beneficiary is described as being within the marriage consideration. . . . This fiction by which a child of the marriage is treated as if he were a party to and as having given consideration for his parents' marriage settlement is no doubt associated with his intimate connection with the marriage which was in fact the consideration for it, and it is, as I understand the law, because he is treated as a party who has given consideration that equity will assist him to enforce any contract to settle property which that settlement may contain. . . . On the other hand, an intended beneficiary who is not issue of the marriage is not within the marriage consideration, is not treated as though any consideration moved from him, and will not be assisted to enforce a contract to make a settlement. Thus the next-of-kin of the covenantor who are intended to take the property which is to be brought into settlement in the event of a failure of issue cannot enforce a covenant to settle (*Re d'Angibau* [(1880) 15 ChD 228]), nor can the children by a previous marriage of one of the parties, unless maybe, their interests are interwoven with those of the children of the marriage (see *Attorney-General* v *Jacobs-Smith* [1895] 2 QB 341), nor can the children of the marriage, if the settlement is a post-nuptial one, for in such a case, though there may be consideration as between the husband and the wife, that consideration would not be their marriage but consideration of some other kind to which their children would be strangers: *Green v Paterson* (1886) 32 ChD 95.

These authorities show that there is an equitable exception to the general rule of law which I have mentioned where the contract is made in consideration of marriage and the intended beneficiary who seeks to have the contract enforced is within the marriage consideration. They do not support the existence of any wider exception save perhaps in the case of a beneficiary who is not within the marriage consideration but whose interests under the intended trusts are closely interwoven with interests of others who are within that consideration. They do not support the view that any such exception exists in favour of a person who was not a party to the contract and is not to be treated as though he had been and who has given no consideration and is not to be treated as if he had given consideration. Where the obligation to settle property has been assumed voluntarily it is clear that no object of the intended trusts can enforce the obligation. Thus in *Re Kay's Settlement* [1939] Ch 329, a spinster made a voluntary settlement in favour of herself and her issue which contained a covenant to settle after-acquired property. She later married and had children who, as volunteers, were held to have no right to enforce the covenant. . . .

Notes

1.   Although it is unusual for the beneficiaries actually to be party to the deed of covenant, where they are they can sue on that and do not need to rely on the intervention of equity.

2.   However, whereas contracts under seal (or covenants by deed) are recognised as valid by the common law, even where no consideration moves from the promisee, they are not recognised as valid in equity (see *Ellenborough* above). The result is that whereas the common law remedy of damages can be obtained, the equitable remedy of specific performance, which would require the settlor actually to constitute the trust, cannot. However, a beneficiary who is party to the deed can obtain substantial damages at common law.

Cannon v Hartley
[1949] Ch 213
Chancery Division

Facts: On the breakdown of a marriage, a father covenanted to make provision for his daughter by settling on her property expected later to be acquired under the will of his parents. When he received the property he refused to settle it on the agreed terms. The daughter was not of course within the marriage consideration, as the covenant itself was not made prior to or in consideration of marriage.

Held: As a party to the deed, the daughter could enforce the contract at common law, and obtain substantial damages.

ROMER J: . . . In the present case the plaintiff, although a volunteer, is not only a party to the deed of separation but is also a direct covenantee under the very covenant upon which she is suing. She does not require the assistance of the court to enforce the covenant for she has a legal right herself to enforce it. She is not asking for equitable relief but for damages at common law for breach of covenant.

Notes
1.   Of course, if the contract is for ordinary common law consideration, conventional contractual principles apply, but this is very rare.
2.   A more likely situation is where there are no issue of the marriage, and action is brought by those entitled in default of issue, typically the next of kin of the wife. They are not within the marriage consideration, and unless otherwise party to the covenant cannot sue.

Re Plumptre's MS, Underhill v Plumptre
[1910] 1 Ch 609
Chancery Division

Facts: The facts of were similar to those in *Pullan* v *Koe*, except that the beneficiaries were not within the marriage consideration.
     The case concerned a marriage settlement made in 1878, covering presently owned and after-acquired property. The settlement was of the conventional type, so that there having been a failure of issue, the intended beneficiaries were the next of kin of the wife. In 1884, the husband made a gift of stock to his wife. On the death of the wife, intestate, in 1909, the intended beneficiaries attempted to enforce the covenant.

Held: Eve J held that the gift of stock should have been settled on the terms of the settlement, so that the husband was in breach of covenant by making an outright gift in favour of his wife. He also held, however, that the next of kin could not enforce the covenant in equity because they were volunteers.
     The result was that the stock represented by the original gift (the original stock having been sold and the money reinvested) went to the husband on the intestacy of his wife, and the next of kin could not enforce the covenant.

EVE J: . . . [The next of kin] are not in my opinion *cestuis que trust* under the settlement, for nothing therein amounts to a declaration of trust, or to anything more than an executory contract on the part of the husband and wife; it is, so far as the next of kin are concerned, . . . a voluntary contract to create a trust as distinguished from a complete voluntary trust such as existed in the case of *Fletcher* v *Fletcher* [below], on which [the next of kin] so strongly relied. The collaterals are no parties to the contract; they are not within the marriage consideration and cannot be considered otherwise than as volunteers, and in these respects it makes no difference that the covenant sought to be enforced is the husband's and that the property sought to be brought within it comes from the wife. For each of the foregoing propositions authority is to be found in the judgment of the Court of Appeal in *Re D'Angibau* (1880) 15 ChD 228; and in the same judgment is to be found this further statement – that where, as in this case, the husband has acquired a legal title as administrator of his wife to property which was subject to the contract to settle, volunteers are not entitled to enforce against that legal title the contract to create a trust contained in the settlement. . . .

Notes

1.   It was also noted, in passing, that the would-be trustees, who were party to the deed of covenant, would be unable to sue at common law, because they were time barred. The breach had occurred in 1884, when the husband had used money which should have been caught by the settlement to make an outright gift to his wife. The case was not brought until after the wife's death in 1909. It is obvious that in cases of this type there is often a long delay between the breach and the case being brought, and that limitation is therefore often a problem (the intended trustees' action would also have been time barred in *Pullan* v *Koe*).'

2.   One can, however, infer from Eve J's judgment (at the bottom of p. 616) that he thought that the trustees would have been able to sue had they not been time barred. It is not a strong inference, but is relevant to the discussion in the following section.

3.   The only way in which would-be beneficiaries in a *Plumptre*-situation could benefit from the covenant would be if there were other beneficiaries who were not volunteers (as in *Pullan* v *Koe*), such as the children of the marriage, who could enforce the covenant on behalf of the would-be beneficiaries as well as on their own behalf, or the would-be beneficiaries were themselves parties to the covenant.

C: Action by Trustee Against Settlor

Re Pryce, Neville v *Pryce*
[1917] 1 Ch 234
Chancery Division

Facts: The case concerned a marriage settlement covering after-acquired property. Consideration moved from both the husband and the wife, but none from the trustees. The main issue concerned the wife's after-acquired property, which ought to have been caught by the covenant. There were no issue of the marriage, and the beneficiaries in default of issue were volunteers. The trustees sought directions whether they should take proceedings to enforce the covenant.

Held: The trustees ought not to take any steps to enforce the covenant.

EVE J: The position of the wife's fund is . . . that her next of kin would be entitled to it on her death; but they are volunteers, and although the Court would probably compel fulfilment of the contract to settle at the instance of any persons within the marriage consideration (see per Cotton LJ in *In re D'Angibau* (1880) 15 ChD 228, 242, 246), and in their favour will treat the outstanding property as subjected to an enforceable trust (*Pullan* v *Koe* [1913] 1 Ch 9), 'volunteers have no right whatever to obtain specific performance of a mere covenant which has remained as a convenant and has never been performed': see per James LJ in *In re D'Angibau*. Nor could damages be awarded either in this Court, or, I apprehend, at law, where, since the Judicature Act, the same defences would be available to the defendant as would be raised in an action brought in this Court for specific performance or damages.

In these circumstances, seeing that the next of kin could neither maintain an action to enforce the covenant nor for damages for breach of it, and that the settlement is not a declaration of trust constituting the relationship of trustee and cestui que trust between the defendant and the next of kin, in which case effect could be given to the trusts even in favour of volunteers, but is a mere voluntary contract to create a trust, ought the Court now for the sole benefit of these volunteers to direct the trustees to take proceedings to enforce the defendant's covenant? I think it ought not; to do so would be to give the next of kin by indirect means relief they cannot obtain by any direct procedure, and would in effect be enforcing the settlement as against the defendant's legal right to payment and transfer from the trustees of the parents' marriage settlement. The circumstances are not unlike those which existed in the case of *In re D'Angibau*, and I think the position here is covered by the judgments of the Lords Justices in that case.

Accordingly, I declare that the trustees ought not to take any steps to compel the transfer or payment to them of the premises assured to the wife by the deed of December 12, 1904. . . .

Notes

1.   Eve J thought that the volunteers would not be able to obtain damages at common law, and since they are not party to the covenant this is clearly correct. If the beneficiaries are party, see *Cannon* v *Hartley*, above, on the common law damages position.

2.   In *Re D'Angibau* the action was (as in *Re Plumptre*) brought by the volunteers, not by the trustee.

Questions

1.   Does it follow that because the next of kin cannot sue, the trustees, who have an independent cause of action, should not be directed to sue on their behalf?

2.   Does it follow that because the next of kin cannot sue, the trustees, who have an independent cause of action, should be directed not to sue on their behalf?

3.   Is it clear which reasoning (*1.* or *2.* above) was actually adopted by Eve J in the above passage?

4.   Does the last paragraph of the above passage follow from what precedes it?

5.   Is there anything in the above passage which suggests that the trustees could not obtain damages for breach of contract, assuming that they could obtain any by suing on the deed of covenant? Or do the words 'compel the transfer or payment' suggest specific performance?

6.   If the trustees had been allowed to sue, could they have obtained specific performance of the covenant?

7.   Given that the trustees were attempting to add property to an existing trust, if they had been directed to take steps to enforce the covenant, or that they may take steps to enforce the covenant, and the action had failed, who would have born the costs of the action?

8.   Is there anything in the above passage which suggests that the position would have been different had the trustees provided consideration? (Note that the next of kin still would have been unable to sue.)

9.   Was Mrs Beswick in *Beswick* v *Beswick* a volunteer? Should anybody have been allowed to sue on her behalf?

Re Kay's Settlement, Adbent v *Macnab*
[1939] Ch 329
Chancery Division

Facts: The case concerns a voluntary settlement by a spinster, who only married much later. There was no marriage consideration, and hence the children of the later marriage were volunteer beneficiaries.

Held: The trustees ought not to take any steps to enforce the covenant. *Re Pryce* was followed, but the trustees were also directed not to sue for damages.

SIMONDS J (after quoting the above passage from *Re Pryce*): . . . It is true that in those last words the learned judge [in Re Pryce] does not specifically refer to an action for damages, but it is clear that he has in mind directions both with regard to an action for specific performance and an action to recover damages at law – or, now, in this Court.

In those circumstances it appears to me that I must follow the learned judge's decision and I must direct the trustees not to take any steps either to compel performance of the covenant or to recover damages through [the settlor's] failure to implement it. . . .

Questions
1.   Do either of these two cases decide what would have been the result had trustees actually sued, in their personal capacity?
2.   If the trustees had sued for damages in *Kay*, would they have been restricted to nominal damages on the basis that they had personally suffered no loss? (See the discussion in chapter 2, and the passage from Goddard, below.)

Re Cook's ST
[1965] Ch 902
Chancery Division

Decision: The facts have already been set out (see p. 72). Buckley J held that the volunteer beneficiaries could not compel the trustees to enforce the covenant on their behalf.

BUCKLEY J: . . . As an alternative argument, Mr Brightman formulated this proposition, which he admitted not to be directly supported by any authority, but he claimed to conflict with non: that where a covenantor has for consideration moving from a third party covenanted with trustees to make a settlement of property, the court will assist an intended beneficiary who is a volunteer to enforce the covenant if he is specially an object of the intended trust or (which Mr Brightman says is the same thing) is within the consideration of the deed. In formulating this proposition Mr

Brightman bases himself on language used by Cotton LJ in *Re d'Angibau* (1880) 15 ChD 228, 242, CA and by Romer J in *Cannon v Hartley* [1949] Ch 213, 223. As an example of a case to which the proposition would apply, Mr Brightman supposes a father having two sons who enters into an agreement with his elder son and with trustees whereby the father agrees to convey an estate to his elder son absolutely in consideration of the son convenanting with his father and the trustees, or with the trustees alone, to settle an expectation on trusts for the benefit of the younger son. The younger son is a stranger to the transaction, but he is also the primary (and special) beneficiary of the intended settlement. A court of equity should, and would, Mr Brightman contends, assist the younger son to enforce his brother's covenant and should not permit the elder son to frustrate the purposes of the agreement by refusing to implement his convenant although he has secured the valuable consideration given for it. This submission is not without attraction, for it is not to be denied that, generally speaking, the conduct of a man who, having pledged his word for valuable consideration, takes the benefits he has so obtained and then fails to do his part, commands no admiration. I have, therefore, given careful consideration to this part of the argument to see whether the state of the law is such as might justify me (subject to the construction point) in dealing with the case on some such grounds.

There was ro consideration for Sir Francis's covenant moving from the trustees; nor, of course, was there any consideration moving from Sir Francis's children [beneficiaries]. . . .

[Buckley J found that there was consideration moving from Sir Herbert, and continued:] . . . Mr Brightman distinguishes [*Kay*] from the present on the grounds that in *Re Kay's Settlement* [1939] Ch 329 the settlement and convenant were entirely voluntary, whereas Sir Francis received consideration from Sir Herbet; but Sir Francis received no consideration from his own children. Why, it may be asked, should they be accorded had Sir Herbert given no consideration? As regards them the convenant must, in my judgment, be regarded as having been given voluntarily. A plaintiff is not entitled to claim equitable relief against another merely because that latter's conduct is unmeritorious. Conduct by A which is unconscientious in relation to B so as to entitle B to equitable relief may not be unconscientious in relation to C so that C will have no standing to claim relief notwithstanding that the conduct in question may affect C. The father in Mr Brightman's fictitious illustration could after performing his part of the contract release his elder son from the latter's covenant with him to make a settlement on the younger son, and the younger son could, I think, not complain. Only the covenant with the trustees would then remain, but this covenant would be a voluntary with the trustees having given no consideration. I can see no reason why in these circumstances the court should assist the younger son to enforce the convenant with the trustees. But the right of the younger son to require the trustees to enforce their convenant could not, I think, depend on whether the father had or had not released his convenant. Therefore, as it seems to me, on principle the younger son would not in any event have an equitable right to require the trustees to enforce their covenant. In other words, the arrangement between the father and his elder son would not have conferred any equitable right or interest upon his younger son.

I reach the conclusion that Mr Brightman's proposition is not well-founded. There is no authority to support it and *Green v Paterson* (1886) 32 ChD 95 is, I think, authority the other way. Accordingly, the second and third defendants are not, in my judgment, entitled to require the trustees to take proceedings to enforce the convenant even if it is capable of being constructed in a manner favourable to them.

Notes
1.   Unlike *Re Pryce* [1917] 1 Ch 234 and *Re Kay's Settlement* [1939] Ch 239, *Re Cook's ST* apparently does not decide that the trustees of the settlement had no remedy, or that they should not themselves enforce the covenant, but only that they could not be compelled to do so by the beneficiaries. However, the actual order was in similar terms to that in *Re Pryce/Re Kay*.
2.   Clearly, a trustee who has provided no consideration cannot sue for specific performance, but he may have an action for damages (at any rate, if he is allowed to use it). We need now to consider further the nature of the damages action.

David Goddard, '*Equity, Volunteers and Ducks*' [1988] Conv 19

Donald has a wealthy uncle, Scrooge, who in an uncharacteristic moment of generosity made a promise, under seal, to pay Donald £100,000 to hold on trust for Donald's nephews, Huey, Duey and Louie. Scrooge, regretting his impulsive behaviour, now refuses to pay.

. . .

It is true that Donald is not, in fact, one penny worse off. . . .

The reason that Donald did not in fact suffer any loss from Scrooge's failure to pay, is that equity would have restrained him from dealing with the money (which he would have had legal title to) otherwise that for the benefit of his nephews. But in a court of common law, prior to the Judicature Act 1873, the fact that a court of equity would have interfered with Donald's use of the money would not have been considered relevant: he would have been legal owner of the £100,000 if the promise had been honoured, but he is not – what is this but a loss *at law* of £100,000? . . .

In considering Donald's claim, a court of common law would have considered neither what Donald would have been required to do with the money by a court of equity, nor what Donald might be required to do with the damages by a court of equity. Worse off at law, he would have been compensated at law. Nor does the Judicature Act affect this: it did not fuse law and equity (the 'fusion fallacy'), but simply conferred jurisdiction in both on all courts. Where rules conflict, equity prevails: but it is not a *conflict* where law assesses damages on the basis of legal title, ignoring equity. Equity will not award such damages, but neither will it prevent them being sought.

Thus, Donald could in any event bring an action for damages, and recover his (legal) loss of £100,000. Such a conclusion is, in fact, hardly surprising: it displays a remarkable degree of tunnel vision to suggest that trustees who make no profit from their trust, so cannot establish loss where the trust funds are diminished by a third party's breach of contract or covenant (or tort, for that matter), cannot therefore recover substantial common law damages. Once look beyond the narrow context of cases 'on' equity and volunteers, and examples of trustees being able to recover are legion. Many trustees – especially large charity trustees – enter into a variety of contracts: they would be amazed to learn that they could not recover damages for breach. In particular, the increasing number of unit trusts would appear far less attractive as investments if it were true that the trustees had no legal remedies against defaulting purchasers and sellers of shares! . . .

Note
Goddard goes on to argue that Donald would be required to hold the damages on trust for the nephews, and that the cases set out above are wrong.

Questions
1. Given that where A contracts with B that B will provide a benefit for C, if B defaults A's damages are nominal (see chapter 2), how does this situation differ from that?
2. Do you find convincing (or relevant) the arguments that trustees can sue on behalf of the trust and claim substantial damages (presumably to be held on trust), given that here the action is brought by someone who is not yet trustee of the disputed property?
3. Let us suppose (as I do) that Goddard is correct in his assertion that Donald can recover damages of £100,000. Do you think that he should be allowed to keep them for himself?
4. If in *3.* you thought that Donald should not be allowed to keep the £100,000, you may have come to the conclusion that equity would impose on his conscience and require him to hold them on trust (perhaps adopting a principle similar to that in *Neste Oy* v *Lloyds Bank plc, The Tiiskeri* [1983] 2 Lloyd's Rep 658, where in a rather different situation the recipient of money could not in all conscience hold on to it, and was required to hold it on constructive trust). But on trust for whom? If for the beneficiaries, then is equity not assisting a volunteer?
5. If you do not favour Donald keeping the damages for himself, and you do not favour equity assisting a volunteer, then a third possible solution is that he holds the damages on resulting trust for Scrooge. But if that solution were to be adopted, do you agree with Goddard that no promise under seal would ever be actionable, because the party suing would always be required to hold the damages on resulting trust for the covenant-breaker? If you do not agree, then how do you distinguish this situation from any other promise under seal?
6. Would your answers to *3.* to *5.* be different if instead of the promise being made under seal, Donald had provided consideration for it? Remember that the nephews are still volunteers, but I would suggest that the resulting trust for the contract-breaker now looks a less attractive solution. Arguably Donald should be allowed to keep the damages for himself, but if you previously came to the conclusion that he should hold them on trust for the nephews, is their position to be weakened merely because Donald has provided consideration?
7. If Donald had provided consideration then he may be able to obtain specific performance. But would this be to seek the intervention of equity (by seeking an equitable remedy) to assist a volunteer? Was Mrs Beswick a volunteer? Did equity assist her?
8. What do you think is meant by the principle that equity will not assist a volunteer? Does it mean anything more than that *specific performance can be obtained* only by beneficiaries under fully constituted trusts, persons within the marriage consideration, and others (like Mr Beswick) who have provided consideration recognised in equity?

SECTION 3: TRUSTS OF PROMISES

There is no reason in principle why a covenant made to trustees to settle property should not of itself form the subject matter of a trust. If there is a fully constituted trust of the promise, the beneficiaries can enforce it directly, even if volunteers, or can require the trustees to sue. *Lloyd's* v *Harper* (see chapter 2) suggests that substantial damages can be obtained by the trustee, which will be held on trust for the beneficiaries.

A: Existing Property

Fletcher v *Fletcher*
(1844) 4 Hare 67
Vice Chancellor

Facts: Ellis Fletcher covenanted with trustees by deed to pay £60,000 to his trustees, on trust for his illegitimate sons, who were outside the marriage consideration and were thus volunteers.

Held: The surviving son, Jacob, was able to compel the trustees to enforce the covenant on his behalf. Though the money was never settled, Wigram V-C held that the *covenant* was held on a fully constituted trust for Jacob. Thus Jacob could enforce it in his own right, despite being a volunteer. Substantial damages were recoverable, amounting to the promised £60,000.

Notes

1. This case has often been criticised on its facts. The trustees knew nothing of the covenant until the death of the settlor, Ellis Fletcher, and then were unwilling to enforce it. Even so, Jacob could compel the trustees to sue. However, it could be argued that the ignorance of the trustees, or their unwillingness to accept the trust, should not be a bar to a finding that Fletcher meant to give his trustees a chose in action rather than the money itself, so creating a valid trust. The relevant intention is surely that of the settlor, not of the trustees. If a trustee is unwilling to act, 'Equity will not allow a trust to fail for want of a trustee', and the courts will appoint another trustee.

2. Accepting that the relevant intention is that of the settlor, however, we still have to ask who this is. After all, this is a trust of the promise, not of the property to be settled. It is arguably the *trustee* of the property who owns the contractual cause of action, since he can enforce it, so surely he rather than the settlor of the property is settlor of the contract. Indeed, on this view the would-be trustee of the property is both settlor and trustee of the promise, declaring himself trustee of it. Yet while there is no doubt that the trustee of the property is the *legal* owner of the contract, it is the beneficial owner who can settle it (perhaps creating a sub-trust). The beneficial owner of the

promise would presumably be the person entitled to benefit from it in equity: this is essentially the same problem as that considered at the end of the previous section.
3. In cases since *Fletcher* v *Fletcher* the courts have demanded much more conclusive evidence that the settlor really did intend to settle the benefit of the covenant, before construing trusts of promises: e.g., *Re Schebsman* [1944] Ch 83, see chapter 2, and see *Smith* [1982] Conv 352. It is probable that were the same facts to arise today, no trust would be construed, and *Fletcher* v *Fletcher* would be considered wrongly decided in this regard.

Re Cavendish-Browne
[1916] WN 341
Chancery Division

Facts: Catherine Cavendish Browne made a voluntary settlement containing a covenant to 'convey and transfer to the trustees all the property, both real and personal, to which she was absolutely entitled by virtue of the joint operation of the wills of' two named persons. She died without having settled property to which she was so entitled in trust.

Held: Younger J, 'without delivering a final judgment, held . . . that the trustees were entitled to recover [from Catherine's administrators] substantial damages for breach of the covenant . . . , and that the measure of damages was the value of the property which would have come into the hands of the trustees if the covenant had been duly performed'.

Note
Although it is not entirely clear, it appears that Catherine was *already* entitled to the property at the time that the contract was made (i.e., this is existing property).

B: After-Acquired Property

There is some authority that only covenants to settle existing property can be held on trust.

Re Cook's ST
[1965] Ch 902
Chancery Division

Decision: The facts have already been set out (see p. 72). The beneficiaries also unsuccessfully argued that there was a fully-constituted trust of the promise, Buckley J taking the view that only promises to settle existing property could be held on trust.

BUCKLEY J: Counsel for the second and third defendants have contended that on the true view of the facts there was an immediate settlement of the obligation created by the covenant, and not merely a covenant to settle something in the future. It was said, as Mr Monckton put it, that by the agreement Sir Herbert bought the rights arising under the covenant for the benefit of the cestuis que trustent under the settlement and that, the convenant being made in favour of the trustees, these rights became assets of the trust. He relied on *Fletcher* v *Fletcher* (1844) 4 Hare 67; *Williamson* v *Codrington* (1750) 1 Ves Sen 511 and *Re Cavendish Browne's ST* [1916] WN 341. I am not able to accept this argument. The covenant with which I am concerned did not, in my opinion, create a debt enforceable at law, that is to say, a property right, which, although to bear fruit only in the future and upon a contingency, was capable of being made the subject of an immediate trust, as was held to be the case in *Fletcher* v *Fletcher*. Nor is this convenant associated with property which was the subject of an immediate trust as in *Williamson* v *Codrington*. Nor did the convenant relate to property which then belonged to the covenantor, as in *Re Cavendish Browne's ST*. In contrast to all these cases, this covenant upon its true construction is, in my opinion, an executory contract to settle a particular fund or particular funds of money which at the date of the covenant did not exist and which might never come into existence. It is analogous to a covenant to settle an expectation or to settle after-acquired property. The case, in my judgment, involves the law of contract, not the law of trusts.

Notes

1. The view that a covenant to settle after-acquired property cannot form the subject matter of a trust has also been taken by Lee (1969) 85 LQR 213, and Barton (1975) 91 LQR 236, but this reasoning has been criticised: e.g., Meagher and Lehane (1976) 92 LQR 427. Nevertheless, it by no means obvious why a *contract* to settle after-acquired property cannot form the subject matter of a trust, even though it is impossible to create an immediate trust of after-acquired property. The contract after all is existing not future property. The reasoning in *Re Ellenborough* [1903] 1 Ch 697 does not apply to it.

2. In the above passage from *Cook*, Buckley J talks of the covenant in *Fletcher* creating a debt enforceable at law, and the same is presumably true in *Re Cavendish Browne's ST*: see also Friend [1982] Conv 280. The trust of the promise constituted the settlor as debtor of the trustees. This reasoning may not be possible where the covenant is to settle after-acquired property, however, since it will be difficult or impossible to assess damages based on the value of property which has not yet been acquired, may never be acquired, and indeed need not even yet exist. Perhaps this is the real reason for limiting the principle in *Fletcher* v *Fletcher* to covenants for existing property (but see the contrary argument by Meagher and Lehane (1976) 92 LQR 427).

SECTION 4:   AUTOMATIC CONSTITUTION

A: Existing Property

Re Ralli's WT
[1964] 1 Ch 288
Chancery Division

Facts: Helen's father left his residue on trust for his wife for her life, thence to his two daughters, Helen and Irene. Helen, by her marriage settlement, covenanted with trustees of whom the plaintiff (Irene's husband) was one, to settle all her existing and after-acquired property on Irene's children.

On Helen's death, in 1956, the plaintiff, who was the sole surviving trustee under the marriage settlement, was also appointed a trustee under Helen's father's will, and hence obtained title to Helen's residuary estate under her father's will, on the death of Helen's mother (in 1961). He brought an action to determine whether he held the property on the terms of Helen's will, or on the trusts of Helen's marriage settlement.

Held: Buckley J held that the trust had become fully constituted by the accident of the trustee obtaining legal title to the property by other means, but he also held that, by entering into the marriage settlement, Helen could be regarded as declaring herself trustee of that property (which was existing and not future property) from that moment.

BUCKLEY J (after interpreting clause 8 of the settlement): For these reasons I think that the plaintiff's submission in this respect is right and that Helen held, and since her death the defendants have held and now hold, her equitable interest in her share of the testator's residue on the trusts of the settlement. If this is so, the rule that equity will not assist a volunteer to enforce an executory contract to make a settlement has no application to this case, for the relevant trust has been completely declared by the defendants' predecessor in title and such declaration is binding on them and is enforceable by and for the benefit of the beneficiaries under the settlement, whether they are volunteers or not. . . .

In my judgment the circumstance that the plaintiff holds the fund because he was appointed a trustee of the will is irrelevant. He is at law the owner of the fund, and the means by which he became so have no effect upon the quality of his legal ownership. The question is: For whom, if anyone, does he hold his fund in equity? In other words, who can successfully assert an equity against him disentitling him to stand upon his legal right? It seems to me to be indisputable that Helen, if she were alive, could not do so, for she has solemnly covenanted under seal to assign the fund to the plaintiff, and the defendants can stand in no better position. It is, of course, true that the object of the covenant was not that the plaintiff should retain the property for his own benefit, but that he should hold it on the trusts of the settlement. It is also true that, if it were necessary to enforce performance of the covenant, equity would not assist the beneficiaries under the settlement, because they are mere volunteers; and that for the same reason the plaintiff, as trustee of the settlement, would not be bound to enforce the covenant and would not be constrained by the court to do so, and indeed, it seems, might be constrained by the court not to do so. As matters stand, however, there is no occasion to invoke the assistance of equity to enforce performance of the covenant. It is for the defendants to invoke the assistance of equity to make good their claim to the fund. To do so successfully they must show that the plaintiff cannot conscientiously withhold it from them. When they seek to do this, he can point to the covenant which, in my judgment, relieves him from any fiduciary obligation he would otherwise owe to the defendants as Helen's representatives. In so doing the plaintiff is not seeking to enforce an equitable remedy against the defendants on behalf of persons who could not enforce such a remedy themselves: he is relying upon the combined effect of his legal ownership of the fund and his rights under the covenant.

That an action on the covenant might be statute-barred is irrelevant, for there is no occasion for such an action.

Notes

1. In this case, the trust was constituted by Helen's entering into the contract to settle, but in general there must be a difference between entering into a contract, which is in principle revocable (should both parties to the contract so agree) and declaring oneself trustee, which is not. In *Re Ralli's Will Trusts*, the case turned upon the precise wording of clause 8 of the covenant, which (in Buckley J's view) indicated an irrevocable intention on Helen's part:

> . . . it being the intention of these presents and of the said parties hereto that by virtue and under the operation of the said covenants all the property comprised within the terms of such covenants shall become subject in equity to the settlement hereby covenanted to be made thereof.

This part of the case should not be taken as being of general application, therefore.

2. In *Re Ralli* the plaintiff was party to the covenant in Helen's marriage settlement, but on the principles discussed in *Re Cook*, above, may not have been able to enforce that covenant. By his second line of reasoning in *Re Ralli*, Buckley J decides that by obtaining the trust property by other means, he is relieved of the necessity of enforcing the covenant, since he already has legal title to the trust property. Helen's intention is irrelevant to this question.

3. The logic of the second line of reasoning in *Re Ralli's WT* extends to all cases where the trustee acquires legal title, and so long as he does so the method of acquisition is irrelevant. Thus, the principle ought still to apply if, for example, he comes by his legal title not as his executor, but as the settlor's trustee in bankruptcy, or even as a judgment creditor, or where the settlor has mortgaged his property to the trustee, and the trustee forecloses. However, it seems likely that transfer of legal title is required, and not merely physical possession.

4. Buckley J reasoned by analogy from *Strong v Bird* (1874) LR 18 Eq 315, where a gift was completed by the donor (testator) appointing the donee executor under his will (see further chapter 9). This is a very different situation from *Strong v Bird*, however, since under the rule in *Strong v Bird* the appointment of the executor is a voluntary act of the donor, and completion of the gift may be easily inferred from that voluntary act, whereas in *Re Ralli* the plaintiff held the after-acquired capacity by a route that was independent of the wishes of the settlor under the covenant. Indeed, *Re Ralli* would presumably allow constitution even against the wishes of the settlor, and even where the covenant was entirely voluntary. Buckley J also cited authority (*Re James* [1935] Ch 449) for the proposition that the rule in *Strong v Bird* operates however the donee obtained the donor's property, but this case was doubted in *Re Gonin* [1979] Ch 16. Even if *Re James* is correct, there is an additional requirement that the donor must have shown an intention to give *inter vivos* until his death, so the *Strong* v *Bird* analogies really do not support the conclusion in *Re Ralli*.

5.   The rule in *Strong* v *Bird* could presumably be relevant if transfer of *legal* title to an executor who was also trustee under a voluntary settlement was perfected by the rule (e.g., if in a case such as *Re Stewart* [1908] 2 Ch 251, the executor was also trustee).

B: After-Acquired Property

Re Ralli could have been decided simply on the basis that Helen had declared herself trustee of *existing* property from the date of the settlement. This line of reasoning is not open with after-acquired property, but the alternative line of reasoning in *Ralli* is, as in the following case.

Re Bowden, Hulbert v Bowden
[1936] 1 Ch 71
Chancery Division

Facts: A settlor covenanted to settle under a voluntary settlement made in 1868 property to which she might become entitled upon the death of her father. Her father died in 1869 and the executors transferred her share of the property to the trustees of the settlement. In 1935 the settlor requested the trustees to transfer the property to her.

Held: Upon transfer of the property to the trustees, it had become impressed with the trusts of the settlement.

BENNETT J: Counsel for the settlor submitted that . . . the property the subject of the trusts of the settlement should be transferred to her. He based his argument on the authority of *Meek* v *Kettlewell* (1842) 1 Ha 464 and *Re Ellenborough* [1903] 1 Ch 697 and contended that the settlement, being a voluntary settlement, was void and altogether unenforceable. Neither of these authorities supports either of his propositions. All that was decided in *Meek* v *Kettlewell* was that where the assistance of the court of equity is needed to enable the trustees of a voluntary settlement to obtain possession of property subjected to the trusts of the voluntary settlement, the property not having been vested in the trustees, a court of equity will render no assistance to the plaintiff.

But here nobody is seeking the assistance of the court of equity to enforce the voluntary settlement. Under a valid authority, unrevoked, the persons appointed trustees under the settlement received the settlor's interest under her father's will, and, immediately after it had been received by them, as a result of her own act and her own declaration, contained in the voluntary settlement, it became impressed with the trusts contained in the settlement.

No assistance is required from a court of equity to put the property into the hands of the trustees.

Note
This case (and the second line of reasoning in *Ralli*) cannot be correct if *Re Brooks*, above, is good law. *Re Bowden* was not cited in *Re Brooks*. *Re Brooks* was not cited in *Ralli*. I would suggest that *Re Brooks* is wrong, but given that all these decisions are at first instance only, it is not possible to reach a clear conclusion.

4   CERTAINTY

SECTION 1:   CERTAINTY OF INTENTION

The question here is what words or conduct are sufficient to lead to the inference that a trust has been created. By about the middle of the nineteenth century, the courts were adopting a fairly strict view, the modern view being derived from the judgment of Cotton LJ in *Re Adams and Kensington Vestry* (1884) 27 ChD 394, 410, where it was established that there would be no trust unless this was the testator's clear intention, and a gift to the widow 'in full confidence that she would do what was right as to the disposal thereof between my children, either in her lifetime or by will after her decease' was treated as giving the widow an absolute interest unfettered by any trust in favour of the children.

It is clear, however, that trusts can be created without express words of trust, as for example in *Re Kayford* considered in chapter 3. In *Cominsky* v *Bowring-Hanbury* [1905] AC 84, the House of Lords found a trust on the basis of words very similar to those employed in *Re Adams and Kensington Vestry*: 'absolutely in full confidence that she [the widow] will make such use of [the property] as I would have made myself and that at her death she will devise it to such one or more of my nieces as she may think fit.' The entire document must be construed, and it therefore cannot be said that words which create a trust in one situation will necessarily do so in another.

If, on the other hand, a testator reproduces the *exact* language of an earlier will which has previously been held to create a trust, it may be possible to infer that he intended to use the earlier will as a precedent. If so, the court in construing the later will should follow the earlier decision, at least unless that decision was clearly wrong: *Re Steele's WT* [1948] Ch 603.

SECTION 2:   CERTAINTY OF SUBJECT MATTER

It is essential that the property comprising the subject matter of the trust is defined with precision, and also that the share that each beneficiary is to receive is ascertainable.

The courts are very strict about defining the trust property precisely. For example, in *Sprange* v *Barnard* (1789) 2 Bro CC 585, a testatrix left £300 in joint stock annuities '. . . for my husband . . . ; and at his death, the remaining part of what is left, that he does not want for his own wants and use, to be divided between . . . ', and Arden MR held that no trust was created, and that the husband was absolutely entitled to the £300. The 'remaining part of what is left, that he does not want for his own wants and use', could not be defined with sufficient certainty.

Another example is *Palmer* v *Simmonds* (1854) 2 Drew 221, where 'the bulk' of the testatrix's residuary estate was held insufficiently precise. The residuary estate was left to one Harrison, 'for his own use and benefit, as I have full confidence in him, that if he should die without issue he will leave the bulk of my residuary estate unto . . . '. Kindersley V-C observed:

> What is the meaning then of bulk? The appropriate meaning, according to its derivation, is something which bulges out . . . Its poplar meaning we all know. When a person is said to have given the bulk of his property, what is meant is not the whole but the greater part, and that is in fact consistent with its classical meaning. When, therefore, the testatrix uses that term, can I say that she has used a term expressing a definite, clear, certain part of her estate, or the whole of her estate? I am bound to say that she has not designated the subject as to which she expresses her confidence; and I am therefore of opinion that there is no trust created; that [the residuary legatee] took absolutely, and those claiming under him now take.

Another example is *Re Kolb's WT* [1962] Ch 531, where an attempt to create a trust of 'Blue chip securities' failed, since although the term was generally understood by investors, no technical or objective definition exists.

By contrast, the courts seem to be more flexible in ascertaining shares of beneficial interests. So long as the courts are capable of arriving at an objective definition, it seems that they will give effect to the disposition. In *Re Golay's WT* [1965] 1 WLR 969, Ungoed-Thomas J upheld a trust which allowed 'Totty' to receive a 'reasonable income' from the testator's properties, since this could be objectively quantified by a court. However, what the testator or a specified person considers to be reasonable would fail, since there the test is subjective.

SECTION 3:   CERTAINTY OF OBJECT

In the following discussion it is worth remembering that a trustee has a duty to distribute, albeit that under a discretionary trust no object can claim entitlement to any part of the fund, whereas a donee of a power does not.

However, a donee of a power may have a duty to consider whether to distribute, which duty must be exercised in a fiduciary manner. The nature of these duties is considered further in section C, below, but see also the discussion in section D, which casts doubt on the rigidity of the above distinction.

If the donees of a power do not appoint, a gift or trust over may have been provided for in default of appointment. A gift or trust over is a gift or trust which takes effect where the property has not otherwise been fully disposed of. It must be provided for in the original trust instrument, and if it has been it will take effect. If not, the property goes on resulting trust to the settlor.

It follows that if the settlor provides for a gift over or trust over in default of appointment, or has otherwise provided for this contingency, a power *must* be intended. This is because a trustee *must* appoint. The converse statement does not follow, however, and the courts will by no means presume a trust because there is no gift over in default. If in this case a power is construed, a failure to appoint leads to a resulting trust in favour of the settlor.

A: Development of the Law Before *McPhail* v *Doulton*

Re Gestetner Settlement
[1953] Ch 672
Chancery Division

Facts: Trustees had power to distribute capital among a very wide class, consisting of four named persons, the descendants, spouse, widow or widower of the settlor's father or uncle, and the directors and employees or former employees of a large number of companies. There being a gift over in default of appointment, this was a power given to a trustee. The validity of the power was challenged.

Held:

(a)   Where a power does not impose a trust on the donee's conscience, it is not necessary to know all the objects in order to appoint, so that a power may be good although it is in favour of an indefinite class.

(b)   But where a trustee is under a duty to select there must be certainty among those recipients.

(c)   The present case concerned a power given to trustees, who had no duty to appoint, only a duty to consider whether to distribute. Although the whole class could not be ascertained, since it was a fluctuating body, the power was valid.

HARMAN J: . . . If, therefore, there be no duty to distribute, but only a duty to consider, it does not seem to me that there is any authority binding on me to say that this whole trust is bad. In fact, there is no difficulty, as has been admitted, in ascertaining whether any given postulant is a member of the specified class. Of course, if that could not be ascertained the matter would be quite different, but of John Doe or Richard Doe it can be postulated easily enough whether he is or is not eligible to receive the settlor's bounty. There being no uncertainty in that sense, I am reluctant to introduce a notion of uncertainty in the other sense, by saying that the trustees must worry their heads to survey the world from China to Peru, when there are perfectly good objects of the class in England. Consequently, I am not minded to upset the scheme put forward by the settlor on the ground indicated, namely, that of uncertainty. There is no uncertainty in so far as it is quite certain whether particular individuals are objects of the power. What is not certain is how many objects there are; and it does not seem to me that such an uncertainty will invalidate a trust worded in this way. I accordingly declare the trust valid.

Notes

1. Harman J in the above passage was concerned with a trust where the trustees had a power to distribute, and the problem related to the objects of the power, not to the objects of the trust.

2. The case effectively decides that the judgment required of donees of a power can be exercised without the need to ascertain the entire class. The case, which was based largely on older authorities, suggests that it is enough to satisfy the individual ascertainability test, but does examine this test with the precision of later authorities.

IRC v *Broadway Cottages Trust*
[1955] Ch 20
Court of Appeal

Facts: £80,000 was settled upon trustees to apply the income within the perpetuity period in their absolute discretion, the objects being a very wide class, mostly of remote issue, contained in a schedule. There was no gift over in default of appointment, so that this was an attempt to set up a trust rather than a power. Two charities (Broadway Cottages Trust and Sunnylands Trust) were among the beneficiaries, and claimed income tax exemption on income received under settlement. The IRC claimed that, the trust being void for uncertainty, the income should be taxed as belonging to the settlor.

The charities admitted that the class was not ascertainable, while the Crown conceded that the individual ascertainability test was satisfied.

Held: The trust was void for uncertainty. The whole range of objects had to be ascertainable. The income therefore belonged in equity to the settlor on resulting trust (on the principles of chapter 8).

JENKINS LJ: It must, we think, follow from the appellants' concession to the effect that the class of 'beneficiaries' is incapable of ascertainment, and we understand them not to dispute, that the trust of the capital of the settled fund for all the beneficiaries living or existing at the termination of the appointed period, and if more than one in equal shares, must be void for uncertainty, inasmuch as there can be no division in equal shares amongst a class of persons unless all the members of the class are known.

We think it must also follow that a trust to divide the income of the trust fund during the appointed period amongst a class consisting of the settlor's wife and all the

beneficiaries for the time being living or in existence, and if more than one in equal
shares, would equally have been void for uncertainty.

. . .

In approaching this question both sides accept the principle stated by Lord Eldon
in *Morice* v *Bishop of Durham* (1805) 10 Ves 522, 539, 540, where he said: 'As it is a
maxim, that the execution of a trust shall be under the control of the court, it must
be of such a nature, that it can be under that control; so that the administration of it
can be reviewed by the court; or, if the trustee dies, the court itself can execute the
trust: a trust therefore, which, in case of maladministration could be reformed; and a
due administration directed; and then, unless the subject and the objects can be
ascertained, upon principles, familiar in other cases, it must be decided, that the court
can neither reform maladministration, nor direct a due administration.' The principle
can be concisely stated by saying that, in order to be valid, a trust must be one which
the court can control and execute. Mr Pennycuick, for the appellants, contends that
it is satisfied by the trust now before the court. Mr Cross, for the Crown, contends
that it is not.

The arguments in support of the Crown's claim that the trust is invalid are to this
effect: First, the court could not compel the trustees to make any distribution of
income . . ., for [the] clause purports to confer on the trustees an uncontrolled
discretion to determine the person or persons falling within the class of beneficiaries
to whom any distribution is to be made, and the shares in which those persons, if more
than one, are to take; and it would be beyond the power of the court to make or
enforce an order upon the trustees to exercise that discretion. Nor could the court
itself exercise the trustees' discretion in the event of their failing or refusing to do so,
for the discretion is conferred on, and exercisable by, the trustees alone. Secondly, if
the class of beneficiaries was an ascertainable class, it would or might be possible to
imply a trust in default of distribution by the trustees for all the members of the class
in equal shares, and that would be a trust which the court could control and execute.
But, as the class is unascertainable, no such trust can be implied. Thirdly, again, if
the class was ascertainable, it would or might be possible for all the beneficiaries to
join in a demand for the execution of the trust by the distribution of the whole income
amongst themselves in equal shares, and proper for the court to recognize and enforce
that demand as made by all the persons beneficially interested in the subject-matter of
the trust. But, as the class is unascertainable, no such demand is possible. Short of
the whole class, no beneficiary or collection of beneficiaries can claim execution of the
trust, for the trustees are under no duty to any particular beneficiary or beneficiaries,
short of the whole class, to make any distribution to him or them of the whole or any
part of the income; and such duty as the trust purports to impose on them towards
the class as a whole is illusory, since the whole class can never be ascertained.

Fourthly, the validity of the trust must be tested by considering its terms and asking
oneself whether the court would be able to control and execute the trust if called upon
to do so. That question must be answered by reference to what might happen, and
not merely by reference to what would be likely to happen. That is to say, the charge
of invalidity cannot be met by making the assumption (in itself reasonable enough)
that trustees undertaking a trust such as this would, in all probability, carry it out, by
distributing the income amongst persons falling within the class of beneficiaries as
defined by the settlement. On the contrary, it must be assumed that the trustees for
some reason or other might fail or refuse to make any distribution, and see whether
the court could execute the trust in that event. Consideration of the case on that
assumption shows that the most the court could do would be to remove the inert or
recalcitrant trustees and appoint others in their place. That, however, would not be

execution of the trust by the court, but a mere substitution for one set of trustees invested with an uncontrollable discretion of another set of trustees similarly invested, who might be equally inert or recalcitrant.

Fifthly, there is a distinction between a trust for distribution amongst all or any one or more exclusively of the others or other of an unascertainable class, with no other disposition (which is this case), and a power to distribute amongst all or any one or more exclusively of the others or other of an unascertainable class, with a trust in default of appointment for an ascertainable class. In the latter case (at all events if the qualification for membership of the unascertainable class is such as to make it possible to decide with certainty whether a given individual is or is not a member of it) there is a valid disposition of the beneficial interest which the court can control and execute in the shape of the trust in default of appointment and, although the execution of the power is beyond the control of the court, except in the negative sense that it can prevent any purported exercise of the power in favour of non-objects, it will nevertheless be a valid power operating, if and so far as exercised, as a defeasance in favour of the appointee or appointees of the interests given in default of appointment.
. . .

Sixthly, the court cannot mend the invalidity of the trust by imposing an arbitrary distribution amongst some only of the whole unascertainable class. . . .

. . . We think the submissions made on behalf of the Crown, to the effect that the trust is not one which the court could control or execute, and that this objection cannot be met by urging the improbability of assistance by the court ever becoming necessary, are well founded. We also agree with the further submission on the same side to the effect that the court would not be executing the trust merely by ordering a change in the trusteeship. . . .

Notes
1. This case has been overruled, but the conventional view is that the reasoning continues to apply to fixed trusts. Another reason for the inclusion of this case is that Jenkins LJ's logic is difficult to fault (I would suggest), and therefore given that the decision must now be regarded as incorrect, the assumptions made by Jenkins LJ must also be considered wrong.
2. The case could be distinguished from *Gestetner*, since there was an *obligation* to distribute. But in Jenkins LJ's view, if the trustees refused to distribute, the court could not itself exercise any discretion on their behalf. It could remove the trustees and appoint others in their place, but in theory it could be impossible to find any other trustees prepared to execute the trust. It followed that however unlikely this eventuality may be, at the end of the day a court had to be prepared to carry out the trust itself. Since it refused to exercise any discretion it could only divide the property equally among all the objects: 'It could not mend the invalidity of the trust by imposing an arbitrary distribution amongst some only of the whole unascertainable class.'
3. Although there is a logic to this conclusion, given the premises, equality of distribution will often not implement the intentions of the settlor, and indeed is quite likely to frustrate them. It seems that the equality principle originated in nineteenth century family settlements (e.g., *Burrough* v *Philcox* (1840) 5 Myl & Cr 72), where it may have been the most reliable method of carrying out the settlor's intention. It is much less likely to be appropriate,

however, in modern settlements, for example, dividing proceeds among employees of a company.

4. Nevertheless, equality of distribution was the rule, and of course it could only be done if it was possible to draw up a list of all the objects. For this reason, *Broadway* applied the class ascertainability test to discretionary trusts. One result of this was that the test for certainty was much more stringent for discretionary trusts than for powers. This had two main consequences: first, many perfectly reasonable trusts failed; secondly, the courts were at pains to construe doubtful dispositions as powers, rather than discretionary trusts.

Question
Was the concession that the class was not ascertainable correctly made?

Re Gulbenkian's Settlements, Whishaw v Stephens
[1970] AC 508
House of Lords

Facts: The case concerned the will of Calouste Gulbenkian (a well-known American oil entrepreneur), made in 1929, under which the trustees had a power to apply income to maintain his son, Nubar Gulbenkian:

> . . . and any person or persons in whose house or apartments or in whose company or under whose care or control or by or with whom the said Nubar Sarkis Gulbenkian may from time to time be employed or residing.

It was observed that the clause (which had apparently found its way into a standard book on precedents) did not make sense as it stood, but it was interpreted as meaning:

(a) any person by whom Mr Gulbenkian may from time to time be employed, and

(b) any person in whose house or in whose company or in whose care he may from time to time be residing.

No difficulties arose over limb (a), but it was argued that limb (b) was void for uncertainty.

Held: A power was not void for uncertainty if it could be said with certainty whether any given individual was or was not a member of the class, and did not fail simply because it was impossible to ascertain every member of the class. *Gestetner* was followed.

Notes
1. The exact formulation of the test is of importance. Note the words 'was or was not' a member of the class.
2. In the Court of Appeal, Lord Denning MR ([1968] Ch 126, at pp. 132–34) had taken the view that a was power void for uncertainty only if it was impossible to identify one single beneficiary. The argument (at p. 134)

is that unless it is impossible to carry out the power, it will not be held bad for uncertainty. In Lord Denning MR's view, therefore, it was enough to be able to identify one individual clearly within the class.

3.   The House of Lords (with Lord Donovan reserving his opinion) rejected Lord Denning MR's view, on the grounds that in order properly to exercise his or her discretion, *any* donee of a power must be able to ascertain whether *any* intended object was within the class of objects of the power. Even where the power gives the trustee 'absolute discretion', the discretion must be exercised in a fiduciary manner, and the donee of the power must at least consider whether to exercise it.

4.   The *Gulbenkian* decision strengthened if anything the view that different tests applied to powers and discretionary trusts.

B: *McPhail* v *Doulton* and the Modern Law

Re Baden's Deed Trusts (No. 1), McPhail v *Doulton*
[1971] AC 424
House of Lords

Facts: The settlor, Bertram Baden, purported by deed to transfer shares in Matthew Hall & Co. Ltd to trustees to form the nucleus of a fund for the benefit of the staff of the company, their relatives and dependants. Clause 9, set out at p. 447, provided:

(a)   The trustees shall apply the net income of the fund in making at their absolute discretion grants to or for the benefit of any of the officers and employees or ex-officers or ex-employees of the company or to any relatives or dependants of any such persons in such amounts at such times and on such conditions (if any) as they think fit and any such grant may at their discretion be made by payment to the beneficiary or to any institution or person to be applied for his or her benefit and in the latter case the trustees shall be under no obligation to see to the application of the money.

(b)   The trustees shall not be bound to exhaust the income of any year or other period in making such grants as aforesaid and any income not so applied shall be dealt with as provided by clause 6(a) hereof. [Clause 6. (a) All moneys in the hands of the trustees and not required for the immediate service of the fund may be placed in a deposit or current account with any bank or banking house in the name of the trustees or may be invested as hereinafter provided.]

(c)   The trustees may realise any investments representing accumulations of income and apply the proceeds as though the same were income of the fund and may also (but only with the consent of all the trustees) at any time prior to the liquidation of the fund realise any other part of the capital of the fund which in the opinion of the trustees it is desirable to realise in order to provide benefits for which the current income of the fund is insufficient.

The executors challenged the deed on behalf of the estate, on the ground that the settlement was void for uncertainty. It was argued that the disposition created a discretionary trust, not a power, and that the applicable test was therefore the class ascertainability test propounded by the Court of Appeal in *IRC* v *Broadway Cottages Trust* [1955] Ch 20, rather than the individual ascertainability test propounded by the House of Lords in *In re Gulbenkian's Settlements* [1970] AC 508. The *Gulbenkian* test, it was argued, applied only to powers.

Held (Lords Hodson and Guest dissenting): The disposition created a discretionary trust, not a power. However, the individual ascertainability test for certainty of objects, as applied to powers, was also the correct test to be applied to discretionary trusts. *IRC* v *Broadway Cottages* was overruled, and the case was remitted to the Chancery Division for application of the correct test.

LORD WILBERFORCE: . . . I therefore agree with Russell LJ and would to that extent allow the appeal, declare that the provisions of clause 9(a) constitute a trust and remit the case to the Chancery Division for determination whether on this basis clause 9 is . . . valid or void for uncertainty.

This makes it necessary to consider whether, in so doing, the court should proceed on the basis that the relevant test is that laid down in *IRC* v *Broadway Cottages Trust* [1955] Ch 20 or some other test.

That decision gave the authority of the Court of Appeal to the distinction between cases where trustees are given a power of selection and those where they are bound by a trust for selection. In the former case the position, as decided by this House, is that the power is valid if it can be said with certainty whether any given individual is or is not a member of the class and does not fail simply because it is impossible to ascertain every member of the class (*Re Gulbenkian's Settlements* [1970] AC 508). But in the latter case it is said to be necessary, for the trust to be valid, that the wide range of objects (I use the language of the Court of Appeal) should be ascertained or capable of ascertainment.

The respondents invited your lordships to assimilate the validity test for trusts to that which applies to powers. Alternatively they contended that in any event the test laid down in the *Broadway Cottages* case [1955] Ch 20 was too rigid, and that a trust should be upheld if there is sufficient practical certainty in its definition for it to be carried out, if necessary with the administrative assistance of the court, according to the expressed intention of the settlor. I would agree with this, but this does not dispense from examination of the wider argument. The basis for the *Broadway Cottages* principle is stated to be that a trust cannot be valid unless, if need be, it can be executed by the court, and (though it is not quite clear from the judgment where argument ends and decision begins) that the court can only execute it by ordering an equal distribution in which every beneficiary shares. So it is necessary to examine the authority and reason for this supposed rule as to the execution of trusts by the court.

Assuming, as I am prepared to do for present purposes, that the test of validity is whether the trust can be executed by the court, it does not follow that execution is impossible unless there can be equal division.

As a matter of reason, to hold that a principle of equal division applies to trusts such as the present is certainly paradoxical. Equal division is surely the last thing the settlor ever intended: equal division among all may, probably would, produce a result beneficial to none. Why suppose that the court would lend itself to a whimsical execution? And as regards authority, I do not find that the nature of the trust, and of the court's powers over trusts, calls for any such rigid rule. Equal division may be sensible and has been decreed, in cases of family trusts, for a limited class; here there is life in the maxim 'equality is equity', but the cases provide numerous examples where this has not been so, and a different type of execution has been ordered, appropriate to the circumstances. . . .

So I think that we are free to review the *Broadway Cottages* case [1955] Ch 20. The conclusion which I would reach, implicit in the previous discussion, is that the wide distinction between the validity test for powers and that for trust powers is unfortunate and wrong, that the rule recently fastened upon the courts by *IRC* v *Broadway Cottages Trust* ought to be discarded, and that the test for the validity of trust powers ought to be similar to that accepted by this House in *Re Gulbenkian's Settlements* [1970] AC 508 for powers, namely, that the trust is valid if it can be said with certainty that any given individual is or is not a member of the class. . . .

Assimilation of the validity test does not involve the complete assimilation of trust powers with powers. As to powers, I agree with my noble and learned friend Lord Upjohn in *Re Gulbenkian's Settlements* that although the trustees may, and normally will, be under a fiduciary duty to consider whether or in what way they should exercise their power, the court will not normally compel its exercise. It will intervene if the trustees exceed their powers, and possibly if they are proved to have exercised it capriciously. But in the case of a trust power, if the trustees do not exercise it, the court will: I respectfully adopt as to this the statement in Lord Upjohn's opinion (p. 525). I would venture to amplify this by saying that the court, if called upon to execute the trust power, will do so in the manner best calculated to give effect to the settlor's or testator's intentions. It may do so by appointing new trustees, or by authorising or directing representative persons of the classes of beneficiaries to prepare a scheme for distribution, or even, should the proper basis for distribution appear, by itself directing the trustees so to distribute. . . . Then, as to the trustees' duty of inquiry or ascertainment, in each case the trustees ought to make such a survey of the range of objects or possible beneficiaries as will enable them to carry out their fiduciary duty (cf. *Liley* v *Hey* (1842) 1 Hare 580). A wider and more comprehensive range of inquiry is called for in the case of trust powers than in the case of powers.

Two final points: first, as to the question of certainty. I desire to emphasise the distinction clearly made and explained by Lord Upjohn ([1970] AC 508, 524) between linguistic or semantic uncertainty which, if unresolved by the court, renders the gift void, and the difficulty of ascertaining the existence or whereabouts of members of the class, a matter with which the court can appropriately deal on an application for directions. There may be a third case where the meaning of the words used is clear but the definition of beneficiaries is so hopelessly wide as not to form 'anything like a class' so that the trust is administratively unworkable or in Lord Eldon's words one that cannot be executed (*Morice* v *Bishop of Durham* (1805) 10 Ves 522, 527). I hesitate to give examples for they may prejudice future cases, but perhaps 'all the residents of Greater London' will serve. I do not think that a discretionary trust for 'relatives' even of a living person falls within this category.

Notes

1. The *ratio* of *Re Baden's Deed Trusts (No. 1)* is that the test for certainty for discretionary trusts is essentially the same as that for powers – the individual ascertainability test, not the class ascertainability test.

2. In reaching its decision, the House rejected the principle of equality of distribution, in a case where equal distribution would have made a nonsense of the settlor's intention, accepting that even in the final analysis (in other words even assuming that no trustee can be found who is prepared to execute the trust), the court could exercise the necessary discretion itself. Therefore, the reasoning in the *IRC* v *Broadway Cottages Trust* [1955] Ch 20 was inapplicable (and indeed, *Broadway Cottages* was overruled).

3. Lord Wilberforce also made the point that in applying the test the courts are concerned only with conceptual uncertainty. A trust will not fail merely because there are evidential difficulties in ascertaining whether or not someone is within the class, as the court is never defeated by evidential uncertainty, and can deal with problems of proof when an application for enforcement arises:

> I desire to emphasise the distinction clearly made . . . between linguistic or semantic uncertainty which, if unresolved by the court, renders the gift void, and the difficulty of ascertaining the existence or whereabouts of members of the class, a matter with which the court can appropriately deal on an application for directions.

4. But there is not total assimilation between the tests for trusts and powers, since in considering the exercise of their discretion, the trustees must, according to Lord Wilberforce in *McPhail* v *Doulton* itself, make a survey of the entire field of objects, and consider each individual case responsibly, on its merits. A trust can fail if it is administratively unworkable, and this test may be more stringent than that for powers.

5. The trust also fails if the definition of beneficiaries is so hopelessly wide as not to form 'anything like a class'. The example given is a gift to 'all the residents of Greater London'.

6. Nothing in this case clearly affects fixed trusts. The House merely assimilated fixed trusts and powers. This aspect is considered further in section 3D.

Re Baden's Trusts (No. 2)
[1973] Ch 9
Court of Appeal

Decision: The deed considered in *Re Baden's Deed Trusts (No. 1)* was remitted to the Chancery Division for application of the test propounded by the House of Lords, and was appealed for a second time to the Court of Appeal. The Court of Appeal held that the trust was valid on the individual ascertainability test.

SACHS LJ: It is first to be noted that the deed must be looked at through the eyes of a businessman seeking to advance the welfare of the employees of his firm and those so connected with the employees that a benevolent employer would wish to help them. He would not necessarily be looking at the words he uses with the same eyes as those of a man making a will. Accordingly, whether a court is considering the concept implicit in relevant words, or whether it is exercising the function of a court of construction, it should adopt that same practical and common-sense approach which was enjoined by Upjohn J in *Re Sayer* [1957] Ch 423, 436, and by Lord Wilberforce in the *Baden* case [1971] AC 424, 452, and which would be used by an employer setting up such a fund.

The next point as regards approach that requires consideration is the contention, strongly pressed by Mr Vinelott, that the court must always be able to say whether any given postulant is not within the relevant class as well as being able to say whether he is within it. In construing the words already cited from the speech of Lord Wilberforce in the *Baden* case (as well as those of Lord Reid and Lord Upjohn in [*Re Gulbenkian's Settlements* [1970] AC 508]), it is essential to bear in mind the difference between conceptual uncertainty and evidential difficulties. That distinction is explicitly referred to by Lord Wilberforce in *Re Baden's Deed Trusts* [1971] AC 424, 457 when he said:

> . . . as to the question of certainty. I desire to emphasise the distinction clearly made and explained by Lord Upjohn [1970] AC 508, 524 between linguistic or semantic uncertainty which, if unresolved by the court, renders the gift void, and the difficulty of ascertaining the existence or whereabouts of members of the class, a matter with which the court can appropriately deal on an application for directions.

As Mr Vinelott himself rightly observed, 'the court is never defeated by evidential uncertainty', and it is in my judgment clear that it is conceptual uncertainty to which reference was made when the 'is or is not a member of the class' test was enunciated. (Conceptual uncertainty was in the course of argument conveniently exemplified, rightly or wrongly matters not, by the phrase 'someone under a moral obligation' and contrasted with the certainty of the words 'first cousins'.) Once the class of persons to be benefited is conceptually certain it then becomes a question of fact to be determined on evidence whether any postulant has on inquiry been proved to be within it: if he is not so proved, then he is not in it. That position remains the same whether the class to be benefited happens to be small (such as 'first cousins') or large (such as 'members of the X Trade Union' or 'those who have served in the Royal Navy'). The suggestion that such trusts could be invalid because it might be impossible to prove of a given individual that he was not in the relevant class is wholly fallacious – and only Mr Vinelott's persuasiveness has prevented me from saying that the contention is almost unarguable.

MEGAW LJ: The main argument of Mr Vinelott was founded upon a strict and literal interpretation of the words in which the decision of the House of Lords in *Re Gulbenkian's Settlements* [1970] AC 508 was expressed. That decision laid down the test for the validity of powers of selection. It is relevant for the present case, because in the previous excursion of this case to the House of Lords [1971] AC 424 it was held that there is no relevant difference in the test of validity, whether the trustees are given a power of selection or, as was held by their lordships to be the case in this trust deed, a trust for selection. The test in either case is what may be called the *Gulbenkian* test. The *Gulbenkian* test, as expressed by Lord Wilberforce at p. 450, and again in almost identical words at p. 454 is this:

> . . . the power is valid if it can be said with certainty whether any given individual is or is not a member of the class and does not fail simply because it is impossible to ascertain every member of the class.

The executors' argument concentrates on the words 'or is not' in the first of the two limbs of the sentence quoted above: 'if it can be said with certainty whether any given individual is or is not a member of the class'. It is said that those words have been used deliberately, and have only one possible meaning; and that however startling or drastic or unsatisfactory the result may be – and Mr Vinelott does not shrink from saying that the consequence is drastic – this court is bound to give effect to the words used in the House of Lords' definition of the test. It would be quite impracticable for the trustees to ascertain in many cases whether a particular person was not a relative of an employee. The most that could be said is: 'There is no proof that he is a relative'. But there would still be no 'certainty' that such a person was not a relative. Hence, so it is said, the test laid down by the House of Lords is not satisfied, and the trust is void. For it cannot be said with certainty, in relation to any individual, that he is not a relative.

I do not think it was contemplated that the words 'or is not' would produce that result. It would, as I see it, involve an inconsistency with the latter part of the same sentence: 'does not fail simply because it is impossible to ascertain every member of the class'. The executors' contention, in substance and reality, is that it does fail 'simply because it is impossible to ascertain every member of the class'.

The same verbal difficulty, as I see it, emerges also when one considers the words of the suggested test which the House of Lords expressly rejected. That is set out by Lord Wilberforce in a passage immediately following the sentence which I have already quoted. The rejected test was in these terms [1971] AC 424, 450:

> . . . it is said to be necessary . . . that the whole range of objects . . . should be ascertained or capable of ascertainment.

Since that test was rejected, the resulting affirmative proposition, which by implication must have been accepted by their lordships, is this: a trust for selection will not fail simply because the whole range of objects cannot be ascertained. In the present case, the trustees could ascertain, by investigation and evidence, many of the objects: as to many other theoretically possible claimants, they could not be certain. Is it to be said that the trust fails because it cannot be said with certainty that such persons are not members of the class? If so, is that not the application of the rejected test: the trust failing because 'the whole range' of objects cannot be ascertained'?

In my judgment, much too great emphasis is placed in the executors' argument on the words 'or is not'. To my mind, the test is satisfied if, as regards at least a substantial number of objects, it can be said with certainty that they fall within the trust; even though, as regards a substantial number of other persons, if they ever for some fanciful reason fell to be considered, the answer would have to be, not 'they are outside the trust', but 'it is not proven whether they are in or out'. What is a 'substantial number' may well be a question of common sense and of degree in relation to the particular trust: particularly where, as here, it would be fantasy, to use a mild word, to suggest that any practical difficulty would arise in the fair, proper and sensible administration of this trust in respect of relatives and dependants.

I do not think that this involves, as Mr Vinelott suggested, a return by this court to its former view which was rejected by the House of Lords in the *Gulbenkian* case. If I did so think, I should, however reluctantly, accept Mr Vinelott's argument and its consequences. But as I read it, the criticism in the House of Lords of the decision of this court in that case related to this court's acceptance of the view that it would be sufficient if it could be shown that one single person fell within the scope of the power or trust. The essence of the decision of the House of Lords in the *Gulbenkian* case, as

I see it, is not that it must be possible to show with certainty that any given person is or is not within the trust; but that it is not, or may not be, sufficient to be able to show that one individual person is within it. If it does not mean that, I do not know where the line is supposed to be drawn, having regard to the clarity and emphasis with which the House of Lords has laid down that the trust does not fail because the whole range of objects cannot be ascertained. I would dismiss the appeal.

Notes

1. The disposition was 'to or for the benefit of any of the officers and employees or ex-officers or ex-employees of the company or to any relatives or dependants of any such persons'. It was argued by John Vinelott QC, who was challenging the disposition on behalf of the executors, that it could not be shown that any person definitely is or *is not* within the class (as required by the *Gulbenkian* test). Had this ingenious argument been accepted it would have meant virtually returning to the rejected class-ascertainability test, as Megaw LJ observed. The Court of Appeal rejected the argument, but not on identical grounds.

2. Sachs LJ avoided the difficulty by emphasising that the court was concerned only with conceptual certainty, so that it should not be fatal that there might be *evidential* difficulties in drawing up John Vinelott QC's list. This effectively destroys the Vinelott argument, which was addressed primarily towards *evidential* difficulties in drawing up the class. Sachs LJ also took the view that the courts would place the burden of proof, in effect, on someone claiming to be within the class. This seems acceptable if ultimate enforcement is the issue, and the test is of the *locus standi* of the claimant, but it does not help the administration of the trust.

3. Megaw LJ adopted a different solution, however, requiring that as regards a substantial number of objects, it can be shown with certainty that they fall within the class. This is rather a vague test – clearly it is not enough to be able to show that *one* person is certainly within the class, as this test was rejected in *Gulbenkian* (see the discussion of powers, above). Presumably, the test requires evidential, as well as conceptual certainty. Maybe Megaw LJ adopted it simply because he could find no other way of rejecting Mr Vinelott's argument without returning either to the rejected *Broadway* test, or to the Denning test which had been rejected in *Gulbenkian*. Indeed, none of the judges in the Court of Appeal was able to find a satisfactory solution to this difficulty. The test may have the merit, however, of ensuring that the trustees will be able to get a feel for the width of the class, which they need properly to be able to exercise their discretion.

4. Stamp LJ's test is probably the strictest of the three, and he seemed to be quite impressed by the Vinelott argument. He emphasised that it must be possible for the trustees to make a comprehensive survey of the range of objects, but he did not think it would be fatal if, at the end of the survey, it was impossible to draw up a list of every single beneficiary. He would have taken the view that the trust failed, had he not felt compelled to follow an early House of Lords authority, which had held that a discretionary trust for 'relations' was valid, 'relations' being defined narrowly as 'next of kin'.

Re Barlow's WT
[1979] 1 WLR 278, [1979] 1 All ER 296
Chancery Division

Decision: Browne-Wilkinson J upheld a direction to an executor to sell a collection of valuable paintings, subject to provision 'to allow any member of my family and any friends of mine who may wish to do so' to purchase them at well below current market value. The issue was whether 'family' and 'friends' were conceptually uncertain, so that the gift should fail for uncertainty.

BROWNE-WILKINSON J: Counsel for the fourth defendant, who argued in favour of the validity of the gift, contended that the tests laid down in the *Gulbenkian* case [1970] AC 508 and *McPhail* v *Doulton* [1971] AC 424 were not applicable to this case. The test, he says, is that laid down by the Court of Appeal in *Re Allen* [1953] Ch 810 as appropriate in cases where the validity of a condition precedent or description is in issue, namely that the gift is valid if it is possible to say of one or more persons that he or they undoubtedly qualify even though it may be difficult to say of others whether or not they qualify.

The distinction between the *Gulbenkian* test and the *Re Allen* test is, in my judgment, well exemplified by the word 'friends'. The word has a great range of meanings; indeed, its exact meaning probably varies slightly from person to person. Some would include only those with whom they had been on intimate terms over a long period; others would include acquaintances whom they liked. Some would include people with whom their relationship was primarily one of business; other would not. Indeed, many people, if asked to draw up a complete list of their friends, would probably have some difficulty in deciding whether certain of the people they knew were really 'friends' as opposed to 'acquaintances'. Therefore, if the nature of the gift was such that it was legally necessary to draw up a complete list of 'friends' of the testatrix, or to be able to say of any person that 'he is not a friend', the whole gift would probably fail even as to those who, by any conceivable test, were friends. But in the case of a gift of a kind which does not require one to establish all the members of the class (e.g., 'a gift of £10 to each of my friends'), it may be possible to say of some people that, on any test, they qualify. Thus in *Re Allen* Evershed MR took the example of a gift to X 'if he is a tall man'; a man 6 feet 6 inches tall could be said on any reasonable basis to satisfy the test, although it might be impossible to say whether a man, say, 5 feet 10 inches high satisfied the requirement.

So in this case, in my judgment, there are acquaintances of a kind so close that, on any reasonable basis, anyone would treat them as being 'friends'. Therefore, by allowing the disposition to take effect in their favour, one would, certainly be giving effect to part of the testatrix's intention even though as to others it is impossible to say whether or not they satisfy the test.

In my judgment, it is clear that Lord Upjohn in *Re Gulbenkian* was considering only cases where it was necessary to establish all the members of the class. He made it clear that the reason for the rule is that in a gift which requires one to establish all the members of the class (e.g., 'a gift to my friends in equal shares') you cannot hold the gift good in part, since the quantum of each friend's share depends on how many friends there are. So all persons intended to benefit by the donor must be ascertained if any effect is to be given to the gift. In my judgment, the adoption of Lord Upjohn's test by the House of Lords in *McPhail* v *Doulton* is based on the same reasoning, even though in that case the House of Lords held that it was only necessary to be able to survey the class of objects of a power of appointment and not to establish who all the members were. But such reasoning has no application to a case where there is a condition or description attached to one or more individual gifts; in such cases, uncertainty as to some other persons who may have been intended to take does not in any way affect the quantum of the gift to persons who undoubtedly possess the qualification. Hence, in my judgment, the different test laid down in *Re Allen*. The recent decision of the Court of Appeal in *Re Tuck's ST* [1978] Ch 49 establishes that the test in *Re Allen* is still the appropriate test in considering such gifts, notwithstanding the *Gulbenkian* and *McPhail* v *Doulton* decisions: see per Lord Russell of Killowen.

Accordingly, in my judgment, the proper result in this case depends on whether the disposition in cl. 5(a) is properly to be regarded as a series of individual gifts to persons answering the description 'friend' (in which case it will be valid), or a gift which requires the whole class of friends to be established (in which case it will probably fail).

Note

Had it been necessary for the executor to ascertain who all the friends of the testator were, the gift would presumably have failed as being conceptually uncertain, because he could not have sensibly surveyed the entire class. Friendship is a matter of degree on which opinions can differ. This did not matter in *Barlow* itself, because friendship was simply a condition of exercising an option, and there was therefore no need for the purposes of the particular disposition to survey the class at all. It was enough, therefore, to place the burden on each person coming forward to prove that he was a friend, and Browne-Wilkinson J laid down certain minimum qualifications.

C: Present-Day Distinction Between Trusts and Powers

In *McPhail* v *Doulton* Lord Wilberforce did not think that there was necessarily a total assimilation between trusts and powers, and it may be that the administrative unworkability tests work differently as between trusts and powers.

Re Manisty's Settlement
[1972] 1 Ch 17
Chancery Division

Facts: The settlement gave trustees a discretionary power to apply the trust fund for the benefit of a small class of the settlor's near relations, save that any member of a smaller 'excepted class' was to be excluded from the class of beneficiaries. The trustees were also given power at their absolute discretion to declare that any person, corporation or charity (except a member of the excepted class or a trustee) should be included in the class of beneficiaries. A summons was brought to determine whether the power was void for uncertainty.

Held: The power to extend the class of beneficiaries was valid.

TEMPLEMAN J: The argument that a discretionary trust in favour of a recognised class can be too wide was considered in *Re Baden's Deed Trusts (No. 2)* [1972] Ch 607, a case known as *Baden (No. 2)*, and a decision which for present purposes must apply to special powers as well as to discretionary trusts. In *Baden (No. 2)* it was submitted that a discretionary trust exercisable in favour of employees and former employees of a company and their relatives and dependants was void for uncertainty because it did not satisfy the test suggested at p. 620 of the judgment of Brightman J, namely, that such a trust is

> invalid if the class is so large or arbitrary that the trustees cannot reasonably estimate the membership, or know how to set about instituting inquiries which will reveal the membership including the membership of its subclasses or categories, and if the trustees cannot therefore properly discharge their duty to consider how the fund should be divided between the subclasses or categories, and what further inquiries they should make.

The suggested test only serves to illustrate how impossible it is to define the circumstances in which a recognised class may be said to be too wide. Brightman J rejected the test and held that the discretionary trust was valid, applying only the test established in *Re Baden's Deed Trusts (No. 1)* [1971] AC 424 that a trust in favour of a recognised class is valid if it can be said with certainty that any given individual is or is not a member of the class. The decision of Brightman J in *Baden (No. 2)* was affirmed by the Court of Appeal [1973] Ch 9 . . . . I conclude from *Re Gestetner* [1953] Ch 672, *Re Gulbenkian's Settlements* [1970] AC 508 and the two *Baden* cases that a power cannot be uncertain merely because it is wide in ambit.

An alternative argument against the validity of an intermediate power conferred on trustees is that a power which is not confined to individuals or to classes recognised by the court is too vague. An intermediate power which does not attempt to classify the beneficiaries but only specifies or classifies excepted persons is therefore, it is said, too vague. It is admitted that it may be difficult to define or describe those classes which would not be recognised by the court, and are therefore also too vague, but the example suggested by Lord Wilberforce in *Baden (No. 1)* [1971] AC 424, 457 [above] of 'all the residents of Greater London' is given as an instance of a class which would not be so recognised. The submission that an intermediate power is too vague because the beneficiaries are not limited to specified individuals or recognised classes is in the final analysis based on the same reasoning as the attack on wide discretionary trusts which was rejected in *Baden (No. 2)* [1972] Ch 607. The argument is that an intermediate power where the beneficiaries are not limited to specified individuals or recognised classes precludes the trustees from considering in a sensible manner whether and how to exercise the power, and prevents the court from judging whether the trustees have surveyed the field of objects and have properly considered whether and how to exercise the power.

Implicit in this argument are two assertions, first, that the terms of a special power in favour of recognised classes necessarily provide some guidance to the trustees with regard to the proper mode of considering how to exercise the power, and secondly, that the terms of a special power in favour of recognised classes enable the court to judge whether the trustees are in breach of their duty. In my judgment neither assertion is well founded. Some powers may give an indication of the expectations of the settlor. In *Gulbenkian* [1970] AC 508 it was plain that the trustees were expected to have regard to the best interests of Mr Nubar Gulbenkian. There are similar powers where all the beneficiaries are equal but some are more equal than others. But . . .

[t]he terms of a special power do not necessarily indicate in themselves how the trustees are to consider the exercise of the power. That consideration is confided to the absolute discretion of the trustees.

The court cannot insist upon any particular consideration being given by the trustees to the exercise of the power. If a settlor creates a power exercisable in favour of his issue, his relations and the employees of his company, the trustees may in practice for many years hold regular meetings, study the terms of the power and the other provisions of the settlement, examine the accounts and either decide not to exercise the power or to exercise it only in favour, for example, of the children of the settlor . . . . In my judgment it cannot be said that the trustees in those circumstances have committed a breach of trust and that they ought to have advertised the power or looked beyond the people who are most likely to be the objects of the bounty of the settlor. . . .

If a person within the ambit of the power is aware of its existence he can require the trustees to consider exercising the power and in particular to consider a request on his part for the power to be exercised in his favour. The trustees must consider this request, and if they decline to do so or can be proved to have omitted to do so, then the aggrieved person may apply to the court which may remove the trustees and appoint others in their place. . . .

The court may also be persuaded to intervene if the trustees act 'capriciously', that is to say, act for reasons which I apprehend could be said to be irrational, perverse or irrelevant to any sensible expectation of the settlor; for example, if they chose a beneficiary by height or complexion or by the irrelevant fact that he was a resident of Greater London. A special power does not show the trustees how to consider the exercise of the power in a sensible manner and does not by its terms enable the court to judge whether the power is being considered in a proper manner. The conduct and duties of trustees of an intermediate power, and the rights and remedies of any person who wishes the power to be exercised in his favour, are precisely similar to the conduct and duties of trustees of special powers and the rights and remedies of any person who wishes a special power to be exercised in his favour. In practice, the considerations which weigh with the trustees will be no different from the considerations which will weigh with the trustees of a wide special power . . . . In both cases the trustees have an absolute discretion and cannot be obliged to take any form of action, save to consider the exercise of the power and a request from a person who is within the ambit of the power . . . . The only difference between an intermediate power and a special power for present purposes is that a settlor by means of a special power cannot be certain that he has armed his trustees against all developments and contingencies. . . .

Logically, in my judgment, there is no reason to bless a special power which prescribes the ambit of the power by classifying beneficiaries and at the same time to outlaw an intermediate power which prescribes the ambit of the power by classifying excepted persons. It may well be that there are some classes of special power which will not be recognised by the court, but this possibility does not affect the validity of intermediate powers. The objection to the capricious exercise of a power may well extend to the creation of a capricious power. A power to benefit 'residents of Greater London' is capricious because the terms of the power negative any sensible intention on the part of the settlor. If the settlor intended and expected the trustees would have regard to persons with some claim on his bounty or some interest in an institution favoured by the settlor, or if the settlor had any other sensible intention or expectation, he would not have required the trustees to consider only an accidental conglomeration of persons who have no discernable link with the settlor or with any institution. A capricious power negatives a sensible consideration by the trustees of the exercise of the power. But a wide power, be it special or intermediate, does not negative or prohibit a sensible approach by the trustees to the consideration and exercise of their powers.

Questions
1.   Is the sensible intention of settlor test part of administrative unworkability, or an additional test?
2.   Suppose that even the class ascertainability test is satisfied. Then it could not be said that the disposition was administratively unworkable, because clearly the trustees could survey the entire class. Could the disposition could still fail if the terms were such as to negative any sensible intention on the part of the settlor?

Re Hay's ST
[1982] 1 WLR 1202, [1981] 3 All ER 786
Chancery Division

Decision: An 'intermediate' or 'hybrid' power of appointment, allowing a trustee to appoint anyone in the world except for a specified number or class of persons did not infringe the certainty of objects requirement.

However, the appointment actually made was void. The trustees simply appointed the trust fund to be held by themselves for 'such person or persons and for such purposes' as the trustees should in their discretion appoint by deed within 21 years of the date of the settlement. This was not a valid appointment, since it had merely set up the mechanism for future appointments. The trustees had in effect purported to delegate their powers of appointment, rather than exercise them, and even though they had delegated them to themselves, they had infringed the rule that a trustee may not delegate his powers, including intermediate powers (*'delegatus non potest delegare'*).

SIR ROBERT MEGARRY V-C (on the certainty point): The starting point must be to consider whether the power created by . . . the settlement is valid. The rival arguments were presented by counsel for the defendants in his primary contention, and by counsel for the Attorney General, in favour of validity, and by counsel for the defendants, in his alternative contention, against validity. The essential point is whether a power for trustees to appoint to anyone in the world except a handful of specified persons is valid. Such a power will be perfectly valid if given to a person who is not in a fiduciary position: the difficulty arises when it is given to trustees, for they are under certain fiduciary duties in relation to the power, and to a limited degree they are subject to the control of the courts. At the centre of the dispute there are *Re Manisty's Settlement* [1974] Ch 17 [above] (in which Templeman J differed from part of what was said in the Court of Appeal in *Blausten* v *IRC* [1972] Ch 256; *McPhail* v *Doulton* [1971] AC 424 (which I shall call *Re Baden (No. 1)* [in this section]; and *Re Baden's Deed Trusts (No. 2)* [1973] Ch 9 [above], which I shall call *Re Baden (No. 2)*. Counsel for the defendants, I may say, strongly contended that *Re Manisty's Settlement* was wrongly decided.

In *Re Manisty's Settlement* a settlement gave trustees a discretionary power to apply the trust fund for the benefit of a small class of the settlor's near relations, save that any member of a smaller 'expected class' was to be excluded from the class of beneficiaries. The trustees were also given power at their absolute discretion to declare that any person, corporation or charity (except a member of the excepted class or a trustee) should be included in the class of beneficiaries. Templeman J held that this power to extend the class of beneficiaries was valid. In *Blausten v IRC* which had been decided some 18 months earlier, the settlement created a discretionary trust of income for members of a 'specified class' and a power to pay or apply capital to or for the benefit of members of that class, or to appoint capital to be held on trust for them. The settlement also gave the trustees power 'with the previous consent in writing of the settlor' to appoint any other person or persons (except the settlor) to be included in the 'specified class'. The Court of Appeal decided the case on a point of construction; but Buckley LJ ([1972] Ch [1972] Ch 256 at 271) also considered a contention that the trustees' power to add to the 'specified class' was so wide that it was bad for uncertainty, since the power would enable anyone in the world save the settlor to be included. He rejected this contention on the ground that the settlor's prior written consent was requisite to any addition to the 'specified class'; but for this, it seems plain that he would have held the power void for uncertainty. Orr LJ simply concurred, but Salmon LJ expressly confined himself to the point of construction, and said nothing about the power to add to the 'specified class'. In *Re Manisty's Settlement* [1974] Ch 17 at 29, Templeman J rejected the view of Buckley LJ on this point on the ground that *Re Gestetner* [1953] Ch 672, *Re Gulbenkian's Settlements* [1970] AC 508 and the two *Baden* cases did not appear to have been fully explored in the *Blausten* case, and the case did not involve any final pronouncement on the point. In general, I respectfully agree with Templeman J.

I propose to approach the matter by stages. First, it is plain that if a power of appointment is given to a person who is not in a fiduciary position, there is nothing in the width of the power which invalidates it *per se*. The power may be a special power with a large class of persons as objects; the power may be what is called a 'hybrid' power, or an 'intermediate' power, authorising appointment to anyone save a specified number or class of persons; or the power may be a general power. Whichever it is, there is nothing in the number of persons to whom an appointment may be made which will invalidate it. The difficulty comes when the power is given to trustees as such, in that the number of objects may interact with the fiduciary duties of the trustees and their control by the court. The argument of counsel for the defendants carried him to the extent of asserting that no valid intermediate or general power could be vested in trustees.

That brings me to the second point, namely, the extent of the fiduciary obligations of trustees who have a mere power vested in them, and how far the court exercises control over them in relation to that power. In the case of a trust, of course, the trustee is bound to execute it, and if he does not, the court will see to its execution. A mere power is very different. Normally the trustee is not bound to exercise it, and the court will not compel him to do so. That, however, does not mean that he can simply fold his hands and ignore it, for normally he must from time to time consider whether or not to exercise the power, and the court may direct him to do this.

When he does exercise the power, he must, of course (as in the case of all trusts and powers) confine himself to what is authorised, and not go beyond it. But that is not the only restriction. Whereas a person who is not in a fiduciary position is free to exercise the power in any way that he wishes, unhampered by any fiduciary duties, a trustee to whom, as such, a power is given is bound by the duties of his office in exercising that power to do so in a responsible manner according to its purpose. It is not enough for him to refrain from acting capriciously; he must do more. He must 'make such a survey of the range of objects or possible beneficiaries' as will enable him to carry out his fiduciary duty. He must find out 'the permissible area of selection and then consider responsibly, in individual cases, whether a contemplated beneficiary was within the power and whether, in relation to the possible claimants, a particular grant was appropriate': per Lord Wilberforce in *Re Baden (No. 1)* [1971] AC 424 at 449, 457.

I pause there. The summary of the law that I have set out above is taken from a variety of sources, principally *Re Gestetner* [1953] Ch 672, *Re Gulbenkian's Settlements* [1970] Ac 508 at 518, 524–5 and *Re Baden (No. 1)* [1971] AC 424 at 456. The last proposition, relating to the survey and consideration, at first sight seems to give rise to some difficulty. It is now well settled that no mere power is invalidated by it being impossible to ascertain every object of the power; provided the language is clear enough to make it possible to say whether any given individual is an object of the power, it need not be possible to compile a complete list of every object: see *Re Gestetner* [1953] Ch 672 at 688; *Re Gulbenkian's Settlements* [1970] AC 508; *Re Baden (No. 1)* [1971] AC 424. As Harman J said in *Re Gestetner* [1953] Ch 672 at 688, the trustees need not 'worry their heads to survey the world from China to Peru, when there are perfectly good objects of the class in England'.

That brings me to the third point. How is the duty of making a responsible survey and selection to be carried out in the absence of any complete list of objects? This question was considered by the Court of Appeal in *Re Baden (No. 2)*. That case was concerned with what, after some divergences of judicial opinion, was held to be a discretionary trust and not a mere power; but plainly the requirements for a mere power cannot be more stringent than those for a discretionary trust. The duty, I think, may be expressed along the following lines: I venture a modest degree of amplification and exegesis of what was said in *Re Baden (No. 2)* [1973] Ch 9 at 20, 27. The trustee must not simply proceed to exercise the power in favour of such of the objects as happen to be at hand or claim his attention. He must first consider what persons or classes of persons are objects of the power within the definition in the settlement or will. In doing this, there is no need to compile a complete list of the objects, or even to make an accurate assessment of the number of them: what is needed is an appreciation of the width of the field, and thus whether a selection is to be made merely from a dozen, or, instead, from thousands or millions. . . . Only when the trustee has applied his mind to 'the size of the problem' should he then consider in individual cases whether, in relation to other possible claimants, a particular grant is appropriate. In doing this, no doubt he should not prefer the undeserving to the deserving; but he is not required to make an exact calculation whether, as between deserving claimants, A is more deserving than B: see *Re Gestetner* [1953] Ch 672 at 688, approved in *Re Baden (No. 1)* [1971] AC 424 at 453.

If I am right in these views, the duties of a trustee which are specific to a mere power seem to be threefold. Apart from the obvious duty of obeying the trust instrument, and in particular of making no appointment that is not authorised by it, the trustee must, first, consider periodically whether or not he should exercise the power; second, consider the range of objects of the power; and third, consider the appropriateness of individual appointments. I do not assert that this list is exhaustive; but as the authorities stand it seems to me to include the essentials, so far as relevant to the case before me.

On this footing, the question is thus whether there is something in the nature of an intermediate power which conflicts with these duties in such a way as to invalidate the power if it is vested in a trustee. . . .

[His lordship considered the Court of Appeal decision in *Blausten v IRC* [1972] Ch 256, and rejected the view that a power of this width would be saved only by a requirement for the consent of the settlor. He continued:]

From what I have said it will be seen that I cannot see any ground on which the power in question can be said to be void. Certainly it is not void for linguistic or semantic uncertainty; there is no room for doubt in the definition of those who are or are not objects of the power. Nor can I see that the power is administratively unworkable. The words of Lord Wilberforce in *Re Baden (No. 1)* [1971] AC 424 at 457 are directed to discretionary trusts, not powers. Nor do I think that the power is void as being capricious. In *Re Manisty's Settlement* [1974] Ch 17 at 27 Templeman J appears to be suggesting that a power to benefit 'residents in Greater London' is void as being capricious 'because the terms of the power negative any sensible intention on the part of the settlor'. In saying that, I do not think that the judge had in mind a case in which the settlor was, for instance, a former chairman of the Greater London Council, as subsequent words of his on that page indicate. In any case, as he pointed out earlier, this consideration does not apply to intermediate powers, where no class which could be regarded as capricious has been laid down. Nor do I see how the power in the present case could be invalidated as being too vague, a possible ground of invalidity considered in *Re Manisty's Settlement* [1974] Ch 17 at 24. Of course, if there is some real vice in a power, and there are real problems of administration or execution, the court may have to hold the power invalid: but I think that the court should be slow to do this. Dispositions ought if possible to be upheld, and the court ought not to be astute to find grounds on which a power can be invalidated. Naturally, if it is shown that a power offends against some rule of law or equity, then it will be held to be void: but a power should not be held void on a peradventure. In my judgment, the power conferred by . . . the settlement is valid.

Note

Sir Robert Megarry V-C's conclusion depends upon the nature of the duties of the trustees in considering whether to exercise the power. The relevant passage is the following:

> Apart from the obvious duty of obeying the trust instrument, and in particular of making no appointment that is not authorised by it, the trustee [in considering whether to exercise the power of appointment] must, first, consider periodically whether or not he should exercise the power; second, consider the range of objects of the power; and third, consider the appropriateness of individual appointments.

It is not entirely clear how far this reasoning also applies to discretionary trusts; in a number of places in the above passage a distinction is drawn between powers and trusts, and it does not necessarily follow that a discretionary trust in similar terms would be valid.

R v District Auditor, ex parte West Yorkshire Metropolitan County Council
[1986] RVR 24
Divisional Court of the Queen's Bench Division

Facts: Prior to the abolition of the Metropolitan County Councils, they were prohibited from incurring expenditure under Local Government Act 1972, s. 137(1):

which in their opinion is in the interests of their area or any part of it or some or all of its inhabitants

after 1 April 1985.

When West Yorkshire Metropolitan County Council realised that they were going to have a large surplus on 1 April 1985, they sought to find ways of ensuring that this money could still be spent after the 1 April deadline. In their attempt to achieve this aim, they purported to set up a discretionary trust of £400,000, having a duration of 11 months, 'for the benefit of any or all or some of the inhabitants of the County of West Yorkshire'. The trust also directed the trustees to use the fund specifically:

(a)   To assist economic development in the county in order to relieve unemployment and poverty.

(b)   To assist bodies concerned with youth and community problems.

(c)   To assist and encourage ethnic and other minority groups.

(d)   To inform all interested persons of the consequences of the proposed abolition of the Council (and the other Metropolitan County Councils) and of other programs affecting local government in the county.

Held: This was held to be administratively unworkable. The inhabitants of the County of West Yorkshire numbered about two and a half million. The range of objects was held to be so hopelessly wide as to be incapable of forming anything like a class.

There are clear statements in the case that trusts may be treated differently from powers in this regard, since a court may be called upon ultimately to execute a trust, whereas it will not of course be required to execute a power.

LLOYD LJ: . . . For the creation of an express private trust three things are required. First, there must be a clear intention to create the trust. Secondly there must be certainty as to the subject matter of the trust; and thirdly there must be certainty as to the persons intended to benefit. Two of the three certainties, as they are familiarly called, were present here. Was the third? Mr Henderson argued that the beneficiaries of the trust were all or some of the inhabitants of the county of West Yorkshire. The class might be on the large side, containing as it does some 2½ million potential beneficiaries. But the definition, it was said, is straightforward and clear cut. There is no uncertainty as to the concept. If anyone were to come forward and claim to be a beneficiary, it could be said of him at once whether he was within the class or not.

I cannot accept Mr Henderson's argument. I am prepared to assume in favour of the council, without deciding, that the class is defined with sufficient clarity. I do not decide the point because it might, as it seems to me, be open to argument what is meant by 'an inhabitant' of the county of West Yorkshire. But I put that difficulty on one side. For there is to my mind a more fundamental difficulty. A trust with as many as 2½ million potential beneficiaries is, in my judgment, quite simply unworkable. The class is far too large. In *Re Gulbenkian's Settlements* [1970] AC 508, [1968] 3 All ER 785 Lord Reid said at page 518: 'It may be that there is a class of case where, although the description of a class of beneficiaries is clear enough, any attempt to apply it to the facts would lead to such administrative difficulties that it would for that reason be held to be invalid.'

In the following year in *Re Baden's Deed Trusts* [1971] AC 424, Lord Wilberforce said . . . [Lloyd LJ quoted the passage on administrative unworkability, and the 'all the residents of Greater London' example]. It seems to me that the present trust comes within the . . . case to which Lord Wilberforce refers. I hope I am not guilty of being prejudiced by the example which he gave. But it could hardly be more apt, or fit the facts of the present case more precisely.

I mention the subsequent decisions in *Re Baden (No. 2)* [1972] Ch 607, and on appeal [1973] Ch 9 and *Re Manisty's Settlement* [1974] Ch 17, with misgiving, since they were not cited in argument. The latter was a case of an intermediate power, that is to say, a power exercisable by trustees in favour of all the world, other than members of an excepted class. After referring to *Gulbenkian* and the two *Baden* cases, Templeman J (as he then was) said: 'I conclude . . . that a power cannot be uncertain merely because it is wide in ambit'. A power to benefit, for example, the residents of Greater London might, he thought, be bad, not on the ground of its width but on the ground of capriciousness, since the settlor could have no sensible intention to benefit 'an accidental conglomeration of persons' who had 'no discernible link with the settlor'. But that objection could not apply here. The council had every reason for wishing to benefit the inhabitants of West Yorkshire. Lord Wilberforce's *dictum* has also been the subject of a good deal of academic comment and criticism, noticeably by L. McKay (1974) 38 Conv 269 and C. T. Emery (1982) 98 LQR 551. I should have welcomed further argument on these matters, but through no fault of Mr Henderson this was not possible. So I have to do the best I can.

My conclusion is that the *dictum* of Lord Wilberforce remains of high persuasive authority, despite *Re Manisty*. *Manisty's* case was concerned with a power, where the function of the court is more restricted. In the case of a trust, the court may have to execute the trust. Not so in the case of a power. That there may still be a distinction between trusts and powers in this connection was recognised by Templeman J himself in the sentence immediately following his quotation of Lord Wilberforce's *dictum*, when he said:

> In these guarded terms Lord Wilberforce appears to refer to trusts which may have to be executed and administered by the court and not to powers where the court has a very much more limited function.

There can be no doubt that the declaration of trust in the present case created a trust and not a power. Following Lord Wilberforce's dictum, I would hold that the definition of the beneficiaries of the trust is 'so hopelessly wide' as to be incapable of forming 'anything like a class'. I would therefore reject Mr Henderson's argument that the declaration of trust can take effect as an express private trust.

D: Fixed Trusts

Questions
1. Does Jenkins LJ's reasoning in *Broadway Cottages* still apply to fixed trusts? See Matthews [1984] Conv 22 and Martin and Hayton [1984] Conv 304.
2. Is the class ascertainability test an evidential or conceptual test? If it is a conceptual test, how (if at all) does it differ from the individual ascertainability test? If it is a conceptual test, were the concessions made by the charities in *Broadway Cottages* correct? Note that where there are evidential difficulties,

the judge may make a *Benjamin* order ([1902] 1 Ch 723) (see, e.g., *Re Green's WT* [1985] 3 All ER 455).

3. If fixed trusts need satisfy only the individual ascertainability test, is the test of administrative unworkability sufficient to strike down unworkable trusts?

4. Michael settles a fund upon trustees to be distributed equally in favour of his three sons, Paul, Quenton and Richard. The existence and whereabouts of all three is known at the date of the settlement. Later, Richard goes on an Antarctic expedition, and much later is thought (but not known definitely) to have perished. The trustees wish to distribute. Discuss.

Would your answer be different if by the time of the settlement, Richard had already embarked upon the expedition, and it was not known whether he was alive or dead?

E: Enforcement of Powers

There may be limited exceptions to the proposition that the courts do not enforce powers, which may, of course, affect the above discussion. In *Klug* v *Klug* [1918] 2 Ch 67, a mother who disapproved of her daughter's marriage without her consent capriciously refused to exercise a power in her favour. On application by the public trustee, the court ordered that the power should be exercised.

Mettoy Pension Trustees v *Evans*
[1991] 2 All ER 513
Chancery Division

Decision: Warner J held, relying on *Klug* v *Klug*, that the court could enforce a fiduciary power in the same manner as a discretionary trust. The case is unusual, however, in that there was nobody else who was capable of exercising the power. The case concerned a pension fund where the employer's powers had ceased on his going into liquidation, and where the fiduciary power did not vest in either the receivers or the liquidator.

WARNER J: The question then arises, if the discretion is a fiduciary power which cannot be exercised either by the receivers or by the liquidator, who is to exercise it? I heard submissions on that point. The discretion cannot be exercised by the directors of the company, because on the appointment of the liquidator all the powers of the directors ceased. I was referred to a number of authorities on the circumstances in which the court may interfere with or give directions as to the exercise of discretions vested in trustees, namely *Gisborne* v *Gisborne* (1877) 2 App Cas 300, *Re Hodges, Dovey* v *Ward* (1878) 7 Ch D 754, *Tabor* v *Brooks* (1878) 10 Ch D 273, *Klug* v *Klug* [1918] 2 Ch 67, *Re Allen-Meyrick's Will Trusts, Mangnall* v *Allen-Meyrick* [1966] 1 All ER 740, [1966] 1 WLR 499, *McPhail* v *Doulton* [1970] 2 All ER 228, [1971] AC 424, *Re Manisty's Settlement* [1973] 2 All ER 1203 at 1209–1211, [1974] Ch 17 at 25–26 and *Re Locker's Settlement Trusts, Meachem* v *Sachs* [1978] 1 All ER 216, [1977] 1 WLR 1323. None of those cases deals directly with a situation in which a fiduciary power is left with no one to exercise it. They point however to the conclusion that in that situation the court must step in. Mr Inglis-Jones and Mr Walker urge me to say that in this case the court should step in by giving directions to the trustees as to the distribution of the surplus in the pension fund. They relied in particular on this passage in the speech of Lord Wilberforce in *McPhail* v *Doulton* [1970] 2 All ER 228 at 247, [1971] AC 424 at 456–457:

> As to powers, I agree with my noble and learned friend Lord Upjohn in *Re Gulbenkian's Settlement* [1968] 3 All ER 785, [1970] AC 508 that although the trustees may, and normally will, be under a fiduciary duty to consider whether or in what way they should exercise their power, the court will not normally compel its exercise. It will intervene if the trustees exceed their powers, and possibly if they are proved to have exercised it capriciously. But in the case of a trust power, if the trustees do not exercise it, the court will; I respectfully adopt as to this the statement in Lord Upjohn's opinion (see [1968] 3 All ER 785 at 793, [1970] AC 508 at 525). I would venture to amplify this by saying that the court, if called upon to execute the trust power, will do so in the manner best calculated to give effect to the settlor's or testator's intentions. It may do so by appointing new trustees, or by authorising or directing representative persons of the classes of beneficiaries to prepare a scheme of distribution, or even, should the proper basis for distribution appear, by itself directing the trustees so to distribute. The books give many instances where this has been done and I see no reason in principle why they should not do so in the modern field of discretionary trusts . . .

. . . In that latter part [of the passage Lord Wilberforce] was indicating how the court might give effect to a discretionary trust when called upon to execute it. It seems to me however that the methods he indicated could be equally appropriate in a case where the court was called upon to intervene in the exercise of a discretion in category 2. In saying that I do not overlook that in *Re Manisty's Settlement* [1973] 2 All ER 1203 at 1210, [1974] Ch 17 at 25 Templeman J expressed the view that the only right and the only remedy of an object of the power who was aggrieved by the trustees' conduct would be to apply to the court to remove the trustees and appoint others in their place. However, the earlier authorities to which I was referred, such as *Re Hodges* and *Klug* v *Klug*, had not been cited to Templeman J. I conclude that, in a situation such as this, it is open to the court to adopt whichever of the methods indicated by Lord Wilberforce appears most appropriate in the circumstances.

Note

If *Klug* v *Klug* and *Mettoy Pension Trustees* v *Evans* are correct, they create limited exceptions to the principle that a court will not enforce a fiduciary power where non-exercise of a power is capricious, and where there is nobody available to exercise a power. The cases do not affect the general principle that where donees of a power make a *bona fide* decision not to exercise it, the courts will not compel them to do so.

Extract from Jill Martin's note on the case
[1991] Conv 364

Many points of interest to the general trusts lawyer arose in *Mettoy Pension Trustees* v *Evans* [1991] 2 All ER 513. The facts, in outline, were that the company had gone into liquidation, with a surplus in its pension fund. Under the rules the company had a power of appointment in favour of the pensioners, any of the surplus not so appointed going to the company. A separate trustee company was trustee of the fund. The question was whether the liquidator could release the power and thus secure the surplus for the creditors, to which the answer was no. The first step was to classify the power as fiduciary or non-fiduciary. The judgment contains a useful summary of the distinctions between fiduciary and bare powers: a bare (non-fiduciary) power can be released, while a fiduciary power cannot; while there is no duty to exercise either kind, the donee of a fiduciary power owes a duty to the objects to consider whether and how to exercise it, while the donee of a bare power owes no such duty to the objects; he merely owes a duty to the default beneficiaries to keep within its terms if it is exercised and not to commit a fraud on the power. Which kind of power has been created is a question of construction. In the present case the power was fiduciary. A relevant consideration was that the benefit to the objects if the power were not fiduciary would be illusory: any 'take-over raider' would be able to get all the surplus, as would the creditors on the company's insolvency. The fact that the objects (the pensioners) were not volunteers, in contrast with traditional powers, made such a conclusion unpalatable and thus tilted the balance in favour of the fiduciary classification.

Thus the liquidator could not release the power, but this did not solve all the problems. According to the traditional approach to powers, the pensioners still had no remedy if the power was not exercised in their favour, and there was no duty to exercise it. Herein lies the significance of the case, for Warner J proceeded to hold that the pensioners should have similar remedies to those available to the objects of discretionary trusts. The position with regard to the latter was laid down in *McPhail* v *Doulton* [1971] AC 424, at 457, where Lord Wilberforce said that the court could execute the trust 'by appointing new trustees, or by authorising or directing representative persons of the classes of beneficiaries to prepare a scheme of distribution, or even, should the proper basis for distribution appear, by itself directing the trustees so to distribute.' Warner J held that the court could adopt whichever of these methods was most appropriate.

In the present case the court's assistance was required because there was nobody to exercise the power: the donee company could not do so after the appointment of the liquidator; the receiver appointed under a debenture could not do so because the fiduciary power was not an asset of the company which could be the subject of any charge created by a debenture; the liquidator could not do so because there would be a conflict between his duties to the pensioners and to the creditors. The way out of the impasse was for the court to intervene in one of the ways mentioned above. Presumably Warner J would hold that the court could also intervene in these ways if the trustees exceeded their powers or acted capriciously. [Jill Martin notes: Regarded as occasions for intervention by Lord Wilberforce in *McPhail* v *Doulton* [1971] AC 424 at 457.] Of course, there is no suggestion that the court could execute a power when the trustees have made a bona fide decision not to do so.

Previous authorities have suggested that the only way the court can intervene in the case of a power is by the appointment of new trustees [Jill Martin notes: see *Re Manisty's Settlement* [1974] Ch 17]. This, for some reason, had not been requested in the present case. [Jill Martin notes: See (1991) 107 LQR 214 (S. Gardner), suggesting that the trustee company was the obvious substitute, and that this would have been the most appropriate means of intervention. Gardner also suggests that one result of the assimilation of remedies might be that 'administrative unworkability' now applies to fiduciary powers as well as to discretionary trusts. There would have been no problem in *Mettoy* itself because the class of pensioners would not give rise to difficulty under this principle.] In upholding the possibility of a more positive intervention,

Warner J relied on *Klug* v *Klug* [Jill Martin notes: [1918] 2 Ch 17, not cited in *Re Manisty's Settlement, supra*. But see (1991) 107 LQR 214 (S. Gardner), where it is considered that the older cases relied on, such as *Klug*, do not give great support to the judicial exercise of fiduciary discretions], where the court in effect directed the exercise of the power of advancement. The appropriate manner of intervention in the present case was deferred until further evidence and submissions had been heard.

5 PRIVATE PURPOSE TRUSTS AND UNINCORPORATED ASSOCIATIONS

This chapter is primarily about private purpose trusts, sometimes referred to as trusts of imperfect obligation. Unincorporated associations also exist to carry out purposes, and it might at first sight be thought that the private purpose trust might also be a good model upon which to base donations to unincorporated association. However, although this can sometimes be the case, usually a contractual analysis will be more appropriate.

SECTION 1: PRIVATE PURPOSE TRUSTS

Purpose trusts may either be for a pure purpose (for example, a trust to advance a cause), where no individual directly benefits, or for the benefit of an ascertainable group of people (for example, a trust to build a school swimming pool). A private (non-charitable) purpose trust of the first type is usually struck down, because it is not enforceable by anyone. Charitable trusts (which are dealt with in chapters 12–14) are always purpose trusts, and are valid, but there problems of enforcement do not arise as the Attorney-General has *locus standi* to sue.

A: The Beneficiary Principle

Re Astor's ST, Astor v Scholfield
[1952] Ch 534, [1952] 1 All ER 1067
Chancery Division

Facts: Trustees were instructed to hold a fund upon various trusts including 'the maintenance of good relations between nations [and] . . . the preservation of the independence of newspapers'. The purposes were not charitable, but the settlement was drafted expressly (by limiting its duration) so as to be valid under the perpetuity rules.

Held: The trust was held by Roxburgh J to be void, because there were no human beneficiaries capable of enforcing it.

ROXBOROUGH J (after observing that it was common ground that none of the purposes offended the rule against perpetuities, and that none was charitable): The question upon which I am giving this reserved judgment is whether the non-charitable trusts of income during 'the specified period' declared by clause 5 and the third schedule of the settlement of 1945 are void. [Counsel] have submitted that they are void on two grounds: (1) that they are not trusts for the benefit of individuals; (2) that they are void for uncertainty.

Lord Parker considered the first of these two questions in his speech in *Bowman* v *Secular Society Ld* [1917] AC 406 and I will cite two important passages. The first is [at p. 437]:

The question whether a trust be legal or illegal or be in accordance with or contrary to the policy of the law, only arises when it has been determined that a trust has been created, and is then only part of the larger question whether the trust is enforceable. For, as will presently appear, trusts may be unforceable and therefore void, not only because they are illegal or contrary to the policy of the law, but for other reasons.

The second is [at p. 441]:

A trust to be valid must be for the benefit of individuals, which this is certainly not, or must be in that class of gifts for the benefit of the public which he courts in this country recognize as charitable in the legal as opposed to the popular sense of that term.

Commenting on those passages [counsel for the trustees] observed that *Bowman* v *Secular Society Ld.* arose out of a will and he asked me to hold that Lord Parker intended them to be confined to cases arising under a will. But they were, I think, intended to be quite general in character. Further, [counsel] pointed out that Lord Parker made no mention of the exceptions or apparent exceptions which undoubtedly exist, and from this he asked me to infer that no such general principle can be laid down. the question is whether those cases are to be regarded as exceptional and anomalous or whether they are destructive of the supposed principle. I must later analyse them. But I will first consider whether Lord Parker's propositions can be attacked from a base of principle.

The typical case of a trust is one in which the legal owner of property is constrained by a court of equity so to deal with it as to give effect to the equitable rights of another. These equitable rights have been hammered out in the process of litigation in which a claimant on equitable grounds has succesfully asserted rights against a legal owner or other person in control of property. Prima facie, therefore, a trustee would not be expected to be subject to an equitable obligation unless there was somebody who could enforce a correlative equitable right, and the nature and extent of that obligation would be worked out in proceedings for enforcement. This is what I understand by Lord Parker's first proposition. At an early stage, however, the courts were confronted with attempts to create trusts for charitable purposes which there was no equitable owner to enforce. Lord Eldon explained in *Attorney General* v *Brown* (1818) 1 Swans 265, 290 how this difficulty was dealt with:

It is the duty of a court of equity, a main part, originally almost the whole, of its jurisdiction, to administer trusts; to protect not the visible owner, who alone can proceed at law, but the individual equitably, though not legally, entitled. From this principle has arisen the practice of administering the trust of a public charity: persons possessed of funds appropriated to such purposes are within the general rule; but no one being entitled by an immediate and peculiar interest to prefer a complaint, who is to compel the performance of their obligations, and to enforce their responsibility? It is the duty of the King, as *parens patriae*, to protect property devoted to charitable uses; and that duty is executed by the officer who represents the Crown for all forensic purposes. On this foundation rests the right of the Attorney-General in such cases to obtain by information the interposition of a court of equity. . . .

But if the purposes are not charitable, great difficulties arise both in theory and in practice. In theory, because having regard to the historical origins of equity it is difficult to visualize the growth of equitable obligations which nobody can enforce, and in practice, because it is not possible to contemplate with equanimity the creation of large funds devoted to non-charitable purposes which no court and no department of state can control, or in the case of maladministration reform. Therefore, Lord Parker's second proposition would prima facie appear to be well founded. Moreover, it gains no little support from the practical considerations that no officer has ever been consituted to take, in the case of non-charitable purposes, the position held by the Attorney-General in connexion with charitable purposes, and no case has been found in the reports in which the court has ever directly enforced a non-charitable purpose against a trustee. Indeed where, as in the present case, the only beneficiaries are purposes and at present unascertainable person, it is difficult to see who could initiate such proceedings. If the purposes are valid trusts, the settlors have retained no beneficial interest and could not initiate them. It was suggested that the trustees might proceed ex parte to enforce the trusts against themselves. I doubt that, but at any rate nobody could enforce the trusts against them. This point, in my judgment, is of importance, because in most of the cases which are put forward to disprove Lord Parker's propositions the court had indirect means of enforcing the execution of the non-charitable purposes.

These cases I must now consider. First of all, there is a group relating to horses, dogs, grave and monuments, among which I was referred to *Pettingall* v *Pettingall* (1842) 11 LJ Ch 176; *Mitford* v *Reynolds* (1846) 16 Sim 105; *In re Dean* (1889) 41 ChD 552; *Pirbright* v *Salwey* [1896] WN 86; and *In re Hooper* [1932] Ch 38.

In *Pettingall* v *Pettingall* a testator made the following bequest by his will:

Having a favourite black mare, I hereby bequeath, that at my death, £50 per annum be paid for her keep in some park in England or Wales; her shoes to be taken off, and she never to be ridden or put in harness; and that my executor consider himself in honour bound to fulfil my wish, and see that she will be well provided for, and removable at his will. At her death all payment to cease.

It being admitted that a bequest in favour of an animal was valid, two questions were made: first, as to the form of the decree on this point; and secondly, as to the disposition of the surplus not required for the mare. Knight Bruce VC said, that so much of the £50 as would be required to keep the mare comfortably, should be applied by the executor, and he was entitled to the surplus. He must give full information, whenever required, respecting the mare; and if the mare were not properly attended to, any of the parties interested in the residue might apply to the court. The decree on this point ought to be, that £50 a year should be paid to the executor during the life of the mare, or until further order; he undertaking to maintain her comfortaably; with liberty for all parties to apply. The points which I wish to make are (1) that it was there admitted that a request in favour of an animal was valid, and (2) that there were persons interested in residue who having regard to the decree made would have had no difficulty in getting the terms of the 'bequest' enforced.

Mitford v *Reynolds* related to a sepulchral monument and to horses, and there again there was a remainderman on behalf of charity to see to the enforcement of the directions, and an administration action was on foot.

In *In re Dean* a testor devised his freehold estates, subject to and charged with an annuity of £750, and to a term of 50 years granted to his trustees, to the use of the plaintiff for life, with remainders over; and he gave to his trustees his horses, ponies and hounds; and he charged his said freehold estates with the payment to his trustees, for the term of 50 years, if any of the said horses and hounds should so long live, of an annual sum of £750. And he declared that his trustees should apply the said annual sum in the maintenance of the horses and hounds for the time being living, and in maintaining the stables, kennels and buildings inhabited by the said animals in such condition of repair as his trustees might deem fit; and in consideration of the maintenance of his horses, ponies, and hounds being a charge upon his said estate as a foresaid, he gave all his personal estate not otherwise disposed of to the plaintiff absolutely. North J said [at p. 556]:

Then it is said, that there is no cestui que trust who can enforce the trust, and that the court will not recognize a trust unless it is capable of being enforced by someone. I do not assent to that view. There is not the least doubt that a man may if he pleases, give a legacy to trustees, upon trust to apply it in erecting a monument to himself, either in a church or in a churchyard, or even in unconsecrated ground, and I am not aware that such a trust is in any way invalid, although it is difficult to say who would be the cestui que trust of the monument. In the same way I know of nothing to prevent a gift of a sum of money to trustees, upon trust to apply it for the repair of such a monument. In my opinion such a trust would be good, although the testator must be careful to limit the time for which it is to last, because, as it is not a charitable trust, unless it is to come to an end within the limits fixed by the rule against perpetuities, it would be illegal. But a trust to lay out a certain sum in building a monument, and the gift of another sum in trust to apply the same to keeping that monument in repair, say, for ten years, is, in my opinion, a perfectly good trust, although I do not see who could ask the court to enforce it. If persons beneficially interested in the estate could do so, then the present plaintiff can do so; but, if such persons could not enforce the trust, still it cannot be said that the trust must fail because there is no one who can actively enforce it.

This is the best case in the series from [counsel for the trustees'] point of view, because North J did undoubtedly uphold the particular directions, whether or not they could be 'actively enforced.' But putting it at its highest, he merely held that there were certain classes of trusts, of which this was one, in which that objection was not fatal. He did not suggest that it was not generally fatal outside the realms of charity.

In *Pirbright* v *Salwey* a testator, after expressing his wish to be buried in the inclosure in which his child lay in a certain churchyard, bequeathed to the rector and churchwardens of the parish church £800 Consols, the interest and dividends to be derived therefrom to be applied, so long as the law for the time being permitted, in keeping up the inclosure and decorating the same with flowers. It was held that the gift was valid for at least a period of 21 years from the testator's death, and *semble* that it was not charitable.

In *In re Hooper* a testator bequeathed to his executors and trustees money out of the income of which to provide, so far as they legally could do so, for the care and upkeep of certain graves a vault and certain monuments. Maugham J. said: 'This point is one to my mind of doubt, and I should have felt some difficulty in deciding it if it were not for *Pirbright* v *Salwey*. . . . That was a decision arrived at by Stirling J, after argument by very eminent counsel. The case does not appear to have attracted much attention in textbooks, but it does not appear to have been commented upon adversely, and I shall follow it.' In this case, and probably also in *Pirbright* v *Salwey*, there was a residuary legatee to bring before the court any failure to comply with the directions. But I think that Maugham J regarded them both as exceptions from general principle.

Last in this group is *In re Thompson* [1934] Ch 342 I have included it in this group because, although it relates to the furtherance of foxhunting and thus moves away from the subject-matter of the group and much nearer to the present case, it is expressly founded on *Pettingall* v *Pettingall*, and it is indeed a most instructive case. The testator bequeathed a legacy of £1,000 to a friend to be applied by him in such manner as he should think fit towards the promotion and furthering of foxhunting, and devised and bequeathed his residuary estate to Trinity Hall in the University of Cambridge. An originating summons was taken out by the executors to determine whether the legacy was valid or failed for want of a definite object or for uncertainty or on other grounds. When counsel, during the course of the argument, observed [at p. 343], 'True, there is no cestui que trust who can enforce the application of the legacy, but that is immaterial: *In re Dean*. The object to which the legacy is to be applied is sufficiently defined to be enforced,' Clauson J interposed: 'The college, as residuary legatees, seem to have an interest in the legacy, as, but for the trust for its application, they would be entitled to it. The procedure adopted by Knight Bruce V-C in *Pettingall* v *Pettingall*, cited in Jarman on Wills, 7th ed., vol. 2, p. 877, might be followed in this case.' And in his judgment he said [at p. 344]:

> In my judgment the object of the gift has been defined with sufficient clearness and is of a nature to which effect can be given. The proper way for me to deal with the matter will be, not to make, as it is asked by the summons, a general declaration, but following the example of Knight Bruce V-C in *Pettingall* v *Pettingall*, to order that, upon the defendant Mr Lloyd [the friend] giving an undertaking (which I understand he is willing to give) to apply the legacy when received by him towards the object expressed in the testator's will, the plaintiffs do pay to the defendant Mr Lloyd the legacy of £1,000; and that, in case the legacy should be applied by him otherwise than towards the promotion and furthering of foxhunting, the residuary legatees are to be at liberty to apply.

I understand Clauson J to have held in effect that there was somebody who could enforce the purpose indicated because the college, as residuary legatees, would be entitled to the legacy but for the trust for its application and they could apply to the court to prevent any misapplication or breach of the undertaking given by Mr Lloyd. I infer from what he said that he would not have upheld the validity of this non-charitable purpose if there had been no residuary legatee, and no possibility of making such an order as was made in *Pettingall* v *Pettingall*.

Lastly, I was referred to *In re Price* [1943] Ch 422, where a testatrix by her will gave one-half of her residuary estate to the Anthroposophical Society in Great Britain 'to be used at the discretion of the chairman and executive council of the society for carrying on the teachings of the founder, Dr Rudolf Steiner.' At first sight this case would appear to be a strong card in [counsel for the trustees'] hand. The first part of the judgment proceeds upon the footing that the purposes were not charitable. The society was the residuary legatee and there was no room for such an order as was made in *In re Thompson*. There was nobody who could have enforced the carrying out of the purposes. On closer inspection, however, it will be found that this point was not raised in argument or referred to in the judgment, and the decision was based upon *In re Drummond* [1914] 2 Ch 90, which is a different class of case. As the present case cannot, on any view, be assimilated to *In re Drummond*, I need not further consider *In re Price*.

Let me then sum up the position so far. On the one side there are Lord Parker's two propositions with which I began. These were not new, but merely re-echoed what Sir William Grant had said as Master of the Rolls in *Morice v The Bishop of Durham* [9 Ves 399, at 405] as long ago as 1804: 'There must be somebody, in whose favour the court can decree performance.' The position was recently restated by Harman J in *In re Wood* [[1949] Ch 498, 501]: 'A gift on trust must have a cestui que trust,' and this seems to be in accord with principle. On the other side is a group of cases relating to horses and dogs, graves and monuments – matters arising under wills and intimately connected with the decreased – in which the courts have found means of escape from these general propositions and also *In re Thompson* and *In re Price* which I have endeavoured to explain. *In re Price* belongs to another field. The rest may, I think, properly be regarded as anomalous and exceptional and in no way destructive of the proposition which traces descent from or through Sir William Grant through Lord Parker to Harman J. Perhaps the late Sir Arthur Underhill was right in suggesting that they may be concessions to human weakness or sentiment (see Law of Trusts, 8th ed., p. 79 [10th ed., p. 97]). They cannot, in my judgment, of themselves (and no other justification has been suggested to me) justify the conclusion that a Court of Equity will recognize as an equitable obligation affecting the income of large funds in the hands of trustees a direction to apply it in furtherance of enumerated non-charitable purposes in a manner which no court or department can control or enforce. I hold that the trusts here in question are void on the first of the grounds submitted by [counsel for the Attorney-General].

[Roxburgh J went on to hold that the trusts were also void for uncertainty.]

Notes

1. This case restates an old principle that a trust will be void unless there are human beneficiaries capable of enforcing it.

2. Roxburgh J recognises that charitable trusts are an exception to this principle, since the Attorney-General can enforce them.

3. Various cases where private purpose trusts appear to have been upheld were explained by Roxburgh J as cases where there is a human beneficiary (entitled to the residue) who can enforce the trust. This is not altogether satisfactory, since the residuary beneficiary will not necessarily have any interest in enforcing it, but they were regarded as anomalous exceptions in *Re Astor's ST*, and similarly in *Re Endacott* [1960] Ch 232, where a gift 'to North Tawton Devon Parish Council for the purpose of providing some useful memorial to myself' was held void by the Court of Appeal. *Dean* and *Thompson* were again regarded as anomalous and not to be extended.

Re Shaw, Public Trustee v Day
[1957] 1 WLR 729, [1957] 1 All ER 745
Chancery Division

Facts: The issue was whether a trust to research into the advantages of a new 40-letter alphabet was valid as a charitable or purpose trust. The facts are stated more fully (and colourfully) in Harman J's judgment, set out in chapter 13.

Held: The trust was not valid as a charity (see chapter 12). Not being charitable, the trust failed, since there were no ascertainable beneficiaries.

HARMAN J: Can, then this project be upheld apart from charity? I feel bound to say at once that, as the authorities stand, I do not think I am at liberty to hold that it can. . . .
Lord Parker of Waddington in *Bowman* v *Secular Society Ltd* categorically states ([1917] AC at p. 441):

A trust to be valid must be for the benefit of individuals . . . or must be in that class of gifts for the benefit of the public which the courts in this country recognise as charitable . . .

In other words, one cannot have a trust, other than a charitable trust, for the benefit, not of individuals, but of objects. The reason has been often stated, that the court cannot control the trust. The principle has been recently restated by Roxburgh J in *Re Astor's Settlement Trusts, Astor* v *Scholfield* ([1952] 1 All ER 1067), where the authorities are copiously reviewed. An object cannot complain to the court, which, therefore, cannot control the trust, and, therefore, will not allow it to continue. . . .
The result is that the alphabet trusts are, in my judgment, invalid, and must fail. It seems that their begetter suspected as much, hence his jibe about failure by judicial decision. I answer that it is not the fault of the law, but of the testator, who failed almost for the first time in his life to grasp the problem or to make up his mind what he wanted.

B: Indirect Methods of Enforcing Private Purposes

It may also be possible to make provision for a pure purpose indirectly, using a device, for example where a gift is made to charity A so long as it maintains the testator's grave to the satisfaction of the testator's trustees with a gift over to charity B. Obviously, the testator wishes his grave to be maintained for a long time, but the gift over is exempt from perpetuity rules, so long as B is a charity. If B is not a charity the gift over will fail for perpetuity unless the gift is appropriately limited in duration: *Re Wightwick* [1950] 1 Ch 260.

Perpetuity rules retain a position of considerable importance in any discussion of private purpose trusts and non-charitable unincorporated associations. Essentially, at common law, a contingent interest (i.e., an interest which will arise only upon the happening of some future event, which may or may not occur) must be certain to vest, if at all, within 21 years from the death of some person who is living at the date when the disposition creating that future interest comes into effect. If there is any possibility that the event in question can happen outside that time, the interest is void right from the outset. This is why the gift over to B fails if B is not a charity, unless the gift to A is limited in duration.

Although the position has been to some extent affected by the Perpetuities and Accumulations Act 1964 (considered in greater detail at the end of the chapter), the common law is a good starting point, because the law was largely developed under a common law regime. We will also need to consider the common law rule when explaining and criticising some of the cases, not only in this chapter, but also in chapter 8, where similar issues arise.

Although a gift over is caught by the perpetuity rule, a determinable fee in real estate has never been caught by the rule, even though the determining event may be postponed until long into the future. A similar principle was applied to personalty in *Re Chardon* [1928] 1 Ch 464, which allowed a non-charitable purpose effectively to be carried on indefinitely.

Re Chardon, Johnson v Davies
[1928] 1 Ch 464
Chancery Division

Facts: A testator's will provided:

> I give unto my trustees the sum of two hundred pounds free of duty upon trust to invest the same upon any of the investments hereinafter authorised and pay the income thereof to the South Metropolitan Cemetery Company West Norwood during such period as they shall continue to maintain and keep the graves of my great grandfather and the said Priscilla Navone in the said Cemetery in good order and condition with flowers and plants thereon as the same have hitherto been kept by me.

Held: Romer J held the gift valid. A trust to pay income to a corporation so long as the corporation maintains the testator's grave to the satisfaction of his trustees is not subject to perpetuity, at any rate at common law. The cemetery was entitled absolutely to the income, and could dispose of it at any time. The interest of the persons interested in the legacy, subject to the interest of the cemetery company (i.e., who took in the event that the graves were no longer satisfactorily maintained), also vested immediately, on analogy with an interest subject to a determinable fee simple.

ROMER J: . . . If this be a bad gift it must be because there is some principle of law or equity that makes it bad. Now there is a rule to the effect that vested interests in property cannot be rendered inalienable. But the interest of the cemetery company under the gift in question is certainly not inalienable; they could dispose of it, if they could find a purchaser, tomorrow. There is also the well known rule against perpetuities which is quite a different rule from that against inalienability, and that rule is that the vesting of property real or personal (and it also applies to interests legal or equitable) cannot be postponed beyond lives in being and twenty-one years. This gift does not appear to offend against that rule. The interest of the cemetery company, such as it is, vests at once. It has been pointed out on more than one occasion . . . that the rule against perpetuities is not dealing with the duration of interests but with their commencement, and so long as the interest vests within lives in being and twenty-one years it does not matter how long that interest lasts. . . .

. . . It is admitted by Mr Crossman [for the crown] that a trust to pay the income to A. his executors administrators and assigns indefinitely, that is to say for ever, would be a good trust, because it would be equivalent to giving an absolute interest, and so it would, but he says that a trust to pay the income to A. for an indefinite period, that is to say until the happening of an event that may never happen, is bad, because that is not equivalent to an absolute interest. While it is true that it is not equivalent to an absolute interest it is very much like, and analogous to, a determinable fee in real estate. . . . I therefore do not know any reason why a trust to pay the income indefinitely to a certain person his executors administrators and assigns until a certain event happens should be bad . . .

. . . The cemetery company and the persons interested in the legacy, subject to the interest of the cemetery company, could combine to-morrow and dispose of the whole legacy. The trust does not, therefore, offend the rule against inalienability. The interest of the cemetery company is a vested interest; the interests of the residuary legatee, it being agreed on all hands that, subject to the interest of the cemetery company, the legacy falls into residue, are also vested. All the interests therefore created in this 200*l*., legal and equitable, are vested interests and, that being so, the trusts do not offend the rule against perpetuity. I know of no other rule which will enable me to come to the conclusion that this is an invalid gift.

Notes
1.   This decision was followed in *Re Chambers* [1950] 1 Ch 267, which Wynn-Parry J regarded as being indistinguishable from *Chardon*. It depended on the gift of the income being absolute (since otherwise the rule against inalienability is infringed): *Re Wightwick* [1950] 1 Ch 260. This is a matter of construction. The latter case concerned a gift of dividends on shares to the treasurer of the National Anti-Vivisection Society, 'such dividends to be at the disposal of the committee for the time being for the purposes of the said association until the time shall arrive that the practice of vivisection be made penal by law within the United Kingdom of Great Britain and Ireland and shall also be made a punishable offence upon the continent of Europe and elsewhere'. There was a gift over to the Royal Society for the Prevention of Cruelty to Animals, which was a charitable body. Had the National Anti-Vivisection Society also been, as the testatrix thought, charitable no problems would have arisen, but the House of Lords held it non-charitable in 1947 (see further chapter 12). In holding the gift void, Wynn-Parry J said:

As regards the primary gift [to the National Anti-Vivisection Society], the fact that it is a gift of income for an indefinite period is not of itself an objection, and *prima facie* it would be good if it does not infringe the rule against inalienability: *Re Chardon*. . . .

That case has been the subject of criticism . . . It is sufficient for my purpose that the learned judge accepted the view, which he pointed out, was common ground, namely, that, subject to the interest of the cemetery company, the legacy to it fell into residue. Romer J was able to hold the gift to the cemetery company valid, first, because he found no context in the terms of the gift which would operate to fetter the right of the cemetery company to dispose of the income, and, secondly, because, on the view which he accepted, those interested in residue, into which the legacy would fall on the determination of the interest of the cemetery company, could join with the cemetery company in disposing of the whole legacy.

The first question, therefore, is to decide whether the National Anti-Vivisection Society could dispose of the income which is the subject of the primary gift. This is, to my mind, a question which depends on the language of the gift. The income is to be paid half-yearly to the treasurer for the time being of the society. In contrast, the direction in *Re Chardon* was to pay the income to the cemetery company *simpliciter*, a direction which would include its assigns. The will in this case further provides that the income is to be at the disposal of the committee for the time being for the purposes of the association. That, to my mind, means that the committee must apply the income received each half-year for a particular purpose, that is, the purposes of the association, with the result that, in my judgment, the association takes the income on a trust, namely to apply it towards the furtherance of its objects.

A trust of income for an indefinite period for a purpose not being charitable is void as a perpetuity or as tending to a perpetuity, because it involves rendering the capital inalienable. Turning to the language of the will, by which a limit is sought to be set upon the period of payment to the association, it appears to me that it can be no overstatement to say that it tends to a perpetuity, because it is hardly possible to imagine that the court could ever be satisfied, on evidence, that the condition on which the payment is to determine had been satisfied. On this short ground the present case is, in my view, distinguishable from *Re Chardon*, and the primary gift is void.

The primary gift having therefore failed, Wynn-Parry J held that the gift over, not being a residuary legacy, was also void.

2. Clearly, a gift subject to a prior determinable interest was not automatically caught by the common law perpetuity rule on that account. It may also be that the common law rule did not apply to interests by way of resulting trust, the residuary interest in *Chardon* being similar to an interest by way of resulting trust. The relevance of all this becomes clearer in chapter 8.

3. *Chardon* was decided on the common law perpetuity rule. The interest in the residue would now be caught under the Perpetuities and Accumulations Act 1964, s. 12, but the 1964 Act applies only to dispositions which are void at common law. If *Chardon* is correct, therefore, it suggests another device for making provision for a pure purpose.

Perpetuities and Accumulations Act 1964

12. Possibilities of reverter, conditions subsequent, exceptions and reservations

(1) In the case of —

(a) a possibility of reverter on the determination of a determinable fee simple, or

(b) the possibility of a resulting trust on the determination of any other determinable interest in property,

the rule against perpetuities shall apply in relation to the provision causing the interest to be determinable as it would apply if that provision were expressed in the form of a condition subsequent giving rise, on breach thereof, to a right of re-entry or an equivalent right in the case of property other than land, and where the provision falls to be treated as void for remoteness the determinable interest shall become an absolute interest.

(2)   Where a disposition is subject to any such provision, or to any such condition subsequent, or to any exception or reservation, the disposition shall be treated for the purposes of this Act as including a separate disposition of any rights arising by virtue of the provision, condition subsequent, exception or reservation.

C: Trust for Benefit of Identifiable Objects

The objection that there must be somebody to enforce the trust loses its force when there are humans interested in its enforcement. Suppose, however, that although objects can be found with an interest in enforcing the trust, none is entitled to a full beneficial interest. Although the contrary view is arguable, it is probable that only where a full beneficial interest is granted to the identifiable objects will the disposition be valid.

Leahy v *Attorney-General for New South Wales*
[1959] AC 457
Privy Council

Facts: The issue arose as to the validity of a trust of property for 'such order of nuns of the Catholic Church or the Christian brothers as my executors and trustees shall select'.

Held: The trust was not charitable, and Viscount Simonds in the Privy Council thought that it would have failed as a private trust on the ground that, even though the individual members had an interest in enforcing the trust, they were not granted a full beneficial interest. The gift was saved by s. 37D of the Conveyancing Act 1919–1954, of New South Wales, but only so far as orders other than contemplative orders of nuns were concerned (the trustees had wished to preserve their right to select such orders).

VISCOUNT SIMONDS; . . . What is meant when it is said [as it had been in the High Court] that a gift is made to the individuals comprising the community and the words are added 'it is given to them for the benefit of the community'? If it is a gift to individuals, each of them is entitled to his distributive share (unless he has previously bound himself by the rules of the society that it shall be devoted to some other purpose). It is difficult to see what is added by the words 'for the benefit of the community.' If they are intended to import a trust, who are the beneficiaries? If the present members are the beneficiaries, the words add nothing and are meaningless. If some other persons or purposes are intended, the conclusion cannot be avoided that the gift is void. For it is uncertain, and beyound doubt tends to a perpetuity.

The question then appears to be whether, even if the gift to a selected Order of Nuns is prima facie a gift to the individual members of that Order, there are other considerations arising out of the terms of the will, or the nature of the society, its organisation and rules, or the subject-matter of the gift which should lead the court to conclude that, though prima facie the gift is an absolute one (absolute both in quality of estate and in freedom from restriction) to individual nuns, yet it is invalid because it is in the nature of an endowment and tends to a perpetuity or for any other reason. This raises a problem which is not easy to solve, as the divergent opinions in the High Court indicate.

The prima facie validity of such a gift (by which term their Lordships intend a bequest or demise) is a convenient starting point for the examination of the relevant law. For as Lord Tomlin (sitting at first instance in the Chancery Division) said in *In re Ogden* [1933] Ch 678, 49 TLR 341, a gift to a voluntary association of persons for the general purposes of the association is an absolute gift and prima facie a good gift. He was echoing the words of Lord Parker in *Bowman's* case [1917] AC 406, 442 that a gift to an unincorporated association for the attainment of its purposes 'may . . . be upheld as an absolute gift to its members.' These words must receive careful consideration, for it is to be noted that it is because the gift can be upheld as a gift to the individual members that it is valid, even though it is given for the general purposes of the association. If the words 'for the general purposes of the association' were held to import a trust, the question would have to be asked, what is the trust and who are the beneficiaries? A gift can be made to persons (including a corporation) but it cannot be made to a purpose or to an object: so also, a trust may be created for the benefit of persons as costuis que trust but not for a purpose or object unless the purpose or object be charitable. For a purpose or object cannot sue, but, if it be charitable, the Attorney-General can sue to enforce it. . . . It is therefore by disregarding the words 'for the general purposes of the association' (which are assumed not to be charitable purposes) and treating the gift as an absolute gift to individuals that it can be sustained. . . .

Notes
1.   This passage is authority for the proposition that a gift to a non-charitable unincorporated association can take effect only as a gift to the present members. If it is given for the purposes of the association it is invalid, although the members of the association have a clear interest in enforcing it.
2.   It seems generally that for a trust to be valid, not only must it benefit individuals (who must be ascertainable within the certainty of object tests), but those individuals must also be the beneficiaries under the trust.

Questions
1.   What exactly is the perpetuity difficulty to which Viscount Simonds refers at the end of the first paragraph set out above? (Note: this issue is discussed in greater detail in the following section.)
2.   Is *Leahy* consistent with the following case?

Re Denley's Trust Deed
[1969] 1 Ch 373
Chancery Division

Decision: A gift of land for use as a sports ground 'primarily for the benefit of the employees of the company and secondarily for the benefit of such other persons as the trustees may allow to use the same' was valid, despite being a private purpose trust, because the class of individuals to benefit was ascertainable.

GOFF J: I think there may be a purpose or object trust, the carrying out of which would benefit an individual or individuals, where that benefit is so indirect or intangible or which is otherwise so framed as not to give those persons any *locus standi* to apply to the court to enforce the trust, in which case the beneficiary principle would, as it seems to me, apply to invalidate the trust, quite apart from any question of uncertainty or perpetuity. Such cases can be considered if and when they arise. The present is not, in my judgment, of that character, and it will be seen that . . . the trust deed expressly states that, subject to any rules and regulations made by the trustees, the employees of the company shall be entitled to the use and enjoyment of the land. Apart from this possible exception, in my judgment the beneficiary principle of *Re Astor's ST* [1952] Ch 534, which was approved in *Re Endacott (decd)* [1960] Ch 232, CA – see particularly by Harman LJ – is confined to purpose or object trusts which are abstract or impersonal. The objection is not that the trust is for a purpose or object *per se*, but that there is no beneficiary or cestui que trust. . . .

Where, then, the trust, though expressed as a purpose, is directly or indirectly for the benefit of an individual or individuals, it seems to me that it is in general outside the mischief of the beneficiary principle.

Notes
1. These passages are not entirely clear. One view is that the test is not whether a full beneficial interest is granted, but whether individuals who are ascertainable have *locus standi* to sue. They will have so long as the benefit is not too indirect or intangible. This view of *Denley* was adopted by Megarry J in *Re Northern Developments (Holdings) Ltd*, unreported, 6 October 1978 (considered in the *Carreras Rothmans* case in chapter 2). Another view of *Denley*, however, is that Goff J construed it as a trust for individuals, and not as a purpose trust at all. If this view is correct then the case breaks no new ground, and all private purpose trusts remain void, apart from the anomalous exceptions discussed in the *Astor* extracts above. This view was taken, for example, by Vinelott J in *Re Grant's WT* [1980] 1 WLR 360 (at p. 370):

That case [*Denley*] on a proper analysis, in my judgment, falls outside the categories of gifts to unincorporated incorporations and purpose trusts. I can see no distinction in principle between a trust to permit a class defined by reference to employment to use and enjoy land in accordance with rules to be made at the discretion of trustees on the one hand, and, on the other hand, a trust to distribute income at the discretion of the settlor. In both cases the benefit to be taken by any member of the class is at the discretion of the trustees, but any member of the class can apply to the court to compel the trustees to administer the trust in accordance with its terms.

A similar view can be found in (1985) 101 LQR 269, at pp. 280–2 (P.J. Millett QC).
2. If the *Northern Developments* view of *Denley* is correct, It is arguable that *Carreras Rothmans* v *Freeman Matthews Treasure Ltd (in liq)* [1985] 1 Ch 207,

set out in chapter 2, is better explained as a *Denley* purpose trust than as an enforceable trust in favour of the third party creditors.

3.   Whatever the case decides, pure purpose trusts, such as *Re Astor's ST* [1952] Ch 534, are unaffected by it.

4.   The duration of the trust in *Denley* was expressly limited (with a gift over to a hospital), so as to ensure that there were no perpetuity difficulties. Compare *Re Hobourn Aero Components Ltd's Air Raid Distress Fund* [1946] Ch 86, in chapter 8.

R v District Auditor, ex parte West Yorkshire Metropolitan County Council
[1986] RVR 24
Divisional Court of the Queen's Bench Division

Decision: The decision in this case has been set out in chapter 4 (see p. 109). An alternative argument, based on *Denley*, also failed because whatever it decides, it depends on the individuals to whom benefit is given being ascertainable within the certainty of object rules.

LLOYD LJ: Since, as I have already said, it was not argued that the trust can take effect as a valid charitable trust, it follows that the declaration of trust is ineffective. What we have here, in a nutshell, is a non-charitable purpose trust. It is clear law that, subject to certain exceptions, such trusts are void: see *Lewin on Trusts*, 16th Edition, page 17–19. The present case does not come within any of the established exceptions. Nor can it be brought within the scope of such recent decisions as *Re Denley's Trust Deed* [1969] 1 Ch 373 and *Re Lipinski's WT* [1976] 1 Ch 235, since there are, for the reasons I have given, no ascertained or ascertainable beneficiaries.

SECTION 2:   DONATIONS TO (NON-CHARITABLE) UNINCORPORATED ASSOCIATIONS

A: Must Take Effect as Gift to Present Members

As we have seen in *Leahy*, there are difficulties in giving property for the purposes of a non-charitable unincorporated association, even though there are humans with an interest in applying the property as the donor intended. If these persons are not beneficiaries the disposition will fail on the beneficiary principle. If the members of the association for the time being are beneficiaries then, unless membership of the association is fixed, it must be contemplated that beneficial interests will move at an unspecified future time, when old members resign or new members join, and there will be perpetuity problems unless the gift is limited to take effect within the perpetuity period, or unless (since 1964) the wait and see principle of the Perpetuities and Accumulations Act 1964 is applicable (see further below). An express limitation (which can, since 1964, be a specified period of up to 80 years) is very rare.

The only alternative is a gift to present members only, but in order to prevent them from severing their share, this is normally subject to their contractual duties as members of the association, under which a member will typically be prevented from severing his share, which will accrue to the other members on his death or resignation. This now seems to be accepted as the usual basis for donations to non-charitable unincorporated associations.

B: Contractual Analysis

Neville Estates v *Madden*
[1962] Ch 832
Chancery Division

Facts: The plaintiffs, Neville Estates Ltd, claimed a declaration that they were entitled to specific performance of a contract for the sale of land owned by the Catford Synagogue. The trustees of the synagogue claimed that the consent of the Charity Commissioners was required.

Held: The plaintiffs' action failed. A gift to the Catford Synagogue, whose objects included maintaining places of worship for persons of the Jewish religion who conform to the German or Polish ritual, could not take effect as a gift to the members beneficially, subject only to their contractual rights and liabilities towards one another as members of the association, but could take effect as a charitable purpose trust. On the charitable aspect, see chapter 12.

CROSS J (on the holding of property by non-charitable unincorporated associations): I turn now at last to the legal issues involved. The question of the construction and effect of gifts to or in trust for unincorporated associations was recently considered by the Privy Council in *Leahy* v *Attorney-General for New South Wales* [1959] AC 457. The position, as I understand it, is as follows. Such a gift may take effect in one or other of three quite different ways. In the first place, it may, on its true construction, be a gift to the members of the association at the relevant date as joint tenants, so that any member can sever his share and claim it whether or not he continues to be a members not as joint tenants, but subject to their respective contractual rights and liabilities towards one another as members of the association. In such a case a member cannot sever his share. It will accrue to the other members on his death or resignation, even though such members include persons who became members after the gift took effect. If this is the effect of the gift, it will not be open to objection on the score of perpetuity or uncertainty unless there is something in its terms or circumstances or in the rules of the association which precludes the members at any given time from dividing the subject of the gift between them on the footing that they are solely entitled to it in equity.

Thirdly, the terms or circumstances of the gift or the rules of the association may show that the property in question is not to be at the disposal of the members for the time being, but is to be held in trust for or applied for the purposes of the association as a quasi-corporate entity. In this case the gift will fail unless the association is a charitable body. If the gift is of the second class, i.e., one which the members of the association for the time being are entitled to divide among themselves, then, even if the objects of the association are in themselves charitable, the gift would not, I think, be a charitable gift. If, for example, a number of persons formed themselves into an association with a charitable object – say the relief of poverty in some district – but if it was part of the contract between them that, if a majority of the members so desired, the association should be dissolved and its property divided between the members at the date of dissolution, a gift to the association as part of its general funds would not, I conceive, be a charitable gift.

Note

A gift to a non-charitable unincorporated association was held valid on the basis of the second of the above methods in *Re Lipinski's WT*, where Oliver J upheld a bequest to the Hull Judeans (Maccabi) Association. The requirement that 'the members at any given time [can divide] the subject of the gift between them on the footing that they are solely entitled to it in equity' can cause difficulties, however: see *Re Recher's WT* [1972] Ch 526.

In *Conservative and Unionist Central Office v Burrell* [1982] 1 WLR 522, the Court of Appeal, applying the reasoning in *Neville Estates*, held that the Conservative Central Office was not an unincorporated association (and therefore did not come within a statutory tax provision). The court held for a body to be an unincorporated association for these purposes, its members must be subject to mutually enforceable obligations, whereas there were no enforceable mutual understandings between the members of the Conservative Central Office. In other words, the passage above, and the passage set out from *Re Recher's WT* in this section, are also used to *define* unincorporated associations for statutory purposes.

Re Recher's WT
[1972] Ch 526
Chancery Division

Facts: The testatrix left some of her residuary estate to a non-charitable unincorporated association which, on the construction of her will, was identified as the London and Provincial Anti-Vivisection Society. By the date of the will, however, that society had ceased to exist, but had amalgamated with the National Anti-Vivisection Society. The question was whether the gift could take effect in favour of the National Anti-Vivisection Society.

Held:

(a)   The gift could not be construed as a trust for the purposes of the London and Provincial Anti-Vivisection Society.

(b)   It would have been possible to construe the gift, on the basis of Cross J's views in *Neville Estates v Madden* [1962] Ch 832 (above), as a gift to the members of the London and Provincial Anti-Vivisection Society, subject to the contract towards each other to which they had bound themselves as members, had the Society been in existence at the date of the testatrix's will. By then it had been dissolved, however, and the contract between the members terminated. The gift could not be construed as a gift to the members of a different association (i.e., the National Anti-Vivisection Society), and accordingly failed.

BRIGHTMAN J: A trust for non-charitable purposes, as distinct from a trust for individuals, is clearly void because there is no beneficiary. It does not, however, follow that persons cannot band themselves together as an association or society, pay subscriptions and validly devote their funds in pursuit of some lawful non-charitable purpose. An obvious example is a members' social club. But it is not essential that the members should only intend to secure direct personal advantage to themselves. The association may be one in which personal advantages to the members are combined with the pursuit of some outside purpose. Or the association may be one which offers no personal benefit at all to the members, the funds of the association being applied exclusively to the pursuit of some outside purpose. Such an association of persons is bound, I would think, to have some sort of constitution; i.e., the rights and the liabilities of the members of the association will inevitably depend on some form of contract *inter se*, usually evidenced by a set of rules. In the present case it appears to me clear that the life members, the ordinary members and the associate members of the London and Provincial Society were bound together by a contract *inter se*. Any such member was entitled to the rights and subject to the liabilities defined by the rules. If the committee acted contrary to the rules, an individual member would be entitled to take proceedings in the courts to compel observance of the rules or to recover damages for any loss he had suffered as a result of the breach of contract. As and when a member paid his subscription to the association, he would be subjecting his money to the disposition and expenditure thereof laid down by the rules. That is to say, the member would be bound to permit, and entitled to require, the honorary trustees and other members of the society to deal with that subscription in accordance with the lawful directions of the committee. Those directions would include the expenditure of that subscription, as part of the general funds of the association, in furthering the objects of the association. The resultant situation, on analysis, is that the London and Provincial Society represented an organisation of individuals bound together by a contract under which their subscriptions became, as it were, mandated towards a certain type of expenditure as adumbrated in r. 1. Just as the two parties to a bipartite bargain can vary or terminate their contract by mutual assent, so it must follow that the life members, ordinary members and associate members of the London and Provincial Society could, at any moment of time, by unanimous agreement (or by majority vote if the rules so prescribe), vary or terminate their multipartite contract. There would be no limit to the type of variation or termination to which all might agree. There is no private trust or trust for charitable purposes or other trust to hinder the process. It follows that if all members agreed, they could decide to wind up the London and Provincial Society and divide the net assets among themselves beneficially. No one would have any *locus standi* to stop them so doing. The contract is the same as any other contract and concerns only those who are parties to it, that is to say, the members of the society. The funds of such an association may, of course, be derived not only from subscriptions of the contracting parties but also from donations from non-contracting parties and legacies from persons who have died. In the case of a donation which is not accompanied by any words which purport to impose a trust, it seems to me that the gift takes effect in favour of the existing members of the association as an accretion to the funds which are the subject-matter of the contract which such members have made *inter se*, and falls to be dealt with in precisely the same way as the funds which the members themselves have subscribed. So, in the case of a legacy. In the absence of words which purport to impose a trust, the legacy is a gift to the members beneficially, not as joint tenants or as tenants in common so as to entitle each member to an immediate distributive share, but as an accretion to the funds which are the subject-matter of the contract which the members have made *inter se*.

Notes

This passage was adopted by Vinelott J in *Re Grant's WT* [1980] 1 WLR 360, where a grant to the Chertsey Constituency Labour Party could not be construed as a grant to the Chertsey and Walton Constituency Labour Party, the old Chertsey CLP having been dissolved in 1971, upon the redistribution of Parliamentary constituency boundaries. These cases show up the difficulties of being unable to construe a grant to a non-charitable unincorporated association as a gift for the *purposes* of the association.

Another difficulty in *Re Grant* was that the members of the Chertsey and Walton Constituency Labour Party did not have control over their own property, because they were also bound by the rules of the Labour Party nationally. Thus, a gift to the CLP could not be construed as a gift to the members of the CLP beneficially, since they could not direct that the bequest be divided among themselves as beneficial owners. The gift could only take effect, if at all, as a private purpose trust, in which case it infringed the rule against perpetuities.

The passage was also adopted by Walton J in *Re Bucks Constabulary Fund (No. 2)* [1979] 1 WLR 936 (see chapter 8).

News Group Newspapers Ltd and Others v *Society of Graphical and Allied Trades 1982*
[1986] ICR 716, [1986] IRLR 227
Court of Appeal

Decision: A writ of sequestration entitling Commissioners 'to sequester all the real and personal property of the defendant Society of Graphical and Allied Trades 82' for contempt of a court order did not apply to the London Branch of Clerical, Administrative and Executive Personnel of the union, since their assets were not to be taken to belong to the national union. *Re Grant's WT* was distinguished on the grounds that the London branch could unilaterally secede from the national union, unlike the Chertsey and Walton Constituency Labour Party, which had no power to secede from the national Labour Party.

LLOYD LJ: Mr Newman [for the Commissioners] submitted that the case cannot be brought within Cross J's second [*Neville Estates*] class because the branch assets are not at the free disposal of the members of the branch. They cannot alter the rules, so as to divide the branch assets among themselves, without the consent of the National Executive Council. He . . . relies on *Re Grant's Will Trusts*, in which Vinelott J held that the gift in question, a gift to the 'Labour Party Property Committee for the benefit . . . of the Chertsey and Walton Constituency Labour Party' could not take effect as an accretion to the funds of the Constituency Labour Party to be held in accordance with its rules. Vinelott J gave two reasons. We are not concerned with the second. But as to the first he said:

I base this conclusion on two grounds. First, the members of the Chertsey and Walton CLP do not control the property, given by subscription or otherwise, to the CLP. The rules which govern the CLP are capable of being altered by an outside body which could direct an alteration under which the general committee of the CLP would be bound to transfer any property for the time being held for the benefit of the CLP to the National Labour Party for national purposes. The members of the Chertsey and Walton CLP could not alter the rules so as to make the property bequeathed by the testator applicable for some purpose other than that provided by the rules; nor could they direct that property to be divided amongst themselves beneficially.

I do not accept Mr Newman's submission, since in the present case the members of the branch do not need to alter the rules in order to divide the branch assets among themselves. Under the rules as they stand, the members of the branch have complete control of the branch assets. However unlikely it may be in practice, they could in theory secede from the union. There is nothing in the rules of the union to prevent them, nor, in the words of Brightman J in *Re Recher's WT*, is there 'any private trust or trust for charitable purposes or other trust to hinder the process'. The vesting of the branch assets in the branch trustees does not hinder the process, since, under the rules, the trustees are expressed to be the agents of the branch committee, and are bound to act in accordance with the branch committee's decisions. *Re Grant's WT* is distinguishable, because in that case the National Executive Committee had power to change the rules governing the Constituency Labour Party, and could therefore have procured transfer of the assets of the Constituency Party against the Constituency Party's wishes, to the National Labour Party for national purposes. I can therefore understand Vinelott J's difficulty in bringing *Grant's* case within the second [*Neville Estates*] class. But there is no such difficulty in the present case. The union has no power, direct or indirect, to procure the transfer of branch assets to the union. I therefore see no objection to the view that the branch assets are held, and held exclusively, pursuant to the contract between the members of the branch for the time being. That would seem to be the sensible and straightforward view. There are no technical rules of equity which would prevent us so holding. Accordingly I would allow the appeal.

Questions

1.   X gives £1,000 to the Plane Truth, an unincorporated society dedicated to the proof of all unproven mathematical theorems. Assume that the Plane Truth is non-charitable. Can X prevent the members of the Plane Truth (at any time) from dissolving the society and spending the assets on beer?

2.   Suppose the gift is conditional upon the Plane Truth continuing to exist as a society, with a gift over to charity if it ceases to exist. Can such a condition be placed upon the gift? If so, does the condition have to be triggered, if at all, within a certain time, and if so, what time (see further below)?

C: Effect of Modern Law of Perpetuities

Perpetuities and Accumulations Act 1964

1.   Power to specify perpetuity period

(1)   Subject to section 9(2) of this Act [on options to purchase land] and subsection (2) below [relating to powers of appointment], where the instrument by

which any disposition is made so provides, the perpetuity period applicable to the disposition under the rule against perpetuities, instead of being of any other duration, shall be of a duration equal to such number of years not exceeding eighty as is specified in that behalf in the instrument. . . .

3. Uncertainty as to remoteness

(1) Where, apart from the provisions of this section and sections 4 [age reduction] and 5 [death of surviving spouse] of this Act, a disposition would be void on the ground that the interest disposed of might not become vested until too remote a time, the disposition shall be treated, until such time (if any) as it becomes established that the vesting must occur, if at all, after the end of the perpetuity period, as if the disposition were not subject to the rule against perpetuities; and its becoming so established shall not affect the validity of anything previously done in relation to the interest disposed of by way of advancement, application of intermediate income or otherwise. . . .

(4) Where this section applies to a disposition and the duration of the perpetuity period is not determined by virtue of section 1 or 9(2) of this Act, it shall be determined as follows:—

(a) where any persons falling within subsection (5) below are individuals in being and ascertainable at the commencement of the perpetuity period the duration of the period shall be determined by reference to their lives and no others, but so that the lives of any description of persons falling within paragraph (b) or (c) [relating to grandchildren] of that subsection shall be disregarded if the number of persons of that description is such as to render it impracticable to ascertain the date of death of the survivor;

(b) where there are no lives under paragraph (a) above the period shall be twenty-one years.

(5) The said persons are as follows:—

(a) the person by whom the disposition was made; . . .

10. Avoidance of contractual and other rights in cases of remoteness

Where a disposition *inter vivos* would fall to be treated as void for remoteness if the rights and duties thereunder were capable of transmission to persons other than the original parties and had been so transmitted, it shall be treated as void as between the person by whom it was made and the person to whom or in whose favour it was made or any successor of his, and no remedy shall lie in contract or otherwise for giving effect to it or making restitution for its lack of effect.

15. Short title, interpretation and extent

(2) In this Act —

'disposition' includes the conferring of a power of appointment and any other disposition of an interest in or right over property, and references to the interest disposed of shall be construed accordingly; . . .

(4) Nothing in this Act shall affect the operation of the rule of law rendering void for remoteness certain dispositions under which property is limited to be applied for purposes other than the benefit of any person or class of persons in cases where the property may be so applied after the end of the perpetuity period.

Notes

1. In chapter 8 we will come across a number of cases which cannot be explained on the basis of the contractual analysis in the previous section, but on the basis of some kind of trust analysis. The perpetuity difficulties of doing this at common law were examined in *Leahy*, above. No case (as far as I am aware) has analysed the effect of the 1964 Act on private purpose trusts and unincorporated associations, so the best I can do here is set out arguments which will also be relevant to chapter 8.

2. Before the 1964 Act it would have been possible to make a gift, including a gift to a non-charitable unincorporated association (on the contractual analysis), determinable upon an uncertain future event (such as the dissolution of the association). The reverter on the determining event was not subject to the rule against perpetuities (see *Re Chardon*, above), but since 1964 is caught by s. 12 of the Act (see also above).

3. Before the 1964 Act it would have been possible to construe a gift to an unincorporated association as a trust in favour of its members for the time being so long as the gift was expressly limited in duration to a life in being plus 21 years. The same limit probably applied to such pure purpose trusts as the courts upheld (as anomalous exceptions).

4. In the case of unincorporated associations, s. 1 of the 1964 Act appears to allow for the substitution of an 80-year period. In the case of pure purpose trusts the position is complicated by the interrelationship between s. 1 and s. 15(4). Section 1 applies only to dispositions, defined in s. 15(2). With a pure purpose trust there is no creation of a beneficial interest, but the transfer of legal title to trustees is presumably sufficient to come under s. 15(2), and hence trigger s. 1.

5. Where no period is expressly specified, it may be thought that s. 3 allows a gift to an unincorporated association to take effect as a trust in favour of its members for the time being until it becomes clear that a disposition of an equitable interest will occur more than 21 years after the death of the donor. However, consider the following argument: by the rules of the association the trustees will have the right to dispose of equitable interests in favour of new members at any future time (say, 1,000 years into the future). This is clear right from the start, and whether or not s. 10 applies, it seems that there is nothing to wait and see for. Against this it might be argued that the society could be dissolved within the perpetuity period, but if it is a trust in favour of present and future members the question is how? The contractual analysis allows for dissolution at any time by the members for the time being, but the *Saunders* v *Vautier* doctrine (on which see further chapter 7) would not allow dissolution on a trust analysis, since the beneficiaries include unascertained (and possibly unborn) future members.

6. If the analysis in the previous paragraph is correct, it follows that a trust analysis is only possible for the holding of property by non-charitable unincorporated associations if a perpetuity period is expressly specified.

7. In question 2 at the end of the previous section, there is no obvious reason why, if the gift to the Plane Truth is made to present members on the contractual analysis, s. 3 should not operate on the triggering of the condition.

Question
The above analysis deals with perpetuity only. Can you envisage any certainty difficulties with any of the proposed scenarios? Consider in particular the wait and see scenario in note 5, assuming my argument on s. 3 is wrong. Who are the beneficiaries under the trust envisaged? Given that the proposed trust is probably a fixed trust, is there any way they can satisfy the certainty of object requirements of the last chapter?

6 FORMALITIES AND PUBLIC POLICY

This chapter considers further requirements for validity, not so far considered.

SECTION 1: FORMALITIES

There are no formality requirements for trusts, except those laid down by statute; these are now contained in the Law of Property Act 1925, s. 53. The important distinctions to bear in mind are between land and other property, and between declarations and dispositions.

Implied, resulting and constructive trusts are expressly exempted from the statutory requirements, and so, it appears, are variations of trust carried out under the Variation of Trusts Act 1958 (on which see chapter 7). As is suggested below, however, the distinction between implied, resulting and constructive trusts on the one hand, and express trusts on the other, may be less important than appears at first sight; it is probable that express trusts can also, in some circumstances, fall outside the operation of s. 53, even though they are not specifically exempted.

A: The Statutory Provisions

Law of Property Act 1925

53. Instruments required to be in writing

(1) Subject to the provisions hereinafter contained [they are contained in s. 54, below] with respect to the creation of interests in land by parol —

(a) no interest in land can be created or disposed of except by writing signed by the person creating or conveying the same, or by his agent thereunto lawfully authorised in writing, or by will, or by operation of law;

(b) a declaration of trust respecting any land or any interest therein must be manifested and proved by some writing signed by some person who is able to declare such trust or by his will;

(c) a disposition of an equitable interest or trust subsisting at the time of the disposition, must be in writing signed by the person disposing of the same, or by his agent thereunto lawfully authorised in writing or by will.

(2) This section does not affect the creation or operation of resulting, implied or constructive trusts.

54. Creation of interests in land by parol

(1) All interests in land created by parol and not put in writing and signed by the persons so creating the same, or by their agents thereunto lawfully authorised in writing, have, notwithstanding any consideration having been given for the same, the force and effect of interests at will only.

Note

Section 53(1)(b) requires no special treatment here, as it, and its relationship with s. 53(2), are considered as they arise throughout the book (see, e.g., chapters 9 and 11).

B: Dispositions of Equitable Interests

Section 53(1)(c) replaced section 9 of the Statute of Frauds 1677, which provided:

AND bee it further enacted that all grants and assignments of any trust or confidence shall likewise be in writeing signed by the partie granting or assigning the same or by such last will or devise or else shall likewise be utterly void and of none effect.

Other sections of the 1677 Act are set out in chapter 11.

Brian Green, 'Grey, Oughtred and Vandervell – A Contextual Reappraisal' (1984) 47 MLR 385

In addressing itself to subsisting equitable interests, section 53(1)(*c*) took up the mantle of section 9 of the Statute of Frauds 1677 [Green sets out the section], and like that provision was designed (i) to prevent hidden oral transactions in equitable interests in fraud of those truly entitled and (ii) to enable trustees to know where the equitable interests behind their trusts reside at any particular time. [Green notes Lord Upjohn in *Vandervell* v *IRC* [1967] 2 AC 291, 311 B–D]. . . .

Section 9 of the 1677 Act, being concerned solely with 'grants and assignments' of subsisting equitable rights, and hence exclusively with dispositions by equitable proprietors themselves, fell squarely within the twin policy objectives noted above. By replacing the words 'grants and assignments' with the single word 'disposition,' the draftsman (as a matter of language at least) potentially extended the requirement of writing to transactions effected by persons other than the equitable owner for the time being, e.g. to trustees exercising a power of revocation and new appointment: a case clearly outside the twin policy objectives in that (i) if the consent of the person entitled in equity pending the revocation and new appointment is (as is usually the case) irrelevant to the trustees exercising their power, divestment of his previously subsisting interest behind his back cannot be a cause for concern and (ii) since it is the trustees who will be exercising the power it can hardly be said that writing is necessary to enable them (at least so long as they are viewed as a single and continuing body of persons) to ascertain to whom their fiduciary duties are owed.

A principal reason for singling out subsisting equitable interests for protection is because evidence of their movement will often be the only indicator of where a particular right resides at any given time. There is no documentary paper title, nor generally is there physical possession . . . : two indicia which facilitate the identification of a legal proprietor. In general there is only an invisible entitlement to certain rights perceived by courts of equity behind the veil of legal title.

Notes

1.   Green notes that there are exceptions to the position in the last paragraph, as where a life tenant has the right to occupy property.

2.   The old section was probably in line with the twin policy objectives suggested by Green, but it seems from the following case that the new section is not to be interpreted as merely consolidatory, and that 'disposition' is considerably wider than 'grants and assignments'. It is not an easy term to define, but probably includes all transfers of equitable interests apart from declarations of trust, disclaimers of equitable interests (*Re Paradise Motor Co. Ltd* [1968] 1 WLR 1125), mergers of legal and equitable title (*Vandervell* v *IRC*, below) and by implication, perhaps, surrenders of equitable interests.

3.   Whether or not the twin policy objectives suggested by Green were the original reasons behind the writing requirements, all the cases considered in detail here are in fact taxation cases.

Grey* v *IRC
[1960] AC 1
House of Lords

Facts: Mr Hunter was beneficial owner of 18,000 shares of £1 each, the legal title being held by nominees. In order to transfer his beneficial interest, Mr Hunter orally directed the nominees (one of whom was Grey) to hold the shares on trust for beneficiaries under six settlements (the nominees were also the trustees under these settlements). Later the trustees/nominees executed six deeds of declaration to this effect, which were in writing.

The issue was whether the equitable title in the shares was transferred by the oral direction, or by the deeds of declaration. If the oral direction had transferred the shares no *ad valorem* stamp duty was payable; if the transfer had been effected by the written declaration, it was.

Held: The transfer of the equitable title was effected by the written declaration. The oral direction transferred the bare legal title only. A direction by a beneficiary to the trustees to transfer his interest to someone else constitutes a disposition and must therefore be in writing, under s. 53(1)(c) of the Law of Property Act 1925.

Lord Radcliffe's view was that s. 53(1) did not merely consolidate the earlier Statute of Frauds: this was a disposition, whether or not it was also within the mischief of s. 9 of the earlier statute.

LORD RADCLIFFE: Where opinions have differed [in the courts below] is on the point whether his direction i.e., Mr Hunter's oral direction to his trustees was a 'disposition' within the meaning of s. 53(1)(c) of the Law of Property Act 1925, the argument for giving it a more restricted meaning in that context being that s. 53 is to be construed as no more than a consolidation of three sections of the Statute of Frauds, ss. 3, 7 and 9. So treated, 'disposition', it is said, is merely the equivalent of the former words of s. 9, 'grants and assignments', except that testamentary disposition has to be covered as well, and a direction to a trustee by the equitable owner of the property prescribing new trusts upon which it is to be held is a declaration of trust but not a grant or assignment. The argument concludes, therefore, that neither before 1 January 1926 nor since did such a direction require to be in writing signed by the disponor or his agent in order to be effective.

In my opinion, it is a very nice question whether a parol declaration of trust of this kind was or was not within the mischief of s. 9 of the Statute of Frauds. The point has never, I believe, been decided and perhaps it never will be. Certainly it was long established at law that while a declaration of trust respecting land or any interest therein required writing to be effective, a declaration of trust respecting personalty did not. Moreover, there is warrant for saying that a direction to his trustee by the equitable owner of trust property prescribing new trusts of that property was a declaration of trust. But it does not necessarily follow from that that such a direction, if the effect of it was to determine completely or *pro tanto* the subsisting equitable interest of the maker of the direction, was not also a grant or assignment for the purposes of section 9 and therefore required writing for its validity. Something had to happen to that equitable interest in order to displace it in favour of the new interests created by the direction: and it would be at any rate logical to treat the direction as being an assignment of the subsisting interest to the new beneficiary or beneficiaries or, in other cases, a release or surrender of it to the trustees.

I do not think, however, that that question has to be answered for the purposes of this appeal. It can only be relevant if s. 53(1) of the Law of Property Act 1925, is treated as a true consolidation of the three sections of the Statute of Frauds concerned and as governed, therefore, by the general principle, with which I am entirely in agreement, that a consolidating Act is not to be read as effecting changes in the existing law unless the words it employs are too clear in their effect to admit of any other construction. If there is anything in the judgments of the majority of the Court of Appeal which is inconsistent with this principle I must express my disagreement with them. But, in my opinion, it is impossible to regard s. 53 of the Law of Property Act 1925 as a consolidating enactment in this sense. It is here that the premises upon which Upjohn J and the Master of the Rolls founded their conclusions are, I believe, unsound.

[Lord Radcliffe examined the history of the 1925 legislation, and continued:]

For these reasons I think that there is no direct link between s. 53(1)(c) of the Act of 1925 and section 9 of the Statute of Frauds. The link was broken by the changes introduced by the amending Act [Law of Property (Amendment) Act] of 1924, and it was those changes, not the original statute, that s. 53 must be taken as consolidating. If so, it is inadmissible to allow the construction of the word 'disposition' in the new Act to be limited or controlled by any meaning attributed to the words 'grant' or 'assignment' in s. 9 of the old Act.

Note

It may be easy to avoid the effects of *Grey*. Had Mr Hunter surrendered his interest this would possibly not have required writing. If the trustees immediately declared new trusts, at Mr Hunter's request, these would also not have required writing. For further discussion and questions, see below.

Question

Is this decision in line with the twin policy objectives suggested by Green, above?

Ian Bamsey, *'Vanwall, A Technical Appraisal'*, Haynes, 1990, pp. 8–9 (chapter entitled 'Seeing Red')

Alfa Romeo, Maserati, Ferrari: as Grand Prix racing got underway in the aftermath of World War . . . , it did so painted blood red. . . .

Before the dust of war settled, Mays, Berthon and Ken Richardson had launched a renewed appeal. In March 1945 Mays argued: 'I feel very strongly that the ultimate in any activity is of direct value to the country achieving it. There is no doubt that the motor and associated industries have achieved it in the mechanisation of our forces. It is only fitting that this superiority should be perpetuated as a gesture to the technicians and Servicemen who had made our victory possible – no less than to the masses who have patiently endured so much. It becomes incumbent upon those of us who have the ability to try to produce a car which will securely uphold our place in the very forefront of international competition'.

These sentiments found favour with a number of key individuals in the British motor industry, including . . . Guy Anthony ('Tony') Vandervell of Vandervell Products Ltd. . . .

Vandervell Products, which the owner had pledged to undertake some of the manufacturing work, was famed for its Thinwall bearings. [Bamsey explains how the thin wall type of bearing had originated in the USA, but that Vandervell had obtained the licence to manufacture it in the UK and Europe.] . . .

By the late Forties Tony Vandervell's Park Royal, Acton (West London) based company was a huge concern. . . . [In] 1949 Vandervell purchased a 1.5 litre Ferrari Grand Prix car . . . for the sport of it. . . .

The 1.5 litre supercharged Ferrari was the first Grand Prix car to be fitted with Thinwall bearings. . . . Vandervell dubbed his Ferrari the 'Thinwall Special' . . . [Bamsey goes on to describe how the car crashed in its first, and presumably only, race].

Notes

1. Since Tony Vandervell and Vandervell Products Ltd are fairly central to this part of the book, readers may be interested to know who Vandervell was. Bamsey goes on to describe the rise of the Vanwall racing car, which succeeded the Thinwall Special, was built by Vandervell Products Ltd, and

which, with Stirling Moss as number 1 driver, won the newly-formed World Constructors' title in 1958. Stirling Moss failed to win the Drivers' Championship, however, by one point, becoming widely known as the best British driver never to win the World Championship. The car was reputed to be an ill-handling machine with a heavy gearbox, but was powerful and obviously very competitive. Its name was an amalgam of 'Vandervell' and 'Thinwall Special'.
2. Tony Vandervell lived from 1896 to 1967, and raced motorcycles and cars in the 1920s. He was obviously passionately interested in, and successful at, motor sport. We are interested in another side of the man in this chapter, of course. On page 57 of his book Bamsey notes:

> Certainly Vandervell now had an armoury to match his equipment's potential: over the winter of '56/'57 he amassed enough equipment to ensure that no single car need be raced twice in succession. Still, for tax reasons, only four cars officially existed but there were two new frames and with that there were sufficient parts from which ten chassis could be assembled, though no more than seven 2.5 litre engines had been produced . . .

It seems probable that Vandervell had no desire to pay more tax than was necessary. It is also reputed that the Thinwall Special was so named to allow Vandervell to set off the not inconsiderable costs associated with Formula 1 motor racing as an advertising expense.

Autocar and Motor
1 November 1989, p. 9

First Brooks auction nets over £6.5 million
Over £6.5 million worth of classic sports cars went under the hammer last Friday. In the richest car auction ever held in this country, the new Brooks auction house confirmed its lead position in this field at its very first sale.

The most breathtaking and valuable car in the 40-lot sale was the ex-Stirling Moss Vanwall VW10. Winner of the Dutch and Portuguese Grand Prix in 1958, it sold for £1.45 million to Hans Thulin on behalf of AB Consolidated Collection in Sweden.

Vandervell v *IRC*
[1967] 2 AC 291
House of Lords

Facts (taken from the judgment of Lord Denning MR in *Vandervell's Trusts (No. 2)* [1974] Ch 269):

The late Mr Vandervell died on 10 March 1967. His affairs have twice been to the House of Lords. The first, *Vandervell* v *Inland Revenue Commissioners* [1967] 2 AC 291. The second, *Re Vandervell's Trusts* [1971] AC 912. The third is now on its way.

During his lifetime Mr Vandervell was a very successful engineer. He had his own private company, Vandervell Products Ltd – the products company, as I will call it –

in which he owned virtually all the shares. It was in his power to declare dividends as and when he pleased.

In 1949 he set up a trust for his children. He did it by forming Vandervell Trustees Ltd – the trustee company, as I will call it. He put three of his friends and advisers in control of it. They were the sole shareholders and directors of the trustee company. Two were chartered accountants. The other was his solicitor. He transferred money and shares to the trustee company to be held in trust for the children. Such was the position at the opening of the first period.

The first period: 1958–1961

The first period covers the three years from October 1958 to October 1961. Mr Vandervell decided to found a chair of pharmacology at the Royal College of Surgeons. He was to endow it by providing £150,000. But he did not do it by direct gift. In November 1958, he transferred to the Royal College of Surgeons 100,000 A shares in his products company. His intention was that his products company should declare dividends in favour of the Royal College of Surgeons which would amount in all to £150,000 or more. But, when that sum had been provided, he wanted to be able to regain the shares – so as to use the dividends for other good purposes. So, about the time of the transfer, on 11 December 1958, he got the Royal College of Surgeons to grant an option to his trustee company. By this option the Royal College of Surgeons agreed to transfer the 100,000 A shares to the trustee company for the sum of £5,000 at any time within the next five years. (This £5,000 was far less than the real value of the shares.) At the time when the option was granted, Mr Vandervell did not state definitely the trusts on which the trustee company were to hold the option. He meant the trustee company to hold the option on trust – not beneficially for themselves – but on trust for someone or other. He did not specify the trusts with any kind of precision. But at a meeting with the chairman of the trustee company it was proposed – and Mr Vandervell approved – that the option should be held either on trust for his children (as an addition to the children's settlement) or alternatively on trust for the employees of his products company (see the particulars declared by the executors). He had not made up his mind which of those should benefit. But one thing he was clear about. He thought that he himself had parted with all interest in the shares and in the option.

Afterwards, during the years from 1958 to 1961, he saw to it that his products company declared dividends on those 100,000 shares which were paid to the Royal College of Surgeons. They amounted to £266,000 gross (before tax), or £157,000 net (after tax). So the Royal College of Surgeons received ample funds to found the chair of pharmacology.

But there were other advantages hoped for. The Royal College of Surgeons thought that, being a charity, they could claim back the tax from the Revenue. And Mr Vandervell thought that, having parted with all interest in the shares, he was not subject to pay surtax on these dividends.

The Revenue authorities, however, did not take that view. They claimed that Mr Vandervell had not divested himself of all interest in the shares. They argued that he was the beneficial owner of the option and liable for surtax on the dividends. Faced with this demand, in 1961, the trustee company, on the advice of counsel, and with the full approval of Mr Vandervell, decided to exercise the option. They did it so as to avoid any question of surtax thereafter being payable by Mr Vandervell. This ended the first period (when the option was in being) and started the second period (after the option was exercised).

Held (Lords Reid and Donovan dissenting): The decision of the House of Lords in this case and that of the Court of Appeal in *Re Vandervell's Trusts (No. 2)*, arose out of the same scheme, but the House of Lords was concerned only with the first period, as described above.

By the end of the first period, the legal title in the shares had been transferred to the RCS. Vandervell Trustees Ltd had the legal title in the option. Vandervell's liability for surtax depended on s. 415 of the Income Tax Act 1952:

> (1) Where, during the life of the settlor, income arising under a settlement . . . is, under the settlement and in the events that occur, payable to or applicable for the benefit of any person other than the settlor, then, unless, under the settlement and in the said events, the income . . . (d) is income from property of which the settlor has divested himself absolutely by way of settlement . . . the income shall be treated for the purposes of surtax as the income of the settlor and not as the income of any other person . . .
>
> (2) The settlor shall not be deemed for the purposes of this section to have divested himself absolutely of any property if that property or any income therefrom or any property directly or indirectly representing proceeds of, or income from, that property is, or will or may become, payable to him or applicable for his benefit in any circumstances whatsoever.

The shares
Vandervell had successfully divested himself of any interest in the shares by his oral direction to his trustees. No writing was required, because s. 53(1)(c) has no application where a beneficial owner, solely entitled, directs his bare trustees with regard to the legal and equitable estate.

The option
Vandervell was nevertheless liable to surtax, because he had not succeeded in divesting himself of the equitable interest in the option, the legal interest of which was now in the trustee company. This was held on resulting trust for him, and he was therefore liable to pay surtax on the dividends.

Vandervell had failed to state where the equitable interest was to go. The trusts upon which the option was supposed to be held were undefined and in the air, possibly to be defined later. The trustee company itself was clearly not a beneficiary, and an equitable interest cannot remain in the air, and so the only possibility was a resulting trust in favour of the settlor. [See further chapter 8.]

Vandervell was therefore not entitled to the benefit of s. 415(1)(d) set out above, because the strict requirements of that section had not been satisfied.

LORD WILBERFORCE: The conclusion, on the facts found, is simply that the option was vested in the trustee company as a trustee on trusts, not defined at the time, possibly to be defined later. But the equitable, or beneficial interest, cannot remain in the air: the consequence in law must be that it remains in the settlor. There is no need to consider some of the more refined intellectualities of the doctrine of resulting trust, nor to speculate whether, in possible circumstances, the shares might be applicable for Mr Vandervell's benefit: he had, as the direct result of the option and of the failure to place the beneficial interest in it securely away from him, not divested himself absolutely of the shares which it controlled.

There remains the alternative point taken by the Crown that in any event, by virtue of s. 53(1)(c) of the Law of Property Act 1925, the appellant never effectively disposed of the beneficial interest in the shares to the Royal College of Surgeons. This argument I cannot accept. Section 53(1)(c), a successor to the dormant s. 9 of the Statute of Frauds, has recently received a new lease of life as an instrument in the hands of the

Revenue. The subsection, which has twice recently brought litigants to this House (*Grey* v *IRC* [1960] AC 1 [above]; *Oughtred* v *IRC* [1960] AC 206 [below]), is certainly not easy to apply to the varied transactions in equitable interests which now occur. However, in this case no problem arises. The shares in question, the 100,000 A shares in Vandervell Products Ltd, were, prior to 14 November 1958, registered in the name of the National Provincial Bank Ltd upon trust for the appellant absolutely. On 14 November 1958, the appellant's solicitor received from the bank a blank transfer of the shares, executed by the bank, and the share certificate. So at this stage the appellant was the absolute master of the shares and only needed to insert his name as transferee in the transfer and to register it to become the full legal owner. He was also the owner in equity. On 19 November 1958, the solicitor (or Mr Robins – the case is ambiguous) on behalf of Mr Vandervell, who intended to make a gift, handed the transfer to the college which, in due course, sealed it and obtained registration of the shares in the college's name. The case should then be regarded as one in which the appellant himself has, with the intention to make a gift, put the college in a position to become the legal owner of the shares, which the college in fact became. If the appellant had died before the college had obtained registration, it is clear that on the principle of *Re Rose* [1949] Ch 78 that the gift would have been complete, on the basis that he had done everything in his power to transfer the legal interest, with an intention to give, to the college. No separate transfer, therefore, of the equitable interest ever came to or needed to be made and there is no room for the operation of the subsection. What the position would have been had there simply been an oral direction to the legal owner (viz. the bank) to transfer the shares to the college, followed by such a transfer, but without any document in writing signed by Mr Vandervell as equitable owner, is not a matter which calls for consideration here. The Crown's argument on this point fails but, for the reasons earlier given, I would dismiss the appeal.

Re Vandervell's Trusts (No. 2)
[1974] Ch 269
Court of Appeal

Facts: The facts follow on from the result of the previous case, and the following statement is a continuation the judgment of Lord Denning MR.

The second period: 1961–1965
In October 1961 the trustee company exercised the option. They did it by using the money of the children's settlement. They paid £5,000 of the children's money to the Royal College of Surgeons. In return the Royal College of Surgeons, on 27 October 1961, transferred the 100,000 A shares to the trustee company. The intention of Mr Vandervell and of the trustee company was that the trustee company should hold the shares (which had replaced the option) on trust for the children as an addition to the children's settlement. They made this clear to the Revenue authorities in an important letter written by their solicitors on 2 November 1961, which I will read:

GA Vandervell, Esq. – Surtax
    Further to our letter of 7 September last, we write to inform you that in accordance with the advice tendered by counsel to Vandervell Trustees Ltd, the latter have exercised the option granted to them by the Royal College of Surgeons of 1 December 1958, and procured a transfer to them of the shares referred to in

the option, with funds held by them upon the trusts of the settlement created by Mr G.A. Vandervell and dated 30 December 1949, and consequently such shares will henceforth be held by them upon the trusts of the settlement.

Mr Vandervell believed that thenceforward the trustee company held the 100,000 A shares on trust for the children. He acted on that footing. He got his products company to declare dividends on them for the years 1962 to 1964 amounting to the large sum of £1,256,458 gross (before tax) and £769,580 10s 9d (after tax). These dividends were received by the trustee company and added to the funds of the children's settlement. They were invested by the trustee company for the benefit of the children exclusively.

But even now Mr Vandervell had not shaken off the demands of the Revenue authorities. They claimed that, even after the exercise of the option, Mr Vandervell had not divested himself of his interest in the 100,000 A shares and that he was liable for surtax on the dividends paid to the children's settlement. Faced with this demand, Mr Vandervell, on the advice of counsel, took the final step. He executed a deed transferring everything to the trustee company on trust for the children. This ended the second period, and started the third.

The third period: 1965–1967
On 19 January 1965, Mr Vandervell executed a deed by which he transferred to the trustee company all right, title or interest which he had on the option or the shares or in the dividends – expressly declaring that the trust company were to hold them on the trusts of the children's settlement. At last the Revenue authorities accepted the position. They recognised that from 19 January 1965, Mr Vandervell had no interest whatever in the shares or the dividends. They made no demands for surtax thenceforward.

On 27 January 1967, Mr Vandervell made his will. It was in contemplation of a new marriage. In it he made no provision for his children. He said expressly that this was because he had already provided for them by the children's settlement. Six weeks later, on 10 March 1967, he died.

Held: The Court of Appeal was concerned only with the law for the second period. Liability to surtax now depended on the whereabouts of the equitable interest in the shares during that period. It was argued that, as before, it remained with Vandervell.

The option
The option was destroyed when it was exercised by the trustee company in 1961, so Vandervell's equitable interest in it (resulting from the earlier litigation, above) was extinguished. This was not a disposition within s. 53.

The shares
The children had the equitable interest. The shares had been placed by the trustee company on the trusts of the children's settlements, and Vandervell had now succeeded in divesting himself of the entire interest in these shares, there being no longer a resulting trust in his favour. The later trusts were precisely defined, in favour of the children's settlements, so that it was no longer necessary for the equitable interest to remain in the settlor.

Lord Denning MR analysed the position as a termination of the resulting trust of the option in favour of Vandervell, and a fresh trust of the shares declared (presumably by the trustee company) in favour of the children. As to the first part, writing is not required to terminate a resulting trust, and since the new trust was not of land no formalities were required for its creation.

LORD DENNING MR:
The law for the second period

In October and November 1961, the trustee company exercised the option. They paid £5,000 out of the children's settlement. The Royal College of Surgeons transferred the legal estate in the 100,000 A shares to the trustee company. Thereupon the trustee company became the legal owner of the shares. This was a different kind of property altogether. Whereas previously the trustee company had only a chose in action of one kind – an option – it now had a chose in action of a different kind – the actual shares. This trust property was not held by the trustee company beneficially. It was held by them on trust. On this occasion a valid trust was created at the time of the transfer. It was manifested in clear and unmistakeable fashion. It was precisely defined. The shares were to be held on the trusts of the children's settlement. The evidence of intention is indisputable: (i) The trustee company used the children's money – £5,000 – with which to acquire the shares. This would be a breach of trust unless they intended the shares to be an addition to the children's settlement. (ii) The trustee company wrote to the Revenue authorities the letter of 2 November 1961, declaring expressly that the shares 'will henceforth be held by them on the trusts of the children's settlement'. (iii) Thenceforward all the dividends received by the trustees were paid by them to the children's settlement and treated as part of the funds of the settlement. This was all done with the full assent of Mr Vandervell. Such being the intention, clear and manifest, at the time when the shares were conveyed to the trustee company, it is sufficient to create a trust.

Mr Balcombe for the executors admitted that the intention of Mr Vandervell and the trustee company was that the shares should be held on trust for the children's settlement. But he said that this intention was of no avail. He said that during the first period, Mr Vandervell had on equitable interest in the property, namely, a resulting trust; that he never disposed of this equitable interest (because he never knew he had it): and that in any case it was the disposition of an equitable interest which, under s. 53 of the Law of Property Act 1925, had to be in writing, signed by him or his agent, lawfully authorised by him in writing (and there was no such writing produced). He cited *Grey v IRC* [1960] AC 1 [above] and *Oughtred v IRC* [1960] AC 206 [below].

There is a complete fallacy in that argument. A resulting trust for the settlor is born and dies without any writing at all. It comes into existence whenever there is a gap in the beneficial ownership. It ceases to exist whenever that gap is filled by someone becoming beneficially entitled. As soon as the gap is filled by the creation or declaration of a valid trust, the resulting trust comes to an end. In this case, before the option was exercised, there was a gap in the beneficial ownership. So there was a resulting trust for Mr Vandervell. But as soon as the option was exercised and the shares registered in the trustees' name, there was created a valid trust of the shares in favour of the children's settlement. Not being a trust of land, it could be created without any writing. A trust of personalty can be created without writing. Both Mr Vandervell and the trustee company had done everything which needed to be done to make the settlement of these shares binding on them. So there was a valid trust: see *Milroy v Lord* (1862) 4 De GF & J 264, 274, per Turner LJ.

Note

In 1965 Vandervell, presumably by now justifiably fed up with his scheme, clearly relinquished by deed any interest, legal or equitable, he may still have had in the shares.

Questions

1. So far as the formality aspects of the *Vandervell* decisions are concerned, at no stage did s. 53 operate to defeat a transaction in either case. Given that none of the transactions could have been kept secret from the trustees, is this in accord with the twin policy objectives suggested by Green, above?

2. X holds shares on trust for Y. Y wishes to transfer his equitable interest to Z, and embarks on an arrangement with X and W, where he directs X to transfer the legal and equitable interest in the shares to W, it being understood that W will declare himself trustee for Z. Is writing required at any stage?

3. Suppose W drops out of the picture, and Y surrenders his equitable interest to X, it being understood that X will declare himself trustee for Z. Can that possibly make any difference to your answer?

4. If no writing is required for *3*, is this an easy way to avoid the consequences of *Grey* v *IRC*?

5. Returning to the facts of *2*, let us suppose that W, having received the legal and equitable title to the shares, refused to declare himself trustee of them for Z. What actions, if any, are available against W, on the assumption that Z is not party to the arrangement? You may care to consider the material in chapter 3, and also whether the doctrines in chapters 10 and 11 may apply.

Oughtred v *IRC*
[1960] AC 206
House of Lords

Facts: Mrs Oughtred owned 72,700 shares in William Jackson and Son Ltd absolutely. 200,000 shares in the same company were held on trust for Mrs Oughtred for life, thence for her son, Peter absolutely. The parties orally agreed to exchange their interests, so that Mrs Oughtred would obtain Peter's reversionary interest (she would then have 200,000 shares outright), and in exchange Peter would obtain Mrs Oughtred's 72,700 shares. The contract was later performed.

The Revenue claimed stamp duty on the transfer of the reversionary interest in the 200,000 shares, the actual transfer of which involved writing. Oughtred's argument was that the equitable interest was transferred on the oral contract for sale, and that the later writing transferred only the bare legal title.

Held (Viscount Radcliffe and Lord Cohen dissenting): The oral contract did not transfer the full equitable interest in the shares, and stamp duty was therefore payable on the written transfer. Although equity can, in appropriate circumstances, grant specific performance of a contract of sale, and although in that case a constructive trust arises immediately in favour of the purchaser, the buyer does not have a full beneficial interest until the formal transfer. The situation is analogous to a sale of land, where the deed of conveyance is the effective instrument of transfer (and so liable to stamp duty).

LORD JENKINS: The provisions of the Stamp Act 1891 directly relevant to the claim are these:

Section 1 (which contains the charge of stamp duties) provides that stamp duties 'upon the several instruments specified in Schedule 1 to this Act shall be the several duties in the said Schedule specified'.

Section 54 provides as follows: 'For the purposes of this Act the expression 'conveyance on sale' includes every instrument . . . whereby any property, or any estate or interest in any property, upon the sale thereof is transferred to or vested in a purchaser, or any person on his behalf or by his direction'.

Schedule 1 imposes under the head of charge 'conveyance or transfer on sale, of any property' (except as therein mentioned) *ad valorem* duty upon 'the amount or value of the consideration for the sale'; and under the head of charge 'conveyance or transfer of any kind not hereinbefore described' a fixed duty of 10s [50p]. . . .

I am unable to accept the conclusion that the disputed transfer was prevented from being a transfer of the shares to the appellant on sale because the entire beneficial interest in the settled shares was already vested in the appellant under the constructive trust, and there was accordingly nothing left for the disputed transfer to pass to the appellant except the bare legal estate. The constructive trust in favour of a purchaser which arises on the conclusion of a contract for sale is founded upon the purchaser's right to enforce the contract in proceedings for specific performance. In other words, he is treated in equity as entitled by virtue of the contract to the property which the vendor is bound under the contract to convey to him. This interest under the contract is no doubt a proprietary interest of a sort, which arises, so to speak, in anticipation of the execution of the transfer for which the purchaser is entitled to call. But its existence has never (so far as I know) been held to prevent a subsequent transfer, in performance of the contract, of the property contracted to be sold from constituting for stamp duty purposes a transfer on sale of the property in question. Take the simple case of a contract for the sale of land. In such a case a constructive trust in favour of the purchaser arises on the conclusion of the contract for sale, but (so far as I know) it has never been held on this account that a conveyance subsequently executed in performance of the contract is not stampable *ad valorem* as a transfer on sale. Similarly, in a case like the present one, but uncomplicated by the existence of successive interests, a transfer to a purchaser of the investments comprised in a trust fund could not, in my judgment, be prevented from constituting a transfer on sale for the purposes of stamp duty by reason of the fact that the actual transfer had been preceded by an oral agreement for sale.

In truth, the title secured by a purchaser by means of an actual transfer is different in kind from, and may well be far superior to, the special form of proprietary interest which equity confers on a purchaser in anticipation of such transfer.

The difference is of particular importance in the case of property such as shares in a limited company. Under the contract the purchaser is no doubt entitled in equity as between himself and the vendor to the beneficial interest in the shares, and (subject to due payment of the purchase consideration) to call for a transfer of them from the vendor as trustee for him. But it is only on the execution of the actual transfer that he becomes entitled to be registered as a member, to attend and vote at meetings, to effect transfers on the register, or to receive dividends otherwise than through the vendor as his trustee.

SECTION 2: PUBLIC POLICY

The courts tread warily where public policy is concerned. There is no doubt that the courts can also strike down capricious or useless trusts, as for example in *Brown* v *Burdett* (1882) 21 ChD 667, which was an attempt to create a trust to block up windows.

Other cases have concerned the validity of conditions.

Blathwayt v *Baron Cawley*
[1976] AC 397
House of Lords

Facts: A large estate (valued in 1975 at £2 million) was left in 1936 on various entailed trusts, but such that any person who became entitled was to forfeit his interest if he became a Roman Catholic (or ceased to use the name and arms of Blathwayt). It was argued that with respect to the present children, the religious condition tended to restrain the carrying out of parental duties, and was therefore void on public policy grounds.

Held: The effect of the clause may have been to force the parents to choose between material and spiritual welfare for their offspring, but this was not necessarily contrary to public policy. In the event, however, the House of Lords held by a 3–2 majority (Lords Wilberforce and Fraser of Tullybelton dissenting) that the clause did not apply on its construction.

LORD WILBERFORCE: . . . Finally, as to public policy. The argument under this heading was put in two alternative ways. First, it was said that the law of England was now set against discrimination on a number of grounds including religious grounds, and appeal was made to the Race Relations Act 1968 which does not refer to religion and to the European Convention of Human Rights of 1950 which refers to freedom of religion and to enjoyment of that freedom and other freedoms without discrimination on ground of religion. My Lords. I do not doubt that conceptions of public policy should move with the times and that widely accepted treaties and statutes may point the direction in which such conceptions, as applied by the courts, ought to move. It may well be that conditions such as this are, or at least are becoming, inconsistent with standards now widely accepted. But acceptance of this does not persuade me that we are justified, particularly in relation to a will which came into effect as long ago as 1936 and which has twice been the subject of judicial consideration, in introducing for the first time a rule of law which would go far beyond the mere avoidance of discrimination on religious grounds. To do so would bring about a substantial reduction of another freedom, firmly rooted in our law, namely that of testamentary disposition. Discrimination is not the same thing as choice: it operates over a larger and less personal area, and neither by express provision nor by implication has private selection yet become a matter of public policy.

. . .

LORD SIMON OF GLAISDALE: My Lords, on all the points dealt with in his speech, save as to the principal issue of construction, I agree with my noble and learned friend, Lord Wilberforce. In particular, I agree with what he has said about public policy as applied by the law to a religious forfeiture clause such as your Lordships are concerned with. The actual personal circumstances can differ so greatly in these matters from case to case that it is difficult to apply a general rule of public policy which is not either practically unreal in many cases or open to some logical objection. Creed or religious observance or sectarian adherence cannot be isolated from other human activities or ideologies. 'Attempt to rule the living from the grave' is a vivid phrase apt to cause revulsion from the conduct referred to: but it is difficult to see why, if public policy is invoked, a particular disposition should be more objectionable if made by will than if made inter vivos. Moreover, it would appear that the policy of English law is to allow a testator considerable freedom in the way in which he disposes of his estate: modern English law knows nothing (apart from taxation and discretionary intervention under the Inheritance (Family Provision) legislation) of a part of a deceased's estate reserved from his disposition. Balancing these various matters, I agree with my noble and learned friend, Lord Wilberforce, that in these days society's interest in a parent's conscientious choice as to what influence should be brought to bear on his own child during minority is sufficiently vindicated by the rule that a forfeiture clause shall not operate till after the lapse of a reasonable period after the child reaches the age of majority. This also accords with the contemporary view that it is for a youth himself to take the crucial decision on such a matter. He cannot hope to do so emancipated from conflicting influences and interests.

I must not be taken thereby to be implying that it is for courts of law to embark on an independent and unfettered appraisal of what they think is required by public policy on any issue. Courts are concerned with public policy only in so far as it has been manifested by parliamentary sanction or embodied in rules of law having binding judicial force. As to such rules of law your Lordships have the same power to declare, to bind and to loose as in regard to any other judicial precedent. Rules of law expressing principles of public policy therefore fall to be treated with the same respect and circumspection, the same common sense and regard to changing circumstances, as any other rules of law. So approaching the authorities expressing public policy with regard to forfeiture clauses – specifically those relating to religious and other ideologies – I agree that the law is as stated by my noble and learned friend, Lord Wilberforce.

. . .

LORD CROSS OF CHELSEA: . . . The summons issued by the trustees of the will on February 23, 1940, asked two questions – first, whether Christopher forfeited his life interest in the property settled by the will on being received into the Roman Catholic Church on November 10, 1939, and, secondly, if the answer to the first question was 'Yes,' how the trustees were to deal with the income of the property pending the birth of a son to Christopher. I do not suppose that the legal advisers of the family at that time expected the first question to be answered otherwise than as Farwell J answered it – that is to say in the affirmative; for before the decision of this House in *Clayton* v *Ramsden* [1943] AC 320 few if any Chancery practitioners would have thought it seriously arguable that a condition subsequent forfeiting a life interest on the life tenant becoming a Roman Catholic was void. The decision in *Clayton* v *Ramsden* turned primarily on a condition for forfeiture on the beneficiary marrying a person 'not of Jewish parentage' but four of the members of the House expressed the view that a condition against marriage with a person 'not of the Jewish faith' was also void for uncertainty. If that be so then it is certainly arguable that a condition for forfeiture on the beneficiary becoming a Roman Catholic is void. That point was not however taken on behalf of Mark on the hearing of the summons taken out after his birth in 1949. That proceeded on the footing that Christopher forfeited his life interest in 1939 and that the only point to be determined was whether the interest in the income to which Justin then became entitled in possession had come to an end on Mark's birth. Your Lordships refused Mark leave to raise the issue of Christopher's forfeiture on this appeal; but the question whether the condition is or is not void emerges again in its application to Mark's estate tail. In agreement, I believe, with all your Lordships, I am clearly of opinion that the condition was not and is not void either for uncertainty or, as applied to a person of full age at the date of the will, on grounds of public policy. I accept, of course, that by the law of England a stricter test of certainty is applied to a condition subsequent than to a condition precedent but I agree with the judges both in the Irish Republic and in Northern Ireland that it would be an affront to common sense to hold that a condition for forfeiture if the beneficiary should become a Roman Catholic is open to objection on the ground of uncertainty: see *In re McKenna* [1947] IR 277 and *McCausland* v *Young* [1948] NI 72; [1949] NI 49. If I had been a member of the House which heard *Clayton* v *Ramsden*, I might well have agreed with Lord Wright that a condition for forfeiture on marriage with a person 'not of the Jewish faith' was valid. But it is a vaguer conception than being or not being a Roman Catholic and acceptance of the view of the majority does not involve the consequence that a condition of forfeiture on becoming a Roman Catholic is open to objection on the score of uncertainty. Turning to the question of public policy, it is true that it is widely thought nowadays that it is wrong for a government to treat some of its citizens less favourably than others because of differences in their religious beliefs; but it does not follow from that that it is against public policy for an adherent of one religion to distinguish in disposing of his property between adherents of his faith and those of another. So to hold would amount to saying that though it is in order for a man to have a mild preference for one religion as opposed to another it is disreputable for him to be convinced of the importance of holding true religious beliefs and of the fact that this religious beliefs are the true ones.

Note

As is clear from the extract from Lord Cross's speech, above, conditions subsequent can alternatively be struck down on the grounds of uncertainty, as in *Clayton* v *Ramsden* [1943] AC 320, which concerned a forfeiture on marriage to a person 'not of Jewish parentage and of the Jewish faith'. This was held to be conceptually uncertain. But it seems that so long as a clause is not uncertain the courts will be slow to strike it down on grounds of public policy, and a somewhat similar clause to the above was upheld by the Court of Appeal in *Re Tuck's ST* [1978] Ch 49, where 'an approved wife' of Jewish blood was precisely defined, cases of dispute being dealt with by the Chief Rabbi in London. Names and arms clauses (such as the other clause in *Blathwayt*) have also been upheld, for example: *Re Neeld* [1962] Ch 643 (CA).

Re Lysaght (decd)
[1966] 1 Ch 191, [1965] 2 All ER 888, [1965] 3 WLR 391
Chancery Division

Decision: The decision is set out in chapter 13 (see p. 409). For present purposes, Buckley J did not regard a racial bar (prior to the Race Relations Act 1965) as contrary to public policy.

BUCKLEY J: In *Clayton* v *Ramsden* [1943] AC 320, a condition subsequent under which a beneficiary was to forfeit a benefit in the event of her marrying a person not of Jewish parentage and of the Jewish faith was held void for uncertainty, but different considerations apply in this respect to a forfeiture provision from those applicable to a condition precedent or a qualification to take a benefit (*Re Allen, Faith v Allen* [1953] Ch 810). In the one case the person liable to suffer a forfeiture must be able to know with certainty what will cause a forfeiture: in the other all that any person claiming to benefit has to do is to establish that the condition or qualification is satisfied in his particular case. The fact that someone else might have difficulty in demonstrating this with certainty does not prevent someone who clearly satisfies the appropriate test from claiming to be entitled or eligible to benefit. In the present case there would be a wide field open to any trustee of the endowment fund for the selection of students who manifestly satisfy the qualification of being neither of the Jewish nor of the Roman Catholic faith. Accordingly, I do not think that this part of the trust is affected by the vice of uncertainty. Nor, in my judgment, is it contrary to public policy, as counsel for the personal representatives suggests. I accept that racial and religious discrimination is nowadays widely regarded as deplorable in many respects, and I am aware that there is a bill dealing with racial relations at present under consideration by Parliament, but I think that it is going much too far to say that the endowment of a charity, the beneficiaries of which are to be drawn from a particular faith or are to exclude adherents to a particular faith, is contrary to public policy. The testatrix's desire to exclude persons of the Jewish faith or of the Roman Catholic faith from those eligible for the studentship in the present case appears to me to be unamiable, and I would accept the suggestion of counsel for the Attorney-General that it is undesirable, but it is not, I think, contrary to public policy.

7 VARIATION OF TRUSTS

Chapters 3 to 6 concerned the requirements for setting up an express trust. Once such a trust is set up it is in principle permanent, but it may be expedient later to vary its terms.

The main reason for wishing to vary trusts is to reduce liability to taxation. Until the Variation of Trusts Act 1958, however, powers to vary were extremely limited, especially where tax planning was the motive.

Most of the jurisdiction considered in this chapter is statutory, but there are circumstances apart from those provided for by statute where variation is possible. The trust instrument itself may have been drafted so as to confer upon the trustees the power to vary the beneficial interests. There is also an inherent equitable jurisdiction considered in the following section.

SECTION 1: INHERENT EQUITABLE JURISDICTION

A: *Saunders* v *Vautier*

In the absence of express powers, it may be possible to effect a variation in the trust by taking advantage of the rule in *Saunders* v *Vautier* (1841) 10 LJ Ch 354. Collectively, the beneficiaries, so long as they are all adult, *sui iuris* and between them entitled to the entirety of the trust property, can bring the trust to an end and resettle the property on any terms they wish. Thus, for example, in a simple settlement of property upon a life interest for X with remainder for Y, X and Y may agree to end the trust and divide the capital between them immediately. They can also collectively consent to any act by the trustees which has the effect of varying the terms of the trust. However there are limits to the application of the *Saunders* v *Vautier* doctrine.

First, it depends on the beneficiaries all being collectively entitled. Thus, donees under a power cannot use it, and though beneficiaries under a discretionary trust usually can, they will not be able to unless the entire class of objects is ascertainable. Secondly, it turns upon all the beneficiaries being able to consent to dissolve the trust, or to what would otherwise be a breach of trust by the trustees. If some of the beneficiaries are infants, or if the settlement creates any interests in favour of persons who are not yet born or ascertained, variation of the trust upon this basis will not be possible. This is a serious limitation when dealing with family settlements of the usual type, which almost invariably give interests to non *sui iuris* persons. As will appear below, this is the difficulty tackled by the Variation of Trusts Act 1958.

Thirdly, unless the trustees also agree, the beneficiaries cannot vary an existing trust, and keep it on foot, instead of dissolving it and resettling the property. In *Re Brockbank* [1948] Ch 206, a trustee wished to retire and the beneficiaries sought to have a trust corporation appointed in place of the remaining trustees, who opposed the change on the ground of the cost to the trust of the trust corporation's fees. The beneficiaries argued that since they were all *sui iuris* and collectively entitled, the trustees were obliged to appoint in accordance with their wishes. Vaisey J rejected this argument. The beneficiaries might terminate the trust if they so wished, but they were not entitled to control the trustees' exercise of their statutory power to appoint while the trust subsisted. Although the *ratio* of the case is confined to the appointment of new trustees under s. 36 of the Trustee Act 1925 (on which see chapter 14), there are remarks by Vaisey J of a much wider scope:

It seems to me that the beneficiaries must choose between two alternatives: either they must keep the trust of the will on foot. In which case those trusts must continue to be executed by trustees . . . not . . . arbitrarily selected by themselves; or they must, by mutual agreement, extinguish and put an end to the trusts . . .

Walton J expressed similar views in *Stephenson v Barclays Bank* [1975] 1 WLR 88. One of the reasons he gave was that otherwise the beneficiaries could force upon the trustees duties quite different to those they had originally accepted.

Stephenson (Inspector of Taxes) v Barclays Bank Trust Co. Ltd
[1975] 1 WLR 882, [1975] 1 All ER 625
Chancery Division

Facts: Under a deed of family arrangement made in 1969, Richard and Charles were the only beneficiaries under a trust of a fund. The trustees (Barclays Bank Trust Co. Ltd) had already (before the arrangement was made) acquired the investments which were to make up the fund, but did not transfer them to Richard and Charles. On the question of the liability of the trustees to capital gains tax, the Crown contended that Richard and Charles were 'absolutely entitled as against the trustee' from 1969, as required by s. 22(5) of the Finance Act 1965. The trustees contended that Richard and Charles did not become absolutely entitled until the fund was actually distributed.

Held (for the Crown): Richard and Charles were 'absolutely entitled as against the trustee' from 1969, and it could not be contended that they did not become absolutely entitled until the fund was actually distributed.

WALTON J: I now turn to a consideration of the phrase 'absolutely entitled as against the trustee', which is now of course fairly closely defined in the Finance Act 1969, sch. 19, para. 9. It is there defined as meaning that the person concerned —

> has the exclusive right, subject only to satisfying any outstanding charge, lien or other right of the trustees to resort to the asset for payment of duty, taxes, costs or other outgoings, to direct how that asset should be dealt with.

Now it is trite law that the persons who between them hold the entirety of the beneficial interests in any particular trust fund are as a body entitled to direct the trustees how that trust fund is to be dealt with, and this is obviously the legal territory from which that definition derives. However, in view of the arguments advanced to me by counsel for the respondents, and more particularly that advanced by him on the basis of the decision of Vaisey J in *Re Brockbank* [1948] Ch 206 [above], I think it may be desirable to state what I conceive to be certain elementary principles. (1) In a case where the persons who between them hold the entirety of the beneficial interest in any particular trust fund are all *sui juris* and acting together ('the beneficial interest holders'), they are entitled to direct the trustees how the trust fund may be dealt with. (2) This does not mean, however, that they can at one and the same time override the pre-existing trusts and keep them in existence. Thus, in *Re Brockbank* itself the beneficial interest holders were entitled to override the pre-existing trusts by, for example, directing the trustees to transfer the trust fund to X and Y, whether X and Y were the trustees of some other trust or not, but they were not entitled to direct the existing trustees to appoint their own nominee as a new trustee of the existing trust. By so doing they would be pursuing inconsistent rights. (3) Nor, I think, are the beneficial interest holders entitled to direct the trustees as to the particular investment they should make of the trust fund. I think this follows for the same reason as the above. Moreover, it appears to me that once the beneficial interest holders have determined to end the trust they are not entitled, unless by agreement, to the further services of the trustees. Those trustees can of course be compelled to hand over the entire trust assets to any person or persons selected by the beneficiaries against a proper discharge, but they cannot be compelled, unless they are in fact willing to comply with the directions, to do anything else with the trust fund which they are not in fact willing to do. (4) Of course, the rights of the beneficial interest holders are always subject to the right of the trustees to be fully protected against such matters as duty, taxes, costs or other outgoings; for example, the rent under a lease which the trustees have properly accepted as part of the trust property.

Note

Walton J went on to hold that Richard and Charles were absolutely entitled from 1969, although the fund was still actually held by the bank.

B: Non *Sui Iuris* Beneficiaries

There are often in any case persons unable to give consent, especially children and unborn persons. The courts have limited power to permit a variation of trust under their inherent jurisdiction, where not all beneficiaries are adult and *sui iuris*.

It has long been recognised that the court may, in the case of necessity, permit the trustees to take measures not authorised by the trust instrument, including varying the beneficial interests. The inherent jurisdiction is narrow, encompassing for the most part only emergency and salvage. Originally, this seems to have been confined to cases where some act of salvage was urgently required, such as the mortgage of an infant's property in order to raise money for vital repairs. Gradually, it was widened to cover other contingencies not foreseen and provided for by the settlor, but the House of Lords reaffirmed in *Chapman* v *Chapman* [1954] AC 429 that some element of emergency still needs to be shown.

The courts may also approve compromises of disputes regarding the beneficial entitlements on behalf of infant or future beneficiaries. In *Chapman* v *Chapman* it was argued that this jurisdiction could be extended to cover situations where no real dispute had arisen, but this broad conception of the inherent jurisdiction was firmly disapproved by the House of Lords, and held to be confined to instances where a genuine element of dispute exists.

Chapman v *Chapman*
[1954] AC 429
House of Lords

Decision: A judge of the Chancery Division has no inherent jurisdiction to approve a rearrangement of a trust the only purpose of which is to reduce liability to estate duty.

LORD SIMONDS LC: My Lords, this appeal raises questions of considerable importance and for that reason, though I have had the privilege of reading the opinion which my noble and learned friend, Lord Morton of Henryton, is about to deliver and agree with it in its reasoning and conclusions, I think it desirable to make some observations upon the main argument of the appellants. By way of preliminary explanation, it is only necessary to say that your Lordships are invited to hold that a judge of the Chancery Division of the High Court of Justice has an inherent jurisdiction in the execution of the trusts of a settlement to sanction on behalf of infant beneficiaries and unborn persons a rearrangement of the trusts of that settlement for no other purpose than to secure an adventitious benefit which may be and, in the present case, is, that estate duty, payable in a certain event as things now stand, will, in consequence of the rearrangement, not be payable in respect of the trust funds.
. . .

My Lords, I am unable to accept as accurate this view of the origin, development and scope of the jurisdiction of the Court of Chancery. I do not propose to embark on the arduous task of tracing to its sources this peculiar jurisdiction. Many volumes have been to it, and I have refreshed my memory by reference to some of them. Nowhere can I find any statement which would support the broad proposition for which the appellants contend. Moreover, the law reports contain many cases in which the scope of the jurisdiction has been discussed, every one of them a work of supererogation if its scope was unlimited.

In my opinion, the true view that emerges from a consideration of this jurisdiction through the centuries is not that at some unknown date it appeared full-fledged and that from time to time timid judges have pulled out some of its feathers, but rather that it has been a creature of gradual growth, though with many setbacks, and that the range of its authority can only be determined by seeing what jurisdiction the great equity judges of the past assumed and how they justified that assumption. It is, in effect, in his way that the majority of the Court Appeal in the present case have approached the problem and, in my opinion, it is the right way. It may well be that the result is not logical, and it may be asked why, if the jurisdiction of the court extended to this thing, it did not extend to that also. But, my Lords, that question is as vain in the sphere of jurisdiction as it is in the sphere of substantive law. We are as little justified in saying that a court has a certain jurisdiction, merely because we think it ought to have it, as we should be in declaring that the substantive law is something different from what it has always been declared to be merely, because we think it ought to be so. It is even possible that we are not wiser than our ancestors. It is for the legislature, which does not rest under that disability, to determine whether there should be a change in the law and what that change should be.

. . . There is no doubt the Chancellor (whether by virtue of the paternal power or in the execution of a trust, it matters not) had and exercised the jurisdiction to change the nature of an infant's property from real to personal estate and vice versa, though this jurisdiction was generally so exercised as to preserve the rights of testamentary disposition and of succession. Equally, there is no doubt that from an early date the court assumed the power, sometimes for that purposes ignoring the direction of a settlor, to provide maintenance, for an infant, and, rarely, for an adult, beneficiary. So, too, the court had power in the administration of trust property to direct that by way of salvage some transaction unauthorized by the trust instrument should be carried out. Nothing is more significant than the repeated assertions by the court that mere expediency was not enough to found the jurisdiction. Lastly, and I can find no other than these four categories, the court had power to sanction a compromise by an infant in a suit to which that infant was a party by next friend or guardian and litem. This jurisdiction, it may be noted, is exercisable alike in the Queen's Bench Division and the Chancery Division and whether or not the court is in course of executing a trust.

This brings me to the question which alone presents any difficulty in this case. It is whether this fourth category, which I may call the compromise category, should be extended to cover cases in which there is no real dispute as to rights and, therefore, no compromise, but it is sought by way of bargain between the beneficiaries to rearrange the beneficial interests under the trust instrument and to bind infants and unborn persons to the bargain by order of the court.

My Lords, I find myself faced at once with a difficulty which I do not see my way to overcome. For though I am not as a rule impressed by an argument about the difficulty of drawing the line since I remember the answer of a great judge that, though he knew not when day ended and night began, he knew that midday was day and midnight was night, yet in the present case it appears to me that to accept this extension in any degree is to concede exactly what has been denied. It is the function of the court to execute a trust, to see that the trustees do their duty and to protect them if they do it, to direct them if they are in doubt and, if they do wrong, to penalize them. It is not the function of the court to alter a trust because alteration is thought to be advantageous to an infant beneficiary. It was, I thought, significant that counsel was driven to the admission that since the benefit of the infant was the test, the court had the power, though in its discretion it might not use it, to override the wishes of a living and expostulating settlor, if it assumed to know better than he what was beneficial for the infant. This would appear to me a strange way for a court of conscience to execute a trust. If, then, the court had not, as I hold it has not, power to alter or rearrange the trusts of a trust instrument, except within the limits which I have defined, I am unable to see how that jurisdiction can be conferred by pleading that the alternation is but a little one.

Notes

1. *Chapman* v *Chapman* applies only to variations in the beneficial interests as such. There is a wider inherent jurisdiction regarding the administration of the trust fund. For example, in *Re Duke of Norfolk's Settlement Trusts* [1982] Ch 61, the court authorised payment of remuneration to a trustee under its inherent jurisdiction. See chapter 14.

2. On the fourth (compromise) category referred to in the above passage, in *Re Powell-Cotton's Resettlement* [1956] 1 All ER 60, the Court of Appeal held that there were no disputed rights where an investment clause was ambiguous and it would have been advantageous to the beneficiaries to replace it with a new clause. In *Mason* v *Farbrother* [1983] 2 All ER 1078, genuine points of difference were found to have arisen where two contending interpretations of an investment clause had widely different implications for the permitted range of investments. The court, however, was reluctant to approve the substitution of a new clause under its inherent jurisdiction, preferring to rely upon s. 57 of the Trustee Act (see below). In *Allen* v *Distillers Co. (Biochemicals) Ltd* [1974] QB 384, the court was asked to approve a settlement of the claims of the child victims of the drug thalidomide, and the question arose as to whether the court could postpone the vesting of capital in the children to an age greater than 18. Eveleigh J, on the basis of the rule in *Saunders* v *Vautier*, held there was no inherent jurisdiction to order such a postponement, but found it to be authorised by the terms of the settlement itself.

SECTION 2:   STATUTORY POWERS TO VARY TRUSTS APART FOR THE VARIATION OF TRUSTS ACT 1958

A: Matrimonial Causes Act 1973

These provisions are further considered in chapter 9. Sections 24 and 25 give a wide power to make orders affecting the property of parties to matrimonial proceedings, so as to avoid the unfairness which sometimes arose where the property of a married couple, in particular the matrimonial home, came under the rules governing resulting trusts (see chapter 9) The court may order provision for either spouse to be made by payments in cash, by transfers of property, or by the creation of a settlement for the benefit of a spouse and children.

More important in the context of variation, s. 24(1)(c) and (d) allow for variation of an ante- or post-nuptial settlement, including settlements made by will or codicil, and also permit the making of an order extinguishing or reducing the interest of either of the spouses under such a settlement. The term 'settlement' has been widely interpreted to include any provision (other than outright gifts) made for the benefit of the parties to a marriage, whether by themselves or by a third party, and the acquisition of a matrimonial home has been held to be a settlement (*Ulrich* v *Ulrich* [1968] 1 WLR 180). Further, the court has the power to vary or discharge any order for a settlement or variation under s. 24(1) made on or after a decree of judicial separation, if the separation order is rescinded or the marriage subsequently dissolved.

B: Mental Health Act 1983

Mental Health Act 1983

96. Powers of the judge as to patient's property and affairs

(1) Without prejudice to the generality of section 95 above, the judge shall have power to make such orders and give such directions and authorities as he thinks fit for the purposes of that section and in particular may for those purposes make orders or give directions or authorities for —

. . .

(d) the settlement of any property of the patient, or the gift of any property of the patient to any such persons . . .

C: General Powers in the 1925 Legislation

Trustee Act 1925

57. Power of court to authorise dealings with trust property

(1) Where in the management or administration of any property vested in trustees, any sale, lease, mortgage, surrender, release or other disposition, or any purchase, investment, acquisition, expenditure, or other transaction, is in the opinion of the court expedient, but the same cannot be effected by reason of the absence of any power for that purpose vested in the trustees by the trust instrument, if any, or by law, the court may by order confer upon the trustees, either generally or in any particular instance, the necessary power for the purpose, on such terms, and subject to such provisions and conditions, if any, as the court may think fit and may direct in what manner any money authorised to be expended, and the costs of any transaction, are to be paid or borne as between capital and income.

(2) The court may, from time to time, rescind or vary any order made under this section, or may make any new or further order.

(3) An application to the court under this section may be made by the trustees, or by any of them, or by a person beneficially interested under the trust.

(4) This section does not apply to trustees of a settlement for the purposes of the Settled Land Act 1925.

Settled Land Act 1925

64. General power of the tenant for life to effect any transaction under an order of the court

(1) Any transaction affecting or concerning the settled land, or any part thereof, or any other land (not being a transaction otherwise authorised by this Act, or by the settlement) which in the opinion of the court would be for the benefit of the settled

land, or any part thereof, or the persons interested under the settlement, may, under an order of the court, be effected by a tenant for life, if it is one which could have been validly effected by an absolute owner.

Note
This section was invoked by Morritt J in *Hambro* v *Duke of Marlborough, The Times*, 25 March 1994, to allow the eleventh Duke of Marlborough (as tenant for life) to execute a conveyance the effect of which was to disinherit the Marquess of Blandford, who (the trustees had concluded) displayed un-businesslike habits and lack of responsibility.

Trustee Act 1925

53. Vesting orders in relation to infants' beneficial interests
Where an infant is beneficially entitled to any property the court may, with a view to the application of the capital or income thereof for the maintenance, education, or benefit of the infant, make an order —
    (a) appointing a person to convey such property; or
    (b) in the case of stock, or a thing in action, vesting in any person the right to transfer or call for a transfer of such stock, or to receive the dividends or income thereof, or to sue for and recover such thing in action, upon such terms as the court may think fit.

Note
This section allows the court to authorise dealings with an infant's property with a view to application of the capital or income for the infant's mainten-ance, education or benefit. 'Benefit' has been interpreted to cover dealings having the effect of reducing estate duty for the benefit of the infant: *Re Meux* [1958] Ch 154.

In that case, the proceeds of sale of property were to be re-settled upon the infant, and so could be regarded as an 'application' for the infant's benefit. However, in *Re Hayworth's Contingent Reversionary Interest* [1956] Ch 364, a proposal to sell an infant's contingent reversionary interest to the life tenant for cash, thus ending the trusts, was thought not to be for the 'benefit' of the infant. Other types of dealing approved under the section have included the barring of entails to exclude remote beneficiaries (*Re Gower's Settlement* [1934] Ch 365) or to simplify a proposed application to the court for approval of a further variation under the Variation of Trusts Act 1958 (*Re Bristol's Settled Estates* [1964] 3 All ER 939).

SECTION 3: VARIATION OF TRUSTS ACT 1958

Following the decision of the House of Lords in *Chapman* v *Chapman*, above, the Law Reform Committee was asked to consider the question of the court's powers to sanction variations (see Law Reform Committee Sixth Report (Court's Power to Sanction Variations of Trusts), Cmnd 310). The Variation of Trusts Act was based on these recommendations, and provides a new statutory jurisdiction independent of the Trustee Act 1925 or the Settled Land Act 1925.

A: The Statutory Provisions

Variation of Trusts Act 1958

1.   Jurisdiction of courts to vary trusts

(1)   Where property, whether real or personal, is held on trusts arising, whether before or after the passing of this Act, under any will, settlement or other disposition, the court may as it thinks fit by order approve on behalf of —

(a)   any person having, directly or indirectly, an interest, whether vested or contingent, under the trusts who by reason of infancy or other incapacity is incapable of assenting, or

(b)   any person (whether ascertained or not) who may become entitled, directly or indirectly, to an interest under the trusts as being at a future date or on the happening of a future event a person of any specified description or a member of any specified class of persons, so however that this paragraph shall not include any person who would be of that description, or a member of that class, as the case may be, if the said date had fallen or the said event had happened at the date of the application to the court, or

(c)   any person unborn, or

(d)   any person in respect of any discretionary interest of his under protective trusts where the interest of the principle beneficiary has not failed or determined, any arrangement (by whomsoever proposed, and whether or not there is any other person beneficially interested who is capable of assenting thereto) varying or revoking all or any of the trusts, or enlarging the trustees' powers of managing and administering any of the property subject to the trusts:

Provided that except by virtue of paragraph (d) of this subsection the court shall not approve an arrangement on behalf of any person unless the carrying out thereof would be for the benefit of that person.

[The remaining subsections are detailed provisions which are not reproduced.]

B: Relationship with Trustee Investments Act 1961

Trustees of the British Museum v *Attorney-General*
[1984] 1 WLR 418, [1984] 1 All ER 337
Chancery Division

Decision: The court's jurisdiction under the Variation of Trusts Act 1958, s. 1 allows, in appropriate circumstances, extension of the powers of investment beyond those prescribed in the Trustee Investments Act 1961.

SIR ROBERT MEGARRY V-C: The main point of importance is whether the court should continue to apply the principle that was laid down in *Re Kolb's WT* [1962] Ch 53] . . . , *Re Cooper's Settlement* [1962] Ch 826, and *Re Porrott's WT* (1961) 105 SJ 931, and was recognised in *Re Clarke's WT* [1961] 1 WLR 1471, and *Re University of London Charitable Trusts* [1964] Ch 282.

As is well known, the instrument establishing a trust may prescribe powers of investment which are either narrower or wider than those laid down by the general law: see the Trustee Act 1925, s. 69(2); Trustee Investments Act 1961, s.1(3). Subject to any such provision in the instrument, statute has prescribed the range of authorised investments for trustees. Under Part I of the Trustee Act 1925, and in particular s. 1 [since repealed by s. 1 of the Trustee Investments Act 1961], the range of authorised investments was in the main confined to what are generally called gilt-edged securities, and other securities which carried interest at fixed rates. It did not extend to industrial equities, no matter how large and prosperous the concerns. However suitable this was before the 1939–45 war, with a stable pound, it had ceased to be satisfactory when the post-war inflation began to emerge; and in establishing new trusts it became increasingly common to insert investment clauses that were markedly wider than the statutory provisions. That, however, did not help pre-existing trusts, and in these cases a number of successful applications to the courts to widen the investment powers were made under the Trustee Act 1925, s. 57, under the Variation of Trusts Act 1958, and, in the case of charities, under the Charitable Trusts Acts 1853 to 1925, as was done in respect of the 1960 scheme in the present case.

In the end, the Trustee Investments Act 1961 was enacted. By this time, the purchasing power of the pound was about half what it had been in 1939. The Act laid down an elaborate code. Under this, a much wider range of investments was authorised if the trustees first divided the trust fund into two equal parts. One part was confined to 'narrower-range' investments, which very roughly corresponded to the investments which were authorised under the Trustee Act 1925. The other part extended to 'wider-range' investments. The most important constituents of these (and I put it very shortly) were fully paid-up securities in United Kingdom companies with a paid-up capital of at least £1 million which were quoted on a recognised United Kingdom stock exchange and each year for the previous five years had paid a dividend on all shares ranking for dividend. Equities in such companies thus became available for trustee investment; but as with all investments authorised by the Act, save only certain narrower-range investments, the trustees were required to obtain proper advice in accordance with the Act before making the investment.

The Act was passed on 3 August 1961; and in October of that year the first three cases that I have cited, *Kolb, Cooper* and *Porrott*, all fell for decision. In each case an application had been made, doubtless before the Act was passed, for an extension of the powers of investment. Each case seems to have been decided without either of the others being cited; but in each case the judge (Cross, Buckley and Pennycuick JJ respectively) reached the same conclusion. In the words of Cross J in *Re Kolb's WT* [1962] Ch 531 at 540:

> . . . the powers given by the [1961] Act must, I think, be taken to be prima facie sufficient and ought only to be extended if, on the particular facts, a special case for extending them can be made out.

Buckley J said in *Re Cooper's Settlement* [1962] Ch 826 at 830:

> . . . from this time this court will have to be satisfied, whenever applications under s. 1 of the Variation of Trusts Act 1958 ask for relaxation of trustees' powers of investment, that there are special grounds which make it right that trustees should have wider powers of investment than the legislature has indicated in the Trustee Investments Act 1961 as the normally appropriate powers.

Pennycuick J said in *Re Porrott's WT* (1961) 105 SJ 931:

> The court should not, in the absence of special circumstances, enlarge the range of investments beyond that prescribed by the Trustee Investments Act 1961.

That was in 1961; and no doubt for some time that doctrine remained soundly based. However, in recent years the court, usually in chambers, has become ready to authorise extensions of the power of investment, often by an increased willingness to accept circumstances as being 'special'. Further, it has become increasingly common for draftsmen of wills and settlements to insert special investment powers which are far wider than those conferred by the 1961 Act. Then in October 1982 the Law Reform Committee made its 23rd report, *The Powers and Duties of Trustees* (Cmnd 8733), this time on the subject of the powers and duties of trustees; and in this the committee reached the conclusion that the 1961 Act has proved to be 'tiresome, cumbrous and expensive in operation', and that 'the present statutory powers are out of date and ought to be revised', see para 3.17. The committee's proposals for reform rejected any scheme for fixed proportions of the trust fund which could be invested in one type of investment or another, and instead proposed that investments should be divided into those which could be made without taking advice and those which could be made only on taking advice. The former category would include all the narrower-range securities, with certain additions, and the latter would include all other investments quoted on the English Stock Exchange. Subject to taking advice when necessary, trustees should be free to invest in such proportions as they choose: see para 3.21, 22. That was the recommendation.

I cite the report not as authority but as showing what the distinguished members of the committee recognised to be the position some 20 years after the 1961 Act was passed. In addition to that, I have before me detailed evidence of changes in the investment market that have occurred since the 1960 scheme was approved.

[Sir Robert Megarry V-C set out the present powers of investment under the trust in some detail, and continued:]

The evidence before me establishes that over the last 20 years significant changes in investment practice have occurred, especially in the case of large trust funds. The main factors producing these changes may be summarised as follows. First, increased rates of inflation have encouraged a movement from fixed interest investments to equities and property. As I have mentioned, by 1960 the purchasing power of the pound had fallen to about half what it had been in 1939; and in the next 20 years it lost some five-sixths of that reduced value. Second, differences in rates of inflation between one country and another have from time to time made it wise to replace investments in one country by those in another. Third, the exploitation of oil and other natural resources in certain countries has markedly affected the value of particular currencies. Fourth, in recent years the rate of economic growth has been greater in some countries (not least Japan) than in the United Kingdom. Fifth, leading companies in the United Kingdom have found it difficult to grow faster than the economy as a whole, whereas some smaller companies with specialist markets have been able to grow faster. There have also been trends away from the manufacture of capital goods towards the service and energy industries, and away from manufacturing 'high-volume' goods towards manufacturing which adds a high value to the goods. Sixth, the abolition of exchange controls in October 1979 has greatly facilitated overseas investment. Coupled with these factors has been an increased volatility in prices, with sharp changes taking place within three or four days, and sometimes a day. Seventh, unit trusts and certain forms of unsecured loans such as Eurobonds now offer valuable investment opportunities.

I feel no doubt that it is in the best interests of the trustees and the trusts that there should be relaxation of the terms of the 1960 scheme which will take account of these changes. At the same time, any scheme must have appropriate safeguards. The main features of the scheme put forward in this case, as it stands revised after discussion, may be stated as follows.

[Sir Robert Megarry V-C set out the proposed variation in some detail, and continued:]

I am conscious that such a scheme gives extremely wide powers of investment to the trustees. At the same time I consider that it is proper and desirable that such powers should be given, and I have made an order accordingly. There are four factors that I should mention in particular. First, there is the eminence and responsibility of the trustees, the machinery for obtaining highly skilled advice, and the success that this machinery has achieved over the past 20 years. Second, there are the changed conditions of investment, conditions which require great liberty of choice if, on skilled advice, advantage is to be taken of opportunities which often present themselves on short notice and for short periods; and for this, the provision for delegation is plainly advantageous. Third, there is obvious advantage in there being freedom to invest in any part of the world. At the same time, there is due recognition of the prudence of maintaining a solid core of relatively safe investments while setting free a substantial part for investments which, though less 'safe', offer greater opportunities for a substantial enhancement of value. Opinions may vary about the precise percentages; certainly my views have fluctuated. However, in the end I have reached the conclusion that the percentages put forward are reasonable. In reaching my conclusion on this and other points I have been reassured by the fact that counsel for the Attorney General has whole-heartedly supported the scheme after it had undergone careful examination.

From what I have said it will be seen that much of what I say depends to a greater or lesser extent on the special position of the trustees and the trust funds in the case before me. On the other hand, there is much that is of more general application, and it may be convenient if I attempt to summarise my views.

1. In my judgment, the principle laid down in the line of cases headed by *Re Kolb's WT* [1962] Ch 531 is one that should no longer be followed, since conditions have changed so greatly in the last 20 years. Though authoritative, those cases were authorities only *rebus sic stantibus*; and in 1983 they bind no longer. However, if Parliament acts on the recommendations of the Law Reform Committee and replaces the 1961 Act with revised powers of investments, the Kolb principle may well become applicable once more. Until then, the court should be ready to grant suitable applications for the extension of trustees' powers of investment, judging each application on its merits, and without being constrained by the provisions of the 1961 Act.

2. In determining what extended powers of investment should be conferred there are many matters which will have to be considered. I shall refer to five, without in any way suggesting that this list is exhaustive, or that anything I say is intended to fetter the discretion that the curl has to exercise in each case.

(i) The court is likely to give greater weight to the width and efficacy of any provisions for advice and control. The wider the powers, the more important these provisions will be. An existing system of proven efficacy, as here, is likely to be especially cogent.

(ii) Where the powers are of great width, as in the present case, there is much to be said for some scheme of fractional division, confining part of the fund to relatively safe investments, and allowing the other part to be used for investments in which the greater risks will be offset by substantial prospects of a greater return. On the other hand, when the powers are appreciably less wide than they are in the present case, I would in general respectfully concur with the views expressed by the Law Reform Committee that no division of the fund into fractions should be required, and that the only division should be into investments which require advice and those which do not. Nevertheless, although a division of the fund into fractions should not be essential, there may well be cases where such a division may be of assistance in obtaining the approval of the court.

(iii)   The width of the powers in the present scheme seems to me to be at or near the extreme limit for charitable funds. Without the fractional division of the fund and the assurance of effective control and advice I very much doubt whether such a scheme could have been approved. What the court has to judge is the combined effect of width, division, advice and control, which all interact, together with the standing of the trustees.

(iv)   The size of the fund may be very material. A fund that is very large may well justify a latitude of investment that would be denied to a more modest fund, for the spread of investments possible for a larger fund may justify the greater risks that wider powers will permit to be taken.

(v)   The object of the trust may be very material. In the present case, the desirability of having an increase of capital value which will make possible the purchase of desirable acquisitions for the museum despite soaring prices does something to justify the greater risks whereby capital appreciation may be obtained.

Note
This decision was based on the changes of investment pattern, including the movement from fixed interest investments to investments in equities and property, that had occurred between 1961 and 1983, and presumably it follows that further changes in patterns of investment could also affect the attitude of the courts.

At the time of this case investing in equities was relatively risk-free, and there had been a more or less continuous bull market for some eight years. The rationale for the restrictions in the 1961 Act was to limit the powers of trustees to make risky investments, and not to act without proper professional advice, unless wider powers had been expressly given by the trust instrument. There have of course been further changes in investment pattern since 1983, and in particular following on from the stock market crash in late-1987, and one wonders whether the outcome would have been the same had the *British Museum* case been decided today.

C: Persons on Whose Behalf the Court May Give its Approval

The 1958 Act allows the court to give consent on behalf of non *sui iuris* beneficiaries, but the principles underlying the rule in *Saunders* v *Vautier* were preserved by the Act, in as much as the court will not provide a consent which ought properly to be sought from an ascertainable adult, *sui iuris* beneficiary. Hence the limits placed on para. (b), above.

The categories of person on whose behalf consent may be given are set out in s. 1. They include infants and other people who are not capable by reason of capacity of assenting (e.g. those who used to be called lunatics), and unborn persons, so long as the proposed arrangement would be for their benefit. Beneficiaries under protective discretionary trusts are also included: in the last case the statute does not expressly require that a benefit be shown.

The difficulty with para. (b) arises with interests which are very remote, such as interests in default of appointment, or in the event of a failure of the trust. It is the words after 'so however' which cause the problem, since those persons have to consent on their own behalf: the court cannot consent for them. There is no problem over, for example, potential future spouses, since they clearly have a mere expectation of succeeding. They clearly come within the first part of para. (b), and the court can consent on their behalf. But if somebody is named in the instrument as having a contingent interest, however unlikely that contingency is to arise, the court cannot consent on their behalf. They must consent themselves to any variation.

This can seriously limit the scope of the 1958 Act, as can be seen from the following case.

Knocker v Youle
[1986] 1 WLR 934, [1986] 2 All ER 914
Chancery Division

Decision: The court could not consent on behalf of persons who would benefit only in the event of failure or determination of the trust.

WARNER J: What is said by counsel on behalf of the plaintiffs, and is supported by counsel for Mrs Youle's children, is that I have power under s. 1(1)(b) of the Variation of Trusts Act 1958 to approve the arrangement on behalf of the cousins.

[Warner J set out the relevant part of s. 1(1) and continued: . . .]

There are two difficulties. First, it is not strictly accurate to describe the cousins as persons 'who may become entitled . . . to an interest under the trusts'. There is no doubt of course that they are members of a 'specified class'. Each of them is, however, entitled now to an interest under the trusts, albeit a contigent one (in the case of those who are under 21, a doubly contigent one) and albeit also that it is an interest that is defeasible on the exercise of the general testamentary powers of appointment vested in Mrs Youle and Mr Knocker. None the less, it is properly described in legal language as an interest, and it seems to me plain that in this Act the word 'interest' is used in its technical, legal sense. Otherwise, the words 'whether vested or contingent' in para. (a) of s. 1(1) would be out of place.

What counsel invited me to do was in effect to interpret the word 'interest' in s. 1(1) loosely, as a layman might, so as not to include an interest that was remote. I was referred to two authorities: *Re Moncrieff's Settlement Trusts* [1962] 3 All ER 838, [1962] 1 WLR 1344 and the earlier case of *Re Suffert's Settlement, Suffert* v *Martyn-Linnington* [1960] 3 All ER 561, [1961] Ch 1. In both those cases, however, the class in question was a class of prospective next of kin, and, of course it is trite law that the prospective or presumptive next of kin of a living person do not have an interest. They have only a spes successionis, a hope of succeeding, and quite certainly they are the typical category of persons who fall within s. 1(1)(b). Another familiar example of a person falling within that provision is a potential future spouse. It seems to me, however, that a person who has an actual interest directly conferred on him or her by a settlement, albeit a remote interest, cannot properly be described as one who 'may become' entitled to an interest.

The second difficulty (if one could think of a way of overcoming the first) is that there are, as I indicated earlier, 17 cousins who, if the failure or determination of the earlier trusts declared by the settlement had occurred at the date of the application to the court, would have been members of the specified class, in that they were then living and over 21. Therefore, they are prima facie excluded from s. 1(1)(*b*) by what has been conveniently called the proviso to it, that is to say the part beginning 'so however that this paragraph shall not include . . . ' They are in the same boat, if I may express it in that way, as the first cousins in *Re Suffert's Settlement* and the adopted son in *Re Moncrieff's Settlement Trusts*. The court cannot approve the arrangement on their behalf; only they themselves can do so.

Counsel for the plaintiffs suggested that I could distinguish *Re Suffert's Settlement* and *Re Moncreieff's Settlement Trusts* in that respect for two reasons.

First, he suggested that the proviso applied only if there was a single event on the happening of which one could ascertain the class. Here, he said, both Mr Knocker and Mrs Youle must die without exercising their general testamentary powers of appointment to the full before any of the cousins could take anything. But it seems to me that what the proviso is referring to is the event on which the class becomes ascertainable, and that that is a single event. It is, in this case, the death of the survivor of Mrs Youle and Mr Knocker, neither of them having exercised the power to the full; in the words of cl 7 of the settlement, it is 'the failure or determination of the trusts hereinbefore declared concerning the trust fund.'

The second reason suggested by counsel for the plaintiffs why I should distinguish the earlier authorities was that the event hypothesised in the proviso was the death of the survivor of Mr Knocker and Mrs Youle on the date when the originating summonses were issued, that is to say on 6 January 1984. There is evidence that on that day there were in existence wills of both of them exercising their testamentary powers to the full. The difficulty about that is that the proviso does not say ' . . . so however that this paragraph shall not include any person who would have become entitled if the said event had happened at the date of the application to the court'. It says:

. . . so however that this paragraph shall not include any person who would be of that description, or a member of that class, as the case may be, if the said date had fallen or the said event had happened at the date of the application to the court.

So the proviso is designed to identify the presumptive members of the class at the date of the application to the court and does not advert to the question whether at that date they would or would not have become entitled.

I was reminded by counsel of the principle that one must construe Acts of Parliament having regard to their purpose, and it was suggested that the purpose here was to exclude the need to join as parties to applications under the Variation of Trusts Act 1958 people whose interests were remote. In my view, however, that principle does not enable me to take the sort of liberty with the language of this statute that I was invited to take. It is noteworthy that remoteness does not seem to be the test if one thinks in terms of presumptive statutory next of kin. The healthy issue of an elderly widow who is on her deathbed, and who has not made a will, have an expectation of succeeding to her estate; that could hardly be described as remote. Yet they are a category of persons on whose behalf the court could, subject of course to the proviso, approve an arrangement under this Act. On the other hand, people in the position of the cousins in this case have an interest that is extremely remote. None the less, it is an interest, and the distinction between an expectation and an interest is one which I do not think that I am entitled to blur. So, with regret, having regard to the particular circumstances of this case, I have to say that I do not think that I have jurisdiction to approve these arrangements on behalf of the cousins.

D: What is Benefit?

Benefit will usually be synonymous with financial advantage but need not be. In *Re Towler's ST* [1964] Ch 158, Wilberforce J was prepared to postpone the vesting of capital to which a beneficiary was soon to become entitled, upon evidence that she was likely to deal with it imprudently. In *Re Steed's WT* [1960] Ch 407, the proposed scheme was for the elimination of the protective element in a trust relating to land. The principal beneficiary, who was a life tenant (but not *sui iuris* because of the protective element), wanted a variation such that the trustees held the property on trust for herself absolutely. Clearly this was in theory to her financial advantage, but evidence suggested that advantage would in fact be taken of the life tenant's good nature by the very persons against whose importuning the settlor had meant to protect her, and the Court of Appeal refused its consent. In *Re Weston's Settlements* [1969] 1 Ch 223, the Court of Appeal refused to approve a scheme which would have removed the trusts to a tax haven (Jersey), where the family had moved three months previously, on the ground that the moral and social benefits of an English upbringing were not outweighed by the tax savings to be enjoyed by the infant beneficiaries. Harman LJ said that 'this is an essay in tax avoidance naked and unashamed', and Lord Denning MR noted (at p. 223) that:

> There are many things in life more worthwhile than money. One of these things is to be brought up in this our England, which is still 'the envy of less happier lands'. I do not believe it is for the benefit of children to be uprooted from England and transported to another country simply to avoid tax . . . Many a child has been ruined by being given too much. The avoidance of tax may be lawful, but it is not yet a virtue.

Finally, In *Re CL* [1969] 1 Ch 587, the Court of Protection held that there was a benefit to an elderly mental patient in giving up, in return for no consideration, her life interests for the benefit of adopted daughters. This was, in effect, giving approval to a straightforward gift by the beneficiary, from which in strictly material terms she could not possibly benefit. The lady's needs were otherwise amply provided for, however, and the court, in approving the arrangement, took the view that it was acting as she herself would have done, had she been able to appreciate her family responsibilities.

E: Risks

More interesting issues arise where the proposed arrangement involves some element of risk to the beneficiary for whom the court is asked to consent. An element of risk will not prevent the court from approving the arrangement, if the risk is one which an adult beneficiary would be prepared to take. Such a test was applied by Danckwerts J in *Re Cohen's WT* [1959] 1 WLR 865.

Re Robinson's ST
[1976] 1 WLR 806, [1976] 3 All ER 61
Chancery Division

Facts: The fund was held on trust for the plaintiff for her life, with remainders over to her children, one of whom was an infant. The plaintiff was 55 and expected to live for many years. The variation proposed was to divide up the fund, giving the plaintiff an immediate capital share of 52 per cent (the actuarial capitalised value of her share), the children dividing the balance in equal shares. The children who got their share immediately, and those who were over 18 consented to the variation. The court was asked to approve variation on behalf of Nicola (who was 17).

Before the introduction of Capital Transfer Tax in 1975, division of the fund in this way, by giving the children their interests immediately rather than on the death of the life tenant, was almost certain to reduce liability to estate duty, because at that time there was no liability to estate duty on any advance made more than seven years before the death of the life tenant. The same is true today under inheritance tax. However, for a short period following the Finance Act 1975, which introduced Capital Transfer Tax, all *inter vivos* gifts were also taxable, albeit that liability was lower so long as the transfer was made more than three years before the death of the life tenant.

At the time of *Re Robinson's ST*, therefore, the division would not necessarily have favoured Nicola. The transfer would have been taxed immediately, so that the value of the fund would be reduced. On the other hand, Nicola would get her share immediately, and not have to wait for the death of her mother. Whether this would be to her benefit or not would depend entirely on how long her mother was likely to live. If she died immediately, Nicola's share would be less than she would have received under the unvaried trust, since tax would have been paid on it. It was calculated, however, that, given the mother's life expectancy, the deficiency would be made up in income on her share between the date of the variation and her mother's death.

Held: The variation would be approved, subject to a policy of insurance to protect the infant's interests.

TEMPLEMAN J: This is an application under the Variation of Trusts Act 1958 which involves the division of a trust fund between life tenant and remaindermen. One of the remaindermen is an infant of about 17.

Under what might be termed the old-fashioned calculations for estate duty, such a division was comparatively simple. The rates of estate duty were such that the amount which a remainderman stood to inherit if nothing was done was usually very small. In most schemes it was possible to make a division whereby the remainderman took more in any event than he would otherwise take on the death of the life tenant.

Into that simple form of division complications were introduced by the abolition of estate duty and its replacement by capital transfer tax. Evidence in these proceedings demonstrates that the old calculations simply do not fit the new tax. For example, whereas in the old days a tax was payable on death and so all one had to do was to find out what would be left on death after deduction of estate duty, now capital transfer tax is payable on the coming into operation of the division effected by the arrangement.

For that and for other reasons it is very difficult to provide for every possible contingency. The impact of the tax has also this quirk, that the actuarial value of the interest of the life tenant is much reduced. In the present instance figures have been produced which show, for example, that if nothing is done and capital transfer tax is paid on the death of the life tenant, the share of the infant will be somewhere between £58,000 and £60,000 if no alterations in the law are made in the meantime. Under the proposed arrangement, produced as a result of the independent advice of actuaries, the share which the remaindermen get is of a gross value of £58,000, and if capital transfer tax is payable – as to which there is a doubt in the present instance – the tax will reduce the share by something like £11,000 or £14,000. This entails a serious possibility of a loss accruing to the remaindermen. I was much pressed by all counsel, including counsel for the third defendant, with the observations of Stamp J in *Re Cohen's Settlement Trusts* [1965] 3 All ER 139 at 144, [1965] 1 WLR 1229 at 1236 and of Danckwerts J in *Re Cohen's Will Trusts* [1959] 3 All ER 523, [1959] 1 WLR 865 to the effect that a reasonable view of a bargain must be taken. It is not necessary to insist that in all possible circumstances the infant is bound to benefit. It is said that capital transfer tax may not be payable and, if it is, then even taking into account the possible shortfall of £14,000, there will be acceleration of the income of the share which the infant is to take, and her mother, the life tenant, is only about 55 years old, and so, in the normal course of events, acceleration will catch up with the shortfall.

Acceleration of income, at present rates of taxation on income, will take a good deal of catching up to compensate for a shortfall of £14,000. I cannot assume that the life tenant will live long enough to procure that the arrangement viewed as a whole will benefit the infant. I must be satisfied that the arrangement is beneficial.

I expressed doubts and sent the parties away to consider insurance. In the old days of estate duty insurance could be effected by the life tenant to make good any shortfall so far as the reversion was concerned. Capital transfer tax introduces a new complication in that an insurance policy effected and kept up by the life tenant may itself be liable to capital transfer tax with disastrous consequences.

Therefore, although it is slightly anomalous, if the infant is to be protected against the possibility of shortfall, that protection can only be, to some extent, at the expense of the infant in that a policy must be kept up out of income.

I am quite satisfied that it would not be sensible to leave matters entirely as they are. There are other people interested besides the infant, and to preserve the present trusts with present, and future, rates of income and capital taxation does not seem sensible. I am satisfied that the life tenant will only receive under the arrangement a reasonable and fair proportion having regard to the value of her life interest in her present situation.

In these circumstances I think I can accept the arrangement, provided that the infant''s income is to a certain extent made available for insurance in order to protect the infant's own share against loss caused by the premature death of the life tenant. A quotation has been obtained, and it would appear that to insure a shortfall of £14,000 would cost about £800 a year. Having regard to the amount of the income that seems to me to be weighing too much on the future and not enough on the present. A policy for £8,000, which with profits will yield something over £11,000 in ten years and more thereafter, will only cost about £400 a year. That will still leave a substantial income for the infant to receive straight away.

It seems to me if insurance of £8,000 with profits is effected, I can, relying on the observations of Stamp [1965] 3 All ER 139 at 144, [1965] 1 WLR 1229 at 1236 and Danckwerts JJ [1959] 3 All ER 523, [1959] 1 WLR 865, approve this arrangement, although I still think it is a borderline case. Great powers of advocacy were used to persuade me that capital transfer tax has made such a change that the possible result of a death must be disregarded, the actuarial division accepted and a risk taken. I do not take that view. I start with the principle that all these schemes should, if possible, prove that an infant is not going to be materially worse off. There are difficulties with capital transfer tax, and borderline cases, and one may then have to take a broad view, but not a galloping, gambling view.

In my judgment, taking a reasonably prudent view, insurance of £8,000 in the present instance will be sufficient, and I am prepared to sanction the arrangement thus amended.

Note

Templeman J took the view that the court should require evidence that the infant would at least not be materially worse off as a result of the variation. He adopted as the test whether an adult beneficiary would have been prepared to take the risk: a 'broad' view might be taken, but not a 'galloping, gambling view'.

Re Cohen's ST, Eliot-Cohen v Cohen
[1965] 1 WLR 1229, [1965] 3 All ER 139
Chancery Division

Facts: A settlement made in 1909 provided that until the death of the settlor's last surviving son, the *income* would be divided equally between his five sons. On the death of each of the first four sons to die, his share of the *income* went to his issue through all degrees. When the last surviving son died, the *capital* was to be held for the grandchildren of the settlor then living, and the issue of any grandchild then dead, but so that the issue of any dead grandchild would take between them only the share that the grandchild himself would have taken had he or she still been living.

Up until the death of the last surviving son, therefore, the beneficiaries were entitled only to a share of the income. After that the same people who had been entitled to income up to the death of the last surviving son became entitled to a share of the capital (otherwise there would have been perpetuity problems). Only those living at the death of the last surviving son would become entitled at all (again, for perpetuity reasons).

The plaintiff was the last surviving son. The income of the other four sons, who were dead, was being enjoyed by their issue. Clearly on the plaintiff's death estate duty would become payable on the capital corresponding to his share of the income, and there was no attempt to avoid that. The worry was, however, that estate duty would become payable on the entire fund at the death of the plaintiff, since the grandchildren (or issue) who would until then be entitled only to income would become entitled to a share of the capital in the fund. The court was therefore asked to approve a scheme under s. 1 of the Variation of Trusts Act 1958, substituting for the plaintiff's death a fixed date on which interests in the capital would vest. 30 June 1973 was proposed, a date beyond which it was unlikely that the plaintiff would live.

Note that those who would become entitled to a share under the proposed variation, being those grandchildren (or issue) living on 30 June 1973, could be different people from those entitled under the unvaried scheme, being those grandchildren (or issue) living on the plaintiff's death.

Held: The court would approve the variation on behalf of the infants, since the scheme was for their benefit, but it was possible to envisage unborn persons who could get no benefit from the scheme, and could only suffer substantial disadvantage. The court had to be satisfied that every individual for whom it was asked to consent would benefit from the scheme, not merely that the class as a whole would benefit. It could not therefore consent for those unborn persons who could clearly not benefit, so approval for the scheme would be refused.

STAMP J: What is proposed is to substitute a fixed date in place of the death of the plaintiff as the date when the persons to take capital are to be ascertained. The fixed date is to be 30 June 1973, and this is a date which the plaintiff is most unlikely to survive. Subject to a qualification which I need not mention, the persons who will take the capital will be the grandchildren of the settlor living on the fixed date and the issue then living of the deceased grandchild, issue taking in the same way as under the settlement. Since the fixed date is likely to be a later date than the actual date of the death of the plaintiff, any infant issue of a grandchild will have a better chance of taking a share of the capital than he has today because his parent is more likely to have died: and when there is the added chance of avoiding a possible and heavy claim for duty, there is no doubt that the proposed variation is for the benefit of each of the infants.

If in fact the plaintiff survives 30 June 1973, some infant may in the event be worse off than he would have been under the settlement as it stands; for an infant child of a grandchild of the settlor who dies on 1 July 1973 would, as matters now stand, take a share in that event, whereas under the variation he would take nothing. Nevertheless, on balance the proposal is largely for his benefit and a good bargain and his chance of taking free from a heavy claim for duty is improved.

I am invited to say that the proposed variation has similar advantages to any person unborn. I do not think that this is so. If I have to consider whether the variation is for the benefit of a person now unborn who comes into existence after 30 June 1973, then I can only answer that question in the negative. The plaintiff may outlive that date and if he does, a person born on or after 1 July 1973, while the plaintiff was still living, would, as the settlement now stands, thereupon become beneficially interested under the trusts of the settlement; but by the effect of the proposed variation such a person would take nothing. Clearly, there may be a person now unborn who will come into existence after 30 June 1973, and if I must consider the variation from the point of view of such a person, I cannot approve it on his behalf for the variation deprives him of any chance of taking and in this respect the position is different from that of one on the infants.

Nevertheless what is said is that I do not have to consider the matter from the point of view of an unborn person having the characteristic that he will be born after 30 June 1973, but must regard the unborn persons on whose behalf I am asked to sanction the variation as having no characteristics at all. All unborn persons it is urged would have a greater chance of taking under the varied settlement than under the original settlement because the period during which they must come into existence in order to become potential beneficiaries is under the variation likely to be a longer period. Moreover each unborn person, so the argument runs, would by the effect of the variation obtain a better chance of being born and so taking an interest than he has at present, and this outweighs the disadvantage that he would suffer by the effect of the variation if he came into existence after 30 June 1973, while the plaintiff was still living. It was put by counsel for the trustees that one of the conditions or contingencies which each person unborn must at present satisfy in order to take is that he should be born during the life of the plaintiff and that for this condition or contingency there is to be substituted a condition or contingency likely to be more easy to satisfy, namely, that of being born during a period which is likely to be a longer period.

Now it is of course perfectly true that as a result of this variation there would be a greater chance of there being some person or persons now unborn becoming beneficially interested in the trust fund, but to say that some particular unborn person will, immediately on the variation taking effect, have a better chance of being born within the qualifying period or a better chance of satisfying the necessary conditions seems to me to involve an excursion into metaphysics, on which I am unwilling to embark. Such a proposition seems to me to involve the logical conclusion that the court must regard one whose body may come into the existence in the future as having nevertheless such a present imaginary existence as to enable the court to ascribe to him a present chance of coming into existence at some specific time or during some specified period. My mind recoils at the idea of the unborn having prior to his birth such an identity as to enable the court to ascribe to him any such chance, or to enable one to say that he can more or less easily satisfy a condition of coming into existence during some particular period.

No doubt the very expression 'unborn persons' which appears in the [Variation of Trusts] Act of 1958 itself gives colour to the arguments which have been put; but no authority has been cited to show that a still unembodied spirit can be regarded as a person under our law; and I cannot think that the legislature used that expression otherwise than in the sense of future persons and to connote those future persons who will, if there is no variation, become interested under the trusts of the instrument which it is sought to vary, and without whose consent the proposed variation may not in some event be binding on him. It cannot be that the court is to approve on behalf of all persons who will come into this world but, in my judgment, only those who do in the event by reason of their birth to such and such a person on such and such a day acquire that legal identity which qualifies them as beneficiaries and the approval which is to be given is in my judgment so to speak an approval *nunc pro tunc*.

[He went on to say that in his view a person born at a different date would be a different person with a different identity.]

Notes

1. Perhaps the most important aspect of this case is that benefit must be shown on the part of *every single individual* for whom approval is sought. It is not sufficient to show merely that the class as a whole can be benefited. It follows that if one infant or unborn person can be found who will clearly not benefit, approval for the variation cannot be given. It was possible to envisage unborn persons who could not possibly benefit, and the fact that unborn persons as a class might benefit was irrelevant.

2.   No problem arose for approval for the existing infants, although any who died between the death of the plaintiff and 30 June 1973 (assuming that the plaintiff did indeed die before that date) would lose out. On balance, however, the risk was worth taking given the likely saving in estate duty, and the increased chance that his parent would have died by 30 June 1973.

3.   The argument was put that any individual unborn spirit would be more likely to benefit under the varied scheme, since he or she would have a greater chance of being born before 30 June 1973: since the life tenant was unlikely to live that long, it was likely that more time would probably be available in which to be born. This argument was rejected on the ground that the court would not ascribe chances to a mere unembodied spirit. Only once birth (albeit in the future) had occurred could chances of benefit be ascribed.

Re Holt's ST
[1969] 1 Ch 100
Chancery Division

Facts: The trust provided for a life interest of personal property for Mrs Wilson, and then to her children at 21 in equal shares. The variation proposed was that Mrs Wilson should surrender the income of one-half of her life interest to the fund, but another effect of the proposed variation was to postpone the vesting of the children's interests until 30. The court was asked to approve the variation on behalf of Mrs Wilson's three children who were 10, 7 and 6.

The surrender of the income (the real purpose of which was to reduce Mrs Wilson's liability to surtax) was also clearly to the advantage of the children, since the value of the trust property would be increased. However, the postponement to 30 (on the grounds that it would be undesirable for Mrs Wilson's children to receive a large income from 21) was clearly to their disadvantage.

Held: The variation would be approved.

MEGARRY J: I can deal with the merits of this application quite shortly. It seems to me that, subject to one reservation the arrangement proposed is for the benefit of each of the beneficiaries contemplated by the Variation of Trusts Act 1958, s. 1(1). The financial detriment to the children is that the absolute vesting of their interests will be postponed from age twenty-one to age thirty. As against that, they will obtain very substantial financial benefits, both in the acceleration of their interests in a moiety of the trust fund and in the savings of estate duty to be expected in a case such as this. Where the advantages of the scheme are overwhelming, any detailed evaluation, or 'balance sheet' of advantages and disadvantages, seems to me to be unnecessary; but I can imagine cases under the Act where it may be important that an attempt should be made to put in evidence a detailed evaluation of the financial and other consequences of the changes proposed to be made, so that it may be seen whether on balance there is a sufficient advantage to satisfy the proviso to s. 1(1) of the Act of 1958. But this is not such a case, and I say no more about it. I should, however, state that I fully concur in the view taken by Mrs Wilson that, speaking in general terms, it is most important that young children 'should be reasonably advanced in a career and settled in life before they are in receipt of an income sufficient to make them independent of the need to work'. The word 'benefit' in the proviso to s. 1(1) of the Act of 1958 is, I think, plainly not confined to financial benefit, but may extend to moral or social benefit, as is shown by *Re Towler's Settlement Trusts* [1964] Ch 158.

The point that at one stage troubled me concerns the unborn issue. Counsel for the trustees, as in duty bound, put before me a contention that it was possible to conceive of an unborn infant who would be so circumstanced that the proposed rearrangement would be entirely to his disadvantage. He postulated the case of a child born to Mrs Wilson next year, and of Mrs Wilson dying in childbirth, or shortly after the child's birth. In such a case, he said the benefit of the acceleration of interest resulting from Mrs Wilson surrendering the moiety of her life interest would be minimal, and there would be no saving of estate duty. All that would happen in regard to such an infant would be that the vesting of his interest would be postponed from age twenty-one to age thirty, and the only possible advantage in that would be the non-financial moral or social advantage to which I have just referred. In support of this contention he referred me to the decision of Stamp J in *Re Cohen's Settlement Trusts*. There, the scheme originally proposed was not approved by the court because there was a possibility of there being a beneficiary who would get no advantage whatsoever from the proposed arrangement; it would merely be to his detriment.

Counsel for the plaintiff, however, points out that there is an essential distinction between that case and this; for there, whatever the surrounding circumstances, the unborn person contemplated could not benefit from the arrangement. In the present case, he says, all that counsel for the trustees has done is to put forward the case of an infant who might be born next year; and it would be a result of the surrounding circumstances, and not of the time of birth or the characteristics of the infant, that that infant might derive no benefit from the arrangement proposed. Counsel for the plaintiff referred me to *Re Cohen's Will Trusts* [1959] 3 All ER 523, where Danckwerts J held that in exercising the jurisdiction under the Act of 1958 the court must, on behalf of those persons for whom it was approving the arrangement, take the sort of risk which an adult would be prepared to take. Accordingly, says counsel for the plaintiff, counsel for the trustee's special infant to be born next year was in the position that although there was the chance that its mother would die immediately afterwards, there was also the alternative chance that its mother would survive his birth for a substantial period of time. In the latter event, which was the more probable, the advantages of the arrangement would accrue to the infant. In short, he distinguished the decision of Stamp J in *Re Cohen's Settlement Trusts* on the footing that that was the case of an unborn person whose prospects were hopeless, whatever the events, whereas in the present case the hypothetical unborn person has the normal prospects of events occurring which will either improve or not improve his position. Such an unborn person falls, he says, into the category of unborn persons on whose behalf the court should be prepared to take a risk if the arrangement appears on the whole to be for their benefit.

It seems to me that this is a proper distinction to make, and I accept it. Accordingly, I hold that the arrangement is for the benefit of the classes of persons specified in s. 1(1) of the Act of 1958, and I approve it.

Notes
1.   If a child was born the year after the variation, and his mother died very soon afterwards, that child could not possibly benefit. The benefit from Mrs Wilson surrendering part of her income under the trust would be minimal if Mrs Wilson died soon after the birth, whereas the postponement would operate entirely to the child's disadvantage.
2.   Megarry J approved the variation on the same test adopted in *Re Robinson*. *Cohen* was distinguished because here two chances had to occur: that of the unborn person being born next year, and secondly, that child having been born (and thus become a legal entity), his or her mother dying shortly afterwards. The first chance could be disregarded on *Cohen* principles, but not the second. Both were independently unlikely possibilities, so approval for the scheme was given. Even once the theoretical unborn child had been born, he or she would still have been well advised to agree to the variation, and accept the slight risk of his or her mother dying shortly afterwards.
3.   It follows that the reasoning in *Cohen* applies only when the date of *vesting in interest* (or in other words the date on closing the class) is altered, and does not apply merely to alterations in *vesting in possession*.
4.   The main part of the case concerned the question whether writing was required for a variation under s. 53(1)(c) of the Law of Property Act 1925. Megarry J, aware that possibly thousands of variations had been acted upon without writing conforming with s. 53(1)(c), accepted, though without enthusiasm, two grounds put forward by counsel in favour of the view that no writing was necessary. First, it might be said that in conferring express power upon the court to make an order, Parliament had impliedly created an exception to s. 53. Secondly and alternatively, the arrangement might be regarded as one in which the beneficial interests passed to their respective purchasers upon the making of the agreement, that agreement itself being specifically enforceable. The original interests under the (unvaried) trusts would thus be held, from the moment of the agreement, upon constructive trusts identical to the new (varied) trusts, and as constructive trusts would be exempt from writing under s. 53(2).
5.   There was also a perpetuities point, turning on whether the 1964 Act applied to the variation, which has no present-day relevance.

F: Variation not Resettlement

Re Ball's ST
[1968] 1 WLR 899
Chancery Division

Decision: Following *Re Towler's ST* [1964] Ch 158, the courts will not approve a proposal for a total resettlement. This is however a question of substance not form. Merely because an arrangement can correctly be described as effecting a revocation and resettlement, it does not follow that it cannot also be correctly described as effecting a variation of the trusts. The test is whether the arrangement alters completely the substratum of the trust. If so, the court cannot approve it.

MEGARRY J: The second point in this case concerns the jurisdiction of the court. The originating summons asks for the approval of the court of an arrangement 'revoking the trusts of the above-mentioned settlement and resettling the subject matter of the above-mentioned settlement'. What s. 1(1) of the Act of 1958 authorises the court to approve is

> any arrangement . . . varying or revoking all or any of the trusts, or enlarging the powers of the trustees of managing or administering any of the property subject to the trusts.

The word 'resettling' or its equivalent nowhere appears. Accordingly, while there is plainly jurisdiction to approve the arrangement insofar as it revokes the trusts, in my view there is equally plainly no jurisdiction to approve the arrangement as regards 'resettling' the property, at any rate *eo nomine*. In this connexion, I bear in mind the words of Wilberforce J in *Re Towler's Settlement Trusts*. He there said [[1964] Ch 158 at p. 162]:

> . . . I have no desire to cut down the very useful jurisdiction which this Act has conferred on the court, but I am satisfied that the proposal as originally made to me falls outside it. Though presented as 'a variation' it is in truth a complete new re-settlement. The former trust funds were to be got in from the former trustee and held on totally new trusts such as might be made by an absolute owner of the funds. I do not think that the court can approve this.

It seems to me that the originating summons correctly describes what is sought to be done in this case, and as so described there is clearly no jurisdiction for the court to approve the arrangement. But it does not follow that merely because an arrangement can correctly be described as effecting a revocation and resettlement, it cannot also be correctly described as effecting a variation of the trusts. The question then is whether the arrangement in this case can be so described. In the course of argument I indicated that it seemed desirable for the summons to be amended by substituting the word 'varying' for the word 'revoking' and deleting the reference to 'resettling', and that I would give leave for this amendment to be made. On the summons as so amended the question is thus whether the arrangement can fairly be said to be covered by the word 'varying' so that the court has power to approve it.

There was some discussion of the ambit of this word in *Re Holt's Settlement* [1968] 1 All ER 470. It was there held that if in substance the new trusts were recognisable as the former trusts, though with variations, the change was comprehended within the word 'varying', even if it had been achieved by a process of revocation and new declaration. In that case, the new trusts were plainly recognisable as the old trusts with variations. In the present case, the new trusts are very different from the old. . . . All that remains of the old trusts are what I may call the general drift or purport, namely that a moiety of the trust fund is to be held on certain trusts for each son and certain of his issue. Is the word 'varying' wide enough to embrace so categorical a change?

. . . If an arrangement changes the whole substratum of the trust, then it may well be that it cannot be regarded merely as varying that trust. But if an arrangement, while leaving the substratum, effectuates the purpose of the original trust by other means, it may still be possible to regard that arrangement as merely varying the original trusts, even though the means employed are wholly different and even though the form is completely changed.

I am, of course, well aware that this view carries me a good deal farther than I went in *Re Holt*. I have felt some hesitation in the matter, but on the whole I consider that this is a proper step to take. The jurisdiction of the Act of 1958 is beneficial and, in my judgment, the court should construe it widely and not be astute to confine its beneficent operation. I must remember that in essence the court is merely contributing on behalf of infants and unborn and unascertained persons the binding assents to the arrangement which they, unlike an adult beneficiary, cannot give. So far as is proper, the power of the court to give that assent should be assimilated to the wide powers which the ascertained adults have.

In this case, it seems to me that the substratum of the original trusts remains. . . . In the events which are likely to occur, the differences between the old provisions and the new may, I think, fairly be said to lie in detail rather than in substance. Accordingly, in my judgment, the arrangement here proposed, with the various revisions to it made in the course of argument, can properly be described as varying the trusts of the settlement. Subject to the summons being duly amended, I therefore approve the revised arrangement. I may add that since the hearing of this case I have considered the speeches of their lordships in *Re Holmden's Settlement Trusts, IRC v Holmden* [1968] 1 All ER 148, but although these suggest certain questions of interest and difficulty, I find in them nothing to make me resile from the views that I have expressed.

8 AUTOMATIC RESULTING TRUSTS AND WINDING UP OF UNINCORPORATED ASSOCIATIONS

Chapters 3 to 6 concerned express trusts, deliberately created by the settlor, or where the settlor has attempted but failed to create a trust. Chapters 8 to 11 concern trusts which may be categorised as resulting or constructive trusts. I have not attempted rigidly to separate the chapters into resulting and constructive heads, partly because in some cases (in particular in chapter 9) there would be little agreement as to which was the appropriate category, and partly because the categorisation usually makes no practical difference. This chapter concerns one of the two categories of resulting trust, however, the other (presumed resulting trusts) being one of the concepts applicable to chapter 9.

Winding up of unincorporated associations is also included in this chapter, because a resulting trust analysis has frequently been applied to them. The analysis is not without problems, however, and you may conclude that a contractual analysis, outside the law of trusts, will usually be more appropriate.

SECTION 1: AUTOMATIC RESULTING TRUSTS

A: Failure to Dispose of Equitable Interest

In *Re Vandervell's Trusts (No. 2)* [1974] Ch 269, Megarry J distinguished between presumed and automatic resulting trusts, as follows:

(a)   The first class of case is where the transfer to B is not made on any trust . . . there is a rebuttable presumption that B holds on resulting trust for A. The question is not one of the automatic consequences of a dispositive failure by A, but one of presumption: the property has been carried to B, and from the absence of consideration and any presumption of advancement B is presumed not only to hold the entire interest on trust, but also to hold the beneficial interest for A absolutely. The presumption thus establishes both that B is to take on trust and also what that trust is. Such resulting trusts may be called 'presumed resulting trusts'.

(b)   The second class of case is where the transfer to B is made on trusts which leave some or all of the beneficial interest undisposed of. Here B automatically holds on resulting trust for A to the extent that the beneficial interest has not been carried to him or others. The resulting trust here does not depend on any intentions or presumptions, but is the automatic consequence of A's failure to dispose of what is vested in him. Since *ex hypothesi* the transfer is on trust, the resulting trust does not establish the trust but merely carries back to A the beneficial interest that has not been disposed of. Such resulting trusts may be called 'automatic resulting trusts'.

An automatic resulting trust can arise for technical reasons, for example, where the necessary formalities for disposing of the equitable interest are not complied with, or where the trust is void for certainty or perpetuity. Alternatively, as with the shares in *Vandervell* v *IRC* [1967] 2 AC 291 (see chapter 6), the settlor may simply have failed to make any provision for the disposal of the equitable interest.

Another possibility is where it is no longer possible to carry out the trust: the surplus will go on resulting trust to the donors in proportion to their donations.

Re Abbott Fund Trusts, Smith v Abbott
[1900] 2 Ch 326
Chancery Division

Decision: A fund was collected for the relief of two deaf and dumb ladies (who had been defrauded out of their rights under an earlier settlement). No provision was made for disposal of the fund on the death of the survivor. A surplus of some £367 remained when they died, and Stirling J held that this should be held on resulting trust for the subscribers.

Note
The decision is partly a matter of interpreting the intention of the donors. In *Re Abbott*, Stirling J held that the ladies themselves never became absolute owners of the fund. Nor did the trustees once the purposes were accomplished. No resulting trust occurs if either beneficiary or trustee is intended to take absolutely, however.

The fund in *Abbott* was subscribed to by various friends of the Abbotts. On the other hand, where the whole of a specific fund is left by a single individual for the maintenance of given individuals, the courts are more likely to construe the transaction as an absolute gift to those individuals, even where the fund is expressed to be left for a particular purpose (although it depends, of course, on the intention of the donor, which is ultimately a question of fact). An example is the Court of Appeal decision in *Re Osoba* [1979] 1 WLR

247, where a testator left the whole of a fund on trust for the education of his daughter up to university level. On completion of the daughter's university education she was held entitled to the surplus beneficially, the educational purpose being regarded merely as a statement of the testator's motive – in other words, there was no resulting trust in favour of the testator's estate.

In *Cunnack* v *Edwards* [1896] 2 Ch 679, an association was established using members' contributions to provide annuities for the widows of deceased members. The Court of Appeal held that the members had disposed of their contributions out-and-out, subject only to contractual rights to obtain benefits for their widows. When the fund was wound up, the Court of Appeal held that its property should go to the Crown as *bona vacantia*. This case is considered in greater detail in the next section.

Anonymous donations, for example to disaster appeal funds, might also be thought to be out-and-out gifts, with the donor retaining no interest.

Re Welsh Hospital (Netley) Fund
[1921] 1 Ch 655
Chancery Division

Facts: A surplus of £9,000 remained after the winding up of a (charitable) hospital erected at Netley, and the question arose what to do with the surplus. Much of the money had been derived from anonymous sources.

Decision: The surplus was applicable cy près. The donors must be taken to have parted with their donations out-and-out to charity.

P. O. LAWRENCE J: In this case the question is whether the plaintiffs, who are the trustees of a fund raised during the war for the establishment and support of the Welsh Hospital at Netley, are at liberty to apply the surplus of such fund now in their hands for the purpose of founding scholarships in the University of Wales for the encouragement of the study of medicine and surgery by persons of Welsh nationality. In order to determine this question the Court must first of all ascertain whether the fund is devoted permanently to charity and can be applied under the doctrine of cy-près. This is turn depends upon what the Court ought in the circumstances to infer to have been the true intention of the subscribers to the fund when they made their contributions. The fund was started in September, 1914. On the first day of that month the Lord Mayor of Cardiff issued an appeal to the inhabitants of Wales for subscriptions towards a Welsh hospital for service with the Expeditionary Force. The appeal shows that the first idea was that the hospital should be one serving with the Expeditionary Force at the Front in France. It also shows that six months' service in France was estimated to cost 15,000l., and it continues: 'But the sum subscribed is not limited to this amount, as further subscriptions can be used for prolonging the service or increasing the accommodation of the hospital,' and it winds up with this expression: 'We believe that Wales will rise to the full height of its responsibilities in this great national crisis, and by subscribing the necessary sum within a few days prove that it is foremost in seeking to relieve and comfort by the hands of their own fellow countrymen our sick and wounded across the seas.'. . .

The first question to be determined is whether there is a resulting trust in favour of the subscribers to the fund. Mr Greene has argued on behalf of the subscribers that there is a resulting trust for them, and that the surplus ought to be paid back to the various subscribers. All the other parties to the summons have argued that in the circumstances it must be inferred that there was a general charitable intent and that the Court is at liberty to apply the surplus cy-près. In my judgment this latter contention is well founded. The fund was created by contributions from various sources and in varying amounts, partly by donations from private individuals of more or less substantial amounts, and partly by the proceeds resulting from concerts and other entertainments given and from collections in streets and at churches made in most of the towns and villages of Wales. So far as regards the contributors to entertainments, street collections, etc., I have no hesitation in holding that they must be taken to have parted with their money out and out. It is inconceivable that any person paying for a concert ticket or placing a coin in a collecting box presented to him in the street should have intended that any part of the money so contributed should be returned to him when the immediate object for which the concert was given or the collection made had come to an end. To draw such an inference would be absurd on the face of it. So far as regards individual subscribers of substantial amounts, the proper inference to be drawn is not quite so plain. In my opinion, however, these subscribers must be taken to have known that they were contributing to a general fund which was being raised in the manner I have described, and that their contributions would be aggregated with the proceeds of entertainments, street collections, etc., and would not in any way be ear-marked. They must, I think, also be taken to have known that the total funds collected from every source would be applied for the purpose of the charity without discriminating between the moneys derived from any particular source. In these circumstances I am of opinion that the true inference to be drawn is that these subscribers intended to part with their contributions out and out, and that they did not intend that the surplus, if any, of their contributions should be returned to them when the immediate object of the charity should have come to an end. In the result I hold that although all the contributions were in the first instance made for the particular purpose of building, equipping and maintaining the Welsh Hospital at Netley, the main underlying object of the contributors was to provide money for the comfort of sick and wounded Welshmen, and that all the subscribers intended to devote their contributions not only to the particular object, but generally to the benefit of their sick and wounded countrymen. That being so, the Court is, in my judgment, at liberty to apply the surplus of the fund cy-près. . . .

Re North Devon and West Somerset Relief Fund Trusts, Hylton v Wright
[1953] 1 WLR 1260, [1953] 2 All ER 1032
Chancery Division

Decision: An appeal fund set up after the Lynmouth flood disaster of 1952 was held charitable as being for the benefit of the community at large, and the surplus would therefore be applied cy près. The charitable aspect of the case is dealt with in chapter 12, but we are here concerned with why there was no resulting trust in favour of the contributors.

WYNN-PARRY J: I confess that I do not find this question altogether easy to answer. I take as the statement of the principles on which the court should proceed the opening passage from the judgment of Parker J, in *Re Wilson*, where he says ([1913] 1 Ch 320):

For the purposes of this case I think the authorities must be divided into two classes. First of all, we have a class of cases where, in form, the gift is given for a particular charitable purpose, but it is possible, taking the will as a whole, to say that, notwithstanding the form of the gift, the paramount intention, according to the true construction of the will, is to give the property in the first instance for a general charitable purpose rather than a particular charitable purpose, and to graft on to the general gift a direction as to the desires or intentions of the testator as to the manner in which the general gift is to be carried into effect. In that case, though it is impossible to carry out the precise directions, on ordinary principles the gift for the general charitable purpose will remain and be perfectly good, and the court, by virtue of its administrative jurisdiction, can direct a scheme as to how it is to be carried out. In fact the will will be read as though the particular direction had not been in the will at all, but there had been simply a general direction as to the application of the fund for the general charitable purpose in question. Then there is the second class of cases, where, on the true construction of the will, no such paramount general intention can be inferred, and where the gift, being in form a particular gift – a gift for a particular purpose – and it being impossible to carry out that particular purpose, the whole gift is held to fail. In my opinion, the question whether a particular case falls within one of those classes of cases or within the other is simply a question of the construction of a particular instrument.

It is to be observed that in that case the court had to construe a will, the instrument by which a single donor had made the disposition which gave rise to the question. A number of authorities were cited to me, and most of them, I think it is true to say, arose substantially in that way. I have to deal with a very different type of case, a case in which I have to discover the intention of many hundreds – it may be thousands – of donors, and the only document that I have to assist me is not a document brought into existence by any one of those donors, but by those who invited them to become donors.

The nearest case to be found in the reports to the present case is *Re Welsh Hospital (Netley) Fund* [1921] 1 Ch 655. That was a decision of P.O. Lawrence J. The facts were that on the outbreak of the war in 1914 a hospital was erected at Netley, and equipped and run during the war, for the benefit of sick and wounded Welsh soldiers by means of large voluntary subscriptions raised in Wales. In 1919 the hospital was closed, the staff disbanded, and the property sold to the War Office, and, after winding-up the affairs of the hospital, there was a surplus of some £9,000. It was held, on the evidence, that there was not a resulting trust of the surplus for the subscribers to the hospital, but a general charitable intention for sick and wounded Welshmen which enabled the court to apply the fund cy-près. In the judgment of P.O. Lawrence J, reference is made to the terms of the appeal by which the subscriptions were invited. He says [Wynn-Parry J set out parts of the judgment above and continued]:

. . . It appears to me, on careful consideration, that it is impossible to draw a distinction of any substance between the facts of that case and the facts of the present case. It appears to me not in the least decisive that there is a reference in the appeal to persons other than local residents who suffered distress by the disaster. The main underlying object of that appeal was to benefit the people of the district in question. The appeal proceeds in this case, as it did in the case of the Welsh hospital, by emphasising what in the Welsh case was called the immediate object, but which might quite easily in either case have been treated, on a strict construction of the appeal, as the only object. In *Re Welsh Hospital (Netley) Fund*, P.O. Lawrence J, found no difficulty in drawing the conclusion, for the reasons which he gives, that there was a more extended object than might be said at first sight to appear on the face of the appeal; and when I apply his reasoning to the appeal in question in this case, I feel driven to exactly the same conclusion, namely, that there was a general charitable intent. All the reasons which militated in the mind of P.O. Lawrence J, to the conclusion to which he came are present in this case, I, therefore, find it impossible to distinguish that case from this case. In those circumstances, it appears to me to be unnecessary to travel through the rest of the authorities. I need only say that I find nothing in the judgment of P.O. Lawrence J, which is in any way inconsistent with the passage from the judgment of Parker J, in *Re Wilson* which I have read. It is true that the latter case was not apparently cited to P.O. Lawrence J, but, no doubt, that learned judge was well aware of its existence. Indeed, the judgment of Parker J, in *Re Wilson* did not more than state the effect of the authorities as it then existed; nor do I find anything in the later cases which carries the matter further. So far as I am aware, no adverse comment has ever been passed on the decision or judgment of P.O. Lawrence J, in *Re Welsh Hospital (Netley) Fund*. I regard it as authority binding on me and as covering this case.

Notes
1.   This approach was also taken in the *West Sussex* case, below, but is inconsistent with the *Gillingham Bus Disaster Fund* case, considered next.
2.   In chapter 13 we will see that if donations are made to a charitable body which subsequently fails, a cy près scheme is the normal outcome (although in *Re Slevin* Kay LJ left open the possibility that a subsequent failure of the object of the charitable gift might occasion a resulting trust for the donor, presumably if the gift were intended from the outset to be conditional rather than out-and-out).

Question
Why is it necessary to go through the reasoning processes in the last two cases? Surely these are simply subsequent failure cases, on the basis of the authorities set out in chapter 13 (see in particular *Re Ulverston and District New Hospital Building Trusts*).

Re Gillingham Bus Disaster Fund
[1958] Ch 300
Chancery Division

Facts: The case concerned a fund collected to defray funeral and other expenses incurred as a result of a disaster involving the deaths of 24 Royal Marine cadets in Gillingham. The town clerk of Gillingham wrote a letter to the *Daily Telegraph* in the following terms:

> Cadets' memorial. To the editor of the '*Daily Telegraph*'. Sir, The mayors of Gillingham, Rochester, and Chatham have decided to promote a Royal Marine Cadet Corps Memorial Fund to be devoted, among other things, to defraying the funeral expenses, caring for the boys who may be disabled, and then to such worthy cause or causes in memory of the boys who lost their lives, as the mayors may determine.

Harman J held that this was not a charitable purpose (see further chapter 12), and that the last purpose, 'to such worthy cause or causes in memory of the boys who lost their lives, as the mayors may determine', was void for uncertainty. The purposes were therefore taken to be defraying the funeral expenses of the boys who lost their lives, and caring for the boys who were disabled.

Far more money (about £9,000) was collected than was necessary for these purposes, especially as there were common law actions available against the bus company. The question therefore was who owned the surplus: was it the donors, represented by the Official Solicitor, or the Crown (represented by the Treasury Solicitor), as *bona vacantia?*

Held: Harman J, following *Re Abbott*, held that the surplus should be held on resulting trust for the donors.

HARMAN J: In December, 1951, there occurred an accident with tragic consequences, in Dock Road, Gillingham, in the county of Kent, when a motor-vehicle ran into a column of cadets marching along the road, killing 24 of them and injuring a further number. There was, of course, widespread concern at so shocking an event, and the three plaintiffs, then mayors of the surrounding areas, namely, Gillingham, Rochester and Chatham, determined to open a memorial fund. According to the evidence of the town clerk of Gillingham before me at the hearing, this was done by making a statement to the press, and the press accounts of the statement were relied upon as constituting the foundations of the so-called charity. I questioned this at the time, and it now turns out that the town clerk of Gillingham wrote a letter to the editor of the 'Daily Telegraph,' and I dare say to some other papers as well. At any rate, this letter appeared in the columns of the 'Daily Telegraph' on December 13, 1951: 'Cadets' Memorial. To the Editor of the 'Daily Telegraph.' Sir, – The Mayors of Gillingham, Rochester and Chatham have decided to promote a Royal Marine Cadet Corps Memorial Fund to be devoted, among other things, to defraying the funeral expenses, caring for the boys who may be disabled, and then to such worthy cause or causes in memory of the boys who lost their lives, as the Mayors may determine.' There follows another observation by the town clerk, which is not relevant, and then are given the addresses of the mayors to which donations may be sent. It was signed 'Yours faithfully, Frank Hill, Town Clerk, Gillingham.' Mr Hill had entirely forgotten the terms of the letter as written, but there it is. This appeal evoked a generous response from the public, whose subscriptions amounted to nearly £9,000, contributed partly in substantial sums by known persons, but mainly anonymously as a result of street collections, and so forth.

The result has shown that emotion is a bad foundation for such an activity. Each of the dead or injured cadets had at common law legal rights against the bus company, which were in due course asserted, with the result that compensation has been paid in full in accordance with the law. The plaintiffs administering the fund for the benefit of the victims have spent £2,368 14s. 9d., and are at a loss what to do with the balance – hence this summons. There are three claimants: first, the donors, who are represented by the Official Solicitor; second, the Crown, represented by the Treasury Solicitor, claiming the unwanted surplus of the fund as bona vacantia; and, third, the Attorney-General, claiming it for charity. It was agreed at the hearing that I should try the issue as to charity first.

Taking the town clerk's letter as the instrument constituting the trusts applicable to this money, I am constrained to say at the outset that it is most unfortunately worded. It begins by saying that the fund is to be devoted, 'among other things,' to certain objects. On the face of it, this would enable the fund to be devoted to any object in the world. I think this cannot be the true meaning, and that the words must be read so as to confine the objects to such worthy causes as shall keep green the memory of the boy victims. The money is to be spent primarily in defraying the funeral expenses of the dead and caring for the disabled, and secondarily on such other worthy causes as the mayors may determine. It was admitted at the Bar that the primary objects, namely, the funeral expenses and care of the boys, were not themselves charitable objects, there being no element of poverty involved, nor any section of the public. Further 'worthy' objects, while no doubt it would include charitable purposes, must include many others. It is perhaps a wider word even than 'benevolent.' It follows that the trust must fail for uncertainty unless the Charitable Trusts (Validation) Act, 1954, can be invoked to support it.

[Harman J concluded that the Act did not apply – see further chapter 13 – and continued: . . .]

I have already decided that the surplus of this fund now in the hands of the plaintiffs as trustees ought not to be devoted to charitable purposes under a cy-près scheme. There arises now a further question, namely, whether, as the Treasury Solicitor claims, this surplus should be paid to the Crown as bona vacantia, or whether there is a resulting trust in favour of the subscribers, who are here represented by the Official Solicitor. The general principle must be that where money is held upon trust and the trusts declared do not exhaust the fund it will revert to the donor or settlor under what is called a resulting trust. The reasoning behind this is that the settlor or donor did not part with his money absolutely out and out but only sub modo to the intent that his wishes as declared by the declaration of trust should be carried into effect. When, therefore, this has been done any surplus still belongs to him. This doctrine does not, in my judgment, rest on any evidence of the state of mind of the settlor, for in the vast majority of cases no doubt he does not expect to see his money back: he has created a trust which so far as he can see will absorb the whole of it. The resulting trust arises where that expectation is for some unforeseen reason cheated of fruition, and is an inference of law based on after-knowledge of the event.

Counsel for the Crown admitted that it was for him to show that this principle did not apply to the present case. Counsel for the subscribers cited to me *In re Abbott* [1900] 2 Ch 326. In that case a fund had been subscribed for the relief of two distressed ladies who had been defrauded of their patrimony. There was no instrument of trust. When the survivor of them died the trustees had not expended the whole of the moneys subscribed and the summons asked whether this surplus resulted to the subscribers or whether it was payable to the personal representatives of the two ladies. Stirling J had no difficulty in coming to the conclusion that the ladies were not intended to become the absolute owners of the fund and therefore their personal representatives had no claim. It was never suggested in this case that any claim by the Crown to bona vacantia might arise. A similar result was reached in *In re Hobourn Aero Components Air Raid Distress Fund* [1946] Ch 86, where the judge found that the objects of the fund were charitable no general charitable intent was shown in the absence of any element of public benefit and decided that the money belonged to the subscribers upon a resulting trust. Here again no claim was made on behalf of the Crown that the surplus constituted bona vacantia.

I was referred to two cases where a claim was made to bona vacantia and succeeded. The first of these was *Cunnack* v *Edwards* [1896] 2 Ch 679. This was a case of a society formed to raise a fund by subscriptions and so forth from the members to provide for widows of deceased members. Upon the death of the last widow of a member it was found that there was a surplus. It was held by the Court of Appeal that no question of charity arose, that there was no resulting trust in favour of the subscribers, but that the surplus passed to the Crown as bona vacantia. A. L. Smith LJ said this [at p. 683]:

> But it was argued that the proper implication is that when the society itself came to an end, as it has done, there was then a resulting trust of what might happen to be in the coffers of the society in favour of all the personal representatives of those who had been members since the year 1810, and Chitty J has so held. Now it was never contemplated that the society would come to an end; but, on the contrary, provision was made for the introduction of new members for its perpetual existence; and the existing members had power to alter and revise the rules, so that, if it was found that the society was too affluent, provision might be made as to what was to be done with that money might not be wanted. As the member paid his money to the society, so he divested himself of all interest in this money for ever, with this one reservation, that if the member left a widow she was to be provided for during her widowhood. Except as to this he abandoned and gave up the money for ever. . . .
> In my opinion there was no resulting trust in favour of all those members who had ever subscribed to the fund.

Rigby LJ said [[1896] 2 Ch 679, 689]:
> The members were not cestuis que trust of the funds or of any part thereof, but persons who, under contracts or quasi-contracts with the society, secured for valuable consideration certain contingent benefits for their widows which could be enforced by the widows in manner provided by the Acts. Any surplus would, according to the scheme of the rules, be properly used up (under appropriate amendments of the rules) either in payment of larger annuities or in reduction of contributions. It is true that no such alterations were made, and it is now too late so to distribute the funds; but I do not think that such omission can give to the contracting parties any benefit which they did not bargain for.

The ratio decidendi seems to have been that having regard to the constitution of the fund no interest could possibly be held to remain in the contributor who had parted with his money once and for all under a contract for the benefit of his widow. When this contract had been carried into effect the contributor had received all that he had contracted to get for his money and could not ask for any more.
. . .

In addition there were cited to me the three hospital cases: *In re Welsh Hospital (Netley) Fund* [1921] 1 Ch 655, *In re Hillier's Trusts* [1954] 2 All ER 59, and *In re Ulverston and District New Hospital Building Trusts* [1956] 3 All ER 164. In the first of these cases P.O. Lawrence J held that all subscribers to the hospital must be taken to have parted with their money with a general intention in favour of charity. This was the only contest in the case, between the subscribers on the one hand and charity on the other. In *Hillier's* case Upjohn J, at first instance, found that certain categories of subscribers were entitled to have their money back but that others, namely, those who had contributed to collections at entertainments and so forth, had no such right. The Court of Appeal varied this order and declared that the whole fund should go to charity but without prejudice to the right of any individual to prove that he had no general intention but only the particular intention in favour of one hospital. In the *Ulverston* case the Court of Appeal decided that the whole fund had been collected with only one object and not for general charitable purposes and that, so far as money had been received from identifiable sources, there was a resulting trust. No claim to bona vacantia was there made, and Jenkins LJ, in explaining the position in *In re Hillier's Trusts, said this* [[1956] Ch 622, 633]:

I appreciate that anonymous contributors cannot expect their contributions back in any circumstances, at all events so long as they remain anonymous. I appreciate also the justice of the conclusion that anonymous contributors must be regarded as having parted with their money out-and-out, though I would make a reservation in the case of an anonymous contributor who was able to prove conclusively that he had in fact subscribed some specified amount to the fund. If the organisers of a fund designed exclusively and solely for some particular charitable purpose send round a collecting box on behalf of the fund, I fail to see why a person who had put £5 into the box, and could prove to the satisfaction of the court he had done so, should not be entitled to have his money back in the event of the failure of the sole and exclusive charitable purpose for which his donation was solicited and made.

Jenkins LJ, in the course of his judgment, threw out the suggestion that donations from unidentifiable donors might in such a case be treated as bona vacantia.

It was argued for the Crown that the subscribers to this fund must be taken to have parted with their money out and out, and that there was here, as in *Cunnack v Edwards* [1896] 2 Ch 679 . . . no room for a resulting trust. But there is a difference between [that case] and this in that [that was a case] of contract and this is not. Further, it seems to me that the hospital cases are not of great help because the argument centred round general charitable intent, a point which cannot arise unless the immediate object be a charity. I have already held there is no such question here. In my judgment the nearest case is the *Hobourn* case, which, however, is no authority for the present because no claim for bona vacantia was made.

In my judgment the Crown has failed to show that this case should not follow the ordinary rule merely because there was a number of donors who, I will assume, are unascertainable. I see no reason myself to suppose that the small giver who is anonymous has any wider intention than the large giver who can be named. They all give for the one object. If they can be found by inquiry the resulting trust can be executed in their favour. If they cannot I do not see how the money could then, with all respect to Jenkins LJ, change its destination and become bona vacantia. It will be merely money held upon a trust for which no beneficiary can be found. Such cases are common and where it is known that there are beneficiaries the fact that they cannot be ascertained does not entitle the Crown to come in and claim. The trustees must pay the money into court like any other trustee who cannot find his beneficiary. I conclude, therefore, that there must be an inquiry for the subscribers to this fund.

Notes
1.   The Attorney-General appealed unsuccessfully on the issue of charitable status. See further chapter 12.
2.   One difficulty in *Gillingham* was that although some of the money had been provided by identifiable people, most had been obtained from street collections. So many of the donors were anonymous, and the trustees were therefore required to hold the fund on resulting trust for unknown people. Obviously this is most inconvenient administratively.

Re West Sussex Constabulary's Widows, Children and Benevolent (1930) Fund
[1971] 1 Ch 1
Chancery Division

Facts: The purpose of the West Sussex Constabulary's Widows, Children and Benevolent (1930) Fund was to provide allowances for the widows and dependants of deceased members. Some of its revenue was derived from contributions from its own members. Some was also raised from outside sources, by:

(a)   entertainments, raffles and sweepstakes,
(b)   collecting boxes,
(c)   donations, including legacies.

The fund was wound up at the end of 1967, upon the amalgamation of the constabulary with other police forces, and the question arose as to how to divide it up.

Held (on the outside contributions):   The outside contributions raised from category (c) were held on resulting trust for the contributors. Those raised by categories (a) and (b) were clearly intended to take effect as out and out gifts to the fund, and therefore the resulting trust doctrine did not apply to them. Having no owner, therefore, these contributions also were bona vacantia. The views of Harman J in *Re Gillingham Bus Disaster Fund* [1958] Ch 300, regarding street collections, were not followed.

GOFF J (on the outside contributions): . . . Then counsel divided the outside moneys into three categories, first, the proceeds of entertainments, raffles and sweepstakes; secondly, the proceeds of collecting-boxes; and thirdly, donations, including legacies if any, and he took particular objections to each.

I agree that there cannot be any resulting trust with respect to the first category. I am not certain whether Harman J in *Re Gillingham Bus Disaster Fund* [1958] Ch 300 meant to decide otherwise. In starting the facts at p. 304 he referred to 'street collections and so forth'. In the further argument at p. 309 there is mention of whist drives and concerts but the judge himself did not speak of anything other than gifts. If, however, he did, I must respectfully decline to follow his judgment in that regard, for whatever may be the true position with regard to collecting-boxes, it appears to me to be impossible to apply the doctrine of resulting trust to the proceeds of entertainments and sweepstakes and such-like-money-raising operations for two reasons: first, the relationship is one of contract and not of trust; the purchaser of a ticket may have the motive of aiding the cause or he may not; he may purchase a ticket merely because he wishes to attend the particular entertainment or to try for the prize, but whichever it be, he pays his money as the price of what is offered and what he receives; secondly, there is in such cases no direct contribution to the fund at all; it is only the profit, if any, which is ultimately received and there may even be none.

In any event, the first category cannot be any more susceptible to the doctrine than the second to which I now turn. Here one starts with the well-known dictum of P.O. Lawrence J in *Re Welsh Hospital (Netley) Fund* [1921] 1 Ch 655, 660 where he said:

So far as regards the contributors to entertainments, street collections etc., I have no hesitation in holding that they must be taken to have parted with their money out-and-out. It is inconceivable that any person paying for a concert ticket or placing a coin in a collecting-box presented to him in the street should have intended that any part of the money so contributed should be returned to him when the immediate object for which the concert was given or the collection made had come to an end. To draw such an inference would be absurd on the face of it.
. . .

In *Re Ulverston and District New Hospital Building Trusts* [1956] Ch 622, 633, Jenkins LJ threw out a suggestion that there might be a distinction in the case of a person who could prove that he put a specified sum in a collecting-box, and, in the *Gillingham* case [1958] Ch 300 Harman J, after nothing this, decided that there was a resulting trust with respect to the proceeds of collections. He said at p. 314:

In my judgment the Crown has failed to show that this case should not follow the ordinary rule merely because there was a number of donors who, I will assume, are unascertainable. I see no reason myself to suppose that the small giver who is anonymous has any wider intention than the large giver who can be named. They all give for one object. If they can be found by enquiry the resulting trust can be executed in their favour. If they cannot I do not see how the money could then, with all respect to Jenkins LJ, change its destination and become *bona vacantia*. It will be merely money held upon a trust for which no beneficiary can be found. Such cases are common and where it is known that there are beneficiaries the fact that they cannot be ascertained does not entitle the Crown to come in and claim. The trustees must pay the money into court like any other trustee who cannot find his beneficiary. I conclude, therefore, that there must be an enquiry for the subscribers to this fund.

It will be observed that Harman J considered that *Re Welsh Hospital (Netley) Fund* [1921] 1 Ch 655; *Re Hiller's Trusts* [1954] 1 WLR 9 and *Re Ulverston and District New Hospital Building Trusts* [1956] Ch 622 did not help him greatly because they were charity cases. It is true that they were, and, as will presently appear, that is in my view very significant in relation to the third category, but I do not think it was a valid objection with respect to the second, and for my part I cannot reconcile the decision of Upjohn J in *Re Hillier's Trusts* with that of Harman J in the *Gillingham* case [1958] Ch 300. As I see it, therefore, I have to choose between them. On the one hand it may be said that Harman J had the advantage, which Upjohn J had not, of considering the suggestion made by Jenkins LJ. On the other hand that suggestion with all respect, seems to me somewhat fanciful and unreal. I agree that all who put their money into collecting-boxes should be taken to have the same intention, but why should they not all be regarded as intending to part with their money out and out absolutely in all circumstances? I observe that P.O. Lawrence J in *Re Welsh Hospital* [1921] 1 Ch 655, 661, used very strong words. He said that any other view was inconceivable and absurd on the face of it. That commends itself to my humble judgment, and I therefore prefer and follow the judgment of Upjohn J in *Re Hillier's Trusts*. This does not appear to me to trangress the principle which Harman J laid down in the *Gillingham* case where he said, at p. 310:

This doctrine does not, in my judgment, rest on any evidence of the state of mind of the settlor, for in the vast majority of cases no doubt he does not expect to see his money back; he has created a trust which so far as he can see will absorb the whole of it. The resulting trust arises when that expectation is for some unforeseen reason cheated of fruition, and is an inference of law based on after-knowledge of the event.

I accept that fully but I also accept the submission of counsel for the Treasury Solicitor that equity will not impute an intention which it considers would be absurd on the face of it.

SECTION 2: WINDING UP OF UNINCORPORATED ASSOCIATIONS

A: When Wound Up?

It is necessary first to consider when a fund may be wound up. According to Brightman J in *Re William Denby & Sons Ltd Sick and Benevolent Fund* [1971] 1 WLR 973, winding up of a fund is not at the discretion of the treasurer or trustees of the fund, but may occur only when:

(a) the rules allow for dissolution, or
(b) all interested parties agree, or
(c) a court orders dissolution, or
(d) the substratum upon which the fund is founded is gone. An example is *Re St Andrew's Allotment Association* [1969] 1 WLR 229, where an allotment association was wound up when the land for allotments was sold to developers for £70,000.

Many of the cases arise when the club or association has simply been inactive for a number of years, but no positive moves have been made to wind it up. The courts are reluctant in these circumstances to infer that the substratum has gone. In *William Denby* itself the substratum had not disappeared, although after an industrial dispute many of the company's employees left, and for some time (about four and a half years) nobody had contributed to the fund. But before the dispute the fund was viable, and indeed increasing, and mere inactivity by the members did not necessarily lead to the conclusion that they had acquiesced in the dissolution of the fund, since a less drastic interpretation was possible, namely that they had acquiesced in the temporary suspension of contributions and grants.

Re GKN Bolts and Nuts (Automotive Division) Birmingham Works, Sports and Social Club
[1982] 1 WLR 774, [1982] 2 All ER 855, noted [1983] Conv 315
Chancery Division

Decision:
(a) A club did not cease to exist by mere inactivity unless the inactivity was so prolonged or so circumstanced that the only reasonable inference was that the club had been dissolved spontaneously.
(b) On the facts, spontaneous dissolution had occurred, but it required a positive act, in this case a resolution to sell the club's only remaining

asset, the sports ground, since after that the club was no longer capable of carrying out its objects in promoting sport and providing facilities for recreation for its members.

(c)   That since there was nothing to the contrary in the rules, distribution of the assets should be on a basis of equality among members at the time of dissolution.

MEGARRY V-C: The starting point is to consider whether there was a dissolution of the club on 18 December 1975, the date of the resolution to sell. The rules of the club do not help, for they are all directed to the operation of the club as a going concern. It is plain that there never was an agreement by the entire membership that the club should be dissolved, and of course there has been no exercise by the court of its inherent jurisdiction to order a dissolution. The question therefore is whether there has been what was called in arguments a spontaneous dissolution of the club.

As a matter of principle I would hold that it is perfectly possible for a club to be dissolved spontaneously. I do not think that mere inactivity is enough: a club may do little or nothing for a long period, and yet continue in existence. A cataleptic trance may look like death without being death. But inactivity may be so prolonged or so circumstanced that the only reasonable inference is that the club has become dissolved. In such cases there may be difficulty in determining the punctum temporis of dissolution: the less activity there is, the greater the difficulty of fastening on one date rather then another as the moment of dissolution. In such cases the court must do the best it can by picking a reasonable date somewhere between the time when the club could still be said to exist, and the time when its existence had clearly come to an end.

. . .

In *Re William Denby & Sons Ltd Sick and Benevolent Fund* [1971] 2 All ER 1196, [1971] 1 WLR 973, Brightman J classified four categories of case in which an unregistered friendly society or benevolent fund should be regarded as having been dissolved or terminated so that its assets became distributable. [Megarry V-C set out the four categories referred to above and continued:] On the facts of the case it was held that the substratum had not gone distributable; but the judgment considered a number of the authorities, and plainly supports the view that there may be a spontaneous dissolution of a society. . . . Brightman J expressed grave doubts whether mere inactivity of the officers of the society or the fund would suffice (see [1971] 2 All ER 1196 at 1204–1205, [1971] 1 WLR 973 at 981–982), and in this I would respectfully concur. Mere inactivity is equivocal: suspended animation may be continued life, not death; and the mere cessation of function . . . would not, I think, suffice per se. But inactivity coupled with other circumstances may demonstrate that all concerned regard the society as having ceased to have any purpose or function, and so as no longer existing. I think that short inactivity coupled with strong circumstances, or long inactivity coupled with weaker circumstances may equally suffice. The question is whether, put together, the facts carry sufficient conviction that the society is at an end and not merely dormant.

For myself, I would hesitate a little about the use of the phrase 'substratum had not gone' in this context. It has a beguiling sound; but it has strong overtones of the Companies Court. There, it may form the basis of a winding-up order, but it does not by itself initiate or complete the termination of the existence of the company. It therefore seems not altogether appropriate for establishing that there has been a spontaneous dissolution. I also hesitate to use the term 'frustration', with all its contractual overtones. However, this is a mere matter of nomenclature, and does not affect the principle. The question is whether on the facts of the present case the society ceased to exist on 18 December 1975.

On that date, the position was that the club had ceased to operate as a club for several months. The picture was not one of mere inactivity alone; there were positive acts towards the winding up of the club. The sale of the club's stock of drinks was one instance, and others were the ending of the registration for value added tax, and the dismissal of the steward. The cessation of any club activities, the ending of the use of the sports ground and the abandonment of preparing accounts or issuing membership cards were all in one sense examples of inactivity; but I think that there was in all probability some element of deliberation in these matters, and not a mere inertia. In the phrase of counsel for the second defendant, there was a systematic dismantling of the club and its activities.

However that may be, the resolution to sell the sports ground seems to me to conclude the matter. Having taken all steps, active or passive, required to terminate the activities of the club, short of passing a formal resolution to wind it up or dissolve it, the general meeting of the club resolved to sell the club's last asset. . . .

. . . The cessation of all club activities, the general knowledge of attempts to get planning permission in order to sell the sports ground, and then the holding of a general meeting to discuss a sale, even with (on this assumption) inadequate notice, seem to me to mark an acceptance by all concerned that the club was a club no more but merely a collection of individuals with expectations of dividing the proceeds of sale of the one remaining asset of the club. Whether it is put in terms of the club ceasing to function, or whether it is expressed as being a case where the substratum has gone or whether it is said that the club had become inactive and the surrounding circumstances sufficiently indicated that those concerned regarded the club as having ceased to have any purpose or function, and so as no longer existing, the answer in each case is the same. The rules of 1974 stated that the objects of the club were 'to promote the different games of sport, to provide facilities for recreation and to encourage good fellowship among all members'; and all must have recognised that the club had become incapable of carrying out any of its objects. If the resolution to sell the sports ground is valid, as I think it is, that merely reinforces my conclusion that the club ceased to exist as such on 18 December 1975.

. . .

That being so, the question is what the basis of distribution should be. For the reasons that I gave in Re Sick and Funeral Society of St John's Sunday School, Golcar [1972] 2 All ER 439, [1973] Ch 51 (a case which was applied by Walton J in Re Bucks Constabulary Widow's and Orphans' Fund Friendly Society (No 2) [1979] 1 All ER 623, [1979] 1 WLR 936), I think that where, as here, there is nothing in the rules or anything else to indicate a different basis, the distribution should be on a basis of equality, irrespective of the length of membership of the amount of the subscriptions paid. . . . Nor do I think that in this case there is any possible nexus between the length of membership or the number of subscription paid and the property rights of members on a dissolution. Each member on 18 December 1975 is entitled to one equal share in the proceeds of sale, whether his membership has lasted 30 years or a single day.

Note

Where the fund is held on a contractual basis the usual assumption is that only those who are members at the time of dissolution are entitled to a share, and that their share will be equal. It may be different if there are categories of membership. In *Re Sick and Funeral Society of St John's Sunday School, Golcar* [1973] Ch 51, referred to above, there were two distinct classes of membership, one class of which (adults) paid and received twice the benefit of the other (children). Division was such that adults received twice as much as children, but all the adults received the same, and all the children received the same. The share does not depend on the length of time one has been a member, nor on the total contribution made to the club. These factors would be relevant, however, if the funds of the association are held on a trust, rather than contract basis. Furthermore, past members would continue to be entitled to a share, whereas on a contractual analysis they are usually regarded as having forfeited any share on resignation from the club.

In chapter 5 we saw how the courts have tended towards a contractual basis in recent years, and that there are serious difficulties with a trust analysis. The issue cannot be regarded as closed, however, as is clear from the following section.

B: Division of Surplus Property

Re Hobourn Aero Components Ltd's Air Raid Distress Fund, Ryan v Forrest
[1946] Ch 86 (affirmed CA [1946] Ch 194; see Chapter 12)
Chancery Division

Facts: From 1940 to 1944 employees of a company situated in Coventry made weekly contributions to a fund to assist employees who had suffered damage as a result of air raids. Only contributors to the fund could benefit. The fund was closed in 1944, and the question arose what to do with surplus moneys.

Held (at first instance):

(a)   These funds were not held on any charitable trust, since there was an insufficient element of public benefit. It followed that a cy-près scheme could not be directed.

(b)   The contributors were entitled to distribute the fund among themselves, in proportion to the total amount each had contributed, on resulting trust principles.

COHEN J: [Cohen J held that the fund was not held on charitable trust. He continued (on the division of the fund among the contributors):]

The Crown does not claim the fund as *bona vacantia*, and the question is as to how it ought to be distributed amongst the contributories thereto. The form of the question suggests that persons who had ceased to contribute before 9 September 1944, the date on which contributions ceased, might be excluded, but counsel whose interest it was to support this argument admitted that there was no valid ground for any such limitation. In my opinion, he was right in making this admission, since the basis on which the contributions are returned is that each donor retained an interest in the amount of his contributions except so far as they are applied for the purposes for which they were subscribed. Moreover, the rule in *Clayton's Case* (1816) 1 Mer 572 is not applicable in such a case (see *Re British Red Cross Balkan Fund* [1914] 2 Ch 419). The question was also raised whether a subscriber who received benefit from the fund was bound to bring the amount of that benefit into hotchpot for the purposes of the distribution. My attention was called to two cases in which orders had been made for distribution of the fund without regard to such contributions. (See *Re Printers and Transferrers Amalgamated Trades Protection Society* [1899] 2 Ch 184 and *Re Lead Company's Workmen's Fund Society* [1904] 2 Ch 196.) But in both those cases the decision to this effect was based on the difficulty and the expense involved in ascertaining the amount of the respective benefits and the persons to whom they were paid. In the present case I was told by Mr Dinham, the company's accountant, that while considerable labour would be involved, there would be no difficulty in ascertaining the amounts of the benefits or the recipients, and I have come to the conclusion that I should not be justified in deviating from the general principle, that a person seeking to participate in the distribution of a fund must bring into hotchpot anything he has already received therefrom. Accordingly, I propose to declare that the fund now available for distribution ought to be distributed amongst all the persons who during their employment by Hobourn Aero Components Ltd, contributed to the fund at any time after 12 December 1940, in proportion to the total amount contributed by them respectively to the fund, each such person bringing into hotchpot any amount received by him by way of benefit out of the fund.

Note

Cohen J said that 'the basis on which the contributions are returned is that each donor retained an interest in the amount of his contributions except so far as they are applied for the purposes for which they were subscribed'. In other words, a proportion of the *total* contribution of each individual contributor is held on resulting trust, the assumption being that he retains an interest in his contribution. The usual analysis, however, is that each contributor parts with his contribution outright, subject only to his or her contractual right to benefit from the fund (the contributors being bound *inter se* by contractual rights and obligations), and to control the assets of the fund: see the discussion of *Re West Sussex Constabulary's Trusts* [1971] Ch 1, in this chapter, and *Re Bucks Constabulary Fund (No. 2)* [1979] 1 All ER 623, in this chapter.

On the usual analysis, anyone ceasing to contribute to the scheme loses any benefits he or she had under the scheme, and also loses any property interest in the fund. All those who are still contributors at the date of closure of the fund are usually entitled to an *equal* share in the surplus, not a share which is based upon their past contributions. See further *Re Bucks Constabulary Fund (No. 2)*.

Questions

1. The fund in *Hobourn Aero* lasted only four years, but nobody knew this at the outset. It was not expressly limited in duration, and there were fluctuations in membership. If each contributor had made his contribution on trust for present and future members of the association, does this not fall foul of the perpetuity difficulties alluded to in *Leahy*, set out in chapter 5?

2.   Could you save the gift by considering it as analogous to *Re Chardon*, also set out in chapter 5? Is a determinable gift a reasonable analysis for this situation?

3.   The case was decided before the Perpetuities and Accumulations Act 1964. If a similar case arose today, what perpetuity difficulties (if any) would be encountered? (See the discussion at the end of chapter 5.)

Note
In the *West Sussex* case, Goff J thought that Cohen J's analysis set out above was not part of the *ratio* of the case (but surely it was?). He also pointed out that there were no contractual benefits in *Hobourn*, so that the usual contractual analysis may well not be applicable, but that does not in any way answer the perpetuity difficulties (if any) inherent in Cohen J's analysis.

Held (in the Court of Appeal):   The Crown appealed (arguing for a cy près scheme to be directed) on the issue of the charitable status of the fund alone. The Court of Appeal upheld Cohen J's decision. See chapter 12.

Re West Sussex Constabulary's Widows, Children and Benevolent (1930) Fund
[1971] 1 Ch 1
Chancery Division

Facts: The facts of this case have already been set out at p. 191.

Decision (on the members' contributions):   The contributions of the members themselves were not held on resulting trust for them, since the money was paid on a contractual, rather than a trust basis. Further, since only third parties could benefit (widows and dependants), the fund could not belong to the members themselves. These contributions having no owner, would therefore go to the Crown as bona vacantia.

GOFF J (on the members' contributions): First, it was submitted that [the fund] belongs exclusively and in equal shares to all those persons now living who were members on 31 December 1967 and the personal representatives of all the then members since deceased, to whom I will refer collectively as 'the surviving members.' The argument is based on the analogy of he members' club cases . . . , and I cannot accept [it] as applicable, for these reasons. First, it simply does not look like it. This was nothing but a pensions or dependent relatives fund not at all akin to a club. Secondly, in all the cases where the surviving members have taken, with the sole exception of *Tierney* v *Tough* [1914] 1 IR 142, the club, society or organisation existed for the benefit of the members for the time being exclusively, whereas in the present case as in *Cunnack* v *Edwards* [1896] 2 Ch 679, only third parties could benefit. Moreover, in *Tierney's* case the exception was minimal and discretionary and can, I think, fairly be disregarded. . . . Then it was argued that there was a resulting trust, with several possible consequences. If this be the right view there must be a primary division into three parts, one representing contributions from former members, another contributions from the surviving members, and the third moneys raised from outside sources. The surviving members then take the second, and possibly by virtue of r. 10 the first also. Rule 10 is as follows:

> Any member who voluntarily terminates his membership shall forfeit all claim to the fund except in the case of a member transferring to a similar fund of another force in which instance the contributions paid by the member to the West Sussex Constabulary's Widows, Children and Benevolent (1930) fund may be paid into the Fund of the force into which the member transfers.

Alternatively, the first may belong to the past members on the footing that r. 10 is operative so long only as the fund is a going concern, or may be *bona vacantia*. The third is distributable in whole or in part between those who provided the money, or again is *bona vacantia*. In my judgment the doctrine of resulting trust is clearly inapplicable to the contributions of both classes. Those persons who remained members until their deaths are in any event excluded because they have had all they contracted for, either because their widows and dependants have received or are in receipt of the prescribed benefits, or because they did not have a widow or dependants. In my view that is inherent in all the speeches of the Court of Appeal in *Cunnack* v *Edwards* [1896] 2 Ch 679. Further, whatever the effect of r. 10 may be on the contribution of those members who left prematurely, they and the surviving members alike are also unable to claim under a resulting trust, because they put up their money on a contractual basis and not one of trust: see per Harman J in *Re Gillingham Bus Disaster Fund, Bowman* v *Official Solicitor* [1958] Ch 300, at 314. The only case which has given me difficulty on this aspect of the matter is *Re Hobourn Aero Components Ltd's Air Raid Distress Fund, Ryan* v *Forrest* [1946] Ch 86 [above], where in somewhat similar circumstances there was a resulting trust. The argument postulated, I think, the distinction between contract and trust but in another connection, namely whether the fund was charitable. There was in that case a resolution to wind up but that was not, at all events as expressed, the *ratio decidendi* (see per Cohen J at 97) but as his lordship observed there was no argument for *bona vacantia*. Moreover no rules or regulations were ever made and although in fact £1 per month was paid or saved for each member serving in the forces, there were no prescribed contractual benefits. In my judgment the case is therefore distinguishable. Accordingly, in my judgment all the contributions of both classes are *bona vacantia*. . . .

Note

An essentially similar issue, although without the complication of outside contributions, arose in *Re Bucks Constabulary Fund (No. 2)* [1979] 1 WLR 936. Walton J refused to follow Goff J on the question of the members' contributions, although the benefit was for third parties, and held that the fund should be divided equally among existing members. He took the view that merely because the benefit of the fund was intended for third parties, it did not follow (in the absence of valid trusts of the assets being declared in favour of the third parties) that the members themselves did not continue to control the assets, and could indeed collectively have divided them up among themselves had they so wished, before the dissolution.

In *Cunnack* v *Edwards* [1896] 2 Ch 679, which is relied upon by Goff J above, the society was registered under the (later repealed) Friendly Societies Act 1829, s. 26 of which prohibited distribution among the members upon dissolution of the fund. It may be difficult to argue that the case has any general application, therefore.

Questions
1.   If the members gave their contributions out and out, subject only to their contractual rights, to whom did they give them? Does the analysis in *Neville Estates* v *Madden or Re Recher's WT* (see chapter 5) assist in answering this?
2.   If those who had contributed by street collecting boxes, raffles, sweepstakes and the like gave their contributions out and out, to whom did they give them? Does the analysis in *Neville Estates* v *Madden* or *Re Recher's WT* (see chapter 5) assist in answering this?
3.   The reasoning in *Re Abbott*, which was followed by Goff J regarding the identifiable donations including legacies, was that the donors had made their contributions on trust, and that when the trust could no longer be carried out, the surplus went back to them on resulting trust. Applying the same principle here, what was the trust upon which these contributions must be assumed to have been given? Who were the beneficiaries? Would there have been any possibility of any beneficial interests vesting outside the perpetuity period? Is it possible for such a trust to be valid given the decision in *Leahy* (see chapter 5)?
4.   Many of the outside contributions may have been made before the Perpetuities and Accumulations Act 1964 came into force. As far as the identifiable donations were concerned, the *Chardon* analysis could theoretically apply to avoid perpetuity difficulties. Could it apply to any post–1964 donations? Given that it may be reasonable to apply such an analysis to a self-help organisation, as in *Hobourn Aero*, where people are contributing for their own benefit, and where there was apparently no possibility of a contractual analysis, is it reasonable to apply it here, where the alternative contractual analysis is possible?

Re Bucks Constabulary Widows' and Orphans' Fund Friendly Society, Thompson v Holdsworth (No. 2)
[1979] 1 WLR 936, [1979] 1 All ER 623
Chancery Division

Facts: The fund, which was registered under the Friendly Societies Act 1896, was made up of voluntary contributions from its members, for the relief of widows and orphans of deceased members of the Bucks Constabulary. Under s. 49(1) of the 1896 Act, property belonging to a registered friendly society was vested in trustees for the benefit of the members and those claiming through them. There was no provision for distribution of the assets of the fund in the event of the society being wound up.

In April 1968 the Bucks Constabulary was amalgamated with other constabularies to form the Thames Valley Constabulary, and in October 1968 the society was wound up. The trustee applied to court to determine how the funds were to be distributed.

Held: The surplus assets were held on trust for the members of the society at the time of its dissolution, to be distributed among them in equal shares.

Re West Sussex Constabulary's Fund Trusts [1971] Ch 1 (in this section), where the contributions of the members went to the Crown as *bona vacantia*, was distinguished.

WALTON J: [Walton J applied the analysis of Brightman J in *Re Recher's WT* [1972] Ch 526, at 538–9 (in chapter 5) of the basis upon which the funds of unincorporated associations are held by their members. He also referred to the passage in the very similar *West Sussex Constabulary* case (set out as the first passage in the extract above, and continued:]

It will be observed that the first reason given by [Goff J] for his decision is that he could not accept the principle of the members' clubs as applicable. . . . If all that Goff J meant was that the purposes of the fund before him were totally different from those of a members' club then of course one must agree, but if he meant to imply that there was some totally different principle of law applicable one must ask why that should be. His second reason is that in all the cases where the surviving members had taken, the organisation existed for the benefit of the members for the time being exclusively. This may be so, so far as actual decisions go, but what is the principle? Why are the members not in control, complete control, save as to any existing contractual rights, of the assets belonging to their organisation? One could understand the position being different if valid trusts had been declared of the assets in favour of third parties, for example charities, but that this was emphatically not the case was demonstrated by the fact that Goff J recognised that the members could have altered the rules prior to dissolution and put the assets into their own pockets. If there was no obstacle to doing this, it shows in my judgment quite clearly that the money was theirs all the time. . . . As I have already indicated, in the light of s. 49(1) of the 1896 Act the case before Goff J is clearly distinguishable, but I regret that, quite apart from that, I am wholly unable to square it with the relevant principles of law applicable.

The conclusion therefore is that, as on dissolution there were members of the society here in question in existence, its assets are held on trust for such members to the total exclusion of any claim on behalf of the Crown. The remaining question under this head which now falls to be argued is, of course, whether they are simply held *per capita*, or as suggested in some of the cases [e.g., *Re Hobourn Aero Components Ltd's Air Raid Distress Fund* [1946] Ch 86, above] in proportion to the contributions made by each. . . .

I think that there is no doubt that, as a result of modern cases . . . , judicial opinion has been hardening and is now firmly set along the lines that the interests and rights of persons who are members of any type of unincorporated association are governed exclusively by contract, that is to say the rights between themselves and their rights to any surplus assets. I say that to make it perfectly clear that I have not overlooked the fact that the assets of the society are usually vested in trustees on trust for the members. But that is quite a separate and distinct trust bearing no relation to the claims of the members *inter se* on the surplus funds so held on trust for their benefit.

That being the case, prima facie there can be no doubt at all but that the distribution is on the basis of equality, because, as between a number of people contractually interested in a fund, there is no other method of distribution if no other method is provided by the terms of the contract, and it is not for one moment suggested here that there is any other method of distribution provided by the contract. We are, of course, dealing here with a friendly society, but that really makes no difference to the principle. The Friendly Societies Acts do not incorporate the friendly society in any way and the only effect that it has is . . . that there is a section which makes it crystal clear in the Friendly Societies Act 1896 that the assets are indeed held on trust for the members.

Notes

1.   Walton J makes it clear that the funds of unincorporated associations are held by the members beneficially, subject only to their contractual rights and obligations *inter se*. The position is the same for members' clubs as it is for friendly societies, since it is clear that Walton J's decision would have been the same whether or not the 1896 Act applied. Furthermore, in the absence of evidence to the contrary, members who resign lose all claim on the fund, and division is made equally among present members only, at the time of the dissolution of the fund.

2.   Although Walton J is careful technically to distinguish the *West Sussex case* (above), on the narrow basis that the 1896 Act did not apply in *West Sussex*, it is quite clear that he thinks Goff J's view (at any rate on the contributions of the members themselves to the fund) wrong. Goff J thought that the contributors had parted with their property out and out, and had retained no interest in the fund since it was held for the benefit of third parties (the widows and dependants of the deceased members). As Walton J points out, however, the mere fact that the members have contracted between themselves to provide benefits for third parties does not mean (in the absence of a valid trust in favour of the third parties) that they have relinquished their property in the fund. They can, after all, collectively agree to distribute the fund among themselves, or to vary the benefits under the scheme. The position is essentially analogous to *Beswick* v *Beswick* (see chapter 2), where although two parties had contracted to provide a benefit for a third party, they could at any time agree to vary the benefit to be provided for the third party, and the third party had no enforceable claim against either of them.

3.   It is still by no means clear whether a trust or contract analysis will usually be adopted, as is shown by the following case.

Davis v Richards and Wallington Industries Ltd
[1990] 1 WLR 1511, [1991] 2 All ER 563
Chancery Division

Decision: On the winding up of a pension fund, the *ratio* of the case was that distribution of the assets was by a definitive deed which was executed by the trustees, but Scott J went on to consider the position if he were wrong. There were three main sources of contributions to the fund: employers, employees and money transferred from other funds. Scott J thought that the employers' contributions should be held on resulting trust for them, since they were similar to the legacies in *West Sussex*. There was no reason to rebut the conclusion that there was a resulting trust.

SCOTT J (on the resulting trust question): Finally I must address myself to the arguments on resulting trust. These arguments arise only if the definitive deed was ineffective and its inefficacy cannot be remedied by the execution of the executory trust.

Mr Charles, arguing for bona vacantia, has drawn a distinction between payments made under contract and payments made under a trust. He suggested that rights arising under pension schemes were, basically, rights of a contractual character rather than equitable rights arising under a trust. As I understood the argument, if the context in which the rights arise is mainly or exclusively contractual, then a resulting trust will be excluded; but, if the context is mainly or exclusively that of trust, a resulting trust may apply. Unincorporated associations, he said, were based in contract, a pension scheme was a species of unincorporated association, the contributions to pension schemes by employees and employers alike were made under contract with one another; so there was no room for any resulting trust to apply to the surplus produced by the contributions.

. . .

In my opinion, the contractual origin of rights under a pension scheme, although relevant to the question whether a resulting trust applies to surplus, is not conclusive. There are a number of authorities where the courts have had to deal with the question whether the assets of a defunct association or the surplus assets of a pension scheme had become bona vacantia or were held on resulting trusts for the subscribers or members.

I can start with *Re West Sussex Constabulary's Widows Children and Benevolent (1930) Fund Trusts* [1970] 1 All ER 544, [1971] Ch 1. The case concerned a benevolent fund raised from various sources, including raffles, sweepstakes, street collections, legacies and donations. The fund had to be wound up and the question was its destination. Goff J held that so much of the fund as derived from raffles, sweepstakes, street collections and the like was not the subject of any resulting trust and was bona vacantia, but that there was a resuting trust in respect of the legacies and donations. As to the proceeds of the raffles and sweepstakes, Goff J said ([1970] 1 All ER 544 at 548, [1971] Ch 1 at 11):

. . . it appears to me to be impossible to apply the doctrine of resulting trust to the proceeds of entertainments and sweepstakes and such-like money raising operations for two reasons. First, the relationship is one of contract and not of trust. The purchaser of a ticket merely because he wishes to attend the particular entertainment or to try for the prize, but whichever it be, he pays his money as the price of what is offered and what he receives . . .

Mr Charles draws attention to the reference to contract. As to the proceeds of the collecting boxes, Goff J referred to various authorities, including, in particular, Harman J's decision in *Re Gillingham Bus Disaster Fund, Bowman v Official Solicitor* [1958] 1 All ER 37, [1958] Ch 300 and Upjohn J's decision in *Re Hillier, Hillier v A-G* [1953] 2 All ER 1547, [1954] 1 WLR 9. He expressed a preference for the latter decision and said ([1970] 1 All ER 544 at 550, [1971] Ch 1 at 13):

I agree that all who put their money into collecting boxes should be taken to have the same intention, but why should they not all be regarded as intending to part with their money out and out, absolutely, in all circumstances?

On that ground he held that a resulting trust did not apply to the proceeds of collecting boxes and that the proceeds were bona vacantia. He declined, however, when dealing with legacies and donations to draw the same inference of intention to part out and out with the money that he had drawn in respect of the collecting boxes and held that resulting trust applied to the part of the fund attributable to legacies and donations.

The principles to be applied in deciding between a resulting trust and bona vacantia were considered by Knox J in *Jones v Williams* (15 March 1988, unreported). In his judgment Knox J says:

The general rule is well settled that where the owner of property conveys it to another to be held on certain trusts which fail, either in whole or in part, the beneficial interest comes back to the person who conveyed the property: . . .

Where a trust deed is silent as to the destination of a surplus the law will supply a resulting trust in favour of the provider of the funds in question. That is something which arises outside the trust deed as an implication of law. The trust deed may include a clause which prevents a resulting trust from operating and in that case it will operate according to its terms.

But he continued: '. . . it is only where it is absolutely clear that in no circumstances is a resulting trust to arise that it will be excluded.'

I respectfully agree with Knox J's approach. I would, however, venture one qualification. The provision in a trust deed necessary to exclude a resulting trust need not, in my opinion, be express. In the absence of an express provision it would, I think, often be very difficult for a sufficiently clear intention to exclude a resulting trust to be established. But, in general, any term that can be expressed can also, in suitable circumstances, be implied. In my opinion, a resulting trust will be excluded not only by an express provision but also if its exclusion is to be implied. If the intention of a contributor that a resulting trust should not apply is the proper conclusion, it would not be right, in my opinion, for the law to contradict that intention.

In my judgment, therefore, the fact that a payment to a payment to a fund has been made under contract and that the payer has obtained all that he or she bargained for under the contract is not necessarily a decisive argument against a resulting trust.

I must apply these principles to the surplus in the present case. The fund was, as I have said, fed from three sources: employees' contributions, transfers from other pension schemes and employers' contributions.

. . .

The . . . question is whether a resulting trust applies to the surplus, or to so much of the surplus as was derived from each of the three sources to which I have referred.

As to the surplus derived from the employers' contributions, I can see no basis on which a resulting trust can be excluded. The equity to which I referred in the previous paragraph demands, in my judgment, the conclusion that the trustees hold the surplus derived from the employers' contributions upon trust for the employers. There is no express provision excluding a resulting trust and no circumstances from which, in my opinion, an implication to that effect could be drawn.

On the other hand, in my judgment, the circumstances of the case seem to me to point firmly and clearly to the conclusion that a resulting trust in favour of the employees is excluded. The circumstances are these.

(i)   Each employee paid his or her contributions in return for specific financial benefits from the fund. The value of these benefits would be different for each employee, depending on how long he had served, how old he was when he joined and how old he was when he left. Two employees might have paid identical sums in contributions but have become entitled to benefits of a very different value. The point is particularly striking in respect of the employees, and there were several of them, who exercised their option to a refund of contributions. How can a resulting trust work as between the various employees inter se? I do not think it can and I do not see why equity should impute to them an intention that would lead to an unworkable result.

(ii)   The scheme was established to take advantage of the legislation relevant to an exempt approved scheme and a contracted-out scheme. The legislative requirements placed a maximum on the financial return from the fund to which each employee would become entitled. The proposed rules would have preserved the statutory requirements. A resulting trust cannot do so. In my judgment, the relevant legislative requirements prevent imputing to the employees an intention that the surplus of the fund derived from their contributions should be returned to them under a resulting trust.

In my judgment, therefore, there is no resulting trust for the employees.

Finally, there are the transferred funds. . . . So far as the employee members of the transferred schemes were concerned there could not, for the same reasons as those I have already given, be a resulting trust in favour of them. So far as the employer contributors to those funds were concerned (ie the companies whose shares had been taken over), they were not all in the same position vis-à-vis the transferred funds. Some of the transferred schemes expressly excluded any refund of assets to the employer contributors. Those employers could not, therefore, assert any resulting trust. As to the others, it is possible to regard the transferred funds as being subject to some contigent resulting trust of surplus in favour of employer contributors. But, as I understand the evidence, it would be virtually impossible now to identify the part of the £3m-odd surplus that represented the surplus (if there was one) inherent in any of the transferred funds. In my judgment, it is reasonable in the circumstances to regard the employer contributors to the transferred funds, as well as the employee contributors, as intending that the funds should vest in the 1975 scheme trustees to the entire exclusion of any claim under the transferred scheme, whether under the rules thereof or by way of resulting trust. Here again, I do not think equity should impute to the parties an impracticable and unworkable intention.

Accordingly, in my judgment, if any part of the surplus has derived from employees' contributions or from the funds transferred from the pension schemes of other companies, that part of the surplus devolves as bona vacantia. Subject thereto, the surplus is, in my judgment, held upon trust for the employer contributors.

Note

The problem is the same as in *West Sussex*. What was the trust upon which the employers' contributions were held prior to the winding up of the fund? It must have been a trust for a fluctuating body of individuals. Surely, similar perpetuity problems arise as before. Note, however, that contributions here would have been subject to the Perpetuities and Accumulations Act 1964, rendering the *Chardon* reasoning in chapter 5 inapplicable.

Re Bucks Constabulary Widows' and Orphans' Fund Friendly Society (No. 2) was not mentioned by Scott J, although according to the report the case was cited, and there was some consideration given to a contractual analysis (at pp. 589–90). No obvious reason was given for its rejection, however.

Extract from Jill Martin's note on the case
[1991] Conv 364, at pp. 366–8

Our next pensions case is *Davis v Richards & Wallington Industries Ltd* [1990] 1 WLR 1511. In resolving the issue of who was entitled to the surplus funds, Scott J makes some general points about resulting trusts. . . .

The case also illustrates the maxim the equity regards as done that which ought to be done. One reason why the definitive deed was said to be invalid was that it had not been executed by the subsidiary companies. But the beneficiaries (the employees) were not volunteers, and could therefore enforce the incompletely constituted trust. The companies were thus obliged to execute the definitive deed, and the effect of the maxim was that the rights of the parties were the same as if they had done so.

As the definitive deed was held effective, its rules governed the surplus. The discussion of resulting trusts was on the basis of what the position would have been if the deed had been ineffective and if the interim deed had not been an executory trust.

The surplus derived from three sources: the employees (by contract – 5 per cent of salary); transfers from other pension schemes; and the employers (by contract – to pay whatever was necessary to fund the scheme). The fund itself was treated as deriving primarily from the employees, and so the surplus was primarily derived from the employers, who had paid more than necessary. (As to the transferred funds, it was held that the trustees of those funds had divested themselves of them once and for all, and so if any of the surplus derived from them, it was *bona vacantia*).

The question was whether the entitlement of the contributors to the surplus should be resolved by the resulting trust doctrine or by some other means. It was argued that, as the pension scheme was a species of unincorporated association, the rights lay in contract, not trusts. Scott J held that the contractual origin of the rights was not conclusive against a resulting trust, nor was the fact that a contributor to the fund had obtained all that he bargained for under the contract. Reference was made to the finding of a resulting trust in *Re West Sussex Constabulary's Widows Children and Benevolent (1930) Fund Trusts* [1971] Ch 1 in favour of those who had given donations or legacies, and the *bona vacantia* solution for those who had given via collecting boxes, raffles and so forth. Strangely, no mention was made of the finding that the members had got all they bargained for in their contracts so that their contribution to the surplus was *bona vacantia*. *Re Bucks Constabulary Widows' and Orphans' Fund Friendly Society (No. 2)* [1979] 1 WLR 936, which casts some doubt on *Re West Sussex*, was cited but not referred to. Walton J there held that the members were entitled (by way of contract, not resulting trust), and that the assets could not be *bona vacantia* unless the society was defunct.

Scott J in the present case preferred the resulting trust solution, but held that it could be excluded, expressly or impliedly, in which case the property would be *bona vacantia* [Relying on Knox J in *Jones v Williams*, 15 March 1988]. There was here no express exclusion, nor, in the case of the employers, any circumstances to found an implied exclusion. In the case of the employees, however, such circumstances were present. First, a resulting trust would be unworkable. [Jill Martin notes: This factor normally tends to support a per capita distribution rather than *bona vacantia*. See, for example, *Re Sick and Funeral Society of St John's Sunday School, Golcar* [1973] Ch 51. Each employee had paid in return for specific benefits, which were all different, depending on length of service, age and so forth. Some had exercised an option to get a refund of contributions. Equity would not impute an intention that would lead to an unworkable result. Secondly, the pension scheme was based on legislation which placed a maximum on the financial return to which employees would be entitled. This prevented imputing an intention to them to have any surplus. [Jill Martin notes: Intention is not normally given such an important role in resulting trusts (other than in the 'presumed' category, involving conveyances to volunteers). For a prime example, see the *Vandervell* litigation.]

So the conclusion was that if any part of the surplus derived from the employees, it was *bona vacantia*. Subject to that, there would be a resulting trust for the employer companies, pro rata according to their contributions. The difficult calculations were avoided, of course, by the decision that the definitive deed, containing rules as to the surplus, was effective.

To the extent that this decision favours the resulting trust approach, it may be seen as out of line with the modern trend, where a contractual per capita distribution has been preferred. The contest is normally regarded as between the resulting trust (entitlement proportionate to contributions) and contractual (per capita distribution among present members) solutions. The latter is now normally preferred, with *bona vacantia* having little scope for operation [Jill Martin notes: *Re Bucks, supra; Re Sick and Funeral Society, supra; Re G.K.N. Bolts & Nuts Ltd (Automotive Division) Birmingham Works, Sports and Social Club* [1982] 1 WLR 774.] The present case shows that this approach can be sidestepped if it would lead to an inconvenient result.

9 MATRIMONIAL PROPERTY; BENEFICIAL INTERESTS OF COHABITEES

SECTION 1: PRESUMPTIONS CONCERNING INTENTION

Beneficial interests of married and unmarried couples in their home largely depend, at any rate in theory, on intention, but often the circumstances are such that no clear intention is expressed. Parties to an ongoing relationship are unlikely to concern themselves overly with the property consequences of a breakdown of that relationship. The law has developed presumptions, which are however very old, and do not always appear to be ideally suited to the present situation.

A: The Presumption of Resulting Trust

We begin with the presumption of resulting trust. Where there is a voluntary transfer of the legal title to property (i.e., not a transfer for value), then unless there is a presumption of advancement (see below), the presumption is that the equitable title does not follow the legal title, but remains in the settlor, i.e., there is a resulting trust. The presumption is very old, going back at least as far as *Dyer* v *Dyer* (1788) 2 Cox Eq Cas 92, where Eyre CB said (at p. 93):

. . . [T]he trust of a legal estate, whether freehold, copyhold, or leasehold; whether taken in the names of the purchasers and others jointly, or in the name of others without that of the purchaser; whether in the name of one or several; whether jointly or successive, results to the man who advances the purchase money. This is a general proposition supported by all the cases, and there is nothing to contradict it; and it goes on a strict analogy to the rule of the common law, that where a feoffment is made without consideration, the use results to the feoffor.

Hodgson v Marks
[1971] Ch 892
Court of Appeal

Facts: An old lady (Mrs Hodgson) was cajoled into making a voluntary conveyance of her house to her lodger (Evans). Evans was registered as absolute owner, and subsequently sold the property to a third party (Marks). Two issues arose: first, did Mrs Hodgson have an equitable interest in the property, enforceable in spite of lack of writing, and secondly, did that interest bind Marks, who was not shown to have notice of the interest?

Held: Both issues were decided in favour of Mrs Hodgson.

RUSSELL LJ (on the formalities point): I turn next to the question whether section 53(1) of the Law of Property Act 1925 prevents the assertion by the plaintiff of her entitlement in equity to the house. Let me first assume that, contrary to the view expressed by the judge, Mr Marks is not debarred from relying upon the section, and the express oral arrangement or declaration of trust between the plaintiff and Mr Evans found by the judge was not effective as such. Nevertheless, the evidence is clear that the transfer was not intended to operate as a gift, and, in those circumstances, I do not see why there was not a resulting trust of the beneficial interest to the plaintiff, which would not, of course, be affected by section 53(1). It was argued that a resulting trust is based upon implied intention, and that where there is an express trust for the transferor intended and declared – albeit ineffectively – there is no room for such an implication. I do not accept that. If an attempted express trust fails, that seems to me just the occasion for implication of a resulting trust, whether the failure be due to uncertainty, or perpetuity, or lack of form. It would be a strange outcome if the plaintiff were to lose her beneficial interest because her evidence had not been confined to negativing a gift but had additionally moved into a field forbidden by section 53(1) for lack of writing. I remark in this connection that we are not concerned with the debatable question whether on a voluntary transfer of land by A to stranger B there is a presumption of a resulting trust. The accepted evidence is that this was not intended as a gift, notwithstanding the reference to love and affection in the transfer, and section 53(1) does not exclude that evidence.

It may be that the same conclusion can be arrived at by the course referred to in point 2(b) of the points that I have listed as being for consideration in this appeal, namely, that the beneficial interest never left the plaintiff with the result that there was no 'creation' or 'disposition' of that interest in the land, nor any 'declaration of trust respecting land or any interest therein,' and, consequently, nothing within section 53(1). But it is not necessary to consider that approach further.

On the above footing it matters not whether Mr Marks was or was not debarred from relying upon section 53(1) by the principle that the section is not to be used as an instrument for fraud. Mr Marks was in fact ignorant of the plaintiff's interest and it is forcefully argued that there is nothing fraudulent in his taking advantage of the section. I do not propose to canvass the general point further, more particularly in the light of the nature of the subject-matter with which we are dealing – an overriding interest. Quite plainly Mr Evans could not have placed any reliance on section 53, for that would have been to use the section as an instrument of fraud. Accordingly, at the moment before the registration of Mr Marks as registered proprietor there was in existence an overriding interest in the plaintiff, and by force of the statute the registration could only take effect subject thereto.

Questions
1.   Is this an express trust, a presumed resulting trust, depending on the presumed intention of the parties, an automatic resulting trust, depending on the principles elaborated on in chapter 8, or a combination of these?
2.   Given that Mrs Hodgson clearly did not intend to convey her equitable title to Evans, do you need a presumption to reach the conclusion in the case?
3.   The reasoning at first instance was that this was an express trust, and the fact that it was unwritten was of no avail to Evans, since equity would not allow a statute to be used as a cloak for fraud (see further chapter 11). Could an unwritten express trust of land have bound Marks?

Notes
1.   Marks was bound because of the application of s. 70(1)(g) of the Land Registration Act 1925. This aspect of the decision was upheld by the House of Lords in *Williams & Glyn's Bank Ltd* v *Boland* [1981] AC 487.
2.   The effect of the presumption of resulting trust, in the present context, is that contributions to the purchase money are of paramount importance, and indeed this appears to be the case. Thus, for example, where Mr A and Ms B contribute half each to a house, legal title to which is conveyed into the name of Mr A alone, the presumption is not that Ms B is giving a half share of the property to A. Equitable title does not follow legal title, the presumption being that it remains where it is. In other words, each will be entitled in equity to a half share.
3.   The presumption is said to be fairly weak and therefore easily rebutted; and indeed it must be rebutted whenever a gift is to take effect. Evidential problems could arise, however, especially when the donor had died. Suppose Mr X marries Mrs X1 and gives her valuable jewellery. The marriage breaks down and X marries again, Mrs X2. X dies intestate. X2 claims the jewellery on the grounds that the equitable title remained in X. It may be difficult to prove that the presumption of resulting trust has been rebutted, and this is a possible explanation for the development (which is again very old) of the presumption of advancement. The opposite presumption (i.e., that the equitable title *does* follow the legal title) prevails where there is a presumption of advancement.

B: Equitable Title Follows Legal Title

Presumptions of advancement occur where the relationship between the parties is such as to impose a moral obligation upon one to provide for the other. Examples are the obligation of a husband to support his wife, and the obligation of a father to support his children. The effect of the presumption is that where there is a voluntary conveyance of the legal title (i.e., without consideration, in effect a gift), the equitable title passes also. In other words, the presumption is that an out-and-out gift is intended, to fulfil the moral obligation to give, whereas in other voluntary conveyances there is a presumption of resulting trust.

The presumption only applies from husband and wife and from father and child (or any other person to whom he stands in *loco parentis*, e.g., an adopted child). It does not apply from wife to husband, nor at all between unmarried couples. There is authority in *Bennett* v *Bennett*, below, for a weak presumption from mother to child, but there is no reliance on a presumption of advancement in *Sekhon* v *Alissa*, below.

Question
Does the presumption of advancement lead to a different conclusion to the example in note *3* above, and if so, which conclusion is to be preferred? What if X had merely lived with X1 as if married, but no marriage had ever taken place? Do you think the presumptions are necessary today, and lead to sensible conclusions?

Bennett v Bennett
(1879) 10 ChD 474
Court of Appeal

Decision: The presumption of advancement from mother to child is weaker than from father to child.

JESSEL MR: . . . The doctrine of equity as regards presumption of gifts is this, that where one person stands in such a relation to another that there is an obligation on that person to make a provision for the other, and we find either a purchase or investment in the name of the other, or in the joint names of the person and the other, of an amount which would constitute a provision for the other, the presumption arises of an intention on the part of the person to discharge the obligation to the other; and therefore, in the absence of evidence to the contrary, that purchase or investment is held to be in itself evidence of a gift.

In other words, the presumption of gift arises from the moral obligation to give.

. . . The father [of a child] is under that obligation from the mere fact of his being the father, and therefore no evidence is necessary to shew the obligation to provide for his child, because that is part of his duty. In the case of a father, you have only to prove the fact that he is the father, and when you have done that the obligation at once arises; but in the case of a person *in loco parentis* you must prove that he took upon himself the obligation.
. . .

We then arrive at this conclusion, that in the case of a mother . . . it is easier to prove a gift than in the case of a stranger: in the case of a mother very little evidence beyond the relationship is wanted, there being very little additional motive required to induce a mother to make a gift to her child.

Sekhon v Alissa
[1989] 2 FLR 94
Chancery Division

Facts: The daughter bought a house which was conveyed into her sole name for £37,500. She contributed £15,000. The mother contributed

£22,500, and the reason it was conveyed into the name of the daughter alone was because the mother thought that there would be a capital gains tax advantage to her.

Held: Hoffman J considered all aspects of intention and came to the conclusion that the mother did not intend the entire beneficial interest to be conveyed to the daughter.

HOFFMAN J: In my judgment neither of the parties thought that the mother's contribution was really a gift. First, it would have meant that she had parted irrevocably with almost the whole of her savings. Secondly, on the only occasion on which there is any suggestion that she spoke of the money as a gift, she said that this was the 'official' version. I construe this to mean that it was not a gift at all. Thirdly, no other member of the family thought that there was any question of the money having been a gift. The mother herself said that she regarded the purchase as a commercial venture which would not only help the daughter but also give her a better return on her money than the building society. The mother said that the payment was never described by the daughter or her mother as a gift or, for that matter, as a loan. The daughter-in-law said that her clear impression was that the property was bought as a joint venture. As an articled clerk at the time, she had thought that in the circumstances it would have been better to convey it into joint names, but she knew that a solicitor was acting and thought that he would do whatever was needed to safeguard the mother's interests. Fourthly, all the purposes for which the daughter said the house had been bought – to provide her with income, to give her a capital asset, to use her mortgage-raising capacity, to improve her marriage prospects – did not necessarily require that the mother's contribution should have been a gift. On any view, it enabled the daughter to acquire an interest in a property which was likely both to increase in capital value and yield her an income or provide her with a home. Fifthly, in April 1982 the daughter and the son had a scheme which involved converting the house into two flats with the aid of an improvement grant and the purchase of one flat at market value by the son with the aid of a mortgage. They went to see the solicitor about this proposal and told him that the purchase price would be used 'to repay certain of the monies lent to the daughter by her mother'. I shall return to the question of whether the transaction was truly a loan, but this incident is not consistent with its having been a gift. Sixthly, for a period after the autumn of 1984 the daughter accounted to her mother for the rent of one of the flats, making deductions for expenses, rate payments and so forth. Seventhly, at some time during 1983 or 1984 the daughter consulted the daughter-in-law about asking her former principal to prepare documents giving the mother an interest in one of the flats. The daughter-in-law thought that the daughter wanted to convey a legal interest in the flat to the mother so that she should be rid of her responsibilities for looking after it and collecting rents. The daughter says that what she had in mind was some kind of security interest to reassure the mother that her money would be safe. Either view is inconsistent with the payment having been a gift.

The daughter's own interpretation of the transaction distinguished between what she regarded as its legal effect, which was to vest the whole beneficial interest in her absolutely, and her moral obligation to repay her mother, which she has never attempted to deny. Most of the conduct which I have mentioned as evidence that the payment was not a gift was in her view explicable as a recognition of purely moral obligations. But the law does not readily accept that the parties intended to distinguish between legal and moral obligations. The parties may of course expressly agree that obligations which would ordinarily be legally enforceable are to be binding only in honour. Normally, however, the object of equitable institutions such as a resulting trust is to give the force of law to moral obligations. In my judgment, whatever the parties may have intended the outward form of the transaction to be, they did not as between themselves intend to distinguish between legal and moral obligations.

The next question is whether the mother's contribution was to be an unsecured loan or to give her a beneficial interest. In my judgment the law presumes a resulting trust in her favour and that presumption has to be rebutted by evidence that she intended a personal loan without acquiring any interest in the property. I am not satisfied on the evidence that a loan was agreed. The elder daughter and daughter-in-law, as I have said, gave evidence that nothing was said about a loan and the latter thought that the purchase was a joint venture. The mother denied any intention to make a loan. She said that she expected to share in the increased value of the house, and obtain a higher income than from her existing investments. On the daughter's evidence, there was never any discussion about the terms of repayment or whether the mother would be entitled to interest. The only conversation relied upon was the one at the solicitors' office in which her mother had said 'very casually' that she expected to be paid her money back. I think that this remark is not sufficient to rebut the presumption of a resulting trust. The mother could easily have meant that she expected to get her investment back, with whatever capital appreciation was appropriate.

Notes

1.   There is no mention of a presumption of advancement anywhere in this judgment.

2.   Even where the presumption does apply it can, of course, be rebutted, for example if a wife is allowed to draw cheques on a joint banking account for the convenience of the husband, perhaps because the husband is ill, as in *Marshal* v *Crutwell* (1875) LR 20 Eq 328. Clearly in such a case there is no intention to make a gift to the wife, unlike for example *Re Figgis* [1969] 1 Ch 123, where an otherwise similar arrangement on a joint account was not merely for convenience. It also appears that bank guarantees, for example where a husband guarantees his wife's overdraft, do not attract the operation of the presumption, but that ordinary rules of contract apply: *Anson* v *Anson* [1953] 1 QB 636.

3.   The rule in *Strong* v *Bird* (1874) LR 18 Eq 315 was originally an example of the presumption that equitable title followed legal title. The defendant borrowed £1,100 from his step-mother. His step-mother lived in his house and paid rent at £212 quarterly. The money borrowed by the defendant was to be repaid by 11 deductions of £100 from quarterly rent. The step-mother made two deductions, but after that made no more, and continued to pay the full £212 until her death. Orally, she forgave the defendant the remainder of debt (but this was ineffective as a release at law). The defendant was appointed executor under her will. The residuary legatees claimed the remainder of debt, but Jessel MR held the defendant not liable. His appointment as an executor extinguished the debt at common law since it is impossible for an executor to sue himself. Equity acquiesced with the common law position, the deceased being presumed to intend this so long as

he or she had shown an intention to forgive the debt during his or her lifetime, and that such intention had continued up to his or her death. From the appointment of the debtor as executor in these circumstances could be inferred a conclusive release of the debt.

In *Re Stewart* [1908] 2 Ch 251, Neville J applied the same principle to perfect an imperfect *inter vivos* gift of bonds by appointment of the intended donee as executor. This is an extension of the rule, and cannot be explained on the basis of a presumption that equitable title would follow legal, since there had been *inter vivos* common law transfer of title.

On the rule in *Strong* v *Bird* generally, see Kodilinye [1982] Conv 14.

SECTION 2:   APPLICATION TO MATRIMONIAL PROPERTY

A: Development of the Law Prior to *Lloyds Bank* v *Rosset*

If the presumption of advancement applies to matrimonial property, then if a husband provides the money for a home which is conveyed into the name of his wife, an out-and-out gift of the home is presumed. Or if it is conveyed into the joint names of husband and wife, the presumption will be that the equitable title also will be jointly held, even if the husband has provided all the purchase money. The presumption does not apply except to married couples, and it may therefore be that application of the presumption of advancement leads to an anomaly.

We need also to consider the effect, if any, of the Married Women's Property Act 1882. Before then, the common law allowed a married woman very little freedom to own her own property, although to a limited extent property could be held for her on trust (see Gardner, *An Introduction to the Law of Trusts*, Clarendon Law Series (1990), p. 30). Extending the trend started by the Married Women's Property Act 1870, the Married Women's Property Act 1882, s. 1 largely abolished restrictions on the right of a married woman to own property, the effect of that section, coupled with the Law Reform (Married Women and Tortfeasors) Act 1935, s. 2 and the Married Women (Restraint upon Anticipation) Act 1949, s. 1, being entirely to remove any remaining fetters on her separate ownership of property.

Section 17 of the Act arguably gave the courts a wide discretion to determine property rights, but it is now clear that this is not the case.

Pettitt v *Pettitt*
[1970] AC 777
House of Lords

Facts: A cottage was purchased in the name of the wife, the wife providing the entirety of the purchase money. The husband significantly improved the property, using his own labour and money. He claimed an equitable interest, one of his arguments being that s. 17 of the Married Women's Property Act 1882 gave the courts a discretion to award him an interest in these circumstances.

Held: The husband had no interest in the cottage.

LORD REID: Many of the cases have been brought by virtue of the provisions of section 17 of the Married Women's Property Act, 1882. That is a long and complicated section: the relevant part is as follows:

> In any question between husband and wife as to the title to or possession of property, either party . . . may apply by summons or otherwise in a summary way to any judge of the High Court of Justice . . . and the judge . . . may make such order with respect to the property in dispute . . . as he thinks fit.

The main dispute has been as to the meaning of the latter words authorising the judge (including a county court judge and now a registrar) to make such order with respect to the property in dispute as he thinks fit. These are words normally used to confer a discretion on the court: where the discretion is limited, the limitations are generally expressed: but here no limitation is expressed. So it has been said that here these words confer on the court an unfettered discretion to override existing rights in the property and to dispose of it in whatever manner the judge may think to be just and equitable in the whole circumstances of the case. On the other hand it has been said that these words do not entitle the court to disregard any existing property right, but merely confer a power to regulate possession or the exercise of property rights, or, more narrowly, merely confer a power to exercise in proceedings under section 17 any discretion with regard to the property in dispute which has already been conferred by some other enactment. And other intermediate views have also been expressed.

I would approach the question in this way. The meaning of the section cannot have altered since it was passed in 1882. At that time the certainty and security of rights of property were still generally regarded as of paramount importance and I find it incredible that any Parliament of that era could have intended to put a husband's property at the hazard of the unfettered discretion of a judge (including a county court judge) if the wife raised a dispute about it. Moreover, this discretion. if it exists, can only be exercised in proceedings under section 17: the same dispute could arise in other forms of action; and I find it even more incredible that it could have been intended that such a discretion should be given to a judge in summary proceedings but denied to the judge if the proceedings were of the ordinary character. So are the words so unequivocal that we are forced to give them a meaning which cannot have been intended? I do not think so. It is perfectly possible to construe the words as having a much more restricted meaning and in my judgment they should be so construed. I do not think that a judge has any more right to disregard property rights in section 17 proceedings than he has in any other form of proceedings.

It was argued that the present case could be decided by applying the presumption regarding advancement. It was said that if a husband spends money on improving his wife's property, then, in the absence of evidence to the contrary, this must be regarded as a gift to the wife. I do not know how this presumption first arose, but it would seem that the judges who first gave effect to it must have thought either that husbands so commonly intended to make gifts in the circumstances in which the presumption arises that it was proper to assume this where there was no evidence, or that wives' economic dependence on their husbands made it necessary as a matter of public policy to give them this advantage. I can see no other reasonable basis for the presumption. These considerations have largely lost their force under present conditions, and, unless the law has lost all flexibility so that the courts can no longer adapt it to changing conditions, the strength of the presumption must have been much diminished. I do not think that it would be proper to apply it to the circumstances of the present case.

And there is another matter I must deal with before coming to the crucial questions. There are at least suggestions in some cases that property rights may be different before and after the break-up of a marriage. I can see no ground for this. There are other occasions for disputes as to rights of property besides break-up of the marriage, and it appears to me that the property rights of the spouses must be capable of determination immediately after the property has been paid for or the improvements carried out and must in the absence of subsequent agreements or transactions remain the same. There are also suggestions that agreements or arrangements made by the spouses may be rendered inoperative by, or may have a different effect after, the breakdown of the marriage. I suppose that an agreement could take an unusual form, but as a general rule I would think that most improbable. The question does not arise in the present case.

It can now come to the main question of how the law does or should deal with cases where the title to property is in one of the spouses and contributions towards its purchase-price have been made or subsequent improvements have been provided by the other. As regards contributions, the traditional view is that, in the absence of evidence to the contrary effect, a contributor to the purchase-price will acquire a beneficial interest in the property: but as regards improvements made by a person who is not the legal owner, after the property has been acquired, that person will not, in the absence of agreement, acquire any interest in the property or have any claim against the owner.

Let me suppose that a house which requires extensive renovation or improvement is acquired by one spouse putting down the deposit and taking the title. Instalments of the purchase-price and the cost of the improvements will then have to be paid. The other spouse may be willing and able to help, and as a pure matter of convenience, without any thought of legal consequences and without making any agreement, one spouse may pay the instalments of the purchase price and the other may pay for the improvements. On this view the legal position will be different according as the contributing spouse pays the instalments or the cost of the improvements. Payment of the instalments will obtain for him or her a proprietary interest in the house, but payment of the cost of the improvements will not give him or her either an interest in the house or a claim against the other spouse. That seems to me to be entirely unsatisfactory. It is true that the court will do its best to spell out an agreement to prevent this, but I shall return to that matter.

Then go a step farther. There is no question of making any improvements, but the wife who wants to contribute pays all the household bills thus enabling the husband who holds the title to the house to pay the instalments. That wife will have no claim of any kind. And go a step farther still. The wife may not be able to make any financial contribution but by good management and co-operation she may make it possible for the husband to pay the instalments regularly. Again on this view she will have no claim. Opinions may differ as to whether in one or both of these cases she should have any claim.

Views have been expressed that the law does give a claim to the contributing spouse in the first, or the first and second, or in all the three cases which I have outlined. But there has been no unanimity as to the legal basis or the legal nature of such claims. I think that broadly there are two views. One is that you ask what reasonable people in the shoes of the spouses would have agreed if they had directed their minds to the question of what claim the contributing spouse ought to have. The other is that all property used for family purposes must, in the absence of agreement, be regarded as the joint property of the spouses or as belonging to them in equal shares, no matter which spouse bought or inherited it or contributed to its acquisition.

We must first have in mind or decide how far it is proper for the courts to go in adapting or adding to existing law. Whatever views may have prevailed in the last century, I think that it is now widely recognised that it is proper for the courts in appropriate cases to develop or adapt existing rules of the common law to meet new conditions. I say in appropriate cases because I think we ought to recognise a difference between cases where we are dealing with 'lawyer's law' and cases where we are dealing with matters which directly affect the lives and interests of large sections of the community and which raise issues which are the subject of public controversy and on which laymen are as well able to decide as are lawyers. On such matters it is not for the courts to proceed on their view of public policy for that would be to encroach on the province of Parliament.

I would therefore refuse to consider whether property belonging to either spouse ought to be regarded as family property for that would be introducing a new conception into English law and not merely developing existing principles. There are systems of law which recognise joint family property or communio bonorum. I am not sure that those principles are very highly regarded in countries where they are in force, but in any case it would be going far beyond the functions of the court to attempt to give effect to them here.

But it is, I think, proper to consider whether, without departing from the principles of the common law, we can give effect to the view that, even where there was in fact no agreement, we can ask what the spouses, or reasonable people in their shoes, would have agreed if they had directed their minds to the question of what rights should accrue to the spouse who has contributed to the acquisition or improvement of property owned by the other spouse. There is already a presumption which operates in the absence of evidence as regards money contributed by one spouse towards the acquisition of property by the other spouse. So why should there not be a similar presumption where one spouse has contributed to the improvement of the property of the other? I do not think that it is a very convincing argument to say that, if a stranger makes improvements on the property of another without any agreement or any request by that other that he should do so, he acquires no right. The improvement is made for the common enjoyment of both spouses during the marriage. It would no doubt be different if the one spouse makes the improvement while the other spouse who owns the property is absent and without his or her knowledge or consent. But if the spouse who owns the property acquiesces in the other making the improvement in circumstances where it is reasonable to suppose that they would have agreed to some right being acquired if they had thought about the legal position, I can see nothing contrary to ordinary legal principles in holding that the spouse who makes the improvement has acquired such a right.

Some reference was made to the doctrine of unjust enrichment. I do not think that that helps. The term has been applied to cases where a person who has paid money sues for its return. But there does not appear to be any English case of the doctrine being applied where one person has improved the property of another. And in any case it would only result in a money claim whereas what a spouse who makes an improvement is seeking is generally a beneficial interest in the property which has been improved.

. . .

In whatever way the general question as to improvements is decided I think that the claim in the present case must fail for two reasons. These improvements are nearly all of an ephemeral character. Redecoration will only last for a few years and it would be unreasonable that a spouse should obtain a permanent interest in the house in return for making improvements of this character. . . .

LORD UPJOHN (after making similar observations to those of Lord Reid on s. 17):
My Lords, the facts of this case depend not upon the acquisition of property but upon
the expenditure of money and labour by the husband in the way of improvement upon
the property of the wife which admittedly is her own beneficial property. Upon this it
is quite clearly established that by the law of England the expenditure of money by A
upon the property of B stands in quite a different category from the acquisition of
property by A and B.

It has been well settled in your Lordships' House (*Ramsden* v *Dyson* (1865) LR 1
HL 129) that if A expends money on the property of B, prima facie he has no claim
on such property. And this, as Sir William Grant MR, held as long ago as 1810 in
Campion v *Cotton* (1810) 17 Ves 263 is equally applicable as between husband and
wife. If by reason of estoppel or because the expenditure would be rewarded, the
person expending the money may have some claim for monetary reimbursement in a
purely monetary sense from the owner or even, if explicitly promised to him by the
owner, an interest in the land (see *Plimmer* v *Wellington Corpn.* (1884) 9 App Cas 699).
But the respondent's claim here is to a share of the property and his money claim in
his plaint is only a qualification of that. Plainly, in the absence of agreement with his
wife (and none is suggested) he could have no monetary claim against her and no
estoppel or mistake is suggested so, in my opinion, he can have no charge upon or
interest in the wife's property.

It may be that as counsel for the Queen's Proctor quite rightly pointed out this case
could be decided somewhat on the *Balfour* v *Balfour* [1919] 2 KB 571 principle, that
the nature of the work done was of the type done by husband and wife upon the
matrimonial home without giving the worker a legal interest in it. See *Button* v *Button*
[1968] 1 WLR 457. But I prefer to decide this appeal upon the wider ground that in
the absence of agreement, and there being no question of any estoppel, one spouse
who does work or expends money upon the property of the other has no claim
whatever upon the property of the other. *Jansen* v *Jansen* [1965] P 478 was a very
good example of that type of case. The husband, putting it briefly, spent his short
married life making very substantial improvements upon the properties of the wife
which greatly increased their value as reflected in their sale price. The wife recognised
that as between husband and wife he should receive some benefit and instructed her
solicitor to draw up an agreement whereby he was to receive monetary recompense
from the proceeds of sale of one of the properties he had improved when such sale
was effected. The husband refused to accept this so the parties in fact and in law never
did agree. In those circumstances it seems to me clear that the husband had no claim
against the wife even personally and certainly no claim against the property itself either
by way of charge or by way of a share in the property. In my opinion *Jansen* v *Jansen*
was wrongly decided.
. . .

LORD DIPLOCK (after making similar observations to those of Lord Reid on s. 17):
I conclude, therefore, that in determining a question of title to property in proceedings
between husband and wife under section 17 the court has no power to apply any
different principles from those which it applies to the same question in any other
proceedings. It must decide them according to law.

What, then, is the law? Ever since 1882 husband and wife have had the legal
capacity to enter into transactions with one another, such as contracts, conveyances
and declarations of trust so as to create legally enforceable rights and obligations,
provided that these do not offend against the settled rules of public policy about
matrimonial relations. Where spouses have done so, the court has no power to ignore

or alter the rights and obligations so created, though the court in the exercise of the discretion which it always has in respect of its own procedure may, in an appropriate case where a matrimonial suit between the spouses is pending or contemplated, adjourn the hearing or defer making an order for the enforcement of the right until the spouses have had an opportunity of applying for ancillary relief in that suit under the provisions of Part III of the Matrimonial Causes Act, 1965, which do confer power upon the court to vary proprietary rights, upon granting a decree of divorce.

But it is comparatively rarely that husband and wife enter into any express agreement as to the proprietary rights which are to subsist in 'family assets' acquired or improved while they are living or contemplating living happily together. Yet any such acquisition or improvement must have some legal consequences. Family assets are not res nullius. When a 'family asset' is first acquired from a third party the title to it must vest in one or other of the spouses, or be shared between them, and where an existing family asset is improved this, too, must have some legal consequence even if it is only that the improvement is an accretion to the property of the spouse who was entitled to the asset before it was improved. Where the acquisition or improvement is made as a result of contributions in money or money's worth by both spouses acting in concert the proprietary interests in the family asset resulting from their respective contributions depend upon their common intention as to what those interests should be.

I have used the neutral expression 'acting in concert' because many of the ordinary domestic arrangements between man and wife do not possess the legal characteristics of a contract. So long as they are executory they do not give rise to any chose in action, for neither party intended that non-performance of their mutual promises should be the subject of sanctions in any court (see *Balfour* v *Balfour* [1919] 2 KB 571). But this is relevant to non-performance only. If spouses do perform their mutual promises the fact that they could not have been compelled to do so while the promises were executory cannot deprive the acts done by them of all legal consequences upon proprietary rights; for these are within the field of the law of property rather than of the law of contract. It would, in my view, be erroneous to extend the presumption accepted in *Balfour* v *Balfour* that mutual promises between man and wife in relation to their domestic arrangements are prima facie not intended by either to be legally enforceable to a presumption of a common intention of both spouses that *no* legal consequences should flow from acts done by them in performanc of mutual promises with respect to the acquisition, improvement or addition to real or personal property – for this would be to intend what is impossible in law.

How, then, does the court ascertain the 'common intention' of spouses as to their respective proprietary interests in a family asset when at the time that it was acquired or improved as a result of contributions in money or money's worth by each of them they failed to formulate it themselves? It may be possible to infer from their conduct that they did in fact form an actual common intention as to their respective proprietary interests and where this is possible the courts should give effect to it. But in the case of transactions between husband and wife relating to family assets their actual common contemplation at the time of its acquisition or improvement probably goes no further than its common use and enjoyment by themselves and their children, and while that use continues their respective proprietary interests in it are of no practical importance to them. They only become of importance if the asset ceases to be used and enjoyed by them in common and they do not think of the possibility of this happening. In many cases, and most of those which come before the courts, the true inference from the evidence is that at the time of its acquisition or improvement the spouses formed no common intention as to their proprietary rights in the family asset. They gave no thought to the subject of proprietary rights at all.

But this does not raise a problem which is peculiar to transactions between husband and wife. It is one with which the courts are familiar in connection with ordinary contracts and to its solution they apply a familiar legal technique. The common situation in which a court has to decide whether or not a term is to be implied in a contract is when some event has happened for which the parties have made no provision in the contract because at the time it was made neither party foresaw the possibility of that event happening and so never in fact agreed as to what its legal consequences would be upon their respective contractual rights and obligations. Nevertheless the court imputes to the parties a common intention which in fact they never formed and it does so by forming its own opinion as to what would have been the common intention of reasonable men as to the effect of that event upon their contractual rights and obligations if the possibility of the event happening had been present to their minds at the time of entering into the contract. In *Davis Contractors Ltd v Fareham UDC* [1956] AC 696 Viscount Radcliffe analyses this technique as applied to cases of frustration. See also Professor Glanville Williams's analysis of the legal doctrine of implied terms in 'Language and the Law' ((1944) 61 LQR 401).

In applying the technique to contracts the court starts with the assumption that prima facie the parties intended that whatever may happen their legal rights and obligations under their contract should be confined to those which they have expressed. Consequently the court will not imply a term unless it is of opinion that no reasonable men could have failed to form the common intention to which effect will be given by the term which it implies. But such an assumption, viz., that prima facie the parties intended at the time of the transaction to express all the legal consequences as to proprietary rights which would flow from it, whatever might happen in the future, is, for the reasons already indicated, inappropriate to transactions between husband and wife in relation to family assets. In most cases they express none and form no actual common intention about proprietary rights in the family asset because neither spouse gave any thought to an event happening, viz., the cesser of their common use and enjoyment of the asset, which alone would give any practical importance to their respective proprietary interests in the asset. Unless it is possible to infer from the conduct of the spouses at the time of their concerted action in relation to acquisition or improvement of the family asset that they did form an actual common intention as to the legal consequences of their acts upon the proprietary rights in the asset the court must impute to them a constructive common intention which is that which in the court's opinion would have been formed by reasonable spouses.

A similar technique is applied in imputing an intention to a person wherever the intention with which an act is done affects its legal consequences and the evidence does not disclose what was the actual intention with which he did it. This situation commonly occurs when the actor is deceased. When the act is of a kind to which this technique has frequently to be applied by the courts the imputed intention may acquire the description of a 'presumption' – but presumptions of this type are not immutable. A presumption of fact is no more than a consensus of judicial opinion disclosed by reported cases as to the most likely inference of fact to be drawn in the absence of any evidence to the contrary – for example, presumptions of legitimacy, of death, or survival and the like. But the most likely inference as to a person's intention in the transactions of his everyday life depends upon the social environment in which he lives and the common habits of thought of those who live in it. The consensus of judicial opinion which gave rise to the presumptions of 'advancement' and 'resulting trust' in transactions between husband and wife is to be found in cases relating to the propertied classes of the nineteenth century and the first quarter of the twentieth century among whom marriage settlements were common, and it was unusual for the wife to contribute by her earnings to the family income. It was not until after World War II that the courts were required to consider the proprietary rights in family assets of a different social class. The advent of legal aid, the wider employment of married women in industry, commerce and the professions and the emergence of a property-owning, particularly a real-property-mortgaged-to-a-building-society-owning, democracy has compelled the courts to direct their attention to this during the last 20 years. It would, in my view, be an abuse of the legal technique for ascertaining or imputing intention to apply to transactions between the post-war generation of married couples 'presumptions' which are based upon inferences of fact which an earlier generation of judges drew as to the most likely intentions of earlier generations of spouses belonging to the propertied classes of a different social era.

I do not propose to examine in detail the numerous cases decided in the last 20 years and cited in the argument before your Lordships' House in which in the absence of evidence that spouses formed any actual intention as to their respective proprietary rights in a family asset, generally the matrimonial home acquired as a result of their concerted action, the courts have imputed an intention to them. I adhere to the view which I expressed in *Ulrich* v *Ulrich and Felton* [1968] 1 WLR 180, 188–190, in the passage which my noble and learned friend Lord Hodson . . . has already cited at length. I think it fairly summarises the broad consensus of judicial opinion disclosed by the post-war cases (none of which has reached your Lordships' House), as to the common intentions which, in the absence of evidence of an actual intention to the contrary, are to be imputed to spouses when matrimonial homes are acquired on mortgage as a result of their concerted acts of a kind which are typical of transactions between husband and wife to-day. And I firmly think that broad consensus of judicial opinion is right. The old presumptions of advancement and resulting trust are inappropriate to these kinds of transactions, and the fact that the legal estate is conveyed to the wife or to the husband or to both jointly though it may be significant in indicating their actual common intention is not necessarily decisive since it is often influenced by the requirements of the building society which provides the mortgage.

In imputing to them a common intention as to their respective proprietary rights which as fair and reasonable men and women they presumably would have formed had they given their minds to it at the time of the relevant acquisition or improvement of a family asset, the court, it has been suggested, is exercising in another guise a jurisdiction to do what it considers itself to be fair and reasonable in all the circumstances and this does not differ in result from the jurisdiction which Lord Denning, in *Appleton* v *Appleton* [1965] 1 WLR 25, considered was expressly conferred on the court by section 17 of the Married Women's Property Act, 1882.

. . .

In the present case we are concerned not with the acquisition of a matrimonial home on mortgage, but with improvements to a previously acquired matrimonial home. There is no question that at the time that it was acquired the matrimonial home was the wife's property. It was bought not with the help of a mortgage, but with the proceeds of sale of the previous matrimonial home which the wife had inherited from her grandmother. The husband made no contribution to its purchase and the conveyance of it was to the wife alone. The conduct of the parties is consistent only with the sole proprietary interest in it being that of the wife. During the four years that the spouses lived together in their new home the husband in his spare time occupied himself, as many husbands do, in laying out the garden with a lawn and patio, putting up a side wall with a gate, and in various jobs of redecoration and the like in the house itself. He claimed that these leisure activities had enhanced the value of the property by £1,000 and that he was entitled to a beneficial interest in it of that amount. The learned registrar declared that the husband had a beneficial interest in the proceeds of sale of the property in the sum of £300. How that sum was arrived at is not wholly clear. It would seem to be the registrar's estimate of the increase in value of the property due to the husband's work. The Court of Appeal with expressed reluctance felt themselves bound by *Appleton* v *Appleton* [1965] 1 WLR 25 to dismiss the wife's appeal from the Registrar's order.

It is common enough nowadays for husbands and wives to decorate and to make improvements in the family home themselves, with no other intention than to indulge in what is now a popular hobby, and to make the home pleasanter for their common use and enjoyment. If the husband likes to occupy his leisure by laying a new lawn in the garden or building a fitted wardrobe in the bedroom while the wife does the shopping, cooks the family dinner or bathes the children, I, for my part, find it quite impossible to impute to them as reasonable husband and wife any common intention that these domestic activities or any of them are to have any effect upon the existing proprietary rights in the family home on which they are undertaken. It is only in the bitterness engendered by the break-up of the marriage that so bizarre a notion would enter their heads.

I agree with the Court of Appeal that the present case cannot be distinguished from that of *Appleton* v *Appleton*, but in my view *Appleton* v *Appleton* was wrongly decided . . .

Notes
1.   It is clear that s. 17 of the 1882 Act gives the courts no discretion to vary the property rights of the parties established on ordinary equitable principles.
2.   Married couples are to be treated no differently from anybody else.
3.   Lord Upjohn is clearly of the view that improving a property, unlike contribution to the purchase price, will not generally give rise to an equitable interest in it. Lord Reid's position is far less clear-cut, and had the improvements been less 'ephemeral' he may perhaps have been prepared to decide the case differently. It is interesting that whereas Lord Upjohn thought that *Jansen* v *Jansen* was wrongly decided, Lord Reid thought it correct. These issues (which have not been finally determined) are further examined below.
4.   The presumptions of advancement have little if any application to this area of law. See, however, *Tinsley* v *Milligan* [1993] 3 WLR 126 (chapter 11), suggesting that the presumption of resulting trust is still alive and well.
5.   The following provision was a legislative reaction to this case.

Matrimonial Proceedings and Property Act 1970

37.   Contributions by spouse in money or money's worth to the improvement of property
It is hereby declared that where a husband or wife contributes in money or money's worth to the improvement of real or personal property in which or in the proceeds of sale of which either or both of them has or have a beneficial interest, the husband or wife so contributing shall, if the contribution is of a substantial nature and subject to any agreement between them to the contrary express or implied, be treated as having then acquired by virtue of his or her contribution a share or an enlarged share, as the case may be, in that beneficial interest of such an extent as may have been agreed or, in default of such agreement, as may seem in all the circumstances just to any

court before which the question of the existence or extent of the beneficial interest of the husband or wife arises (whether in proceedings before them or in any other proceedings).

Note

This section applies only to husbands, wives, and by virtue of s. 2(1) of the Law Reform (Miscellaneous Provisions) Act 1970, fiancées.

Gissing v Gissing
[1971] AC 886
House of Lords

Facts: Mrs Gissing had been married to Mr Gissing for 16 years, and had paid a substantial sum towards furniture and the laying of a lawn, but the house had been conveyed into the name of Mr Gissing alone, and Mrs Gissing had made no direct contributions towards its purchase. On their divorce, she claimed a beneficial interest.

Held: The House of Lords held that she had no interest.

LORD DIPLOCK: Any claim to a beneficial interest in land by a person, whether spouse or stranger, in whom the legal estate in the land is not vested must be based upon the proposition that the person in whom the legal estate is vested holds it as trustee upon trust to give effect to the beneficial interest of the claimant as cestui que trust. The legal principles applicable to the claim are those of the English law of trusts and in particular, in the kind of dispute between spouses that comes before the courts, the law relating to the creation and operation of 'resulting, implied or constructive trusts.' Where the trust is expressly declared in the instrument by which the legal estate is transferred to the trustee or by a written declaration of trust by the trustee, the court must give effect to it. But to constitute a valid declaration of trust by way of gift of a beneficial interest in land to a cestui que trust the declaration is required by section 53(1) of the Law of Property Act, 1925, to be in writing. If it is not in writing it can only take effect as a resulting, implied or constructive trust to which that section has no application.

A resulting, implied or constructive trust – and it is unnecessary for present purposes to distinguish between these three classes of trust – is created by a transaction between the trustee and the cestui que trust in connection with the acquisition by the trustee of a legal estate in land, whenever the trustee has so conducted himself that it would be inequitable to allow him to deny to the cestui que trust a beneficial interest in the land acquired. And he will be held so to have conducted himself if by his words or conduct he has induced the cestui que trust to act to his own detriment in the reasonable belief that by so acting he was acquiring a beneficial interest in the land.

This is why it has been repeatedly said in the context of disputes between spouses as to their respective beneficial interests in the matrimonial home, that if at the time of its acquisition and transfer of the legal estate into the name of one or other of them an express agreement has been made between them as to the way in which the beneficial interest shall be held, the court will give effect to it – notwithstanding the absence of any written declaration of trust. Strictly speaking this states the principle too widely, for if the agreement did not provide for anything to be done by the spouse in whom the legal estate was not to be vested, it would be a merely voluntary declaration of trust and unenforceable for want of writing. But in the express oral agreements contemplated by these dicta it has been assumed sub silentio that they provide for the spouse in whom the legal estate in the matrimonial home is not vested to do something to facilitate its acquisition, by contributing to the purchase price or to the deposit or the mortgage instalments when it is purchased upon mortgage or to make some other material sacrifice by way of contribution to or economy in the general family expenditure. What the court gives effect to is the trust resulting or implied from the common intention expressed in the oral agreement between the spouses that if each acts in the manner provided for in the agreement the beneficial interests in the matrimonial home shall be held as they have agreed.

An express agreement between spouses as to their respective beneficial interests in land conveyed into the name of one of them obviates the need for showing that the conduct of the spouse into whose name the land was conveyed was intended to induce the other spouse to act to his or her detriment upon the faith of the promise of a specified beneficial interest in the land and that the other spouse so acted with the intention of acquiring that beneficial interest. The agreement itself discloses the common intention required to create a resulting, implied or constructive trust.

But parties to a transaction in connection with the acquisition of land may well have formed a common intention that the beneficial interest in the land shall be vested in them jointly without having used express words to communicate this intention to one another; or their recollections of the words used may be imperfect or conflicting by the time any dispute arises. In such a case – a common one where the parties are spouses whose marriage has broken down – it may be possible to infer their common intention from their conduct.

As in so many branches of English law in which legal rights and obligations depend upon the intentions of the parties to a transaction, the relevant intention of each party is the intention which was reasonably understood by the other party to be manifested by that party's words or conduct notwithstanding that he did not consciously formulate that intention in his own mind or even acted with some different intention which he did not communicate to the other party. On the other hand, he is not bound by any inference which the other party draws as to his intention unless that inference is one which can reasonably be drawn from his words or conduct. It is in this sense that in the branch of English law relating to constructive, implied or resulting trusts effect is given to the inferences as to the intentions of parties to a transaction which a reasonable man would draw from their words or conduct and not to any subjective intention or absence of intention which was not made manifest at the time of the transaction itself. It is for the court to determine what those inferences are.

In drawing such an inference, what spouses said and did which led up to the acquisition of a matrimonial home and what they said and did while the acquisition was being carried through is on a different footing from what they said and did after the acquisition was completed. Unless it is alleged that there was some subsequent fresh agreement, acted upon by the parties, to vary the original beneficial interests created when the matrimonial home was acquired, what they said and did after the acquisition was completed is relevant if it is explicable only upon the basis of their having manifested to one another at the time of the acquisition some particular common intention as to how the beneficial interests should be held. But it would in my view be unreasonably legalistic to treat the relevant transaction involved in the acquisition of a matrimonial home as restricted to the actual conveyance of the fee simple into the name of one or other spouse. Their common intention is more likely to have been concerned with the economic realities of the transaction than with the unfamiliar technicalities of the English law of legal and equitable interests in land. The economic reality which lies behind the conveyance of the fee simple to a purchaser in return for a purchase price the greater part of which is advanced to the purchaser upon a mortgage repayable by instalments over a number of years, is that the new freeholder is purchasing the matrimonial home upon credit and that the purchase price is represented by the instalments by which the mortgage is repaid in addition to the initial payment in cash. The conduct of the spouses in relation to the payment of the mortgage instalments may be no less relevant to their common intention as to the beneficial interests in a matrimonial home acquired in this way than their conduct in relation to the payment of the cash deposit.

It is this feature of the transaction by means of which most matrimonial homes have been acquired in recent years that makes difficult the task of the court in inferring from the conduct of the spouses a common intention as to how the beneficial interest in it should be held. Each case must depend upon its own facts but there are a number of factual situations which often recur in the cases.

Where a matrimonial home has been purchased outright without the aid of an advance on mortgage it is not difficult to ascertain what part, if any, of the purchase price has been provided by each spouse. If the land is conveyed into the name of a spouse who has not provided the whole of the purchase price, the sum contributed by the other spouse may be explicable as having been intended by both of them either as a gift or as a loan of money to the spouse to whom the land is conveyed or as consideration for a share in the beneficial interest in the land. In a dispute between living spouses the evidence will probably point to one of these explanations as being more probable than the others, but if the rest of the evidence is neutral the prima facie inference is that their common intention was that the contributing spouse should acquire a share in the beneficial interest in the land in the same proportion as the sum contributed bore to the total purchase price. This prima facie inference is more easily rebutted in favour of a gift where the land is conveyed into the name of the wife: but as I understand the speeches in *Pettitt* v *Pettitt* four of the members of your Lordships' House who were parties to that decision took the view that even if the 'presumption of advancement' as between husband and wife still survived today, it could seldom have any decisive part to play in disputes between living spouses in which some evidence would be available in addition to the mere fact that the husband had provided part of the purchase price of property conveyed into the name of the wife.

Similarly when a matrimonial home is not purchased outright but partly out of moneys advanced on mortgage repayable by instalments, and the land is conveyed into the name of the husband alone, the fact that the wife made a cash contribution to the deposit and legal charges not borrowed on mortgage gives rise, in the absence of evidence which makes some other explanation more probable, to the inference that their common intention was that she should share in the beneficial interest in the land conveyed. But it would not be reasonable to infer a common intention as to what her share should be without taking account also of the sources from which the mortgage instalments were provided. If the wife also makes a substantial direct contribution to the mortgage instalments out of her own earnings or unearned income this would be prima facie inconsistent with a common intention that her share in the beneficial interest should be determined by the proportion which her original cash contribution bore either to the total amount of the deposit and legal charges or to the full purchase price. The more likely inference is that her contributions to the mortgage instalments were intended by the spouses to have some effect upon her share.

Where there has been an initial contribution by the wife to the cash deposit and legal charges which points to a common intention at the time of the conveyance that she should have a beneficial interest in the land conveyed to her husband, it would be unrealistic to regard the wife's subsequent contributions to the mortgage instalments as without significance unless she pays them directly herself. It may be no more than a matter of convenience which spouse pays particular household accounts, particularly when both are earning, and if the wife goes out to work and devotes part of her earnings or uses her private income to meet joint expenses of the household which would otherwise be met by the husband, so as to enable him to pay the mortgage instalments out of his moneys this would be consistent with and might be corroborative of an original common intention that she should share in the beneficial interest in the matrimonial home and that her payments of other household expenses were intended by both spouses to be treated as including a contribution by the wife to the purchase price of the matrimonial home.

Even where there has been no initial contribution by the wife to the cash deposit and legal charges but she makes a regular and substantial direct contribution to the mortgage instalments it may be reasonable to infer a common intention of the spouses from the outset that she should share in the beneficial interest or to infer a fresh agreement reached after the original conveyance that she should acquire a share. But it is unlikely that the mere fact that the wife made direct contributions to the mortgage instalments would be the only evidence available to assist the court in ascertaining the common intention of the spouses.

Where in any of the circumstances described above contributions, direct or indirect, have been made to the mortgage instalments by the spouse into whose name the matrimonial home has not been conveyed, and the court can infer from their conduct a common intention that the contributing spouse should be entitled to *some* beneficial interest in the matrimonial home, what effect is to be given to that intention if there is no evidence that they in fact reached any express agreement as to what the respective share of each spouse should be?

I take it to be clear that if the court is satisfied that it was the common intention of both spouses that the contributing wife should have a share in the beneficial interest and that her contributions were made upon this understanding, the court in the exercise of its equitable jurisdiction would not permit the husband in whom the legal estate was vested and who had accepted the benefit of the contributions to take the whole beneficial interest merely because at the time the wife made her contributions there had been no express agreement as to how her share in it was to be quantified.

In such a case the court must first do its best to discover from the conduct of the spouses whether any inference can reasonably be drawn as to the probable common understanding about the amount of the share of the contributing spouse upon which each must have acted in doing what each did, even though that understanding was never expressly stated by one spouse to the other or even consciously formulated in words by either of them independently. It is only if no such inference can be drawn that the court is driven to apply as a rule of law, and not as an inference of fact, the maxim 'equality is equity,' and to hold that the beneficial interest belongs to the spouses in equal shares.

The same result however may often be reached as an inference of fact. The instalments of a mortgage to a building society are generally repayable over a period of many years. During that period, as both must be aware, the ability of each spouse to contribute to the instalments out of their separate earnings is likely to alter, particularly in the case of the wife if any children are born of the marriage. If the contribution of the wife in the early part of the period of repayment is substantial but is not an identifiable and uniform proportion of each instalment, because her contributions are indirect or, if direct, are made irregularly, it may well be a reasonable inference that their common intention at the time of acquisition of the matrimonial home was that the beneficial interest should be held by them in equal shares and that each should contribute to the cost of its acquisition whatever amounts each could afford in the varying exigencies of family life to be expected during the period of repayment. In the social conditions of today this would be a natural enough common intention of a young couple who were both earning when the house was acquired but who contemplated having children whose birth and rearing in their infancy would necessarily affect the future earning capacity of the wife.

The relative size of their respective contributions to the instalments in the early part of the period of repayment, or later if a subsequent reduction in the wife's contribution is not to be accounted for by a reduction in her earnings due to motherhood or some other cause from which the husband benefits as well, may make it a more probable inference that the wife's share in the beneficial interest was intended to be in some proportion other than one-half. And there is nothing inherently improbable in their acting on the understanding that the wife should be entitled to a share which was not to be quantified immediately upon the acquisition of the home but should be left to be determined when the mortgage was repaid or the property disposed of, on the basis of what would be fair having regard to the total contributions, direct or indirect, which each spouse had made by that date. Where this was the most likely inference from their conduct it would be for the court to give effect to that common intention of the parties by determining what in all the circumstances was a fair share.

Difficult as they are to solve, however, these problems as to the amount of the share of a spouse in the beneficial interest in a matrimonial home where the legal estate is vested solely in the other spouse, only arise in cases where the court is satisfied by the words or conduct of the parties that it was their common intention that the beneficial interest was not to belong solely to the spouse in whom the legal estate was vested but was to be shared between them in some proportion or other.

Where the wife has made no initial contribution to the cash deposit and legal charges and no direct contribution to the mortgage instalments nor any adjustment to her contribution to other expenses of the household which it can be inferred was referable to the acquisition of the house, there is in the absence of evidence of an express agreement between the parties no material to justify the court in inferring that it was the common intention of the parties that she should have any beneficial interest in a matrimonial home conveyed into the sole name of the husband, merely because she continued to contribute out of her own earnings or private income to other expenses of the household. For such conduct is no less consistent with a common intention to share the day-to-day expenses of the household, while each spouse retains a separate interest in capital assets acquired with their own moneys or obtained by inheritance or gift. There is nothing here to rebut the prima facie inference that a purchaser of land who pays the purchase price and takes a conveyance and grants a mortgage in his own name intends to acquire the sole beneficial interest as well as the legal estate: and the difficult question of the quantum of the wife's share does not arise.

In the instant appeal the matrimonial home was purchased in 1951 for £2,695 and conveyed into the sole name of the husband. The parties had by then been married for some 16 years and both were in employment with the same firm, the husband earning £1,000 and the wife £500 per annum. The purchase price was raised as to £2,150 on mortgage repayable by instalments, as to £500 by a loan to the husband from his employers, and as to the balance of £45 and the legal charges was paid by the husband out of his own moneys. The wife made no direct contribution to the initial deposit or legal charges, nor to the repayment of the loan of £500 nor to the mortgage instalments. She continued earning at the rate of £500 per annum until the marriage broke down in 1961. During this period the husband's salary increased to £3,000 per annum. The husband repaid the loan of £500, and paid the mortgage instalments. He also paid the outgoings on the house, gave to his wife a housekeeping allowance of £8 to £10 a week out of which she paid the running expenses of the household and he paid for holidays. The only contribution which the wife made out of her earnings to the household expenses was that she paid for her own clothes and those of the son of the marriage and for some extras. No change in this arrangement was made when the house was acquired. Each spouse had a separate banking account, the wife's in the Post Office Savings Bank, and each made savings out of their respective earnings. There was no joint bank account and there were no joint savings. There was no express agreement at the time of the purchase or thereafter as to how the beneficial interest in the house should be held. The learned judge was prepared to accept that after the marriage had broken down the husband said to the wife: 'Don't worry about the house – it's yours', but this has not been relied upon, at any rate in your Lordships' House, as an acknowledgment of a pre-existing agreement on which the wife had acted to her detriment so as to give rise to a resulting, implied or constructive trust, nor can it be relied upon as an express declaration of trust as it was oral only.

On what then is the wife's claim based? In 1951 when the house was purchased she spent about £190 on buying furniture and a cooker and refrigerator for it. She also paid about £30 for improving the lawn. As furniture and household durables are depreciating assets whereas houses have turned out to be appreciating assets it may be that she would have been wise to have devoted her savings to acquiring an interest in the freehold; but this may not have been so apparent in 1951 as it has now become. The court is not entitled to infer a common intention to this effect from the mere fact that she provided chattels for joint use in the new matrimonial home; and there is nothing else in the conduct of the parties at the time of the purchase or thereafter which supports such an inference. There is no suggestion that the wife's efforts or her earnings made it possible for the husband to raise the initial loan or the mortgage or that her relieving her husband from the expense of buying clothing for herself and for their son was undertaken in order to enable him the better to meet the mortgage instalments or to repay the loan. The picture presented by the evidence is one of husband and wife retaining their separate proprietary interests in property whether real or personal purchased with their separate savings and is inconsistent with any common intention at the time of the purchase of the matrimonial home that the wife, who neither then nor thereafter contributed anything to its purchase price or assumed any liability for it, should nevertheless be entitled to a beneficial interest in it.

Both Buckley J and Edmund Davies LJ in his dissenting judgment in the Court of Appeal felt unable on this evidence to draw an inference that there was any common intention that the wife should have any beneficial interest in the house. I think that they were right. Like them I, too, come to this conclusion with regret, because it may well be that had husband and wife discussed the matter in 1951 when the house was bought he would have been willing for her to have a share in it if she wanted to. But this is speculation, and if such an arrangement had been made between them there might well have been also a different allocation of the house-hold expenses between them in the ensuing years. . . .

Notes
1.   The distinction drawn in the above passage between express agreement and inferred intention is essentially the same as that drawn by Lord Bridge in *Lloyds Bank* v *Rosset* (below).

2. The interests of the parties were determined on the basis of their inferred intentions at the time of acquisition of the property, and not by their subsequent conduct. In the absence of express agreement, only conduct relevant to the acquisition of the property will generally be relevant.

3. As in *Pettitt* v *Pettitt*, the fact that the parties were married made no difference. The following legislation was a reaction to the decision in *Gissing* v *Gissing*.

Matrimonial Causes Act 1973

24. Property adjustment in connection with divorce proceedings, etc.

(1) On granting a decree of divorce, a decree of nullity of marriage or a decree of judicial separation or at any time thereafter (whether, in the case of a decree of divorce or of nullity of marriage, before or after the decree is made absolute), the court may make any one of the following orders, that is to say —

(a) an order that a party to the marriage shall transfer to the other party, to any child of the family or to such person as may be specified in the order for the benefit of such a child such property as may be so specified, being property to which the first-mentioned party is entitled, either in possession or reversion;

(b) an order that a settlement of such property as may be so specified, being property to which a party to the marriage is so entitled, be made to the satisfaction of the court for the benefit of the other party to the marriage and of the children of the family or either or any of them;

(c) an order varying for the benefit of the parties to the marriage and of the children of the family or either or any of them any ante-nuptial or post-nuptial settlement (including such a settlement made by will or codicil) made on the parties to the marriage;

(d) an order extinguishing or reducing the interest of either of the parties to the marriage under any such settlement; . . .

(2) The court may make an order under subsection (1)(c) above notwithstanding that there are no children of the family.

(3) Without prejudice to the power to give a direction under section 30 below for the settlement of an instrument by conveyancing counsel, where an order is made under this section on or after granting a decree of divorce or nullity of marriage, neither the order nor any settlement made in pursuance of the order shall take effect unless the decree has been made absolute.

25. Matters to which the court is to have regard in deciding how to exercise its powers under [section 24]

(1) It shall be the duty of the court in deciding whether to exercise its powers under section . . . 24 above in relation to a party to the marriage and, if so, in what manner, to have regard to all the circumstances of the case including the following matters, that is to say —

(a) the income, earning capacity, property and other financial resources which each of the parties to the marriage has or is likely to have in the foreseeable future;

(b) the financial needs, obligations and responsibilities which each of the parties to the marriage has or is likely to have in the foreseeable future;

(c) the standard of living enjoyed by the family before the breakdown of the marriage;

(d) the age of each party to the marriage and the duration of the marriage;

(e)   any physical or mental disability of either of the parties to the marriage;

(f)   the contributions made by each of the parties to the welfare of the family, including any contribution made by looking after the home or caring for the family;

(g)   in the case of proceedings for divorce or nullity of marriage, the value to either of the parties to the marriage of any benefit (for example, a pension) which, by reason of the dissolution or annulment of the marriage, that party will lose the chance of acquiring;

and so to exercise those powers as to place the parties, so far as it is practicable and, having regard to their conduct, just to do so, in the financial position in which they would have been if the marriage had not broken down and each had properly discharged his or her financial obligations and responsibilities towards the other.

(2)   Without prejudice to subsection (3) below, it shall be the duty of the court in deciding whether to exercise its powers under section . . . 24 above in relation to a child of the family and, of so, in what manner, to have regard to all the circumstances of the case including the following matters, that is to say—

(a)   the financial needs of the child;

(b)   the income, earning capacity (if any), property and other financial resources of the child;

(c)   any physical or mental disability of the child;

(d)   the standard of living enjoyed by the family before the breakdown of the marriage;

(e)   the manner in which he was being and in which the parties to the marriage expected him to be educated or trained;

and so to exercise those powers as to place the child, so far as is practicable and, having regard to the considerations mentioned in relation to the parties to the marriage in paragraph (a) and (b) of subsection (1) above, just to do so, in the financial position in which the child would have been if the marriage had not broken down and each of those parties had properly discharged his or her financial obligations and responsibilities towards him.

(3)   It shall be the duty of the court in deciding whether to exercise its powers under section 23 . . . 24 above against a party to a marriage in favour of a child of the family who is not the child of that party and, if so, in what manner, to have regard (among the circumstances of the case) —

(a)   to whether that party had assumed any responsibility for the child's maintenance and, if so, to the extent to which, and the basis upon which, that party assumed such responsibility and to the length of time for which that party discharged such responsibility;

(b)   to whether in assuming and discharging such responsibility that person did so knowing that the child was not his or her own;

(c)   to the liability of any other person to maintain the child.

Notes

1.   The Court of Appeal held in *Browne* v *Browne* [1989] 1 FLR 291 that the financial resources of the wife for the purposes of s. 25(1)(a) included large interests she had in trust funds in Jersey and Switzerland. The case depended on her having effective control over (or immediate access to) those funds, so most interests under discretionary trusts would be excluded from consideration for these purposes, as (presumably) would interests in remainder or reversion.

2. It has also been held (in *Jones* v *Jones and Croall* [1989] 2 WLR 852) that a child's interest under a discretionary trust is a financial resource under s. 25(3)(b), for the purposes of determining the amount of maintenance to be paid by the child's father, so long as payments are such as the trustees would (in the exercise of their discretion) make to the child without being subjected to undue pressure.

3. These sections apply only in the event of marital breakdown, and do not alter the law as stated in *Pettitt* v *Pettitt* [1970] AC 777 and *Gissing* v *Gissing* [1971] AC 866 where the parties are unmarried (as in *Burns* v *Burns* and *Grant* v *Edwards*, below), or where the parties continue to be happily married. This last situation is only likely to arise where the dispute involves a third party, as in *Lloyds Bank* v *Rosset*, below.

4. It is obvious from the above discussion that, if the statutory provisions do not apply, great significance is attached by the courts to financial contributions, which are referable to the acquisition of the property. These contributions may take the form of provision of the initial deposit, or payment of mortgage instalments.

By comparison, other contributions are arguably undervalued. Generally speaking, this operates to the disadvantage of the woman living in the home, since it is far more likely that the man will earn more money than the woman, and it is accordingly likely that his financial contributions will be the greater. On the other hand, the woman may contribute in other ways. She may, for example, give up her job to bring up the children, pay the household expenses, or provide furniture or domestic services. Because it undervalues these other contributions, the law appears to work unjustly against the woman (which is presumably why legislation was thought necessary for married couples).

A number of Court of Appeal decisions appeared subsequently to water down the effect of *Gissing* v *Gissing*. The basis of these decisions was the following passage from Lord Diplock's speech in *Gissing* v *Gissing* [1971] AC 886:

> A resulting, implied or constructive trust – and it is unnecessary for present purposes to distinguish between these three classes of trust – is created . . . whenever the trustee has so conducted himself that it would be inequitable to deny to the *cestui que trust* a beneficial interest in the land acquired.

The Court of Appeal took the view that this passage allowed them a great degree of flexibility. The nature of the interest depended on all the equities of the case, and the law might consider not merely financial contributions at the time of acquisition of the property, but all types of contribution, whether at that time or subsequently. It was also argued that equity is a flexible instrument. 'Equity,' said Lord Denning MR in *Eves* v *Eves* [1975] 1 WLR 1338, at p. 1340, 'is not past the age of child bearing'.

However, the Court of Appeal restated the conventional view in *Burns* v *Burns* [1984] Ch 317.

Burns v Burns
[1984] Ch 317, [1984] 1 All ER 244
Court of Appeal

Facts: The plaintiff, Valerie Burns, had been living with the defendant for 19 years, 17 in the house which was the subject of the dispute. She and the defendant, Patrick Burns, had never married, however. The house had been purchased in the name of the defendant, and he paid the purchase price. The plaintiff made no contribution to the purchase price or the mortgage repayments, but had brought up their two children, performed domestic duties and recently contributed from her own earnings towards household expenses. She also bought various fittings, and a washing machine, and redecorated the interior of the house. The plaintiff left the defendant and claimed a beneficial interest in the house.

Held: Since the couple had never married the provisions of the Matrimonial Causes Act 1973, ss. 24 and 25 (see above) did not apply, and the plaintiff's case rested on orthodox property principles. In the absence of a financial contribution which could be related to the acquisition of the property, for example to the mortgage repayments, or a contribution enabling Patrick Burns to pay the mortgage instalments, she was not entitled to a beneficial interest in the house.

FOX LJ: For present purposes I think that such a trust could only arise (a) by express declaration or agreement or (b) by way of a resulting trust where the claimant has directly provided part of the purchase price or (c) from the common intention of the parties.

In the present case (a) and (b) can be ruled out. There was no express trust of an interest in the property for the benefit of the plaintiff; and there was no express agreement to create such an interest. And the plaintiff made no direct contribution to the purchase price. Her case, therefore, must depend on showing a common intention that she should have a beneficial interest in the property. Whether the trust which would arise in such circumstances is described as implied, constructive or resulting does not greatly matter. If the intention is inferred from the fact that some indirect contribution is made to the purchase price, the term 'resulting trust' is probably not inappropriate. Be that as it may, the basis of such a claim, in any case, is that it would be inequitable for the holder of the legal estate to deny the claimant's right to a beneficial interest.

In determining whether such a common intention exists it is, normally, the intention of the parties when the property was purchased that is important. As to that I agree with the observations of Griffiths LJ in *Bernard v Josephs* [1982] Ch 391 at 404. As I understand it, that does not mean that for the purpose of determining the ultimate shares in the property one looks simply at the factual position as it was at the date of acquisition. It is necessary for the court to consider all the evidence, including the contributions of the parties, down to the date of separation (which in the case of man and mistress will generally, though not always, be the relevant date). Thus the law proceeds on the basis that there is nothing inherently improbable in the parties acting on the understanding that the woman —

should be entitled to a share which was not to be quantified immediately on the acquisition of the home but should be left to be determined when the mortgage was repaid or the property disposed of, on the basis of what would be fair having regard to the total contributions, direct or indirect, which each spouse had made by that date. (See *Gissing* v *Gissing* [1971] AC 886 at 900 per Lord Diplock.)

That approach does not, however, in my view preclude the possibility that while initially, there was no intention that the claimant should have any interest in the property, circumstances may subsequently arise from which the intention to confer an equitable interest on the claimant may arise (e.g., the discharge of a mortgage or the effecting of capital improvements to the house at his or her own expense). Further, subsequent events may throw light on the initial intention.

MAY LJ: At the hearing of this appeal our attention was drawn to a number of authorities, to some of which I shall briefly refer, and thereafter state what I think is the general approach adopted by the courts to these disputes which can be deduced from the two leading cases in 1970 and 1971 and those which have followed them.

In *Falconer* v *Falconer* [1970] 3 All ER 449, [1970] 1 WLR 1333 the couple were married in 1960. About a year later a building plot was bought in the wife's name as a site for a house. Part of the purchase price was provided by the wife's mother and the balance was borrowed on mortgage in which the husband joined as surety. A house was then built on the plot with money raised by another mortgage of the plot with the partially erected house on it. As the plot was in the wife's name she was the mortgagor. However her husband again and surety. The husband's father also guaranteed the repayments under the mortgage. After they moved into the house, the husband paid his wife a regular sum by way of housekeeping money. The wife herself went out to work and paid the mortgage instalments out of the total of her own earnings and her housekeeping money. About 18 months later the marriage began to go wrong and the husband moved out of the house. From that time and for two years thereafter he paid one half of the mortgage instalments and the rates on the property. Subsequently the wife formed an association with another man and the husband stopped his payments. The marriage was ultimately dissolved. On the husband's summons under s. 17 of the Married Women's Property Act 1882, the county court judge held that the land itself belonged to the wife but that the husband had a half interest in the house. The wife's appeal to the Court of Appeal was dismissed and in the course of his judgment Lord Denning MR referred to the decision in *Gissing* v *Gissing* and said ([1970] 3 All ER 449 at 452, [1970] 1 WLR 1333 at 1336):

> It stated the principles on which a matrimonial home, which stands in the name of husband or wife alone, is nevertheless held to belong to them both jointly (in equal or unequal shares). It is done, not so much by virtue of an agreement, express or implied, but rather by virtue of a trust which is *imposed* by law. The law imputes to husband and wife an intention to create a trust, the one for the other. It does so by way of an *inference* from their conduct and the surrounding circumstances, even though the parties themselves made no agreement on it. This inference of a trust, the one for the other, is readily drawn when each has made a financial contribution to the purchase price or to the mortgage instalments. The financial contribution may be *direct*, as where it is actually stated to be a contribution towards the price or the instalments. It may be *indirect*, as where both go out to work, the one pays the housekeeping and the other the mortgage instalments. It does not matter which way round it is. It does not matter who pays what. So long as there is a substantial financial contribution towards the family expenses, it raises the inference of a trust. But where it is insubstantial, no such inference can be drawn, see the cases collected in the dissenting judgment of Edmund Davies LJ ([1969] 1 All ER 1043 at 1049,

[1969] 2 Ch 85 at 97), which was upheld by the House. The House did, however, sound a note of warning about proportions. It is not in every case that the parties hold in equal shares. Regard must be had to their respective contributions. This confirms the practice of this court. In quite a few cases we have not given half-and-half but something different. (Lord Denning MR's emphasis).

Megaw LJ ([1970] 3 All ER 449 at 454, [1970] 1 WLR 1333 at 1338) in his judgment quoted a passage from Lord Pearson's speech in *Gissing* v *Gissing* [1970] 2 All ER 780 at 788, [1971] AC 886 at 903 which was to this effect:

I think also that the decision of cases of this kind has been made more difficult by excessive application of the maxim. 'Equality is equity'. No doubt it is reasonable to apply the maxim in a case where there have been very substantial contributions (otherwise than by way of advancement) by one spouse to the purchase of property in the name of the other spouse but the proportion borne by the contributions to the total price or cost is difficult to fix. But if it is plain that the contributing spouse has contributed about one-quarter, I do not think it is helpful or right for the Court to feel obliged to award either one-half or nothing.

In the next case, *Hazell* v *Hazell* [1972] 1 All ER 923, [1972] 1 WLR 301, the couple were again husband and wife. They bought a house for the matrimonial home which was conveyed into the husband's name. The purchase price was obtained in part by a loan from the husband's parents and the remainder by a mortgage from a building society. In order to meet the increased expenditure involved it was agreed between the parties that the wife should go out to work and she used her earnings to supplement the limited housekeeping moneys which her husband gave her, including clothing for herself and the children. The top floor of the house was let and the rent was received by the husband. After 15 years the wife left the husband who stayed on in the house and continued to pay the outgoings. Four years later the parties were divorced. The wife applied under the 1882 Act claiming that she was entitled to a share in the matrimonial home. The deputy county court judge found that she had indeed made substantial contributions to the family expenses but decided that she was not entitled to any share of the house because there was no express or implied agreement to give her one. He went on, however, to hold that if he was wrong in so deciding on that basis, then the wife should have a share amounting to one-fifth. On the wife's appeal, this court held that she was entitled to a share in the ultimate value of the matrimonial home by virtue of the contributions which she made to supplement the housekeeping expenses. On the facts, her earnings had helped her husband to pay the mortgage instalments. In his judgment Lord Denning MR referred to what he had said in *Falconer* v *Falconer* and his reference there to *indirect* contributions by one member of a couple to the purchase price of the matrimonial home, and a little later said ([1972] 1 All ER 923 at 927, [1972] 1 WLR 301 at 305):

Stephenson LJ suggested that it might be inferred that [the wife's] contributions were referable to the acquisition of the house. That seems to be sufficient ground from which the court could and should impute a trust. It would be inequitable for the husband to take the whole when she has helped him so much to acquire it. So I would reverse the decision of the judge and hold that the wife is entitled to a share in the house.

Lord Denning MR then upheld the deputy county court judge's assessment of one-fifth. Megaw LJ agreed and in the course of his judgment, dealing with the question of contributions, said ([1972] 1 All ER 923 at 928, [1972] 1 WLR 301 at 306):

In my judgment it is sufficient if as a matter of common sense the wife's contribution ought to be treated as being a contribution towards the expenses of the acquisition of the matrimonial home.

In *Cooke v Head* [1972] 2 All ER 38, [1972] 1 WLR 518 the couple were not married. They planned to build a bungalow in which they could live after the man's wife had divorced him and they were able to get married. A plot of land was purchased in the man's name and he paid the deposit and arranged the mortgage. Both the man and the woman helped to build the bungalow, the woman's part of the work including demolishing a building, removing hard core and rubble, working a cement-mixer and painting. They both saved each week as much as they could from their earnings. They pooled their savings and used these for mortgage repayments and buying furniture. However, theirs was a relatively short-lived association, for when the bungalow was near completion but not entirely finished they separated and the man alone continued to live in it repaying the mortgage. It seems that the parties lived together for between two and three years. On an application by the woman for a declaration that the bungalow was owned jointly by herself and the man, Plowman J held that she had a one-twelfth interest in the property. She was dissatisfied and appealed. I quote brief passages from the judgment of Lord Denning MR, again with which Karminski and Orr LJJ agreed:

> The particular case of man and mistress came before the Court of Appeal in *Diwell v Farnes* [1959] 2 All ER 379, [1959] 1 WLR 624. The court was divided in opinion. The majority thought that a mistress was not in the same position as a wife. She could recover her actual contributions to the purchase price, but could not claim any part of the windfall on resale. Willmer LJ approached the case much as we approach cases between husband and wife. He would have given the mistress one-half. His approach is more in accord with recent development. . . . In the light of recent developments, I do not think it is right to approach this case by looking at the money contributions of each and dividing up the beneficial interest according to those contributions. The matter should be looked at more broadly, just as we do in husband and wife cases.
>
> We look to see what the equity is worth at the time when the parties separate. We assess the shares as at that times. If the property has been sold, we look at the amount which it has realised, and say how it is to be divided between them. Lord Diplock in *Gissing v Gissing* [1970] 2 All ER 780 at 793, [1971] AC 886 at 909 intimated that it is quite legitimate to infer that 'the wife should be entitled to a share which was not to be quantified immediately on the acquisition of the home but should be left to be determined when the mortgage was repaid or the property disposed of'. Likewise with a mistress.
>
> . . .

Lord Denning MR then considered the various matters which should be taken into account in assessing the parties' share in the family home in these circumstances and ultimately held that the woman plaintiff was entitled to one-third of the net proceeds of sale, instead of the one-twelfth found by the judge at first instance.

Richards v Dove [1974] 1 All ER 888 also concerned an unmarried couple. They first lived as man and mistress in rented accommodation and then in a house which was bought and taken in the man's name. He paid £350 by way of deposit, of which £150 had been lent to him by his mistress. The balance of £3,150 was obtained by a mortgage to the man from the local authority. After the couple moved in, as had been the situation in their earlier rented accommodation, the mistress continued to pay for the household food and gas; the man paid all other bills including the mortgage repayments. Walton J dismissed the woman's application for a declaration that the house was vested in the man on trust for both of them. In his view it did not follow that the application of the relevant principles produced the same result whether the parties were married or not, because it was impossible to leave out of the picture the fact that as between husband and wife the former has certain legal duties relating to the maintenance of his wife, whereas between man and mistress the whole relationship is consensual, with no legal obligations imposed. In his view all that the mistress had done in the case before him was to provide the loan of £150 towards the deposit and then to carry on as they had for a number of years in rented accommo-dation, with the man paying off the mortgage. In truth, as the judge held, his mistress made no 'real' or 'substantial' contribution to the acquisition of the matrimonial home and accordingly was not entitled to any share of it.

Eves v *Eves* [1975] 3 All ER 768, [1975] 1 WLR 1338 also concerned an unmarried couple living together. They bought a house in the man's name partly by the sale of his previous house and partly by a mortgage which he obtained. At the time of the purchase the man told his mistress that if she had been 21 years of age he would have had the house put into their joint names as it was to be their joint home. At the subsequent trial he said that he had used the plaintiff's age as an excuse for not having had the house put into joint names. At the outset the house was in a very dirty and dilapidated condition and the couple each worked hard to improve it. Ultimately, some three years later, the man left the house and married another woman. Penny-cuick V-C held that the plaintiff woman had not established a claim to be entitled to any share of the property and dismissed her application. She successfully appealed. On my reading of the judgments in this court the basis for Lord Denning MR's view that the woman was entitled to a declaration was that the untrue statement by the man that but for her age he would have put the house into their joint names amounted to a recognition by him that, in all fairness, she was entitled to a share in the house, equivalent in some way to a declaration of trust. He went on to say that the declaration was not for a particular share but for such share as was fair in view of all that she had done and was doing for the man and their children and would thereafter do. In this judgment, however, Brightman J, with whom Browne LJ agreed, referred to *Gissing* v *Gissing* and expressed his view that the actual decision in that case was that the wife had made no contribution to the acquisition of the title to the matrimonial home from which it could be inferred that the parties intended her to have any beneficial interest in it. He went on to hold that the case then before his court was different: the man clearly led the plaintiff to believe that she was to have some undefined interest in the property. That, of course, he said, was not enough by itself to create a beneficial interest in his favour but if it was part of the bargain between the parties, expressed or to be implied, that the plaintiff should contribute her labour towards the reparation of a house in which she was to have some beneficial interest, then in his view the arrangement became one to which the law could give effect. Although Pennycuick V-C had been unable to find any link in the evidence, Brightman J disagreed and found it in these circumstances ([1975] 3 All ER 768 at 774, [1975] 1 WLR 1338 at 1345):

> The house was found by them jointly. It was in poor condition. What needed to be done was plain for all to see, and must have been discussed. The plaintiff was to have some interest in the house, or so she was led to believe, although her name would not be on the deeds. They moved in. They both set to and put the house to rights. I find it difficult to suppose that she would have been wielding the 14-pound

sledgehammer, breaking up the large area of concrete, filling the skip and doing other things which were carried out when they moved in, except in pursuance of some expressed or implied arrangement and on the understanding that she was helping to improve a house in which she was to all practical intents and purposes promised that she had an interest.

In the result the court held that the woman was entitled to a one-quarter share in the family home.

Of all the authorities to which our attention was drawn, I think that the facts of *Hall* v *Hall* (1981) 3 FLR 379 are the closest to those of the instant case. In *Hall's* case the couple were unmarried. The woman left her husband and went to live with the man, who was divorced. They bought a flat in the man's name, the woman contributing to the furnishings and the general household expenses. Subsequently a house was bought in the man's name, the purchase money coming partly from the proceeds of the sale of the flat, partly from the man's savings and partly by way of mortgage. Within a year the couple separated. On the woman's application to the county court for a share in the family home, she was awarded one-fifth and her appeal to the Court of Appeal against this award was dismissed. At first sight the decision in *Hall* v *Hall* might not seem to be in accord with the principles applied in the earlier authorities. However, having read the judgments in the case it is clear that the decision proceeded on a concession by counsel for the man, both before the county court and in the Court of Appeal, that in the events which had occurred there had been a resulting trust of the family house in favour of the woman. In these circumstances, save to the extent that the members of the Court of Appeal in *Hall's* case did not expressly say that they thought that this concession had been wrongly made, I think that one should be careful about reaching the conclusion that *Hall's* case extended the basis of the woman's entitlement in man/mistress cases of the type with which we are concerned. With the greatest respect and particularly having regard to the reference to *Falconer* v *Falconer* in the judgments, I think that the concession in *Hall* v *Hall* was wrongly made.

Notes

1. The importance of this case lies in the return to conventional resulting trust principles, after a number of decisions of the Court of Appeal where the court adopted a much more discretionary approach, considering other matters apart from simply the contributions of the parties towards the acquisition of the property.

2. Only *Hall* v *Hall* was actually disapproved, however. It must be assumed that the remaining cases are correct, albeit not necessarily on the grounds originally given. In particular, the decisions in both *Cooke* v *Head* and *Eves* v *Eves* must still be regarded as correct, although the reasoning of Lord Denning MR should now be treated with caution.

3. *Burns* v *Burns* was upheld by the House of Lords in *Winkworth* v *Edward Baron Development Co. Ltd* [1988] 1 WLR 1512. The House refused to infer that Mrs Wing had an equitable interest in the (Hayes Lane) matrimonial home, and the case is a restatement of conventional orthodoxy. She and her husband were the sole directors of Edward Baron Development Co. Ltd, which owned the Hayes Lane house in which they lived. Mr and Mrs Wing had sold their former matrimonial home, which they owned jointly, but the

proceeds (£8,600 after the mortgages had been redeemed) had not gone directly to the acquisition of the new matrimonial home in Hayes Lane, but to pay off the overdraft of Edward Baron Development Co. Ltd.

The reason the case arose was because Edward Baron Development Co. Ltd mortgaged Hayes Lane to Winkworth. Mrs Wing knew nothing of this, and her signature, which was necessary to effect the mortgage, was forged by Mr Wing. The company subsequently became insolvent, and Winkworth brought an action for possession of the property. Mr Wing did not attempt to claim an interest based on his *own* contribution (which was the same as his wife's, i.e., half the proceeds from the sale of the previous property), presumably because his claim was tainted with fraud. No such fraud affected Mrs Wing. She nevertheless lost, because the payment of the £8,600 was not referable to the acquisition of the house in Hayes Lane. Lord Templeman, whose speech was the only speech of substance, expressly followed the reasoning in *Burns* v *Burns*.

An interesting point to note about the *Winkworth* case is that although the parties were married, the legislation outlined above did not apply, and indeed it is unlikely that the Matrimonial Causes Act will ever apply where a beneficial interest is claimed against a third party.

4.   It is clear from Fox LJ's judgment that conduct subsequent to the initial purchase can relate to initial acquisition. It is less clear whether improvements to the property after acquisition can give rise to a beneficial interest. Arguably the respective beneficial interests of the parties should be capable of being varied after acquisition, for example had Valerie Burns after 10 years paid for an extension, doubling the value of the property, although it may well be that the courts would require very strong evidence before inferring a variation in beneficial interests. Another possibility is proprietary estoppel. Both these are examined below.

Thomas v *Fuller-Brown*
[1988] 1 FLR 237, [1988] Fam Law 53
Court of Appeal

Decision: A man had no interest in the house in which he lived with a woman (who had legal title), in spite of making very substantial improvements to it, since the work was not referable to the acquisition of the property.

SLADE LJ: . . . I do not think that we are concerned with the details of the work that [the plaintiff] did, but in fairness to him it should be said that the work was obviously quite substantial. He himself summarized features of the work which he did in an affidavit. In it he said that, *inter alia*, he designed and constructed a two-storey extension, created a through lounge, carried out minor electrical and plumbing works, replastered and redecorated the property throughout, landscaped and reorganized the garden, laid a driveway, carried out repairs to the chimney and the roof and repointed the gable end of the property, constructed an internal entry hall at the property rebuilt the kitchen and installed a new stairway. . . .

At this point I interpose a brief reference to the law. It is perhaps understandable that the defendant, having devoted a substantial amount of labour to the house, though no money, and having seen it correspondingly increase in value, should consider that he should be entitled in law to claim some interest in it. However, it must be said that under English law the mere fact that A expends money or labour on B's property does not by itself entitle A to a interest in the property. In the absence of express agreement or a common intention to be inferred from all the circumstances or any question of estoppel, A will normally have no claim whatever on the property in such circumstances. The decision in the House of Lords in *Pettitt* v *Pettitt* [1970] AC 777 makes this clear. That was a case in which a husband claimed to be beneficially entitled to a share in the proceeds of sale of the former matrimonial home. The house in question had been purchased out of the proceeds of sale of a previous house belonging to the wife, and had been conveyed into her name alone. The husband's claim was based on his having done work on the house by way of redecoration and improvement which he said had enhanced its value by £1,000. Apart from the fact that the parties were in that case husband and wife, the case therefore bears some similarities to the present case.

The House of Lords held (I quote again from the headnote) that:

... upon the facts disclosed by the evidence it was not possible to infer any common intention of the parties that the husband by doing work and expending money on materials for the house should acquire any beneficial proprietary interest therein; and that, accordingly, in the circumstances the husband's claim failed.

I would refer further only to a passage from the speech of Lord Upjohn at p. 818 of the report, where he said:

My Lords, the facts of this case depend not upon the acquisition of property but upon the expenditure of money and labour by the husband in the way of improvement upon the property of the wife which admittedly is her own beneficial property. Upon this it is quite clearly established that by the law of England the expenditure of money by A upon the property of B stands in quite a different category from the acquisition of property by A and B.

I pause there to say that the present case likewise is not a case where the defendant had made any direct contribution to the purchase price of the acquisition of the property. Lord Upjohn continued:

It has been well settled in your Lordships' House (*Ramsden* v *Dyson* (1865) LR 1 HL 129) that if A expends money on the property of B, prima facie he has no claim on such property. And this, as Sir William Grant MR held as long ago as 1810 in *Campion* v *Cotton* (1810) 17 Ves 263, is equally applicable as between husband and wife. If, by reason of estoppel or because the expenditure was incurred by the encouragement of the owner that such expenditure would be rewarded, the person expending the money may have some claim for monetary reimbursement in a purely monetary sense from the owner or even, if explicitly promised to him by the owner, and interest in the land (see *Plimmer* v *Wellington Corporation* (1884) 9 App Cas 699). But the respondent's claim here is to a share of the property and his money claim in his plaint is only a qualification of that. Plainly, in the absence of agreement with his wife (and none is suggested) he could have no monetary claim against her and no estoppel or mistake is suggested so, in my opinion, he can have no charge upon or interest in the wife's property.

In my judgment, with respect, this passage in Lord Upjohn's speech accurately states the law, save that I think that an implicit, as well as an explicit, promise by the owner might suffice to confer on the other party an interest in the land in the circumstances which Lord Upjohn was discussing.

Questions
1.   Would the Court of Appeal have come to the same conclusion if Lord Reid's rather than Lord Upjohn's speech had been relied upon from *Pettitt* v *Pettitt*?
2.   Is any reason given for adopting the views of Lord Upjohn in preference to those of his brethren in *Pettitt* v *Pettitt*?
3.   Why should one not in principle be able to infer an intention to vary beneficial interests from a substantial improvement made after acquisition, and not referable to acquisition?

Passee v *Passee*
[1988] 1 FLR 263
Court of Appeal

Decision: In an appeal on quantification of an aunt's shares in a house purchased by her nephew, the Court of Appeal held that the judge had been entitled to take the cost of subsequent capital improvements incurred by her nephew into account in calculating the parties' shares in the property since it could be inferred from all the evidence that it had been their intention that the share of each should be determined when the property ceased to be theirs on a basis of what was fair, and having regard to the total contributions each had made, including the cost of capital improvements as well as contributions to the purchase price and mortgage.

NICHOLLS LJ: Fourthly, with regard to improvements, the judge made no specific findings on the cost of the work undertaken by the plaintiff, but there is documentary evidence, and it is not disputed, that substantial sums were spent by the plaintiff. A sum of £485 was borrowed on a further mortgage in October 1973 in respect of the cost of reroofing part of the house. That borrowing was repaid with interest by 1978. In June 1980 the plaintiff obtained a loan of £4,000 on a further mortgage from the Greater London Council which, with an improvement grant of £2,500, was for work consisting of rewiring, replumbing and some attention to woodwork in the house. In addition, in 1976, £670 was spent on labour and materials for central heating, and £3,000 was borrowed and used for double glazing in 1983. That sum is still in the course of being repaid.

Mr Jones submitted it was right to give credit for the sums expended, but that this expenditure by itself did not give rise to any change in the beneficial interests. He submitted that, in so far as the judge used the cost to the plaintiff of carrying out these works of improvement as a way of assessing the extent of the beneficial interests, he was in error, because there was no finding by him that the parties had agreed, or might be said to have agreed, that the cost of improvements was to increase the extent of one share to the detriment of the others' shares. He submitted that the judge should have brought the money spent on improvements into account, if at all, by giving the plaintiff credit for the sums actually spent. Mr Jones further submitted that at the trial the plaintiff did not advance such a case, and since the judge made no findings on the amount of the money spent by the plaintiff this item must fall out of the picture.

Reliance was placed on a passage in the judgment of Griffiths LJ in *Bernard* v *Josephs* (1983) 4 FLR 178. At p. 188E Griffiths LJ said this:

It might in exceptional circumstances be inferred that the parties agreed to alter their beneficial interests after the house was bought; an example would be if the man brought the house in the first place and the woman years later used a legacy to build an extra floor to make room for the children. In such circumstances the obvious inference would be that the parties agreed that the woman should acquire a share in the greatly increased value of the house produced by her money. But this depends upon the court being able to infer an intention to alter the share in which the beneficial interest was previously held; the mere fact that one party has spent time and money on improving the property will not normally be sufficient to draw such an inference: see *Pettitt* v *Pettitt* [1970] AC 777. In the absence of any special circumstances, I agree with the judge in this case that the time at which the beneficial interest crystallizes is the time of the acquisition, but to ascertain this he must look at all the evidence including all the contributions made by the parties.

Mr Jones also referred to passages in the speeches in *Pettitt* v *Pettitt* [1970] AC 777. I need not refer to that case because in my view there is a helpful summary of the present state of the law, so far as it is applicable to the present case, by Fox LJ in *Burns* v *Burns* (1984) 5 FLR 216. At p. 224 Fox LJ said this:

The house with which we are concerned in this case was purchased in the name of the defendant and the freehold was conveyed to him absolutely. That was in 1963. If, therefore, the plaintiff is to establish that she has a beneficial interest in the property she must establish that the defendant holds the legal estate upon trust to give effect to that interest. That follows from *Gissing* v *Gissing* [1971] AC 886. For present purposes I think that such a trust could only arise (a) by express declaration or agreement, or (b) by way of a resulting trust where the claimant has directly provided part of the purchase price, or (c) from the common intention of the parties.

In the present case (a) and (b) can be ruled out. There was no express trust of an interest in the property for the benefit of the plaintiff; and there was no express agreement to create such an interest. And the plaintiff made no direct contribution to the purchase price. Her case, therefore, must depend upon showing a common intention that she should have a beneficial interest in the property. Whether the trust which would arise in such circumstances is described as implied, constructive or resulting does not greatly matter. If the intention is inferred from the fact that some indirect contribution is made to the purchase price, the term 'resulting trust' is probably not inappropriate. Be that as it may, the basis of such a claim, in any case, is that it would be inequitable for the holder of the legal estate to deny the claimant's right to a beneficial interest.

In determining whether such common intention exists it is, normally, the intention of the parties when the property was purchased that is important. As to that I agree with the observations of Griffiths LJ in *Bernard* v *Josephs* (1983) 4 FLR 178, at p. 188. As I understand it, that does not mean that for the purpose of determining the ultimate shares in the property one looks simply at the factual position as it was at the date of acquisition. It is necessary for the court to consider all the evidence, including the contributions of the parties, down to the date of separation (which in the case of man and mistress will generally , though not always, be the relevant date). Thus the law proceeds on the basis that there is nothing inherently improbable in the parties acting on the understanding that the woman —

should be entitled to a share which was not to be quantified immediately upon the acquisition of the home but should be left to be determined when the mortgage was repaid or the property disposed of, on the basis of what would be fair having regard to the total contributions, direct or indirect, which each spouse had made by that date.' (See *Gissing* v *Gissing* [1971] AC 886, per Lord Diplock at p. 909).

That approach does not, however, in my view preclude the possibility that while, initially, there was no intention that the claimant should have any interest in the property, circumstances may subsequently arise from which the intention to confer an equitable interest upon the claimant may arise (e.g., the discharge of a mortgage or the effecting of capital improvements to the house at his or her expense). Further, subsequent events may throw light on the initial intention.

It seems to me that the judge in this case was entitled to take into account the cost of subsequent capital improvements incurred by the plaintiff as a factor, if he took the view that, having regard to all the circumstances, it was to be inferred that there was an intention on the part of the parties that their shares in the property were to be arrived at, taking into account not only the initial contributions, but also the sums that were later expended by the plaintiff on the effecting of capital improvements.

Notes
1.   This case is very difficult to reconcile with *Thomas* v *Fuller-Brown*. One possibility is that improvements are more likely to be considered when an interest has been clearly established, and the only issue is quantification. However, nothing in the judgment itself supports this distinction (although support for this approach can be found in the later Court of Appeal decision in *Stokes* v *Anderson* [1991] 1 FLR 391).
2.   It cannot be said that the law is clear on the effect of improvements. If *Passee* v *Passee* is correct, it may be possible to infer that the parties agreed to alter their beneficial interests after the house was bought, but only in exceptional circumstances.
3.   This discussion brings us to the end of one particular type of case. In the cases so far considered, it has been possible to infer intention only from the conduct of the parties. Where there is an express agreement, or where the courts can construe one, the position is quite different, as in the next case.

Grant v Edwards
[1986] Ch 638, [1986] 2 All ER 426
Court of Appeal

Facts: In 1969 a house was purchased for the plaintiff, Mrs Linda Grant, and the defendant, George Edwards, to live in as if married (although Linda Grant was actually married to someone else). The house was purchased in the name of Edwards and his brother. Edwards told Grant that her name would not go on the title for the time being because it would cause prejudice in the matrimonial proceedings pending between Mrs Grant and her husband. In reality, he had no intention of conveying any legal title to the plaintiff.

The defendant paid the deposit on the house, and most, but not all, of the repayments on the two mortgages. The plaintiff also contributed towards general household expenses, provided housekeeping and brought up the children. In 1980 the couple separated, and the plaintiff claimed a beneficial interest in the property.

Held: Edwards's statement that Mrs Grant's name would have appeared on the title except that it could cause prejudice in the matrimonial proceedings was evidence of a common intention that Mrs Grant should have beneficial interest (a half share) in the property. Mrs Grant had relied to her detriment on the common intention, so that she was entitled to a half share on a resulting or constructive trust.

NOURSE LJ: In most of these cases the fundamental, and invariably the most difficult, question is to decide whether there was the necessary common intention, being something which can only be inferred from the conduct of the parties, almost always from the expenditure incurred by them respectively. In this regard the court has to look for expenditure which is referable to the acquisition of the house: see *Burns* v *Burns* [1984] 1 All ER 244 at 252–253, [1984] Ch 317 at 328–329 per Fox LJ. If it is found to have been incurred, such expenditure will perform the twofold function of establishing the common intention and showing that the claimant has acted on it.

There is another and rarer class of case, of which the present may be one, where, although there has been no writing, the parties have orally declared themselves in such a way as to make their common intention plain. Here the court does not have to look for conduct from which the intention can be inferred, but only for conduct which amounts to an acting on it by the claimant. And, although that conduct can undoubtedly be the incurring of expenditure which is referable to the acquisition of the house, it need not necessarily be so.

. . .

It seems therefore, on the authorities as they stand, that a distinction is to be made between conduct from which the common intention can be inferred on the one hand and conduct which amounts to an acting on it on the other. There remains this difficult question: what is the quality of conduct required for the latter purpose? The difficulty is caused, I think, because, although the common intention has been made plain, everything else remains a matter of inference. Let me illustrate it in this way. It would be possible to take the view that the mere moving into the house by the woman amounted to an acting on the common intention. But that was evidently not the view of the majority in *Eves* v *Eves*. And the reason for that may be that, in the absence of evidence, the law is not so cynical as to infer that a woman will only go to live with a man to whom she is not married if she understands that she is to have an interest in their home. So what sort of conduct is required? In my judgment it must be conduct on which the woman could not reasonably have been expected to embark unless she was to have an interest in the house. If she was not to have such an interest, she could reasonably be expected to go and live with her lover, but not, for example, to wield a 14-lb sledge hammer in the front garden. In adopting the latter kind of conduct she is seen to act to her detriment on the faith of the common intention.

MUSTILL LJ: I believe that the following propositions, material to this appeal, can be extracted from the authorities. (For convenience it is assumed that the 'proprietor', viz. the person who has the legal title is male and the 'claimant' who asserts a beneficial interest is female.)

(1)   The law does not recognise a concept of family property, whereby people who live together in a settled relationship *ipso facto* share the rights of ownership in the assets acquired and used for the purposes of their life together. Nor does the law acknowledge that by the mere fact of doing work on the asset of one party to the relationship the other party will acquire a beneficial interest in that asset.

(2)   The question whether one party to the relationship acquires rights to property the legal title to which is vested in the other party must be answered in terms of the existing law of trusts. There are no special doctrines of equity applicable in this field alone.

(3)   In a case such as the present the inquiry must proceed in two stages. First, by considering whether something happened between the parties, in the nature of bargain, promise or tacit common intention, at the time of the acquisition. Second, if the answer is yes, by asking whether the claimant subsequently conducted herself in a manner which was (a) detrimental to herself and (b) referable to whatever happened on acquisition. (I use the expression 'on acquisition' for simplicity. In fact, the event happening between the parties which, if followed by the relevant type of conduct on the part of the claimant, can lead to the creation of an interest in the claimant may itself occur after acquisition. The beneficial interests may change in the course of the relationship.)

(4)   For present purposes, the event happening on acquisition may take one of the following shapes: (a) an express bargain whereby the proprietor promises the claimant an interest in the property, in return for an explicit undertaking by the claimant to act in a certain way; (b) an express but incomplete bargain whereby the proprietor promises the claimant an interest in the property, on the basis that the claimant will do something in return. The parties do not themselves make explicit what the claimant is to do. The court therefore has to complete the bargain for them by means of implication; when it comes to decide whether the proprietor's promise has been matched by conduct falling within whatever undertaking the claimant must be taken to have given *sub silencio*; (c) an explicit promise by the proprietor that the claimant will have an interest in the property, unaccompanied by any express or tacit agreement as to a quid pro quo; (d) a common intention, not made explicit, to the effect that the claimant will have an interest in the property if she subsequently acts in a particular way.

(5)   In order to decide whether the subsequent conduct of the claimant serves to complete the beneficial interest which has been explicitly or tacitly promised to her the court must decide whether the conduct is referable to the bargain, promise or intention. Whether the conduct satisfied this test will depend on the nature of the conduct and the bargain, promise or intention.

(6)   Thus, if the situation falls into category (a) above, the only question is whether the claimant's conduct is of the type explicitly promised. It is immaterial whether it takes the shape of a contribution to the cost of acquiring the property or is of a quite different character.

(7)   The position is the same in relation to situations (b) and (d). No doubt it will often be easier in practice to infer that the quid pro quo was intended to take the shape of a financial or other contribution to the cost of acquisition or of improvement, but this need not always be so. Whatever the court decides the quid pro quo to have been, it will suffice if the claimant has furnished it.

(8)   In considering whether there was a bargain or common intention, so as to bring the case within categories (b) and (d), and, if there was one, what were its terms, the court must look at the true state of affairs on acquisition. It must not imute to the parties a bargain which they never made or a common intention which they never possessed.

(9) The conduct of the parties, and in particular of the claimant, after the acquisition may provide material from which the court can infer the existence of an explicit bargain or a common intention, and also the terms of such a bargain or intention. Examining the subsequent conduct of the parties to see whether an inference can be made as to a bargain or intention is quite different from examining the conduct of the claimant to see whether it amounts to compliance with a bargain or intention which has been proved in some other way. (If this distinction is not observed, there is a risk of circularity. If the claimant's conduct is too readily assumed to be explicable only by the existence of a bargain, she will always be able to say that her side of the bargain has been performed.)

The propositions do not touch two questions of general importance. The first, is whether in the absence of a proved or inferred bargain or intention the making of subsequent indirect contributions, for instance in the shape of a contribution to general household expenses, is sufficient to found an interest. I believe the answer to be that it does not. The routes by which the members of the House reached their common conclusion in *Gissing* v *Gissing* [1971] AC 886 were not, however, the same and the point is still open. Since it does not arise here, I prefer to express no conclusion on it.

The second question is closer to the present case: namely whether a promise by the proprietor to confer an interest, but with no element of mutuality (i.e., situation (c) above), can effectively confer an interest if the claimant relies on it by acting to her detriment. This question was not directly addressed in *Gissing* v *Gissing*, although the speech of Lord Diplock supports an affirmative answer (see [1971] AC 886 at 905). The plaintiff's case was not argued on this footing in the present appeal, and, since the appeal can be decided on other grounds, I prefer not to express an opinion on this important point.

Notes

1. At first sight it seems difficult to reconcile this case with *Burns* v *Burns* [1984] Ch 317, above, but it is clear that, like *Burns* v *Burns*, the case was decided on conventional property reasoning, and not on any special doctrines applicable in this area alone. The crucial element here was the statement by the defendant as to why the plaintiff's name would not go on to the title. This could only be explained on the basis of a common intention that she was to have a half share.

2. Because there was evidence of a common intention (independent of the contributions themselves), Linda Grant's contributions (unlike those of Valerie Burns) were relevant only in order to get round the formality provisions of s. 53 of the Law of Property Act 1925. Resulting and constructive trusts are excluded by virtue of s. 53(2), and in *Grant* v *Edwards* it was necessary only for Linda Grant to show that she had relied on the agreement to her detriment for a constructive trust to arise in her favour.

3. In cases like *Burns* v *Burns* by contrast, where there is no independent evidence of any agreement, evidence of intention can only be inferred from the contributions themselves. This requires a substantial contribution referable to the acquisition of the property, whereas in *Grant* v *Edwards* all Mrs Grant had to show was that she had acted in a manner which was explicable only on the basis that she was to have an interest in the house. This is a far

less stringent requirement. Further, the value of the beneficial interest was determined by the common intention (as evidenced by the defendant's statement), and not by the value of Linda Grant's contributions. In cases like *Burns*, by contrast, where there is no express evidence of a common intention, the value of the contributions will also determine the *size* of the beneficial interest (if any).

Simon Gardner, '*Rethinking Family Property*' (1993) 109 LQR 263, at 264–5

[Note that footnotes have been incorporated as far as possible into the text.]

In *Eves* v *Eves* [1975] 1 WLR 1338 and *Grant* v *Edwards* [1986] Ch 638, the court found an *express* agreement that a woman should have a share in a house owned by her partner. In both, the woman's only hope of success lay with the finding of an express agreement, because she had not made the direct financial contribution needed to allow discovery of an implied agreement. But in both, the partner had explicitly told the woman that she was not to have a share. So on the face of it, there was most decidedly no agreement that she should. The courts based their contrary finding on the fact that in each case the man had added a reason for this refusal to let the woman share the house, which was in truth a bad reason. In one case, it was that at 20 years of age the woman was legally too young to have an interest in land; in the other, it was that any share she had would cause prejudice in the matrimonial proceedings she was currently undergoing with her estranged husband. In each case the court characterised this as an 'excuse,' and went on to say that the man's giving an excuse showed that he actually acknowledged the existence of an agreement that the woman should have a share [per Browne-Wilkinson V-C and Nourse LJ; Gardner notes that Mustill LJ took a slightly different position].

But the fact that the men's statements were excuses (i.e., neither objectively valid nor even sincerely uttered) does not mean that the men were thereby acknowledging an agreement whereby the woman should have a share. If I give an excuse for rejecting an invitation to what I expect to be a dull party, it does not mean that I thereby agree to come: on the contrary, it means that I do not agree to come, but for one reason or another find it hard to say so outright. The fallacious quality of the reasoning in *Eves* v *Eves* and *Grant* v *Edwards* is thus clear. It is hard to think that the judges concerned really believed in it. . . .

Note
Gardner contrasts *Hammond* v *Mitchell*, below, where there was clearer evidence of an express agreement.

Questions
1. Should the crucial factor be the man's actual intention, or the objective inference of that intention on the basis of his words or conduct?
2. If a man wishes to communicate to a woman that her name will not be on the title because the house is to be solely his, does he need to make an excuse?
3. If I make an excuse for not going to a party, am I trying to communicate to the host that I would or that I would not have liked to go?

B: *Rosset* and Post-*Rosset* Litigation

Lloyds Bank v *Rosset*
[1991] 1 AC 107, [1991] 1 All ER 1111
House of Lords

Facts: Mr and Mrs Rosset decided to purchase a semi-derelict farmhouse for £57,000. Mrs Rosset understood that the entire purchase money was to come out of a family trust fund, the trustees of which insisted that the house be purchased in the husband's sole name (this appears to have been the only reason for the legal title being vested in Mr Rosset alone). The house required renovation, and it was intended that this should be a joint venture. The vendors allowed Mr and Mrs Rosset to enter the property a number of weeks before completion in order to begin repairs, and render the house habitable.

During this period Mrs Rosset spent a lot of time at the house, urging on the builders and attempting to coordinate their work (until her husband insisted that he alone should give instructions), going to builders' merchants to obtain material required by the builders, delivering the materials to the site, assisting her husband in planning the renovation and decoration of the house (she was a skilled painter and decorator), wallpapering two bedrooms, arranging the insurance of the house, arranging a crime prevention survey, and assisting in arranging the installation of burglar alarms.

Unbeknown to Mrs Rosset, Mr Rosset was unable to fund the purchase and repairs entirely from the trust fund, and obtained an overdraft of £18,000 from Lloyds Bank, executing a legal charge on the property in their favour on the same day as completion. He later defaulted on the repayments, and the bank sought possession. Mrs Rosset claimed a beneficial interest in the property, binding the bank by virtue of her actual occupation, as an overriding interest under the Land Registration Act 1925, s. 70(1)(g).

Held: Mrs Rosset had no beneficial interest. There was no evidence of any agreement between the parties to share the beneficial interest, and the wife's contributions were regarded as *de minimis*. The principles discussed in this section were applied.

LORD BRIDGE OF HARWICH: . . . [The judge] said:

The decision to transfer the property into the name of [Mr Rosset] alone was a disappointment to [Mrs Rosset], but I am satisfied that she genuinely believed that [Mr Rosset] would hold the property in his name as something which was a joint venture, to be shared between them as the family home and that the reason for it being held by [him] alone was to ensure that [his] uncle would sanction the export of trust funds from Switzerland to England for the purchase. As so often happens [Mr and Mrs Rosset] did not pursue their discussion to the extent of defining precisely what their respective interests in the property should be. It was settled that the property should be transferred into the name of [Mr Rosset] alone to achieve the provision of funds from Switzerland, but *in the period from August 1982 to the 23 November 1982 when the contracts were exchanged, [the parties] did not decide whether [Mrs Rosset] should have any interest in the property.* On one occasion [Mrs Rosset] heard [her husband] say to her parents that he had put the house in their joint names, but she knew that he could not do that and treated what he said as an expression of what he would like to do. In these circumstances I am satisfied that the outcome of the discussions between the parties as to the name into which the property should be transferred did not exclude the possibility that [Mrs Rosset] should have a beneficial interest in the property.

. . .

Even if there had been the clearest oral agreement between Mr and Mrs Rosset that Mr Rosset was to hold the property in trust for them both as tenants in common, this would, of course, have been ineffective since a valid declaration of trust by way of gift of a beneficial interest in land is required by s. 53(1) of the Law of Property Act 1925 to be in writing. But if Mrs Rosset had, as pleaded, altered her position in reliance on the agreement this could have given rise to an enforceable interest in her favour by way either of a constructive trust or of a proprietary estoppel. . . .

[The judge continued:]

Up to 17 December 1982 [Mrs Rosset's] contribution to the venture was: (1) to urge on the builders and to attempt to co-ordinate their work, until her husband insisted that he alone should give instructions; (2) to go to builders' merchants and obtain material required by the builders . . . and to deliver the materials to the site. This was of some importance because Mr Griffin and his employees did not know the Thanet area; (3) to assist her husband in planning the renovation and decoration of the house. In this, she had some skill over and above that acquired by most housewives. She was a skilled painter and decorator who enjoyed wallpapering and decorating, and, as her husband acknowledged, she had good ideas about this work. In connection with this, she advised on the position of electric plugs and radiators and planned the design of the large breakfast room and the small kitchen of the house; (4) to carry out the wallpapering of Natasha's bedroom and her own bedroom, after preparing the surfaces of the walls and clearing up the rooms concerned before the papering began; (5) to begin the preparation of the surfaces of the walls of her son's bedroom, the den, the upstairs lavatory and the downstairs washroom for papering. All this wallpapering was completed after 17 December 1982 but by 31 December 1982; (6) to assist in arranging the insurance of the house by the Minster Insurance Co Ltd home cover policy, in force from 3 November 1982; (7) to assist in arranging a crime prevention survey on 23 November 1982; (8) to assist in arranging the installation of burglar alarms described in a specification dated 3 December 1982.

. . .

The first and fundamental question which must always be resolved is whether, independently of any inference to be drawn from the conduct of the parties in the course of sharing the house as their home and managing their joint affairs, there has at any time prior to acquisition, or exceptionally at some later date, been any agreement, arrangement or understanding reached between them that the property is to be shared beneficially. The finding of an agreement or arrangement to share in this sense can only, I think, be based on evidence of express discussions between the partners, however imperfectly remembered and however imprecise their terms may have been. Once a finding to this effect is made it will only be necessary for the partner asserting a claim to a beneficial interest against the partner entitled to the legal estate to show that he or she has acted to his or her detriment or significantly altered his or her position in reliance on the agreement in order to give rise to a constructive trust or proprietary estoppel.

In sharp contrast with this situation is the very different one where there is no evidence to support a finding of an agreement or arrangement to share, however reasonable it might have been for the parties to each such an arrangement if they had applied their minds to the question, and where the court must rely entirely on the conduct of the parties both as the basis from which to infer a common intention to share the property beneficially and as the conduct relied on to give rise to a constructive trust. In this situation direct contributions to the purchase price by the partner who is not the legal owner, whether initially or by payment of mortgage instalments, will readily justify the inference necessary to the creation of a constructive trust. But, as I read the authorities, it is at least extremely doubtful whether anything less will do.

The leading cases in your Lordships' House are *Pettitt* v *Pettitt* [1969] 2 All ER 385, [1970] AC 777 and *Gissing* v *Gissing* [1970] 2 All ER 780, [1971] AC 886. Both demonstrate situations in the second category to which I have referred and their Lordships discuss at great length the difficulties to which these situations give rise. The effect of these two decisions is very helpfully analysed in the judgment of Lord MacDermott LCJ in *McFarlane* v *McFarlane* [1972] NI 59.

Outstanding examples on the other hand of cases giving rise to situations in the first category are *Eves* v *Eves* [1975] 3 All ER 768, [1975] 1 WLR 1338 and *Grant* v *Edwards* [1986] 2 All ER 426, [1986] Ch 638. In both these cases, where the parties who had cohabited were unmarried, the female partner had been clearly led by the male partner to believe, when they set up home together, that the property would belong to them jointly. In *Eves* v *Eves* the male partner had told the female partner that the only reason why the property was to be acquired in his name alone was because she was under 21 and that, but for her age, he would have had the house put into their joint names. He admitted in evidence that this was simply an 'excuse'. Similarly, in *Grant* v *Edwards* the female partner was told by the male partner that the only reason for not acquiring the property in joint names was because she was involved in divorce proceedings and that, if the property were acquired jointly, this might operate to her prejudice in those proceedings. As Nourse LJ put it ([1986] 2 All ER 426 at 433, [1986] Ch 638 at 649):

Just as in *Eves* v *Eves*, these facts appear to me to raise a clear inference that there was an understanding between the plaintiff and the defendant, or a common intention, that the plaintiff was to have some sort of proprietary interest in the house; otherwise no excuse for not putting her name onto the title would have been needed.

The subsequent conduct of the female partner in each of these cases, which the court rightly held sufficient to give rise to a constructive trust or proprietary estoppel supporting her claim to an interest in the property, fell far short of such conduct as would by itself have supported the claim in the absence of an express representation by the male partner that she was to have such an interest. It is significant to note that the share to which the female partners in *Eves* v *Eves* and *Grant* v *Edwards* were held entitled were one-quarter and one-half respectively. In no sense could these shares have been regarded as proportionate to what the judge in the instant case described as a 'qualifying contribution' in terms of the indirect contributions to the acquisition or enhancement of the value of the houses made by the female partners.

Question
What, if any, is the difference between proprietary estoppel and constructive trust? *Note*: You may care to consider the Court of Appeal decision in *Baker* v *Baker* (1993) 25 HLR 408, and compare it with *Bannister* v *Bannister* and *Binions* v *Evans* in the following chapter. The differences may be quite marked, especially if Lord Denning's views in *Binions* v *Evans* on the application of the Settled Land Act 1925 are wrong.

Note
Given that it is normally (but see *Springette* v *Defoe*, below) far more difficult for an interest to be acquired in the *Burns* or *Rosset* situation than where an independent agreement, or common intention, can be inferred, it is not surprising that post-*Rosset* disputes have essentially been about into over which category a particular case falls.

It is obvious from the discussion in the previous section that evidence for the independent agreement, or common intention, need not be in writing (otherwise no detrimental reliance would be required at all), and indeed it is not even necessary for the parties expressly to have agreed to share the property. In neither *Grant* v *Edwards* and *Eves* v *Eves* was there any evidence of the parties sitting down to make such an agreement, and indeed, in both cases a common intention was inferred from an excuse being made for *not* putting the woman's name on the title. Since the cases often arise many years after the acquisition of the property (in *Burns* v *Burns*, the parties had been living together for 19 years), recollection of old conversations is likely to be extremely scanty. Yet it is upon such recollections that the outcome of the case will probably depend.

Ungurian v Lesnoff
[1990] Ch 206, [1989] 3 WLR 840, [1990] Fam Law 93
Chancery Division

Facts: Mrs Lesnoff, who was a Polish academic, gave up a flat in Poland of which she could have remained in occupation for life, her Polish nationality and her career, in order to live with Mr Ungurian. Ungurian bought a house in London, registered in his sole name, in which he and Mrs Lesnoff lived as man and wife for four years. During that time Mrs Lesnoff installed or supervised the installation of central heating, and the re-wiring and re-plumbing of the house, in addition to other works of improvement and redecoration. Mrs Lesnoff remained in occupation, and Ungurian brought an action for possession and the case finally came to court many years later.

Held: Vinelott J held that Mrs Lesnoff had an interest, but the case depended upon obscure recollections of conversations which were over 20 years old.

VINELOTT J: . . . The words spoken are . . . set out [in Mrs Lesnoff's defence] in the following terms:

In Beirut, over Christmas 1968 and subsequently in London by the plaintiff to the first defendant on a number of different occasions, *inter alia*, the plaintiff used the following words of which the following are a translation from Polish to that effect, 'We will have to look for and buy a house for us in London so that you will feel secure and happy, having lost your house in Poland', and 'You'll have to decide and find the house which you like. I want you to feel that you have something to rely on if anything happens to me'.

The words said to have been spoken and which are reported in those particulars do not support a claim that there was a clear statement by Mr Ungurian that it was to be her absolute property sufficient to found the claim that he constituted himself a bare trustee. They are consistent with the property being bought simply as a home for them both and for Mrs Lesnoff if anything should happen to Mr Ungurian.

. . .

If that is the right conclusion, then the house became settled land within the Settled Land Act 1925 and Mrs Lesnoff is tenant for life and entitled to call for the execution of a vesting deed and for the appointment of trustees. Any understanding that Mr Ungurian was not to be entitled with her consent to sell the house and apply the proceeds, in whole or in part, towards the purchase of another house would be avoided by section 106 of the Settled Land Act 1925.

Notes

1.   From this obscure recollection, and other circumstances surrounding the purchase of the house, and the subsequent conduct of the parties, was inferred a common intention, not that Mrs Lesnoff should have a share of the fee simple, but that she should have the right to reside in the house for life.

The consequences of this were that, because Ungurian's interest was subject to Mrs Lesnoff's prior life interest, there were thereby necessarily successive interests in the property, and the house therefore became settled land within the Settled Land Act 1925. Accordingly, Mrs Lesnoff as tenant for life was entitled to call for the execution of a vesting deed and the appointment of trustees, and, once the house was vested in her, to sell it and to re-invest the proceeds in the purchase of another house or to enjoy the income therefrom.

In reaching this view (which was not necessary for the actual decision) Vinelott J followed the majority view, and not the view of Lord Denning MR in *Binions* v *Evans* [1972] Ch 359, a case which is considered in detail in chapter 10. If he is correct, then Mrs Lesnoff was entitled to sell the house, a consequence certainly infinitely more far-reaching than anything envisaged in the obscurely-recollected conversation that took place in Beirut in December 1968.

Whether or not Vinelott J's view on the application of the Settled Land Act *is* correct is considered further in chapter 11.

The case should be contrasted with the next, where proprietary estoppel reasoning gives the party claiming the benefit of the estoppel no more than the minimum equity necessary to do justice.

2.   For either an estoppel or a constructive trust to succeed there must be evidence of discussions between the parties, however obscure and imperfectly

remembered. It is usually greatly in the interests of the person claiming the beneficial interest to show the existence of some kind of agreement, since then it is the agreement and not the share of the purchase money which determines the extent of the beneficial interest.

Hammond v Mitchell
[1991] 1 WLR 1127, [1992] 2 All ER 109, [1991] FCR 938,
noted [1992] Conv 218
Family Division

Decision: A woman who had not contributed to the purchase price of the property was granted a half share, the case turning on the following statements made by the man:

> I'll have to put the house in my name because I have tax problems due to the fact that my wife burnt all my account books and my caravan was burnt down with all the records of my car sales in it. The tax man would be interested, and if I could prove my money had gone back into a property I'd be safeguarded.
>
> Don't worry about the future because when we are married it will be half yours anyway and I'll always look after you and [the boy].

WAITE J: The template for that analysis has recently been restated by the House of Lords and the Court of Appeal in *Lloyds Bank* v *Rosset* [1990] 1 All ER 1111, [1991] 1 AC 107 and *Grant* v *Edwards* [1986] 2 All ER 426, [1986] Ch 638. The court first has to ask itself whether there have at any time prior to acquisition of the disputed property, or exceptionally at some later date, been discussions between the parties leading to any agreement, arrangement or understanding reached between them that the property is to be shared beneficially. Any further investigation carried out by the court will vary in depth according to whether the answer to that initial inquiry is Yes or No. If there have been discussions of that kind and the answer is therefore Yes, the court then proceeds to examine the subsequent course without legal title referable to a reliance upon the arrangement in question. If there have been no such discussions and the answer to that initial inquiry is therefore No, the investigation of subsequent events has to take the form of an inferential analysis involving a scrutiny of all events potentially capable of throwing evidential light on the question whether, in the absence of express discussion, a presumed intention can be spelt out of the parties' past course of dealing. This operation was vividly described by Dickson J in Canada as: 'The judicial quest for the fugitive or phantom common intention' (see *Pettkus* v *Becker* (1980) 117 DLR (3d) 257), and by Nourse LJ in England as a climb up 'the familiar ground which slopes down from the twin peaks of *Pettitt* v *Pettitt* [1969] 2 All ER 385, [1970] AC 777 and *Gissing* v *Gissing* [1970] 2 All ER 780, [1971] AC 886': see *Grant* v *Edwards* [1986] 2 All ER 426 at 431, [1986] Ch 638 at 464. The process is detailed, time-consuming and laborious.

[Waite J examined the facts in some detail and continued: . . .]

That completes the account of the material to which the law requires me in determining beneficial title to apply the principles enunciated in *Lloyds Bank plc* v *Rosset* [1990] 1 All ER 1111, [1991] 1 AC 107 and *Grant* v *Edwards* [1986] 2 All ER 426, [1986] Ch 638. It will involve asking this question first: is there any, and if so which, property which has been the subject of some agreement, arrangement or understanding reached between the parties on the basis of express discussion to the effect that such property is to be shared beneficially; and (if there is) has Miss Mitchell shown herself to have acted to her detriment or significantly altered her position in reliance on the agreement so as to give rise to a constructive trust or proprietary estoppel?

The answer to that question should, in my judgment, in both its parts be Yes. In relation to the bungalow there was express discussion on the occasions I have already described which, although not directed with any precision as to proprietary interests, was sufficient to amount to an understanding at least that the bungalow was to be shared beneficially. It will, of course, be a question of fact and degree in every case where A and B acquire Blackacre in A's sole name with a mutual expectation of a shared beneficial interest thereafter enlarge it by extension of existing premises or the purchase in A's sole name of an adjoining property Whiteacre, whether B's beneficial interest was intended to extend to the enlarged hereditament. That can only be determined on a review of the whole course of dealing between the parties. I am satisfied in the present case that the parties intended the bungalow, as it became successively enlarged by addition to its own original structure and by the purchase of the adjoining parcels of land and barns, to be subject to the same understanding as governed the original property. Miss Mitchell, by her participation wholeheartedly in what may loosely be called the commercial activities based on the bungalow, not only acted consistently with the view of the situation but also acted to her detriment in that she gave her full support on two occasions to speculative ventures which, had they turned out unfavourably, might have involved the entire bungalow property being sold up to repay the bank an indebtedness to which the house and land were all committed up to the hilt.

There remains the question in relation to the bungalow of what the proportion of Miss Mitchell's, by beneficial interest should be held to be. This is not an area where the maxim that 'equality is equity' falls to be applied unthinkingly. That is plain from the lesser proportions awarded in both *Grant v Edwards* [1986] 2 All ER 426, [1986] Ch 638 and in *Eves v Eves* [1975] 3 All ER 768, [1975] 1 WLR 1338. Nevertheless, when account is taken of the full circumstances of this unusual case, and when Miss Mitchell's contribution as mother/helper/unpaid assistant and at times financial supporter to the family prosperity generated by Mr Hammond's dealing activities is judged for its proper effect, it seems right to me that her beneficial interest in the bungalow should be held to be one-half.

The next question, arising under the *Lloyds Bank plc v Rosset* formula, is whether there is any property in regard to which an intention to share a beneficial ownership should be imputed to the parties in the absence of any express discussion leading to an agreement or understanding to that effect. Miss Mitchell asserts that there is such a property, namely the Spanish house. She acknowledges that there was no previous discussion remotely touching upon the terms of its ownership, but her counsel, Miss Gill, claims that when the parties' whole course of dealing is examined (even according to the more rigorous standards which apply when intention has to be inferred from conduct alone) the intention to constitute Mr Hammond a constructive trustee for Miss Mitchell of part of the beneficial interest in the Spanish house becomes manifest. To support that she relies on the cases (both involving married couples and neither of which was cited in *Lloyds Bank plc v Rosset*) of *Nixon v Nixon* [1969] 3 All ER 1133, [1969] 1 WLR 1676 and *Muetzel v Muetzel* [1970] 1 All ER 443, [1970] 1 WLR 188. I reject that submission. Useful at times though her activities may have been in Spain during the fulfilment of the Soriano venture, Miss Mitchell's activities generally fell a long way short of justifying any inference of intended proprietary interest.

Notes

1. Unlike *Eves* v *Eves* and *Grant* v *Edwards*, there was a genuine agreement where, at any rate as liberally construed in the case.

2. Although a great deal may depend on obscure recollections of old conversations, *Rosset* clearly envisages that the finding of an agreement to share must be based on discussions however imperfectly remembered and however imprecise. If there are no discussions at all then whatever the parties might have assumed, division will be on *Burns* principles. This was the problem in the following case.

Springette v *Defoe*
24 HLR 552, [1992] 2 FCR 561, [1992] Fam Law 459,
noted [1992] Conv 347
Court of Appeal

Facts: No actual discussion had taken place at all, although there was evidence that the parties assumed that they would share equally.

Decision: No common intention to share could be inferred; therefore ordinary resulting trust principles were applied, based on contributions.

DILLON LJ: . . . [I]n *Stokes* v *Anderson* [1991] 1 FLR 391, but so far as I am aware not yet reported, Nourse LJ, in giving the leading judgment with which Lloyd and Ralph Gibson LJJ agreed, said at p. 16B of the transcript that 'the court must supply the common intention by reference to that which all the material circumstances have shown to be fair.' Nicholls LJ used a similar expression in *Passee* v *Passee* [1988] 1 FLR 263 at p. 271A where he said: —

> They intended, or are to be taken to have intended, that each would be entitled to a share to be determined . . . on the basis of what would be fair, having regard to the contributions which in total each had . . . made.

The common intention must be founded on evidence such as would support a finding that there is an implied or constructive trust for the parties in proportions to the purchase price. The court does not as yet sit, as under a palm tree, to exercise a general discretion to do what the man in the street, on a general overview of the case, might regard as fair. But the common intention of the parties must, in my judgment, mean a shared intention communicated between them. It cannot mean an intention which each happened to have in his or her own mind but had never communicated to the other. I find some assistance in this respect in the observation of Lord Bridge of Harwich in *Lloyds Bank* v *Rosset* where he said at p. 132F in relation to the question whether there had been any agreement, arrangement or understanding reached between the parties to the effect that a property was to be shared beneficially:—

> The finding of an agreement or arrangement to share in this sense can only, I think, be based on evidence of express discussions between the partners, however imperfectly remembered and however imprecise their terms may have been.

It is not enough to establish a common intention which is sufficient to found an implied or constructive trust of land that each of them happened at the same time to have been thinking on the same lines in his or her uncommunicated thoughts, while neither had any knowledge of the thinking of the other.

Since therefore it is clear in the present case that there never was any discussion between the parties about what their respective beneficial interests were to be, they cannot, in my judgment, have had in any relevant sense any common intention as to the beneficial ownership of 49, St Andrews Road. I cannot therefore support the conclusion of the Recorder that the beneficial interest was held by Miss Springette and Mr Defoe in equal shares. The presumption of a resulting trust is not displaced. Accordingly I would allow this appeal and would declare instead that they are beneficially entitled in the proportions of 75 per cent to Miss Springette and 25 per cent to Mr Defoe.

Notes

1. It seems that communication must take place, therefore, and it is not enough for a consensus to be arrived at by telepathy. The case can be contrasted with *Hammond* v *Mitchell*, above, where *Grant* v *Edwards* was followed. There was no question in *Hammond* v *Mitchell* of inferring an intention to create a beneficial interest based on contributions or conduct, but unlike *Springette* v *Defoe*, discussions had taken place which were sufficient to amount to an understanding that the bungalow was to be shared beneficially.

2. It can be concluded that although Lord Bridge's speech in *Rosset* has done much to clarify an area of law that was previously rather obscure, the detailed application of Rosset principles might still be fraught with difficulties.

10   SECRET TRUSTS AND MUTUAL WILLS

SECTION 1:   SECRET TRUSTS IN GENERAL

A: Formality Requirements for Wills

Administration of Justice Act 1982

17.   Relaxation of formal requirements for making wills
The following section shall be substituted for section 9 of the Wills Act 1837 —

'**9.   Signing and attestation of wills**
No will shall be valid unless —
    (a)   it is in writing, and signed by the testator, or by some other person in his presence and by his direction; and
    (b)   it appears that the testator intended by his signature to give effect to the will; and
    (c)   the signature is made or acknowledged by the testator in the presence of two or more witnesses present at the same time; and
    (d)   each witness either —
        (i)   attests and signs the will; or
        (ii)   acknowledges his signature,
in the presence of the testator (but not necessarily in the presence of any other witness),
but no form of attestation shall be necessary.'

Note
This relaxes the original provision which additionally required the signature to be at the end of the will, both witnesses to be present simultaneously, and each witness to sign the will in the presence of the testator. The witnesses

may now sign separately, so long as they later acknowledge their signatures in the testator's presence.

The courts have long held that the Wills Act 1837 did not apply to the doctrine which long pre-dated that Act, *donatio mortis causa*. A *donatio mortis causa* is a gift made in contemplation of death, for example where X, on his death bed, hands jewellery to Y, his mistress, intending her to have it if he dies. He does not want the jewellery to go to his 'legitimate heirs' if he dies, but equally, he wants it back if he lives. Y's title to the property arises only on X's death, but the courts do not regard this as a testamentary gift requiring compliance with the Wills Act. In *Sen v Headley* [1991] 2 All ER 636 the Court of Appeal held that the doctrine applied to land, where the keys to a steel box containing the title deeds were handed over, X saying to Y: 'The house is yours, Margaret. You have the keys. They are in your bag. The deeds are in the steel box.' Not only did this *donatio mortis causa* avoid the Wills Act provisions, but also the formality provisions for the transfer of land, Nourse LJ observing (at p. 647):

> Every such gift is a circumvention of the Wills Act 1837. Why should the additional statutory formalities for the creation and transmission of interests in land be regarded as some larger obstacle?

These words seem equally appropriate to secret and half-secret trusts considered in this chapter, whether they be classified as express or constructive trusts.

The purpose of s. 9 (as amended) is to prevent fraud. To make a will is to enter into a major transaction. This must not be done in a light-hearted manner, but must be the result of a deliberate act. Formality requirements are supposed to ensure this. It is also more important than with *inter vivos* gifts to remove the possibility of false claims, as the testator himself obviously cannot refute them. As in other areas, however, formalities can sometimes encourage fraud. But 'equity will not permit a statute to be used as a cloak for fraud', and the doctrines of secret and half-secret trusts have evolved in this area to prevent this.

B: Avoiding the Formality Requirements

There are various reasons why a testator may wish to avoid formality provisions (on this see, e.g., Sheridan (1951) 67 LQR 314). He would certainly wish the identity of the beneficiary to remain secret in the nineteenth century, if a gift of land to a charity was intended, when the Statutes of Mortmain (which prevented testamentary gifts of land to charities between 1736 and 1891) were in force. Another common situation was (and still is) where the beneficiary is to be a lover or mistress, or an illegitimate child.

Possibly the need for secrecy in this situation has diminished since 1969, because until then there was a presumption that a gift to 'children' in a will excluded illegitimate children. Thus it was necessary to identify them to include them. That presumption was reversed in 1969, so that a gift to 'children' on its own will now include illegitimate children (the relevant provisions can be found in the Family Law Reform Act 1987 – see below).

A fully secret trust is where A leaves property by will to B, in a manner which complies with the provisions of the Act, but having come to an understanding with B that he is merely trustee of it in favour of C. The understanding does not comply with the formality requirements of the Act.

A half-secret trust is where A leaves property by a valid will 'to B on trust', but where the beneficial interest under the trust (for example, in favour of C) is undeclared. While the details of the trust are secret, it is made clear that B holds as trustee, and not beneficially.

C: Presumptions Concerning Illegitimate Children

Family Law Reform Act 1987

1.   General principle
(1)   In this Act and enactments passed and instruments made after the coming into force of this section, references (however expressed) to any relationship between two persons shall, unless the contrary intention appears, be construed without regard to whether or not the father and mother of either of them, or the father or mother of any persons through whom the relationship is deduced, have or had been married to each other at any time.

SECTION 2: FULLY SECRET TRUSTS

A: Original Fraud Requirement

McCormick v *Grogan*
(1869) LR 4 HL 82
House of Lords

Facts: In 1851 the testator had left all his property by a three-line will to his friend Mr Grogan. In 1854 he was struck down by cholera. With only a few hours to live he sent for Mr Grogan. He told Mr Grogan in effect that his will and a letter would be found in his desk. The letter named various intended beneficiaries and the intended gifts to them. The letter concluded with the words:

> I do not wish you to act strictly on the foregoing instructions, but leave it entirely to your own good judgment to do as you think I would, if living, and as the parties are deserving.

An intended beneficiary (an illegitimate child) whom Mr Grogan thought it right to exclude sued.

Held: Although in principle the courts will enforce secret trusts, the terms of the letter in this particular case were not such as that equity would impose on the conscience of Mr Grogan, and the secret trust alleged would not be enforced.

LORD HATHERLEY LC: Now this doctrine has been established, no doubt, a long time since upon a sound foundation with reference to the jurisdiction of courts of equity to interpose in all cases of fraud; and therefore if, for example, an heir said to a person who was competent to dispose of his property by will, 'Do not dispose of it by will, I undertake to carry into effect all such wishes as you may communicate to me'. And if the testator, acting on that representation, did not dispose of his property by will, and the heir has kept the property for himself, without carrying those instructions into effect, the court of equity has interposed on the ground of the fraud thus committed by the heir in inducing the testator to die intestate, upon the faith of the heir's representations that he would carry all such wishes as were confided to him into effect. And the court has said that the heir shall not be allowed to hold the property otherwise than as trustee for those with regard to whom the testator gave him the directions in question. So again, if a legatee states to the testator that upon the testator's confiding his property, apparently disposing of it, to him, the legatee, by a regular and formal instrument, he will carry into effect all such intentions as the testator shall confide to him, then that legatee, although he apparently may be held in law to take the whole interest, shall have fastened upon his conscience the trust of carrying into full effect those instructions which he received upon such representations as I have described. And, farther than that, such an undertaking or promise on the part of the legatee has been held, in some cases, to be capable of being inferred from the conduct of the person when secret instructions have been communicated to him by the testator, which conduct has been held by the court to be equivalent to an undertaking or promise on his part that he will abide by the instructions so communicated to him.

But this doctrine evidently requires to be carefully restricted within proper limits. It is in itself a doctrine which involves a wide departure from the policy which induced the Legislature to pass the Statute of Frauds, and it is only in clear cases of fraud that this doctrine has been applied – cases in which the court has been persuaded that there has been a fraudulent inducement held out on the part of the apparent beneficiary in order to lead the testator to confide to him the duty which he so undertook to perform.

Now, in the case before us, Mr Grogan, the respondent, undoubtedly stands in a very favourable position in this matter. The will was made three years before it was communicated to him. He in no way induced the testator to appoint him sole executor and sole legatee of the whole property. On the contrary, it appears from the evidence that he was somewhat surprised when he was informed of the fact. There is therefore no anterior act on the part of Mr Grogan which should induce the court to come to the conclusion upon imperfect evidence of any fraud having been meditated and perpetrated on his part. He is therefore entitled to the benefit of having his conduct regarded as that of a man who stands perfectly *rectus in curia* at the outset of the transaction.

LORD WESTBURY: My lords, the jurisdiction which is invoked here by the appellant is founded altogether on personal fraud. It is a jurisdiction by which a court of equity, proceeding on the ground of fraud, converts the party who has committed it into a trustee for the party who is injured by that fraud. Now, being a jurisdiction founded on personal fraud, it is incumbent on the court to see that a fraud, *a malus animus*, is proved by the clearest and most indisputable evidence. It is impossible to supply presumption in the place of proof, nor are you warranted in deriving those conclusions in the absence of direct proof, for the purpose of affixing the criminal character of fraud, which you might by possibility derive in a case of simple contract. The court of equity has, from a very early period, decided that even an Act of Parliament shall not be used as an instrument of fraud; and if in the machinery of perpetrating a fraud an Act of Parliament intervenes, the court of equity, it is true, does not set aside the Act of Parliament but it fastens on the individual who gets a title under that Act, and imposes upon him a personal obligation, because he applies the Act as an instrument for accomplishing a fraud. In this way the court of equity has dealt with the Statute of Frauds, and in this manner, also, it deals with the Statute of Wills. And if an individual on his deathbed, or at any other time, is persuaded by his heir-at-law, or his next of kin, to abstain from making a will, or if the same individual, having made a will, communicates the disposition to the person on the face of the will benefited by that disposition, but, at the same time, says to that individual that he has a purpose to answer, which he has not expressed in the will, but which he depends on the disponee to carry into effect, and the disponee assents to it, either expressly, or by any mode of action which the disponee knows must give to the testator the impression and belief that he fully assents to the request, then, undoubtedly, the heir-at-law in the one case, and the disponee in the other, will be converted into trustees, simply on the principle that an individual should not be benefited by his own personal fraud. You are obliged, therefore, to show most clearly and distinctly that the person you wish to convert into a trustee acted *malo animo*. You must show distinctly that he knew that the testator or the intestate was beguiled and deceived by his conduct. If you are not in a condition to affirm that without any misgiving, or possibility of mistake, you are not warranted in affixing on the individual the *delictum* of fraud, which you must do before you convert him into a trustee.

Note

Lord Westbury's speech is in much stronger terms than that of Lord Hatherley, requiring a *malus animus* to be proved in the clearest and most indisputable terms. Yet his speech seems most strongly to have influenced academics who have commented on the case, and to have had the greater influence on the subsequent development of the law relating to secret trusts. Recently, however, the courts have been moving away from so strict a requirement: see especially *Ottaway* v *Norman* [1972] Ch 698 (below).

On one view, the passage from Lord Westbury's speech above requires that a deliberate intention to deceive must be shown on B's part (for example, where B had deliberately induced the testator to leave the property to him in the will, on the clear representation that he would hold it in trust for C), and it could also be argued that the standard of proof is as in common law fraud; in other words, a very high standard indeed is required. It may well be that this was indeed what Lord Westbury meant. However, the statement has recently been explained in different terms: '*Malus animus*' may mean no more than the state of mind required for equity to impose a constructive trust on B's conscience, a very different proposition from common law fraud. Further, clearest and most indisputable evidence may mean no more than the standard of proof which the court will require before rectifying a written instrument. This is, at any rate, how the passage was interpreted by Brightman J in *Ottaway* v *Norman* [1972] Ch 698.

B: Modern Interpretations

Ottaway v Norman
[1972] Ch 698
Chancery Division

Facts: Miss Hodges' employer, Mr Ottaway, left her his bungalow in his will, on terms that she would leave it by her own will to Mr Ottaway's son. Miss Hodges later changed her mind and left her property to a cousin.

According to the evidence given by the son and his wife, Miss Hodges also undertook to leave them the furniture and other contents, including her money.

Held: Brightman J accepted that there had been an arrangement between old Mr Ottaway and Miss Hodges that she should leave the bungalow to the son, and imposed a constructive trust upon the bungalow in the hands of Miss Hodges' executor. He also accepted that the secret trust comprised such furnishings and fixtures as Miss Hodges had received under Mr Ottaway's will, but not that it included all Miss Hodges' other property and cash from whatever source.

BRIGHTMAN J: It will be convenient to call the person upon whom such a trust is imposed the 'primary donee' and the beneficiary under that trust the 'secondary donee'. The essential elements which must be proved to exist are: (i) the intention of the testator to subject the primary donee to an obligation in favour of the secondary donee, (ii) communication of that intention to the primary donee; and (iii) the acceptance of that obligation by the primary donee either expressly or by acquiescence. It is immaterial whether these elements precede or succeed the will of the donor. I am informed that there is no recent reported case where the obligation imposed on the primary donee is an obligation to make a will in favour of the secondary donee as distinct from some form of *inter vivos* transfer. But it does not seem to me that there can really be any distinction which can validly be taken on behalf of the defendant in the present case. The basis of the doctrine of a secret trust is the obligation imposed on the conscience of the primary donee and it does not seem to me that there is any materiality in the machinery by which the donor intends that that obligation shall be carried out.

Mr Buckle, for Mr Norman, relied strongly on *McCormick v Grogan* (1869) LR 4 HL 82 [above].

[Brightman J set out the facts of *McCormick v Grogan*, and extracts from the speech of Lord Westbury, the effect of which was that the equitable jurisdiction is founded on personal fraud, and that a *malus animus* must be proved by the clearest and most indisputable evidence. He continued:]

Founding himself on Lord Westbury Mr Buckle sought at one stage to deploy an argument that a person could never succeed in establishing a secret trust unless he could show that the primary donee was guilty of deliberate and conscious wrongdoing of which he said there was no evidence in the case before me. That proposition, if correct, would lead to the surprising result that if the primary donee faithfully observed the obligation imposed on him there would not ever have been a trust at any time in existence. The argument was discarded, and I think rightly. Mr Buckle then fastened on the words 'clearest and most indisputable evidence' and he submitted that an exceptionally high standard of proof was needed to establish a secret trust. I do not think that Lord Westbury's words mean more than this: that if a will contains a gift which is in terms absolute, clear evidence is needed before the court will assume that the testator did not mean what he said. It is perhaps analogous to the standard of proof which this court requires before it will rectify a written instrument, for there again a party is saying that neither meant what they have written.

Notes

1. This was a rather unusual variety of secret trust, in that Miss Hodges's undertaking was to leave property received under a will in her own will, but it had been established in *Re Gardner (No. 1)* [1920] 2 Ch 523 that an agreement to make provision for beneficiaries after one's death could be enforced. In that case, a wife had left her estate to her husband who had agreed to divide the property among beneficiaries on his death, but he died before making his will. The Court of Appeal thought that he held the property for himself for life, and for the beneficiaries after his death.

2. At the time of the arrangement between Miss Hodges and the testator Ottaway, she clearly intended to carry out her promise to leave the land to Ottaway's son in her own will. There was therefore no fraud in the sense required, at any rate by Lord Westbury, in *McCormick v Grogan*.

3. The standard of proof was the ordinary civil standard of balance of probabilities. See further *Re Snowden* [1979] Ch 528 (below).

4. The fact that the trust was oral was not a bar to its enforcement, despite the Law of Property Act 1925, s. 53(1)(b), because the executor was held to be a constructive trustee of the bungalow.

Re Snowden (deceased)
[1979] Ch 528, [1979] 2 All ER 172
Chancery Division

Facts: The testatrix, an elderly widow living with a wealthy older brother decided to change her will, although she was not clear as to how her estate should be disposed of. The evidence suggested that she thought that the easiest method of disposal would be to leave it 'to her brother to split up the remainder as he thought best'. There was evidence that she intended that the residue should be left to her brother to distribute 'between her nephews and nieces equally' and that the brother 'could then see everybody and look after the division for her'. There was other evidence that she wanted 'to be fair to everyone' and that her brother 'would know what to do', and that the brother had agreed 'to deal with everything' for her.

Under the will, the residue of the testatrix's estate was left to the brother absolutely. The testatrix died six days after signing the will, and six days later the brother also died, leaving all his estate to his only son. One of the executors of the testatrix's will sought the determination of the court on how the residue of the testatrix's estate should be distributed.

Held: There was no secret trust in this case. The brother therefore took the residue free from any trust, and on his death it passed to his son absolutely.

In the absence of fraud or other special circumstances, the standard of proof that was required to establish a secret trust was merely the ordinary civil standard of proof required to establish an ordinary trust. Although the testatrix had executed the will on the basis of some arrangement between herself and her brother regarding disposition of the residue, on the evidence it was merely a moral or family obligation imposed on the brother and not a secret trust.

SIR ROBERT MEGARRY V-C: Now it seems perfectly clear that the will was executed by the testatrix on the basis of some arrangement that was made between her and her brother regarding the gift of residue to him. The question is what that arrangement was. In particular, did it impose a trust, or did it amount to a mere moral or family obligation? If it was a trust, what were the terms of that trust? Although these questions are distinct, they are obviously interrelated to some degree. The more uncertain the terms of the obligation, the more likely it is to be a moral obligation rather than a trust: many a moral obligation is far too indefinite to be enforceable as a trust. . . .

I cannot say that there is no evidence from which it could be inferred that a secret trust was created. At the same time, that evidence is far from being overwhelming. One question that arises is thus whether the standard of proof required to establish a secret trust is merely the ordinary civil standard of proof, or whether it is a higher and more cogent standard. If it is the latter, I feel no doubt that the claim that there is a secret trust must fail. On this question, *Ottaway v Norman* [1972] Ch 698 [above] was cited; it was, indeed, the only authority that was put before me. According to the headnote, the standard of proof 'was not an exceptionally high one but was analogous to that required before the court would rectify a written instrument'. When one turns to the judgment, one finds that what Brightman J said was that Lord Westbury's words in *McCormick v Grogan* (1869) LR 4 HL 82 at 97 [above], a case on secret trusts, did not mean that an exceptionally high standard of proof was needed, but meant no more than that —

if a will contains a gift which is in terms absolute, clear evidence is needed before the court will assume that the testator did not mean what he said. It is perhaps analogous to the standard of proof which this court requires before it will rectify a written instrument, for there again a party is saying that neither meant what they have written.

On this, I would make four comments. . . .

Fourth, I am not sure that it is right to assume that there is a single, uniform standard of proof for all secret trusts. The proposition of Lord Westbury in *McCormick v Grogan* with which Brightman J was pressed in *Ottaway v Norman* was that the jurisdiction in cases of secret trust was —

founded altogether on personal fraud. It is a jurisdiction by which a court of equity, proceeding on the ground of fraud, converts the party who has committed it into a trustee for the party who is injured by that fraud. Now, being a jurisdiction founded on personal fraud, it is imcumbent on the court to see that a fraud, a *malus animus*, is proved by the clearest and most indisputable evidence.

Of that, it is right to say that the law on the subject has not stood still since 1869, and that it is now clear that secret trusts may be established in cases where there is no possibility of fraud. *McCormick* v *Grogan* has to be read in the light both of earlier cases that were not cited, and also of subsequent cases, in particular *Blackwell* v *Blackwell* [1929] AC 318 [below]. It seems to me that fraud comes into the matter in two ways. First, it provides a historical explanation of the doctrine of secret trusts; the doctrine was invoked as a means of preventing fraud. That, however, does not mean that fraud is an essential ingredient for the application of the doctrine: the reason for the rule is not part of the rule itself. Second, there are cases within the doctrine where fraud is indeed involved. There are cases where for the legatee to assert that he is a beneficial owner, free from any trust, would be a fraud on his part.

It is to the latter aspect of fraud that it seems to me that Lord Westbury's words are applicable. If a secret trust can be held to exist in a particular case only by holding the legatee guilty of fraud, then no secret trust should be found unless the standard of proof suffices for fraud. On the other hand, if there is no question of fraud, why should so high a standard apply? In such a case, I find it difficult to see why the mere fact that the historical origin of the doctrine lay in the prevention of fraud should impose the high standard of proof for fraud in a case in which no issue of fraud arises. In accordance with the general rule of evidence, the standard of proof should vary with the nature of the issue and its gravity. . . .

Now in the present case there is no question of fraud. . . . The question is simply that of the ordinary standard of evidence required to establish a trust.

Note

This case appears at first sight to water down the general statements of Brightman J in *Ottaway* v *Norman* (above) on the standard of proof required to establish a secret trust. Sir Robert Megarry V-C appears to envisage two (or more) standards of proof depending on whether or not it is necessary to allege fraud in order to establish the trust.

The approach only makes sense, I would suggest, if fraud in the criminal law sense is ever required to establish a secret trust, for it is only to common law fraud that the higher standard of proof is appropriate. It is very unlikely, however, that common law fraud need ever be proved to establish a secret trust.

In any case, Sir Robert Megarry's remarks are only dicta, since in the case there was no evidence of a trust, whatever standard was required.

C: Nature of the Fraud

If the defeat of the intended trustee's (B's) fraudulent profit is all that is desired, it should be sufficient merely to compel him to hold the property on a resulting trust for the testator's estate. This solution would deprive B of his personal gain, and the policy of the Wills Act would appear to be effected. Why should equity further disregard the requirements of the Wills Act 1837 (as later amended), to the extent of giving effect to the testator's oral instruction that the property should go to someone not named in the will?

It should be remembered, however, that the gift to B depended in the first place on B's promise to carry out the wishes of the testator. Hodge [1980]

Conv 341 argues that the nature of B's fraud lies not simply in keeping the property personally, but in the fact that it was the promise to carry out the testator's wishes *in their exact terms* which induced the testator to leave his property to the intended trustee. It is the intended trustee's (B's) failure to do this which makes the fraud, not the element of greed.

B's fraud then, in equity, lies in the defeat of the testator's wishes, not necessarily in his own personal gain. He would be just as fraudulent with regard to the testator's confidence if he gave the property to a charity, as he would be if he kept it for himself. And the testator would be no less defrauded if the intended trustee were (say) to hand over the gift intended for the testator's mistress to his innocent and long-suffering wife. On this argument, nothing less than the enforcement of the testator's wishes will suffice to avert the fraud.

D: Limitations on Enforcement of Fully Secret Trusts

It is clear that once B has received a gift absolutely, any subsequently imposed obligations cannot deprive him of that gift. Apart from the principle that gifts are irrevocable, there is no reason, in such a case, to impose on B's conscience.

Equally, of course, if the intended trustee knew nothing about the trust until after the testator's death, there could have been no fraud in the procuring of the bequest, and thus no reason for the court to compel the intended trustee to do anything in particular with what is now his own property.

Wallgrave v Tebbs
(1855) 2 K & J 313
Vice Chancellor

Facts: The existence of the secret trust, in favour of a charity, was not communicated to B until after A's death. The testator had left property to close friends (B) without informing them in his lifetime that he wished the land to be used for a religious charitable purpose (i.e., in favour of C).

Held: B was entitled to the property absolutely.

Notes
1.   If a secret trust had been found to exist it would have been void under the (now repealed) Statutes of Mortmain. As it was, the friends were free to carry out the testator's wishes. If, as the testator's relatives had argued, a secret trust had been created, they would have had to hold the property on resulting trust *for those relatives*, the purpose of the trust being unlawful. Hence the surprising situation that the very last people who might be expected to argue for a secret trust (the relatives) did so in that case, and in other cases to which the Statutes of Mortmain applied.
2.   The case is authority for the proposition that for a fully secret trust to be enforced, the intended trustee must be told of the existence of the trust before the testator's death. There is no particular difficulty in justifying the decision

in *Wallgrave* v *Tebbs*, since if the intended trustee knew nothing about the trust until after the testator's death, there could have been no fraud in the procuring of the bequest, and thus no reason for the court to compel the intended trustee to do anything in particular with what is now his own property.

3.   The decision seems correct in principle, anyway, because any other decision would have permitted the testator (A) to derogate from his grant. A bequest ought not to be 'snatched back' after it has been made, any more than a birthday present could be later reclaimed.

Re Boyes, Boyes v Carritt
(1884) 26 ChD 531
Chancery Division

Facts: A legacy was given to the testator's solicitor, who was told, before the testator's death, that he was to hold the residuary estate upon trust. However, he was not told its terms until a letter was found, after the death of the testator, which directed him to hold the residuary estate on behalf of a lady who was not the testator's wife. The solicitor wished to carry out the testator's wishes, but the validity of the trust was challenged by the testator's family.

Held: The solicitor held the property as trustee, but on resulting trust for the testator's estate.

KAY J: The result is that Mr Carritt [the solicitor] admits that he is a trustee of all the property given to him by the will. He desires to carry out the wishes of the testator as expressed in the two letters, but of course he can only do so if they constitute a binding trust as against the next of kin.

If it had been expressed on the face of the will that the defendant was a trustee, but the trusts were not thereby declared, it is quite clear that no trust afterwards declared by a paper not executed as a will could be binding. . . . In such a case the legatee would be trustee for the next of kin. [See also *Re Keen* [1937] Ch 236, below and *Re Bateman's WT* [1970] 1 WLR 1463, below.]

There is another well-known class of cases where no trust appears on the face of the will, but the testator has been induced to make the will, or, having made it, has been induced not to revoke it by a promise on the part of the devisee or legatee to deal with the property, or some part of it in a specified manner. In these cases the court has compelled discovery and performance of the promise, treating it as a trust binding the conscience of the donee, on the ground that otherwise a fraud would be committed, because it is to be presumed that if it had not been for such promise the testator would not have made or would have revoked the gift. The principle of these decisions is precisely the same as in the case of an heir who has induced a testator not to make a will devising the estate away from him by a promise that if the estate were allowed to descend he would make a certain provision out of it for a named person: . . . *Wallgrave* v *Tebbs* (1855) 2 K & J 313; *McCormick* v *Grogan* (1869) LR 4 HL 82. But no case has ever yet decided that a testator can by imposing a trust upon his devisee or legatee, the objects of which he does not communicate to him, enable himself to evade the Statute of Wills by declaring those trusts in an unattested paper found after his death.

The essence of all those decisions is that the devisee or legatee accepts a particular trust which thereupon becomes binding upon him, and which it would be a fraud in him not to carry into effect.

If the trust was not declared when the will was made, it is essential in order to make it binding, that it should be communicated to the devisee or legatee in the testator's lifetime and that he should accept that particular trust. It may possibly be that he would be bound if the trust had been put in writing and placed in his hands in a sealed envelope, and he had engaged that he would hold the property given to him by the will upon the trust so declared although he did not know the actual terms of the trust: *McCormick* v *Grogan*. But the reason is that it must be assumed if he had not so accepted the will would be revoked.

Note

Re Boyes extends the principle of *Wallgrave* v *Tebbs* by requiring the *precise terms* of the secret trust to be communicated before the testator's death. It is enough, however, for the intended trustee to be aware of where the terms of the trust could be found (for example, if the terms of the trust are to be placed in a sealed letter to be opened only after the testator's death). Then it could be said that he accepted those terms and was bound by them. In this situation, he would hold the property on the terms of the secret trust: *Re Keen* [1937] Ch 236, 242 (see below).

Although the principle in *Re Boyes* is said to be fraud, the result arguably perpetrated a fraud on the testator, because A obviously did not intend the property to go to his estate. There is nothing in the fraud basis of enforcement which would require that an intended trustee must know the terms of the trust by the time the will is executed. There is no real difference between making a bequest on the strength of the intended trustee's promise, and leaving that bequest unrevoked on the strength of his later assurance. So, there is no reason to refuse to enforce the trust where the intended trustee becomes aware of its terms only after the execution of the will. All that is necessary is that he should be aware of them, or where they are to be found, before the bequest takes effect, i.e., upon the testator's death.

Further, in *Re Boyes* the intended trustee (B) was willing to carry out those terms. It seems that the case must be explained (if indeed it is correct at all) as one in which the scope of any possible fraud was limited to denying the existence of the trust. The intended trustee could hardly be said to have procured the bequest by a promise to adhere to its terms, since he did not know them. All he knew was that the testator wished him to take the property in the capacity of trustee and not beneficially, so by compelling him to hold as trustee the court had done all it needed to in order to make him comply with the terms on which the bequest had been granted.

SECTION 3: HALF-SECRET TRUSTS

A: Basis of Enforcement

Half-secret trusts, like fully-secret trusts, can also in principle be enforced by the intended beneficiary. The leading House of Lords authority is *Blackwell* v *Blackwell* [1929] AC 318. The justification for enforcement of half-secret trusts is the same as that for fully secret trusts, that equity imposes upon the conscience of the secret trustee for the prevention of fraud.

It is sometimes argued that the fraud theory ought to draw a distinction between fully secret and half-secret trusts, on the ground that there is no possibility of an intended trustee of a half-secret trust claiming the property for himself, since the fact of the trust is plain from the will. All that is needed to avert fraud, it is argued, is to compel him to hold on resulting trust for the testator's estate. However, Hodge's reasoning (above) applies as much to half-secret trusts as to their fully secret cousins, and the following extract is consistent with Hodge's view.

Blackwell v *Blackwell*
[1929] AC 318
House of Lords

Facts: By a codicil to his will a testator transferred £12,000 to five trustees, to apply the income 'for the purposes indicated by me to them', with power to pay over the capital sum of £8,000 'to such person or persons indicated by me to them'. He had given detailed oral instructions on the codicil to one of the trustees, and all five knew the general object of the codicil before its execution. The trustees accordingly proposed to pay the income to a lady who was not the testator's wife. The testator's legitimate family challenged the validity of the half-secret trust.

Held: The half-secret trust was valid.

VISCOUNT SUMNER: For the prevention of fraud equity fastens on the conscience of the legatee a trust, a trust, that is, which otherwise would be inoperative; in other words it makes him do what the will in itself has nothing to do with; it lets him take what the will gives him and then makes him apply it, as the court of conscience directs, and it does so in order to give effect to wishes of the testator, which would not otherwise be effectual.

To this two circumstances must be added to bring the present case to the test of the general doctrine, first, that the will states on its face that the legacy is given on trust but does not state what the trusts are, and further contains a residuary bequest, and, second, that the legatees are acting with perfect honesty, seek no advantage to themselves, and only desire, if the court will permit them, to do what in other circumstances the court would have fastened it on their conscience to perform.

Since the current of decisions down to *Re Fleetwood* (1880) 15 ChD 594 and *Re Huxtable* [1902] 2 Ch 793 has established that the principles of equity apply equally when these circumstances are present as in cases where they are not, the material question is whether and how the Wills Act affects this case. It seems to me that, apart from legislation, the application of the principle of equity, which was made in *Fleetwood's* and *Huxtable's* cases, was logical, and was justified by the same consider-ations as in the cases of fraud and absolute gifts. Why should equity forbid an honest trustee to give effect to his promise, made to a deceased testator, and compel him to pay another legatee, about whom it is quite certain that the testator did not mean to make him the object of this bounty? In both cases the testator's wishes are incompletely expressed in his will. Why should equity, over a mere matter of words, give effect to them in one case and frustrate them in another? No doubt the words 'in trust' prevent the legatee from taking beneficially, whether they have simply been declared in conversation or written in the will, but the fraud, when the trustee, so called in the will, is also the residuary legatee, is the same as when he is only declared a trustee by word of mouth accepted by him. I recoil from interfering with decisions of long standing, which reject this anomaly, unless constrained by the statute. . . .

The limits, beyond which the rules as to unspecified trusts must not be carried, have often been discussed. A testator cannot reserve to himself a power of making future unwitnessed dispositions by merely naming a trustee and leaving the purposes of the trust to be supplied afterwards, nor can a legatee give testamentary validity to an unexecuted codicil by accepting an indefinite trust, never communicated to him in the testator's lifetime: *Johnson v Ball* (1851) 5 De G & Sm 85; *Re Boyes* (1884) 26 ChD 531; *Riordan v Banon* (1876) IR 10 Eq 469; *Re Hetley* [1902] 2 Ch 866. To hold otherwise would indeed be to enable the testator to 'give the go-by' to the requirements of the Wills Act, because he did not choose to comply with them. It is communication of the purpose to the legatee, coupled with acquiescence or promise on his part, that removes the matter from the provision of the Wills Act and brings it within the law of trusts, as applied in this instance to trustees, who happen also to be legatees. If I am right in thinking that there is no contradiction of the Wills Act in applying the same rule, whether the trustee is or is not so described in the will, and the whole topic is detached from the enforcement of the Wills Act itself, then, whether the decisions in equity are or are not open to doubt in themselves, I think that, in view of the subject-matter of these decisions and the length of time during which they have been acquiesced in, your lordships may well in accordance with precedent refuse to overrule them lest titles should be rendered insecure and settlements, entered into in reliance on their authority, should now be disturbed.

Note
From the first paragraph, above, three propositions can be gleaned. First, the reason equity fastens on the conscience of the legatee is for the prevention of fraud. Secondly, the effect of the trust is to make the legatee 'do what the will in itself has nothing to do with'; in other words, the trust operates independently of the will. Thirdly, in order to prevent fraud, equity directs the legatee to give effect to wishes of the testator. This point is of some importance. The fraud whose commission is being prevented is not the taking of the property beneficially by the legatee, but having taken it, not giving effect to the wishes of the testator.

B: Limitations on Enforcement

It appears that half-secret trusts differ from their fully secret cousins in one respect. It is necessary for their enforcement, for B to have accepted the obligation before the will is made. This distinction is difficult to justify in principle, because a will is a revocable instrument having no legal status until death. And if it is argued that the contrary result allows the testator to alter the identity of the beneficiaries every day, at any time up his death, then why not have the same rule for fully secret trusts?

Nevertheless, there are dicta which appear to support the distinction in *Blackwell* itself, where Viscount Sumner observed (at p. 339):

A testator cannot reserve to himself a power of making future unattested dispositions by merely naming a trustee and leaving the purposes of the trust to be supplied afterwards, nor can a legatee give testamentary validity to an unexecuted codicil by accepting an indefinite trust, never communicated to him in the testator's lifetime . . .

It is possible that Viscount Sumner meant no more here than to restate the general principle that there must be acceptance by the secret or half-secret trustee and that such acceptance must take place within the lifetime of the testator, but this passage clearly can be taken to support the distinction made in the previous paragraph. *Blackwell v Blackwell* was used as authority for that distinction in *Re Keen* [1937] Ch 236. It is arguable that the time of communication was not the true basis of the decision in *Re Keen*, since the alleged communication did not anyway match the description given in the will, but the rule derived from *Re Keen* has since been applied in *Re Bateman's WT* [1970] 1 WLR 1463.

Re Keen, Evershed v Griffiths
[1937] Ch 236
Court of Appeal

Facts: By clause 5 of the testator's will:

I give to the said Charles Arthur Cheshyre Hazelhurst, and his friend Edward Evershed the sum of £10,000 free of duty to be held upon trust and disposed of by them among such person, persons or charities as may be notified by me to them or either of them during my lifetime and in default of such notification and so far as such notification shall not extend I declare that the sum of £10,000 or such part thereof as shall not be disposed of in manner aforesaid shall fall into and form part of my residuary estate.

Some months prior to the will, the testator had given Evershed a sealed envelope containing a sheet of paper on which he had written the name and address of the proposed secret beneficiary (a lady to whom the testator was not married).

Held: No valid half-secret trust had been created. Accordingly, the £10,000 fell into residue.

LORD WRIGHT MR: [Lord Wright set out the basis of enforcement upon which half-secret trusts are enforced, and continued]:

But [Lord Sumner in *Blackwell* v *Blackwell* [1929] AC 318, above, at 339] goes on to add qualifications which are essentially relevant for the determination of the present case. These are qualifications which flow from the circumstance that the will is not completely silent as to the trust, as is the case in wills of the type discussed in *McCormick* v *Grogan* (1869) LR 4 HL 82 [above], but does in express terms indicate that there is a trust. The qualifications are thus stated by Lord Sumner [1929] AC at p. 339:

[Lord Wright referred to the last of the paragraphs in the extract set out from *Blackwell* v *Blackwell* above, in which Lord Sumner had said that a testator cannot reserve to himself the power of making future unwitnessed dispositions by merely naming a trustee and leaving the purposes of the trust to be supplied afterwards, since to hold otherwise would indeed be to enable the testator to 'give the go-by' to the requirements of the Wills Act, and continued:]

As in my judgment cl. 5 should be considered as contemplating future dispositions and as reserving to the testator the power of making such dispositions without a duly attested codicil simply by notifying them during his lifetime, the principles laid down by Lord Sumner must be fatal to the appellant's claim. Indeed they would be equally fatal even on the construction for which Mr Roxburgh contended, that the clause covered both anterior or contemporaneous notifications as well as future notifications. The clause would be equally invalid, but, as already explained, I cannot accept that construction. In *Blackwell* v *Blackwell* . . . the trusts had been specifically declared to some or all of the trustees at or before the execution of the will and the language of the will was consistent with that fact. There was in [that case] no reservation of a future power to change the trusts, in whole or in part. Such a power would involve a power to change a testamentary disposition by an unexecuted codicil and would violate s. 9 of the Wills Act. . . .

But there is still a further objection which in the present case renders the appellant's claim unenforceable; the trusts which it is sought to establish by parol evidence would be inconsistent with the express terms of the will. . . .

In the present case, while cl. 5 refers solely to a future definition or to future definitions of the trust subsequent to the date of the will, the sealed letter relied on as notifying the trust was communicated (as I find the facts) before the date of the will. That it was communicated to one trustee only and not to both would not, I think, be an objection (see Lord Warrington's observation in the *Blackwell* case at p. 341). But the objection remains that the notification sought to be put in evidence was anterior to the will and hence not within the language of cl. 5, and inadmissible simply on that ground as being inconsistent with what the will prescribes.

It is always with reluctance that a Court refuses to give effect to the proved intention of the testator. In the present case it may be said that the objection is merely a matter of drafting and that the decision in *Blackwell* v *Blackwell* would have been applicable if only cl. 5 had been worded as applying to trusts previously indicated by the testator. The sealed letter would then have been admissible, subject to proof of the communication and acceptance of the trust. This may be true, but the court must deal with the matter as in fact it is. It would be impossible to give effect to the appellant's contention without not merely extending the rule laid down in *Blackwell* v *Blackwell*, but actually contravening the limitations which have been placed on that rule as necessarily arising from the Wills Act and, in addition, from the fact that the conditions prescribed by the will cannot be contradicted.

Note

Until *Re Bateman's WT* (below), it would have been possible to explain this case on the narrow view set out in the last two paragraphs above, that the notification referred to in clause 5 cannot refer to the sealed letter at all, since that was a communication made *prior to* the will. On this view, the case does not seriously limit the enforcement of half-secret trusts. Unfortunately, a much wider view of the case was adopted in *Re Bateman's WT*.

Re Bateman's WT, Brierley v Perry
[1970] 1 WLR 817, [1970] 3 All ER 817
Chancery Division

Facts: Clause 7 of a will provided:

I direct my Trustees to set aside from my estate the sum of Twenty four thousand pounds and to pay the income thereof to such persons and in such proportions as shall be stated by me in a sealed letter in my own handwriting and addressed to my Trustees and on the death of each person so named and in the case of females on marriage I direct the share of income so given shall be divided between my said daughters during their respective lives or to the survivor of them or their issue as aforesaid AND in default of issue then I direct the capital so set aside shall fall into the residue of my Estate.

The trustees received a sealed letter after the will, but before the death of the testator. The estate was insufficient to allow the trustees both to set aside £24,000 as required by clause 7, and also to satisfy the requirements of clause 6, which required two further sums of £20,000 to be set aside on other trusts.

Held: The direction to trustees in clause 7 was invalid. There was also an issue on the interpretation of clause 6, which is not relevant to any of the areas covered in this book.

PENNYCUICK V-C: Clause 7 has given rise to a good deal more difficulty. It will be remembered that the direction in that clause is to set aside a sum of £24,000 and pay the income 'to such persons and in such proportions as shall be stated by me in a sealed letter . . . to my Trustees'. Now those words are on their plain meaning future. There is no evidence whether a sealed letter had been written and addressed to the trustees by the testator at the date that he made his will. The only thing that does appear clear is that after his death some sealed letter or, at any rate, some document was in existence on which the trustees acted. Whatever the facts, the direction to pay the income 'to such persons and in such proportions as shall be stated by me in a sealed letter' clearly imports that the testator may, in the future after the date of the will, give a sealed letter to his trustees. It is impossible to confine the words to a sealed letter already so given. If that be the true construction of the wording it is not in dispute that the direction is invalid.

I was referred to one or two cases on the point, in particular, *Re Keen's Estate, Evershed* v *Griffiths* [1937] Ch 236 [see the extract above], in the Court of Appeal, and *Re Jones' WT, Jones* v *Jones* [1942] Ch 328, a decision of Simonds J. I do not think it is necessary to go further into those cases because it is clear, that once one must construe the direction as admitting of a future letter then the direction is invalid, as an attempt to dispose of the estate by a non-testamentary instrument. I interpose that I am not concerned on this summons with the application of income down to 1962. All sorts of matters of fact may arise in that context, such as the consent of the various beneficiaries, limitation, and so forth.

Note
This case goes further than *Re Keen* (above). It is possible to explain *Keen* on the narrow basis that the will did not refer to any document that was not

already in existence, and so could not on its construction refer to a later document. This explanation is not possible in *Bateman*, however, and the case is authority for the general proposition that a half-secret trust is enforceable only where its terms are known at the date of the will.

The distinction drawn in *Keen* and *Bateman* has not been adopted in the Republic of Ireland: *Re Prendiville (decd)*, Irish High Court, 5 December 1990, noted [1992] Conv 202, where the alternative view of the *Blackwell* dictum, above, was adopted.

Question

Given that a codicil republishes the will, and that in *Blackwell* v *Blackwell* [1929] AC 318 itself, the gift which was subject to the half-secret trust was contained in a codicil (albeit that the gift was created for the first time by the codicil, and the trustees had been duly informed in advance), consider the following:

(a)   In 1992 A makes a will leaving £5,000 to B 'on the trusts which will be communicated to him'. In 1993 A communicates the trusts to B. In 1994 A adds a further £5,000 by codicil. In 1995 A dies. Is there a valid half-secret trust, and if so of how much? Would your answer be different if the original will had left the £5,000 to B 'on the trusts which will be communicated to him sometime after 31 December 1992'?

(b)   In 1992 A makes a will leaving £5,000 to B 'on the trusts which have been communicated to him'. In 1993 A communicates the trusts to B. In 1994 A adds a further £5,000 by codicil. In 1995 A dies. Is there a valid half-secret trust, and if so of how much?

Note

In favour of allowing the trust of the first £5,000 in the latter example, it can be argued that the policy of the *Re Keen rule* ([1937] Ch 236) is merely to ensure that the trust is communicated prior to some properly executed testamentary disposition which indicates its terms, and that therefore the mention of the trust in the codicil should be good enough. A codicil has the effect of republishing a will, in other words it is as though the will itself had been made at the date of the later codicil.

Different issues arise regarding the second £5,000.

Re Colin Cooper, Le Neve-Foster v *National Provincial Bank*
[1939] 1 Ch 811
Court of Appeal

Facts: A testator had left £5,000 to trustees on half-secret trust in his will, having duly informed them in advance and obtained their agreement, and in a later testamentary document added a further £5,000 to this trust.

Held: The Court of Appeal held that only the first amount mentioned in the will could be subject to the half-secret trust, and that the amount added by the codicil fell into residue.

SIR WILFRED GREENE MR: In the present case there is no question that when the testator made his will of February 10, 1938, the legacy of £5000. thereby bequeathed to the two named trustees was effectively given and the giving of it complied with the requirements of a secret trust; the terms had been communicated, the trustees had acquiesced and the testator made his will upon the faith of that acquiescence. But the only trust which was in the picture on that occasion was one which related to a defined and stated sum of £5000. That was the legacy the intention to bequeath which was communicated to the trustees; that was the legacy in respect of which they gave their acceptance; that was the legacy which the testator, induced by that acceptance, in fact bequeathed. At a later date when . . . the testator made a will on March 27, 1938, he had no communication with those trustees with regard to the dispositions which he thereby made; there was no acquiescence by the trustees in the dispositions in question: he made that will not induced by any such acquiescence by the trustees . . . . The substance of the matter is that, having imposed on the conscience of these two trustees the trust in relation to the legacy of £5000. and having written that legacy into his will of February, 1938, by this will he in effect is giving another legacy of the same amount to be held upon the same trusts. It seems to me that upon the facts of this case it is impossible to say that the acceptance by the trustees of the onus of trusteeship in relation to the first and earlier legacy is something which must be treated as having been repeated in reference to the second legacy or the increased legacy, whichever way one chooses to describe it. . . . . I cannot myself see that the arrangement between the testator and the trustees can be construed as though it had meant '£5000 or whatever sum I may hereafter choose to bequeath.' That is not what was said and it was not with regard to any sum other than the £5000 that the consciences of the trustees (to use a technical phrase) were burdened. . . .

CLAUSON LJ: I agree. Crossman J [at first instance] asked himself, as it appears to me, the relevant and the crucial question as to whether he could on the evidence arrive at the conclusion that the trustees ever accepted a trust, either impliedly or expressly, with regard to the second £5000. He came to the conclusion that the evidence did not show that they had ever accepted such a trust, and I cannot see my way to differ from him. For those reasons I agree that the appeal must be dismissed.

Questions
1.   What would have been the result if the trustees had agreed to hold £5,000 or whatever sum the testator finally chose to bequeath, on the trusts that had been communicated to them?
2.   What would have been the result if the trustees had agreed to hold the amount stated in a letter in a sealed envelope, on the trusts stated in the same letter?

SECTION 4: SECRET AND HALF-SECRET TRUSTS TAKE EFFECT INDEPENDENTLY OF THE WILL

A: Beneficiary Witnesses Will

It is clear from *Blackwell* v *Blackwell* [1929] AC 518 that secret and half-secret trusts operate independently of the will. It is possible that they operate as express trusts created *inter vivos* by the agreement reached between the testator and the intended trustee, the function or relevance of the will being to vest the property in the intended trustee at the agreed time for the assumption of his office. From the passage in Viscount Sumner's speech, however, above, it seems more likely that after the will has transferred legal title to the legatee, the court fastens on the conscience of the legatee by imposing on him a trust. This is probably best analysed as a constructive trust, imposed in order to prevent fraud.

A similar analysis was adopted by Lord Westbury in *McCormick* v *Grogan* (at p. 97):

> The Court of Equity has, from a very early period, decided that even an Act of Parliament shall not be used as an instrument of fraud; and if in the machinery of perpetrating a fraud an Act of Parliament intervenes, the Court of Equity, it is true, does not set aside the Act of Parliament but it fastens on the individual who gets a title under that Act, and imposes upon him a personal obligation, because he applies the Act as an instrument for accomplishing a fraud.

Whichever analysis is correct, whether secret and half-secret trusts are express *inter vivos* trusts or constructive trusts imposed once the legatee has received the property (on which, see below), the will does no more than constitute the trust, transferring the legal property to the secret trustee. It seems likely that the trust could also be constituted by intestacy, in the absence of any will, if the settlor refrains from making a will in the knowledge that the property will pass to the intended trustee by virtue of the Administration of Estates Act 1925, rather than using a more usual form of transfer for an *inter vivos* trust.

It is sometimes argued that if secret and half-secret trusts are ordinary *inter vivos* trusts, the Wills Act has no application to them. If this is so, then fraud ought not to be strictly necessary for their enforcement. The mere fact of an existing trust should be enough for equity to intervene to enforce it, irrespective of any '*malus animus*' on the part of the trustee.

Yet while it is undoubtedly correct to say that the *mechanism* by which secret and half-secret trusts are enforced has nothing to do with the will, merely to describe the mechanism is not the same thing as providing a reason for their enforcement. The reason that equity imposes on the conscience of the legatee is fraud, and the mere fact that the mechanism operates independently of the will in no way affects that requirement.

Wills Act 1837

15. Gifts to an attesting witness to be void

If any person shall attest the execution of any will to whom or to whose wife or husband any beneficial devise, legacy, estate, interest, gift, or appointment, of or affecting any real or personal estate (other than and except charges and directions for the payment of any debt or debts), shall be thereby given or made, such devise, legacy, estate, interest, gift, or appointment shall, so far only as concerns such person attesting the execution of such will, or the wife or husband of such person, or any person claiming under such person of wife or husband, be utterly null and void, and such person so attesting shall be admitted as a witness to prove the execution of such will, or to prove the validity or invalidity thereof, notwithstanding such devise, legacy, estate, interest, gift, or appointment mentioned in such will.

Wills Act 1968

1. Restriction of operation of Wills Act 1837, s. 15

(1) For the purposes of section 15 of the Wills Act 1837 (avoidance of gifts to attesting witnesses and their spouses) the attestation of a will by a person to whom or to whose spouse there is given or made any such disposition as is described in that section shall be disregarded if the will is duly executed without his attestation and without that of any such other person.

(2) This section applies to the will of any person dying after the passing of this Act, whether executed before or after the passing of this Act.

Re Young (decd), Young v *Young*
[1951] 1 Ch 344
Chancery Division

Facts: The testator left an estate worth £94,000 to his widow on half-secret trusts. She understood that his chauffeur should receive a legacy of £2,000. The chauffeur had witnessed the testator's will. If a beneficiary witnesses a will, under s. 15 of the Wills Act 1837 any legacy to him is null and void.

Held: The half-secret trust would be enforced. The chauffeur took outside the will, by virtue of the half-secret trust imposed on the testator's widow. It followed that s. 15 of the Wills Act 1837 did not apply. Nor did the fact that the trusts were intended to take effect only after the death of the widow invalidate them.

DANCKWERTS J: It was also said that the trusts in question, being obviously intended to take effect after the widow's death, must be ineffective because she could not be a trustee for any purpose after she was dead. At first sight that seems a reasonable statement, but when it is examined it is, in my view, found to be based upon a fallacy. The widow is, and, if he had survived, the co-executor would have been, a trustee for purposes which were to take effect upon the testator's death as soon as the will came into effect. True the purposes related to future interests and future purposes, but they would have been none the less trustees for those purposes.

A good example of a secret trust being founded in that way is *Re Gardner* [1920] 2 Ch 523. There the testatrix by her will, made in 1909, bequeathed all her real and personal estate to her husband for his use and benefit during his life 'knowing that he will carry out my wishes'. Four days after the date of the will she signed an unattested memorandum expressing her wish that 'the money I leave to my husband' should, on his death, be equally divided among certain named beneficiaries. She died in 1919 and her husband died four days later. After the wife's death a memorandum was found in his safe and there was parol evidence that shortly after the execution of the will the testatrix had said, in his presence, that her property after his death was to be divided equally between the named beneficiaries and that he had assented to that. Those were held to be effective trusts binding upon his estate.

There, the trusts in question were only operative after the husband was dead, and they were operative in respect of an estate which devolved upon him not by reason of the dispositions contained in the will, for she gave him only a life interest: they were interests which vested in him by operation of law. Accordingly there is no difficulty in regard to the fact that these trusts are to operate after the death of the widow. . . .

There is one other point, which is rather interesting, concerning the validity of one of these legacies. The widow has testified that the testator's intention, as communicated to her, was that the man who had been employed by the testator for many years as chauffeur and general factotum should receive a legacy of £2,000. The chauffeur was one of the two attesting witnesses to the will, and if he takes the legacy under the terms of the will the result of s. 15 of the Wills Act 1837 is to make the legacy ineffective. The question is whether he takes the legacy under the will. Mr Christie, on behalf of the next of kin, referred to *Re Fleetwood* (1880) 15 ChD 594, a case of a secret trust, decided by Hall, V-C, where it was held that, as a woman intended to be a beneficiary was one of the attesting witnesses to the fourth codicil, the trust for her failed as to the beneficial interest, as it would have done, Hall V-C said, had it been declared in the codicil. It appears that the point was not argued in that particular case, which was concerned with a number of other points; and it seems to me that that particular decision is contrary to principle. The whole theory of the formation of a secret trust is that the Wills Act has nothing to do with the matter because the forms required by the Wills Act are entirely disregarded, since the persons do not take by virtue of the gift in the will, but by virtue of the secret trusts imposed upon the beneficiary, who does in fact take under the will.

Note
The reasoning of Danckwerts J there also applies in principle to fully secret trusts.

SECTION 5: MISCELLANEOUS ISSUES

A: Joint Tenants and Tenants in Common

In *Re Stead* [1900] 1 Ch 237, Farwell J (at p. 241) made various distinctions where property was given to two or more persons (let us suppose B1 and B2) as joint tenants or tenants in common, but where only one (B1) had promised to hold the property on a secret trust. The question at issue is whether B2 is bound by the trust.

Where a gift is made to trustees as joint tenants, the orthodox view, as stated in *Re Stead*, is that if communication is made before the execution of the will, all will be bound, whereas if communication is made after the execution of the will but before the death of the testator, only those who have accepted the trust are bound by it, on the basis that the gift to an intended trustee who does not consent is not tainted with any fraud in procuring the execution of the will. Where the gift is to the intended trustees as tenants in common, only those who are aware of the trust are bound, whether they obtain this knowledge before or after the will is executed.

The distinctions were said to be based on older cases, but are difficult to support as a matter of policy. B. Perrins argues, however (1972) 85 LQR 225 at p. 228, that Farwell J's distinctions are wrong, and that the true rule rests on the principle of *Huguenin* v *Baseley* (1807) 14 Ves 273, that no man may profit from the fraud of another. On this argument, B2 would be bound if the testator was induced to leave the property to him on the strength of B1's promise, but not otherwise, and the question of when communication occurred would be a matter of evidence only. The argument has much to commend it, and if Perrins is correct, then these cases fit into the general scheme of things, so long as the criteria for enforcement advanced in *Ottaway* v *Norman* (above) are correct.

B: Absence of Intended Trustee, or Renunciation by Him of the Legacy

Suppose B has died before A. This makes it necessary to consider whether a secret trust can be enforced in the absence of the intended trustee (B). It is undoubted law that a legacy cannot take effect where the legatee pre-deceases the testator, and there are statements in *Re Maddock* [1902] 2 Ch 220 which suggest that the trust will not be enforced in this case, nor where the secret trustee renounces the legacy. For example, Collins MR said (at p. 226):

But the right of the [beneficiary] is wholly dependent on whether the legatee accepts the legacy with knowledge of the mandate, and no right for them arises at all unless and until the legatee has, with notice, accepted the legacy.

Cozens-Hardy LJ took a similar view (at p. 231):

Now, the so-called trust does not affect the property except by reason of a personal obligation binding the individual devisee or legatee. If he renounces and disclaims, or dies in the lifetime of the testator, the persons claiming under the memorandum can take nothing against the heir-at-law or next of kin or residuary devisee or legatee.

These statements clearly imply that the trust is not constituted until the testator has died, and the legatee has accepted the trust property.

On the other hand, the fraud on the testator is no less in these cases than in the conventional situation, and there is a general principle that 'equity will not allow a trust to fail for want of a trustee'. It might be thought, therefore, that where the intended trustee has pre-deceased the testator, a trust should be imposed upon the property in the hands of A's executor.

Blackwell v *Blackwell*
[1929] AC 318
House of Lords

Decision: The facts and decision of the House have already been set out at p. 268.

LORD BUCKMASTER: The real difficulty lies in considering whether the fact that in the will itself it is made plain that the gift is fiduciary destroys the principle upon which verbal evidence has been admitted to show the nature of a gift purporting to be absolute and beneficial [i.e., fully-secret trusts].

. . . It is . . . urged that the underlying principle admitting extraneous evidence is that the legatee cannot profit by his own fraud, a principle that does not apply where, on the face of the will, his interest is fiduciary.

This principle is easily understood and may also be stated by saying that he cannot defraud beneficiaries for whom he has consented to act by keeping the money for himself. Apart, however, from the personal benefit accruing to the trustee, the real beneficiaries are equally defrauded in both cases, and the faith on which the testator relied is equally betrayed. Further, if the trustee was the heir or one of the next of kin or a residuary legatee, the fraud would be just the same. The counsel for the appellants seemed at one time to argue that in such a case and to such an extent as to defeat the beneficial interest of the trustee the outside evidence might be admitted, but it is difficult to see on what principle of reasoning the evidence can be admitted in the one case and rejected in the other, when in both cases the fact of the trust appears in the will itself. Again, in the case where no trusts are mentioned the legatee might defeat the whole purpose by renouncing the legacy and the breach of trust would not in that case enure to his own benefit, but I entertain no doubt that the Court, having once admitted the evidence of the trust, would interfere to prevent its defeat. If this be so the personal benefit of the legatee cannot be the sole determining factor in considering the admissibility of the evidence.

Notes

1.   These statements are consistent with the view of fraud advanced by Hodge, above.

2.   The dicta in *Re Maddock* cannot be reconciled with the statement in the above passage that the intended trustee will not be allowed to defeat the testator's purpose by renouncing the legacy.

3.   *Re Maddock* concerned a fully secret trust, whereas the trust in *Blackwell* v *Blackwell* was half-secret. One could argue for a distinction on that basis, since the trust is plain on the face of the will in the latter but not the former case. It is clear, however, that both sets of dicta are intended to apply to both types of trust (indeed, Lord Buckmaster is clearly referring to the fully secret trust, and is mostly concerned to equate the two types).

4.   If the secret trustee cannot renounce the legacy, then on the assumption that the trust is not fully constituted before the death of the testator, there must be a general principle that a trustee cannot renounce his obligations once he has accepted trusteeship, even before the trust is fully constituted. Alternatively, perhaps the trust is constituted earlier.

Re Gardner (No. 2)
[1923] 2 Ch 230
Chancery Division

Decision: A secret trust in favour of a beneficiary who had predeceased the testator was upheld.

ROMER J: The rights of the parties appear to me to be exactly the same as though the husband [secret trustee], after the memorandum had been communicated to him by the testatrix . . . , had executed a declaration of trust binding himself to hold any property that should come to him upon his wife's [settlor's] partial intestacy upon trust as specified in the memorandum.

Notes

1.   It is not possible to leave property to a dead person by will, and the usual analysis is that the will constitutes the trust by transferring legal title to the secret trustee, but in the above passage Romer J saw no reason why a declaration of trust by the secret trustee should not have occurred at the moment of communication of the trust to him.

2.   If Romer J's view is correct, then the consequences are not limited to an ability to make a secret or half-secret trust in favour of a beneficiary who predeceases the testator. If the trust comes into force from the moment of communication, then it must also follow that it is irrevocable from that moment, and that neither the testator nor the secret trustee would be able later to change his or her mind. This is arguably an unfortunate consequence if the communication was made many years before the testator's death and circumstances had changed radically in the meantime (but the same problem could also arise with ordinary *inter vivos* trusts which provide for distribution after a long period of time).

3.   Romer J's view is clearly inconsistent with the views expressed in the Court of Appeal in *Re Maddock* [1902] 2 Ch 220, to the effect that the trust only becomes binding once the legatee accepts the legacy, but would provide a mechanism for putting Lord Buckmaster's views into effect.

Questions

1.   Is the fraud merely deceiving the testator, or deceiving the testator into leaving property in favour of the secret trustee? *Blackwell* argues for the first, *Maddock* for the second.

2.   Do Lord Buckmaster's comments, above, form part of the *ratio* of *Blackwell v Blackwell*?

3.   What is the trust property on Romer J's analysis in *Gardner (No. 2)*? Note that only on the testator's death, and acceptance by the legatee of the legacy, is legal title vested in him. Is the trust property therefore future property, and hence tainted by *Re Ellenborough* (see chapter 3)? Would your answer be different if the agreement had covered only specified property (such as a grandfather clock)?

4.   If the secret beneficiary ran off with the secret trustee's wife, could the secret trustee inform the testator that he was longer prepared to accept the property on the original terms? Or, if he were no longer able to get in touch with the testator, could he refuse to take the property under the will? Are your answers consistent with the views expressed by Romer J?

SECTION 6:   MUTUAL WILLS

A: B Taking Property Under A's Will on the Understanding that it will be Left to C in B's Will

There is no reason in principle why A should not leave property to B on the understanding that B will leave the same property in his will to C. That was the result in *Ottaway v Norman*, above, regarding the land. B simply obtains a life interest in the property. This is also a possible explanation of *Re Oldham* [1925] Ch 75, a mutual wills case. A more problematic situation is where A and B agree that each will leave all his property to the survivor on the understanding that the survivor will leave all his property to C. *Re Hagger* suggests (contrary to *Re Oldham*) that a trust attaches to all the survivor's property, as long as the survivor accepts the legacy under the other's will.

B: Floating Constructive Trusts

The secret trust of land in *Ottaway v Norman* was considered above. According to the evidence given by the son and his wife, Miss Hodges also undertook to leave them the furniture and other contents, including her money. Brightman J accepted that the secret trust comprised such furnishings and fixtures as Miss Hodges had received under Mr Ottaway's will, but not that it included all Miss Hodges's other property and cash from whatever source.

In respect of the last, it seems that he was not convinced that so far-reaching an obligation had in fact been envisaged in the agreement, but if the intended trustee (B) has clearly accepted such an obligation, he accepted that this obligation also could be enforced against her estate. He employed the concept of a 'floating trust', derived from the Australian case of *Birmingham v Renfrew* (1937) 57 CLR 666, which would remain in suspense during the life of the trustee and crystallise on her death, attaching to whatever property was comprised within her estate. This, as the learned judge noted, would seem to preclude Miss Hodges from making even a small pecuniary legacy in favour of her relatives or friends. Similar reasoning was also adopted in the following case.

Re Cleaver
[1981] 1 WLR 939, [1981] 2 All ER 1018
Chancery Division

Decision: Mutual wills could be enforced using the 'floating trust' concept described above. Husband and wife made wills by which each left the estate to the other, subject to various legacies in favour of relatives and other gifts over. The husband died first and his widow received the whole of his net estate. She then made a new will. Nourse J held that the doctrine of mutual wills applied and that the estate of the widow was held on a constructive trust on the terms of the mutual will of the wife which she had revoked.

NOURSE J: This is a case in which it is alleged that mutual wills are enforceable. By that I mean that it is one where it is alleged that two persons (in this case husband and wife) made an enforceable agreement as to the disposal of their property and executed wills in substantially identical terms in pursuance thereof. The husband died first without having revoked his will. The wife accepted benefits under the husband's will and later made her last will in substantially different terms. She is now dead. The question is whether the persons who would have been the beneficiaries under the wife's original will can claim that her estate should be held on the trusts of that will and not of her last will.

. . .

The foundations of the plaintiff's claim is the well-known case of *Dufour v Pereira* (1769) 1 Dick 419, 21 ER 332. That case is fully discussed in Hargrave's Juridical Arguments (1799, vol 2, pp 304ff). That was a case where Lord Camden, relying as it appears only on the terms of a joint will executed by a husband and wife, concluded that there had been a prior agreement. There have not been so very many cases on the subject since, but in one of them, *Gray v Perpetual Trustee Co Ltd* [1928] AC 391, [1928] All ER Rep 758, the Privy Council decided in clear terms that the mere simultaneity of the wills and the similarity of their terms are not enough taken by themselves to establish the necessary agreement. I will read what appear to me to be the material passages in the judgment of the Board, which was delivered by Viscount Haldane. The first reads as follows ([1928] AC 391 at 399–400, [1928] All ER Rep 758 at 761):

> In *Dufour v Pereira* the conclusion reached was that if there was in point of fact an agreement come to that the wills should not be revoked after the death of one of the parties without mutual consent, they were binding. That they were mutual wills to the same effect was at least treated as a relevant circumstance, to be taken into account in determining whether there was such an agreement. But the mere simultaneity of the wills and the similarity of their terms do not appear, taken by themselves, to have been looked on as more than some evidence of an agreement not to revoke. The agreement, which does not restrain the legal right to revoke, was the foundation of the right in equity which might emerge, although it was a fact which had in itself to be established by evidence, and in such cases the whole of the evidence must be looked at.

Their Lordships then proceeded to mention two authorities, the second of which was the decision of Astbury J in *Re Oldham* [1925] Ch 75. The judgment continues ([1928] AC 391 at 400, [1928] All ER Rep 758 at 762):

> Their Lordships agree with the view taken by Astbury J. The case before them is one in which the evidence of an agreement, apart from that of making the wills in question, is so lacking that they are unable to come to the conclusion that an agreement to constitute equitable interests has been shown to have been made. As they have already said, the mere fact of making wills mutually is not, at least by the law of England, evidence of such an agreement having been come to. And without such a definite agreement there can no more be a trust in equity than a right to damages at law.

As to the penultimate sentence of that passage it must, in the light of the earlier passage, be read as meaning that the mere fact of making mutual wills is not by itself sufficient evidence of such an agreement having been come to.

It is therefore clear that there must be a definite agreement between the makers of the two wills, that that must be established by evidence, that the fact that there are mutual wills to the same effect is a relevant circumstance to be taken into account, although not enough of itself, and that the whole of the evidence must be looked at.

I do not find it necessary to refer to any other English case, but I have derived great assistance from the decision of the High Court of Australia in *Birmingham* v *Renfrew* (1936) 57 CLR 666. That was a case where the available extrinsic evidence was held to be sufficient to establish the necessary agreement between two spouses. It is chiefly of interest because both Latham CJ and more especially Dixon J examined with some care the whole nature of the legal theory on which these and other similar cases proceed. I would like to read three passages from the judgment of Dixon J, which state, with all the clarity and learning for which the judgment of that most eminent judge are renowned, what I believe to be a correct analysis of the principles on which a case of enforceable mutual wills depends. First (at 682–683):

> I think the legal result was a contract between husband and wife. The contract bound him, I think, during her lifetime not to revoke his will without notice to her. If she died without altering her will, then he was bound after her death not to revoke his will at all. She on her part afforded the consideration for his promise by making her will. His obligation not to revoke his will during her life without notice to her is to be implied. For I think the express promise should be understood as meaning that is she died leaving her will unrevoked then he would not revoke his. But the agreement really assumes that neither party will alter his or her will without the knowledge of the other. It has long been established that a contract between persons to make corresponding will gives rise to equitable obligations when one acts on the faith of such an agreement and dies leaving his will unrevoked so that the other takes property under its dispositions. It operates to impose upon the survivor an obligation regarded as specifically enforceable. It is true that he cannot be compelled to make and leave unrevoked a testamentary document and if he dies leaving a last will containing provisions inconsistent with his agreement it is nevertheless valid as a testamentary act. But the doctrines of equity attach the obligation to the property. The effect is, I think, that the survivor becomes a constructive trustee and the terms of the trust are those of the will which he undertook would be his last will.

Next (at 689):

> There is a third element which appears to me to be inherent in the nature of such a contract or agreement, although I do not think it has been expressly considered. The purpose of an arrangement for corresponding wills must often be, as in this case, to enable the survivor during his life to deal as absolute owner with the property passing under the will of the party first dying. That is to say, the object of the transaction is to put the survivor in a position to enjoy for his own benefit the full ownership so that, for instance, he may convert it and expend the proceeds if he choose. But when he dies he is to bequeath what is left in the manner agreed upon. It is only by the special doctrines of equity that such a floating obligation, suspended, so to speak, during the life-time of the survivor can descend upon the assets at his death and crystallize into a trust. No doubt gifts and settlements, *inter vivos*, if calculated to defeat the intention of the compact, could not be made by the survivor and his right of disposition, *inter vivos*, is, therefore, not unqualified. But, substantially, the purpose of the arrangement will often be to allow full enjoyment for the survivor's own benefit and advantage upon condition that at his death the residue shall pass as arranged.

Finally (at 690):

> In *In re Oldham*, Astbury J, pointed out, in dealing with the question whether an agreement should be inferred, that in *Dufour* v *Pereira* the compact was that the

survivor should take a life estate only in the combined property. It was, therefore, easy to fix the corpus with a trust as from the death of the survivor. But I do not see any difficulty in modern equity in attaching to the assets a constructive trust which allowed the survivor to enjoy the property subject to a fiduciary duty which, so to speak, crystallized on his death and disabled him only from voluntary dispositions *inter vivos*.

I interject to say that Dixon J was there clearly referring only to voluntary dispositions inter vivos which are calculated to defeat the intention of the compact. No objection could normally be taken to ordinary gifts of small value. He went on:

On the contrary, as I have said, it seems rather to provide a reason for the intervention of equity. The objection that the intended beneficiaries could not enforce a contract is met by the fact that a constructive trust arises from the contract and the fact that testamentary dispositions made upon the faith of it have taken effect. It is the constructive trust and not the contract that they are entitled to enforce.

It is also clear from *Birmingham* v *Renfrew* that these cases of mutual wills are only one example of a wider category of cases, for example secret trusts, in which a court of equity will intervene to impose a constructive trust. A helpful and interesting summary of that wider category of cases will be found in the argument of counsel for the plaintiffs in *Ottaway* v *Norman* [1972] Ch 698 at 701–702. The principle of all these cases is that a court of equity will not permit a person to whom property is transferred by way of gift, but on the faith of an agreement or clear understanding that it is to be dealt with in a particular way for the benefit of a third person, to deal with that property inconsistently witht that agreement or understanding. If he attempts to do so after having received the benefit of the gift equity will intervene by imposing a constructive trust on the property which is the subject matter of the agreement or understanding. I take that statement of principle, and much else which is of assistance in this case, from the judgment of Slade J in *Re Pearson Fund Trusts* (21st October 1977, unreported; the statement of principle is at p. 52 of the official transcript). The judgment of Brightman J in *Ottaway* v *Norman* is to much the same effect.

I would emphasise that the agreement or understanding must be such as to impose on the donee a legally binding obligation to deal with the property in the particular way and that the other two certainties, namely those as to the subject matter of the trust and the persons intended to benefit under it, are as essential to this species of trust as they are to any other. In spite of an argument by counsel for Mr and Mrs Noble to the contrary, I find it hard to see how there could be any difficulty about the second or third certainties in a case of mutual wills unless it was in the terms of the wills themselves. There, as in this case, the principal difficulty is always whether there was a legally binding obligation or merely what Lord Loughborough LC in *Lord Walpole* v *Lord Orford* (1797) 3 Ves 402 at 419, 30 ER 1976 at 1084 described as an honourable engagement.

Before turning in detail to the evidence which relates to the question whether there was a legally binding obligation on the testatrix in the present case or not I must return once more to *Birmingham* v *Renfrew*. It is clear from that case, if from nowhere else, that an enforceable agreement to dispose of property in pursuance of mutual wills can be established only by clear and satisfactory evidence. That seems to me to be no more than a particular application of the general rule that all claims relating to the property of deceased persons must be scrutinised with very great care. However, that does not mean that there has to be a departure from the ordinary standard of proof required in civil proceedings. I have to be satisfied on the balance of probabilities that the alleged agreement was made, but before I can be satisfied of that I must find clear and satisfactory evidence to that effect.

[Nourse J reviewed the evidence and continued:]

In the result, and perhaps contrary to my expectation when the case was opened, I am driven to the conclusion that the plaintiffs are entitled to succeed in this action. . .

Note

It is not clear from the report whether the trust imposed actually bound any property not received under Arthur Cleaver's will. If it did not then the *ratio* goes no further than *Re Oldham* [1925] Ch 75, above (the widow would simply have enjoyed a life interest in the property received under Arthur Cleaver's will). However, in *Re Dale* [1993] 4 All ER 129, Morritt J applied the mutual wills doctrine where the second testator had received no benefit at all under the first testator's will, the mutual agreement having been that their children should share equally. There the trust clearly applied to the whole of the widow's estate.

Questions

1. X marries his first wife X1 and they make mutual wills at age 20, each agreeing to settle the whole of his/her estate on the other party at his/her death. At this time they are both childless and poor, and when X1 dies she leaves X property worth £1,000. Later in life, X marries X2, has a number of children by his second wife, and becomes wealthy. Suppose the reasoning in *Cleaver* is correct. To what extent, if at all, can X spend his wealth during his lifetime on himself, X2 and his children?

2. Presumably there is no reason in principle why B should not contract that in consideration for A leaving B property in his will, B will leave all his property in his will to C. On the assumption that A dies before B, who (if anybody) can enforce the contract against B? (Note: You may care to consider *Beswick* v *Beswick* [1968] AC 58 (chapter 2) and *Re Plumptre's Marriage Settlement* [1910] 1 Ch 609 (chapter 3).) Is it likely that anybody would bring a contract action, and what remedies would be available if he or she did?

Notes

1. In question 2 above, you may wish to consider the following passage from *Re Dale*, where Morritt J (at p. 133) appears to take the view that specific performance of such a contract would never be possible:

> The doctrine of mutual wills is to the effect that where two individuals have agreed as to the disposal of their property and have executed mutual wills in pursuance of the agreement, on the death of the first (T1) the property of the survivor (T2), the subject matter of the agreement, is held on an implied trust for the beneficiary named in the wills. The survivor may thereafter alter his will, because a will is inherently revocable, but if he does his personal representatives will take the property subject to the trust. The

basic doctrine is not in dispute. The dispute is as to the circumstances in which the doctrine applies.

. . . There is no doubt that for the doctrine to apply there must be a contract at law. It is apparent from all the cases, to which I shall refer later, but in particular from *Gray* v *Perpetual Trustee Co. Ltd* [1928] AC 391, [1928] All ER Rep 758, that it is necessary to establish an agreement to make and not revoke mutual wills, some understanding or arrangement being insufficient 'without such a definite agreement there can no more be a trust in equity than a right to damages at law' (see [1928] AC 391 at 400, [1928] All ER Rep 758 at 762 *per* Viscount Haldane). . . .

. . . What is necessary to obtain a decree of specific performance of a contract in favour of a third party is not, in my judgment, a relevant question when considering the doctrine of mutual wills. A will is by its very nature revocable (cf *Re Heys's Estate, Walker* v *Gaskill* [1914] P 192). It seems to me to be inconceivable that the court would order T2 to execute a will in accordance with the agreement at the suit of the personal representatives of T1 or to grant an injunction restraining T2 from revoking it. The principles on which the court acts in imposing the trust to give effect to the agreement to make and not revoke mutual wills must be found in the cases dealing with that topic, not with those dealing with the availability of the remedy of specific performance.

2.   The mutual wills doctrine, which appears to be anomalous, clearly has its origins in the law of contract, and may perhaps be justified on the grounds that the floating constructive trust is the only way of enforcing this particular type of contract.

11   INEQUITABLE CONDUCT

SECTION 1:   CRIMINAL ACTS

A: Forfeiture

Equity will not allow a person to retain the benefit of criminal activities, and holds property so received on constructive trust for those entitled to it.

Re Crippen (decd)
[1911] P 108
Probate Division

Facts: Crippen murdered his wife and attempted to escape abroad with his mistress, Miss Ethel le Nève. He was apprehended while at sea, convicted and sentenced to death. After his conviction and sentence, but before he was hanged, he made a will appointing Miss le Nève his executrix and universal legatee. The question arose regarding that part of Crippen's property to which he was entitled on the death (intestate) of his murdered wife.

Held: Evans P held that Crippen could not take the property, and that it could not therefore pass to Miss le Nève. Instead it passed to his wife's next of kin.

EVANS P: It is clear that the law is, that no person can obtain, or enforce, any rights resulting to him from his own crime; neither can his representative, claiming under him, obtain or enforce any such rights. The human mind revolts at the very idea that any other doctrine could be possible in our system of jurisprudence.

Notes

1. Evans P footnotes *Cleaver* v *Mutual Life Reserve Fund Life Association* [1892] 1 QB 147.

2. It must be assumed that if Crippen had actually received the property he would have held it on constructive trust for his victim. There was no evidence, incidentally, that the murder was in any way motivated by a desire to inherit Mrs Crippen's property, indeed, rather the contrary. This was a notorious trial, perhaps because Crippen was the first murderer to be brought to justice as a result of a wireless communication, and is included in Famous Trials, selected from the Penguin *Famous Trials* series by John Mortimer (Penguin: 1984). Filson Young, who wrote the selected piece on Crippen, thought that the most likely explanation for the murder was that Mrs Crippen had threatened to leave Crippen, taking with her all the money from the joint account to which Crippen himself had contributed the bulk, and that Crippen acted as he did to protect his own capital. He concedes that the official explanation was that Crippen was motivated solely by his feelings for Miss le Nève, but there was never any suggestion that Crippen committed murder in order to steal Mrs Crippen's property.

3. The principle applies not only to property inherited directly by the killer, but also where killer and victim are joint tenants, so that the victim's share passes to the killer by virtue of the right of survivorship.

It is clear from *Re K (decd)* (see the extracts below) that the forfeiture principle was not limited to murder but extended to other forms of culpable homicide. The rigours of the principle were mitigated by the Forfeiture Act 1982, which allows the court a discretion to grant relief from forfeiture except in a case of murder.

Forfeiture Act 1982

1. The 'forfeiture rule'

(1)   In this Act, the 'forfeiture rule' means the rule of public policy which in certain circumstances precludes a person who has unlawfully killed another from acquiring a benefit in consequence of the killing.

(2)   References in this Act to a person who has unlawfully killed another include a reference to a person who has unlawfully aided, abetted, counselled or procured the death of that other and references in this Act to unlawful killing shall be interpreted accordingly.

2. Power to modify the rule

(1)   Where a court determines that the forfeiture rule has precluded a person (in this section referred to as 'the offender') who has unlawfully killed another from acquiring any interest in property mentioned in subsection (4) below, the court may make an order under this section modifying the effect of that rule.

(2)   The court shall not make an order under this section modifying the effect of the forfeiture rule in any case unless it is satisfied that, having regard to the conduct of the offender and of the deceased and to such other circumstances as appear to the court to be material, the justice of the case requires the effect of the rule to be so modified in that case.

(3)   In any case where a person stands convicted of an offence of which unlawful killing is an element, the court shall not make an order under this section modifying the effect of the forfeiture rule in that case unless proceedings for the purpose are brought before the expiry of the period of three months beginning with his conviction.

(4)   The interests in property referred to in subsection (1) above are —

(a)   any beneficial interest in property which (apart from the forfeiture rule) the offender would have acquired —

(i)   under the deceased's will (including as respects Scotland, any writing having testamentary effect) or the law relating to intestacy or by way of *ius relicti*, *ius relictae* or *legitim*;

(ii)   on the nomination of the deceased in accordance with the provisions of any enactment;

(iii)   as a *donatio mortis causa* made by the deceased; or

(iv)   under a special destination (whether relating to heritable or moveable property; or

(b)   any beneficial interest in property which (apart from the forfeiture rule) the offender would have acquired in consequence of the death of the deceased, being property which, before the death, was held in trust for any person.

(5)   An order made under this section may modify the effect of the forfeiture rule in respect of any interest in property to which the determination referred to in subsection (1) above relates and may do so in either or both of the following ways, that is—

(a)   where there is more than one such interest, by excluding the application of the rule in respect of any (but not all) of those interests; and

(b)   in the case of any such interest in property, by excluding the application of the rule in respect of part of the property.

(6)   On the making of an order under this section, the forfeiture rule shall have effect for all purposes (including purposes relating to anything done before the order is made) subject to the modifications made by the order.

(7)   The court shall not make an order under this section modifying the effect of the forfeiture rule in respect of any interest in property which, in consequence of the rule, has been acquired before the coming into force of this section by a person other than the offender or a person claiming through him.

(8)   In this section —

'property' includes any chose in action or incorporeal moveable property; and 'will' includes codicil.

5.   Exclusion of murderers

Nothing in this Act or in any order made under section 2 . . . of this Act shall affect the application of the forfeiture rule in the case of a person who stands convicted of murder.

Re K (decd)
[1986] Fam 180, [1985] 3 WLR 234, [1985] 2 All ER 833;
[1985] 1 Ch 85, [1985] 2 WLR 262, [1985] 1 All ER 403
Court of Appeal affirming Vinelott J
Chancery Division

Facts: The case concerned a wife (whose name was not disclosed) who killed her husband with a shotgun, after suffering many years of violent attacks from him. She was convicted of manslaughter, and sentenced to two years' probation. She was residuary legatee under her husband's will, and also entitled to succeed as joint tenant to the matrimonial home.

Held: Vinelott J held that both the money inherited under the husband's will and his share as joint tenant of the matrimonial home were subject to the forfeiture rule. The principle will not always apply to manslaughter, which does not necessarily require any subjective element of intention, but here the killer had deliberately threatened the victim with a loaded gun with the safety catch removed, and this was sufficient to attract the equitable forfeiture rule. He was however prepared to grant relief under the Act, forming a view based on degree of moral culpability in view of the violence the killer had suffered at the hands of her victim. A question also arose on the construction of s. 2(7), as to whether the Act applied at all, but that has no present-day relevance.

The case went to the Court of Appeal on the application of the 1982 Act only, and Vinelott J's decision was affirmed. Ackner LJ also observed that there is nothing in the Act restricting the offender to the amount that he or she would have obtained on divorce.

VINELOTT J (on the equitable doctrine): Counsel for the widow submitted that the forfeiture rule should apply (apart from cases of murder) only to cases of voluntary manslaughter, i.e. to cases where what would otherwise be murder is reduced to manslaughter by provocation or diminished responsibility or because the death occurred in pursuance of a suicide pact, and not to cases of involuntary manslaughter, i.e. where an unlawful killing is reduced to manslaughter because there was no intent to kill or to do grievous bodily harm. He submitted in the alternative that the rule should only apply to cases of voluntary manslaughter and to cases of involuntary manslaughter where there is something more than a threat sufficient to raise a fear of violence, that is to cases where actual force is employed. I do not think that that is a possible view. In *Gray* v *Barr* [1971] 2 All ER 949, [1971] 2 QB 554 on the evidence of Mr Barr, which was held sufficient to found the conclusion that he had been guilty of manslaughter (though acquitted at the trial), he did not intend to use the gun to injure Mr Gray but the Court of Appeal clearly thought that the forfeiture rule applied. In my judgment the facts of this case fall clearly within the test propounded by Geoffrey Lane J in the passage which I have cited from his judgment in *Gray* v *Barr* [1970] 2 All ER 702 at 710, [1970] 2 QB 626 at 640. The widow, like Mr Barr, was guilty of a threat of violence which was deliberate in that she intended to frighten and so deter the deceased. The death, though I accept wholly unintended, was the unfortunate consequence of her conduct in threatening the deceased with a loaded gun and disengaging the safety catch. Given that the death was the consequence, albeit unintended, of that deliberate threat the court cannot go further and evaluate the degree of moral culpability to be attributed to her conduct in order to say whether the forfeiture rule applies or not.

. . .

ACKNER LJ (on the discretion of the court under the 1982 Act): Another criticism that counsel for the fourth defendant makes is that the judge should not in this case, nor as a general rule, as I understand the position, should any judge, so modify the operation of the forfeiture rule as to enable an offender to inherit more than she would have obtained if she had obtained a divorce from the deceased or made an application under the Inheritance (Provision for Family and Dependants) Act 1975. The court is obliged to give no more than the needs of the offender demand.

The short answer to that submission is that, if that was what Parliament intended to be the limit of the discretion, it would have been very easy to say so, particularly in an Act where the 1975 Act is specifically referred to. I have read s. 2(2) of the 1982 Act and it shows the great width of the discretion given to the court. I can see no justification, either from the terms of the 1982 Act or on any basis of sound sense in restricting the result of the modification of the rule to what it might be thought an offender would have received as a result of obtaining a decree of divorce. There must be many cases, and this could well be one, where it was a great tribute to the wife to continue to live with a husband who behaved in such an intolerable way and, as a result, any suggestion that she should be limited to the sum that she might have got had she taken the easy way out, seems to me to have no sound basis in justice. Since the 1982 Act says nothing about need and does not refer in the subsection to the 1975 Act, although it does in another context in the next section, I can see no validity in this submission.

B: He Who Comes to Equity Must Come With Clean Hands

We saw in chapter 1 that equitable remedies were discretionary, and that the behaviour of the party claiming equitable relief might be relevant to the question whether it is granted. However, established property rights are unaffected by the principle. This can lead to rather fine distinctions, as in the following case.

Tinsley v Milligan
[1993] 3 WLR 126, [1993] 3 All ER 65
House of Lords

Facts: Stella Tinsley and Kathleen Milligan were an unmarried couple who jointly purchased a home which was registered in Tinsley's name alone. On the principles set out in chapter 9 the beneficial interest would have been shared between Tinsley and Milligan in equal shares, but to both Tinsley and Milligan's knowledge, the home was registered in Tinsley's name alone to enable Milligan to make false claims to the Department of Social Security for benefits. After a quarrel Tinsley moved out, and claimed possession from Milligan. Milligan counterclaimed, seeking a declaration that the house was held by Tinsley on trust for both of them in equal shares. Tinsley argued that Milligan's claim was barred by the common law doctrine *ex turpi causa non oritur actio* and by the principle that he who comes to equity must come with clean hands.

Held (Lord Keith and Lord Goff dissenting): Because the presumption of resulting trust applied, Milligan could establish her equitable interest without relying on the illegal transaction, and was therefore entitled to succeed.

LORD JAUNCEY OF TULLICHETTLE: At the outset it seems to me to be important to distinguish between the enforcement of executory provisions arising under an illegal contract or other transaction and the enforcement of rights already acquired under the completed provisions of such a contract or transaction. Your Lordships were referred to a very considerable number of authorities, both ancient and modern, from which certain propositions may be derived.

First: it is trite law that the court will not give its assistance to the enforcement of executory provisions of an unlawful contract whether the illegality is apparent ex facie the document or whether the illegality of purpose of what would otherwise be a lawful contract emerges during the course of the trial (see *Holman v Johnson* (1775) 1 Cowp 341 at 343, [1775–1802] All ER Rep 98 at 99 per Lord Mansfield CJ, *Pearce v Brooks* (1866) LR 1 Exch 213 at 217–218, [1861–73] All ER Rep 102 at 103 per Pollock CB, *Alexander v Rayson* [1936] 1 KB 169 at 182, [1935] All ER Rep 185 at 191 and *Bowmakers Ltd v Barnet Instruments Ltd* [1944] 2 All ER 579 at 582, [1945] KB 65 at 70).

Second: it is well established that a party is not entitled to rely on his own fraud or illegality in order to assist a claim or rebut a presumption. Thus when money or property has been transferred by a man to his wife or children for the purpose of defrauding creditors and the transferee resists his claim for recovery he cannot be heard to rely on his illegal purpose in order to rebut the presumption of advancement (see *Gascoigne v Gascoigne* [1918] 1 KB 223 at 226, *Chettiar v Chettiar* (No. 2) [1962] 1 All ER 494 at 498, [1962] AC 294 at 302 and *Tinker v Tinker* (No. 2) [1970] 1 All ER 540 at 543, [1970] P 136 at 143 per Salmon LJ).

Third: it has, however, for some years been recognised that a completely executed transfer of property or of an interest in property made in pursuance of an unlawful agreement is valid and the court will assist the transferee in the protection of his interest provided that he does not require to found on the unlawful agreement (see *Ayerst v Jenkins* (1873) LR 16 Eq 275 at 283, *Alexander v Rayson* [1936] 1 KB 169 at 184–185, [1935] All ER Rep 185 at 191, *Bowmakers Ltd v Barnet Instruments Ltd* [1944] 2 All ER 579, [1945] KB 65, *Sajan Singh v Sardara Ali* [1960] 1 All ER 269 at 272–273, [1960] AC 167 at 176). To the extent, at least, of his third proposition it would appear that there has been some modification over the years of Lord Eldon LC's principles [in *Muckleston v Brown* (1801) 6 Ves 52 and *Curtis v Perry* (1802) 6 Ves 739].

The ultimate question in this appeal is, in my view, whether the respondent in claiming the existence of a resulting trust in her favour is seeking to enforce unperformed provisions of an unlawful transaction or whether she is simply relying on an equitable proprietary interest that she has already acquired under such a transaction. The nature of a resulting trust was described by Lord Diplock in *Gissing v Gissing* [1970] 2 All ER 780 at 790, [1971] AC 886 at 905 as follows:

A resulting, implied or constructive trust – and it is unnecessary for present purposes to distinguish between these three classes of trust – is created by a transaction between the trustee and the cestui que trust in connection with the acquisition by the trustee of a legal estate in land, whenever the trustee has so conducted himself that it would be inequitable to allow him to deny to the cestui que trust a beneficial interest in the land acquired. And he will be held so to have conducted himself if by his words or conduct he has induced the cestui que trust to act to his own detriment in the reasonable belief that by so acting he was acquiring a beneficial interest in the land.

I find this a very narrow question but I have come to the conclusion that the transaction whereby the claimed resulting trust in favour of the respondent was created was the agreement between the parties that, although funds were to be provided by both of them, nevertheless the title to the house was to be in the sole name of the appellant for the unlawful purpose of defrauding the Department of Social Security. So long as that agreement remained unperformed neither party could have enforced it against the other. However, as soon as the agreement was implemented by the sale to the appellant alone she became trustee for the respondent who can now rely on the equitable proprietary interest which has thereby been presumed to have been created in her favour and has no need to rely on the illegal transaction which led to its creation.

My Lords, I have had the advantage of reading in draft the speech of my noble and learned friend Lord Browne-Wilkinson. I agree with it and for the reasons contained therein as well as for the reasons in this speech I would dismiss the appeal.

Notes

1. Lord Browne-Wilkinson in fact went further than Lord Jauncey in the above passage, taking the view that the equitable principle operated in exactly the same way as the common law illegality doctrine, and that there was no difference between common law and equity in this regard.

2. In *Rowan* v *Dann* (1992) 64 P & CR 202, the Court of Appeal enforced a *Quistclose* trust of land (see further on *Quistclose* trusts chapter 2), using resulting trust reasoning. A farmer (Rowan) in financial difficulties entered into sham leases of his land with Dann, with whom he intended to go into a joint business venture (cattle-embryo transplanting). His sole intention in granting the leases was to keep the land out of hands of creditors, and no rent was ever paid, but no creditors were in the event actually defrauded. When the joint venture failed to get off the ground, the farmer got his land back on *Quistclose* principles. Dann argued that a resulting trust should not be available to aid Rowan as he did not have clean hands, since he had intended to defeat his creditors by the transaction. The case was heard before the decision of the House of Lords in *Tinsley* v *Milligan*, but is in line with it. Scott LJ, distinguishing a number of cases where the fraud principle had operated, observed:

> In each of these cases the plaintiff could not succeed without rebutting the presumption of advancement. The present case is quite different. There is a resulting trust in favour of Mr Rowan by reason of the failure of the joint venture project. This conclusion of a proprietary equitable interest in favour of Mr Rowan is consistent with a long line of authorities of which *Quistclose Investments* v *Rolls Razor Ltd* is a well-known example.
>
> Mr Rowan did not have anything to rebut. He did not have to rely on his dishonest intention to defeat his creditors in order to establish the equitable interest under the resulting trust. . . .

Woolf LJ took a similar approach:

> The important feature of this case is that subject to the issue of legality it is not in dispute that the land, the subject of the tenancy, would revert to

the plaintiff under a resulting trust. This is because of the non-implemen-
tation of the joint venture pursuant to which the tenancy agreement was
entered into. Because of this the plaintiff could succeed in the action
without reference to the illegality of purpose. All he needed to prove was

(1)   that he was the freehold owner;
(2)   that the tenancy was entered into for the purposes of the joint
venture;
(3)   the joint venture had been abandoned.

The situation was one where the defendants and not the plaintiffs had to
raise the illegality of purpose. If the defendants were putting forward a
claim to any interest in land, then it would be necessary for the court to
investigate the illegality on which the defendants sought to rely. However,
in my judgment, there was no need to go into the question of illegality in
this case because the defendants could not rely on the illegality to avoid the
effect in law and in equity of what happened. The position was no different
from the situation which would have existed if the tenancy had been subject
to a condition subsequent which terminated the tenancy on the abandonment of the joint venture.

SECTION 2:   GENERAL FRAUD JURISDICTION

A: Equity Will Not Allow a Statute to be Used as a Cloak for Fraud

Statute of Frauds 1677

**IV.   No action against executors, &c. upon a special promise, or upon any
agreement, or contract for sale of lands, &c. unless agreement, &c. be in
writing, and signed**
And bee it further enacted by the authoritie aforesaid that . . . noe action shall be brought
. . . upon any agreement made upon consideration of marriage or upon any contract or
sale of lands tenements or hereditaments or any interest in or concerning them or upon
any agreement that is not to be performed within the space of one yeare from the
makeing thereof unlesse the agreement upon which such action shall be brought or
some memorandum or note thereof shall be in writeing and signed by the partie to be
charged therewith or some other person thereunto by him lawfully authorized.

Note
The purpose of this provision, which was replaced by s. 40(1) of the Law of
Property Act 1925 (see below), was to prevent fraudulent claims upon
non-existent contracts, by requiring the contracts covered by the section to
be evidenced by writing. Where oral contracts were made and acted upon,
however, the section could potentially be used actively to promote fraud, by
allowing fraudulent denials of the existence of the contract by a party who
may already have received a benefit from it. The equitable doctrine of part
performance developed to prevent this section from being used as a cloak for
fraud.

Detailed discussion of part performance is beyond the scope of this book, but the leading case is *Steadman* v *Steadman* [1976] AC 536, where Lord Simon of Glaisdale described the development of the doctrine as follows (at pp. 558–559):

This is one of those difficult situations where two legal principles are in competition. The first legal principle is embodied in section 40(1) of the Law of Property Act 1925, which states: [Lord Simon set out the section, which is also set out below, and continued:]

This provision replaced that part of section 4 of the Statute of Frauds 1677 which related to interests in land. The preamble to the Statute of Frauds explained its object: 'For prevention of many fraudulent practices, which are commonly endeavoured to be upheld by perjury and subornation of perjury; . . .' The 'mischief' for which the statute was providing a remedy was, therefore, that some transactions were being conducted orally in such a way that important interests were liable to be adversely affected by a mode of operation that invited forensic mendacity. The remedy was to require some greater formality in the record of such transaction than mere word of mouth if it was to be enforced. The continuing need for such a remedy for such a mischief was apparently recognised as subsisting when the law of landed property was recast in 1925.

The second, competing, legal principle was evoked when, almost from the moment of passing of the Statute of Frauds, it was appreciated that it was being used for a variant of unconscionable dealing, which the statute itself was designed to remedy. A party to an oral contract for the disposition of an interest in land could, despite performance of the reciprocal terms by the other party, by virtue of the statute disclaim liability for his own performance on the ground that the contract had not been in writing. Common Law was helpless. But Equity, with its purpose of vindicating good faith and with its remedies of injunction and specific performance, could deal with the situation. The Statute of Frauds did not make such contracts void but merely unenforceable; and, if the statute was to be relied on as a defence, it had to be specifically pleaded. Where, therefore, a party to a contract unenforceable under the Statute of Frauds stood by while the other party acted to his detriment in performance of his own contractual obligations, the first party would be precluded by the Court of Chancery from claiming exoneration, on the ground that the contract was unenforceable, from performance of his reciprocal obligations; and the court would, if required, decree specific performance of the contract. Equity would not, as it was put, allow the Statute of Frauds 'to be used as an engine of fraud.' This became known as the doctrine of part performance – the 'part' performance being that of the party who had, to the knowledge of the other party, acted to his detriment in carrying out irremediably his own obligations (or some significant part of them) under the otherwise unenforceable contract. This competing principle has also received statutory recognition, as regards contracts affecting interests in land, in section 40(2) of the Law of Property Act 1925.

But what was in origin a rule of substantive law designed to vindicate conscientious dealing seems to have come in time sometimes to have been considered somewhat as a rule of evidence. It is easy to appreciate how this happened. Part performance could be viewed as a way of proving an agreement falling within section 4 notwithstanding the absence of writing. Seen as such, it was no doubt considered necessary to frame stringent requirements to prevent the doctrine from carting a sedan chair through the provisions of the statute. If part performance was to be evidence of a contract which could not otherwise and directly be proved, the acts of part performance should themselves intrinsically be capable of proving some such contract as that alleged. Oral evidence was not admissible to connect them with the alleged contract: otherwise, it was held, the statutory object would be defeated by allowing an interest in land to pass on mere oral testimony. As the Earl of Selborne LC put it in *Maddison* v *Alderson* (1883) 8 App Cas 467, 478, 479 . . .:

> The doctrine . . . has been confined . . . within limits intended to prevent a recurrence of the mischief which the statute was passed to suppress. . . . All the authorities show that the acts relied upon as part performance must be unequivocally, and in their own nature referable to some such agreement as that alleged.

It may be questionable whether it was direct respect for the statute which led to such confinement of the doctrine, or whether it was not rather because part performance seems sometimes to have been regarded as an alternative way of proving an oral agreement; for Equity allowed a person to prove by parol evidence that land conveyed to another was so conveyed on trust for himself, notwithstanding section 7 of the Statute of Frauds: *Rochefoucauld* v *Boustead* [1897] 1 Ch 196, 206 [set out in the judgment in *Hodgson* v *Marks*, below] *Bannister* v *Bannister* [1948] 2 All ER 133, 136 [below] – the passages show that here, too, the guiding rule was that the court would not allow the statute to be used as a cloak for fraud. However that may be, the speech of the Earl of Selborne LC has always been regarded as authoritative, notwithstanding that what he said about part performance was, strictly, obiter.

Lord Reid observed (at p. 540):

> This matter has a very long history. Section 40 replaced a part of section 4 of the Statute of Frauds 1677 (29 Car. 2, c. 3), and very soon after the passing of that Act authorities on this matter began to accumulate. It is now very difficult to find from them any clear guidance of general application. But it is not difficult to see at least one principle behind them. If one party to an agreement stands by and lets the other party incur expense or prejudice his position on the faith of the agreement being valid he will not then be allowed to turn round and assert that the agreement is unenforceable. Using fraud in its older and less precise sense, that would be fraudulent on his part and it has become proverbial that courts of equity will not permit the statute to be made an instrument of fraud.
>
> It must be remembered that this legislation did not and does not make oral contracts relating to land void: it only makes them unenforceable. And the statutory provision must be pleaded; otherwise the court does not apply it. So it is in keeping with equitable principles that in proper circumstances a person will not be allowed 'fraudulently' to take advantage of a defence of this kind. There is nothing about part performance in the Statute of Frauds. It is an invention of the Court of Chancery and in deciding any case not clearly covered by authority I think that the equitable nature of the remedy must be kept in mind.

Law of Property Act 1925

40. Contracts for sale, etc., of land to be in writing

(1) No action may be brought upon any contract for the sale or other disposition of land or any interest in land, unless the agreement upon which such action is brought, or some memorandum or note thereof, is in writing, and signed by the party to be charged or by some other person thereunto by him lawfully authorised.

(2) This section applies to contracts made before or after the commencement of this Act and does not affect the law relating to part performance, or sales by the court.

Question
Suppose that s. 2 below had never been enacted. In the light of the above passages from *Steadman v Steadman*, do you think that would have made any difference, and if so, what difference?

Law of Property (Miscellaneous Provisions) Act 1989

2. Contracts for sale etc. of land to be made by signed writing
(1) A contract for the sale or other disposition of an interest in land can only be made in writing and only by incorporating all the terms which the parties have expressly agreed in one document or, where contracts are exchanged, in each.

(2) The terms may be incorporated in a document either by being set out in it or by reference to some other document.

(3) The document incorporating the terms or, where contracts are exchanged, one of the documents incorporating them (but not necessarily the same one) must be signed by or on behalf of each party to the contract.

(4) Where a contract for the sale or other disposition of an interest in land satisfies the conditions of this section by reason only of the rectification of one or more documents in pursuance of an order of a court, the contract shall come into being, or be deemed to have come into being, at such time as may be specified in the order.

(5) This section does not apply in relation to —

(a) a contract to grant such a lease as is mentioned in section 54(2) of the Law Property Act 1925 (short leases);

(b) a contract made in the course of a public auction; or

(c) a contract regulated under the Financial Services Act 1986;

and nothing in this section affects the creation or operation of resulting, implied or constructive trusts.

(6) In this section —

'disposition' has the same meaning as in the Law of Property Act 1925;

'interest in land' means any estate, interest or charge in or over land or in or over the proceeds of sale of land.

(7) Nothing in this section shall apply in relation to contracts made before this section comes into force.

(8) Section 40 of the Law of Property Act 1925 (which is superseded by this section) shall cease to have effect.

Questions
1. What are the differences between s. 2(1) of the 1989 Act and s. 40(1) of the 1925 Act?

2. Is the doctrine of part performance expressly abolished by this statute?

Professor P. H. Pettit, *'Farewell Section 40'* [1989] Conv 441

As is well-known, section 40 replaced provisions first contained in section 4 of the Statute of Frauds 1677, the purpose of which was to prevent the injustice that was thought likely to occur from perjury or fraud when oral evidence was admitted. Although the Court of Chancery was bound by statute, it nevertheless regarded itself as having power to intervene where the strict application of the statute would actually operate to promote fraud rather than to prevent it. It became clear soon after the Statute was passed that this could well happen. There might in fact be a genuine contract, but no proper memorandum, and one of the parties might fraudulently seek to evade liability by reason of the absence of writing. Cases began to appear in the reports within 10 years of the Statute being passed, and the doctrine of part-performance was conclusively established by the House of Lords in *Lester* v *Foxcroft* (1701) Colles PC 108 as early as 1701. It is hardly necessary to repeat here that that doctrine was to the effect that a plaintiff who was unable to produce the required evidence in writing, might nevertheless succeed in obtaining the equitable remedy of specific performance where he had done some act or acts in relation to the contract in reliance on the defendant's promise, provided that the acts of part-performance were such as to indicate on a balance of probabilities that they were performed in reliance on a contract with the defendant which was consistent with the contract alleged.

It is an inevitable consequence of section 2 that the doctrine of part-performance no longer has a role to play in contracts concerning land. The simple fact is that under the new law if section 2 is not complied with there is no contract for either party to perform.

Note

As authority for the statement at the end of the first paragraph above, Pettit cites *Steadman* v *Steadman*, above, and *Re Gonin* [1979] Ch 16, and also refers to (1974) 38 Conv 388 and [1979] Conv 402.

Law of Property Act 1925

53. Instruments required to be in writing

(1) . . .

(b) a declaration of trust respecting any land or any interest therein must be manifested and proved by some writing signed by some person who is able to declare such trust or by his will; . . .

(2) This section does not affect the creation or operation of resulting, implied or constructive trusts.

Note

A non-compliant disposition is rendered void by this provision, which is the successor to ss. 7 and 8 of the Statute of Frauds 1677:

AND bee it further enacted by the authoritie aforesaid that . . . all declarations or creations of trusts or confidences of any lands tenements or hereditaments shall be manifested and proved by some writeing signed by the partie who is by law enabled to declare such trust or by his last will in writeing or else they shall be utterly void and of none effect.

PROVIDED alwayes that where any conveyance shall bee made of any lands or tenements by which a trust or confidence shall or may arise or result by the implication or construction of law or bee transferred or extinguished by an act or operation of law then and in every such case such trust or confidence shall be of like force and effect as the same would have beene if this statute had not beene made. Any thing herein before contained to the contrary notwithstanding.

Just as with s. 2 of the 1989 Act, there is no contract unless it is in writing, so with s. 53(1)(b) there is no trust unless it is in writing. However, the decisions of *Rochefoucauld* v *Boustead* [1897] 1 Ch 196 and *Hodgson* v *Marks* (below) suggest that this form of wording does not preclude the operation of an equitable fraud doctrine.

Hodgson v *Marks*
[1970] 3 WLR 956, [1970] 3 All ER 513
Chancery Division
Reversed on other grounds by the Court of Appeal [1971] 1 Ch 892

Decision: The facts and decision are set out at the beginning of chapter 9.

UNGOED-THOMAS J (set out the facts and continued on the s. 53 point): My conclusion, therefore, is that the transfer of the house by Mrs Hodgson to Mr Evans was under an oral arrangement between them, under which no beneficial interest was to pass to Mr Evans, and was on trust for Mrs Hodgson.

. . .

The question now arises whether the trust in favour of Mrs Hodgson, absolutely beneficially, under the oral arrangement in accordance with which the house was transferred to Mr Evans, is void or ineffective by reason of section 53 of the Law of Property Act, 1925. Section 53 reads [Ungoed-Thomas J set out ss. 53 and 54(1) (see chapter 6) and continued:]

The provisions of section 53 replace corresponding provisions of sections 3, 7, 8 and 9 of the Statute of Frauds. As argued before me, nothing turns on section 54 or on there being any resulting implied or constructive trust within section 53(2). So the question as argued became: Did the principle that the Statute of Frauds should not be used as an instrument of fraud dispense with the writing that would otherwise be essential under section 53 to establish the trust in Mrs Hodgson's favour?

In the leading case *Rochefoucauld* v *Boustead* [1897] 1 Ch 196, the defendant bought property on an express oral trust for the plaintiff, subject to specified advances. The defendant subsequently spent money on developing the property. He also raised money for himself personally by mortgages of the property; and later he or his mortgagees sold the property without the plaintiff's knowledge. Despite the absence of writing required by the Statute of Frauds, the plaintiff successfully contended that the property was bought in trust for her, subject to the specified advances and the defendant's outlays on the property; and for an account on that footing. The purchaser and mortgagees, from whom the defendant raised money, for his personal purposes, were not parties to the proceedings. No order was made with regard to the property itself; and as the property is said to have been sold by the defendant or his mortgagees, presumably those mortgagees were paid off out of the proceeds of sale.

The evidential character of the writing is emphasised, at p. 206:

But it is not necessary that the trust should have been declared by such a writing in the first instance; it is sufficient if the trust can be proved by some writing signed by the defendant, and the date of the writing is immaterial.

Then the judgment goes on to state the principle on which oral evidence of the trust is admitted.

It is further established by a series of cases, the propriety of which cannot now be questioned, that the Statute of Frauds does not prevent the proof of a fraud; and that it is a fraud on the part of a person to whom land is conveyed as a trustee, and who knows it was so conveyed, to deny the trust and claim the land himself. Consequently, notwithstanding the statute, it is competent for a person claiming land conveyed to another to prove by parol evidence that it was so conveyed upon trust for the claimant, and that the grantee, knowing the facts, is denying the trust and relying upon the form of conveyance and the statute, in order to keep the land himself.

It was submitted for the defendants that the principle was limited to cases in which the person relying on the statute was himself the person who had accepted the conveyance of the land as trustee and who nevertheless claimed the land free from the trust. The quoted statement of the principle is expressed in terms compatible with this submission and so lends colour to it. But such statements have to be considered in the light of their facts. In *Rochefoucauld v Boustead* [1897] 1 Ch 196 the grantee who himself took the land on the oral trust had transferred the land in breach of the trust and in fraud of the plaintiff. So there was no occasion in that case to state the principle, except with reference to such a person. In *In re Duke of Marlborough* [1894] Ch 133 the principle was stated at p. 145 in terms to the same effect as in *Rochefoucauld v Boustead* [1897] 1 Ch 196 but those who unsuccessfully relied on the statute in that case were not the original grantee trustee but his executors. So either the principle applies to them as standing in the original grantee's place or it is to be understood more widely than the defendants submit.

Whoever relies upon the statutory requirement of writing is himself using the statute as an instrument to avoid cognisance being taken of the trust. This might occur in circumstances in which establishment of the trust would establish fraud, for example, where, as here, a transfer on oral trust would be taken free of the trust. No other defence is in the least affected by thus dispensing with the statutory requirement of writing. The oral evidence in our case is directed to establishing the trust, i.e., the true nature of the transfer to Mr Evans, and does not affect such defences as those which have been based upon what subsequently happened and estoppel. The statute is thus only a material defence when there is no other effective defence. So if there is other effective defence, the defendant is not defeated; and if there is none, then if he succeeds by relying on the statute, he succeeds only by excluding the evidence of the trust and thus of the fraud. This is so, whether the defendant be, for example, a volunteer or a purchaser for value without notice. So to the extent to which a person relies on the statutory defence to exclude the establishment of fraud, he uses the statute as an instrument of fraud – to succeed by using the statute to exclude evidence of fraud.

In *Rochefoucauld v Boustead* [1897] 1 Ch 196 such a case as that now before me was treated as falling exclusively within the section corresponding to section 53(1)(b) of the Law of Property Act 1925, and the defendants did not attempt to rely on any of the other provisions of section 53 to escape the operation of the principle.

It was further submitted for the defendants that the inclusion in the transfer by Mrs Hodgson to Mr Evans of its being made in consideration of her love and affection for him excluded any resulting trust. Lord Upjohn's observations in *Vandervell v Inland Revenue Commissioners* [1967] 2 AC 291, 312 were referred to. Those observations were made in reference exclusively to resulting trusts; but, as I have said, Mrs Hodgson expressly disclaimed relying on any resulting trust. It did not appear to me that the defendants relied on this reference to consideration of love and affection to defeat the admission of oral evidence of the trust, although counsel for Mrs Hodgson did seem concerned at one stage to rebut such an argument. It seems to me that such a submission would be contrary to the well-established principle that extrinsic evidence is always admissible of the true nature of any transaction, for example, to establish that conveyances, despite their terms, are according to the true nature of the transaction mortgages. *Lincoln* v *Wright* (1859) 4 De G & J 16, itself a Statute of Frauds case, was a conveyance in form which it was agreed should operate as a mortgage. In *Haigh* v *Kaye* (1872) 7 Ch App 469 a conveyance was expressed to be in consideration of a money payment and was of an estate described as absolute. There was in fact no consideration. (The plaintiff thus conveyed the estate, because he had feared an adverse decision in a pending suit, but it was held that that did not affect the position.) It was held that, although the defendant invoked the Statute of Frauds, the plaintiff was entitled to have the estate reconveyed to him.

My conclusion, therefore, is that the defendants are not entitled to exclude parol evidence of the trust.

Notes

1. As we saw at the start of chapter 9, Russell LJ thought that Mrs Hodgson's interest was by way of resulting trust. Mrs Hodgson did not argue a resulting trust, however, but an express trust, and this was the basis of Ungoed-Thomas J's decision in the High Court. It should be noted that although Ungoed-Thomas J was reversed in the Court of Appeal, the reversal was only as to the interpretation of the Land Registration Act, not on the question of the existence of a trust. Ungoed-Thomas J relied on *Rochefoucauld* v *Boustead* [1897] 1 Ch 196. Note that in neither case was any reliance placed on s. 53(2), or its precursor in the 1677 Act.

2. The reasoning of Lindley LJ, who delivered the judgment of the court in *Rochefoucauld* v *Boustead*, does not expressly extend beyond the particular statute: the court 'will not allow the Statute of Frauds to be made an instrument of fraud'. Nevertheless, it would probably apply where there is an attempt to use any statute intended to prevent fraud as a means of perpetrating a fraud. Thus the reasoning probably applies to any statutory formality requirement.

3. Russell LJ seemed unsure whether the *Rochefoucauld* v *Boustead* principle could apply to Marks, the third party purchaser. This is why he preferred to base his decision on resulting trust reasoning, but he would have been happy to apply Ungoed-Thomas J's reasoning to Mr Evans, the original lodger:

Quite plainly Mr Evans could not have placed any reliance on s. 53, for that would have been to use the section as an instrument of fraud.

4. The cases considered so far in this chapter are authority for the proposition that equity will not allow a statute whose purpose is to prevent fraud to be used as a means of perpetrating fraud. Secret and half-secret trusts considered in the last chapter are further examples of the same principle. It

is important to note the limits of the doctrine. No contract has ever been created by the part performance doctrine. In all the cases there has been a valid offer, acceptance, consideration and intention to create legal relations, and the contract would have been enforceable in all respects apart from the statutory formality provisions. Similarly with secret and half-secret trusts, there would have been a valid trust but for the operation of the Wills Act. The doctrine does not create trusts out of nothing. It provides a mechanism for enforcing trusts that are unenforceable only because of the operation of the Wills Act.

The doctrine may amount to no more than an interpretation of the statutory provisions. All the provisions originate with the Statute of Frauds 1677, whose preamble begins:

FOR prevention of many fraudulent practices which are commonly endeavoured to be upheld by perjury and subornation of perjury . . .

It would be odd for the courts to interpret the provisions, or those of successor statutes, in such a way as to allow perpetration of the very fraudulent practices which the 1677 statute sought to prevent.

However, the fraud principle adopted in these cases probably does not apply to every statutory provision. Indeed, it would be difficult to argue that it applies to the Land Charges Act 1925 (which was intended to simplify conveyancing, not prevent fraud), following the House of Lords decision in *Midland Bank Trust Co.* v *Green* [1981] AC 513 (set out in chapter 1). There a sham sale between husband and wife, intended specifically to defeat a third party's valuable option to purchase a farm, succeeded in its purpose, solely because the option had not been properly registered under the Act. Lord Wilberforce said (at p. 531a) that in general it is not 'fraud' to rely on legal rights conferred by Act of Parliament.

Questions
1.   In the light of the discussion on s. 53(1)(b), and its precursor in the 1677 Act, which render dispositions which do not comply void, do you agree with Professor Pettit's conclusion that part performance no longer has a role to play in contracts concerning land? Does your answer depend on whether the Law of Property (Miscellaneous Provisions) Act 1989 was intended to prevent fraud or to promote certainty in conveyancing?
2.   Was Russell LJ correct to doubt whether the *Rochefoucauld* v *Boustead* principle could apply to the third party, Marks?
3.   Section 90 of the Copyright, Designs and Patents Act 1988 provides that '[a]n assignment of copyright is not effective unless it is in writing signed by or on behalf of the assignor', and under the Consumer Credit Act 1974 many consumer credit agreements must be in a prescribed written form and signed. Do you think that it would be possible to apply a doctrine based on part performance if these provisions were not complied with?

B: Wider Fraud Jurisdiction?

This section considers the extent to which, if at all, there is an equitable fraud jurisdiction of more general application than that considered in the previous section.

In addition to the cases considered below, the authorities on floating constructive trusts at the end of chapter 10 are also relevant to this discussion. I suggested there that the authorities for the existence of the floating constructive trust are probably not conclusive, or alternatively that their application to mutual wills may perhaps be justified on the grounds that the floating constructive trust is the only way of enforcing this particular type of contract.

I would suggest that there is no general equitable fraud jurisdiction, and that the cases below which suggest the contrary can be explained in other ways, as ordinary express or resulting trusts, or on a contractual analysis. Certainly there are statements in the cases suggesting a far wider jurisdiction, but where the cases have been subsequently considered, the courts have generally preferred a narrow interpretation. It may be that there is an unwillingness to use a property concept, such as the constructive trust, to do justice in a particular case, given all the other consequences of creating property rights.

Neste Oy v *Lloyds Bank plc, The Tiiskeri*
[1983] 2 Lloyd's Rep 658
Queen's Bench Division (Commercial Court)

Facts: The plaintiff shipowners made a series of payments to PSL (their agents) to discharge liabilities relating to their vessels. PSL were a customer of the defendant bank. They got into financial difficulties and by the time the sixth and last payment was made PSL had resolved to cease trading. The defendant bank claimed to set off the last payment against PSL's debts, and the plaintiffs challenged their right to set off.

Held: The last payment was held on constructive trust for the plaintiffs. The defendant bank was also bound because it had the requisite knowledge (see further on this chapter 19), and therefore these funds were not available for set-off.

BINGHAM J: My conclusion that there was no express trust in respect of the first five payments must, if correct, apply to the last payment also. But Counsel for the plaintiffs contended that PSL were constructive trustees of this last payment, whether or not they were constructive trustees of the earlier payments. He founded this distinction not on a mistake of fact by the plaintiffs (which he was refused leave to amend to allege) but on the fact that this payment was credited to PSL at a time when Peckston Group Ltd had already resolved that it and its group companies should cease trading immediately (one of the directors supporting that resolution being a director of PSL), at a time when PSL had not paid for the services for which the funds had been remitted and at a time when, in all the circumstances, there was no chance that PSL could pay for the services in question. This, submitted Counsel, was a case falling within the statement of Mr Justice Cardozo in *Beatty* v *Guggenheim Exploration Co.* 225 NY 380 (1919) at p. 386, and quoted in Snell's *Principles of Equity* (28th ed.) at p. 192:

> . . . A constructive trust is the formula through which the conscience of equity finds expression. When property has been acquired in such circumstances that the holder of the legal title may not in good conscience retain the beneficial interest, equity converts him into a trustee.

Counsel also relied on the general principles contained in a passage from Story's Commentaries on Equity Jurisprudence, 2nd ed. (1839) vol. 2, par. 1255, accepted as correctly stating the law of England by Goulding J in *Chase Manhattan Bank NA* v *Israel-British Bank (London) Ltd* [1981] Ch 105 [see chapter 17], at pp. 117C and 118E:

> 1255. One of the most common cases in which a Court of Equity acts upon the ground of implied trusts *in invitum*, is where a party has received money which he cannot conscientiously withhold from another party. It has been well remarked, that the receiving of money which consistently with conscience cannot be retained is, in Equity, sufficient to raise a trust in favour of the party for whom or on whose account it was received. This is the governing principle in all such cases. And therefore, whenever any controversy arises, the true question is, not whether money has been received by a party of which he could not have compelled the payment, but whether he can now, with a safe conscience, *ex aequo et bono*, retain it. Illustrations of this doctrine are familiar in cases of money paid by accident, or mistake, or fraud. And the difference between the payment of money under a mistake of fact, and a payment under a mistake of law, in its operation upon the conscience of the party, presents the equitable qualifications of the doctrine in a striking manner.

Counsel for the bank contended that no relevant distinction could be drawn between the first five payments and the last. While naturally diffident at entering seas so little chart, and regarded with great caution by mariners much more expert than I, it seems to me that there is a relevant distinction. Given the situation of PSL when the last payment was received, any reasonable and honest directors of that company (or the actual directors had they known of it) would, I feel sure, have arranged for the repayment of that sum to the plaintiffs without hesitation or delay. It would have seemed little short of sharp practice for PSL to take any benefit from the payment, and it would have seemed contrary to any ordinary notion of fairness that the general body of creditors should profit from the accident of a payment made at a time when there was bound to be a total failure of consideration. Of course it is true that insolvency always causes loss and perfect fairness is unattainable. The bank, and other creditors, have their legitimate claims. It nonetheless seems to me that at the time of its receipt PSL could not in good conscience retain this payment and that accordingly a constructive trust is to be inferred.

I thus answer this first question: No, but PSL became constructive trustees for the plaintiffs of the last payment of £21,327.50 made on Feb. 22, 1980.

[Bingham J continued on the question of notice:]

If so, did the bank have such notice that the funds were so held as to preclude it from exercising any right of set-off in respect of these funds?

If the answer I have already given is correct, this question arises for decision only in respect of the last payment. But in case I am wrong I should indicate the answer I would give to the question on that hypothesis.

Counsel for the plaintiffs submitted (in my judgment rightly) that if PSL held these funds as trustee the bank was not entitled to take the benefit of them unless the bank was at the time of doing so a *bona fide* purchaser for value without notice of the trust. Counsel further submitted, with reference to the recent judgment of Peter Gibson J in *Baden Delvaux and Lecuit v Société General pour Favouriser le Développement du Commerce et du l'Industrie en France SA* [1983] BCLC 325, that it was enough for the plaintiffs to establish the requisite notice by showing, as he contended they did here, that the bank wilfully shut its eyes to the obvious or wilfully and recklessly failed to make such enquiries as an honest and reasonable man would have made or knew of circumstances which would have indicated the facts to an honest and reasonable man. As the source of such notice the plaintiffs relied on the bank's knowledge (through Mr Martin) of PSL's mode of business and (from Mr Barrows) of PSL's pre-funding; on the daily contact between Mr Martin and Mr Lambert; on the transfer of (on the whole) round sums, not suggestive of precisely calculated invoice amounts; and on the details accompanying the payments, particularly where the word 'advance' was used. Reliance was naturally placed on an answer by Mr Martin in cross-examination when he agreed that the use of the word 'advance' showed that a payment was being made in advance, not in arrears, as would have occurred to him had he seen the documents (which he had not done at the time). . . .

[Bingham J considered the first five payments and continued:]

It remains to consider the last payment, which I have held to have been subject to a constructive trust. This payment cannot in all probability have been credited to PSL's main account before the bank had learned of the Peckston Group Ltd. decision that it and the group companies should cease trading at once and seek appointment of a receiver. The bank did not then know all the facts but it did know that PSL would trade no more and I think it was at that point clearly put on enquiry. An enquiry then would have elicited the facts which have led me to conclude that a constructive trust arose. It had not at that point given value. By the time the set-off was effected the bank was even more clearly on notice. The result is, in my opinion, that the bank cannot assert its right to set-off in respect of this last payment held by PSL upon a constructive trust for the plaintiffs.

Notes

1. It might be argued that this case is similar to the *Quistclose* decision in chapter 2, in which case it is of interest that the money was not paid into a separate account.

2. Although there are indeed factual similarities between this case and *Quistclose*, the reasoning here is not in *Quistclose* terms, but in terms of imposition of a constructive trust. Yet although the reasoning is in terms of constructive rather than resulting trust, this case is (I would suggest) effectively the same as *Vandervell v IRC* (chapter 8), or perhaps the Court of Appeal decision in *Hodgson v Marks* (chapter 9). It is clear that the grantee was not intended to take beneficially, and no provision had been made for the disposal of the equitable interest. It therefore reverted to the settlor.

3. This case does not therefore seem to be authority for a wide general principle for the imposition of a constructive trust to prevent fraud. We saw

in the previous chapter that mutual wills are enforced in order to prevent fraud, but special features are present there and it would be difficult to argue from those cases to a general jurisdiction based on fraud.

Bannister v *Bannister*
[1948] 2 All ER 133
Court of Appeal

Facts: The defendant was negotiating to sell two cottages to the plaintiff, her brother in law, and it was understood that after the sale she would be able to continue to live in one of the cottages rent free for as long as she wished. Because of this oral arrangement the plaintiff obtained the cottages for only £250, as compared with their true market value of around £400.

No written agreement giving rights to the defendant was included in the conveyance, however. She relied on his oral statement: 'I do not want to take any rent, but will let you stay' in one of the cottages 'as long as you like rent free',

After the sale, the plaintiff claimed possession of the cottage.

Held: The plaintiff held the cottage as constructive trustee of the defendant for her life.

SCOTT LJ: The conclusion . . . reached by the learned county court judge was attacked in this court on substantially the following three grounds:— First, it was said that the oral undertaking found by the learned county court judge to have formed part of the agreement – namely, that the plaintiff would let the defendant stay in No. 30 as long as she liked rent free – did not, as a matter of construction of the language used, amount to a promise that the defendant should retain a life interest in No. 30, but amounted merely to a promise that the plaintiff would allow the defendant to remain in No. 30 rent free as his tenant at will. Secondly, it was said that, even if the terms of the oral undertaking were such as to amount to a promise that the defendant should retain a life interest in No. 30, a tenancy at will free of rent was, nevertheless, the greatest interest she could claim in view of the absence of writing and the provisions of ss. 53 and 54 of the Law of Property Act, 1925. Thirdly, it was said that a constructive trust in favour of the defendant (which the absence of writing admittedly would not defeat) could only be raised by findings to the effect that there was actual fraud on the part of the plaintiff and that the property was sold and conveyed to him on the faith of an express oral declaration of trust which it would be fraudulent in him to deny. It was, accordingly, submitted that the learned county court judge's conclusion that there was a constructive trust could not stand since it was negatived by his finding that there was no fraud in the case and by the absence of any evidence of anything amounting to an express oral declaration of trust.

[Scott LJ rejected the first objection and continued:]

As will be seen from what is said below, the second objection (based on want of writing) in effect stands or falls with the third, and it will, therefore, be convenient to deal with that next. It is, we think, clearly a mistake to suppose that the equitable principle on which a constructive trust is raised against a person who insists on the absolute character of a conveyance to himself for the purpose of defeating a beneficial interest, which, according to the true bargain, was to belong to another, is confined to cases in which the conveyance itself was fraudulently obtained. The fraud which brings the principle into play arises as soon as the absolute character of the conveyance

is set up for the purpose of defeating the beneficial interest, and that is the fraud to cover which the Statute of Frauds or the corresponding provisions of the Law of Property Act, 1925, cannot be called in aid in cases in which no written evidence of the real bargain is available. Nor is it, in our opinion, necessary that the bargain on which the absolute conveyance is made should include any express stipulation that the grantee is in so many words to hold as trustee. It is enough that the bargain should have included a stipulation under which some sufficiently defined beneficial interest in the property was to be taken by another. The above propositions are, we think, clearly borne out by . . . *Rochefoucauld* v *Boustead*. We see no distinction in principle between a case in which property is conveyed to a purchaser on terms that the entire beneficial interest in some part of it is to be retained by the vendor . . . and a case, like the present, in which property is conveyed to a purchaser on terms that a limited beneficial interest in some part of it is to be retained by the vendor. We are, accordingly, of opinion that the third ground of objection to the learned county court judge's conclusion also fails. His finding that there was no fraud in the case cannot be taken as meaning that it was not fraudulent in the plaintiff to insist on the absolute character of the conveyance for the purpose of defeating the beneficial interest which he had agreed the defendant should retain. The conclusion that the plaintiff was fraudulent, in this sense, necessarily follows from the facts found, and, as indicated above, the fact that he may have been innocent of any fraudulent intent in taking the conveyance in absolute form is for this purpose immaterial. The failure of the third ground of objection necessarily also destroys the second objection based on want of writing and the provisions of ss. 53 and 54 of the Law of Property Act 1925.
. . .

In the result, we hold that the appeal fails and the order of the learned county court judge should be affirmed, but in the interests of accuracy we think his order should be varied by substituting a declaration to the effect that the plaintiff holds No. 30 in trust during the life of the defendant to permit the defendant to occupy the same for so long as she may desire to do so and subject thereto in trust for the plaintiff. A trust in this form has the effect of making the beneficiary a tenant for life within the meaning of the Settled Land Act, 1925, and, consequently, there is a very little practical difference between such a trust and a trust for life *simpliciter*. The appeal will be dismissed with that variation in the form of the order. The plaintiff must pay the costs of the appeal.

Note

Although few would doubt that the defendant should have been protected against a possession order by the plaintiff, the conclusion that she should be treated as a tenant for life within the Settled Land Act 1925 (on which, see further chapter 1) is perhaps regrettable, but it may be the inevitable consequence of the constructive trust reasoning, giving her a full beneficial life tenancy in the property.

The questions are directed towards the possibility of finding alternative routes to protecting the defendant, without the need to develop a general fraud doctrine leading to the imposition of a constructive trust.

Questions

1. If you take property expressly subject to a condition that you hold it for the benefit of somebody else, why are you not an express trustee?

2.   If this case is merely an example of an express declaration of trusteeship by the plaintiff, could he have relied on s. 53(1)(b) given the decision in *Rochefoucauld* v *Boustead*, above?

3.   If this is really an express trust, is the defendant a tenant for life under the Settled Land Act 1925?

4.   Given that there was no third party involved, could the defendant have been adequately protected on the basis of a contractual or estoppel licence? Do such licences have to be in writing?

5.   If the defendant were merely a contractual or estoppel licensee, would she be a tenant for life under the Settled Land Act 1925?

Sir Nicholas Browne-Wilkinson, '*Constructive Trusts and Unjust Enrichment*' Holdsworth Club Address, 1991

According to the conventional equitable principles, the consequences of holding that there is a constructive trust go far beyond making the constructive trustee himself personally liable to the beneficiary. The essence of the constructive trust is that the property held by the constructive trustee is itself trust property. The beneficiary . . . has an equitable interest . . . from the date when the constructive trust arises: that equitable interest . . . is enforceable against the [property] even in the hands of third parties unless the third party is a purchaser for value without notice. Therefore, according to the conventional law of trusts, the imposition of a constructive trust may have an effect far beyond requiring someone who has been unjustly enriched to disgorge his unjust enrichment. Third parties who have not been unjustly enriched may suffer as a result of holding that there is a constructive trust.

Note

The next case is an example of the imposition of a constructive trust on a purchaser. In considering whether it gives rise to any potential conveyancing difficulties, you may care to give thought to the position of a subsequent purchaser, in the event that Mr and Mrs Binions sell the property on in Mrs Evans's lifetime.

Binions v *Evans* [1972] Ch 359 Court of Appeal

Facts: Mrs Evans's husband was employed by the Tredegar Estate (near Newport in South Wales) and lived rent-free in a cottage owned by the estate. The husband died when the defendant (Mrs Evans) was 73.

The trustees of the estate then entered into an agreement with the defendant that she could continue to live in the cottage during her lifetime as tenant at will rent-free; she undertook to keep the cottage in good condition and repair.

Subsequently the estate sold the cottage to the plaintiffs. The contract provided that the property was sold subject to the 'tenancy agreement'. In consequence of that provision, the plaintiffs paid a reduced price for the cottage.

The plaintiffs sought to eject the defendant, claiming that she was a tenant at will.

Held: That plaintiffs' claim failed. Megaw and Stephenson LJJ decided the case on the grounds that the defendant was a tenant for life under the Settled Land Act 1925. Lord Denning MR held that the plaintiffs took the property subject to a constructive trust for the defendant's benefit.

LORD DENNING MR: Suppose, however, that the defendant did not have an equitable interest at the outset, nevertheless it is quite plain that she obtained one afterwards when the Tredegar Estate sold the cottage. They stipulated with the plaintiffs that they were to take the house 'subject to' the defendant's rights under the agreement. They supplied the plaintiffs with a copy of the contract: and the plaintiffs paid less because of her right to stay there. In these circumstances, this court will impose on the plaintiffs a constructive trust for her benefit: for the simple reason that it would be utterly inequitable for the plaintiffs to turn the defendant out contrary to the stipulation subject to which they took the premises. That seems to me clear from the important decision of *Bannister* v *Bannister* [1948] 2 All ER 133, which was applied by the judge, and which I gladly follow.

This imposing of a constructive trust is entirely in accord with the precepts of equity. As Cardozo J once put it: 'A constructive trust is the formula through which the conscience of equity finds expression', see *Beatty* v *Guggenheim Exploration Co.* (1919) 225 NY 380, 386: or, as Lord Diplock put it quite recently in *Gissing* v *Gissing* [1971] AC 886, 905, a constructive trust is created 'whenever the trustee has so conducted himself that it would be inequitable to allow him to deny the cestui que trust a beneficial interest in the land acquired'.

I know that there are some who have doubted whether a contractual licensee has any protection against a purchaser, even one who takes with full notice. We were referred in this connection to Professor Wade's article 'Licences and third parties' in (1952) 68 LQR 337, and to the judgment of Goff J in *Re Solomon, a Bankrupt, ex parte Trustee of the Bankrupt* v *Solomon* [1967] Ch 573. None of these doubts can prevail, however, when the situation gives rise to a constructive trust. Whenever the owner sells the land to a purchaser, and at the same time stipulates that he shall take it 'subject to' a contractual licence, I think it plain that a court of equity will impose on the purchaser a constructive trust in favour of the beneficiary. . . .

In many of these cases the purchaser takes expressly 'subject to' the rights of the licensee. Obviously the purchaser then holds the land on an imputed trust for the licensee. But, even if he does not take expressly 'subject to' the rights of the licensee, he may do so impliedly. At any rate when the licensee is in actual occupation of the land, so that the purchaser must know that he is there, and of the rights which he has: see *Hodgson* v *Marks* [1971] Ch 892. Whenever the purchaser takes the land impliedly subject to the rights of the contractual licensee, a court of equity will impose a constructive trust for the beneficiary. So I still adhere to the proposition I stated in *Errington* v *Errington and Woods* [1952] 1 KB 290, 299; and elaborated in *National Provincial Bank* v *Hastings Car Mart* [1964] Ch 665, 686–9, namely, that, when the licensee is in actual occupation, neither the licensor nor anyone who claims through him can disregard the contract except a purchaser for value without notice.

MEGAW LJ: In my view, Judge Bulger was right in holding that the effect was the same as the effect of the agreement considered by this court in *Bannister* v *Bannister* [1948] 2 All ER 133.

[Megaw LJ set out the facts of *Bannister* v *Bannister* (above), and continued:]
The court (Scott LJ, Asquith LJ and Jenkins J) held, at p. 137:

... the plaintiff holds No. 30 in trust during the life of the defendant to permit the defendant to occupy the same for so long as she may desire to do so and subject thereto in trust for the plaintiff. A trust in this form has the effect of making the beneficiary a tenant for life within the meaning of the Settled Land Act 1925, and, consequently, there is very little practical difference between such a trust and a trust for life *simpliciter*.

As was said by the court, at p. 136:

Similar words in deeds and wills have frequently been held to create a life interest determinable (apart from special considerations introduced by the Settled Land Act 1925) on the beneficiary ceasing to occupy the premises.

I confess that I have had difficulty in seeing precisely how the Settled Land Act of 1925 was applicable. But the court in *Bannister* v *Bannister* [1948] 2 All ER 133 so held, and I am certainly content, and we are probably bound, to follow that authority. I see no relevant distinction. The fact that the transaction – the creation of the trust – was there effected orally, whereas here there is an agreement in writing, surely cannot be a ground for saying that the principle is not here applicable. The fact that there is here express provision for determination by the beneficiary cannot provide a relevant distinction. The defendant in *Bannister* v *Bannister* [1948] 2 All ER 133 was free to give up occupation whenever she wished. The fact and nature of the obligations imposed upon the defendant by the agreement in the present case must tend in favour of, rather than adversely to, the creation of an interest in land, as compared with *Bannister's* case.

I realise that the application of the Settled Land Act 1925 may produce some odd consequences; but no odder than those which were inherent in the decision in *Bannister* v *Bannister* [1948] 2 All ER 133. I do not find anything in the possible, theoretical, consequences to lead me to the conclusion that *Bannister's* case should not be followed.

The plaintiffs took with express notice of the agreement which constitutes, or gives rise to, the trust. They cannot turn the defendant out of the house against her will; for that would be a breach of the trust which binds them.

If for some reason *Bannister* v *Bannister* [1948] 2 All ER 133 did not apply, so that there would then be no trust and the defendant would possibly have no 'interest in land' within the technical meaning of those words, there would none the less be a continuing contractual obligation as between the trustees and the defendant. It would then be what is sometimes called an irrevocable licence. It would be irrevocable – that is not determinable by the licensors, the trustees, without the consent of the licensee, the defendant – because it is founded on a contract. The agreement was based on consideration – the provisions made by the defendant as her side of the agreement. That irrevocable licence, that contractual right to continue in occupation, remained binding upon the trustees. They could not, and did not, free themselves from it unilaterally by selling the land to the plaintiffs. As the plaintiffs took with express notice of, and indeed expressly subject to, the agreement between the trustees and the defendant, the plaintiffs would, on ordinary principles, be guilty of the tort of interference with existing contractual rights if they were to evict the defendant. For that would be knowingly to interfere with her continuing contractual rights with a third party, the trustees. In the ordinary way, the court would intervene to prevent the plaintiffs from interfering with those rights. I should have thought that ordinary principles of equity would have operated in the same way. However, it may be that there are special technical considerations in the law relating to land which would require to be reviewed before one could confidently assert that the ordinary principles as to the protection of known contractual rights would apply. There are, for example, passages in the speech of Lord Upjohn in *National Provincial Bank* v *Hastings Car Mart* [1965] AC 1175, 1239, which indicate doubts and difficulties in this sphere. Since, in my opinion, this case is governed by *Bannister* v *Bannister* [1948] 2 All ER 133 I do not think it is necessary to pursue that topic further.

Notes

1. Lord Denning MR started with the assertion that Mrs Evans had a contractual licence, which bound the purchasers with notice. If his reasoning were correct, then it would have been unnecessary for the Court of Appeal to consider whether Mrs Evans also had a beneficial interest, and there would have been no need for any discussion of constructive trusts at all. This line of reasoning was not very promising at the time, but looks especially unpromising in the light of the *Ashburn Anstalt* decision, below. Whereas in *Bannister* v *Bannister* a contractual licence may have sufficed, it seems likely that a property interest is required to protect Mrs Evans.

2. Lord Denning MR alternatively reasoned that because Mr and Mrs Binions had purchased expressly subject to the agreement, equity would impose upon their conscience, and require them to hold the property on constructive trust for Mrs Evans. The Master of the Rolls himself thought that to take *impliedly* subject to an enforceable agreement would also be enough. He also thought that a constructive trust could be imposed whenever the trustee had conducted himself in an inequitable manner.

3. Lord Denning MR also thought that the Settled Land Act 1925 would not apply, since the words 'limited in trust' in s. 1 (see chapter 1) should be construed as 'expressly limited in trust', and did not therefore apply to a constructive trust.

4. The reasoning of Megaw and Stephenson LJJ was entirely different. In their view, the original agreement between the trustees and the defendant created a life tenancy. Thus, even at this stage the trustees held the property on trust for Mrs Evans for her life, thereafter for the Tredegar Estate in fee simple. Because this was a succession of equitable interests, Mrs Evans had an interest in land coming within the provisions of the Settled Land Act 1925 (see again s. 1, set out in chapter 1). The purchasers were therefore bound by an existing trust, on the ordinary principles of the equitable notice doctrine.

5. Note the alternative economic torts reasoning of Megaw LJ.

6. The constructive trust reasoning of Lord Denning MR (at any rate where the purchaser takes expressly subject to the agreement) and the economic torts reasoning of Megaw LJ were both applied, in a different context, by Browne-Wilkinson J in *Swiss Bank Corporation* v *Lloyds Bank* [1979] Ch 548. *Swiss Bank Corporation* v *Lloyds Bank* was reversed on its facts ([1982] AC 584), but no doubt was cast on Browne-Wilkinson J's views on these questions.

7.   On the views expressed here on the operation of the Settled Land Act 1925, see also *Ungurian* v *Lesnoff* [1990] Ch 206, in chapter 9, where Vinelott J was unconvinced by Lord Denning MR's views above, preferring those of Megaw and Stephenson LJJ.

Questions
1.   Subsequent cases (below) have adopted aspects of Lord Denning MR's reasoning, but have tended to limit it to where the purchaser takes expressly subject to the agreement. What, if any, is the difference between that and express trusteeship?
2.   Do you think that conveyancing difficulties are caused by imposing the obligations of trusteeship only on someone who takes expressly subject to the beneficiary's rights? Would conveyancing difficulties be caused by adopting Lord Denning MR's reasoning in full? Once a trust is created, what is the position of a subsequent purchaser? Could a subsequent purchaser be bound on the basis of constructive notice alone? If the Settled Land Act 1925 applied, could a subsequent purchaser without notice be bound (see *Weston* v *Henshaw* [1950] Ch 510, referred to at the end of chapter 1)?
3.   If Megaw and Stephenson LJJ are right about the application of the Settled Land Act 1925, when did Mrs Evans become a tenant for life? What conclusions should have been drawn about the sale to Mr and Mrs Binions in that event (see Settled Land Act 1925, s. 18, set out in chapter 1, and *Weston* v *Henshaw*)?
4.   On Megaw LJ's alternative reasoning, the plaintiffs would be restrained from interfering with the contractual rights of the defendant. The authorities on interference with contract suggest that it would apply only where the purchaser had express notice of the contract, and constructive notice of its terms. Given that the tort action does not create any property rights, does it give rise to any conveyancing difficulties? What is the position of a purchaser who knows nothing of the contract at the time of purchase, but is told of it later?

Lyus v *Prowsa Developments*
[1982] 1 WLR 1044
Chancery Division

Facts: The plaintiffs contracted to buy a plot of land from a firm of builders, who were to build a house to be occupied by the plaintiffs. The plaintiffs paid a deposit to the firm of builders, which afterwards became insolvent before the house was built. The builder's bank (the National Westminster Bank) held a legal charge, granted before the plaintiffs' contract, over the property.

It is clear that at this point the plaintiffs were entirely at the mercy of the bank, and no longer had any enforceable rights. The bank was under no liability to complete the plaintiffs' contract. In fact, the bank exercised its power of sale as mortgagee, and sold the land to the first defendant. By the contract of sale it was provided that the land was sold subject to and with the benefit of the plaintiffs' contract. Subsequently the first defendant contracted to sell the plot to the second defendant. The contract provided that the land was sold subject to the plaintiffs' contract so far, if at all, as it might be enforceable against the first defendant. The contract was duly completed.

In the action the plaintiffs sought a declaration that their contract was binding on the defendants, and an order for specific performance.

Held: The action succeeded. Dillon J held, on the basis of *Binions* v *Evans*, that the defendants held the benefit of the original estate contract on trust for the plaintiffs, and that Mr and Mrs Lyus were entitled to specific performance of it.

Note

In one respect *Lyus* v *Prowsa Developments* represents an extension of *Binions* v *Evans*; the plaintiffs had no rights at all before the purchase from the bank, as they were before then entirely at the mercy of the bank. Here the right was apparently created by the sale. However, Dillon J limited *Binions* v *Evans* to cases where the purchaser took *subject to* a right. It is not enough that he merely knew of it.

This case, creating as it does new rights on the sale itself, looks wrong in principle.

Re Sharpe
[1980] 1 WLR 219
Chancery Division

Facts: An 82-year-old lady, who was not in good health, loaned a large sum of money (£12,000) to her nephew to enable him to purchase a house in which they could both live. The nephew later went bankrupt, and the question arose whether the old lady's money was secured, or whether it formed part of the nephew's assets, to be divided among his general creditors.

Held: Browne-Wilkinson J found for the old lady, on the basis that she was a beneficiary under a constructive trust, which bound the trustee in bankruptcy.

Note

Browne-Wilkinson J's views on when a constructive trust might arise were, like those later expressed in *Re Basham* (below), very wide. He thought that a constructive trust can be imposed simply because a licensee expends money or otherwise acts to his detriment. If the reasoning in this case is correct, almost any reliance on a promise relating to the occupation of property could give rise to a constructive trust.

Re Sharpe may well be better explained on other grounds. For example, if it was the intention of the aunt and nephew that the old lady should have an interest in the property, then she may well have an interest on conventional resulting trust principles.

Alternatively, it has been argued by Jill Martin in [1980] Conv 207, that an estoppel licence or proprietary estoppel was created, and that this is the true explanation of the decision.

I would suggest that there are problems with this approach, in particular whether estoppel licences can in fact be proprietary, so as to bind a trustee in bankruptcy.

The constructive trust reasoning in *Re Sharpe* was treated dismissively by Fox LJ in *Ashburn Anstalt* v *Arnold* [1988] 2 All ER 147 (below), but he did not elaborate, since the case before him was sufficiently different not to be affected directly by *Re Sharpe*.

Re Basham (deceased)
[1987] 1 All ER 405
Chancery Division

Facts: The plaintiff worked for her stepfather without payment for about 30 years, on the understanding that his estate would go to her on his death. On the intestacy of her stepfather, the plaintiff sought a declaration that she was entitled to his estate.

Held: Edward Nugee QC followed *Re Cleaver* [1981] 1 WLR 939 (see chapter 10), and held that a proprietary estoppel giving rise to a constructive trust arose, the plaintiff thereby obtaining the conveyance of the estate to her. He said that proprietary estoppel was a form of constructive trust which arose when A acted to his detriment on the faith of a belief known to and encouraged by B that he had or was going to have a right over B's property, so that B was prevented by equity from insisting on his strict legal rights if to do so would be inconsistent with A's belief.

Note
If this case is correct, then any act by the plaintiff, in reliance upon an alleged agreement (or even a mere representation by the defendant), would enable the plaintiff to succeed on constructive trust reasoning, whether or not the act would also constitute a sufficient act of part performance.

The reasoning in *Re Basham* is also similar to that adopted in *Re Sharpe (a bankrupt)* [1980] 1 WLR 219, although that case is not mentioned in Edward Nugee's judgment.

Ashburn Anstalt v Arnold
[1988] 2 All ER 147
Court of Appeal

Facts: Arnold & Co. had agreed in February 1973 with Matlodge (Ashburn Anstalt's predecessors in title), on the sale of a sublease on the property (shop premises) to Matlodge, that Arnold & Co. could remain in occupation 'as licensees'. Matlodge had no immediate need for the premises, but wished eventually to demolish it for development. The agreement allowed Arnold & Co. to remain, rent-free but paying all outgoings, until 29 September 1973, and thereafter until Matlodge gave three months' notice, certifying that it was ready forthwith to demolish the property for development.

By October 1985, as a result of various transactions, both the head-lease and sub-lease on the property had merged in the freehold, which was purchased by Ashburn Anstalt. Arnold & Co. was still in occupation, and claimed to be entitled to remain on the terms of the original agreement. The land was registered, and they claimed that the agreement gave them an overriding interest, under s. 70(1)(g) of the Land Registration Act 1925 (see chapter 1), which was binding on Matlodge's successors in title. In other words, they claimed that Ashburn Anstalt were bound by the 1973 agreement, despite not being party to it. Ashburn Anstalt, on the other hand, sought possession.

Only interests 'subsisting in reference' to land come within s. 70(1)(g), so the main issue was whether the agreement created such an interest.

Held:

(a) The agreement created a lease, rather than a contractual licence. This disposed of the case, because a lease is undeniably an interest in land, and hence within s. 70(1)(g).

(b) If, however, the agreement did not create a lease (i.e. if the court was wrong on the main issue), but created only a contractual licence, contractual licences are not interests in land, and do not bind third party purchasers.

(c) No constructive trust would be imposed on Ashburn Anstalt. A constructive trust would only be imposed where the court was satisfied that the conscience of the purchaser was affected. This required more than mere notice, even express notice of the contractual licence. Even a purchaser who took 'subject to' a contractual licence would not necessarily be bound. There must be a clear undertaking on the part of the purchaser, and the obligation must be imposed expressly in the conveyance.

FOX LJ: The constructive trust principle to which we now turn has been long established and has proved to be highly flexible in practice. It covers a wide variety of cases from that of a trustee who makes a profit out of his trust or a stranger who knowingly deals with trust property, to the many cases where the courts have held that a person who directly or indirectly contributes to the acquisition of a dwelling-house purchased in the name of and conveyed to another has some beneficial interest in the property. The test, for present purposes, is whether the owner of the property has so conducted himself that it would be inequitable to allow him to deny the claimant an interest in the property (see *Gissing* v *Gissing* [1971] AC 886 at 905 per Lord Diplock).

[Fox LJ set out the facts of *Bannister* v *Bannister* [1948] 2 All ER 133, above and continued:]

The Court of Appeal (Scott, Asquith LJJ and Jenkins J) held that [the plaintiff was not entitled to eject the defendant]. Scott LJ, giving the judgment of the court, said (at 136):

> It is, we think, clearly a mistake to suppose that the equitable principle on which a constructive trust is raised against a person who insists on the absolute character of a conveyance to himself for the purpose of defeating a beneficial interest, which, according to the true bargain, was to belong to another, is confined to cases in which the conveyance itself was fraudulently obtained. The fraud which brings the principle into play arises as soon as the absolute character of the conveyance is set up for the purpose of defeating the beneficial interest. . . . Nor is it, in our opinion, necessary that the bargain on which the absolute conveyance is made should include any express stipulation that the grantee is in so many words to hold as trustee. It is enough that the bargain should have included a stipulation under which some sufficiently defined beneficial interest in the property was to be taken by another.

In *Re Schebsman, ex parte Official Receiver, The Trustee v Cargo, Superintendents (London) Ltd* [1944] Ch 83 at 89 Greene MR said:

> It is not legitimate to import into the contract the idea of a trust when the parties have given no indication that such was their intention.

Du Parcq LJ said that the court ought not to be astute to discover indications of such an intention (see [1943] 2 All ER 768 at 779, [1944] Ch 83 at 104). We do not, however, regard either of these observations as differing from what Scott LJ said in *Bannister* v *Bannister*. It is, we think, in every case a question of what is the reasonable inference from the known facts.

We come then to four cases in which the application of the principle to particular facts has been considered. In *Binions* v *Evans* [1972] Ch 359 [in this chapter] . . . [Fox LJ set out the facts of the case and continued:] Lord Denning MR . . . held that the plaintiffs took the property subject to a constructive trust for the defendant's benefit. In our view that is a legitimate application of the doctrine of constructive trusts. The estate would certainly have allowed the defendant to live in the house during her life in accordance with their agreement with her. They provided the plaintiffs with a copy of the agreement they made. The agreement for sale was subject to the agreement, and they accepted a lower purchase price in consequence. In the circumstances it was a proper inference that on the sale to the plaintiffs, the intention of the estate and the plaintiffs was that the plaintiffs should give effect to the tenancy agreement. If they had failed to do so, the estate would have been liable in damages to the defendant.

In *DHN Food Distributors Ltd* v *Tower Hamlets London Borough Council* [1976] 1 WLR 852 premises were owned by one company (Bronze Investments Ltd) but occupied by an associated company (DHN) under an informal agreement between them: they were part of a group. The premises were subsequently purchased by the council and the issue was compensation for the disturbance. It was said that Bronze was not disturbed and that DHN had no interest in the property. The Court of Appeal held that DHN had an irrevocable licence to occupy the land. Lord Denning MR said ([1976] 1 WLR 852 at 859):

> It was equivalent to a contract between the two companies whereby Bronze granted an irrevocable licence to DHN to carry on their business on the premises. In this situation counsel for the claimants cited to us *Binions* v *Evans* [1972] Ch 359, to which I would add *Bannister* v *Bannister* [1948] 2 All ER 133 and *Siew Soon Wah alias Siew Pooi Tong* v *Yong Tong Hong* [1973] AC 836. Those cases show that a

contractual licence (under which a person has the right to occupy premises indefinitely) gives rise to a constructive trust under which the legal owner is not allowed to turn out the licensee. So here. This irrevocable licence gave to DHN a sufficient interest in the land to qualify them for compensation for disturbance.

Goff LJ made this a ground for his decision also.

On that authority, Browne-Wilkinson J in *Re Sharpe (a bankrupt), ex parte the trustee of the bankrupt v Sharpe* [1980] 1 WLR 219 felt bound to conclude that, without more, an irrevocable licence to occupy gave rise to a property interest. He evidently did so with hesitation. For the reasons which we have already indicated, we prefer the line of authorities which determine that a contractual licence does not create a property interest. We do not think that the argument is assisted by the bare assertion that the interest arises under a constructive trust.

In *Lyus v Prowsa Developments* [1982] 1 WLR 1044 [Fox LJ set out the facts (see above) and continued:] . . . This again seems to us to be a case where a constructive trust could justifiably be imposed. The bank were selling as mortgagees under a charge prior in date to the contract. They were therefore not bound by the contract and on any view could give a title which was free from it. There was, therefore, no point in making the conveyance subject to the contract unless the parties intended the purchaser to give effect to the contract. Further, on the sale by the bank, a letter had been written to the bank's agents, Messrs Strutt & Parker, by the first defendant's solicitors, giving an assurance that their client would take reasonable steps to make sure the interests of contractual purchasers were dealt with quickly and to their satisfaction.

How far any constructive trust so arising was on the facts of that case enforceable by the plaintiffs against the owners for the time being of the land we do not need to consider.

Re Sharpe seems to us a much more difficult case in which to imply a constructive trust against the trustee in bankruptcy and his successors, and we do not think it could be done. Browne-Wilkinson J did not, in fact, do so. He felt (understandably we think) bound by the authorities to hold that an irrevocable licence to occupy was a property interest. In *Re Sharpe*, although the aunt provided money for the purchase of the house, she did not thereby acquire any property interest in the ordinary sense, since the judge held that it was advanced by way of a loan (though no doubt she may have had some rights of occupation as against the debtor). And when the trustee in bankruptcy, before entering into the contract of sale, wrote to the aunt to find out what rights, if any, she claimed in consequence of the provision of funds by her, she did not reply. The trustee in bankruptcy then sold with vacant possession. These facts do not suggest a need in equity to impose constructive trust obligations on the trustee or his successors.

We come to the present case. It is said that when a person sells land and stipulates that the sale should be 'subject to' a contractual licence, the court will impose a constructive trust on the purchaser to give effect to the licence (see *Binions v Evans* [1972] Ch 359 at 368 per Lord Denning MR). We do not feel able to accept that as a general proposition. We agree with the observations of Dillon J in *Lyus v Prowsa Developments Ltd* [1982] 1 WLR 1044 at 1051 as follows:

By contrast, there are many cases in which land is expressly conveyed subject to possible incumbrances when there is no thought at all of conferring any fresh rights on third parties who may be entitled to the benefit of the incumbrances. The land is expressed to be sold subject to incumbrances to satisfy the vendor's duty to disclose all possible incumbrances known to him, and to protect the vendor against any possible claim by the purchaser if a third party establishes an overriding right to the benefit of the incumbrance against the purchaser. So, for instance, land may be contracted to be sold and may be expressed to be conveyed subject to the restrictive covenants contained in a conveyance some 60 or 90 years old. No one would suggest that by accepting such a form of contract or conveyance a purchaser is assuming a new liability in favour of third parties to observe the covenants if there was for any reason before the contract or conveyance no one who could make out a title as against the purchaser to the benefit of the covenants.

The court will not impose a constructive trust unless it is satisfied that the conscience of the estate owner is affected. The mere fact that land is expressed to be conveyed 'subject to' a contract does not necessarily imply that the grantee is to be under an obligation, not otherwise existing, to give effect to the provisions of the contract. The fact that the conveyance is expressed to be subject to the contract may often, for the reasons indicated by Dillon J be at least as consistent with an intention merely to protect the grantor against claims by the grantee as an intention to impose an obligation on the grantee. The words 'subject to' will, of course, impose notice. But notice is not enough to impose on somebody an obligation to give effect to a contract into which he did not enter. Thus, mere notice of a restrictive covenant is not enough to impose upon the estate owner an obligation or equity to give effect to it: see *London CC* v *Allen* [1914] 3 KB 642.

The material facts in the present case are as follows. (i) There is no finding that the plaintiffs paid a lower price in consequence of the provision that the sale was subject to the 1973 agreement. (ii) The 1973 agreement was not contractually enforceable against Legal and General who were not, therefore, exposed to the risk of any contractual claim for damages if the agreement was not complied with. The 1973 agreement was enforceable against Cavendish and it seems that, in 1973, Cavendish was owned by Legal and General. There is no finding as to the relationship between Cavendish and Legal and General in August 1985, when Legal and General sold to the plaintiffs. And there is no evidence before the deputy judge as to the circumstances or the arrangements attending the transfer by Cavendish to Legal and General. (iii) While the letter of 7 February 1985 is not precisely worded, it seems that Legal and General was itself prepared to give effect to the 1973 agreement.

In matters relating to the title to land, certainty is of prime importance. We do not think it desirable that constructive trusts of land should be imposed in reliance on inferences from slender materials. In our opinion the available evidence in the present case is insufficient. The deputy judge, while he did not have to decide the matter, was not disposed to infer a constructive trust, and we agree with him.

Notes

1.   The 'lease' was, to say the least, very unusual. The difficulty was not so much that rent was not payable, because in principle it is possible to lease property rent-free, but that the agreement did not appear to be for a certain duration after 29 September 1973. It could only be terminated (on three months' notice) in certain circumstances (intention to demolish the property for redevelopment), which may never have occurred. Thus, it seemed that one of the most fundamental requirements for a lease, certainty of maximum duration, was not present. Nor was Arnold & Co. under any obligation to remain in occupation of the property. Nevertheless, relying heavily on the

three-month notice provision, Fox LJ held that a periodic tenancy had been created.

2. The lease reasoning in this case has subsequently been criticised in the House of Lords. Indeed, the case was overruled in *Prudential Assurance Co. Ltd* v *London Residuary Body and others* [1992] 2 AC 386 (House of Lords). However, although the decision itself no longer stands, Fox LJ's reasoning above is still cited with approval, and it may be assumed that the contractual licence and constructive trust aspects of the case still stand.

3. There is a categorical statement that contractual licences are not interests in land, and that they bind only the parties to them, and not third parties. Statements of Lord Denning MR to the contrary in *Errington* v *Errington* [1952] 1 KB 290 were disapproved, and Fox LJ thought that if the decision in *Errington* was correct, it could only be justified on grounds other than those adopted by Lord Denning MR. In *Errington* v *Errington*, a father purchased a house on a mortgage, and agreed with his son and her new wife that if they occupied the house and paid all the instalments, he would then transfer the property to them. The young couple went into occupation, and paid the instalments. Later, the father died, and his widow inherited the property. The the son left his wife, who continued to live in the house, paying the mortgage instalments. The widow sought possession from the daughter-in-law, and lost.

The case raises a number of difficulties, but for present purposes we are only concerned with why the widow was bound by an arrangement that had been made not by herself, but by her predecessor in title, assuming that Lord Denning's views are indeed incorrect. A possible explanation is the agreement was to convey the house to the young couple upon payment of all the instalments, and was therefore an estate contract, which is clearly an interest in land, capable of binding the widow.

The contract was oral, so to succeed on this basis the daughter-in-law would have to argue part performance (see above). The couple went into occupation, and started to pay off the mortgage instalments. Even on the traditional reasoning, these acts surely point to the existence of a contract, referable to land.

Estate contracts need to be registered (in *Errington* under the provisions of the Land Charges Act, now 1972), in order to bind purchasers, but the widow was not a purchaser. She had simply inherited the house. Non-registration is no objection to the estate contract theory, therefore, and I would suggest that this is the true explanation of *Errington* v *Errington*.

4. While Fox LJ supported the decision in *Binions* v *Evans*, he would virtually have limited it to its facts. On his view, a constructive trust will only be imposed where the conveyance to the purchaser is made *expressly* subject to the contractual licence, and he also thought that the fact that the purchaser had paid a reduced price in *Binions* v *Evans* significant. None of these factors was present in *Ashburn Anstalt*, so no constructive trust arose.

12 LEGAL DEFINITION OF CHARITY

SECTION 1: INTRODUCTION

A: Sources of Law

Statute of Charitable Uses 1601

Preamble

Whereas Lands, Tenements, Rents, Annuities, Profits, Hereditaments, Goods, Chattels, Money and Stocks of Money, have been heretofore given, limited, appointed and assigned, as well as by the Queen's most excellent Majesty, and her most noble Progenitors, as by sundry other well disposed persons; some for Relief of aged, impotent and poor People, some for the Maintenance of sick and maimed Soldiers and Mariners, Schools of Learning, Free Schools, and Scholars in Universities, some for the Repair of Bridges, Ports, Havens, Causeways, Churches, Sea-Banks and Highways, some for the Education and Preferment of Orphans, some for or towards Relief, Stock or Maintenance for Houses of Correction, some for the Marriages of Poor Maids, some for Supportation, Aid and Help of young Tradesmen, Handicraftsmen and Persons decayed, and others for the Relief or Redemption of Prisoners or Captives, and for Aid or Ease of any poor Inhabitants concerning Payments of Fifteens [a tax on moveable property], setting out of Soldiers and other Taxes; which Lands, Tenements, Rents, Annuities, Profits, Hereditaments, Goods, Chattels, Money and Stocks of Money, nevertheless have not been employed according to charitable Intent of the givers and Founders thereof, by reason of Frauds, Breaches of Trust, and Negligence in those that should pay, deliver and employ the same: For Redress and Remedy whereof, Be it enacted . . .

Note

There is no formal statutory definition of charity, despite occasional proposals. Nor does it appear likely that a statutory definition will appear in the near future. The courts in the past, however, used the Preamble to the Statute of Charitable Uses 1601, sometimes referred to as the Statute of Elizabeth (which was part of a scheme intended to curb abuses), as a guideline to simplify their task of determining which purposes were charitable. The Preamble listed those purposes which were regarded as charitable at the time. Purposes which fell within the 'spirit and intendment' of the Preamble were accepted by the courts as being charitable. Those which did not were not, however much they may have been regarded as beneficial to the public.

By operation of the doctrine of precedent, what had originally been simply a convenient practice by the courts crystalised into rigid legal doctrine, and thus the Preamble came, in effect, to have direct legal force. The Statute of Charitable Uses was repealed by s. 13(1) of the Mortmain and Charitable Uses Act 1888, but the Preamble itself was recited in s. 13(2).

Mortmain and Charitable Uses Act 1888

13. Repeal
(2) Whereas by the preamble of the Act of the forty-third year of Elizabeth, chapter four (being one of the enactments hereby repealed), it is recited as follows: [The preamble is then set out verbatim]: and whereas in divers enactments and documents reference is made to charities within the meaning, purview, and interpretation of the said Act:

Be it therefore enacted that references to such charities shall be construed as references to charities within the meaning, purview, and interpretation of the said preamble.

Note
This Act was itself repealed by Charities Act 1960, s. 38, most of which has itself subsequently been repealed. However, the following provision remains.

Charities Act 1960

38. Repeal of law of mortmain
(4) Any reference in any enactment or document to a charity within the meaning, purview and interpretation of the Charitable Uses Act 1601 or of the preamble to it, shall be construed as a reference to a charity within the meaning which the word bears as a legal term according to the law of England and Wales.

Note
The purposes laid down in the Preamble are many and diverse, but fortunately in the House of Lords in *Commissioners for Special Purposes of Income Tax* v *Pemsel* [1891] AC 531, Lord Macnaughten categorised them under four main heads:

1. Relief of poverty.
2. Advancement of education.
3. Advancement of religion.
4. Other purposes which are beneficial to the community.

Any given charitable purpose may, of course, fall within more than one of these heads.

Generally, therefore, there is no need to go back before 1891 for a judicial definition of charity. However, for head 4 the test still depends on the spirit and intendment of the preamble: *Scottish Burial Reform and Cremation Society Ltd* v *Glasgow Corporation* [1968] AC 138. In that case, Lord Wilberforce also sounded a general note of caution about over-rigorous application of the *Pemsel* heads (see further below), noting in particular that the law of charity is a moving subject which may well have evolved even since 1891.

B: Overseas Benefits

In *Re Niyazi's WT* [1978] 1 WLR 910 (below), a trust to construct a hostel for working men in Cyprus was held charitable as being for the relief of poverty, and there is nothing to prevent the benefits of a charity being directed overseas, as opposed to being confined within the UK, or primarily directed within the UK. Missionary societies operating abroad always seem to have been regarded as religious charities, and these will often involve advancement of education also. However, although the Charity Commissioners (Annual Report for 1963, paras 69–76) take the view that trusts to relieve poverty or to advance religion will be charitable wherever found, a trust which falls within the fourth head must involve a benefit, even if indirect, to persons within the UK.

C: Purposes Must be Exclusively Charitable

To be charitable, a trust must not merely be capable of application to charitable purposes; it must be exclusively so. If it is possible to benefit an object which is not charitable, then the trust will fail as a charity unless the courts feel able to sever the offending objects from the main corpus of the otherwise charitable purpose, as in *Re Hetherington* [1990] Ch 1, below, or to declare that the non-charitable purposes are merely subsidiary.

There are various principles of construction. For example, if a purpose is described as 'charitable *and* benevolent', it is probable that these will be construed conjunctively: 'benevolent' merely qualifies 'charitable', so only charitable purposes are included. But in *Chichester Diocesan Fund* v *Simpson* [1944] AC 341, the words 'charitable *or* benevolent' would have permitted the trustees to devote all the funds to benevolent ends which were not also charitable. The trust therefore failed, leading to further litigation because funds had already been distributed by the trustees: *Re Diplock, Minister of Health* v *Simpson* [1951] AC 251.

As a general guide, a comma, or the word 'or', is likely to lead to the listed purposes being interpreted disjunctively (i.e., as alternatives), while the word 'and' is usually read conjunctively: 'charitable and . . . ' succeeds; 'charitable or . . . ' fails. This is not invariably the case, however.

Attorney-General of the Bahamas v *Royal Trust Co.*
[1986] 3 All ER 323
Privy Council

Decision: The Privy Council held not charitable a bequest for 'any purposes for and/or connected with the education and welfare of Bahamian children and young people', on the grounds that education and welfare should be interpreted disjunctively, and that a trust for welfare was not charitable. Paragraph (t) substituted by the third codicil referred to in the passage below was in these terms:

All the rest residue and remainder of my trust estate I direct my trustees to pay over to the manager of the Nassau Branch of the Royal Bank of Canada for the time being the manager of the Nassau Branch of Barclays Bank (Dominion, Colonial and Overseas) for the time being and the said Stafford Lofthouse Sands upon trust to invest the same in any investments for the time being authorised by law for the investment of trust moneys or on mortgage of any real or personal estate situate within the Colony and in their absolute and uncontrolled discretion to use the income therefrom and any part of the capital thereof for any purposes for and/or connected with the education and welfare of Bahamian children and young people either within or without the Colony and in all respects as they shall in their absolute discretion deem fit.

LORD OLIVER OF AYLMERTON: Thus the sole question on this appeal is one of the true construction of para (t) and it is common ground between the parties that if the trusts declared in this paragraph were trusts solely for the 'welfare' of Bahamian children and young persons they would not, as the authorities stand, be valid charitable trusts. It follows that if, as both Blake CJ and the Court of Appeal held, the words 'education and welfare' in the paragraph are to be construed disjunctively (ie as embracing two distinct purposes) this appeal must necessarily fail, since the fund will then be capable of being applied in perpetuity to purposes some of which may be non-charitable. It is, however, the contention of counsel for the Attorney General that, reading the will and codicils as a whole, the true construction of the paragraph is one which involves reading the word 'and' in its conjunctive sense, that is to say, that the only purposes for which the trust moneys are authorised to be disbursed by the paragraph are purposes which are not merely for the welfare of Bahamian children and young persons but are also educational. To put it another way the word 'education' limits the word 'welfare' and there is only one overall purpose of the trust and that is the purpose of educational welfare.

In approaching the question it is helpful to bear in mind the analysis of Sargant J in *Re Eades, Eades* v *Eades* [1920] 2 Ch 353. He was there concerned to decide whether a gift for 'religious, charitable and philanthropic objects' constituted a good charitable bequest. In the course of his judgment, after observing that there were only two possible constructions (that is to say, either that the objects must possess all three characteristics or that there were three distinct, but possibly overlapping, characteristics the possession of any one of which would qualify an object for selection as a proper object of the trusts) he observed (at 356):

Such a construction as the second is sometimes referred to as a disjunctive construction, and as involving the change of the word 'and' into 'or'. This is a short and compendious way of expressing the result of the construction, but I doubt whether it indicates accurately the mental conception by which the result is reached. That conception is one, I think, which regards the word 'and' as used conjunctively and by way of addition, for the purpose of enlarging the number of objects within the area of selection; and it does not appear to be a false mental conception, or one really at variance with the ordinary use of language, merely because it involves in the result that the qualifications for selection are alternative or disjunctive. Further, the greater the number of the qualifications or characteristics enumerated, the more probable, as it seems to me, is a construction which regards them as multiplying the kind or classes of objects within the area of selection, rather than as multiplying the number of qualifications to be complied with, and so diminishing the objects within the area of selection.

It would be a work of supererogation to rehearse yet again the numerous reported decisions in which testators have used somewhat similar, although not identical, expressions. They have been fully and helpfully reviewed in the judgment of Blake CJ and in the judgments in the Court of Appeal and have been drawn to their Lordships' attention by counsel for the Attorney General in the course of his able argument. In the end, however, the question is one of the construction of the particular dispositions of this testator and references to the construction placed on different expressions in the wills of other testators, whilst perhaps useful as guidelines, are necessarily of limited assistance.

It is true that in the instant case there are two, and only two objects, specified, so that, to that extent, it is the easier to adopt the conjunctive construction for which counsel for the Attorney General contends. But there are a number of formidable difficulties about this, and not least that it is not easy to imagine a purpose connected with the education of a child which is not also a purpose for the child's welfare. Thus if 'welfare' is to be given any separate meaning at all it must be something different from and wider than mere education, for otherwise the word becomes otiose. Counsel has sought to meet this by the submission that, in the context of the paragraph as a whole, 'welfare' is used in the sense of 'welfare ancillary to education'. But 'welfare' is a word of the widest import and when used in connection with a class of 'children and young people' generally is capable of embracing almost anything which would lead to the enhancement of the quality of life of any member of the class. Counsel's difficulty then is to find any context, either in the paragraph itself or in other parts of the will, for subordinating this wide concept to the object of education. Despite the helpful argument of counsel for the Attorney General, their Lordships have been unable to discern any context from which the inference of subordination can be drawn and that difficulty would remain even if the trustees had been directed simply to apply the income for 'education and welfare'. The difficulty is, however, compounded by the additional and not unimportant words 'for any purposes for and/or connected with', for, if counsel were otherwise able to link the word 'welfare' with the preceding word 'education' in a conjunctive sense, it would then be impossible to find a purpose which was connected with 'welfare' (used in this ancillary sense) which was not also 'connected with' education, so that the reference to 'welfare' would again become otiose.

The point is not one which is susceptible of a great deal of elaboration and their Lordships need say no more than that they agree with Blake CJ and the Court of Appeal that the phrase 'education and welfare' in this will inevitably falls to be construed disjunctively. It follows that, for the reasons which were fully explored in the judgments in the courts below, and as is now conceded on the footing of a disjunctive construction, the trusts in para (t) do not constitute valid charitable trusts and that, accordingly, the residue of the trust estate falls into the residuary gift in cl 16 of the will.

Notes
1. This case shows that although it may be possible to draw up guidelines to construction, categoric statements should be treated with caution.
2. The Charitable Trusts Validation Act 1954 provided a limited exception to the principles discussed in this section. The Attorney-General argued unsuccessfully that this Act applied in *Re Gillingham Bus Disaster Fund* [1959] Ch 62. The case went to the Court of Appeal on this issue alone, and the Court of Appeal decision does not affect the views of Harman J set out in chapter 8. The Charitable Trusts Validation Act 1954 has no present-day application, so although it generated a body of quite interesting case law, space does not permit further discussion of it here, except to note that the disposition in *Leahy* v *A-G for New South Wales* (see chapter 5) would have failed had it not been saved by s. 37D of the Conveyancing Act 1919–1954, which was the Australian equivalent of the Charitable Trusts (Validation) Act 1954.

D: Profit-seeking

Generally speaking, it is incompatible with charitable status actively to seek profit as a primary objective, although fees may be charged, and incidental acquisition of profit should not disqualify. See further *Scottish Burial Reform and Cremation Society Ltd* v *Glasgow Corporation* [1968] AC 138, below.

E: Role of the Charity Commissioners

Charities Act 1993

3. The register of charities
(1) The Commissioners shall continue to keep a register of charities, which shall be kept by them in such manner as they think fit.
(2) There shall be entered in the register every charity not excepted by subsection (5) below; and a charity so excepted (other than one excepted by paragraph (a) of that subsection) may be entered in the register at the request of the charity, but (whether or not it was excepted at the time of registration) may at any time, and shall at the request of the charity, be removed from the register.
(3) The register shall contain —
    (a) the name of every registered charity; and
    (b) such other particulars of, and such other information relating to, every such charity as the Commissioners think fit.
(4) Any institution which no longer appears to the Commissioners to be a charity shall be removed from the register, with effect, where the removal is due to any change in its purposes or trusts, from the date of that change; and there shall also be removed from the register any charity which ceases to exist or does not operate.
(5) The following charities are not required to be registered —

(a)   any charity comprised in Schedule 2 to this Act (in this Act referred to as an 'exempt charity');

(b)   any charity which is excepted by order or regulations;

(c)   any charity which has neither —

(i)   any permanent endowment, nor

(ii)   the use or occupation of any land,

and whose income from all sources does not in aggregate amount to more than £1,000 a year;

and no charity is required to be registered in respect of any registered place of worship.

(6)   With any application for a charity to be registered there shall be supplied to the Commissioners copies of its trusts (or, if they are not set out in any extant document, particulars of them), and such other documents or information as may be prescribed by regulations made by the Secretary of State or as the Commissioners may require for the purpose of the application.

(7)   It shall be the duty —

(a)   of the charity trustees of any charity which is not registered nor excepted from registration to apply for it to be registered, and to supply the documents and information required by subsection (6) above; and

(b)   of the charity trustees (or last charity trustees) of any institution which is for the time being registered to notify the Commissioners if it ceases to exist, or if there is any change in its trusts or in the particulars of it entered in the register, and to supply to the Commissioners particulars of any such change and copies of any new trusts or alterations of the trusts.

(8)   The register (including the entries cancelled when institutions are removed from the register) shall be open to public inspection at all reasonable times . . .

4.   Effect of, and claims and objections to, registration

(1)   An institution shall for all purposes other than rectification of the register be conclusively presumed to be or to have been a charity at any time when it is or was on the register of charities.

(2)   Any person who is or may be affected by the registration of an institution as a charity may, on the ground that it is not a charity, object to its being entered by the Commissioners in the register, or apply to them for it to be removed from the register; and provision may be made by regulations made by the Secretary of State as to the manner in which any such objection or application is to be made, prosecuted or dealt with.

(3)   An appeal against any decision of the Commissioners to enter or not to enter an institution in the register of charities, or to remove or not to remove an institution from the register, may be brought in the High Court by the Attorney General, or by the persons who are or claim to be the charity trustees of the institution, or by any person whose objection or application under subsection (2) above is disallowed by the decision.

(4)   If there is an appeal to the High Court against any decision of the Commissioners to enter an institution in the register, or not to remove an institution from the register, then until the Commissioners are satisfied whether the decision of the Commissioners is or is not to stand, the entry in the register shall be maintained, but shall be in suspense and marked to indicate that it is in suspense; and for the purposes of subsection (1) above an institution shall be deemed not to be on the register during any period when the entry relating to it is in suspense under this subsection.

(5)   Any question affecting the registration or removal from the register of an institution may, notwithstanding that it has been determined by a decision on appeal

under subsection (3) above, be considered afresh by the Commissioners and shall not be concluded by that decision, if it appears to the Commissioners that there has been a change of circumstances or that the decision is inconsistent with a later judicial decision, whether given on such an appeal or not.

Note

The role of the courts in deciding whether a body is charitable has been diminished by these sections, replacing with amendments the equivalent sections from the Charities Act 1960. An organisation seeking charitable status must normally apply for registration to the Charity Commissioners, who have power under the Act to grant or withhold registration according to their decision as to whether the proposed purposes are, in law, charitable. Registration is conclusive evidence of charitable status.

However, refusal by the Commissioners to register an organisation gives rise to a right of appeal under s. 4, which is in the first instance an informal appeal to the board of Charity Commissioners. Such appeals are rare, usually single figures each year. Further appeal lies through the courts (as in, e.g., *Incorporated Council of Law Reporting for England and Wales* v *Attorney-General* [1972] Ch 73, and *McGovern* v *Attorney-General* [1982] Ch 321), initially the High Court, and thence to the Court of Appeal and House of Lords. The legal definition of charity is still a matter for the courts, therefore, but only as the end product of a complex administrative process.

SECTION 2:   RELIEF OF POVERTY

A: Aged, Impotent and Poor Read Disjunctively

The original basis for this head of charity was the reference to 'relief of aged, impotent and poor people' in the Preamble to the Statute of Charitable Uses 1601. It is clear that it is not necessary for the recipients of benefit to be aged, impotent and poor for a bequest to be charitable: any one will do.

Joseph Rowntree Memorial Trust Housing Association Ltd v *Attorney-General*
[1983] 1 Ch 159, [1983] 2 WLR 284, [1983] 1 All ER 288
Chancery Division

Decision: Provision of housing for the aged was charitable, notwithstanding that the schemes operated by way of bargain rather than bounty.

PETER GIBSON J: The views of the Charity Commissioners on schemes such as these were set out in para. 102 to 108 of the Charity Commissioners' report for 1980 (HC Paper (1979–80) no 608). . . . I hope I summarise the objections of the Charity Commissioners fairly as being the following: (1) the schemes provide for the aged only by way of bargain on a contractual basis rather than by way of bounty; (2) the benefits provided are not capable of being withdrawn at any time if the beneficiary subsequently ceases to qualify; (3) the schemes are for the benefit of private individuals, not for a charitable class; (4) the schemes are a commercial enterprise capable of producing profit for the beneficiary.

Before I deal with these objections it is appropriate to consider the scope of the charitable purpose which the plaintiffs claim the scheme carries out, that is to say in the words of the preamble to the Statute of Elizabeth (43 Eliz I c 4, the Charitable Uses Act 1601) 'the relief of aged persons'. That purpose is indeed part of the very first set of charitable purposes contained in the preamble: 'the relief of aged, impotent and poor people.' Looking at those words without going to authority and attempting to give them their natural meaning, I would have thought that two inferences therefrom were tolerably clear. First, the words 'aged, impotent and poor' must be read disjunctively. It would be as absurd to require that the aged must be impotent or poor as it would be to require the impotent to be aged or poor, or the poor to be aged or impotent. There will no doubt be many cases where the objects of charity prove to have two or more of the three qualities at the same time. Second, essential to the charitable purpose is that it should relieve aged, impotent and poor people. The word 'relief' implies that the persons in question have a need attributable to their condition as aged, impotent or poor persons which requires alleviating, and which those persons could not alleviate, or would find difficulty in alleviating, themselves from their own resources. The word 'relief' is not synonymous with 'benefit'.

Those inferences are in substance what both counsel submit are the true principles governing the charitable purpose of the relief of aged persons. Counsel for the plaintiffs stresses that any benefit provided must be related to the needs of the aged. Thus a gift of money to the aged millionaires of Mayfair would not relieve a need of theirs as aged persons. Counsel for the Attorney General similarly emphasises that to relieve a need of the aged attributable to their age would be charitable only if the means employed are appropriate to the need. He also points out that an element of public benefit must be found if the purpose is to be charitable. I turn then to authority to see if there is anything that compels a different conclusion.

[Peter Gibson J reviewed the authorities and continued:]

These authorities convincingly confirm the correctness of the proposition that the relief of the aged does not have to be relief for the aged poor. In other words the phrase 'aged, impotent and poor people' in the preamble must be read disjunctively. The decisions in Re Glyn's Will Trusts [[1950] 2 All ER 1150n], Re Bradbury [[1950] 2 All ER 1150], Re Robinson [[1951] Ch 198], Re Cottam's Will Trusts [[1955] 1 WLR 1299]and Re Lewis [[1955] Ch 106]give support to the view that it is a sufficient charitable purpose to benefit the aged, or the impotent, without more. But these are all decisions at first instance and with great respect to the judges who decided them they appear to me to pay no regard to the word 'relief'. I have no hesitation in preferring the approach adopted in Re Neal and Le Cras v Perpetual Trustee Co Ltd that there must be a need which is to be relieved by the charitable gift, such need being attributable to the aged or impotent condition of the person to be benefited. My attention was drawn to Picarda The Law and Practice Relating to Charities (1977) p. 79, where a similar approach is adopted by the learned author.

In any event in the present case, as I have indicated, the plaintiffs do not submit that the proposed schemes are charitable simply because they are for the benefit of the aged. The plaintiffs have identified a particular need for special housing to be provided for the elderly in the ways proposed and it seems to me that on any view of the matter that is a charitable purpose, unless the fundamental objections of the charity commissioners to which I have referred are correct. To these I now turn.

The first objection is, as I have stated, that the scheme makes provision for the aged on a contractual basis as a bargain rather than by way of bounty. This objection is sometimes expressed in the form that relief is charitable only where it is given by way of bounty and not by way of bargain (see 5 Halsbury's Laws (4th edn) para 516). But as the learned editors recognise this does not mean that a gift cannot be charitable if it provides for the beneficiaries to contribute to the cost of the benefits they receive. There are numerous cases where beneficiaries only receive benefits from a charity by way of bargain. *Re Cottam* and *Le Cras v Perpetual Trustee Co Ltd* provide examples. Another class of cases relates to fee-paying schools (see for example *The Abbey, Malvern Wells Ltd v Minister of Town and Country Planning* [1951] 2 All ER 154, [1951] Ch 728). Another example relates to a gift for the provision of homes of rest for lady teachers at a rent (*Re Estlin, Prichard v Thomas* (1903) 72 LJ Ch 687). It is of course crucial in all these cases that the services provided by the gift are not provided for the private profit of the individuals providing the services.

The source of the statement that charity must be provided by way of bounty and not bargain is to be found in some remarks of Rowlatt J in *IRC v Society for the Relief of Widows and Orphans of Medical Men* (1926) 136 LT 60 at 65. This was a case relating to the statutory provisions allowing tax relief for income applicable to charitable purposes only of trusts or bodies established for charitable purposes only. Rowlatt J said:

> It seems to me that when it is said that the relief of poverty is a charity within the meaning of the rule which we are discussing that does mean the relief of poverty by way of bounty; it does not mean the relief of poverty by way of bargain. A purely mutual society among very poor people whose dependants would quite clearly always be very poor would not, I think, be a charity: it would be a business arrangement, as has been said in one of the cases, whereby contractual benefits accrued to people whose poverty makes them very much in need of them. That would not be a charity. I think, therefore, that the crux of this case is whether this is a case of that sort.

He went on to hold that the case before him was not that of a mutual society: the beneficiaries had no right to anything.

In my judgment Rowlatt J's remarks must be understood in their limited context. They are entirely appropriate in determining whether a mutual society conferring rights on members is charitable. If a housing association were a co-operative under which the persons requiring the dwellings provided by the housing association had by that association's constitution contractual rights to the dwellings, that would no doubt not be charitable, but that is quite different from bodies set up like the trust and the association. The applicants for dwellings under the schemes which I am considering would have no right to any dwelling when they apply. The fact that the benefit given to them is in the form of a contract is immaterial to the charitable purpose in making the benefit available. I see nothing in this objection of the charity commissioners.

The second objection was that the schemes do not satisfy the requirement that the benefits they provide must be capable of being withdrawn at any time if the beneficiary ceases to qualify. No doubt charities will, so far as practical and compatible with the identified need which they seek to alleviate, try to secure that their housing stock becomes available if the circumstances of the persons occupying the premises change. But it does not seem to me to be an essential part of the charitable purpose to secure that this should always be so. The nature of some benefits may be such that it will endure for some time, if benefits in that form are required to meet the particular need that has been identified. Thus, in *Re Monk, Giffen v Wedd* [1927] 2 Ch 197, [1927]

All ER Rep 157 a testatrix set up a loan fund whereby loans for up to nine years were to be made available to the poor. This was held to be charitable. No doubt the circumstances of the borrower might change whilst the loan was outstanding. If the grant of a long-term leasehold interest with the concomitant security of tenure that such an interest would give to the elderly is necessary to meet the identified needs of the elderly, then in my judgment that is no objection to such a grant. The plaintiffs have put in evidence that they oppose the inclusion in a lease of any provision entitling the plaintiffs to determine the lease in the event of a change in financial circumstances of the tenant. Their main reason, which to my mind is a cogent one, is the unsettling effect it could have on aged tenants. In any event the distinction between what prima facie is a short-term letting and a long lease has been rendered somewhat illusory by statute. A charity may find it no less difficult to recover possession from weekly tenants whose circumstances have changed than it would to recover possession from a tenant under a long lease.

The third objection was that the schemes were for the benefit of private individuals and not for a charitable class. I cannot accept that. The schemes are for the benefit of a charitable class, that is to say the aged having certain needs requiring relief therefrom. The fact that, once the association and the trust have selected individuals to benefit from the housing, those individuals are identified private individuals does not seem to me to make the purpose in providing the housing a non-charitable one any more than a trust for the relief of poverty ceases to be a charitable purpose when individual poor recipients of bounty are selected.

The fourth objection was that the schemes were a commercial enterprise capable of producting a profit for the beneficiary. I have already discussed the cases which show that the charging of an economic consideration for a charitable service that is provided does not make the purpose in providing the service non-charitable, provided of course that no profits accrue to the provider of the service. It is true that a tenant under the schemes may recover more than he or she has put in, but that is at most incidental to the charitable purpose. It is not a primary objective. The profit (if it be right to call the increased value of the equity a profit as distinct from a mere increase avoiding the effects of inflation, as was intended) is not a profit at the expense of the charity, and indeed it might be thought improper, if there be a profit, that it should accrue to the charity which has provided no capital and not to the tenant which has provided most if not all the capital. Again, I cannot see that this objection defeats the charitable character of the schemes.

I turn then to a consideration of the schemes themselves. . . .

Note

On the distinction between bargain and bounty, see further below. Notice the distinction drawn by Peter Gibson J between mutual societies and this type of case.

B: Definition of Poverty; Extent to which Poverty Inferred

Where poverty needs to be shown we must consider its definition. In *Re Coulthurst* [1951] Ch 661, Evershed MR said of poverty (at pp. 665–6):

It is quite clearly established that poverty does not mean destitution: it is a word of wide and somewhat indefinite import; it may not be unfairly paraphrased for present purposes as meaning persons who have to 'go short' in the ordinary acceptance of that term, due regard being had to their status in life, and so forth.

Poverty, therefore, is a relative matter, depending on one's status in life, and the courts have been willing to allow trusts to assist such categories as 'distressed gentlefolk'.

Subject to the width of the definition of poverty, it is essential that poverty should be imposed as a qualification for benefit, and that only the poor can benefit. A trust which may benefit rich persons as well as poor will fail under this head. The courts are reluctant to infer a limitation to the poor, the best example of this reluctance being perhaps *Re Sanders' WT* [1954] Ch 265, where Harman J thought that the provision of dwellings for 'the working classes' in the Pembroke Dock area was not sufficient to limit the benefit to poor persons. However, whereas the courts are reluctant to infer exclusion of the rich in the absence of an express limitation to the poor, it would be wrong to assume that they never do so.

Re Niyazi's WT
[1978] 1 WLR 910, [1978] 3 All ER 785
Chancery Division

Decision: Megarry V-C held charitable a bequest of £15,000 'for the construction of or as a contribution towards the cost of a working men's hostel' in Famagusta, Cyprus, although there was no express limitation to the poor. He accepted that persons requiring such accommodation would necessarily be poor.

MEGARRY V-C: Certain points seem reasonably plain. First, 'poverty' is not confined to destitution, but extends to those who have small means and so have to 'go short'. Second, a gift which in terms is not confined to the relief of poverty may by inference be thus confined. In *Re Lucas* [1922] 2 Ch 52 there was a gift of 5s per week to the oldest respectable inhabitants of a village. As the law then stood, Russell J was unable to hold that a gift merely to the aged was charitable; but he held that the limitation to 5s a week indicated quite clearly that only those to whom such a sum would be of importance and a benefit were to take, and so the gift was charitable as being for the relief of poverty. I do not think that it can be said that nothing save the smallness of the benefit can restrict an otherwise unrestricted benefit so as to confine it within the bounds of charity. I think that anything in the terms of the gift which by implication prevents it from going outside those bounds will suffice. In *Re Glyn's Will Trusts* [1950] 2 All ER 1150 Danckwerts J held that a trust for building free cottages for old women of the working classes aged 60 or more provided a sufficient context to show an intention to benefit indigent persons, and so was charitable.

Thus far, I do not think that there is any serious difference between counsel for the Attorney-General and counsel for the Greek mayor on the one hand and counsel for the next-of-kin on the other. The main dispute is whether in this case there is enough in the words and their context to confine the gift to the relief of poverty. Not surprisingly, counsel for the next-of-kin strongly relied on *Re Sanders' Will Trusts* [1954] Ch 265. There the trust was to provide 'dwellings for the working classes and their families' living within five miles of Pembroke Dock. Harman J rejected the contention that this was a charitable gift, since 'working classes' was not a phrase which connoted poverty, and there was nothing about old age which might indicate those who had ceased to work. An appeal from this decision was compromised [1954] *The Times*, 22nd July. . . .

As the arguments finally emerged, counsel for the Attorney-General's main contention was that, even if neither 'working men' nor 'hostel', by itself, could be said to confine the trust to what in law was charity, the use of these expressions in conjunction sufficed for his purpose. They were enough to distinguish *Re Sanders' Will Trusts*, especially as Harman J had not had the advantage which I have had of being able to consider what had been said in the *Guinness* case [*Guinness Trust (London Fund) founded 1890, registered 1902* v *Green* [1955] 1 WLR 872]. I think that the adjectival expression 'working mens' plainly has some flavour of 'lower income' about it, just as 'upper class' has some flavour of affluence, and 'middle class' some flavour of comfortable means. Of course there are impoverished members of the 'upper' and 'middle' classes, just as there are some 'working men' who are at least of comfortable means, if not affluence: one cannot ignore the impact of such things as football pools. But in construing a will I think that I am concerned with the ordinary or general import of words rather than exceptional cases; and, whatever may be the future meaning of 'working men' or 'working class', I think that by 1967 such phrases had not lost their general connotation of 'lower income'. I may add that nobody has suggested that any difficulty arose from the use of 'working men' as distinct from 'working persons' or 'working women'.

The connotation of 'lower income' is, I think, emphasised by the word 'hostel'. No doubt there are a number of hostels of superior quality; and one day, perhaps, I may even encounter the expression 'luxury hostel'. But without any such laudatory adjective the word 'hostel' has to my mind a strong flavour of a building which provides somewhat modest accommodation for those who have some temporary need for it and are willing to accept accommodation of that standard in order to meet the need. When 'hostel' is prefixed by the expression 'working mens', then the further restriction is introduced of the hostel being intended for those with a relatively low income who work for their living, especially as manual workers. The need, in other words, is to be the need of working men, and not of students or battered wives or anything else. Furthermore, the need will not be the need of the better paid working men who can afford something superior to mere hostel accommodation, but the need of the lower end of the financial scale of working men, who cannot compete for the better accommodation but have to content themselves with the economies and shortcomings of hostel life. It seems to me that the word 'hostel' in this case is significantly different from the word 'dwellings' in *Re Sanders' Will Trusts*, a word which is appropriate to ordinary houses in which the well-to-do may live, as well as the relatively poor.

Has the expression 'working mens hostel' a sufficient connotation of poverty in it to satify the requirements of charity? On any footing the case is desperately near the borderline, and I have hesitated in reaching my conclusion. On the whole, however, for the reasons that I have been discussing, I think that the trust is charitable, though by no great margin. This view is in my judgment supported by two further considerations. First, there is the amount of the trust fund, which in 1969 was a little under £15,000. I think one is entitled to assume that a testator has at least some idea of the probable value of his estate. The money is given for the purpose 'of the construction of or as a contribution towards the cost of the construction of a working mens hostel'. £15,000 will not go very far in such a project, and it seems improbable that contributions from other sources towards constructing a 'working mens hostel' would enable or encourage the construction of any grandiose building. If financial constraints point towards the erection of what may be called an 'economy hostel', decent but catering for only the more basic requirements, then only the relatively poor would be likely to be occupants. There is at least some analogy here to the 5s per week in *Re Lucas* [1922] 2 Ch 52. Whether the trust is to give a weekly sum that is small enough to indicate that only those in straitened circumstances are to benefit, or whether it is to give a capital sum for the construction of a building which will be of such a nature that it is likely to accommodate only those who are in straitened circumstances, there will in each case be an implied restriction to poverty.

The other consideration is that of the state of housing in Famagusta. Where the trust is to erect a building in a particular area, I think that it is legitimate, in construing the trust, to erect some regard to the physical condition existing in that area. Quite apart from any question of the size of the gift, I think that a trust to erect a hostel in a slum or in an area of acute housing need may have to be construed differently from a trust to erect a hostel in an area of housing affluence or plenty. Where there is a grave housing shortage, it is plain that the poor are likely to suffer more than the prosperous, and that the provision of a 'working mens hostel' is likely to help the poor and not the rich.

In the result, then, I hold that the trust is charitable. With some hesitation I would hold this without the aid of the two further considerations that I have just mentioned, the first of which was not discussed in argument. With the aid of these considerations I remain hesitant, though less so. . . .

Notes

1. *Niyazi* may well be exceptional and not of general application. The amount of money left for the purpose was relatively small, and the word 'hostel', rather than 'dwelling' suggested very inferior accommodation. 'Working men' is more limited than 'working classes', excluding for example battered wives and students, and Megarry V-C had regard to the deplorable housing shortage in Famagusta.

2. Note that the benefit of this charity was entirely directed overseas.

Question

Do you think that Megarry V-C thought that *Re Sanders' WT* was correct?

SECTION 3: ADVANCEMENT OF EDUCATION

A: What Constitutes Education?

The preamble to the Act of 1601 (set out above) speaks only of 'schools of learning, free schools, scholars in universities' and the 'education and preferment of orphans', but in modern times this category has grown to cover a very wide range of educational and cultural activities extending far beyond the administration of formal instruction.

Schools and universities are clearly charitable, and so now are nursery schools, adult education centres, and societies dedicated to promoting training and standards within a trade or profession. Education is not limited to teaching, however, and learned societies which bring together experts in a field to share and exchange knowledge may be charitable. Museums, zoos, and public libraries may be educational to the public at large, quite apart from their research activities. Even cultural activities such as drama, music, literature and fine arts can come within this head: see, e.g., *Re Delius* [1957] Ch 299.

Learned societies are charitable, and professional and vocational bodies which advance education, such as the Royal College of Surgeons, are also charitable, even though one of the ancillary purposes is the protection and assistance of its members. Other examples include the Royal College of Nursing, the Institute of Civil Engineers, and the Incorporated Council of Law Reporting (in *Incorporated Council of Law Reporting for England and Wales v Attorney-General* [1972] Ch 73, the Attorney-General tried unsuccessfully to argue that the citation of law reports in court could not be educational because judges are deemed to have complete knowledge of the law). Bodies whose chief purpose is to further the interests of the members and to promote the status of the profession will not, however, be charitable, for example the General Nursing Council (see *General Nursing Council for England and Wales v St Marylebone BC* [1959] AC 540).

Questions
1.   About once a year I give a talk (for a fee) at a conference run by a commercial company for businessmen, lawyers and the like, the principal aim of the conference being to keep the delegates up to date on some area of law. Anybody can go to the conference (subject to paying a fee), and I would hope that my talks are educational. Why are the conferences not charitable?
2.   Is it charitable to write or publish legal textbooks?

B: Research

Re Shaw (deceased), Public Trustee v Day
[1957] 1 WLR 729, [1957] 1 All ER 745
Chancery Division

Facts: The issue was whether a trust to research into the advantages of a new 40-letter alphabet was valid as a charitable or purpose trust. The facts are stated more fully (and colourfully) in Harman J's judgment.

Held: The trust was not valid as an educational charity, because increase of knowledge is not a charitable purpose unless combined with an element of teaching or education. Nor was the trust within the category of charitable trusts for other purposes beneficial to the community, because the object of the research was to convince the public that the new alphabet would be beneficial and, analogously to the cases of trusts for political purposes advocating a change in the law (see below), the court was not in a position to judge whether the adoption of the new alphabet in fact would be beneficial.

Not being charitable, the trust failed, since there were no ascertainable beneficiaries. See further on this point chapter 5.

HARMAN J: All his life long Bernard Shaw was an indefatigable reformer. He was already well-known when the present century dawned, as novelist, critic, pamphleteer, playwright; and during the ensuing half century he continued to act as a kind of itching powder to the British public, to the English-speaking peoples, and indeed to an even wider audience, castigating their follies, their foibles and their fallacies and bombarding them with a combination of paradox and wit that earned him in the course of years the status of an oracle: the Shavian oracle; and the rare distinction of adding a word to the English language. Many of his projects he lived to see gain acceptance and carried into effect and become normal. It was natural that he should be interested in English orthography and pronunciation. These are obvious targets for the reformer. It is as difficult for the native to defend the one as it is for the foreigner to compass the other. The evidence shows that Shaw had for many years been interested in the subject. Perhaps his best known excursion in this field is 'Pygmalion' in which the protagonist is a professor of phonetics: this was produced as a play in 1914 and has held the stage ever since and invaded the world of the film. It is indeed a curious reflexion that this same work, tagged with versicles which I suppose Shaw would have detested, and tricked out with music which he would have eschewed (see the preface to 'The Admirable Bashville'), is now charming huge audiences on the other side of the Atlantic and has given birth to the present proceedings. I am told that the receipts from this source have enabled the executor to get on terms with the crushing death duties payable on the estate, thus bringing the interpretation of the will into the realm of practical politics.

The testator, whatever his other qualifications, was the master of a pellucid style, and the reader embarks on his will confident of finding no difficulty in understanding the objects which the testator had in mind. This document, moreover, was evidently originally the work of a skilled equity draftsman. As such, I doubt not, it was easily to be understood, if not of the vulgar, at any rate by the initiate. Unfortunately the will bears ample internal evidence of being in part the testator's own work. The two styles, as ever, make an unfortunate mixture. It is always a marriage of incompatibles: the delicate testamentary machinery devised by the conveyancer can but suffer when subjected to the *cacoethes scribendi* of the author, even though the latter's language, if it stood alone, might be a literary masterpiece.

This will is a long and complicated document made on June 12, 1950, when the testator was already ninety-four years old, though it is fair to say that it is rather youthful exuberance than the circumspection of old age that mars its symmetry. . . .

Clause 35 . . . I must read in full.

35. I devise and bequeath all my real and personal estate not otherwise specifically disposed of by this my will or any codicil hereto and all property over which I have general power of appointment unto my trustee upon trust that my trustee shall (subject to the power of postponing the sale and conversion thereof hereinafter contained) sell my real estate and sell call in or otherwise convert into money as much as may be needed of my personal estate (other than any copyrights which as provided by cl. 7 of this my will are not to be sold) to increase the ready moneys of which I may be possessed at my death to an amount sufficient to pay my funeral and testamentary expenses and debts estate duty legacy duty and all the duties payable on my death in respect of my estate or the bequests hereby made free of duty (other than testamentary expenses) and the legacies bequeathed by this

my will or any codicil hereto or to make such other payments or investments or change of investments as in his opinion shall be advisable in the interest of my estate and shall invest the residue of such moneys in manner hereinafter authorised. And shall stand possessed of the said residuary trust moneys and the investments for the time being representing the same and all other investments for the time being forming part of my residuary estate (herein called my residuary trust funds) and the annual income thereof upon the trusts hereby declared of and concerning the same. (1) To institute and finance a series of inquiries to ascertain or estimate as far as possible the following statistics (a) the number of extant persons who speak the English language and write it by the established and official alphabet of twenty-six letters (hereinafter called Dr. Johnson's alphabet); (b) how much time could be saved per individual scribe by the substitution for the said alphabet of an alphabet containing at least forty letters (hereinafter called the proposed British alphabet) enabling the said language to be written without indicating single sounds by groups of letters or by diacritical marks, instead of by one symbol for each sound; (c) how many of these persons are engaged in writing or printing English at any and every moment in the world; (d) on these factors to estimate the time and labour wasted by our lack of at least fourteen unequivocal single symbols; (e) to add where possible to the estimates of time lost or saved by the difference between Dr. Johnson's alphabet and the proposed British alphabet estimates of the loss of income in British and American currency. The inquiry must be confined strictly to the statistical and mathematical problems to be solved without regard to the views of professional and amateur phoneticians, etymologists, spelling reformers, patentees of universal languages, inventors of shorthand codes for verbatim reporting or rival alphabets, teachers of the established orthography, disputants about pronunciation, or any of the irreconcilables whose wranglings have overlooked and confused the single issue of labour saving and mode change impossible during the last hundred years. The inquiry must not imply any approval of or disapproval of the proposed British alphabet by the inquirers or by my trustee. (2) To employ a phonetic expert to transliterate my play entitled 'Androcles and the Lion' into the proposed British alphabet assuming the pronunciation to resemble that recorded of His Majesty our late King George V, and sometimes described as Northern English. (3) To employ an artist-calligrapher to fair-copy the transliteration for reproduction by lithography photography or any other method that may serve in the absence of printers' types. (4) To advertise and publish the transliteration with the original Dr. Johnson's lettering opposite the transliteration page by page and a glossary of the two alphabets at the end and to present copies to public libraries in the British Isles, the British Commonwealth, the American States North and South and to national libraries everywhere in that order.
. . .

The first two [residuary legatees] now claim that what I may call the alphabet trusts are entirely void and that the claimants are entitled, therefore, to come into their inheritance at once and to stop the accumulation of income. The grounds of this claim are two: first, that the trusts, being for an object and not for a person, are void trusts; secondly, that they are void for uncertainty.

The Attorney-General appears as parens patriae to uphold the trusts as being charitable trusts, and counsel for the Attorney-General at my request also supported the proposition of the executor that, even if not charitable, these trusts, not being tainted with the vice of perpetuity (as it is called), are a valid exercise by a man of his power of disposing of his own money as he thinks fit. The claimants retort that these trusts are not charitable trusts, and it seems to me that I should address myself first to that question. It is notorious that the word 'charitable', when used by a lawyer, covers many objects which a layman would not consider to be included under that word, but excludes benevolent or philanthropic activities which the layman would consider charitable. In construing a will the lawyer's sense must prevail in the absence of some special context. The four heads of charity are set out by Lord Macnaghten in *Commissioners for Special Purposes of Income Tax* v *Pemsel* ([1891] AC 531 at p. 583). His words, as has often been pointed out, are not original, being drawn from the argument of Sir Samuel Romilly in his reply in *Morice* v *Bishop of Durham* ((1805), 10 Ves 522 at p. 532). They are almost too familiar to need repetition. Shortly stated the four heads are (i) religion, (ii) poverty, (iii) education, and (iv) 'other purposes beneficial to the community'. Sir Samuel Romilly describes the last head as being 'the most difficult', and the phrase he uses is 'the advancement of objects of general public utility'. Here, again, it is trite law that not every object coming within one or other of these categories is charitable – a college for pickpockets is no charity – but that every object which is to rank as charitable must either fit into one or more of the first three categories, or, if not, may still be held charitable because of general public utility.

The first object of the alphabet trusts is to find out by inquiry how much time could be saved by persons who speak the English language and write it, by the use of the proposed British alphabet and so to show the extent of the time and labour wasted by the use of our present alphabet, and, if possible, further to state this waste of time in terms of loss of money. The second is to transliterate one of the testator's plays, 'Androcles and the Lion', into the proposed British alphabet, assuming a given pronunciation of English, and to advertise and publish the transliteration in a page by page version in the proposed alphabet on one side and the existing alphabet on the other, and, by the dissemination of copies and, in addition, by advertisement and propaganda, to persuade the government or the public or the English speaking world to adopt it. This was described by the Attorney-General as a useful piece of research beneficial to the public, because it would facilitate the education of the young and the teaching of the language and show a way to save time and, therefore, money. It was suggested that the objects could thus be brought within the third category and that a parallel could be found in the decision of Danckwerts, J, in *Crystal Palace Trustees* v *Minister of Town & Country Planning* ([1950] 2 All ER 857, n.), where trusts 'for the promotion of industry, commerce and art' were held charitable. So they were, but only in the context provided by the instrument (An Act of Parliament) in which they appeared. In my opinion, if the object be merely the increase of knowledge, that is not in itself a charitable object unless it be combined with teaching or education (see the speech of Rigby, LJ, in *Re Macduff, Macduff* v *Macduff* [1896] 2 Ch 451 at p. 472). . . .

The research and propaganda enjoined by the testator seem to me merely to tend to the increase of public knowledge in a certain respect, namely, the saving of time and money by the use of the proposed alphabet. There is no element of teaching or education combined with this, nor does the propaganda element in the trusts tend to more than to persuade the public that the adoption of the new script would be 'a good thing', and that, in my view, is not education. Therefore I reject this element . . . .

Notes

1.   Harman J went on to reject the trust as valid under the fourth category: see below.

2.   Harman J also held that the disposition failed as a valid non-charitable purpose trust. See further chapter 5.

3.   It would be wrong to conclude that research without a teaching element can never be charitable. The cases below suggest that research with a view to publication can be charitable, so long as the results of the research (if any) are likely to be of value.

4.   George Bernard Shaw may have been under-ambitious, to judge from the following passage, taken from an article about speech recognition by computers. It would be difficult to learn a 40,000-letter alphabet, however.

John McCrone, *'Computers that listen'*
New Scientist, 4 December 1993, at p. 34

. . . [I]t was found that there were a lot more than forty or so phonemes, or standing and syllabic sounds, that linguists had traditionally believed to be the building blocks of a language like English. In fact, a large vocabulary recogniser like that of Dragon Systems has to use more than 40,000 sound fragments known as phonemes in context (PICs) to capture the fine detail of all the possible pronunciations of words.

'The C sound at the beginning of a word like cat is very different from the C sound of a word like coat,' says Bridle [a director of Dragon Systems and formerly a pioneer of speech research at what was then the Royal Signals and Radar Establishment at Malvern]. 'Most linguists would treat the sound as being the same, but in spoken language where every phoneme is affected by the sounds directly before and after it, you need to be able to include the difference in your models.'

Re Hopkins
[1965] Ch 669, [1964] 3 WLR 840, [1964] 3 All ER 46
Chancery Division

Decision: Wilberforce J upheld as charitable a bequest to the Francis Bacon society for the purposes of finding the Bacon-Shakespeare manuscripts.

WILBERFORCE J (after stating the facts): What, then, of the practical possibility of discovering any manuscripts, Shakespearian, Baconian, or of other authorship? The experts who have given evidence on the side of the next of kin are not encouraging, but are also not very specific. [Wilberforce J reviewed the expert evidence and continued:] On this evidence, should the conclusion be reached that the search for the Bacon-Shakespeare manuscripts is so manifestly futile that the court should not allow this bequest to be spent on it as on an object devoid of the possibility of any result? I think not. The evidence shows that the discovery of any manuscript of the plays is unlikely; but so are many discoveries before they are made. (One may think of the Codex Sinaiticus, or the Tomb of Tutankhamen, or the Dead Sea Scrolls.) I do not think that that degree of improbability has been reached which justifies the court in placing an initial interdict on the testatrix' benefaction.

I come, then, to the only question of law: is the gift of a charitable character? The society has put its case in the alternative under the two headings of education and of general benefit to the community and has argued separately for each. This compartmentalisation is derived from the accepted classification into four groups of the miscellany found in the Statute of Elizabeth. That statute, preserved as to the preamble only by the Mortmain and Charitable Uses Act 1888, lost even that precarious hold on the Statute Book when the Act of 1888 was repealed by the Charities Act 1960, but the somewhat ossificatory classification to which it gave rise survives in the decided cases. It is unsatisfactory because the frontiers of 'educational purposes' (as of the other divisions) have been extended and are not easy to trace with precision, because, under the fourth head, it has been held necessary for the court to find a benefit to the public within the spirit and intendment of the obsolete Elizabethan statute. The difficulty of achieving that, while at the same time keeping the law's view of what is charitable reasonably in line with modern requirements, explains what Lord Simonds accepted as the case to case approach of the courts (see *National Anti-Vivisection Society* v *Inland Revenue Comrs* [1948] AC 31 at p. 65). There are in fact examples of accepted charities which do not decisively fit into one rather than the other category. Examples are institutes for scientific research (see *National Anti-Vivisection Society* v *Inland Revenue Comrs, per* Lord Wright [1948] AC at p. 42), museums (see *Re Pinion, Westminster Bank, Ltd* v *Pinion* [1964] 1 All ER 890), the preservation of ancient cottages (*Re Cranstoun, National Provincial Bank* v *Royal Society for the Encouragement of Arts, Manufactures and Commerce* [1932] 1 Ch 537), and even the promotion of Shakespearian drama (*Re Shakespeare Memorial Trust, Lytton (Earl)* v *A-G* [1923] 2 Ch 398). The present may be such a case.

Accepting, as I have the authority of Lord Simonds for doing, that the court must decide each case as best it can, on the evidence available to it, as to benefit; and within the moving spirit of decided cases, it would seem to me that a bequest for the purpose of search, or research, for the original manuscripts of England's greatest dramatist (whoever he was) would be well within the law's conception of charitable purposes. The discovery of such manuscripts, or of one such manuscript, would be of the highest value to history and to literature. It is objected, against this, that as we already have the test of the plays, from an almost contemporary date, the discovery of a manuscript would add nothing worth while. This I utterly decline to accept. Without any undue exercise of the imagination, it would surely be a reasonable expectation that the revelation of a manuscript would contribute, probably decisively, to a solution of the authorship problem, and this alone is benefit enough. It might also lead to improvements in the text. It might lead to more accurate dating.

Is there any authority, then, which should lead me to hold that a bequest to achieve this objective is not charitable? By counsel for the next of kin much reliance was placed on the decision on Bernard Shaw's will, the *British alphabet* case (*Re Shaw, Public Trustee* v *Day* [1957] 1 All ER 745). Harman J held that the gift was not educational because it merely tended to the increase of knowledge, and that it was not within the fourth charitable category because it was not itself for a beneficial purpose but for the purpose of persuading the public by propaganda that it was beneficial. The gift was very different from the gift here. But the learned judge did say this [1957] 1 All ER at p. 752:

> . . . if the object be merely the increase of knowledge, that is not in itself a charitable object unless it be combined with teaching or education

And he referred to the House of Lords decision in *Whicker* v *Hume* (1858) 7 HL Cas 124 where, in relation to a gift for advancement of education and learning, two of the learned lords read 'learning' as equivalent to 'teaching', thereby in his view implying that learning, in its ordinary meaning, is not a charitable purpose.

This decision certainly seems to place some limits on the extent to which a gift for research may be regarded as charitable. Those limits are that either it must be 'combined with teaching or education', if it is to fall under the third head, or it must be beneficial to the community in a way regarded by the law as charitable, if it is to fall within the fourth category. The words 'combined with teaching or education', though well explaining what the learned judge had in mind when he rejected the gift in *Re Shaw* [1957] 1 All ER 745, are not easy to interpret in relation to other facts. I should be unwilling to treat them as meaning that the promotion of academic research is not a charitable purpose unless the researcher were engaged in teaching or education in the conventional meaning; and I am encouraged in this view by some words of Lord Greene MR in *Re Compton, Powell v Compton* [1945] Ch 123. The testatrix there had forbidden the income of the bequest to be used for research, and Lord Greene MR treated this as a negative definition of the education to be provided. It would, he said [1945] Ch at p. 127, exclude a grant to enable a beneficiary to conduct research on some point of history or science. This shows that Lord Greene considered that historic research might fall within the description of 'education'. I think, therefore, that the word 'education' as used by Harman J in *Re Shaw* [1957] 1 All ER 745 must be used in a wide sense, certainly extending beyond teaching, and that the requirement is that, in order to be charitable, research must either be of educational value to the researcher or must be so directed as to lead to something which will pass into the store of educational material, or so as to improve the sum of communicable knowledge in an area which education may cover – education in this last context extending to the formation of literary taste and appreciation: (compare *Royal Choral Society* v *Inland Revenue Comrs* [1943] 2 All ER 101). Whether or not the test is wider than this, it is, as I have stated it, amply wide enough to include the purposes of the gift in this case.

As regards the fourth category, Harman J is evidently leaving it open to the court to hold, on the facts, that research of a particular kind may be beneficial to the community in a way which the law regards as charitable, 'beneficial' here not being limited to the production of material benefit (as through medical or scientific research) but including at least benefit in the intellectual or artistic fields.

So I find nothing in this authority to prevent me from finding that the gift falls under either the third or fourth head of the classification of charitable purposes.

On the other side there is *Re British School of Egyptian Archaeology, Murray v Public Trustee* [1954] 1 All ER 887, also a decision of Harman J, a case much closer to the present. The trusts there were to excavate, to discover antiquities, to hold exhibitions, to publish works and to promote the training and assistance of students – all in relation to Egypt. Harman J held that the purposes were charitable, as being educational. The society was one for the diffusion of a certain branch of knowledge, namely, knowledge of the ancient past of Egypt; and it also had a direct educational purpose, namely, to train students. The conclusion reached that there was an educational charity was greatly helped by the reference to students, but it seems that Harman J must have accepted that the other objects – those of archaeological research – were charitable too. They were quite independent objects on which the whole of the society's funds could have been spent, and the language [1954] 1 All ER at p. 891 'the school has a direct educational purpose, namely, to train students' seems to show that the learned judge was independently upholding each set of objects.

Counsel for the next of kin correctly pointed out that in that case there was a direct obligation to diffuse the results of the society's research, and said that it was this that justified the finding that the archaeological purposes were charitable. I accept that research of a private character, for the benefit only of the members of a society, would not normally be educational – or otherwise charitable – as did Harman J [1954] 1 All ER at p. 890, but I do not think that the research in the present case can be said to be of a private character, for it is inherently inevitable, and manifestly intended, that the result of any discovery should be published to the world. I think, therefore, that *Re British School of Egyptian Archaeology* [1954] 1 All ER 887 supports the society's contentions. . . .

. . .

One final reference is appropriate, to *Re Shakespeare Memorial Trust* [1923] 2 Ch 398. The scheme there was for a number of objects which included the performance of Shakespearian and other classical English plays and stimulating the art of acting. I refer to it for two purposes, first as an example of a case where the court upheld the gift either as educational or for purposes beneficial to the community – an approach which commends itself to me here – and secondly as illustrative of the educational and public benefit accepted by the court as flowing from a scheme designed to spread the influence of Shakespeare as the author of the plays. The gift is not that, but it lies in the same field, for the improving of our literary heritage, and my judgment is for upholding it.

Notes

1. Where research is concerned, the courts will presumably assess the value of the ultimate aim of the project, but on the assumption that any findings would be of value, it does not seem to be a bar to charitable status that nothing might be found at all. Of course, it is often difficult to know in advance whether or not the results of research will be useful (after all, if you did know the conclusions, the research would be pointless).

2. Though he observed that if found the discovery would be 'of the highest value to history and to literature', the search could equally have been futile, as not only were the manuscripts not known to exist, but Wilberforce J thought their discovery unlikely. Value judgments are very difficult to operate when the outcome of the quest is uncertain, as will usually be the case where genuine research is concerned.

3. Secret research is clearly not charitable.

C: Sport and Recreation

Re Dupree's Deed Trusts
[1945] Ch 16
Chancery Division

Decision: Vaisey J held charitable a gift of £5,000 to be applied by the trustees in promoting an annual chess tournament open to boys and young men under 21 resident in the City of Portsmouth.

VAISEY J: In this case I have to decide whether the encouragement and promotion of chess-playing among the boys and young men of the city of Portsmouth is a good charitable object.

The game of chess (which, by those who follow it, as well, perhaps, as by those who do not follow it, is regarded as something rather more than a mere game) is an institution with a very long history behind it, and it possesses the somewhat notable feature that it is essentially a game of skill into which elements of chance enter, if at all, only to a negligible extent. It is a game which, I suppose, is played all over the civilized world. I have some evidence which enables me to say – and, indeed, I think I might have said it even without that evidence – that the nature of the game is such as to encourage the qualities of foresight, concentration, memory and ingenuity. Even unguided by actual evidence, I should not have been surprised if the conclusion could have been reached that the game is essentially one which does possess an educational value.

There are many pursuits possessing an educational value which may be followed to excess, and the matter is in no way concluded by any such consideration. Chess players may become so obsessed by the interest of their pursuit that they may neglect other duties, but the same thing may be said of those who range the mysterious country of the higher mathematics or indulge in the study of classical authors. I am not surprised to learn from the evidence that there are schoolmasters and persons actually concerned with the business of education who regard the playing of chess as something of so much value educationally that in some places it is actually a part of a school curriculum. . . .

I think that the case before me may be a little near the line, and I decide it without attempting to lay down any general propositions. One feels, perhaps, that one is on rather a slippery slope. If chess, why not draughts? If draughts, why not bezique, and so on, through to bridge and whist, and, by another route, to stamp collecting and the acquisition of birds' eggs? Those pursuits will have to be dealt with if and when they come up for consideration in connexion with the problem whether or no there is in existence an educational charitable trust. Nor do I say whether, if this trust had been without a geographical limitation, if it had been for the promotion of chess playing *in vacuo* or at large, the area of what is regarded as charitable would or would not have been over-stepped. Having regard to the evidence before me and to what is known about the game of chess by everybody, and, in particular, to the fact that the encouragement of chess playing here is for the benefit of young persons living within a well-defined area, and also that it is of the essence of the constitution of the trusteeship that two of the trustees should be persons closely connected with educational activities in the borough, I think I am bound, in the present case, to hold that there is a good charitable trust, and answer the question by declaring that the trusts constituted by the deed of June 30, 1932, are valid charitable trusts.

IRC v *McMullen and others*
[1981] AC 1, [1980] 1 All ER 884
House of Lords

Facts: The issue was whether the Football Association Youth Trust, whose objects were as follows, was charitable:

(a) To organise or provide or assist in the organisation and provision of facilities which will enable and encourage pupils of Schools and Universities in any part of the United Kingdom to play Association Football or other games or sports and thereby to assist in ensuring that due attention is given to the physical education and development of such pupils as well as the development and occupation of their minds and with a view to furthering this object (i) to provide or assist in the provision of Association Football or games or sports equipment of every kind for the use of such pupils as aforesaid (ii) to provide or assist in the provision of courses lectures demonstrations and coaching for pupils of Schools and

Universities in any part of the United Kingdom and for teachers who organise or supervise playing and coaching of Association Football or other games or sports at such Schools and Universities as aforesaid (iii) to promote provide or assist in the promotion and provision of training colleges for the purposes of training teachers in the coaching of Association Football or other games or sports at such Schools and Universities as aforesaid (iv) to lay out manage equip and maintain or assist in the laying out management equipment and maintenance of playing fields or appropriate indoor facilities or accommodation (whether vested in the Trustees or not) to be used for the teaching and playing of Association Football or other sports or games by such pupils as aforesaid.

(b) To organise or provide or assist in the organisation or provision of facilities for physical recreation in the interests of social welfare in any part of the United Kingdom (with the object of improving the conditions of life for the boys and girls for whom the same are provided) for boys and girls who are under the age of twenty-one years and who by reason of their youth or social and economic circumstances have need of such facilities.

It was argued that it was charitable either as an educational charity, or under the provisions of the Recreational Charities Act 1958.

Held: The trust charitable for the advancement of education, even though the sports and games were not required to be enjoyed as part of a school or university curriculum. The House left open the question whether it was also charitable under the Recreational Charities Act 1958.

LORD HAILSHAM LC: [Lord Hailsham quoted from Eve J in *Re Mariette* [1915] 2 Ch 284, where he said (at 288):

No one of sense could be found to suggest that between those ages [10 to 19] any boy can be properly educated unless at least as much attention is given to the development of his body as is given to the development of his mind.

and continued:]

Apart from the limitation to the particular institution I would think that these words apply as well to the settlor's intention in the instant appeal as to the testator's in *Re Mariette*, and I regard the limitation to the pupils of schools and universities in the instant case as a sufficient association with the provision of formal education to prevent any danger of vagueness in the object of the trust or irresponsibility or capriciousness in application by the trustees. I am far from suggesting either that the concept of education or of physical education even for the young is capable of indefinite extension. On the contrary, I do not think that the courts have as yet explored the extent to which elements of organisation, instruction or the disciplined inculcation of information, instruction or skill may limit the whole concept of education. I believe that in some ways it will prove more extensive, in others more restrictive that has been thought hitherto. But it is clear at least to me that the decision in *Re Mariette* is not to be read in a sense which confines its application for ever to gifts to a particular institution. It has been extended already in *Re Mellody* [1918] 1 Ch 228, to gifts for annual treats for schoolchildren in a particular locality (another decision of Eve J), to playgrounds for children (*Re Chesters*, 25 July 1934 unreported, possibly not educational, but referred to in *IRC* v *Baddeley* [1955] AC 572 at 596); to a children's outing (*Re Ward's Estate* (1937) 81 SJ 397), to a prize for chess to boys and young men resident in the City of Portsmouth (*Re Dupree's Deed Trusts* [1945] Ch 16, a decision of Vaisey J), and for the furthering of the Boy Scouts' movement by helping to purchase sites for camping, outfits etc. (*Re Webber* [1954] 1 WLR 1500, another decision of Vaisey J).

Note
The Court of Appeal ([1979] 1 WLR 130), whose decision was reversed, had held by a majority that this trust was not charitable under the Recreational Charities Act 1958, because the recipients of benefit were not deprived. Because the House held that it was a valid educational charity, they did not need to decide this issue, and left it open. On the 1958 Act generally, see further below.

D: Value Judgments

It is perhaps inevitable with such a wide range of educational purposes that occasionally the courts will have to make value judgments, or 'a school for prostitutes or pickpockets' would be charitable.

Re Pinion (decd)
[1965] Ch 85
Court of Appeal

Facts: The testator left his 'studio' for the purposes of a museum to display his collection of what were claimed to be 'fine arts'. However, expert witnesses thought that the paintings were 'atrociously bad', and one 'expresse[d] his surprise that so voracious a collector should not by hazard have picked up even one meritorious object'. The question arose as to the validity of the trust, and this depended on whether it was charitable.

Held: Harman LJ described the collection as 'a mass of junk', and reversing Wilberforce J, the Court of Appeal held the trust void.

HARMAN LJ: Where a museum is concerned and the utility of the gift is brought in question it is, in my opinion, and herein I agree with the judge, essential to know at least something of the quality of the proposed exhibits in order to judge whether they will be conducive to the education of the public. So I think with a public library, such a place if found to be devoted entirely to works of pornography or of a corrupting nature, would not be allowable. Here it is suggested that education in the fine arts is the object. For myself a reading of the will leads me rather to the view that the testator's object was not to educate anyone, but to perpetuate his own name and the repute of his family, hence perhaps the direction that the custodian should be a blood relation of his. However that may be, there is a strong body of evidence here that as a means of education this collection is worthless. The testator's own paintings, of which there are over 50, are said by competent persons to be in an academic style and 'atrociously bad' and the other pictures without exception worthless. Even the so-called 'Lely' turns out to be a 20th century copy.

Apart from pictures there is a haphazard assembly – it does not merit the name collection, for no purpose emerges, no time nor style is illustrated – of furniture and objects of so-called 'art' about which expert opinion is unanimous that nothing beyond the third-rate is to be found. Indeed one of the experts expresses his surprise that so voracious a collector should not by hazard have picked up even one meritorious object. The most that skilful cross-examination extracted from the expert witnesses was that there were a dozen chairs which might perhaps be acceptable to a minor provincial museum and perhaps another dozen not altogether worthless, but two dozen chairs do not make a museum and they must, to accord with the will, be exhibited stifled by a large number of absolutely worthless pictures and objects.

It was said that this is a matter of taste, and de gustibus non est disputandum, but here I agree with the judge that there is an accepted canon of taste on which the court must rely, for it has itself no judicial knowledge of such matters, and the unanimous verdict of the experts is as I have stated. The judge with great hesitation concluded that there was that scintilla of merit which was sufficient to save the rest. I find myself on the other side of the line. I can conceive of no useful object to be served in foisting upon the public this mass of junk. It has neither public utility nor educative value. I would hold that the testator's project ought not to be carried into effect and that his next-of-kin is entitled to the residue of his estate.

RUSSELL LJ: The first question for consideration is whether [counsel] for the Attorney-General, is correct in contending that the judge should not have received the expert evidence . . . on the aesthetic merits of the testator's collection of objects and its tendency if exhibited to the public to promote or advance education in aesthetic appreciation. [Counsel] argued that the court could not inquire into such matters: that an exhibition to the public of a collection of objects such as these must be assumed to have that tendency. I cannot agree.

The mere fact that a person makes a gift of chattels to form a public museum cannot establish that its formation will have a tendency to advance education in aesthetic appreciation or in anything else. Inquiry must first be made, what are the chattels? Five hundred balls of string could not have that tendency. Nor is the inquiry ended on finding that the chattels are household furniture, carpets, light fittings, paintings, china and so forth: otherwise the contents of any dwelling-house in the land, if displayed to the public, could be said to have a tendency to advance education in aesthetic appreciation – which would, I think, be absurd. Some further judicial inquiry is needed directed to the quality of those chattels. The judge cannot conduct that inquiry on his own, unless the matter be so obvious as to call for no hesitation. He may be lacking in aesthetic appreciation. He is, I consider, entitled to the assistance of people expert in such matters, and to arrive at a conclusion based on such assistance. If the conclusion so based is that the quality of the articles is such that their exhibition to the public cannot be reasonably supposed to have the tendency mentioned, there is no charitable gift.

Accordingly, I would reject the submission that the judge should not have entertained the evidence . . . on the quality and the potential educational value of this gift.

Note

In *Re Hummeltenberg* [1923] 1 Ch 237 the court held void a trust to train spiritualistic mediums (though perhaps disciplined research into the paranormal, undertaken on scientific principles, could be charitable). On the other hand, in *Re Delius* [1957] Ch 299 a trust for the appreciation of the works of the composer was held charitable, but Roxburgh J made it clear that the undoubted merit of Delius's music was critical.

Questions
1. In *The Emperor's New Mind*, Vintage (1990), Winner of the 1990 Science Book Prize, Roger Penrose sets out (at p. 76):

> The famous statement known as 'Fermat's last theorem', made in the margin of Diophantus's *Arithmetica*, by the great seventeenth century mathematician Pierre de Fermat (1601–1665) . . .

He continues:

> . . . Though a lawyer by profession (and a contemporary of Descartes), Fermat was widely regarded as the finest mathematician of his time. He claimed to have 'a truly wonderful proof' of his assertion, which the margin was too small to contain; but to this day no-one has been able to reconstruct such a proof nor, on the other hand, to find any counter-example of Fermat's assertion!

Fermat's last theorem is part of number theory, the common view of which is admitted by David Burton in the preface to *Elementary Number Theory*, 2nd ed., William Brown Publishers (1980) to be 'the most obviously useless branch of pure mathematics'. In June 1993 Fermat's last theorem was finally proved, after nearly 350 years, by Andrew Wiles, an English mathematician working at Princeton University (see *New Scientist*, 3 July 1993, p. 14).

In the light of *Re Pinion*, and also *Re Hopkins*, above, would an unincorporated association set up in 1990 (the year of publication of *The Emperor's New Mind*) to prove Fermat's last theorem have been charitable?
2. The whole of the modern computer industry depends on quantum mechanics, and without quantum mechanics there would be no lasers, CDs or micro-processors. Yet in the 1920s quantum mechanics was regarded as the purest form of science with no possible practical application, and even when the laser was invented much later, it was seen as a solution looking for a problem. So would an association set up in the 1920s to research into quantum mechanics have been charitable?
3. Do you think it is possible to make value judgments in the area of research?

SECTION 4: ADVANCEMENT OF RELIGION

A: What Constitutes Religion?

The law adopts a tolerant stance towards religion, and seems reluctant to enter into value judgments in this area. As Cross J remarked in *Neville Estates* v *Madden* [1962] Ch 832, below, in which a trust for the members of the

Catford Synagogue was held charitable: 'As between different religions the law stands neutral, but it assumes that any religion is at least likely to be better than none.' Another example is *Church of the New Faith* v *Commissioner of Payroll Tax (Victoria)* (1983) 83 AJC 4652, a case concerning Australian Scientology, where the High Court of Australia held that:

There can be no acceptable discrimination between institutions which take their character from religions which the majority of the community recognises as religions and institutions which take their character from religions which lack that general recognition.

Generally speaking, it seems, the courts are unprepared to engage in value judgments as to the relative worth of different religions.

In *Bowman* v *Secular Society Ltd* [1917] AC 406, Lord Parker of Waddington thought that a trust for the purpose of any kind of monotheistic theism would be a good charitable trust.

The preamble to the Statute of Charitable Uses 1601 gave little support for the tolerant approach the law has taken, the only reference to religion within it concerning the repair of churches. It may be that the explanation lies in the mortmain legislation in force from 1736 to 1891, which as we have seen rendered many gifts to charity void. Religious tolerance in this area, therefore, may have been used simply as a device to strike down testamentary gifts, the authorities from that period still having validity today.

In *Thornton* v *Howe* (1862) 31 Beav 14, for example, charitable status was extended to a devise of land to promote the writings of Joanna Southcote, the founder of a small but fervent sect in the West of England, who had proclaimed that she was with child by the Holy Ghost and would give birth to a second Messiah. The practical effect of the decision was to bring the trust within the invalidating provisions of the mortmain legislation, but the case is still seen as a landmark in establishing that any theistic belief, however obscure or remote, will fall within the meaning of religion for the purposes of charity law. The case is discussed and applied in *Re Watson* [1973] 1 WLR 1472.

Re Watson (decd), Hobbs v Smith
[1973] 1 WLR 1472, [1973] 3 All ER 678
Chancery Division

Decision: Plowman J held charitable a trust to publish the religious writings of a retired builder who was virtually the sole remaining adherent of a small, fundamentalist group of believers. Expert testimony regarded the theological merits of the works as very small, but confirmed the genuineness of the writers' beliefs.

PLOWMAN J (after stating the facts): So much for the evidence. There are two questions to consider. The first is, what are the purposes of the trust expressed by the will, and, secondly, whether that trust is a charitable trust. Now as to the first point, the work of God which is referred to in a number of passages in the will which I have read, to quote the will, is 'the work of God as it has been maintained by Mr H.G. Hobbs and myself since 1942 . . . in propagating the truth as given in the Holy Bible'. And I accept counsel for the Attorney-General's submission that, on the true construction of the will, read in the light of the evidence of surrounding circumstances, the trust is one for the publication and distribution to the public of the religious works of Mr H.G. Hobbs. If that is right, to get one point out of the way, that trust will not, in my judgment, fail for impracticability, as counsel for the next-of-kin suggested on one view of the will that it must. On the second question, whether that trust, namely the trust for the publication and distribution to the public of the religious works of Mr Hobbs, is charitable, counsel for the next-of-kin submitted that it was not. He submitted that not every religious trust is charitable, that to be charitable there must be an element of public benefit, that whether or not there is a sufficient public benefit is a matter for the court to decide on evidence, irrespective of the opinion of the donor and that there is no sufficient element of public benefit in this case.

Counsel's submissions were based primarily on *National Anti-Vivisection Society* v *Inland Revenue Comrs* [1948] AC 31 [below] and *Gilmour* v *Coats* [1949] AC 426 [below], and he submitted that the approach of the House of Lords in those cases was inconsistent with the decision of Romilly MR in *Thornton* v *Howe* (1862) 31 Beav 14. *Thornton* v *Howe* was a well-known case about the writings of Joanna Southcote. The sidenote reads:

> A trust 'for printing, publishing and propagating the sacred writings' of Joanna Southcote, is a charitable trust, which if given out of pure personalty will be enforced and regulated. In respect to charitable trusts for printing and circulating works of a religious tendency, this Court makes no distinction between one sect and another, unless their tenets include doctrines adverse to the foundation of all religion or be subversive of all morality, in which case this Court will declare the bequest void.

After referring to the gift in the will Romilly MR said (1862) 31 Beav at 18:

> In the first place, it is said that this, if a lawful and legitimate purpose, is a charity and therefore void, so far as the real estate is concerned, by reason of the Statute of Mortmain; and, secondly, it is also said that this is wholly void, both as to realty and personalty, by reason of the immorality and irreligious tendency of the writings of Joanna Southcote, which, by this disposition of her property, the testatrix intended to circulate and make more extensively known. On the latter point, being unacquainted with the writings of Joanna Southcote, it became my duty to look into them, for the purpose of satisfying myself on this point, and the result of my investigation is, that there is nothing to be found in them which, in my opinion, is likely to corrupt the morals of her followers, or make her readers irreligious.

And I may pause there to say that, in my judgment, is equally true of the writings of Mr H.G. Hobbs in this case. Romilly MR then went on to express his opinion of Joanna Southcote, saying that, in his opinion, she was —

> a foolish, ignorant woman, of an enthusiastic turn of mind, who had long wished to become an instrument in the hands of God to promote some great good on earth.

He said (1862) 31 Beav at 19, 20, 21:

> In the history of her life, her personal disputations and conversations with the devil, her prophecies and her inter-communings with the spiritual world, I have found

much that, in my opinion, is very foolish, but nothing which is likely to make persons who read them either immoral or irreligious. I cannot, therefore, say that this devise of the testatrix is invalid by reason of the tendency of the writings of Joanna Southcote. On the other hand, the contention raised, that this is a gift to promote objects which are within the meaning of what this Court, for shortness, terms 'charitable objects', and that, consequently, it is within the provisions of the Statute of Mortmain, presents a more serious objection to this devise . . .

I am of opinion, that if a bequest of money be made for the purpose of printing and circulating works of a religious tendency, or for the purpose of extending the knowledge of the Christian religion, that this is a charitable bequest, and this Court will, upon a proper application being made to it, sanction and settle a scheme for this purpose, and, in truth, it is but lately that I have had in Chambers to settle and approve of a scheme of this description. In this respect, I am of opinion that the Court of Chancery makes no distinction between one sort of religion and another. They are equally bequests which are included in the general terms of charitable bequests. Neither does the Court, in this respect, make any distinction between one sect and another. It may be that the tenets of a particular sect inculcate doctrines adverse to the very foundations of all religion, and that they are subversive of all morality. In such a case, if it should arise, the Court will not assist the execution of the bequest, but will declare it to be void; but the character of the bequest, so far as regards the Statute of Mortmain, would not be altered by this circumstance. The general immoral tendency of the bequest would make it void, whether it was to be paid out of pure personalty or out of real estate. But if the tendency were not immoral, and although this Court might consider the opinions sought to be propagated foolish or even devoid of foundation, it would not, on that account, declare it void, or take it out of the class of legacies which are included in the general terms charitable bequests. The words of the bequest here are, 'to propagate the sacred writings of Joanna Southcote'. The testatrix, it is clear, was a disciple or believer in Joanna Southcote, who, from her writings, it is clear, was a very sincere Christian; but she laboured under the delusion that she was to be made the medium of the miraculous birth of a child at an advanced period of her life, and that thereby the advancement of the Christian religion on earth would be occasioned. But her works, as far as I have looked at them, contain but little upon this subject, and nothing which could shake the faith of any sincere Christian. In truth, though her works are in a great measure incoherent and confused, they are written obviously with a view to extend the influence of Christianity. I cannot say that the bequest of a testator to publish and propagate works in support of the Christian religion is a charitable bequest, and, at the same time, say, that if another testator should select for this purpose some three or four authors, whose works will, in his opinion, produce that effect, such a bequest thereupon ceases to be charitable. Neither can I do so if a testator should select one single author whose works he thinks will produce that result. If a testator were to leave a fund for the purpose of propagating, at a very reduced price, the religious writings of Dr Paley or Dr Butler, I should be of opinion that the bequest was charitable in its character, and I must hold the same in respect of what the testatrix has called 'the sacred writings of the late Joanna Southcote'.

The question then arises whether *Thornton* v *Howe* is still good law. It has been treated as good law on a considerable number of occasions since it was decided and I mention certain examples which were cited to me in the course of the arguments. The first one, I think, is *Bowman* v *Secular Society Ltd* [1917] AC 406. The reference

to *Thornton* v *Howe* is in the speech of Lord Parker of Waddington, where he said
[1917] AC at 442:

> . . . a trust for the attainment of political objects has always been held invalid, not
> because it is illegal, for every one is at liberty to advocate or promote by any lawful
> means a change in the law, but because the Court has no means of judging whether
> a proposed change in the law will or will not be for the public benefit, and therefore
> cannot say that a gift to secure the change is a charitable gift. The same
> considerations apply when there is a trust for the publication of a book. The Court
> will examine the book, and if its objects be charitable in the legal sense it will give
> effect to the trust as a good charity: *Thornton* v *Howe*.

[Plowman J reviewed a number of other authorities, and concluded:]
   Now the result of those cases, including the *Anti-Vivisection* case to which counsel
for the next-of-kin referred, in my judgment, is this. First of all, as Romilly MR said
in *Thornton* v *Howe*, the court does not prefer one religion to another and it does not
prefer one sect to another. Secondly, where the purposes in question are of a religious
nature – and, in my opinion, they clearly are here – then the court assumes a public
benefit unless the contrary is shown. In the *Anti-Vivisection* case, Lord Wright said
[1948] AC at 42:

> The test of benefit to the community goes through the whole of Lord Macnaghten's
> classification [in the *Pemsel* case [1891] AC 531], though, as regards the first three
> heads [which of course includes religion], it may be prima facie assumed unless the
> contrary appears.

And Lord Simonds, in his speech, said [1948] AC at 65:

> I would rather say that, when a purpose appears broadly to fall within one of the
> familiar categories of charity, the court will assume it to be for the benefit of the
> community and therefore charitable unless the contrary is shown, and further that
> the court will not be astute in such a case to defeat upon doubtful evidence the
> avowed benevolent intention of a donor.

   And thirdly, that having regard to the fact that the court does not draw a distinction
between one religion and another or one sect and another, the only way of disproving
a public benefit is to show, in the words of Romilly MR in *Thornton* v *Howe*, that the
doctrines inculcated are – 'adverse to the very foundations of all religion, and that they
are subversive of all morality'. And that in my judgment, as I have said already, is
clearly not the case here, and I therefore conclude that this case is really on all fours
with *Thornton* v *Howe* and for that reason is a valid charitable trust.

Notes
1.   Far from benefiting Joanna Southcote, the result of *Thornton* v *Howe* was
to render a testamentary disposition of land void under the Mortmain
legislation. Today, of course, the effect of the decision is that you pay more
tax so that minority religious sects can pay less.
2.   Both Joanna Southcote and Mr H.G. Hobbs were Christians, but it is
not necessary that the religious beliefs in question be Christian. Certainly the
Jewish, Sikh, Hindu and Muslim faiths have been accepted (see also *Neville
Estates* v *Madden*, below). Religion implies a supernatural element, however.

It is not charitable merely to advance ethics or morality, since those concern man's relations with man, not man's relations with God.

Re South Place Ethical Society, Barralet v Attorney-General
[1980] 3 All ER 918
Chancery Division

Decision: The South Place Ethical Society was not a religious charity, because although its objects included 'the study and dissemination of ethical principles', and 'the cultivation of a rational religious sentiment', its beliefs were non-theistic.

However, the society was charitable as being for the advancement of education and for purposes beneficial to the community. Advancement of education was to be construed widely: *IRC v McMullen* [1981] AC 1 (above) applied.

DILLON J (on the issue of religion): I propose therefore to consider first the claim that the society is charitable because its objects are for the advancement of religion. In considering this, as in considering the other claims, I keep very much in mind the observation of Lord Wilberforce in the *Scottish Burial Reform and Cremation Society Ltd v Glasgow City Corpn* [1968] AC 138 at 154, that the law of charity is a moving subject which may well have evolved even since 1891. The submissions of counsel for the society seek to establish that this is indeed so, having regard to current thinking in the field of religion.

Of course it has long been established that a trust can be valid and charitable as for the advancement of religion although the religion which is sought to be advanced is not the Christian religion. In *Bowman v Secular Society Ltd* [1917] AC 406 at 448–50, Lord Parker of Waddington gave a very clear and valuable summary of the history of the approach of the law to religious charitable trusts. He said ([1917] AC 406 at 449):

It would seem to follow that a trust for the purpose of any kind of monotheistic theism would be a good charitable trust.

Counsel for the society accepts that, so far as it goes, but he submits that Lord Parker should have gone further, even in 1917 (because the society's beliefs go back before that date) and the court should go further now. The society says that religion does not have to be theist or dependent on a god; any sincere belief in ethical qualities is religious, because such qualities as truth, love and beauty are sacred, and the advancement of any such belief is the advancement of religion. . . .

In a free country . . . it is natural that the court should desire not to discriminate between beliefs deeply and sincerely held, whether they are beliefs in a god or in the excellence of man or in ethical principles or in Platonism or some other scheme of philosophy. But I do not see that that warrants extending the meaning of the word 'religion' so as to embrace all other beliefs and philosophies. Religion, as I see it, is concerned with man's relations with God, and ethics are concerned with man's relations with man. The two are not the same, and are not made the same by sincere inquiry into the question, What is God? If reason leads people not to accept Christianity or any known religion, but they do believe in the excellence of qualities such as truth, beauty and love, or believe in the Platonic concept of the ideal, their beliefs may be to them the equivalent of a religion, but viewed objectively they are not religion.

Note
In an old case in the Privy Council, *Yeap Cheah Neo* v *Ong Chen Neo* (1875)
LR 6 PC 381, a provision for the performance of ancestor worship was held
non-charitable. High ethical principles or moral philosophy, being concerned
with man's relations with man, cannot amount to a religion, though they may
of course be educational, and so charitable under that head. Plowman J also
thought in *Re Watson*, considered above, that doctrines which were averse to
the foundations of all religion, and subversive of all morality, would not be
charitable under this head.

Buddhism poses a problem in this context, since although it is generally
accepted as being a religion, it is not clear (at any rate to the judiciary)
whether or not Buddhists believe in a supernatural or supreme being. It is
possible that it should be treated as an exception, since a trust to advance
Buddhism is clearly charitable. Difficulties could also presumably arise where
a human being sets himself up as a deity, and is worshipped as such – such
religions exist, and it is unclear whether or not their advancement is
charitable.

It seems that the gift must be exclusively for religious purposes, so that a
gift for 'missionary work' or 'parish work' will be too wide, since such work
may involve elements not wholly religious. On the other hand, in *Re
Simson* [1946] Ch 299, a gift to a named clergyman 'for his work in the parish'
was held to be impliedly confined to his religious duties.

B: Advancement of Religion

As with education, the means by which religion may be advanced may be
many and various. Apart from the provision and maintenance of churches,
and provision of or for the benefit of clergymen, such matters as church
choirs, Sunday school prizes, and even exorcism, have all been held to
advance religion.

Religion must be advanced, however. This seems to require some positive
action. For example, in *United Grand Lodge of Ancient Free & Accepted Masons
of England and Wales* v *Holborn BC* [1957] 1 WLR 1080, Donovan J, in
denying charitable status to freemasons (who attempted to claim rates
advantages), commented (after setting out the objects of the lodge) that:

Admirable though these objects are it seems to us impossible to say that they add up
to the advancement of religion. Indeed, as already stated, the first Antient Charge,
headed 'Concerning God and Religion' says, among other things, this: 'Let a man's
religion or mode of worship' (the contrast is not perhaps without significance) 'be
what it may, he is not excluded from the Order, provided he believe in the glorious
architect of heaven and earth, and practise the sacred duties of morality'. Thus it
would seem that no Mason need practise any religion, but, provided that he believes
in a Supreme Being and lives a moral life, he may be and remain a Mason.
    Accordingly, one cannot really begin to argue that the main object of Freemasonry
is to advance religion, except perhaps by saying that religion can be advanced by
example as well as by precept, so that the spectacle of a man leading an upright moral

life may persuade others to do likewise. The appellants did not in fact advance this argument, but even if it were accepted, it leads to no useful conclusion here. For a man may persuade his neighbour by example to lead a good life without at the same time leading him to religion. And there is nothing in the 'Constitutions', nor, apparently, in the evidence tendered to quarter sessions, to support the view that the main object of Masonry is to encourage Masons to go out in the world, and by their example lead persons to some religion or another. When one considers the work done by organisations which admittedly do set out to advance religion, the contrast with Masonry is striking. To advance religion means to promote it, to spread its message ever wider among mankind; to take some positive steps to sustain and increase religious belief; and these things are done in a variety of ways which may be comprehensively described as pastoral and missionary. There is nothing comparable to that in Masonry. This is not said by way of criticism. For Masonry really does something different. It says to a man, 'Whatever your religion or your mode of worship, believe in a Supreme Creator and lead a good moral life'. Laudable as this precept is, it does not appear to us to be the same thing as the advancement of religion. There is no religious instruction, no programme for the persuasion of unbelievers, no religious supervision to see that its members remain active and constant in the various religions they may profess, no holding of religious services, no pastoral or missionary work of any kind.

Religion may have been a necessary qualification for membership of the lodge, as it might be for a church squash club, for example, but the lodge did not advance religion, any more than a church squash club would.

There is also a public benefit requirement under this head of charity, on which see further below.

C: Reform of the Law?

Charities: A Framework for the Future HMSO (May 1989)

2.18 Although, for historical reasons, it received only indirect mention in the preamble to the 1601 statute, the advancement of religion has always been a charitable object. Indeed, the very concept of charity is essentially religious in origin.

2.19 With the growth in religious toleration, and with the development of a multi-cultural society in the United Kingdom, the courts have progressively admitted to charitable status a variety of Christian and other religious faiths. Gifts to dissenting Protestant churches and for the advancement of the Jewish and Roman Catholic faiths have been upheld by the courts as being of charitable purpose. The Commissioners have also registered trusts for the advancement of the Hindu, Sikh, Islamic and Buddhist religions.

2.20 The present position is that any religious body is entitled to charitable status so long as its tenets are not morally subversive and so long as its purposes are directed to the benefit of the public. The modern attitude of the courts is summed up in the often quoted remark of Mr Justice Cross, later Lord Cross of Chelsea: 'As between religions the law stands neutral, but it assumes that any religion is at least likely to be better than none.' [*Neville Estates* v *Madden* [1962] Ch 832, at 853 is footnoted.] More recently, in the Australian Scientology Case [*Church of the New Faith* v *Commissioner of Payroll Tax (Victoria)* (1983) 83 AJC 4652], Mason ACJ and Brennan J of the High

Court of Australia held that: 'There can be no acceptable discrimination between institutions which take their character from religions which the majority of the community recognises as religious and institutions which take their character from religions which lack that general recognition'. These dicta are important in drawing attention to the understandable reluctance of the courts to judge the relative worth of different religions or the truth of competing religious doctrines, all of which may have a place in a tolerant and culturally diverse society.

2.21   The importance of religion as a fundamental spring of charity can scarcely be overestimated. It is part of the make up of Man to want to give. It is part of the ethics of most religions to encourage that.

2.22   Trusts for the advancement of religion have contributed much to the spiritual welfare of generations of individuals and to the sound development of our society. Nevertheless, the question has been raised from time to time as to whether trusts which are set up to further certain religious groups should be entitled to charitable status. Anxieties have been expressed, in particular, about a number of organisations whose influence over their followers, especially the young, is seen as destructive of family life and, in some cases, as tantamount to brainwashing.

2.23   The Government have considerable sympathies for these anxieties. They have considered whether it might be possible to amend the law in such a way as to exclude those religious organisations whose activities are deemed undesirable. Their conclusion is that there are great difficulties in the way of doing so, but they would welcome views as to how this might be achieved, and in particular on the suggestions which follow.

2.24   It has been suggested that the problem would be solved if charitable status were removed from all trusts which are established to advance religion – of whatever type and without exception. This proposal has, at least, the merit of simplicity. It would also avoid the need to make invidious comparisons between different religions. While the advancement of religion might cease to be a charitable object, religious organisations would still remain free to propagate their doctrines and, if they so wished, to promote and to administer trusts for such purposes as the relief of poverty which would remain charitable as before.

2.25   The Government finds the whole concept of removing charitable status from religious trusts unattractive and believes that it would be resisted vigorously, not just by the religious bodies who would be affected, but also by the great majority of the public. The removal of religion as a head of charity would leave many existing trusts, some of which are of considerable antiquity, in an impossible legal limbo. The legal difficulties of resolving the subsequent uncertainties would be immense and might well prove insuperable. It is true that these difficulties could largely be avoided if trusts which were already in existence were preserved, and loss of charitable status was confined to organisations which were established after legislation. Drawing a line under religion in this way would, though, be difficult to justify: there would be little justification for denying charitable status to new trusts for religious purposes of an existing denomination. Such a policy would, in any event, do nothing to deal with the problems presented by organisations which already exist and which have acquired charitable status.

2.26   Alternative suggestions for tightening the law concentrate on the criterion of 'public benefit'. A trust for the advancement of religion is presumed to be for the public benefit unless that presumption is rebutted by evidence to the contrary. This presumption reflects the reluctance of the courts to enter into questions of the comparative worth of different religions. Although the courts will not prefer one religion to another, they will decide in the light of evidence which is placed before them whether or not there is a benefit to the community from the religious activity in question.

2.27 For some critics the neutrality of the law is objectionable, and suggestions have been made from time to time that the presumption of public benefit should be removed and that it should be replaced with a positive test of worth. The Goodman Committee, for example, suggested that those who seek charitable status for the promotion of religious movements should be required to satisfy the Charity Commissioners or the court that their advancement was for the benefit of the community 'according to certain basic concepts which should be established'. In summing up, the Committee proposed that religions which were 'considered detrimental to the community's moral welfare' should be excluded from charitable status. However, the Committee offered no guidance on the content of the 'basic concepts' which it had in mind. The Government would not regard it as satisfactory, nor do they consider that it would be likely to be acceptable to Parliament, that these concepts should be undefined and that they should be left to the interpretation of the Charity Commissioners or to the courts.

2.28 The difficulties of principle which the Goodman Committee encountered, in considering what criteria might be applied to religions, are formidable. So also are the practical difficulties which vary with the nature of the particular movement in question. If its aims are clearly not for the public benefit, that is in itself sufficient reason for refusing to register as a charity any trust which is established in order to advance them.

2.29 In some cases the undesirability of a doctrine may be clear enough. Sometimes, however, the objectionable feature may be only one element in a complex body of doctrine. The question would then arise whether that one element alone should be enough to justify refusal to register, bearing in mind that, in religious matters, it is often a single doctrinal element which is the cause of controversy.

2.30 Furthermore, with religious movements of the kind about which public anxiety has been expressed, it is not usually a question of whether their *objects* are contrary to the public interest. The question is whether, if the actual *conduct* of the movement causes harm, a trust which is set up to advance its beliefs should be deprived of charitable status on the grounds that they are not of public benefit.

2.31 The Charity Commissioners already have powers of inquiry available to them under section 6 of the 1960 Act. Where it appears that the charity's conduct is not in accord with its objects, and there has, therefore, been a breach of trust, the Commissioners can refer the matter to the Attorney General or use their powers under section 20. Chapter 5 of this White Paper outlines the Government's proposals for strengthening these powers.

2.32 Where conduct is in breach of trust, or is marginal to the pursuit of an organisation's objects, action can generally be taken to restrain the trustees or their agents. Action of this kind does not affect an organisation's charitable status. But in exceptional cases where from a careful examination of *all the circumstances* the activities complained of appeared to them to be directly and essentially expressive of the objects and tenets of a particular movement, the Charity Commissioners might nevertheless conclude that the pursuit of those objects was not beneficial, and hence not therefore being directed to charitable purposes. Should they reach this conclusion the Commission could remove the organisation from the register of charities under section 4(3) of the 1960 Act on the grounds that it no longer appeared to them to be a charity. Under section 5(3) of the Act the Attorney General can appeal against any decision of the Commissioners to remove or not to remove an organisation from the register.

2.33 The trustees of any organisation which is removed from the register may themselves appeal against that decision to the High Court under section 5(3). The

Commissioners cannot take action under section 4(3) unless there is evidence which shows that such an exceptional course is justified. This is a sensitive area. Some religious movements evidently demand uncritical adherence from their members. Evidence of sufficient weight and cogency to justify removal from the register can be difficult to obtain.

2.34 Frustration with the difficulty of obtaining evidence against undesirable religious movements has led some commentators to suggest a change in the law. But no acceptable or relevant change in the law on charitable status would remove the need for evidence. Indeed, evidence which would be sufficient to refuse registration as a charity would be more, not less, difficult to obtain at the pre-registration stage when for practical purposes the organisation might not yet have begun to operate. In the light of this, the Government doubt whether it would be wise to attempt to introduce any new principle into the law. Their view is that the existing law is adequate. What is needed now is the determined pursuit of evidence in order to justify the bold use by the Commissioners of their powers of investigation and remedy.

2.35 The Government acknowledge the concern which underlies much of the recent public comment on the position of cults. Calls to strengthen the law may, however, rest on a mistaken view of what the law allows. This may be a reflection not just of the undoubted complexity of charity law, especially where it concerns charitable status, but also of the present wording of section 4(3) of the 1960 Act.

2.36 It is important both for the Commissioners and for trustees that the law in this area should be fully understood. The Government will, therefore, be considering whether it would be possible, whilst preserving the underlying principles involved, to amend section 4(3) in order to make it explicit that the Commissioners have the power to remove a body from the register where there is evidence that it is acting in pursuit of its objects in ways which are not for the public benefit.

SECTION 5:   OTHER PURPOSES BENEFICIAL TO THE COMMUNITY

A: Reference Back to Preamble

What the law admits as charitable under this head is still governed by the general statement of charitable purposes which was set out in the preamble to the Statute of Charitable Uses 1601. If some wholly novel purpose appears, the question is not whether it is beneficial in some general sense, but whether it falls within the 'spirit and intendment' of the Preamble, or can be held to by analogy with the principles developed through the cases.

Scottish Burial Reform and Cremation Society, Ltd v *Glasgow City Corporation*
[1968] AC 138, [1967] 3 All ER 215, [1967] 3 WLR 1132
House of Lords

Decision: The House of Lords held a society charitable for rating purposes (under the fourth *Pemsel* head), whose main object was the promotion of sanitary methods of disposal of the dead. The society charged fees but was not profit-making.

LORD WILBERFORCE: My Lords, the Scottish Burial Reform and Cremation Society Ltd. was formed in 1890 with the following main objects, as stated in clause 3 of its memorandum of association:—

(a) To promote reform in the present methods of burial in Scotland, both as regards the expense involved and the dangerous effects on the public health. (b) To promote inexpensive and at the same time sanitary methods of disposal of the dead, which shall best tend to render the remains innocuous; and, in particular to promote the method known as cremation.

The company is non-profit-making in the sense that its income and property must be applied solely towards the promotion of its objects and that its members receive no dividends nor any distribution on a winding up.

In 1890 the company was, no doubt, a pioneering venture; it must have been one of the earliest undertakings offering to provide a service of cremation for the inhabitants of Glasgow and of Scotland. Though its first object is stated as the promotion of reform in burial methods, its activity in this direction has not been by way of propaganda, but rather by way of providing services of a kind and in a manner which would progressively persuade the public of their advantages. . . .

Was, then, the company established for charitable purposes only? I interpret its objects clause as meaning that the company was formed for a general and a particular purpose: the general purpose was to promote methods of disposal of the dead which should be inexpensive and sanitary; the particular purpose (to which the company has in fact confined itself) to promote the method known as cremation. It is this combination of purposes which has to be examined in order to see whether it satisfies the legal test of charitable purposes.

On this subject, the law of England, though no doubt not very satisfactory and in need of rationalisation, is tolerably clear. The purposes in question, to be charitable, must be shown to be for the benefit of the public, or the community, in a sense or manner within the intendment of the preamble to the statute 43 Eliz. I, c. 4. The latter requirement does not mean quite what it says; for it is now accepted that what must be regarded is not the wording of the preamble itself, but the effect of decisions given by the courts as to its scope, decisions which have endeavoured to keep the law as to charities moving according as new social needs arise or old ones become obsolete or satisfied. Lord Macnaghten's grouping of the heads of recognised charity in *Pemsel's* case [1891] AC 531, 583 is one that has proved to be of value and there are many problems which it solves. But three things may be said about it, which its author would surely not have denied: first that, since it is a classification of convenience, there may well be purposes which do not fit neatly into one or other of the headings; secondly, that the words used must not be given the force of a statute to be construed; and thirdly, that the law of charity is a moving subject which may well have evolved even since 1891.

With this in mind, approach may be made to the question whether the provision of facilities for the disposal of human remains, whether, generally, in an inexpensive and sanitary manner, or, particularly, by cremation, can be considered as within the spirit of the statute. Decided cases help us, at any rate, to the point of showing that trusts for the repair or maintenance of burial grounds connected with a church are charitable.

. . .

Then in *In re Eighmie* [1935] Ch 524, a trust for the maintenance of a cemetery owned and managed by a local authority was held charitable. The cemetery was an extension of a closed churchyard so that the decision can be regarded as a logical step rather than a new departure. Now what we have to consider is whether to take the further step of holding charitable the purpose of providing burial, or facilities for the disposal of mortal remains, without any connection with a church, by an independent body. I have no doubt that we should. I would regard the earlier decisions as falling on the borderline between trusts for the advancement of religion and trusts otherwise beneficial to the community. One may say either that burial purposes fall within both, or that the categories themselves shade one into the other. So I find no departure in principle in saying that purposes such as the present – which, though the company in fact provides the means for religious observance, should be regarded as independent of any religious basis – are to be treated as equally within the charitable class.

It was argued for the respondents that the company's purposes were neither for the benefit of the community nor, in any event, within the intendment of the preamble to the Statute of Elizabeth I. One or other of these arguments was accepted by the Lord Ordinary and by three members of the Inner House. As to the first of these, there was some suggestion that the necessary basis of fact had not been shown, and that the appellants should have averred, and if necessary proved, that their services were more inexpensive and more sanitary than normal methods of burial. In my opinion, the appellants rightly made no such averment, for no such comparison was called for. All they had to do was to show that the provision of inexpensive and sanitary methods, and of cremation in particular, was for the benefit of the community. As to this, the facts speak for themselves; for, it being admitted by joint minute that the company had used its premises in carrying out its objects, the scale on which the company's services were resorted to clearly showed that they met a need of the public. And it can hardly be said that to meet a need of this character is not beneficial. The second argument can be met in two ways. First, it may be said that the same evolutionary process which has carried charity from the 'repair of churches' to the maintenance of burial grounds (i) in a churchyard and (ii) in a cemetery extended from a churchyard should naturally carry it further so as to embrace the company's objects. Secondly, and more generally, the company's objects themselves may directly be seen to be within the preamble's spirit. The group 'repair of bridges, ports, havens, causeways, churches, sea banks and highways' has within it the common element of public utility and it is of interest to note that the original label of Lord Macnaghten's fourth category 'other purposes beneficial to the community' affixed by Sir Samuel Romilly in *Morice v Bishop of Durham* (1805) 10 Ves 522, 532 was ' . . . the advancement of objects of general public utility.' In this context I find it of significance that Parliament in 1902 by the Cremation Act of that year placed cremation, as a public service, on the same footing as burial.

I regard, then, the provision of cremation services as falling naturally, and in their own right, within the spirit of the preamble.

One other point requires mention. The company makes charges for its services to enable it, in the words of the joint agreed minute, to fulfil effectively the objects for which it was formed. These charges, though apparently modest, are not shown to be higher or lower than those levied for other burial services. In my opinion, the fact that cremation is provided for a fee rather than gratuitously does not affect the charitable character of the company's activity, for that does not consist in the fact of providing financial relief but in the provision of services. That the charging for services for the achievement of a purpose which is in itself shown to be charitable does not destroy the charitable element was clearly, and, in my opinion, rightly, decided in *Inland Revenue Commissioners* v *Falkirk Temperance Café Trust* 1927 SC 261 as well as in English authorities.

I am therefore of opinion that the appellant makes good its claim to rating relief and I would allow the appeal.

Note

The most important point about the fourth head is the continued reference back to the preamble to the Statute of Charitable Uses 1601. It is a truly miscellaneous head, covering private hospitals and nursing homes, museums, parks, community centres, orphanages and many other purposes. Animal charities also come under head 4, at any rate as long as they confer a benefit upon mankind, and not merely on the animals themselves.

B: Range of Activities Covered

Re Moss (decd), Hobrough v *Harvey*
[1949] 1 All ER 495, 65 TLR 299, [1949] WN 93
Chancery Division

Decision: A gift for the welfare of cats and kittens needing care was a charitable gift because of the beneficial effects it had on mankind. The testatrix's will had been challenged by the next-of-kin.

ROMER J: Inasmuch as I am satisfied that this is a valid charitable object, the bequest does not fail, and I propose to base my decision on that ground. Russell LJ, in *Re Grove-Grady* [1929] 1 Ch 557 laid it down clearly that a gift in favour of animals depends for its validity on the question whether such a gift produces a benefit to mankind. He said ([1929] 1 Ch 582):

So far as I know there is no decision which upholds a trust in perpetuity in favour of animals upon any other ground than this, that the execution of the trust in the manner defined by the creator of the trust must produce some benefit to mankind. I cannot help feeling that in some instances matters have been stretched in favour of charities almost to bursting point: and that a decision benevolent to one doubtful charity has too often been the basis of a subsequent decision still more benevolent in favour of another.'

Later he said (*ibid.*, 588):

In my opinion, the court must determine in each case whether the trusts are such that benefit to the community must necessarily result from their execution.'

The observations of the Lord Justice on those matters received recognition in the House of Lords in *Inland Revenue Comrs* v *National Anti-Vivisection Society* [1948] AC 31 [below].

Therefore, one has to see whether the present case passes that test, namely, the test whether the gift produces some benefit to mankind. In my judgment, it passes that test with honours. It seems to me that the care of and consideration for animals which through old age or sickness or otherwise are unable to care for themselves are manifestations of the finer side of human nature, and gifts in furtherance of these objects are calculated to develop that side and are, therefore, calculated to benefit mankind. That is more especially so, perhaps, where the animals are domestic animals. That appears to have been the view of the matter taken by Lord Hanworth

MR, in *Re Grove-Grady* [1929] 1 Ch 557 where, after referring to certain authorities, he said ([1929] 1 Ch 570):

> From these authorities it seems clear that if the object be to enhance the condition of animals that are useful to mankind, or to secure good treatment for animals, whether those animals are useful to mankind or not (see *per* Chatterton V-C, in *Armstrong* v *Reeves* (1890) 25 LR Ir 325 and *per* Wood V-C, in *Marsh* v *Means* (1857) 30 LTOS 89, or to insure humane conduct towards, and treatment of, them whether in respect of a particular subjection of them to the use of mankind, as for food (*Re Cranston* [1898] 1 IR 431), or in what is called vivisection, such objects are to be deemed charitable.

It appears to me that, taking a fair view of this lady's activities as they emerge from her affidavit, it may truthfully be said of them that they conform to all those tests and criteria to which Lord Hanworth draws attention. I need, I think, only add that a gift to the Institution of the Home for Lost Dogs was regarded as a charitable gift in *Re Douglas* (1887) 35 ChD 472.

Counsel for the next-of-kin has urged that this is not a trust for the protection of cats and kittens or protection from cruelty, but is merely a gift for their welfare. I do not take that view of the matter. The gift in the will is not merely a gift to be used at the lady's discretion for the welfare of cats and kittens. It is for the welfare of cats and kittens needing care and attention. It is plain that a gift to prevent cruelty in relation to cats and kittens would be good as having an elevating effect on mankind. For my part, I can see no difference between that and a gift the object of which is to alleviate distress among cats and kittens. It seems to me that, that being the object which the testatrix had in mind, the object which she intended to benefit, and it being, in substance, the object of the work which this lady has carried out and is now carrying out, the gift is perfectly good as being a valid charitable bequest, and I so hold.

C: Social and Recreational Activity

Until the 1950s it was assumed that while some recreational purposes, such as boys' clubs, women's institutes and parish halls, were potentially charitable, sporting facilities were not, unless they were either educational, or promoted efficiency in the armed forces. A series of cases in the 1950s, however, suggested that no recreational purpose will be charitable at common law. As we shall see below, however, a fifth (limited) head of recreational charities has now been added by statute.

IRC v *City of Glasgow Police Athletic Association*
[1953] AC 380
House of Lords

Facts: The question arose as to the charitable status of the City of Glasgow Police Athletic Association, membership of which was restricted to officers and ex-officers of the force. The objects of the association were to encourage and promote all forms of athletic sports and general pastimes. The Special Commissioners found that the association was regarded as an essential part of the police organization, that played an important part in the maintenance of health, morale and *esprit de corps* within the police force, that it attracted recruits to the force and that it helped to induce members of the force to continue in the force rather than leave it.

Held: The purposes were not exclusively charitable because of the inclusion of a social element.

LORD REID: [Lord Reid set out the objects of the association, and continued:]

I do not doubt that the purpose of increasing or maintaining the efficiency of a police force is a charitable purpose within the technical meaning of those words in English law. It appears to me to be well established that the purpose of increasing the efficiency of the army or a part of it is a charitable purpose. It may be that in some cases the facts hardly justified the conclusion that this was the purpose of the gift in question, but that does not affect the principle. I can see no valid distinction between the importance or character of the public interest of maintaining the efficiency of the army and that of maintaining the efficiency of the police.

But it is not enough that one of the purposes of a body of persons is charitable: the Act requires that it must be established for charitable purposes only. This does not mean that the sole effect of the activities of the body must be to promote charitable purposes, but it does mean that that must be its predominant object and that any benefits to its individual members of a non-charitable character which result from its activities must be of a subsidiary or incidental character.

It was argued that this association could not be regarded as established for charitable purposes because its revenue is all spent on activities in which its members alone take part. I am not satisfied that in every case that would be enough by itself to prevent the body from being held to be established for charitable purposes only, and I prefer to base my opinion on the facts of this case.

The peculiarity of this case is that the same activities have a double result. They are beneficial to the public by increasing the efficiency of the force and they are beneficial to the members themselves in affording them recreation and enjoyment: and all the relevant facts appear to me to indicate that the purpose was to produce this double result. It may well be that considerations of public interest were the primary cause of the association being established and maintained: but I think that it is clear that all or most of the activities of the association are designed in the first place to confer benefits on its members by affording them recreation and enjoyment. It is only as a result of these benefits that the purpose of increasing the efficiency of the police force is achieved. In some cases where the end is a charitable purpose the fact that the means to the end confer non-charitable benefits may not matter; but in the present case I have come to the conclusion that conferring such benefits on its members bulks so large in the purposes and activities of this association that it cannot properly be said to be established for charitable purposes only. I therefore agree that this appeal should be allowed.

Note

In *Williams Trustees* v *IRC* [1947] AC 447, The London Welsh Association, whose objects were to promote social and recreational purposes among Welsh people living in London, had also been held non-charitable, partly on the basis that purely social activities could not be charitable within the spirit of the preamble to the Statute of Charitable Uses 1601. Finally, in *IRC* v *Baddeley* [1955] AC 572, a reduction in stamp duty on a conveyance of land was refused because the purposes of the conveyance were not charitable. The conveyance was to a Methodist mission, and the purposes were essentially those of promoting the 'religious, social and physical well-being' of residents of an area by providing facilities for 'religious services and instruction; and for the social and physical training and recreation' of such people. The inclusion of purely social purposes prevented these purposes from being exclusively charitable.

SECTION 6:   RECREATIONAL CHARITIES ACT 1958

We have seen above how doubt was cast by a number of decisions about 40 years ago, on the charitable status of a number of social trusts which had always been assumed to be charitable. The Recreational Charities Act 1958 was enacted to restore what was assumed to be the *status quo ante* in respect of those trusts. The London Welsh Association (above), for example, was validated by the Charity Commissioners in 1977.

Recreational Charities Act 1958

1.   General provision as to recreational and similar trusts, etc.

(1)   Subject to the provisions of this Act, it shall be and be deemed always to have been charitable to provide, or assist in the provision of, facilities for recreation or other leisure-time occupation, if the facilities are provided in the interests of social welfare:

Provided that nothing in this section shall be taken to derogate from the principle that a trust or institution to be charitable must be for the public benefit.

(2)   The requirements of the foregoing subsection that the facilities are provided in the interests of social welfare shall not be treated as satisfied unless —

(a)   the facilities are provided with the object of improving the conditions of life for the persons for whom the facilities are primarily intended; and

(b)   either —

(i)   those persons have need of such facilities as aforesaid by reason of their youth, age, infirmity or disablement, poverty or social and economic circumstances; or

(ii)   the facilities are to be available to the members or female members of the public at large.

(3)   Subject to the said requirement, subsection (1) of this section applies in particular to the provision of facilities at village halls, community centres and women's institutes, and to the provision and maintenance of grounds and buildings to be used for purposes of recreation or leisure-time occupation, and extends to the provision of facilities for those purposes by the organising of any activity.

2.   Miners' welfare trusts

(1)   Where trusts declared before the seventeenth day of December, nineteen hundred and fifty-seven, required or purported to require property to be held for the purpose of activities which are social welfare activities within the meaning of the Miners' Welfare Act, 1952, and at that date the whole or part of the property held on those trusts or of any property held with that property represented an application of moneys standing to the credit of the miners' welfare fund or moneys provided by the Coal Industry Social Welfare Organisation, those trusts shall be treated as if they were and always had been charitable.

(2) For the purposes of this section property held on the same trusts as other property shall be deemed to be held with it, though vested in different trustees.

Note

Section 1 states that it shall be and be deemed always to have been charitable to provide, or assist in the provision of, facilities for recreation or other leisure-time occupation, if the facilities are provided in the interests of social welfare. A proviso adds that nothing in the section shall be taken to derogate from the principle that a trust or institution to be charitable must be for the public benefit. Under s. 1(2), the requirement that the facilities are provided in the interests of social welfare is not to be satisfied unless the facilities are provided with the object of improving the conditions of life for the persons for whom the facilities are primarily intended, and either:

(a) those persons have need of such facilities as aforesaid by reason of their youth, age, infirmity or disablement, poverty or social and economic circumstances; or

(b) the facilities are to be available to the members or female members of the public at large.

Subject to the requirement of social welfare, there is specific reference to the provision of facilities at village halls, community centres and women's institutes, and to the provision and maintenance of grounds and buildings to be used for the purposes of recreation or leisure-time occupation, extending to the provision of facilities for these purposes by the organising of any activity.

Section 1(2)(b) above allows for the provision of facilities for recreation or other leisure-time occupation where the facilities are made available to the public at large, but under subsection (1) they have also to be provided in the interests of social welfare. In *IRC* v *McMullen* (considered in a different context above), Walton J at first instance ([1978] 1 WLR 664, [1978] 1 All ER 230) held that the requirement of social welfare in subsection (1) implied that for a charity to succeed under the Act, the recipients must be limited to those who are in some way 'deprived persons'. The Court of Appeal ([1979] 1 WLR 130, [1979] 1 All ER 588) split on the issue, the majority (Stamp and Orr LJJ) holding that the class to be benefited must be disadvantaged in such a way as to have a special need for the facilities. There was no such limitation in *McMullen* itself, where the gift was to the Football Association Youth Trust. Bridge LJ dissented, preferring a wider view that social welfare may be promoted by benefits which extend to the better off as well as the socially deprived. The House of Lords ([1981] AC 1) left the issue open, allowing the appeal on the grounds that the trust was charitable under head 2 (above). Indeed, their Lordships expressly refused to decide which of the approaches adopted in the Court of Appeal was correct, but the issue has now been resolved in *Guild* v *IRC* [1992] 2 All ER 10, where the House of Lords came down in favour of Bridge LJ's view.

Guild v *IRC*
[1992] 2 All ER 10
House of Lords

Decision: A gift of a sports centre was a valid charitable gift for tax purposes, although the benefit was not limited to deprived persons.

LORD KEITH OF KINKEL: A Scottish court, when faced with the task of construing and applying the words 'charity' and 'charitable' in a United Kingdom tax statute, must do so in accordance with the technical meaning of these words in English law (see *Special Comrs of Income Tax* v *Pemsel* [1891] AC 531 and *IRC* v *Glasgow Police Athletic Association* [1953] AC 380). For tax purposes, and for them alone, the English law of charity is to be regarded as part of the law of Scotland. Lord Jauncey's decision in the action of multiplepoinding proceeded on the general law of Scotland as regards charities, and, as the *Glasgow Police Athletic* case shows, the decision under the corresponding English common law rules would have been different. However, the *Glasgow Police Athletic* case and that of *IRC* v *Baddeley* [1955] AC 572 led to the Recreational Charities Act 1958 (the 1958 Act), and it is that Act which the executor invokes in his claim to the charitable exemption from capital transfer tax.
[Lord Keith set out s. 1 of the 1958 Act and continued:]
In the course of his argument in relation to the first branch of the bequest counsel for the Crown accepted that it assisted in the provision of facilities for recreation or other leisure time occupation within the meaning of sub-s. (1) of s. 1 of the 1958 Act, and also that the requirement of public benefit in the proviso to the subsection was satisfied. It was further accepted that the facilities of the sports centre were available to the public at large so that the condition of sub-s. (2)(b)(ii) was satisfied. It was maintained, however, that these facilities were not provided 'in the interests of social welfare' as required by sub-s. (1), because they did not meet the condition laid down in sub-s. (2)(a), namely that they should be 'provided with the object of improving the conditions of life for the persons for whom the facilities are primarily intended'. The reason why it was said that this condition was not met was that on a proper construction it involved that the facilities should be provided with the object of meeting a need for such facilities in people who suffered from a position of relative social disadvantage. Reliance was placed on a passage from the judgment of Walton J in *IRC* v *McMullen* [1978] 1 WLR 664. That was a case where the Football Association had set up a trust to provide facilities to encourage pupils of schools and universities in the United Kingdom to play association football and other games and sports. Walton J held that the trust was not valid as one for the advancement of education nor did it satisfy s. 1 of the 1958 Act. He said (see [1978] 1 WLR 664 at 675) in relation to the words 'social welfare' in sub-s. (1):

In my view, however, these words in themselves indicate that there is some sort of deprivation – not, of course, by any means necessarily of money – which falls to be alleviated; and I think that this is made even clearer by the terms of subsection (2)(a). The facilities must be provided with the object of improving the conditions of life for persons for whom the facilities are primarily intended. In other words, they must be to some extent and in some way deprived persons.

When the case went to the Court of Appeal (see [1979] 1 WLR 130) the majority (Stamp and Orr LJJ) affirmed the judgment of Walton J on both points, but Bridge LJ dissented. As regards the 1958 Act point he said ([1979] 1 WLR 130 at 142):

I turn therefore to consider whether the object defined by clause 3(1) is charitable under the express terms of section 1 of the Recreational Charities Act 1958. Are the facilities for recreation contemplated in this clause to be 'provided in the interests of social welfare' under s. 1(1)? If this phrase stood without further statutory elaboration, I should not hesitate to decide that sporting facilities for persons undergoing any formal process of education are provided in the interests of social welfare. Save in the sense that the interests of social welfare can only be served by the meeting of some social need, I cannot accept the judge's view that the interests of social welfare can only be served in relation to some 'deprived' class. The judge found this view reinforced by the requirement of subsection (2)(a) of s. 1 that the facilities must be provided 'with the object of improving the conditions of life for the persons for whom the facilities are primarily intended; . . . ' Here again I can see no reason to conclude that only the deprived can have their conditions of life improved. Hyde Park improves the conditions of life for residents in Mayfair and Belgravia as much as for those in Pimlico or the Portobello Road, and the village hall may improve the conditions of life for the squire and his family as well as for the cottagers. The persons for whom the facilities here are primarily intended are pupils of schools and universities, as defined in the trust deed, and these facilities are in my judgment unquestionably to be provided with the object of improving their conditions of life. Accordingly the ultimate question on which the application of the statute to this trust depends, is whether the requirements of s. 1(2)(b)(i) are satisfied on the ground that such pupils as a class have need of facilities for games or sports which will promote their physical education and development by reason either of their youth or of their social and economic circumstances, or both. The overwhelming majority of pupils within the definition are young persons and the tiny minority of mature students can be ignored as *de minimis*. There cannot surely be any doubt that young persons as part of their education do need facilities for organised games and sports both by reason of their youth and by reason of their social and economic circumstances. They cannot provide such facilities for themselves but are dependent on what is provided for them.

In the House of Lords the case was decided against the Crown on the ground that the trust was one for the advancement of education, opinion being reserved on the point under the 1958 Act. Lord Hailsham LC said ([1981] AC 1 at 11) —

. . . I do not wish my absence of decision on the third or fourth points to be interpreted as an indorsement of the majority judgments in the Court of Appeal nor as necessarily dissenting from the contrary views contained in the minority judgment of Bridge LJ.

. . .

The fact is that persons in all walks of life and all kinds of social circumstances may have their conditions of life improved by the provision of recreational facilities of suitable character. The proviso requiring public benefit excludes facilities of an undesirable nature. In my opinion the view expressed by Bridge LJ (see [1979] 1 WLR 130 at 142) in *IRC* v *McMullen* is clearly correct and that of Walton J (see [1978] 1 WLR 664 at 675) in the same case is incorrect. . . . I would therefore reject the argument that the facilities are not provided in the interests of social welfare unless they are provided with the object of improving the conditions of life for persons who suffer from some form of social disadvantage. It suffices if they are provided with the object of improving the conditions of life for members of the community generally.

Note
Presumably, social welfare indicates some element of provision for others, so that a group acting purely to benefit themselves would fail to qualify. In any event, such an enterprise would lack the necessary element of public benefit preserved by the Act.

Question
Are private flying clubs charitable? Assume that anybody can join, and that the club's charges are set primarily with a view to covering the high costs of private flying (around £100–£150 per hour), rather than with a view to making a profit. Would your answer be different if the society ran only jet aircraft costing £10,000 per hour?

SECTION 7: PUBLIC BENEFIT

In the case of religious charities the issue of public benefit and the issue of advancement are inextricably mixed, so that the public benefit issues have already been discussed. For the other heads, however, it is not enough merely to fall within one of the classifications described above. There is an additional public benefit test, which must also be satisfied.

The leading modern decision on public benefit is the *Oppenheim* case (below), which applies directly to education charities. We shall start with that case and then consider the extent to which, if at all, it also applies to other heads of charity.

A: The *Oppenheim* Personal Nexus Test

In the case of relief of poverty, even benefiting a small number of people may be regarded as conferring a public benefit (see below). Yet whereas education is clearly a benefit to those in immediate receipt of it, it is not self-evident that educating a few people constitutes a benefit to the general public. Indeed, given that many of the cases under this head are in reality disputes over tax relief, it would be quite wrong if the education of a privileged few were to be regarded as charitable. Under this head it is therefore necessary that there is some additional benefit to the general public, or some appreciable sector thereof.

That is not to say that a particular form of education has to be capable of being enjoyed by everyone, so long as access to it is reasonably open. Thus public schools may be charitable as long as they are not operated as profit-making ventures, although their fees may place them beyond the means of the majority. Even scholarships or endowed chairs, which can be enjoyed only by one person at a time, present no difficulty. The problems arise where it is sought to limit range of the potential beneficiaries within a class which is insufficiently wide to constitute a section of the public.

It is clear that it may be charitable to provide (e.g.) scholarships, open to:

(a) persons following a common profession or calling, or their children and dependants; or

(b) people of common nationality, religion or sex; or

(c) the inhabitants of a given area, provided this is reasonably large, such as a town or county.

Special provisions for people suffering disability are also permissible, since they are a section of the public in a meaningful sense.

However, under head 2, and probably under all the *Pemsel* heads except relief of poverty, it will be fatal that the class of potential beneficiaries (however large) be defined in terms of relation to particular individuals, or a company. This approach originated in *Re Compton* [1945] Ch 123, where charitable status was denied to a trust to educate the children of three named families. It is understandable that the courts are reluctant to allow an essentially private arrangement to enjoy charitable privileges, especially tax advantages, but it seems that the principle extends to cases where the class of potential beneficiaries is defined in terms of a relationship with an employer, even where the employer is a substantial concern.

Oppenheim v Tobacco Securities Trust Co.
[1951] AC 297
House of Lords

Facts: The income of a trust fund was directed to be applied 'in providing for . . . the education of children of employees or former employees of the British-American Tobacco Co. Ltd . . . or any of its subsidiary or allied companies in such manner . . . as the acting trustees shall in their absolute discretion . . . think fit'. The number of present employees alone exceeded 110,000.

Held (Lord MacDermott dissenting): The trust was not charitable, under the second head in *Pemsel's* case as being for the advancement of education, there being an insufficient element of public benefit. Although the number of potential beneficiaries was considerable, it was not charitable because of the personal nexus rule (because all the potential beneficiaries were connected with the same company).

LORD SIMONDS: It is a clearly established principle of the law of charity that a trust is not charitable unless it is directed to the public benefit. This is sometimes stated in the proposition that it must benefit the community or a section of the community. Negatively it is said that a trust is not charitable if it confers only private benefits. In the recent case of *Gilmour v Coates* [1949] AC 426 this principle was reasserted. It is easy to state and has been stated in a variety of ways, the earliest statement that I find being in *Jones v Williams* (1767) 2 Amb 651, in which Lord Hardwicke LC, is briefly reported as follows: 'Definition of charity: a gift to a general public use, which extends to the poor as well as to the rich'. With a single exception, to which I shall refer, this applies to all charities. We are apt now to classify them by reference to Lord

Macnaughten's division in *Commissioners for Special Purposes of Income Tax* v *Pemsel* [1891] AC 531, 583 and, as I have elsewhere pointed out, it was at one time suggested that the element of public benefit was not essential except for charities falling within the fourth class, 'other purposes beneficial to the community'. This is certainly wrong except in the anomalous case of trusts for the relief of poverty with which I must specifically deal. In the case of trusts for educational purposes the condition of public benefit must be satisfied. The difficulty lies in determining what is sufficient to satisfy the test. . . .

The difficulty arises where the trust is not for the benefit of any institution either then existing or by the terms of the trust to be brought into existence, but for the benefit of a class of persons at large. Then the question is whether that class of persons can be regarded as such as a 'section of the community' as to satisfy the test of public benefit. The words 'section of the community' have no special sanctity, but they conveniently indicate first, that the possible (I emphasise the word 'possible') beneficiaries must not be numerically negligible, and secondly, that the quality which distinguishes them from other members of the community, so that they form a section of it, must be a quality which does not depend on their relationship to a particular individual. . . . A group of persons may be numerous, but, if the nexus between them is their personal relationship to a single *propositus* or to several *propositi*, they are neither the community nor a section of the community for charitable purposes. . . .

It must not, I think, be forgotten that charitable institutions enjoy rare and increasing privileges, and that the claim to come within that privileged class should be clearly established. With the single exception of *Re Rayner* (1920) 89 LJ Ch 369, which I must regard as of doubtful authority, no case has been brought to the notice of the House in which such a claim as this has been made, where there is no element of poverty in the beneficiaries, but just this and no more, that they are the children of those in common employment.

Learned counsel for the appellant sought to fortify his case by pointing to the anomalies that would ensue from the rejection of his argument. For, he said, admittedly those who follow a profession or calling, clergymen, lawyers, colliers, tobacco workers and so on, are a section of the public; how strange then it would be if, as in the case of railwaymen, those who follow a particular calling are all employed by one employer. Would a trust for the education of railwaymen be charitable, but a trust for the education of men employed on the railways by the Transport Board not be charitable? And what of service of the Crown whether in the civil service or the armed forces? Is there a difference between soldiers and soldiers of the King? My lords, I am not impressed by this sort of argument and will consider on its merits, if the occasion should arise, the case where the description of the occupation and the employment is in effect the same, where in a word, if you know what a man does, you know who employs him to do it. It is to me a far more cogent argument, as it was to my noble and learned friend in the *Hobourn* case [1946] Ch 194, that if a section of the public is constituted by the personal relations of employment, it is impossible to say that it is not constituted by 1,000 as by 100,000 employees, and, if by 1,000, then by 100, and if by 100, then by 10. I do not mean merely that there is a difficulty in drawing the line, though that too is significant: I have it also in mind that, though the actual numbers of employees at any one moment might be small, it might increase to any extent, just as, being large, it might decrease to any extent. If the number of employees is the test of validity, must the court take into account potential increase or decrease, and if so, as at what date?

. . . I would also, as I have previously indicated, say a word about the so-called 'poor relations' cases. I do so only because they have once more been brought forward as an argument in favour of a more generous view of what may be charitable. It would not be right for me to affirm or to denounce or to justify these decisions: I am concerned only to say that the law of charity, so far as it relates to 'the relief of aged, impotent and poor people' (I quote from the statute) and to poverty in general, has followed its own line, and that it is not useful to try to harmonise decisions on that branch of the law with the broad proposition on which the determination of this case must rest. It is not for me to say what fate might await those cases if in a poverty case this House had to consider them.

LORD MACDERMOTT (dissenting): But can any really fundamental distinction, as respects the personal or impersonal nature of the common link, be drawn between those employed, for example, by a particular university and those whom the same university has put in a certain category as the result of individual examination and assessment? Again, if the bond between those employed on a particular railway is purely personal, why should the bond between those who are employed as railwaymen be so essentially different? Is a distinction to be drawn in this respect between those who are employed in a particular industry before it is nationalised and those who are employed therein after that process has been completed and one employer has taken the place of many? Are miners in the service of the National Coal Board now in one category and miners at a particular pit or of a particular district in another? Is the relationship between those in the service of the Crown to be distinguished from that obtaining between those in the service of some other employer? Or, if not, are the children of, say, soldiers or civil servants to be regarded as not constituting a sufficient section of the public to make a trust for their education charitable?

It was conceded in the course of the argument that, had the present trust been framed so as to provide for the education of the children of those engaged in the tobacco industry in a named county or town, it would have been a good charitable disposition, and that even though the class to be benefited would have been appreciably smaller and no more important than is the class here.

Notes
1.   As well as standing for the personal nexus test, the case requires that the recipients of benefit must be a section of the community. This aspect of the case was applied in *Davies* v *Perpetual Trustee Co.* [1959] AC 459, where the Privy Council held non-charitable a trust which was confined to Presbyterian youths who were descended from settlers in New South Wales who had originated from the North of Ireland. Although quite large in number, this category of potential beneficiaries was held not to be a section of the public.
2.   Lord Simonds apparently took the view that the test of public benefit may vary between the four heads of charity in *Pemsel's* case, and in particular excluded the 'poor relations' cases from consideration. For the question of whether the same test applies to other heads of charity, see *Inland Revenue Commissioners* v *Baddeley* [1955] AC 572 (below). For the test to be applied in the 'poor relations' cases, see *Dingle* v *Turner* [1972] AC 602 (below).
3.   Lord Simonds expressly refers to the tax concessions given to charities, and this clearly influenced his decision. This passage was also referred to with approval in *Davies* v *Perpetual Trustee* [1959] AC 459.

Questions
1.   Suppose that the trustees had decided to use the fund to pay 15 per cent of the fees of those employees who decided to send their children to

fee-paying schools. How many employees do you suppose could have benefited in practice from such a scheme? Do you feel that the real problem in this case is the extent of the discretion given to the trustees?

2. How would you feel about paying more tax so that a trust to send the sons and daughters of a private company to public school could pay less?

3. Do you think that Lord MacDermott's railwaymen example has any force now that it looks as though the railways are going to be privatised? Given that a trust for railwaymen set up in 1951 could have continued indefinitely whatever corporate structure was later adopted by the railway industry, do you think they have ever had any force?

B: Preference Cases

In *Re Koettgen's WT* [1954] Ch 252, an educational trust succeeded despite a direction that the trustees should give preference to the families of employees, up to a maximum of 75 per cent of income. On the other hand, doubts have been expressed, and for example a preference for the grantor's family rendered a gift non-charitable in *Caffoor v Income Tax Commissioner, Colombo* [1961] AC 584. In *IRC v Educational Grants Association Ltd* [1967] Ch 123, affirmed [1967] Ch 993, between 76 per cent and 85 per cent of the income of a fund (varying from year to year) was paid out for the education of persons connected with the Metal Box Co. Ltd. In a dispute with the Inland Revenue, it was held that the money had not been paid exclusively for charitable purposes. Pennycuick J found 'considerable difficulty in the *Koettgen* decision', and thought that a preference for a private class might always be fatal (although he did not need actually to decide that).

Question
Is a possible solution to this problem that the trust is valid, albeit that (following *Oppenheim*) it allows the trustees to use the property for both charitable and non-charitable purposes, but that they will be constrained to use it for charitable purposes only (as in *Hetherington*, below)?

C: Public Benefit and Utility Charities

Lord Simonds thought in *Oppenheim* that the test of public benefit may vary between the four heads of charity (in particular he excluded the 'poor relations' cases entirely from consideration). It is clear that the personal nexus test applies to the fourth head, but arguably the requirement that the trust benefits a section of the public is more stringent under the fourth head than under the second.

For example, in *Williams' Trustees v IRC* [1947] AC 447, doubt was expressed by Lord Simonds as to whether Welsh people living in London could be a section of the public under the fourth head. In *IRC v Baddeley* [1955] AC 572 (see also above), the House of Lords held that the persons to be benefited must either be the whole community or the inhabitants of a particular area. If some further restriction is imposed, thus creating in effect a class within a class, the test of public benefit will not be satisfied.

IRC v *Baddeley*
[1955] AC 572
House of Lords

Facts: Land was conveyed for the benefit of the Stratford Newtown Methodist Mission, '. . . for the promotion of the religious social and physical well-being of persons resident in the County Boroughs of West Ham and Leyton in the County of Essex by the provision of facilities for religious services and instruction and for the social and physical training and recreation of such . . . persons who for the time being are in the opinion of such leaders members or likely to become members of the Methodist Church and of insufficient means otherwise to enjoy the advantages provided by these presents and by promoting and encouraging all forms of such activities as are calculated to contribute to the health and well-being of such persons'. . . .

Further land was conveyed on similar terms, but for the promotion of moral, rather than religious, welfare, but with the same additional social element, and for the benefit of the same class of people as above (persons resident in the County Boroughs of West Ham and Leyton in the County of Essex who for the time being are in the opinion of such leaders members or likely to become members of the Methodist Church . . .). Provision of intoxicating liquor was firmly prohibited.

The question arose whether the gift was charitable.

Held: This was not a charitable donation. The purposes were not exclusively charitable because of the inclusion of a social element. Also, the purposes did not satisfy the public benefit requirement for the fourth head of charity.

VISCOUNT SIMONDS (on the public benefit issue): This brings me to another aspect of the case, which was argued at great length and to me at least presents the most difficult of the many difficult problems in this branch of the law. Suppose that, contrary to the view that I have expressed [in a part of his lordship's opinion not reproduced here], the trust would be a valid charitable trust, if the beneficiaries were the community at large or a section of the community defined by some geographical limits, is it the less a valid trust if it is confined to members or potential members of a particular church within a limited geographical area?

The starting point of the argument must be, that this charity (if it be a charity) falls within the fourth class in Lord Macnaughten's classification. It must therefore be a trust which is, to use the words of Sir Samuel Romilly in *Morice* v *Bishop of Durham* (1805) 10 Ves 522, 532, of 'general public utility', and the question is what these words mean. It is, indeed, an essential feature of all 'charity' in the legal sense that there must be in it some element of public benefit, whether the purpose is educational, religious or eleemosynary: see the recent case of *Oppenheim* v *Tobacco Securities Trust Co.* [1951] AC 297 [above], and, as I have said elsewhere, it is possible, particularly in view of the so-called 'poor relations' cases, the scope of which may one day have to be considered, that a different degree of public benefit is requisite according to the class in which the charity is said to fall. But it is said that if a charity falls within the fourth class, it must be for the benefit of the whole community or at least of all the inhabitants of a sufficient area.

LORD REID (dissenting): In *Oppenheim's case* [1951] AC 297 [above] the trust was for the advancement of education, but the decision of this House was that it is not enough that the class of beneficiaries is numerous, it must also be a section of the community, and the *ratio decidendi* applies equally to a trust for the advancement of religion. So if . . . the members of a religious denomination do not constitute a section of the public (or the community) then a trust solely for the advancement of religion or of education would not be a charitable trust if limited to members of a particular church. Of course, the appellants do not contend that is right: they could not but admit that the members of a church are a section of the community for the purpose of such trusts. But they maintain that they cease to be a section of the community when it comes to trusts within the fourth class . . . the appellants cannot succeed on this argument unless that contention is sound. Poverty may be in a special position but otherwise I can see no justification in principle for holding that when dealing with one deed for one charitable purpose the members of the Methodist or any other church are a section of the community, but when dealing with another deed for a different charitable purpose they are only a fluctuating body of private individuals.

Notes
1.   The inclusion of a social element had the same effect as in *IRC* v *Glasgow* (above). It would not necessarily be fatal today, due to the subsequent enactment of the Recreational Charities Act 1958 (see above).
2.   The essential difference between the approaches of Viscount Simonds and Lord Reid is that whereas the former would allow different tests of public benefit for the different heads of charity, Lord Reid would apply the same test for each head (except possibly the 'poor relations' cases). From Viscount Simonds's approach it seems that the public benefit requirement under the fourth head is at least as stringent as the *Oppenheim* test (above), which applies to the second head (advancement of education).
3.   The 'poor relations' have now been reconsidered – see *Dingle* v *Turner* (below).
4.   The *Baddeley* test seems therefore to be a different, and additional, test to that adopted in *Davies* v *Perpetual Trustee Co.* [1959] AC 459, above, for the second head. Indeed, the very definition of charity under the fourth head (purposes beneficial to the community) would seem to demand a more stringent test of public benefit than under any other head. However, Lord Reid thought otherwise in his dissenting speech in *IRC* v *Baddeley*.
5.   It is also likely that what constitutes a section of the public depends on the purposes of the particular trust, and the courts are more likely to strike down arbitrary restrictions which are irrelevant to those purposes, but which simply serve to exclude other sections of the public. For example, in *IRC* v *Baddeley*, the limitation was to Methodists living in West Ham and Leyton, and the trust included the provision of playing fields. Lord Simonds clearly

thought that the restriction to Methodists living in West Ham and Leyton was completely irrelevant to the provision of playing fields. Referring (at p. 592) to a rhetorical question put in argument: 'Who has ever heard of a bridge to be crossed only by impecunious Methodists?', he went on to say that what is true of a bridge for Methodists is equally true of any other public purpose falling within the fourth head, and of the adherents of any other creed. The limitation merely operated to prevent the purpose from being a public purpose; it could have had no other effect. A purpose which is not a public purpose cannot be charitable within the fourth head.

6. There is some authority that the test of public benefit can vary even within the fourth head itself. In *Re Dunlop (decd)* (1984) Northern Irish Judgments Bulletin (noted by Norma Dawson [1987] Conv 114), Carswell J upheld as charitable a bequest 'to hold the remainder of my residuary estate for the Presbyterian Trust . . . to found or help to found a home for Old Presbyterian persons', and a cy près scheme (see chapter 13) was ordered. There was earlier Northern Irish authority that the Presbyterians of Londonderry were not a sufficient section of the public under the fourth head, and it was accepted that there was no difference between Irish and English definitions of charity. Carswell J took the view, however, that public benefit depended upon the nature of 'the advantage which the donor intends to provide for the benefit of all of the public'. A 'bridge to be used only by Methodists should clearly fail to qualify, whereas a gift for the education of the children of members of that church might be a valid charity'. But he was also prepared to distinguish between purposes within the fourth head itself.

7. It should perhaps finally be observed that neither *IRC v Baddeley* nor *Williams' Trustees v IRC* actually turned on the issue of public benefit. In the former case the purposes were not exclusively religious, but included social purposes and the provision of playing fields; and in the latter case purposes were exclusively social and recreational. They would therefore have failed because of the inclusion of a social content, whatever view had been taken on the public benefit issue.

D: Public Benefit and Poverty Charities

It is unquestioned law that to relieve poverty is to confer a benefit upon the public at large, if only by mitigating the burden of support for the poor which would otherwise fall upon the community. The House of Lords in *Oppenheim* exempted 'poor relations' cases as anomalous, and left open the question whether the personal nexus test applies to them.

The 'poor relations' anomaly stems from the practice of Chancery in the nineteenth century when faced with trusts expressed to be for poor relations; rather than allow these to fail for uncertainty (at a time when the class ascertainability test applied) or perpetuity, the courts rescued such trusts by holding them charitable. Since then the 'poor relations' cases have been consistently followed, which is probably why the House of Lords left them alone in *Oppenheim*. Since then the House of Lords has considered them directly in *Dingle* v *Turner* [1972] AC 601, and expressly upheld them. In that case a trust for 'poor employees of E. Dingle and Co.' was held charitable, although it would have failed under the personal nexus test. The same reasoning must apply to 'poor relation'. It is clear, therefore, that the personal nexus test does not apply to this head of charity.

In order for a trust to be charitable under this head, it is however necessary that the trust should be intended to benefit a class of persons, and not simply to make a gift to an individual, or group of individuals, who happen to be poor. In *Re Scarisbrick* [1951] 1 Ch 662 Jenkins LJ stated the rule thus:

I think the true question in each case has really been whether the gift was for the relief of poverty amongst a class of persons, or . . . a particular description of the poor, or was merely a gift to individuals, albeit with the relief of poverty amongst those individuals as the motive of the gift, or with a selective preference for the poor or the poorest amongst those individuals.

This statement received the approval of Lord Cross in the leading case of *Dingle* v *Turner*, considered below. In *Scarisbrick* itself the class of potential recipients was sufficiently wide as to be incapable of exhaustive ascertainment ('such relations of my said son and daughters as shall be in needy circumstances . . .'), so the trust was charitable.

Assuming that Jenkins LJ's test is satisfied, however, the public benefit requirements are less stringent under this head than under the others, and the class to be benefited can be quite small.

Dingle v *Turner*
[1972] AC 601, [1972] 1 All ER 878
House of Lords

Decision: A trust to invest a large sum of money, and apply the income in paying pensions to poor employees and ex-employees of E. Dingle & Co. Ltd was a valid charitable bequest for the relief of poverty. The *Oppenheim* personal nexus test (above) does not apply to poverty charities.

LORD CROSS: The status of some of the 'poor relations' trusts as valid charitable trusts was recognised more than 200 years ago and a few of those then recognised are still being administered as charities today. In *Re Compton* [1945] Ch 123 Lord Greene MR said that it was 'quite impossible' for the Court of Appeal to overrule such old decisions and in the *Oppenheim* case [1951] AC at 309 [above]. Lord Simonds in speaking of them remarked on the unwisdom of —

[casting] doubts on decisions of respectable antiquity in order to introduce a greater harmony into the law of charity as a whole.

Indeed counsel for the appellant hardly ventured to suggest that we should overrule the 'poor relations' cases. His submission was that which was accepted by the Court of Appeal in Ontario in *Re Cox* [1951] OR 205 – namely that while the 'poor relations' cases might have to be left as long standing anomalies there was no good reason for sparing the 'poor employees' cases which only date from *Re Gosling* (1900) 48 WR 300 decided in 1900 and which have been under suspicion ever since the decision in *Re*

Compton in 1945. But the 'poor members' and the 'poor employees' decisions were a natural development of the 'poor relations' decisions and to draw a distinction between different sorts of 'poverty' trusts would be quite illogical and could certainly not be said to be introducing 'greater harmony' into the law of charity. Moreover, although not as old as the 'poor relations' trusts, 'poor employees' trusts have been recognised as charities for many years; there are now a large number of such trusts in existence; and assuming, as one must, that they are properly administered in the sense that benefits under them are only given to people who can fairly be said to be, according to current standards, 'poor persons' to treat such trusts as charities is not open to any practical objection. So it seems to me it must be accepted that wherever else it may hold sway the *Compton* rule has no application in the field of trusts for the relief of poverty and that the dividing line between a charitable trust and a private trust lies where the Court of Appeal drew it in *Re Scarisbrick* [1951] Ch 622.

The *Oppenheim* case was a case of an educational trust and although the majority evidently agreed with the view expressed by the Court of Appeal in the *Hobourn Aero* case [1946] Ch 194 [below], that the *Compton* rule was of universal application outside the field of poverty, it would no doubt be open to this House without overruling *Oppenheim* to hold that the scope of the rule was more limited. If ever I should be called on to pronounce on this question – which does not arise in this appeal – I would as at present advised be inclined to draw a distinction between the practical merits of the *Compton* rule and the reasoning by which Lord Greene MR sought to justify it. That reasoning – based on the distinction between personal and impersonal relationships – has never seemed to me very satisfactory and I have always – if I may say so – felt the force of the criticism to which my noble and learned friend Lord MacDermott subjected it in his dissenting speech in the *Oppenheim* case. For my part I would prefer to approach the problem on far broader lines. The phrase 'a section of the public' is in truth a vague phrase which may mean different things to different people. In the law of charity judges have sought to elucidate its meaning by contrasting it with another phrase 'a fluctuating body of private individuals'. But I get little help from the supposed contrast for as I see it one and the same aggregate of persons may well be describable both as a section of the public and as a fluctuating body of private individuals. The ratepayers in the Royal Borough of Kensington and Chelsea, for example, certainly constitute a section of the public; but would it be a misuse of language to describe them as a 'fluctuating body of private individuals'? After all, every part of the public is composed of individuals and being susceptible of increase or decrease is fluctuating. So at the end of the day one is left where one started with the bare contrast between 'public' and 'private'. No doubt some classes are more naturally describable as sections of the public than as private classes while other classes are more naturally describable as private classes than as sections of the public. The blind, for example, can naturally be described as a section of the public; but what they have in common – their blindness – does not join them together in such a way that they could be called a private class. On the other hand, the descendants of Mr Gladstone might more reasonably be described as a 'private class' than as a section of the public, and in the field of common employment the same might well be said of the employees in some fairly small firm. But if one turns to large companies employing many thousands of men and women most of whom are quite unknown to one another and to the directors the answer is by no means so clear. One might say that in such a case the distinction between a section of the public and a private class is not applicable at all or even that the employees in such concerns as ICI or GEC are just as much 'sections of the public' as the residents in some geographical area. In truth the question whether or not the potential beneficiaries of a trust can fairly be said to constitute a section of the public is a question of degree and cannot be by itself decisive of the question whether the trust is a charity. Much must depend on the purpose of the trust. It may well be that, on the one hand, a trust to promote some purpose, prima facie charitable, will constitute a charity even though the class of potential beneficiaries might fairly be called a private class and that, on the other hand, a trust to promote another purpose, also prima facie charitable, will not constitute a charity even though the class of potential beneficiaries might seem to some people fairly describable as a section of the public.

In answering the question whether any given trust is a charitable trust the courts – as I see it – cannot avoid having regard to the fiscal privileges accorded to charities. As counsel for the Attorney-General remarked in the course of the argument the law of charity is bedevilled by the fact that charitable trusts enjoy two quite different sorts of privilege. On the one hand, they enjoy immunity from the rules against perpetuity and uncertainty and although individual potential beneficiaries cannot sue to enforce them the public interest arising under them is protected by the Attorney-General. If this was all there would be no reason for the courts not to look favourably on the claim of any 'purpose' trust to be considered as a charity if it seemed calculated to confer some real benefit on those intended to benefit by it whoever they might be and if it would fail if not held to be a charity. But that is not all. Charities automatically enjoy fiscal privileges which with the increased burden of taxation have become more and more important and in deciding that such and such a trust is a charitable trust the court is endowing it with a substantial annual subsidy at the expense of the taxpayer. Indeed, claims of trusts to rank as charities are just as often challenged by the Revenue as by those who would take the fund if the trust was invalid. It is, of course, unfortunate that the recognition of any trust as a valid charitable trust should automatically attract fiscal privileges, for the question whether a trust to further some purpose is so little likely to benefit the public that it ought to be declared invalid and the question whether it is likely to confer such great benefits on the public that it should enjoy fiscal immunity are really two quite different questions. The logical solution would be to separate them and to say – as the Radcliffe Commission proposed – that only some charities should enjoy fiscal privileges. But as things are, validity and fiscal immunity march hand in hand and the decisions in the *Compton* and *Oppenheim* cases were pretty obviously influenced by the consideration that if such trusts as were there in question were held valid they would enjoy an undeserved fiscal immunity. To establish a trust for the education of the children of employees in a company in which you are interested is no doubt a meritorious act; but however numerous the employees may be the purpose which you are seeking to achieve is not a public purpose. It is a company purpose and there is no reason why your fellow taxpayer should contribute to a scheme which by providing 'fringe benefits' for your employees will benefit the company by making their conditions of employment more attractive. The temptation to enlist the assistance of the law of charity in private endeavours of this sort is considerable – witness the recent case of the Metal Box scholarships – *IRC* v *Educational Grants Association Ltd* [1967] Ch 993 – and the courts must do what they can to discourage such attempts. In the field of poverty the danger is not so great as in the field of education – for while people are keenly alive to the need to give their children a good education and to the expense of doing so, they are generally optimistic enough not to entertain serious fears of falling on evil days much before they fall on them. Consequently the existence of company 'benevolent funds', the income of which is free of tax does not constitute a very attractive 'fringe benefit'. This is a practical justification – although not, of course, the historical explanation – for the special treatment accorded to poverty trusts in charity law. For the same sort of reason a trust to promote some religion among the employees of a company might perhaps safely be held to be charitable provided that it was clear that the benefits were to be purely spiritual. On the other hand, many 'purpose' trusts falling under Lord Macnaughten's fourth head if confined to a class of employees would clearly be open to the same sort of objection as educational trusts. As I see it, it is on these broad lines rather than for the reasons actually given by Lord Greene MR that the *Compton* rule can best be justified.

Note
In the light of the comments made in the last paragraph set out above, note that only the validity of the bequest was at issue, and tax advantages were not claimed.

E: Public Benefit and Religion

There is also a public benefit requirement for religious charities. The leading case is *Gilmour v Coats* [1949] AC 426, where the House of Lords had to consider a gift of £500 towards a Carmelite priory. The priory housed about 20 cloistered nuns who devoted themselves to intercessory prayer, and had no contact at all with the outside world. This was held non-charitable on the grounds that there was no contact with the outside world. Arguments based on Catholic doctrine, to the effect that everyone benefited from the intercessory prayers, were rejected as being not susceptible to legal proof. Nor could any benefit be found merely in the example of the piousness of the women, as it was too vague and intangible. The House of Lords also rejected the argument that, entry being open to all women, the priory should be treated on analogy with an educational institution offering scholarship entry, holding that an educational establishment which required its members to withdraw from the world and leave no record of their studies would not be charitable either.

On the other hand, in *Re Caus* [1934] Ch 162, Catholic masses for the dead were held charitable. This case was doubted in *Gilmour v Coats*, but in principle the case seems correct, since Catholic masses are normally said in public, and *Caus* was applied by Browne-Wilkinson V-C in *Re Hetherington* [1990] Ch 1.

Re Hetherington
[1990] Ch 1
Chancery Division

Decision: A gift for the saying of masses is charitable as long as the masses are said in public. The gift (which on a literal interpretation could be used for the saying of either private or public masses) must therefore be construed as a gift for public masses only, private masses not being permissible since it would not be a charitable application of the fund for a religious purpose.

SIR NICHOLAS BROWNE-WILKINSON V-C: In my judgment the cases establish the following propositions.

(1) A trust for the advancement of education, the relief of poverty or the advancement of religion is prima facie charitable and assumed to be for the public benefit. *National Anti-vivisection Society* v *Inland Revenue Commissioners* [1948] AC 31, 42 and 65. This assumption of public benefit can be rebutted by showing that in fact the particular trust in question cannot operate so as to confer a legally recognised benefit on the public, as in *Gilmour* v *Coats* [1949] AC 426.

(2) The celebration of a religious rite in public does confer a sufficient public benefit because of the edifying and improving effect of such celebration on the members of the public who attend. As Lord Reid said in *Gilmour* v *Coats* [1949] AC 426, 459:

> A religion can be regarded as beneficial without it being necessary to assume that all its beliefs are true, and a religious service can be regarded as beneficial to all those who attend it without it being necessary to determine the spiritual efficacy of that service or to accept any particular belief about it.

(3) The celebration of a religious rite in private does not contain the necessary element of public benefit since any benefit by prayer or example is incapable of proof in the legal sense, and any element of edification is limited to a private, not public, class of those present at the celebration: see *Gilmour* v *Coats; Yeap Cheah Neo* v *Ong Cheng Neo* (1875) LR 6 PC 381 and *Hoare* v *Hoare* (1886) 56 LT 147.

Where there is a gift for a religious purpose which could be carried out in a way which is beneficial to the public (i.e. by public Masses) but could also be carried out in a way which would not have sufficient element of public benefit (i.e. by private Masses) the gift is to be construed as a gift to be carried out only by the methods that are charitable, all non-charitable methods being excluded: see *In re White* [1893] 2 Ch 41, 52–53; and *In re Banfield* [1968] 1 WLR 846.

Applying those principles to the present case, a gift for the saying of Masses is prima facie charitable, being for a religious purpose. In practice, those Masses will be celebrated in public which provides a sufficient element of public benefit. The provision of stipends for priests saying the Masses, by relieving the Roman Catholic Church pro tanto of the liability to provide such stipends, is a further benefit. The gift is to be construed as a gift for public Masses only on the principle of *In re White*, private Masses not being permissible since it would not be a charitable application of the fund for a religious purpose.

Neville Estates v *Madden*
[1962] Ch 832
Chancery Division

Facts and decision: The facts of this case have already been set out in chapter 5. The decision was that a gift to the Catford Synagogue, whose objects included maintaining of places of worship for persons of the Jewish religion who conform to the German or Polish ritual, could take effect as a charitable purpose trust. The consent of the Charity Commissioners was therefore required before an order for the sale of land could be made.

In order to hold the Catford Synagogue charitable, Cross J had to distinguish *Gilmour* v *Coates*.

CROSS J (on the question whether the purposes of the Catford Synagogue were charitable): If, as I have held, this £3,250 and the land bought with it was held by the trustees for the purposes of this synagogue, then the plaintiffs contend that the trust is not a charitable trust on two grounds. First, because the objects of the synagogue are not wholly religious. Secondly, because if the objects are wholly religious, a trust for the benefit of an unincorporated association of this sort is not a charitable trust but a private trust for the benefit of the members from time to time.

The chief purposes which a synagogue exists to achieve are the holding of religious services and the giving of religious instruction to the younger members of the congregation. But just as today church activity overflows from the church itself to the parochial hall, with its whist drives, dances and bazaars, so many synagogues today organise social activities among the members. A new clause added to the scheme of the United Synagogue in October, 1926, authorised, or purported to authorise, that body to establish, *inter alia*, halls for religious and social purposes, and the Catford Synagogue, as I have said, has erected a communal hall near the synagogue building in which social functions are held. The plaintiffs, fastening on these facts and on the wording of cl. 2 of the trust deed, argue that the trust in this case is open to the objections which proved fatal to the trust for the foundation of a community centre which came before the court in *IRC* v *Baddeley* [1955] AC 572 [above]. But in my judgment there is a great difference between that case and this. Here, the social activities are merely ancillary to the strictly religious activities. In the *Baddeley* case, on the other hand, no one sought to argue – indeed it was manifestly impossible to argue – that the trust was for the advancement of religion. No doubt it had a religious flavour in that the beneficiaries were confined to Methodists or persons likely to become Methodists, and the premises and the activities in which the beneficiaries were to engage were to be under the control of the leaders of a Methodist mission. Nevertheless the activities in themselves were directed predominantly to the social and not to the religious well-being of the beneficiaries.

In my judgment the purposes of the trust with which I am concerned are religious purposes – the social aspect is merely ancillary.

I turn now to the argument that this is a private, not a public trust. In an article which he contributed in 1946 to volume 62 of the *Law Quarterly Review*, Professor Newark argued that the courts ought not to concern themselves with the question whether or not a trust for a religious purpose confers a public benefit. Even assuming that such questions can be answered at all, judges, he said, are generally ill-equipped to answer them and their endeavours to do so are apt to cause distress to the faithful and amusement to the cynical. I confess that I have considerable sympathy with Professor Newark's views; but the decision of the House of Lords in *Gilmour* v *Coats* [1949] AC 426 has made it clear that a trust for a religious purpose must be shown to have some element of public benefit in order to qualify as a charitable trust. In that case it was held that a trust to apply the income of a fund for all or any of the purposes of a community of Roman Catholic nuns living in seclusion and spending their lives in prayer, contemplation and penance, was not charitable because it could not be shown that it conferred any benefit on the public or on any section of the public. The trust with which I am concerned resembles that in *Gilmour* v *Coats* in this, that the persons immediately benefited by it are not a section of the public but members of a private body. All persons of the Jewish faith living in or about Catford might well constitute a section of the public, but the members for the time being of the Catford Synagogue are no more a section of the public than the members for the time being of a Carmelite Priory. The two cases, however, differ from one another in that the members of the Catford Synagogue spend their lives in the world, whereas the

members of a Carmelite Priory live secluded from the world. If once one refuses to
pay any regard – as the courts refused to pay any regard – to the influence which these
nuns living in seclusion might have on the outside world, then it must follow that no
public benefit is involved in a trust to support a Carmelite Priory. As Lord Greene
said in the Court of Appeal ([1948] Ch 340, 354): 'Having regard to the way in which
the lives of the members are spent, the benefit is a purely private one'. But the court
is, I think, entitled to assume that some benefit accrues to the public from the
attendance at places of worship of persons who live in this world and mix with their
fellow citizens. As between different religions the law stands neutral, but it assumes
that any religion is at least likely to be better than none.

Note
On this view, religion can be advanced by example, so long as one mixes in
the world in a *physical* sense. *Neville Estates* is authority that no more is
required. It is not easy, however, to reconcile this position with the views of
Harman J in the following case.

Question
Given that freemasons also mix in the world, how does this case differ from
United Grand Lodge of Ancient Free & Accepted Masons of England and Wales
v *Holborn BC* [1957] 1 WLR 1080, above?

Re Warre's WT, Wort v Salisbury Diocesan Board of Finance
[1953] 1 WLR 725, [1953] 2 All ER 99
Chancery Division

Decision: Harman J refused to accord charitable status to an Anglican
house of retreat open to all members of the public wishing to retire from
the world for a short period of meditation and spiritual renewal. Technically this is probably *obiter dicta*, since the gift in question was also void for
uncertainty, the trustees being given a wide discretion, including using the
property for purposes which were undoubtedly non-charitable.

HARMAN J (after stating the facts and holding the disposition void for uncertainty):
Should I be wrong in that view, and the so-called wishes are mandatory, then it
remains to be seen whether those wishes themselves are exclusively charitable. . . .
   The testatrix proposed . . . what she called a retreat house, and this phrase is
explained as meaning a house devoted to a form of religious activity or inactivity which
is known as a 'retreat', and that is a form of religious experience well understood in
the Church of England. It is a retirement from the activities of the world for a space
of time for religious contemplation and the cleansing of the soul. No doubt that is a
highly beneficial activity for the person who undertakes it, but it is not in English law
a charitable activity. In *Cocks v Manners* (1871) LR 12 Eq 574, which was recently
confirmed by the House of Lords in *Gilmour v Coats* [1949] AC 426, Sir John Wickens
V-C said (LR 12 Eq 585):

   A voluntary association of women for the purpose of working out their own
   salvation by religious exercises and self-denial seems to me to have none of the
   requisites of a charitable institution, whether the word 'charitable' is used in its

popular sense or in its legal sense. It is said, in some of the cases, that religious purposes are charitable, but that can only be true as to religious services tending directly or indirectly towards the instruction or the edification of the public . . .

Gilmour v *Coats* was concerned with a trust for a certain Roman Catholic priory which consisted of cloistered nuns, who devoted their life to prayer, contemplation, penance and self-sanctification within their convent and engaged in no exterior works. There was evidence as to the doctrine of the Roman Catholic Church with regard to the benefit conferred by the contemplative life, not only on those who followed it themselves, but also through the efficacy of their intercessory prayers. The House of Lords held that the element of public benefit essential to render a purpose charitable applied equally to religious as to other charities. By that decision, therefore, the House declined to go beyond the doctrine of *Cocks* v *Manners*.

Activities which do not in any way affect the public or any section of it are not charitable. Pious contemplation and prayer are, no doubt, good for the soul, and may be of benefit by some intercessory process, of which the law takes no notice, but they are not charitable activities. It follows, then, that if the purposes indicated by way of confining the absolute discretion given to the trustees include a purpose which is not charitable, the trustees are, on this view, enjoined to embark on a purpose which is not charitable.

Note

On Cross J's reasoning in *Neville Estates*, above, one might have expected this to be charitable, because the meditators would return to the world after their spiritual renewal. It is not possible to state a clear conclusion, therefore, on the question of short-term private meditation, since there are conflicting High Court views. Nevertheless, Cross J's view seems more in accord with recent High Court decisions, and the recent practice of the Charity Commissioners.

SECTION 8: PURPOSES WHICH CREATE PROBLEMS UNDER ANY HEAD

A: Political Purposes

A trust cannot be charitable under any head if its purposes are, directly or indirectly, political. A trust to promote the aims of a particular political party is clearly not capable of being charitable, and attempts to disguise such objectives as educational trusts have generally failed.

The definition of political in this context is somewhat wider than the layman might expect, however. Where the objectives involve attempting to bring about a change in the law, they will be considered political and therefore non-charitable, unless change in the law is merely ancillary to the main purpose of the trust. This was one of the reasons for the failure of the National Anti-Vivisection Society to achieve charitable status in *National Anti-Vivisection Society* v *IRC* [1948] AC 31. Lord Simonds gave as the ostensible rationale that it is for Parliament, not the courts, to decide whether any change would be in the public benefit. He also rejected the contention that alteration in the law was merely ancillary to the purposes of the trust, since in order to abolish vivisection it would have been necessary to repeal the Cruelty of Animals Act 1876 (since replaced by the Animals (Scientific Procedures) Act 1986), and replace it with a new enactment prohibiting vivisection altogether.

(a) Change in the law in the UK

National Anti-Vivisection Society v Inland Revenue Commissioners
[1948] AC 31
House of Lords

Decision: The National Anti-Vivisection Society was not a charity within the fourth head, because its purposes were not beneficial for the community. The special commissioners for income tax had found that any assumed public benefit in the advancement of morals was outweighed by a detriment to medical science and research. Also, its objects (*necessarily* requiring an alteration in the law) were political. It followed that the society, not being 'a body of persons . . . established for charitable purposes only', was not exempt from income tax by virtue of s. 37(1)(b) of the Income Tax Act 1918.

LORD SIMONDS (on the question whether the object to be obtained was political): My lords, if I may deal with this second reason first, I cannot agree that in this case an alteration in the law is merely ancillary to the attainment of a good charitable object. In a sense no doubt, since legislation is not an end in itself, every law may be regarded as ancillary to the object which its provisions are intended to achieve. But that is not the sense in which it is said that a society has a political object. Here, the finding of the Commissioners is itself conclusive. 'We are satisfied', they say, 'that the main object of the society is the total abolition of vivisection . . . and (for that purpose) the repeal of the Cruelty to Animals Act 1876 [now replaced by the Animals (Scientific Procedures) Act 1986], and the substitution of a new enactment prohibiting vivisection altogether.' This is a finding that the main purpose of the society is the compulsory abolition of vivisection by Act of Parliament. What else can it mean? And how else can it be supposed that vivisection is to be abolished? Abolition and suppression are words that connote some form of compulsion. It can only be by Act of Parliament that that element can be supplied. . . .

Lord Parker uses slightly different language but means the same thing when he says that the court has no means of judging whether a proposed change in the law will or will not be for the public benefit. It is not for the court to judge and the court has no means of judging. The same question may be looked at from a slightly different angle. One of the tests, and a crucial test, whether a trust is charitable, lies in the competence of the court to control and reform it. I would remind your lordships that it is the King as *parens patriae* who is the guardian of charity and that it is the right and duty of his Attorney-General to intervene and inform the court, if the trustees of a charitable trust fall short of their duty. So too it is his duty to assist the court, if need be, in the formulation of a scheme for the execution of a charitable trust. But, my lords, is it for a moment to be supposed that it is the function of the Attorney-General on behalf of the Crown to intervene and demand that a trust shall be established and administered by the court, the object of which is to alter the law in a manner highly prejudicial, as he and His Majesty's government may think, to the welfare of the State? . . . I conclude upon this part of the case that a main object of the society is political and for that reason the society is not established for charitable purposes only.

[His lordship continued on the question of benefit:] It is to me a strange and bewildering idea that the court must look so far and no farther, must see a charitable purpose in the intention of the society to benefit animals and thus elevate the moral character of men but must shut its eyes to the injurious results to the whole human and animal creation. I will readily concede that, if the purpose is within one of the heads of charity forming the first three classes in the classification which Lord Macnaughten borrowed from Sir Samuel Romilly's argument in *Morice* v *Bishop of Durham* (1805) 10 Ves 522, 531, the court will easily conclude that it is a charitable purpose. But even here to give the purpose the name of 'religious' or 'education' is not to conclude the matter. It may yet not be charitable, if the religious purpose is illegal or the educational purpose is contrary to public policy. Still there remains the overriding question: Is it *pro bono publico*? It would be another strange misreading of Lord Macnaughten's speech in [*Commissioners for Special Purposes of Income Tax* v *Pemsel*] [1891] AC 531 . . . to suggest that he intended anything to the contrary. I would rather say that, when a purpose appears broadly to fall within one of the familiar categories of charity, the court will assume it to be for the benefit of the community and, therefore, charitable, unless the contrary is shown, and further that the court will not be astute in such a case to defeat on doubtful evidence the avowed benevolent intention of a donor. But, my lords, the next step is one that I cannot take. Where on the evidence before it the court concludes that, however well-intentioned the donor, the achievement of his object will be greatly to the public disadvantage, there can be no justification for saying that it is a charitable object. If and so far as there is any judicial decision to the contrary, it must, in my opinion, be regarded as inconsistent with principle and be overruled.

Question
Would Lord Simonds's reasoning in the first of the above passages apply to a society whose objects were to:

(a) Campaign for a change in the law brought about by statutory instrument, such as raising of financial limits?

(b) Campaign against a change in the law which was being proposed by the Government?

(c) Campaign against a change in the law which was not being proposed by the Government or anybody else? Can the question of charitable status (which is permanent) depend on the views of the Government (which is not)?

(d) Campaign for a change in local bye-laws (e.g., to create a dog-free zone in a public park)?

(e) Campaign to alter the law overseas?

Notes
1. On the question of political objects, see further *McGovern* v *A-G* [1982] Ch 321 (below), where similar principles were applied to a body (Amnesty International) whose objects included altering the laws of overseas jurisdictions, and *Re Koeppler's WT* [1986] Ch 423 (below), where alteration in the

law was only an incidental object, and was not a bar to the body being an educational charity.

2.   On the question of public benefit, this was treated as a question of fact, and if an object is not for the benefit of the public it cannot be charitable under any head (although Lord Simonds conceded in the last passage set out above that if the object fell within one of the first three heads public benefit would usually be assumed). Lord Simonds also recognised (at p. 74) that public benefit is not static, but may alter over time.

3.   It follows, therefore, that any trust whose main object includes a change in the law of the United Kingdom cannot be charitable. In *Re Bushnell* [1975] 1 WLR 1596, money was left to advance awareness of the benefits of socialised medicine and to show that its realisation was fully possible only in a socialist state. The testator had died in 1941, before the introduction of the National Health Service. One of the grounds upon which the trust was held void was its political bias in favour of socialism. Another ground for the failure of the trust in *Re Bushnell* was that in 1941 legislation would have been needed (and was of course later enacted) to introduce socialised medicine.

4.   This was also an additional reason for the failure of Shaw's 40-letter alphabet (see below), and accounts for the inability of (e.g.) the Campaign against Racial Discrimination and the National Council for Civil Liberties to be registered.

Re Shaw, Public Trustee v Day
[1957] 1 WLR 729, [1957] 1 All ER 745
Chancery Division

Decision: The facts and decision have already been set out at p. 121.

HARMAN J (on the fourth head): It seems to me that the objects of the alphabet trusts are analogous to trusts for political purposes, which advocate a change in the law. Such objects have never been considered charitable. In his celebrated speech in *Bowman* v *Secular Society Ltd* [1917] AC 406 Lord Parker of Waddington said (*ibid.*, at p. 442):

Now if your Lordships will refer for a moment to the society's memorandum of association you will find that none of its objects, except, possibly, the first, are charitable. The abolition of religious tests, the disestablishment of the Church, the secularisation of education, the alteration of the law touching religion or marriage, or the observation of the Sabbath, are purely political objects. Equity has always refused to recognise such objects as charitable. It is true that a gift to an association formed for their attainment may, if the association be unincorporated, be upheld as an absolute gift to its members, or, if the association be incorporated, as an absolute gift to the corporate body; but a trust for the attainment of political objects has always been held invalid, not because it is illegal, for every one is at liberty to advocate or promote by any lawful means a change in the law, but because the court has no means of judging whether a proposed change in the law will or will not be for the public benefit, and therefore cannot say that a gift to secure the change is a charitable gift.

I, therefore, do not reach the further inquiry whether the benefit is one within the spirit or intendment (as it is called) of the Statute of Elizabeth, but, if I had to decide that point, I should hold that it was not.

Chesterman, Charities, Trusts and Social Welfare
Weidenfeld & Nicholson Law in Context Series (1979), pp. 359–360

Long-established charities which are overtly concerned to promote or oppose changes in the law have not been denied charitable status. Three instances already referred to are the Howard League for Penal Reform, the Anti-Slavery Society and the Lord's Day Observance Society. All three of these do not conceal their involvement in legislative matters: the last of them, for instance, is empowered by its constitution to 'promote or oppose or join in promoting or opposing legislation, parliamentary, municipal, or other measures affecting any of the objects of the society'. This form of indulgence towards such charities is attributable to the comparatively recent growth of the ban on political activity and the fact that the charity commissioners are not disposed to refuse registration to organisations long believed to be charitable.

Notes
1. Chesterman footnotes: An undertaking to this effect was in fact given when the Charities Act 1960 was going through Parliament: see Expenditure Committee Report, paras 57–9 (where the implications of this are criticised); Evidence to the Expenditure Committee, Qs 1563–4.
2. Chesterman goes on to point out that there is no ban on officers of charities making their personal views known, allowing it to be known that they happen to be officers, and that quite a number of activist groups employ organisational fission, separate legal structures being set up which do not engage in political activity, and which can therefore enjoy charitable status.

(b) Change in the law overseas

Lord Simonds' reasoning in *National Anti-Vivisection Society* v *IRC*, applies only to changes to the law in the United Kingdom, but in *McGovern* v *Attorney-General* [1982] Ch 321, Slade J frustrated Amnesty International's attempt to procure charitable status for some of its activities by creating a trust of those parts which were thought most likely to be accepted as charitable, on the ground that a main object of the trust was to secure the alteration of the laws of foreign countries.

McGovern v Attorney-General
[1982] Ch 321, [1981] 3 All ER 493
Chancery Division

Facts: The objects of Amnesty International were:

(a) The relief of needy persons within any of the following categories: (i) prisoners of conscience (ii) persons who have recently been prisoners of conscience (iii) persons who would in the opinion of the trustees be likely to become prisoners of conscience if they returned to their country of ordinary residence (iv) relatives or dependants of the foregoing persons; by the provision of appropriate charitable (and in particular financial educational or rehabilitational) assistance.

(b)   Attempting to secure the release of prisoners of conscience.

(c)   Procuring the abolition of torture or inhuman or degrading treatment or punishment.

(d)   The undertaking promotion and commission of research into the maintenance and observance of human rights.

(e)   The dissemination of the results of such research by (i) the preparation and publication of the results of such research (ii) the institution and maintenance of a library accessible to the public for the study of matters connected with the objects of this trust and of the results of research already conducted into such matters (iii) the production and distribution of documentary films showing the results of such research.

(f)   The doing of all such other things as shall further the charitable purposes set out above provided always that the foregoing objects shall be restricted to those which are charitable according to the law of the United Kingdom but subject thereto they may be carried out in all parts of the world.

The trustees applied to the Charity Commissioners for registration as a charity under s. 4 of the Charities Act 1960 (now s. 3 of the 1993 Act), and the Commissioners refused. Amnesty appealed under s. 5(3) (now s. 4).

Held: Because of the inclusion of objects (b) and (c), Amnesty International was not a charitable body: a direct and main object of the trust was to secure changes in the laws of foreign countries. The decision represents an extension of the principles laid down in the House of Lords in *National Anti-Vivisection Society* v *IRC* [1948] AC 31 (above).

SLADE J: I now turn to consider the status of a trust of which a main object is to secure the alteration of the laws of a foreign country. The mere fact that the trust was intended to be carried out abroad would not by itself necessarily deprive it of charitable status. A number of trusts to be executed outside this country have been upheld as charities, though the judgment of Evershed MR in *Camille and Henry Dreyfus Foundation Inc.* v *IRC* [1954] Ch 672 at 684–5 illustrates that certain types of trust, for example trusts for the setting out of soldiers or the repair of bridges or causeways, might be acceptable as charities only if they were to be executed in the United Kingdom. The point with which I am at present concerned is whether a trust of which a direct and main object is to secure a change in the laws of a foreign country can ever be regarded as charitable under English law. Though I do not think that any authority cited to me precisely covers the point, I have come to the clear conclusion that it cannot.

I accept that the dangers of the court encroaching on the functions of the legislature or of subjecting its political impartiality to question would not be nearly so great as when similar trusts are to be executed in this country. I also accept that on occasions the court will examine and express an opinion on the quality of a foreign law. Thus, for example, it has declined to enforce or recognise rights conferred or duties imposed by a foreign law, in certain cases where it has considered that, on the particular facts, enforcement or recognition would be contrary to justice or morality. I therefore accept the particular point made by Mr Tyssen (about the law stultifying itself) has no application in this context. There is no obligation on the court to decide on the principle that any foreign law is *ex hypothesi* right as it stands; it is not obliged for all purposes to blind itself to what it may regard as the injustice of a particular foreign law.

In my judgment, however, there remain overwhelming reasons why such a trust still cannot be regarded as charitable. All the reasoning of Lord Parker in *Bowman* v *Secular Society Ltd* [1917] AC 406 seems to me to apply *a fortiori* in such a case. *A fortiori* the court will have no adequate means of judging whether a proposed change in the law of a foreign country will or will not be for the public benefit. Evershed MR in *Camille and Henry Dreyfus Foundation Inc.* v *IRC* [1954] Ch 672 at 684 expressed the prima facie view that the community which has to be considered in this context, even in the case of a trust to be executed abroad, is the community of the United Kingdom. Assuming that this is the right test, the court in applying it would still be bound to take account of the probable effects of attempts to procure the proposed legislation, or of its actual enactment, on the inhabitants of the country concerned, which would doubtless have a history and social structure quite different from that of the United Kingdom. Whatever might be its view as to the content of the relevant law from the standpoint of an English lawyer, it would, I think, have no satisfactory means of judging such probable effects on the local community.

Furthermore, before ascribing charitable status to an English trust of which a main object was to secure the alteration of a foreign law, the court would also, I conceive be bound to consider the consequences for this country as a matter of public policy. In a number of such cases there would arise a substantial prima facie risk that such a trust, if enforced, could prejudice the relations of this country with the foreign country concerned. . . . The court would have no satisfactory means of assessing the extent of such risk, which would not be capable of being readily dealt with by evidence and would be a matter more for political than for legal judgment. For all these reasons, I conclude that a trust of which a main purpose is to procure a change in the laws of a foreign country is a trust for the attainment of political objectives within the spirit of Lord Parker's pronouncement and, as such, is non-charitable.

Thus far, I have been considering trusts of which a main purpose is to achieve changes in the law itself or which are of a party political nature. Under any legal system, however, the government and its various authorities, administrative and judicial, will have wide discretionary powers vested in them, within the framework of the existing law. If a principal purpose of a trust is to procure a reversal of government policy or of particular administrative decisions of governmental authorities, does it constitute a trust for political purposes falling within the spirit of Lord Parker's pronouncement? In my judgment it does. If a trust of this nature is to be executed in England, the court will ordinarily have no sufficient means of determining whether the desired reversal would be beneficial to the public, and in any event could not properly encroach on the functions of the executive, acting *intra vires*, by holding that it should be acting in some other manner. If it is a trust which is to be executed abroad, the court will not have sufficient means of satisfactorily judging, as a matter of evidence, whether the proposed reversal would be beneficial to the community in the relevant sense, after all its consequences, local and international, had been taken into account.

Notes

1. See also *Re Koeppler's WT* [1986] Ch 423 below, where *McGovern* was distinguished.

2. The decision represents an extension of the principles laid down in the House of Lords in *National Anti-Vivisection Society* v *IRC* [1948] AC 31. The reasoning adopted by Lord Simonds could not be applied directly here, but Slade J thought that to grant charitable status to such purposes might prejudice the relations of the British Government with foreign countries, and this consideration of policy could not be overlooked by the court.

3. A political taint will in any case be fatal to charitable status, whether or not a trust's direct and main object is to secure a change in the law of the United Kingdom, or of a foreign country. This can apply even to trusts seeking to promote aims which most civilised nations hold to be high aspirations. In *Re Strakosch* [1949] Ch 529, the promotion of racial harmony between English and Africaans communities in South Africa was held non-charitable, and registration of community councils is refused where their principal aim is the promotion of inter-racial accord. The same will apply where the aims are harmony and peace, if such movements overtly or covertly call upon governments to promote specific policies, such as disarmament. One reason sometimes given for denying charitable status to attempts to promote moral objectives is that they necessarily involve a propagandist element biased in favour of only one side of the argument.

(c)   Discussion of political issues, and campaigning

On the other hand, it is legitimate for an educational charity to discuss political issues, and a political object which is merely incidental will not be fatal. In *Re Koeppler's WT* [1986] Ch 423, a testamentary gift to Wilton Park, whose main function was to organise educational conferences, was upheld by the Court of Appeal as a gift for charitable purposes, although Wilton Park's objects included the promotion of informed international public opinion and the promotion of greater cooperation between East and West.

Re Koeppler's WT, Barclays Bank Trust Co. plc v *Slack*
[1986] Ch 423, [1985] 2 All ER 869
Court of Appeal

Facts: The issue arose over the validity of a testamentary gift to the warden of the institution known as Wilton Park. At the time of the testator's death there was no entity called Wilton Park, nor was there a warden of Wilton Park, but there was a Wilton Park project, which consisted of a series of conferences. It was accepted that the gift could only be valid if it was construed as a gift for charitable purposes.

Held: The gift was construed as a gift for the purposes of the Wilton Park project (applying the reasoning in *Re Finger's WT* [1972] 1 Ch 286, in chapter 13). These purposes were charitable, being for the advancement of education. The political purposes of Wilton Park were of only an incidental nature, and did not invalidate the gift.

SLADE LJ (on the political issue): The organisation and conduct of the conferences which had been held since 1950 at Wiston House were clearly the central features of the Wilton Park project. The 'specific aspects' dealt with at each conference covered a wide range of topics. Examples of these specific aspects are to be found in the programmes for the four conferences immediately preceding the date of the testator's will and those for the four conferences immediately preceding his death. They were as follows:

(1) An enquiry into the 'quality of life'; ecology and the environment; participation in government and industry; tensions in free societies; (2) Europe and the emergent pattern of superpower relationships; (3) the unification of Europe; a balance sheet; (4) the requirements of Western defence and the possibilities of arms control; (5) the European Community and its external relations; (6) the media, public opinion and the decision-making process in government; (7) security issues as a factor in domestic and international politics; (8) labour and capital and the future of industrial society.

As the judge observed, those specific themes are self-evidently matters on which persons of differing political persuasions might have differing views and some of the speakers invited to speak at plenary sessions of the conferences were politicians. However, he found that 'it is clear that Wilton Park has taken pains to avoid inculcating any particular political viewpoint' (see [1984] Ch 243 at 251). There is therefore no question of the Wilton Park conferences being intended to further the interests of a particular political party. . . .

There are two particular points which have caused me to hesitate before finally concluding that this gift is of a charitable nature. First, I have already mentioned the wide range of topics which are discussed at Wilton Park conferences, some of which could be said to have a political flavour. We were referred to a decision of my own in *McGovern v Attorney-General* [1982] Ch 321 [above], where I held, *inter alia*, that though certain trusts, declared in a trust deed, for research into the observance of human rights and the dissemination of the results of such research would have been charitable if they had stood alone, they failed because, read in their context, they were merely adjuncts to the political purposes declared by the earlier provisions of the deed.

However, in the present case, as I have already mentioned, the activities of Wilton Park are not of a party political nature. Nor, so far as the evidence shows, are they designed to procure changes in the laws or governmental policy of this or any other country: even when they touch on political matters, they constitute, so far as I can see, no more than genuine attempts in an objective manner to ascertain and disseminate the truth. In these circumstances I think that no objections to the trust arise on a political score, similar to those which arose in the *McGovern* case. The trust is, in my opinion, entitled to what is sometimes called a 'benignant construction', in the sense that the court is entitled to presume that the trustees will only act in a lawful and proper manner appropriate to the trustees of a charity and not, for example, by the propagation of tendentious political opinions, any more than those running the Wilton Park project so acted in the 33 years predating the testator's death: compare *McGovern v Attorney-General* [1982] Ch 321 at 353.

Note
Another authority that discussion of political issues is not necessarily fatal to charitable status is *Attorney-General v Ross* [1986] 1 WLR 252, where Scott J commented, at p. 263, that 'there is nothing the matter with an educational

charity in the furtherance of its educational purposes encouraging students to develop their political awareness or to acquire knowledge of and to debate and to form views on political issues'. He also observed that there is no reason why a charitable student organisation should not affiliate to a non-charitable organisation if that enables it to further its own charitable activities for the benefit of students. That is the basis upon which student unions are entitled to affiliate to the National Union of Students, a non-charitable organisation. It is, however, essential that the purpose of the affiliation should be to benefit the student body in their capacity as students.

There are limits to the extent to which a charity can go in this direction, however. Political discussion may not be fatal to charitable status, but campaigning, in the sense of seeking to influence public opinion on political matters, undoubtedly is.

Webb v O'Doherty and others
The Times 11 February 1991
Chancery Division

Decision: Hoffman J, distinguishing *Attorney-General v Ross*, granted an injunction restraining the officers of a students' union, which was an educational charity, from making any payments to the National Student Committee to Stop War in the Gulf, or to the Cambridge Committee to Stop War in the Gulf.

HOFFMAN J: This is a motion for an interlocutory injunction to restrain the Anglia Student Union (Cambridge) from expending money in support of a campaign against the Gulf War and from affiliating to national and local organisations carrying on such a campaign. The Student Union is an educational charity. Its purposes are wholly charitable and its funds can be devoted to charitable purposes only. Charitable educational purposes undoubtedly include discussion of political issues. As Scott J said in *A-G v Ross* [1986] 1 WLR 252 at page 263, 'there is nothing the matter with an educational charity in the furtherance of its educational purposes encouraging students to develop their political awareness or to acquire knowledge of and to debate and to form views on political issues.'

There is, however, a clear distinction between the discussion of political matters, or the acquisition of information which may have a political content, and a campaign on a political issue. There is no doubt that campaigning, in the sense of seeking to influence public opinion on political matters, is not a charitable activity. It is, of course, something which students are, like the rest of the population, perfectly at liberty to do in their private capacities, but it is not a proper object of the expenditure of charitable money.

There are some cases in which it is not altogether easy to distinguish between political discussion carried on for educational purposes and political campaigning. The Amnesty International case (*McGovern v A-G* [1982] Ch 321) provides illustration of how difficult that distinction may sometimes be. Campaigning against disregard of human rights by foreign governments or our own is not charitable, but research into the observance of human rights may well be, even though an incidental effect of the publication of the research is to provide material for people campaigning against human rights abuses. The law will only permit charitable money to be spent on what might be regarded as political persuasion if that is a mere incidental effect of expenditure for proper charitable educational purposes.

In this case the Student Union passed a resolution on the 22nd of January, 1991 which began by expressing various views about the Gulf War and the situation in the Middle East and then mandated the executive in the following terms: '1. To affiliate to the National Student Committee to Stop the War in the Gulf and the Cambridge Committee to stop the War in the Gulf. 2. To campaign on the above issues. 3. To support and publicise national and local demonstrations, speaker meetings and non-violent direct actions organised by CND and Committee To Stop War in the Gulf. 4. To support the teach-in on the Gulf Crisis organised by the Student Committee To Stop War this Thursday. 5. To allocate £100 from the Campaign budget to the anti-Gulf War campaign. 6. To write to the Prime Minister and Ministry of Defence outlining this policy.' All those aims are, as I have said, perfectly legitimate aims for citizens of this country to espouse, but I have absolutely no doubt that there is no way in which they can be described as 'charitable'. The whole thrust of the resolutions is to commit the Union and the expenditure of the Union's money to what is no doubt perfectly accurately described as a 'campaign against the War in the Gulf.' So far from that being an education purpose with incidental political effects, it seems to me that any educational effect which it may have (and I do not dispute that it may) is incidental to the main purpose of attempting to influence public opinion.

Mr O'Doherty, who is the President of the Union, has sworn an affidavit in which he says that he undertakes to seek advice as to how the £100 authorised by the resolution should be spent so as to ensure that it is not spent on non-charitable purposes. It seems to me, however, that at present there is nothing within the mandate which has been given to him which could be described as a charitable purpose, and consequently the seeking of advice on this point would be superfluous. If the Union were minded to authorise activities of an exclusively educational character but which nonetheless related to the War in the Gulf, the position might be different, but that would in my judgment require the passing of a wholly different resolution and would give rise to questions which obviously cannot be considered today.

A separate aspect of the application is the question of whether the Union should affiliate to the two organisations, one national and one in Cambridge, which are mentioned in the resolution. Affiliation involves a contribution to the funds of these organisations in a fairly modest amount and an indication of general support for their objectives. The fact that a body to which the Union affiliates is not itself formed for charitable purposes is not necessarily an objection to the affiliation. As Mr Justice Scott said in *A-G v Ross*, there is no reason why a charitable student organisation should not affiliate to a non-charitable organisation if that enables it to further its own charitable activities for the benefit of students. That is the basis upon which the union is entitled to affiliate to the National Union of Students, a non-charitable organisation, and no doubt to other non-charitable organisations as well. It is, however, essential for this purpose that the purpose of the affiliation should be to benefit the student body in their capacity as students. What is not permitted is to affiliate to a wholly non-charitable organisation simply as a way of furthering a non-charitable purpose or of channelling funds into non-charitable activities. It is said here that one of the effects of affiliation to these two organisations is that the Union will receive materials of educational value. I am bound to say that no particulars are given in the evidence as to what such materials may be, and the only literature which has so far been exhibited is a hand bill summoning students to a demonstration in London. On the face of it, these two organisations are of a wholly political and non-charitable character and there is no evidence before me which could provide an educational ground for the affiliation of the student union. For those reasons, it appears to me that not only do the plaintiffs have the necessary arguable case, but there is not a seriously arguable case for the respondents. The injunction must go.

(d)   Reform of the law?

Chesterman, *Charities, Trusts and Social Welfare*
Weidenfeld & Nicholson Law in Context Series (1979), pp. 357–358

. . . Many charities are conscious of the fact that while to seek out undiscovered needs and 'pioneer' new modes of welfare provision will in the short term tend to a more equitable distribution of resources and a more humane society, long-lasting determination to 'hold on' at all costs to the particular form of provision which they have pioneered has ultimately conservative implications. Such charities may thus try to restrict their role to that of a 'catalyst': having led the way within a particular context of welfare provision, they abdicate in favour of the state. The irony here, however, is that if they are too vociferous in urging the state to take over from them, they risk being deemed non-charitable because they are 'political' in one of the senses which charity law does not recognize. In the eyes of the law, a statement by a charity such as Shelter that 'it exists to put itself out of business' has non-charitable implications.

This dilemma for the 'progressive' charity has become particularly evident in recent times amongst international relief charities such as Oxfam and War on Want. Many such charities appreciate too well that merely to distribute food and other basic amenities amongst the poor inhabitants of developing countries will at best relieve in the short term the immediate symptoms of poverty. Ultimately, more progress towards cure will be achieved if projects to stimulate local food production, distribution of locally-manufactured goods, or the building of essential amenities are undertaken; better still may be to try to persuade the foreign government to distribute the country's resources more equitably or the British government to grant more foreign aid. Yet these approaches to the problem fall foul of either or both of two rules of charity law: (a) that charities must not be 'political' in an activist sense; and (b) that activities within the fourth category of charitable purpose are not charitable if carried out abroad (except perhaps within the British Commonwealth), because such 'public' purposes fall properly within the province of the relevant foreign government. International relief charities may thus have to choose between two courses of 'political' action: continuing to hand out 'international doles', with all their politically conservative implications, or encountering opposition from the Charity Commission by pursuing courses of action which they consider much more fruitful in the long run.

Charities: A Framework for the Future
HMSO (May 1989)

2.37   There is a crucial difference between charities and non-charitable voluntary bodies. Any non-charitable voluntary organisation is entirely, and quite properly, free to support any cause which it wishes to support, and in any manner in which it wishes to do so, as long as it keeps within the law. In contrast, charities cannot have political objects. They are constrained by law to the reasonable advocacy of causes which directly further their non-political objects and which are ancillary to their achieving those. In this context, 'politics' does not mean only 'party politics' but political activity as it has been defined by the High Court in many cases which have been decided over the years. Charities may not, therefore, seek improperly to influence the policies of local or central Government either at home or abroad. Nor may they advocate changes in the existing law, or even its retention, in a way which would not be in furtherance of their purposes.

2.38   The precise extent to which a charity may properly seek to influence Government and public attitudes is a difficult question. It turns, in individual cases, on the trusts of the particular charity concerned and on the manner and the context in which it proposes to bring issues into public discussion. The courts have, however, laid down certain basic principles. These were set out in the Charity Commissioners' Annual Report for 1981 and they have since been issued in the form of a booklet 'Political Activities by Charities' which is intended for the guidance of trustees.

2.39   The Charity Commission's guidance is, broadly, to the effect that:

— governing instruments should not include a power to exert political pressure except in a way which is ancillary to a charitable purpose;
— the powers and purposes of a charity should not include the power to bring pressure to bear on the Government to adopt, to alter, or to maintain a particular line of action, although charities may present reasoned argument and information to Government;
— where the objects of a charity include the advancement of education or the power to conduct research, care must be taken to ensure that both objectivity and balance is maintained and that propaganda is avoided.

2.40   It follows from this guidance that charities are precluded from direct or indirect financial or other support of, or opposition to, any political party or individual or group which seeks elective office or any organisation which has a political object. Charities must not allow the proportion of effort and resources which are devoted to persuasion to become greater than that which is devoted directly to meeting its objects. In other respects, the guidance at present allows considerable latitude. Charities can, for example, quite properly respond to invitations from Government to comment on proposed changes in the law. Where a Bill is being debated, they can legitimately supply members of either House with such relevant information and arguments as they believe will assist the attainment of their objects. Where this kind of action is in furtherance of their purposes, charities are free to present to government departments reasoned memoranda advocating changes in the law.

2.41   The Government believe that the safeguards which the law provides are indispensable to prevent what are essentially political factions or pressure groups from assuming the guise of charity. It is vital, in the long term interests of the public and charities alike, that political and charitable purposes should remain distinct. It would be wrong if taxpayers, through the Government, were to find themselves unwittingly distorting the democratic process by subsidising bodies whose true purpose was to campaign not so much for their beneficiaries as for some political end. Nor do the Government believe that the public would for long continue to display their generosity if charities were to ally themselves to causes with which individual donors might well differ strongly on political grounds.

2.42   There is no reason to believe that the vast majority of charities experience any great difficulty in complying with the law. There are, however, some signs that the public is anxious that the behaviour of a few charities may, on occasions, stray beyond the bounds of what is permissible or desirable. The Government have accordingly considered whether the law could with advantage be tightened.

2.43   Ministers welcome the advice and the guidance which charities can offer to Members of Parliament, to central and local government, and to other public authorities on a wide range of social problems. Charities should feel free to take the initiative in offering advice and opinions and in proposing changes in the law and should not need to wait to be invited to do so. The Government firmly believe, however, that such activities must remain ancillary to a charity's primary purposes, which must be clearly charitable and nonpolitical. Such activities must be kept subordinate to the non-political work of the organisation. They must not be allowed to predominate.

2.44   The Government's view is that this approach commands general agreement. The guidance issued by the Charity Commission, which derives from the present law, provides an adequate framework for the future. There is bound to be difficulty, and room for dispute, over the application of general guidance to particular instances. But to alter the guidance by legislation could well have the disadvantage of laying down inflexible rules, instead of allowing the law to develop in the light of particular cases which may present features which cannot now be foreseen. Of course, there are at present some difficult borderline cases, but that would be so whatever general rules might be laid down.

2.45   The Government's view is, therefore, that a rigid approach would not be sensible. The decision on what is permissible in the way of political activity is best left to the good judgment of the trustees of individual charities, who know that, in cases where the restrictions appear to be breached, the Charity Commissioners will take vigorous action with the support of the Attorney General.

2.46   In cases of doubt, trustees can seek the guidance of the Charity Commission. Such guidance should be freely given, as it is at present. For trustees who unwisely insist on engaging in illegitimate political activity the powers of the Commissioners and the Attorney General are considerable. Trustees who stray too far can be held personally liable to repay to the charity any funds which have been spent on political activities. The Government's proposals to sharpen the Commissioners' powers of investigation, in order to enforce a remedy, will greatly strengthen their hand in imposing the proper degree of control. These proposals are set out in Chapter 5.

B: Self-help Organisations

Although self-help organisations may possibly have been regarded as charitable in the nineteenth century, when for example friendly societies contributed considerably to the then limited provisions for welfare, Hall V-C held in *Re Clark* (1875) 1 ChD 497 that a friendly society was not charitable because of the absence of any stipulation that benefits should be restricted to those members who were poor as well as old, disabled or sick.

If they are not poverty charities, self-help organisations clearly fail on the *Oppenheim* personal nexus test (above). Hall V-C envisaged that they may succeed as poverty charities, where as we have seen public benefit tests are less stringent, but there may be a second principle that the benefits of charity must be provided by bounty and not bargain (but note the views of Peter Gibson J in *Joseph Rowntree Memorial Trust Housing Association Ltd v A-G*, above). Where, as is the case with many friendly societies, the beneficiaries have, in effect, bought their entitlement in a contractual arrangement, the element of altruism essential to charity is lacking.

Re Hobourn Aero Components Ltd's Air Raid Distress Fund, Ryan v Forrest
[1946] Ch 86
affirmed [1946] Ch 194 (CA)
Court of Appeal

Facts: From 1940 to 1944 employees of a company situated in Coventry made weekly contributions to a fund to assist employees who had suffered damage as a result of air raids. Only contributors to the fund could benefit. The fund was closed in 1944, and the question arose what to do with surplus moneys.

Held at first instance:

(a) These funds were not held on any charitable trust, since there was an insufficient element of public benefit. It followed that a cy près scheme could not be directed.

(b) The contributors were entitled to distribute the fund among themselves, in proportion to the total amount each had contributed, on resulting trust principles (see chapter 8).

Held in the Court of Appeal: The Crown appealed (arguing for a cy près scheme to be directed) on the issue of the charitable status of the fund alone. The Court of Appeal upheld Cohen J's decision.

LORD GREENE MR: We are not dealing with a fund put up by outside persons, although, even if we were, I should on the authority of *Re Compton* [1945] Ch 123 feel constrained to hold that such a fund would not be a good charity. The point to my mind which really puts this case beyond reasonable doubt is the fact that a number of employees of this company, actuated by motives of self-help, agreed to a deduction from their wages to constitute a fund to be applied for their own benefit without any question of poverty coming into it. Such an arrangement seems to me to stamp the whole transaction as one having a personal character, money put up by a number of people, not for the general benefit, but for their own individual benefit. I am not concerned to dispute the proposition that a fund put up for air raid distress in Coventry generally would be a good charitable gift. I have very little doubt that it would be. But there is all the difference in the world between such a fund and a fund put up by a dozen inhabitants of a street, or, it may be, a thousand employees of a firm, to provide for themselves out of the moneys subscribed by themselves some kind of immediate relief in case they suffered from an air raid.

MORTON LJ: . . . there is no element of poverty in the present case. That, of course, does not prevent a trust from coming within the fourth head of Lord Macnaughten's classification in *Pemsel's case* [1891] AC 531, but the relevance of it in the present case is this: where poverty is essential in the qualification for benefits under a particular fund, there have been cases where trusts which would appear to be of a private nature have been held to be charitable. An example of this is the case of *Spiller v Maude* (1881) 32 ChD 158 n, which has been already mentioned. The reason, as was suggested by the Master of the Rolls in *Re Compton* [1945] Ch 123, may be that the relief of poverty is regarded as being in itself beneficial to the community. That element being absent in the present case, the appellant cannot rely on these cases. Mr Upjohn has argued that the provision of relief for air raid distress should be elevated to the same position as trusts for the relief of poverty. No doubt the provision of relief for air raid distress is a most excellent object, and I should not myself doubt that a fund for the relief of air raid distress in Coventry was a fund held upon charitable trusts. But I do not feel inclined to extend the somewhat anomalous line of cases where poverty has been held to take a trust out of the category of a private trust and into the category of a trust which is charitable in the legal sense.

Note
Morton LJ suggests that the self-help reasoning in *Hobourn Aero* may not apply to poverty trusts, where the public benefit requirement is less stringent (see, e.g. *Dingle* v *Turner*, above), but Lord Greene MR seemed rather less sure. Whatever may be the position regarding poverty charities, however, it is clear that a self-help scheme can never be charitable, unless it is for the relief of poverty.

C: Disaster Appeals

These will be valid if for the relief of poverty, otherwise (like self-help organisations) they will fail on the grounds of public benefit (unless they are drawn up so as to benefit a large section of the community: see *Re North Devon and West Somerset Relief Fund Trusts*, below). This leaves the organisers of such funds with two alternatives. One possibility is that they can apply a means test criterion to the receipt of benefit, which they may regard as invidious. For example, in the Aberfan coal-tip disaster of 1966, the majority of victims were children, and far from it being easy to show that their deaths produced material deprivation among the relatives, one could actually argue that the cost of rearing the children had been saved. In fact, the Commissioners eventually held that the fund was charitable, when money was paid to enable people to move away from the area altogether. Chesterman, *Charities, Trusts and Social Welfare*, gives an extremely comprehensive coverage of this appeal (see the extract below), and see also (1982) 132 NLJ 223.

The other possibility, often favoured by fund organisers (e.g., Penlee lifeboat disaster fund in 1982), is to avoid the means test and draft the appeal in such a way as to avoid charitable status altogether. In that event, of course, the tax concessions will also be forgone. Perhaps more importantly, the cy près doctrine described in the next chapter will not apply, and there may be difficulties over distribution of any surplus left over after the purposes have been achieved (see chapter 8). It may even be, as we have seen, that the Crown will take some or all of the surplus as *bona vacantia*, not perhaps the most fitting consequence of the altruism of the donors.

One of the problems with disaster appeals is that they are usually set up very quickly after the disaster has occurred, often before the full legal consequences have been considered. They may well be described as charitable, and donors may believe that their contributions are going to a charitable fund, only for the organisers later to change their minds and draft the purposes so as to avoid charitable status. An interesting question might then arise as to what happens to the money already contributed, in the (probably unlikely) event of a dispute (for example, if somebody who had contributed on the assumption that the fund was charitable objected when he discovered that it was not).

Chesterman, *Charities, Trusts and Social Welfare*
Weidenfeld & Nicholson Law in Context Series (1979), pp. 339–43

On 21 October 1966, a huge coal-tip belonging to the National Coal Board collapsed, crushing a school-house and about forty other buildings in the small Welsh village of Aberfan. One hundred and sixteen children (belonging to 99 families) and 28 adults were killed, and another 29 children injured. A public appeal launched almost immediately by the local mayor attracted nearly 90,000 separate donations. Within about two months, the fund totalled £1.5 million and it ultimately closed at nearly £1.75 million, of which about £83,000 was earmarked for specific purposes such as the benefit of bereaved families, memorials to the dead victims and building a play-ground for the surviving children, and the balance was for the general purposes of the appeal.

. . . If the legal concept of charity was based solely on the notion of disinterested giving with a view to relieving the unhappiness of others, the Aberfan trust would have been indisputably charitable . . . In fact, as the charity commissioners had warned in their report for 1965, disaster funds are not automatically charitable. . . . 'those responsible for drawing up appeals and trust deeds should use words to show that no person will receive assistance unless he is in need' . . . .

The commissioners' comments in their 1965 report clearly originated from the *Gillingham* and *Hobourn* decisions. Their view was a cautious one, because (a) the lack of 'public benefit' was conceded, without being argued, in *Gillingham* and (b) where the victims of a disaster are numerous, as in the *West Somerset* case [below] but not in *Gillingham*, the *Gillingham* dictum may not be appropriate. Nevertheless, when the Aberfan trust deed was drawn up, both the lawyers involved and the commissioners took the view that a restriction of benefit to victims 'in need' should be included. This placed the committee in something of a quandary. Neither the local community nor the donors (to whose wishes the committee, in their capacity as agents, were bound by law to pay some respect . . .) were in favour of anything in the nature of a means test. On the other hand, liability to taxation on the fund's substantial investment income and the possibility that, as in the *Gillingham* case itself, any surplus undisposed of might have to be returned to the donors on resulting trust constituted disincentives against drafting a trust which was not charitable.

. . . [E]ventually the charity commissioners' sanction had to be obtained to the distribution of a flat sum of £5,000 to each bereaved family, irrespective of its financial circumstances. This figure was thought sufficient to enable any family to move out of Aberfan if it so wished, or at least to start a new mode of life as an aid towards overcoming its grief. . . .

Re North Devon and West Somerset Relief Fund Trusts, Hylton v Wright
[1953] 1 WLR 1260, [1953] 2 All ER 1032
Chancery Division

Decision: An appeal fund set up after the Lynmouth flood disaster of 1952 was held charitable as being for the benefit of the community at large, and the surplus would therefore be applied cy près.

WYNN-PARRY J: The first question which I have to decide on this summons is whether the trusts affecting the funds mentioned in the evidence are valid charitable trusts. I accept, as, indeed, I am bound to do, that in the case such as this where the trust is clearly of a public nature, for the trusts to be good charitable trusts they must be shown not only to be beneficial to the community, or a defined section of the community, but beneficial in the way which the law regards as charitable. For that I need refer to no other authority than the opinion of Lord Simonds in *Williams' Trustees v Inland Revenue Comrs* [1947] AC 447.

The method by which such a question as this should be approached is, I conceive, laid down authoritatively by Chitty J, in *Re Foveaux*, where he says ([1895] 2 Ch 501):

Cases arise, such as the present, in which it is not easy to ascertain whether a particular institution is or is not a charity. Charity in law is a highly technical term. The method employed by the court is to consider the enumeration of charities in the statute of Elizabeth, bearing in mind that the enumeration is not exhaustive. Institutions whose objects are analogous to those mentioned in the statute are admitted to be charities; and, again, institutions which are analogous to those already admitted by reported decisions are held to be charities. The pursuit of these analogies obviously requires caution and circumspection. After all, the best that can be done is to consider each case as it arises, upon its own special circumstances.

Before turning to the vital document in this case, I would observe in passing, that in the recent case of *Re Hobourn Aero Components, Ltd's Air Raid Distress Fund* [1946] 1 All ER 501. . . .

[Wynn-Parry J quoted from the case and continued:]

With those considerations in view, I turn to the appeal for contributions which was launched in this case, because, in my judgment, the question is solely one of construction of this comparatively short document. In the first place, it is, I think, legitimate, and, indeed, necessary, to remember that this appeal was issued only three days after the disaster of Aug. 15, 1952, and it bears the stamp of having as its authors people who had not had time, if, indeed, the desirability ever crossed their minds, of consulting their legal advisers. I say that because in the case of such a document issued in such circumstances it does not appear to me proper that the court should be astute to fix on any particular word and give to it too wide or, in some circumstances, too narrow a meaning.

The appeal is headed: 'Appeal by the Lords Lieutenant of Devon and Somerset', and it opens with these words:

We invite not only the people of the west country, but everyone who has known and loved Lynmouth and the quiet villages of north Devon and west Somerset, which have suffered so grievously in this disaster, to contribute to a fund for the relief of all who have suffered.

In my view, too much emphasis can very easily be put on that word 'all', and, indeed, reliance was sought to be placed on the use of that word by counsel for the first defendant in their respective arguments. I think that that sentence, applying the elementary rule of construction, must be read together with the whole of the rest of the document. The document proceeds:

These villages have been overwhelmed by a tragedy terrible in its suddenness and completeness. Homes have been swept away with whole families. Others are bereaved, or homeless, or have nothing left. In the darkness of a single night part of the town of Lynmouth itself has disappeared for ever.

That, if may say so, with all respect, is a most dramatic and, for the purposes of the appeal, well-framed paragraph, and the whole emphasis there is on the results of the disaster so far as concerns distress, either through pecuniary suffering or through bodily suffering. The document goes on:

> The material damage will run into a figure far beyond the resources of the inhabitants of these stricken valleys.

That is a sentence which, in my judgment, it is most material to bear in mind, because it places great emphasis on the circumstances taken into consideration by the authors of the document and put by them before those to whom they appeal, and shows that the intention is to help financially those who, by reason of the magnitude of the disaster, are, whatever otherwise would have been their means, unable adequately to help themselves.

The document then condescends to a number of details as regards material damage, and mentions the serious loss of human life and human suffering, and proceeds:

> We hope and believe that this fund will meet a generous response far beyond the confines of the west country, for in its romantic beauty and appeal Lynmouth in particular was a possession not of one county, but of the nation.

In my view, in so far as that sentence could, on a strict view, be regarded as an intimation that the funds are required merely to restore amenities, it should not be given that construction in so far as that construction might tend to defeat what might otherwise have been said to be capable of being extracted from the document, viz., an intention to help relieve hardship and suffering by the charity of the community. It is merely a paragraph, to my mind, put in to emphasise that this distress and suffering which the appeal is designed to relieve has fallen on a district which was particularly beautiful. The document goes on:

> But those who have suffered are not only the local people. Many holiday-makers, notably the boy scouts who were camping at Filleigh, have suffered grievously. These need help every bit as much as our own people, and for that reason we do ask the whole country to support this fund.

The reasoning there is that it is desirable to put forward some ground which will help to justify an appeal to the whole country, and the ground put forward is that persons who could not be regarded as local people, but who, being in the area at the time of the disaster, themselves have suffered grievously, need help; and the help that is appealed for is, of course, financial help, because that is of the essence of the appeal. Then comes a general statement:

> This countryside, that has given pleasure to so many, will, we feel sure, be generously remembered in its hour of need by all those who have known it in happier days.

The last paragraph is one which deals merely with machinery and which, for this purpose, I need not read.

Looking at that document as a whole, I extract from it an intention on the part of the authors to apply the money which may be subscribed at their invitation to relieve hardship and suffering which has been experienced both by what are called 'the local people' and others who were within the area at the time of the disaster and to achieve that by the charity of the community. I am unable to dissect this document in such a way as to discover in it, either by looseness of phrasing, and, therefore, by inference, or by express words, any intention to benefit this part of the community in a way which the law would not regard as charitable.

For those reasons, I propose in answer to question (i) of the summons to declare that the trusts affecting the fund are valid charitable trusts.

Note
On the issue why the donations did not go to the donors on resulting trust, see chapter 8.

13   CY PRÈS

SECTION 1:   GENERAL PRINCIPLES

This Anglo-Norman phrase (which is sometimes hyphenated) meant something like 'as near as possible', and the doctrine of cy près in charity law lays down that where property given on trust for charitable purposes cannot be used in the precise manner intended by the donor, the court (and since about 130 years ago the Charity Commissioners) may make a scheme for the application of the property to purposes resembling as closely as possible the donor's original intention. The idea, in other words, is not to frustrate the intention of the donor (who cannot be consulted if the gift is testamentary) any more than necessary. The doctrine dates back at least as far as the seventeenth century. It only applies to charities – if private purposes fail, the results are as discussed in chapter 8.

The question whether cy près can be applied can arise either because it is clear from the outset that the donor's intention cannot be fulfilled, as where the organisation which he has singled out for benefit has already ceased to exist, or because at some later time, during the continuance of the trust, it turns out that the purposes cannot be achieved. Cy près is more easily invoked in the latter case, for once property has been dedicated to charity, there is no possibility of a resulting trust to the donor.

Where, however, a gift fails from the start, the courts have since the early-nineteenth century insisted that before the property can be applied cy près, a general or 'paramount' charitable intention must be shown.

SECTION 2:   INITIAL FAILURE

The question turns on whether the intention of the donor was specific or general. If it was to further some specific purpose which cannot be carried out, or benefit some specific institution no longer in existence, then the gift fails and the property will return to the settlor, or his estate, on a resulting trust, as discussed in chapter 8.

If, however, the intention is a more general one, which might be satisfied by applying the property to a purpose or institution similar to that specified, a cy près scheme may be ordered. The test, then, is whether a general or 'paramount' charitable intention can be found.

A: Charity Never Existed at All

(a)   Finding general charitable intention

In *Re Rymer* [1895] 1 Ch 19, a gift for a specific seminary which had ceased to exist failed. This is the general position where no paramount (or general) charitable intention can be found. Whether a general charitable intention can be shown is a question of fact, and the cases in this section are illustrations of the factors that can be taken into account, and are not cited as authorities.

If the charity specified by the donor has never existed at all, it is usually easier to discover a general charitable intention than where the charity once existed but has since ceased (as in *Re Rymer*), since only a general intention can be attributed to the donor who fails correctly to specify the beneficiary. For example, in *Re Harwood* [1936] Ch 285, a gift was made to the Peace Society in Belfast, which could not be shown ever to have existed. Farwell J found that there was an intention to benefit societies aimed at promoting peace, and the gift was therefore applied cy près. A second gift in the will, in favour of the Wisbech Peace Society, which had once existed but had ceased to do so prior to the testatrix's death, was held, however, to have lapsed.

Another possibility, suggested by the following case, is what is sometimes termed 'charity by association'. The authority for the existence of this doctrine cannot be said to be conclusive, however.

Re Satterthwaite's WT, Midland Bank Executor & Trustee Co. v *Royal Veterinary College*
[1966] 1 WLR 277, [1966] 1 All ER 919
Court of Appeal

Facts: Under the testatrix's will, her residuary estate was to be divided in approximately equal proportions among nine organisations, all of whose names appeared to show that they were concerned with animal welfare. One was unidentifiable; six were charities; another was the Animal Defence and Anti-Vivisection Society, which for long was considered to be a charity (but not, of course, since the *National Anti-Vivisection Society* case considered in the last chapter), and another was the 'London Animal Hospital'. The list had been thoughtlessly compiled from the London telephone directory, the testatrix's chief concern being to divert her estate to animal charities, because she hated the whole human race. The London Animal Hospital had never existed as a charity.

Held: The Court of Appeal held that the gift to the London Animal Hospital should be applied cy près.

HARMAN LJ: There remains the claim of the Attorney-General that a general charitable intent is shown. On this I have felt the gravest doubts. If a particular donee were intended which cannot be identified, no general intent would follow. When one looks at the whole of the residuary bequest, however, it seems plain that each share is intended to go to some object connected with the care or the cure of animals. That anti-vivisection has been declared not to be in law a charitable object (see *National Anti-Vivisection Society v Inland Revenue Comrs* [1948] AC 31) is irrelevant. The society exists to save animals from suffering. The other names make the same sort of suggestion, though it is true that the evidence suggested that the word 'clinic' often indicated a place where the business of animal surgery was carried on rather than a charitable organisation.

The judge has held that there is a general charitable intent sufficient to cause share No. (8) to be applied cy près, and it would be inconsistent to come to a different conclusion in the case of share No. (4) if, as I have held, the object there too is not identifiable. It follows that a scheme must in this instance also be settled.

RUSSELL LJ (after stating the facts): What is the result in law of this? I have already indicated that she is to be taken as intending to benefit a charitable activity; but the organisation picked by name was not such. *Prima facie*, therefore, the bequest would fail and there would be a lapse, with the result in this case in fact – owing to the incidence of liabilities and death duties – of mere relief of other residuary objects. My assumption, however, is that the testatrix was pointing to a particular charitable application of this one-ninth of residue. If a particular mode of charitable application is incapable of being performed as such, but it can be discerned from his will that the testator has a charitable intention (commonly referred to as a general charitable intention) which transcends the particular mode of application indicated, the court has jurisdiction to direct application of the bequest to charitable purposes cy près. Here I have no doubt from the nature of the other dispositions by this testatrix of her residuary estate that a general intention can be discerned in favour of charity through the medium of kindness to animals. I am not in any way deterred from this conclusion by the fact that one-ninth of residue was given to an anti-vivisection society which in law – unknown to the average testator – is not charitable (see *National Anti-Vivisection Society v Inland Revenue Comrs* [1948] AC 31).

Accordingly in my judgment the correct answer in this case is that the one-ninth share in question is not payable to the third defendant but should be applied cy près and to that end the matter should be referred to chambers for settlement of a scheme.

DIPLOCK LJ: With that humility which is becoming in a common law lawyer when confronted with such an arcane branch of the Chancery law, I agree with the judgments which have been delivered.

Notes

1. The authority for the doctrine of charity by association comes from Russell LJ's opinion, which was that a general intention to benefit animal charities could be inferred from the testatrix's known attitude towards the human race, and from the fact that all but one the other dispositions were made in favour of genuine animal charities. But Harman LJ expressed 'the gravest doubts', and seems to have been swayed more by Plowman J's finding (at first instance) of a general charitable intent regarding one of the other gifts. Diplock LJ agreed with both viewpoints!

2.   Limited additional authority for the doctrine of charity by association may be found in *Re Finger's WT* (below) regarding the gift to the National Council for Maternity and Child Welfare (the incorporated body), but there were additional factors and the decision was distinguished in *Re Spence* (below).

3.   A better explanation of *Re Satterthwaite* may be that, as with the Peace Society in Belfast in *Re Harwood* [1936] Ch 285, the London Animal Hospital had never existed as a charity. In *Re Jenkins' WT* [1966] Ch 249, Buckley J declined to hold that a gift to the British Union for the Abolition of Vivisection (which did exist but was not charitable) could be taken as charitable simply by being included in a list of gifts to unquestionably charitable organisations.

4.   Sir Robert Megarry V-C refused to apply what he described as the doctrine of 'charity by association' in *Re Spence* [1979] Ch 483, on the grounds that the *Re Satterthwaite* only applied where the body had never existed.

Re Spence (decd), Ogden v Shackleton
[1979] Ch 483, [1978] 3 WLR 483, [1978] 3 All ER 92
Chancery Division

Decision: A gift to an old folks home failed because it was a gift for a specific charitable purpose which, though possible when the will was made, had become impossible before the testatrix died. No general charitable intention could be inferred.

MEGARRY V-C: Counsel's other contention for the Attorney-General was that the will displayed a sufficient general charitable intention for the moiety to be applied cy-près. In doing this he had to contend with *Re Harwood* [1936] Ch 285. This, and cases which apply it, such as *Re Stemson's WT* [1970] Ch 16, establish that it is very difficult to find a general charitable intention where the testator has selected a particular charity, taking some care to identify it, and the charity then ceases to exist before the testator's death. This contrasts with cases where the charity described in the will has never existed, when it is much easier to find a general charitable intention.

These cases have been concerned with gifts to institutions, rather than gifts for purposes. The case before me, on the other hand, is gift for a purpose, namely, the benefit of the patients at a particular old folks home. It therefore seems to me that I ought to consider the question, of which little or nothing was said in argument, whether the principle in *Re Harwood*, or a parallel principle, has any application to such a case. In other words, is a similar distinction to be made between, on the one hand, a case in which the testator has selected a particular charitable purpose, taking some care to identify it, and before the testator dies that purpose has become impracticable or impossible of accomplishment, and on the other hand a case where the charitable purpose has never been possible or practicable?

As at present advised I would answer Yes to that question. I do not think that the reasoning of the *Re Harwood* line of cases is directed to any feature of institutions as distinct from purposes. Instead, I think the essence of the distinction is in the difference between particularity and generality. If a particular institution or purpose is specified, then it is that institution or purpose, and no other, that is to be the object of the benefaction. It is difficult to envisage a testator as being suffused with a general glow of broad charity when he is labouring, and labouring successfully, to identify some particular specified institution or purpose as the object of his bounty. The specific displaces the general. It is otherwise where the testator has been unable to specify any particular charitable institution or practicable purpose, and so, although his intention of charity can be seen, he has failed to provide any way of giving effect to it. There, the absence of the specific leaves the general undisturbed. It follows that in my view in the case before me, where the testatrix has clearly specified a particular charitable purpose which before her death become impossible to carry out, counsel for the Attorney-General has to face that level of great difficulty in demonstrating the existence of a general charitable intention which was indicated by *Re Harwood*.

One way in which counsel sought to meet that difficulty was by citing *Re Finger's WT* [1972] 1 Ch 286. There, Goff J distinguished *Re Harwood* and held that the will before him displayed a general charitable intention. He did this on the footing that the circumstances of the case were 'very special'. The gift that failed was a gift to an incorporated charity which had ceased to exist before the testatrix died. The 'very special' circumstances were, first, that apart from a life interest and two small legacies, the whole estate was devoted to charity, and that this was emphasised by the direction to hold the residue in trust for division 'between the following charitable institutions and funds'. Second, the charitable donee that had ceased to exist was mainly, if not exclusively, a coordinating body, and the judge could not believe that the testatrix meant to benefit that body alone. Third, there was evidence that the testatrix regarded herself as having no relatives.

In the case before me neither of these last two circumstances applies, nor have any substitute special circumstances been suggested. As for the first, the will before me gives 17 pecuniary legacies to relations and friends, amounting in all to well over one-third of the net estate. Further, in *Re Rymer* [1895] 1 Ch 19, which does not appear to have been cited, the will had prefaced the disputed gift by the words 'I give the following charitable legacies to the following institutions and persons respectively'. These words correspond to the direction which in *Re Finger's WT* was regarded as providing emphasis, and yet they did not suffice to avoid the conclusion of Chitty J and the Court of Appeal that a gift to an institution which had ceased to exist before the testator's death lapsed and could not be applied cy-près. I am not sure that I have been able to appreciate to the full the cogency of the special circumstances that appealed to Goff J; but however that may be, I can see neither those nor any other special circumstances in the present case which would suffice to distinguish *Re Harwood*.

The other way in which counsel for the Attorney-General sought to meet his difficulty was by relying on *Re Satterthwaite's WT* [1966] 1 WLR 277 (which he said was his best case), and on *Re Knox* [1937] Ch 109, which I think may possibly be better. The doctrine may for brevity be described as charity by association. If the will gives the residue among a number of charities with kindred objects, but one of the apparent charities does not in fact exist, the court will be ready to find a general charitable intention and so apply the share of the non-existent charity cy-près. I have not been referred to any explicit statement of the underlying principle, but it seems to me that in such cases the court treats the testator as having shown the general intention of giving his residue to promote charities with that type of kindred objects, and then, when he comes to dividing the residue, as casting round for particular charities when that type of objects to name as donees. If one or more of these are non-existent, then the general intention will suffice for a cy-près application. It will be observed that, as stated, the doctrine depends, at least to some extent, on the detection of 'kindred objects' (a phrase which comes from the judgment of Luxmoore J in *Re Knox* [1937] Ch 109 at 113) in the charities to which the shares of residue are given; in this respect the charities must in some degree be *ejusdem generis*.

In *Re Satterthwaite's WT* the residuary gift was to nine charitable bodies which were all concerned with kindness to animals; but the gifts to two of them failed as no bodies could be found which sufficiently answered the descriptions in the will. Harman LJ said [1966] 1 WLR 277 at 284 that he 'felt the gravest doubts' whether a general charitable intent had been shown. However, at first instance the judge had held that in respect of one of the bodies a sufficient general charitable intention had been displayed, and as there had been no appeal as to that share, he (Harman LJ) would reach the same conclusion in respect of the other share, which was the subject of the appeal. On the other hand, Russell LJ had no doubt that a general charitable intention had been shown [1966] 1 WLR 277 at 286. Diplock LJ delivered a single sentence judgment agreeing with both the other judgments. The support which this case provides for counsel for the Attorney-General accordingly seems to me to be a trifle muted.

In *Re Knox* Luxmoore J distilled a general charitable intention out of a residuary gift in quarters to two named infirmaries, a named nursing home and Dr Barnado's Homes. No institution existed which correctly answered the description of the nursing home, and it was held that the quarter share that had been given to it should be applied cy-près. I am not entirely sure what genus the judge had in mind as embracing the infirmaries and Dr Barnado's Homes when he said [1937] Ch 109 at 113 that 'the object of each of the other charities is a kindred object to that which is to be inferred from the name' of the nursing home: perhaps it was the provision of residential accommodation for those in need. Perhaps I should also mention *Re Hartley (decd)* (15th March 1978) unreported, a decision of mine in a case in which the Attorney-General was one of the parties. In that case, *Re Knox* was applied to a will when the residue was given in quarters between service charities of a benevolent nature. It was held that a general charitable intention had been shown which sufficed for the cy-près application of the share given to a body of that nature which did not exist at the date of the will. A body which might have answered the description in the will had existed some years earlier.

It will be observed that these are all cases of gifts to bodies which did not exist. In such cases, the court is ready to find a general charitable intention: see *Re Davis* [1902] 1 Ch 876 at 884. The court is far less ready to find such an intention where the gift is to a body which existed at the date of the will but ceased to exist before the testator died, or, as I have already held, where the gift is for a purpose which, though possible and practicable at the date of the will, has ceased to be so before the testator's death. The case before me is, of course, a case in this latter category, so that counsel for the Attorney-General has to overcome this greater difficulty in finding a general charitable intention. Not only does counsel have this greater difficulty: he also has, I think, less material with which to meet it. He has to extract the general charitable intention for the gift which fails from only one other gift: the residue, of course, was simply divided into two. In *Re Knox* and *Re Hartley (decd)* the gifts which failed were each among three other gifts, and in *Re Satterthwaite's WT* there were seven or eight other gifts. I do not say that a general charitable intention or a genus cannot be extracted from a gift of residue equally between two: but I do say that larger numbers are likely to assist in conveying to the court a sufficient conviction both of the genus and of the generality of the charitable intention.

Notes

1. In addition to distinguishing *Re Satterthwaite* on the basis that the London Animal Hospital did not exist at all, Megarry V-C noted that both there and in *Re Knox*, all the objects named were 'kindred objects': charity by association, if it applies at all, requires more than merely that all the objects be charitable.
2. It must be emphasised that the question is ultimately one of fact, and the above cases should be treated as examples rather than authorities.

(b) Non-existent body, but no initial failure

Even where the charity specified does not exist, it may be possible to save the gift if the institution can be said to continue to exist in some other form. In recent years many small charities have amalgamated, and it is sometimes possible to regard the new body thus formed as being the same as the old. In *Re Faraker* [1912] 2 Ch 488, for example, a gift to 'Mrs Bailey's charity, Rotherhithe' (which was taken to mean 'Hannah Bayly's Charity') passed to the new charity formed by an amalgamation of Hannah Bayly's Charity with several others.

Another approach is to find that the gift was made for the *purpose* of the named charity, rather than for the body itself. If the body is unincorporated, then by definition the gift cannot be to it but must be to its purposes, and if those purposes can still be fulfilled, the gift will not fail. Since there is no failure, there is no need to show a general charitable intention. Indeed, this is not an application of cy près as such, but rather an instance of finding a substitute trustee to carry out the purposes of the trust. Where the body is a corporation, however, a gift to it will *prima facie* lapse if the corporation has ceased to exist, just as a gift to a human individual would lapse if the person concerned had died before the gift was made. The gift may be rescued only on the cy près principles already outlined, i.e., if the court is able to find a general charitable intention going beyond the specific aim of benefiting the named corporate charity.

Re Finger's WT, Turner v Ministry of Health
[1972] 1 Ch 286
Chancery Division

Facts: Testamentary gifts were made to the National Radium Commission, an unincorporated association, and to the National Council for Maternity and Child Welfare, which was a corporate charity. Both had ceased to exist by the time the testatrix died.

Held: The gift to the National Radium Commission was interpreted as a gift to its purposes, and since these still continued, the gift did not fail. The gift to the National Council for Maternity and Child Welfare would have failed, except that in the case it was possible to discern a general charitable intention which allowed for the application of the gift cy-près.

GOFF J: If the matter were *res integra* I would have thought that there would be much to be said for the view that the status of the donee, whether corporate or incorporate, can make no difference to the question whether as a matter of construction a gift is absolute or on trust for purposes. Certainly drawing such a distinction produces anomalous results.

In my judgment, however, on the authorities a distinction between the two is well established, at all events in this court. I refer first to *Re Vernon's WT* [1972] Ch 300 where Buckley J said at p. 303C–G:

> Every bequest to an unincorporated charity by name without more must take effect as a gift for a charitable purpose. No individual or aggregate of individuals could claim to take such a bequest beneficially. If the gift is to be permitted to take effect at all, it must be as a bequest for a purpose, viz., that charitable purpose which the named charity exists to serve. A bequest which is in terms made for a charitable purpose will not fail for lack of a trustee but will be carried into effect either under the Sign Manual or by means of a scheme. A bequest to a named unincorporated charity, however, may on its true interpretation show that the testator's intention to make the gift at all was dependent upon the named charitable organisation being available at the time when the gift takes effect to serve as the instrument for applying the subject-matter of the gift to the charitable purpose for which it is by inference given. If so and the named charity ceases to exist in the lifetime of the testator, the gift fails: *Re Ovey* (1885) 29 ChD 560. A bequest to a corporate body, on the other hand, takes effect simply as a gift to that body beneficially, unless there are circumstances which show that the recipient is to take the gift as a trustee. There is no need in such a case to infer a trust for any particular purpose. The objects to which the corporate body can properly apply its funds may be restricted by its constitution, but this does not necessitate inferring as a matter of construction of the testator's will a direction that the bequest is to be held in trust to be applied for those purposes: the natural construction is that the bequest is made to the corporate body as part of its general funds, that is to say, beneficially and without the imposition of any trust. That the testator's motive in making the bequest may have undoubtedly been to assist the work of the incorporated body would be insufficient to create a trust.

. . .

As I read the dictum in *Re Vernon's WT* [1972] Ch 300, the view of Buckley J was that in the case of an unincorporated body the gift is *per se* a purpose trust, and provided that the work is still being carried on will have effect given to it by way of a scheme notwithstanding the disappearance of the donee in the lifetime of the testator, unless there is something positive to show that the continued existence of the donee was essential to the gift. Then Buckley J put his dictum into practice and decided *Re Morrison* (1967) 111 SJ 758 on that very basis, for there was nothing in that case beyond the bare fact of a gift to a dissolved unincorporated committee. In the case of a corporation, however, *Re Vernon* shows that the position is different as there has to be something positive in the will to create a purpose trust at all. . . .

Accordingly I hold that the bequest to the National Radium Commission being a gift to an unincorporated charity is a purpose trust for the work of the commission which does not fail but is applicable under a scheme, provided (1) there is nothing in the context of the will to show – and I quote from *Re Vernon's WT* – that the testatrix's intention to make a gift at all was dependent upon the named charitable organisation being available at the time when the gift took effect to serve as the instrument for applying the subject matter of the gift to the charitable purpose for which it was by inference given; (2) that charitable purpose still survives; but that the gift to the National Council for Maternity and Child Welfare, 117 Piccadilly, London being a gift to a corporate body fails, notwithstanding the work continues, unless there is a context in the will to show that the gift was intended to be on trust for that purpose and not an absolute gift to the corporation.

[He went on to hold that the gift to the National Council for Maternity and Child Welfare failed (at 299A), but that a cy près scheme could be applied since a general charitable intention was shown.] See further on this aspect of the case *Re Spence*, above.

Notes

1. If the body is unincorporated, then by definition the gift cannot be to it but must be to its purposes. Where the body is a corporation, however, a gift to it will *prima facie* lapse if the corporation has ceased to exist, just as a gift to a human individual would lapse if the person concerned had died before the gift was made. The gift may be rescued only on the cy-près principles applicable to initial failure, i.e., if the court is able to find a general charitable intention going beyond the specific aim of benefiting the named corporate charity. This was the outcome of the case itself, so far as the National Council for Maternity and Child Welfare was concerned.

2. Since the gift to the National Radium Commission was construed as a gift to its purposes, all the court needed to do was to settle a scheme to apply the property elsewhere. This is not a cy-près scheme as such, but rather an instance of finding a substitute trustee to carry out the purposes of the trust. It would not have been necessary to look for any general charitable intention above and beyond those purposes.

3. Similar principles were applied in *Re Koeppler's WT* [1986] Ch 423, chapter 13, where Slade LJ construed a gift to a non-existent body as a valid trust for educational purposes. The non-existent body there was treated as analogous to the National Radium Commission in this case.

B: Gifts with Conditions Attached

It is possible for there to be an initial failure even where the institution to whom the donation is made exists, but where there is a condition in the gift which the donee body finds unacceptable.

Re Lysaght (decd)
[1966] 1 Ch 191, [1965] 2 All ER 888, [1965] 3 WLR 391
Chancery Division

Facts: The testatrix left £5,000 to the Royal College of Surgeons in order to establish and maintain one or more studentships. There was a condition, contained in clause 11(d) of the will, which would have disqualified Jews and Roman Catholics, and the College declined to accept the gift on these terms. They were happy to accept the gift without the conditions.

Held:

(a)   The conditions could not be struck out on grounds of uncertainty or public policy.

(b)   The gift was saved nonetheless, because the court found a general charitable intention on the part of the testatrix, to establish medical studentships. The cy près doctrine therefore operated; the condition could be deleted as not being essential to the fulfilment of the general intention. A scheme was ordered on the terms of the will as it stood without the condition.

BUCKLEY J: The question in this case is whether a bequest for charitable purposes which was contained in the will, dated June 22, 1960, of a testatrix who died on January 2, 1962 is effective or whether it fails on the grounds that it is impracticable to carry it into effect. [Buckley J, stated the facts and continued]: The first question for decision is whether the trust declared by clause 11 of the will in respect of the endowment fund are effective, or whether on the true construction of the will and in the events which have happened they fail. The Royal College of Surgeons, which I shall refer to as 'the college,' when informed by the executors of the bequest, stated, through their solicitors, that the college could not accept it in the terms stated in the will because the provision that a student must not be of the Jewish or Roman Catholic faith was, as they put it, 'so invidious and so alien to the spirit of the college's work as to make the gift inoperable in that form,' but they went on to say that the college would be most happy to accept the bequest with that one provision deleted.

Mr Morris Smith for the college has submitted that the condition that a student must be not of the Jewish or Roman Catholic faith is void for uncertainty, citing *Clayton* v *Ramsden* [1943] AC 320 and *In re Wolffe* [1953] 2 All ER 697. He further submits that, since a charitable trust cannot fail for uncertainty (*In re Gott* [1944] Ch 193) the trusts of the endownment fund are valid.

Mr Balcombe for the personal representatives of Henry Lysaght says that, although the court can by means of a scheme cure any uncertainty in a charitable gift, it should depart no further from the terms of the will than is necessary to achieve that end, and that any scheme which the court could devise in the present case to eliminate any uncertainty in the offending provision would still leave a provision involving religious discrimination in the trusts which would consequently still be unacceptable to the college. He goes on to say that, since it was an essential feature of the testatrix's intention that the college and no one else should be the trustee of the endowment fund, it would remain impossible to carry her intention into effect, notwithstanding any such scheme, if the college were still to refuse to act as the trustee, as it is common ground that they would so long as the trusts involve religious discrimination. Mr Balcombe further says that by reason of the element of religious discrimination the trusts are void as contrary to public policy.

The Attorney-General, while he concedes on the one hand that the will discloses no general charitable intent, submits on the other that the primary object of the gift is the establishment of a medical studentship; that the detailed provisions of clause 11 are machinery and are not essential parts of that primary object; that the provision requiring religious discrimination is at least undesirable and militates against the beneficial effect of the charity, and that the court can accordingly by way of scheme eliminate it. In making such a concession and at the same time presenting such submissions, I think that the Attorney-General is giving with one hand and taking away with the other.

Let me consider for a moment the meaning of the term 'general charitable intent.' Whether a donor has or has not evinced such an intent is relevant in any case in which the donor has made a charitable gift in terms which cannot be carried out exactly. In such a case the court has to discover whether the donor's true intention can be carried out notwithstanding that it is impracticable to give effect to some part of his particular directions. I take by way of example four imaginary testators. The first bequeaths a fund for charitable purposes generally, the second for the relief of poverty, the third for the relief of poverty in the parish of 'X,' the fourth for the relief of a particular class of poor (for example, of a particular faith or of a particular age group) in the parish of 'X.' Each of them couples with his bequest an indication of a particular manner in which the gift should be carried into effect, say, by paying the fares of poor persons travelling by rail from the village of 'X' to the town of 'Y' to obtain medical advice and attention. Between the dates of the wills and of the deaths of the four testators the railway between 'X' and 'Y' is closed, so that it becomes impossible for anyone to travel by rail from the one to the other. In each case the court must consider whether it was an essential part of the testator's intention that his benefaction should be carried into effect in all respects in the particular manner indicated and no other, or whether his true intention was, in the first case to make a gift for charitable purposes without qualification; in the second, to relieve poverty; in the third, to relieve poverty in the parish of 'X' and in the fourth, to relieve the poverty of the particular class of persons in the parish of 'X'; the specification of a particular mode of giving effect to such intention being merely an indication of a desire on his part in this respect: see the well-known passage in the judgment of Parker J in *In re Wilson* [1913] 1 Ch 314 at 320, 321. If on the true construction of any of the wills the latter is the true view, the court will, if it can, carry the testator's true intention into effect in some other way cy-près to the impracticable method indicated by the testator. In so doing the court is not departing from the testator's intention but giving effect to his true paramount intention. Such an intention is called a general, charitable intention. It is not general in the sense of being unqualified in any way or as being confined only to some general head of charity. It is general in contrast with the particular charitable intention which would have been shown by any of the four supposed testators who upon the true construction of his will intended to benefit poor people by paying their railway fares when travelling by rail between 'X' and 'Y' to obtain medical advice and attention and in no other way. Such a general intention would not avail if the court could find no practical or legal method of giving effect to it – if, for instance, it could be shown in respect of the bequest of the fourth testator that at the relevant time there were no poor people of the particular class specified in his will to be found in the parish of 'X' and there was no reasonable likelihood of there being any such at any foreseeable time in the future. The question would then arise whether the testator's true intention was restricted to benefiting this particular class of poor people or whether he had some yet more general charitable intent to which the court could give effect.

A general charitable intention, then, may be said to be a paramount intention on the part of a donor to effect some charitable purpose which the court can find a method of putting into operation, notwithstanding that it is impracticable to give effect to some direction by the donor which is not an essential part of his true intention – not, that is to say, part of his paramount intention.

In contrast, a particular charitable intention exists where the donor means his charitable disposition to take effect if, but only if, it can be carried into effect in a particular specified way, for example, in connection with a particular school to be established at a particular place, *In re Wilson*, or by establishing a home in a particular house: *In re Packe* [1918] 1 Ch 437. The alternatives are neatly stated by Younger LJ in *In re Willis* [1921] 1 Ch 44, 54:

> The problem which in this case we have to solve is to say by which of two different principles the construction of this gift has to be controlled. The first of these principles is that if a testator has manifested a general intention to give to charity, whether in general terms or to charities of a defined character or quality, the failure of the particular mode in which the charitable intention is to be effectuated shall not imperil the charitable gift. If the substantial intention is charitable the court will substitute some other mode of carrying it into effect. The other principle which I paraphrase from the judgment of Kay J in *Biscoe* v *Jackson* (1887) 35 ChD 460 at 463 is this. If on the proper construction of the will the mode of application is such an essential part of the gift that you cannot distinguish any general purpose of charity but are obliged to say that the prescribed mode of doing the charitable act is the only one the testator intended or at all contemplated, then the court cannot, if that mode fails, apply the money cy près.

When, therefore, the Attorney-General submits that the primary intention of the testatrix in the present case was to found a medical studentship and that the detailed directions contained in clause 11 are not essential to that intention, he is, I think, contending, notwithstanding his concession to the contrary, that the testatrix had a general charitable intention, that is to say, a paramount intention to which the court can give effect, notwithstanding that it may be impracticable or, as Mr Clauson suggests, impolitic to give effect to that part of those detailed directions which requires religious discrimination. I proceed, therefore, to consider how far (a) the selection of the college as the trustee of the endowment fund and (b) the provision for religious discrimination, are essential parts of the testatrix's intention.

The recital with which clause 11 opens is an expression of the testatrix's motive for making a charitable gift and no more, but as such it is, I think, very relevant to the ascertainment of her true intention. It shows that her aim was to establish medical studentships in the gift of the president and council of the college. . . . In my judgment, upon the proper construction of clause 11 of the testatrix's will the essentials of her intention expressed in that clause were (a) to found medical studentships which (b) should be administered by the governing body of the college (c) for the purposes set out in paragraph (E) of clause 11 [para. (E) set out the purposes of the studentships]. These parts of the clause state her objective, and in them, in my judgment, the heart of her intention is to be found. The remaining provisions of clause 11 may not unfairly be said to deal with the machinery of the trust. This is . . . less clearly so in the cases of paragraphs (D) and (F) dealing with eligibility [para. (f) required a student to be married and between 19 and 30], but I can find nothing . . . which suggests that these regulations as to eligibility were essential parts of her objective. . . . I recognise that . . . the whole clause should be taken in its entirety, but in doing so I am left with the clear impression that the testatrix's true and overriding intention is to be found in the recital . . . and that paragraphs (D) and (F) contain directions to which the testatrix had doubtless given anxious and careful thought but which do not form essential parts of that intention. . . . This does not mean that, so far as they can be given effect consistently with giving effect to the paramount intention of the testatrix, they need not be complied with. It does, however, mean that, in so far as it is impossible to give effect to them, or impossible to do so consistently with carrying out the paramount intention, this will not jeopardise the validity of the bequest.

On these grounds I think that the Attorney-General is justified in his submission that clause 11 (D) is not an essential part of the primary and paramount object of the testatrix in respect of the endowment fund.

As regards the trusteeship it is noteworthy that the testatrix confers important discretionary powers upon the college . . . to regulate the object which each student shall be required to pursue and the quality and conduct of students. Although another trustee could, no doubt, be found capable of exercising these discretions, the college is obviously a body particularly suited to exercise them. This circumstance alone would, I think, be insufficient to establish that the personality of the trustee was of the essence of the testatrix's intention, but, coupled with the recital of the testatrix's wish to found studentships 'within the gift of the President and Council of this College,' it satisfies me that it was the particular wish of the testatrix that the college should be the trustee of this fund because of its peculiar aptitude for the office, and that it was to the college and to no one else that she meant to confide these discretionary powers.

In my judgment, the present case is to be distinguished from cases like *Moggridge* v *Thackwell* (1803) 7 Ves 36 and *In re Willis* [1921] 1 Ch 44 where bequests were made to charities to be selected by a named person who predeceased the testator. In each of those cases the testator was held to have shown an intention to benefit charitable purposes generally, leaving only the mode of application to the selection of the named person. Selection by that person having become impossible, the court carried the testator's intention into effect by way of a scheme. In the present case, on the other hand, I reach the conclusion that the intention of the testatrix was confined to establishing a charitable trust of which the college should be the trustee and so was conditional upon the college being able and willing to accept that office.

Are, then, the circumstances such as to justify the court in permitting the trusts of the endowment fund to be administered without regard to so much of clause 11 (D) as requires religious discrimination?

[Buckley J concluded that the discrimination clauses were neither uncertain nor affected by public policy (see chapter 6) and continued, on the issue of practicability:]

I do not understand the college to assert that it would be legally incapable of accepting the trusts of the endowment and giving them effect with due regard to the provision for religious discrimination. It is not suggested that this would be ultra vires the college. What I understand from their solicitor's letter which is in evidence and from what counsel has stated in court is that on account of the character of the college and of the purposes which it exists to serve, the college would be unalterably opposed to accepting and administering a trust containing any provision for religious discrimination.

Obviously a trustee will not normally be permitted to modify the terms of his trust on the ground that his own opinions or convictions conflict with them. If his conscience will not allow him to carry out the trust faithfully in accordance with its terms, he must make way for a trustee who can and will do so. But how, if the identity of the trustee selected by the settlor is essential to his intention? If it is of the essence of a trust that the trustees selected by the settlor and no one else shall act as the trustees of it and those trustees cannot or will not undertake the office, the trust must fail: *In re Lawton* [1936] 3 All ER 378 and see *Reeve* v *Attorney-General* (1843) 3 Hare 191 at 197 and Tudor on Charities, 5th ed., (1929), p. 128. I have already reached the conclusion that it is an essential part of the testatrix's intention that the college should be the trustee of the endowment fund. The college is, as I have said, unalterably opposed to accepting the trust if any provision for religious discrimination is an effective part of it. That part or paragraph (D) which requires religious discrimination, if it is to be insisted upon, will consequently defeat the testatrix's intention entirely, for in that case the college must disclaim the trust with the result that it will fail.

The impracticability of giving effect to some inessential part of the testatrix's intention cannot, in my judgment, be allowed to defeat her paramount charitable intention.

In *In re Robinson* [1923] 2 Ch 332 P.O. Lawrence J had to deal with a fund bequeathed many years earlier for the endowment of a church of an evangelical character to which conditions were attached, including what was called an 'abiding' condition that a black gown should be worn in the pulpit unless this should become illegal. The evidence showed that in 1923 the wearing of a black gown in the pulpit, though not illegal, would be detrimental to the teaching and practice of evangelical doctrines and services in the church in question. Lawrence J had to determine whether a scheme could properly be sanctioned dispensing with the observance of this condition.

[Buckley J set out part of the judgment, which is given in greater detail in the extract from the case, below, and continued: . . .] The judge held on the evidence that the effect of insisting upon the condition would be to defeat the main intention of the testatrix. He held that, although compliance with the condition was not impossible in an absolute sense, it was impracticable and ought to be dispensed with.

In that case compliance with the condition relating to the black gown was not impracticable at the inception of the trust in 1889, but had become so by 1923. In the present case, if the trust is impracticable, this is due to an initial difficulty, not to any change of circumstances. Since *In re Robinson* [1923] 2 Ch 332 was decided it has been recognised that different considerations govern the application of the cy près doctrine when impracticability supervenes after a charitable trust has once taken effect from those which apply in cases of initial impracticability. In cases of supervening impracticability it matters not whether the original donor had or had not a general charitable intention (see *In re Wright* [1954] Ch 347 at 362). It was not, however, on any such ground as this that the decision in *In re Robinson* was based. The passage which I have read from the judgment of P.O. Lawrence J makes it clear that he decided as he did because, in his opinion, the testatrix's dominant intention was to endow a church and that the condition as to wearing a black gown was not an essential part of that intention but merely subsidiary.

If I am right in the view that I have formed, that it was an essential part of the testatrix's intention in the present case that the college should be the trustee of the endowment fund, then I think that the reasoning in *In re Robinson* is precisely applicable to the present case. Just as insistence on the black gown condition would in *In re Robinson* have defeated the paramount intention of the testatrix, so insistence on the provision for religious discrimination would defeat the paramount intention of the testatrix in the present case: indeed it would destroy the trust, for it would result in the college disclaiming the trusteeship, which would occasion the failure of the trust.

Accordingly, in my judgment, the court can and should enable the college to carry the trust into effect without any element of religious discrimination.

Notes

1. *Re Robinson* is a case on subsequent failure and is considered further below. In that case, the gift towards an endowment for a proposed evangelical church had taken effect, and the condition was held subsequently to have become impracticable. Since there was therefore no initial failure in *Robinson*, there was no need to find a general or paramount charitable intention. In

Lysaght, by contrast, there would be an initial failure unless a general charitable intention could be found. But once a general charitable intention could be found a cy près scheme could be adopted, and then the conditions could be struck out on the same basis as in *Robinson.*

2.   *Re Lysaght*was followed in *Re Woodhams* [1981] 1 WLR 493, where a general charitable intention to foster musical education was found, allowing the court to remove the restriction which would have limited scholarships to boys from two named children's homes, and which also prevented the donees from accepting the gift.

3.   It may be wondered why the gift fails unless the conditions are deleted. 'Equity will not allow a trust to fail for want of a trustee', and in principle it might be thought that the court should find a trustee who is prepared to carry out the terms of the trust on the settlor's terms. In other words, it should not be necessary to delete the repugnant condition.

In a case like *Re Lysaght,* however, the identity of the donee is essential to the purposes of the trust, and were the Royal College to decline the gift another trustee simply could not be found to carry out the testatrix's intention.

Question
In the light of the detailed provisions in the will in *Re Lysaght,* and the fact that the gift was clearly intended for a particular institution, can it really be said that the testatrix had displayed a general charitable intention?

Harris v Sharp
(unreported) 21 March 1989
Court of Appeal

Facts: Mr Sharp had left £50,000 with his solicitors, and executed a memorandum giving them irrevocable authority to make a gift of that sum to provide a fellowship in paediatric surgery at Liverpool Royal Children's Hospital. It seems that the motivation for this memorandum was that he had been guilty of embezzling the funds of another charitable trust, and wished to use the memorandum in mitigation against sentence.

The Liverpool Health Authority, which had authority to act for the hospital, believed that the £50,000 was part of the fruits of the embezzlement, and indicated that it intended to refuse the gift. Sharp, who had by now been sentenced, thereupon decided he wanted the money back, whereupon the Health Authority promptly changed its mind and claimed to keep the gift. Mervyn Davies J (see [1988] Conv 288) held that the memorandum had created a charitable trust, and that neither the hospital nor the Health Authority had any standing to disclaim the gift, since neither was donee. Hence the purported disclaimer by the Health Authority was ineffective. Sharp appealed.

Held: The appeal would be dismissed.

FOX LJ: This is an appeal by the first defendant, Mr Robert Sharp, from a decision of Mervyn Davies J. On 6th September 1982 Mr Sharp pleaded guilty at Preston Crown Court to all of five counts on an indictment of conspiracy to defraud a charity known as the National Heart Research Fund of unspecified sums of money. On 8th September 1982 Mr Sharp signed and handed to his solicitors a memorandum in writing dated 8th September 1982, together with a bankers draft for the sum of £50,000. The memorandum was in the following terms – and for convenience I have numbered the paragraphs:

(1) I Robert Roy Sharp instruct you my solicitors Messrs Leslie Harris Priestly & Fisher of my free choice and will having discussed the matter with you and Counsel to receive from me a bankers draft herewith in the sum of £50,000. This sum is to be held by you in your Client account or other appropriate investment. I give you Leslie Harris Priestly & Fisher irrevocable authority to make a gift of that sum to provide a Fellowship in Paediatric Surgery at the Liverpool Royal Children's Hospital, Myrtle Street, Liverpool.

(2) This Fellowship is to be set up and its scope determined, under the guidance of Mr David Hamilton Consultant Paediatrician at the said hospital (if he so agrees or in the alternative the Head for the time being of the Department of Paediatric Surgery at the University of Liverpool). The said sum is to be regarded as being held by you my solicitors for the said charitable purpose.

(3) I express the wish that it should be so utilised, if possible, by consideration of the incidence of taxation so as to produce the maximum financial benefit to the said charitable cause by whatever legal means are appropriate by, for example, deed of covenant or otherwise in order to achieve the said purpose and create a charitable trust.

(4) I further authorise you my solicitors and hereby give you sole, absolute and irrevocable discretion to appoint two or more trustees as you think fit for the purpose of carrying out and executing the said charitable purpose.

(5) I have been advised by yourselves and Counsel, and I accept the position, that the aforesaid may be of no benefit whatsoever to me as regards any sentence that I may receive at the Preston Crown Court upon the indictment to which I have pleaded guilty.

On 13th September 1982 Mr Sharp was sentenced at the Preston Crown Court to 30 months imprisonment.

In his plea of mitigation on behalf of Mr Sharp, leading Counsel referred to the transaction involving the memorandum and the payment of £50,000. On 15th September 1982 the plaintiffs wrote to the Liverpool Royal Children's Hospital (the 'hospital'), enclosing a copy of the memorandum, and asking for instructions.

On 8th November 1982 the Mersey Regional Health Authority – to which the matter had been referred by the hospital – wrote to the plaintiffs stating that the Liverpool Health Authority would be delighted to accept the £50,000 for the purpose of providing a Fellowship in Paediatric Surgery at the hospital. The letter then continued:

However, the point occurs to me as to the source from which the funds of £50,000 are derived. As I understand it, your client was charged with various fraud offences in relation to a charity which was formed for the purpose of providing monies for heart research.

On 19th November 1982 the plaintiffs wrote stating that their instructions were '. . . that the £50,000 represented Mr Sharp's life savings over many years' and was certainly not part of any ill-gotten gains.

On 6th December 1982 the Legal Adviser to the Mersey Regional health Authority wrote that he was 'taking formal instructions from the Authority in the light thereof'.

On 30th October 1983, no further communication having been received from the Health Authority in the meantime, Mr Sharp wrote to the Health Authority saying he understood that the source of the sum of £50,000 was the subject of investigation and that, in the circumstances, it might be advisable for the Authority to decline the gift.

On 19th December 1983 the Legal Adviser to the Mersey Regional Health Authority wrote saying that the delay had been caused by the inability to obtain proper instructions from the Liverpool Health Authority. In the second paragraph of the letter the Legal Adviser said this:

Fortunately, these are now to hand and I quote from a recent letter from the Authority: 'The Authority would be pleased to accept the donation, provided there is an assurance that the money is from *bona fide* sources. This point would, I think, need to be re-affirmed. It would, however, be necessary to modify to some extent the purpose of the donation, originally identified by Mr Sharp.'

I interpose here to say that the proposed variation arose from the fact that the estimated income from the sum of £50,000 – that is to say £5,000 per annum – was half the salary required to pay a Fellow. Therefore it was suggested as there was an existing Fellowship in its ninth year but owing to restricted funds its continuation was uncertain – Mr Sharp's fund should be utilised in supporting a second Fellow in alternate years and also as a back-up for the existing Fellowship.

On 7th February 1984 Mr Sharp replied stating that he was not prepared to give any assurance as to the source of the money, or to allow any change to the purpose or terms of the trust.

On 2nd April 1984 the Mersey Regional Health Authority wrote to the solicitors stating:

In view of the latest developments, and particularly in view of the contents of Mr Sharp's letter to yourselves dated 7th February, Liverpool Health Authority does not wish to accept your client's offer.

On 31st October 1985 the originating summons, from which this appeal is brought, was issued by the plaintiffs. On 24th February 1986 the Treasury Solicitor, acting on behalf of HM Attorney-General (who is the second defendant to the originating summons) wrote to the Mersey Regional Health Authority stating that the trustees of the National Heart Research Fund had now agreed 'pursuant to Section 15 of the Trustee Act, 1925 that they would abandon any claim they might have to the £50,000 paid by Mr Sharp'.

Regarding the matter of the sufficiency of funds, the Treasury Solicitor said: 'Counsel had advised that £50,000 was sufficient to fund a Fellowship for several years if both capital and income were resorted to; alternatively, the Fellowship might suffice to give sufficient support to a Fellow who had additional income from some other charitable or other source.' In these circumstances, the Authority was asked to reconsider its decision.

On 11th June 1986 the Mersey Regional Health Authority wrote to the Treasury Solicitor stating that the Liverpool Authority was now prepared to change its views and accept the necessary monies to set up the trust.

On 9th October 1986 the Treasury Solicitor wrote to the Mersey Regional Health Authority asking for confirmation

(1) that the Liverpool Authority and the hospital would recognise the Fellowship in paediatric surgery created and endowed by Mr Sharp's fund; would permit

Mr David Hamilton, or alternatively the Head of the Department of Paediatric Surgery in the University to determine the scope of the Fellowship; and

(2)   the income of the fund would be sufficient to enable the Fellowship to be created – for example, by supporting a Fellow in alternate years.

These confirmations were given by the Mersey Regional Health Authority in its letter of 8th January 1987. The Authority stated that the fund would not be sufficient to enable the Fellowship to be filled continuously, and that Liverpool Health Authority proposed to offer the Fellowship on an *ad hoc* basis for a fixed term, or possibly on alternate years.

The originating summons asks:

(1)   That it may be determined: (a) Whether the said Memorandum and the transfer of £50,000 to them by the first defendant constituted the plaintiffs (a) trustees or (b) agents for the first defendant

(b)   Whether, if the said Memorandum created a trust, that trust is a valid charitable trust or failed for initial impossibility

(c)   Whether, if the said Memorandum created a charitable trust which failed for initial impossibility the said Fund is nevertheless applicable cy-pres or results to the First Defendant.

Mervyn Davies J held:

(1)   that the Memorandum and the transfer constituted the plaintiffs trustees;

(2)   that the Memorandum created a valid charitable trust;

(3)   that if the trust had failed for initial impossibility, the trust fund would result to Mr Sharp.

Mr Sharp appeals against determinations (1) and (2), and the Attorney General appeals against determination (3).

It is submitted on behalf of Mr Sharp that the memorandum merely created an agency which authorised the plaintiffs to apply the £50,000 for the establishment of the Fellowship. It is accepted that had the plaintiffs exercised that agency by transferring the £50,000 to trustees to apply it to create the Fellowship, Mr Sharp could not have recovered the monies thereafter. But it is said that what has been created is a revocable agency, and that the agency has been revoked before the £50,000 was applied for or irrevocably settled upon trusts for the Fellowship. The word 'irrevocable' in paragraph (1) of the Memorandum it is said is meaningless or misconceived in the context. Accordingly, the monies have resulted to Mr Sharp.

I am unable to accept this submission. Paragraph (1) of the Memorandum, beginning: 'I Robert Roy Sharp . . . ' is, I agree, expressed in terms of authority and if it stood alone might be said to constitute an agency only. But it does not stand alone. Paragraph (2) ends with the words 'The said sum is to be regarded as being held by you my solicitors for the said charitable purpose'. In my view those words are a clear indication of an intention to dedicate the money to the charitable purpose and to create an immediate trust. Thus the words are expressed in the present tense; 'The said sum is to be regarded . . . ' and indicate that the plaintiffs are to hold the money for a specified charitable purpose. If there is a direction to hold money for a specified charitable purpose, in my opinion that it a trust. The charitable purpose is identified in paragraph (1), that is to say, to provide a Fellowship – and the trustees are to hold the fund for that purpose.

The intention to create a charitable trust is again emphasised by the concluding words of paragraph (3), namely '. . . in order to achieve the said purpose and create a charitable trust.'

Again, in paragraph (4), the plaintiffs are authorised '. . . for the purpose of carrying out and executing the said charitable purpose'.

I appreciate that paragraphs (3) and (4) related to matters to be carried out in the future, but they are subordinate to the final sentence contained in paragraph (2) '. . . the said sum is to be regarded as held by you my solicitors for the said charitable purpose'. Similarly, I regard the irrevocable authority to make a gift for the establishment of the Fellowship as mere machinery to carry out the intention of the donor to create an immediate charitable trust. The fact that further steps may have to be taken in order to effectuate the charitable intention which is expressed in the Memorandum – namely, to dedicate the fund to charity irrevocably – is not inconsistent with the immediate establishment of the trust. That circumstance, in my view, is merely an example of the principle of an executory trust.

That principle is stated in *Snell's Principles of Equity*, 28th Edition, page 119, in the following terms:

> 1. Distinction between executed and executory trusts. Although the objects of a trust must be certain, it is not essential that the instrument creating the trust should mark out precisely the interests which the objects are to take in the trust property; that may be left to be done by a formal settlement to be prepared afterwards. For instance, on the marriage of H and W it may be agreed between them that certain property shall be settled on trust for them and their children . . . In these cases, although a valid trust is created, a further instrument is necessary to carry into effect the general intention expressed in the first instrument . . .

That principle in my view applies as well to a charitable trust as it does to a private trust.

In the present case, so far as the general purpose is concerned, that is clearly expressed in paragraphs (1) and (2) of the Memorandum. I do not think the fact that the £50,000 was paid by Mr Sharp to his solicitors, and that it was to be held by them upon client account, is of any consequence. In my view these provisions are consistent with the existence of the trust.

So far as concerns the client account, the actual words are 'client account or other appropriate investment'. What is being dealt with is a temporary arrangement for holding the money in question, and is not inconsistent with the existence of a trust. If there was a trust, there is no reason why the trust, through its trustees, should not be the client.

In determining the effect of the Memorandum the Court is not limited to the language of the document itself. The Court is entitled to look at the circumstances in which the Memorandum was brought into being.

Mr Sharp pleaded guilty to conspiracy to defraud a charity; he was awaiting sentence. The transaction represented by the transfer of the sum of £50,000 and the signing of the Memorandum was intended to be brought to the attention of the Crown Court when Mr Sharp came up for sentence. Whilst it is evident from the concluding words of the Memorandum that Mr Sharp was aware that the transaction might not, in the event, be of help to him in relation to the question of the sentence he would receive, it is difficult to imagine that it would have had any impact at all upon the sentencing court if it were merely a revocable authority to Mr Sharp's solicitors which could be revoked and so bring the money back to him after sentence. To produce an impact upon the sentencing court the creation of a trust, or other irrevocable disposition to charity, was necessary in my view.

It is therefore no surprise to discover that Mr Carman, QC, appearing for Mr Sharp, informed the court that Mr Sharp had transferred '... a large proportion of his life's savings to solicitors to hold irrevocably and to make a gift of £50,000 to provide a Fellowship in Paediatric Surgery at the Liverpool Royal Children's Hospital'. Mr Carman's opinion as to the construction of the Memorandum is irrelevant; but the effect of the payment and of the Memorandum is in my view correctly stated by him, as it appears in the transcript of his plea in mitigation which is before the Court.

In my view there was an irrevocable gift of the sum of £50,000 to the plaintiffs for the purpose stated in the memorandum. I do not think that the word 'irrevocable' was mis-used in the memorandum; there was an irrevocable dedication of £50,000 to a charitable purpose immediately. And in my view, reading the document as a whole, that was the intention of the donor.

In my judgment the result is that Mervyn Davies J correctly concluded that the Memorandum created a valid charitable trust and constituted the plaintiffs the initial trustees of that trust.

The next matter argued before us was whether, on the assumption that a valid charitable trust was created by the transfer of £50,000 and the signing of the memorandum, there has been an effective disclaimer of the trust. On the basis that a charitable trust was created, the plaintiffs were, as I have said, initial trustees of that trust. The trust property was vested in them; they have not sought to make any disclaimer of that trust.

However, on 2nd April 1984, the Mersey Regional Health Authority wrote to the plaintiffs stating that the Liverpool Health Authority did not wish to accept the gift. It is said on behalf of Mr Sharp that that letter constituted a disclaimer by the Liverpool Royal Children's Hospital who were represented by the Liverpool Health Authority, so that the trust was disclaimed and the fund resulted to Mr Sharp.

A disclaimer is a rule of property law to prevent property being thrust upon persons who do not wish to receive it. A trustee can no doubt disclaim before accepting the trust; if he does so, the trust property will not vest in him – it will either vest in the other trustees or, if there are none, it will be held by the settlor and it will result on the settlor to give effect to the trust.

In my view neither the hospital nor either of the Health Authorities were trustees of this fund at any time. The Memorandum does not constitute any of them trustees. Initially the trustees were the plaintiffs; they were given power, by the Memorandum, to appoint other trustees if they thought fit, but they did not do so. Disclaimer by the hospital, or by the Health Authorities, does not in my view, therefore, arise as an issue in this case. They were not trustees and the property was not vested in them – there was nothing for them to disclaim. But in any event what we have here is a trust. A trustee may, before acceptance, be able to disclaim the trust, but he cannot, by disclaimer, bring an end to the beneficial limitations which are contained in the trust (see *Mallott* v *Wilson* [1903] 2 Ch 494). The trust will continue and if the trustee disclaims the trusteeship, the court will, if necessary, appoint a new trustee to execute the trust; but the trustee cannot, by something which is called a 'disclaimer' (or by any other method which is not provided for in the trust itself) bring the trust to an end.

The result in my view is that neither the hospital nor the Authorities had any standing to destroy a valid charitable trust by disclaimer. They had no power, in pursuance of any authority given to them by the Memorandum or by the general law, to determine this trust or to disclaim it so that the charitable trust ceased to take effect. A beneficiary can disclaim a beneficial interest which is given to him by a trust purpose, but neither the hospital nor the Health Authorities were beneficiaries in that sense. The beneficiary of Mr Sharp's disposition was 'charity' and there can be no question of the hospital or the Health Authorities disclaiming the benefit of the charitable trust so as to prevent the Attorney-General insisting upon the execution of a trust.

It may be that the refusal of a person to co-operate in effecting a trust purpose could make that trust purpose impracticable; however, that has nothing to do with disclaimer. Practicability is a separate matter, to which I now turn.

The question is whether, at the date of the Memorandum, it was practicable to carry the charitable purpose into effect, or whether there was a reasonable prospect that it would be possible to do so at some future date (see Re Tacon [1958] 1 Ch 447, [1958] 1 All ER 163, and Re White's Will Trusts [1955] 1 Ch 188, 193).

In the latter case the enquiry directed by Upjohn J was whether, at the date of the death of the testatrix, it was practicable to carry the intention of the testatrix into effect, or whether, at the said date, there was any reasonable prospect that it would be possible to do so at some future time.

At the date when the memorandum was signed, it would be necessary for enquiries to be made about the effectuating of the purposes contained in the Memorandum, and I agree with the judge that the real question is whether there was a reasonable prospect that the gift would be practicable at some time in the future. The onus of proving impracticability, prima facie at any rate, is upon the person who is asserting it (see Re Tacon [1958] 1 Ch 447, 453).

The Memorandum provides that a Fellowship is to be set up under the guidance of Mr David Hamilton (if he agrees); or, alternatively, the Head of the Department of Paediatric Surgery at the University. There is no evidence that either of those gentlemen regarded the gift as being likely to be impracticable to carry out, either at the date of the Memorandum or at some time thereafter. In November 1982 the Mersey Regional Health Authority wrote stating that the Liverpool Health Authority 'would be delighted to accept the gift'. The Mersey Regional Health Authority, however, then raised the question of the source of the money.

On 19th November 1982 the plaintiffs replied that their instructions were that the whole of the monies were raised by means of a legitimate occupation. In December 1983 the Mersey Regional Health Authority wrote stating that the Liverpool Health Authority would be pleased to accept the gift, but (1) asked for an assurance as to the source of the money (i.e. that it was lawful) and (2) that since the income of the fund was not sufficient by itself to support a Fellow, the fund should be used to support a second Fellow in alternate years. I see no reason to infer impracticability from that correspondence.

As regards the aspect of a tainted source, Mr Sharp, having instructed his solicitors in 1982 that the money came from legitimate sources, chose to throw doubt upon that in 1983 in refusing to give the assurance which was asked for without giving any explanation as to his refusal. It was always quite possible in my view – and indeed it was ultimately proved to be the case – that the Heart Foundation charity (which was the likely source of any misappropriation of monies, if indeed any of the monies were misappropriated) would agree (if the Attorney General had no objection) to the money being applied for the charity stated in the Memorandum. The money was being given to charity, and an improper source might well have been very difficult to identify in any event at that point in time.

As to the adequacy of the fund, it has to be borne in mind that the trust was not rigid. Paragraph (2) of the Memorandum directed that a Fellowship was to be set up and its scope determined under the guidance of Mr Hamilton, or the Head of the Department of Paediatric Surgery in the University. Under those powers, it would have been possible to declare the duration of the appointment – that is to say, yearly, or bi-annually, or in co-operation with some other Fellowship or fund, so as to tailor the structure of the Fellowship to the money which was available in the trust.

Mr Sharp, having set up the trust, was not thereafter entitled to dictate its administration. He had set up the trust and the matter had left his hands altogether.

There is no evidence that these methods, to which I have referred, were likely to be or were thought to be impracticable in 1982, or at any date thereafter. In the letter of 8th January 1987, the Mersey Regional Health Authority states '. . . I also confirm that the income of the fund would be sufficient to enable a Fellowship to be created, although it would not be sufficient to enable a Fellowship to be funded continuously.' The Liverpool Health Authority therefore proposed that they should be given discretion to offer a Fellowship on an *ad hoc* basis for a fixed period of years or possibly alternate years.

Thus far in the circumstances I do not think that Mr Sharp discharges the onus which is upon him of showing that at the date of the Memorandum, or indeed thereafter, it was impracticable to carry the trust into effect.

The trust is flexible and was intended to be flexible, and it could easily be moulded to meet the needs of the situation presented by the nature of the Fellowship to the amount of money available for this endowment.

There is, however, a further aspect of the matter. By their letter of 2nd April 1984, the Mersey Regional Health Authority stated that the Liverpool Health Authority did not wish to accept Mr Sharp's offer. That it is said is conclusive and unequivocal evidence that the hospital was not prepared to co-operate, so that impracticability was, at any rate by that date, firmly established. Let it be assumed that the co-operation of the hospital was necessary. The question is whether the letter of 2nd April 1984 does (as Mr Sharp contends) conclude the question of impracticability. I agree that the question of whether a person, whose co-operation is necessary or important to the effectuating of the trust, will in fact co-operate, but the matter should not be allowed to drag on indefinitely. On the other hand where, as here, co-operation is in the end shown to be possible, the Court should be slow to assume that a valid charitable trust was terminated because of an initial refusal of co-operation. Persons whose co-operation is necessary may, in good faith, reach conclusions which are simply wrong and which, with further investigation, can be shown to be wrong. In the present case, the experience of the Treasury Solicitor in charity matters enabled him to obtain the consent of the Heart Foundation Charity without great difficulty.

Moreover, there are two further considerations to which I should refer: first, the refusal (if it be a refusal) of co-operation by the hospital was, at any rate in part, due to the refusal by the person who is now claiming to be entitled to the fund – that is to say Mr Sharp – to confirm the assurance which had been given previously on his instructions that the money had a lawful origin.

Mr Carman, QC, appearing for Mr Sharp, asserted it to be the fact that the money represented 'a large proportion of Mr Sharp's life savings'. Secondly, nobody has changed their position in reliance upon the letter of 2nd April 1984. Therefore, in all the circumstances, I can see no valid reason for treating that letter of 2nd April as conclusive; the reality of the matter is that the hospital has now changed its mind and in my view effect should be given to that. It seems to me the reality is that this trust was never impracticable of performance, and there is no justification for declaring that the charitable purpose has been destroyed and that the fund results to Mr Sharp.

In my judgment, therefore, the memorandum created a valid charitable trust; the plaintiffs were the trustees of that trust; there was no disclaimer, either of trusteeship or of any interest arising under the trust – either by the Health Authorities, or the hospital, or anybody else.

In those circumstances it is not necessary for me to investigate the question of general charitable intention.

The result in my view is that this appeal fails and should be dismissed.

Note

Although it appears that a body whose cooperation is required for the gift to operate cannot disclaim it, the case turns on the fact that the trust had been set up by the memorandum to solicitors, and that the Liverpool Health Authority never became either trustee or beneficiary. By the time the case came to court there was no impracticality, so the trust would be enforced.

C: Miscellaneous Problems

National Lottery Act 1993

38. Grants to charities etc.

(1) The Charities Board may make out of any money they receive grants for meeting the expenditure of charities or of institutions such as are mentioned in paragraph (b) of the definition of 'charitable expenditure' in section 44(1).

(2) In making a grant under this section, the Charities Board may impose such conditions as they think fit, including conditions requiring the amount of a grant to be repaid forthwith on breach of any condition.

44. Interpretation of Part II [Distribution of the Net Proceeds of the National Lottery]

(1) In this Part —

'charitable expenditure' means expenditure —

(a) by charities, or

(b) by institutions, other than charities, that are established for charitable purposes (whether or not those purposes are charitable within the meaning of any rule of law), benevolent purposes or philanthropic purposes;

. . .

Questions

1. The National Lottery Charities Board makes a grant in favour of X institution believing it to be charitable. Later, the House of Lords holds that X is not charitable, although it pursues benevolent purposes. Later still, X is wound up. The Charity Commissioners wish to apply the surplus cy près. The National Lottery Charities Board argues for a resulting trust so that it can redistribute it to a benevolent but non-charitable body. Discuss.

2. In 1995 an American space satellite falls to Earth, out of control. Large sections of the satellite survive re-entry into the Earth's atmosphere, one of which lands on a crowded cinema in Bradford. 500 people are killed, and many more injured.

The Bradford Cinema Disaster Appeal Fund is immediately launched, and is described on TV news programmes, and in newspapers reporting on the disaster, as charitable. Contributions are invited by the organisers, who say nothing to negate the impression that the fund is to be charitable, and a great deal of money is collected. Alan, believing the fund to be charitable, writes a cheque for £500 to the organisers.

Four days later, the organisers appreciate the consequences of the fund having charitable status, and decide to draft the purposes in such a way as to avoid it.

Alan is furious, and demands the return of his £500. The Charity Commissioners, arguing that Alan clearly intended his money to be donated for a charitable purpose, wish to apply his £500 cy près. The fund organisers wish to apply the £500 to the purposes of the fund.

Discuss.

SECTION 3: SUBSEQUENT FAILURE

Once property has been dedicated to charitable purposes, it remains so, and if those purposes cease to be capable of achievement, there can be no resulting trust to the settlor or his estate unless the terms on which the gift was originally made provide for this to happen. It is not necessary to search for a general charitable intention on the part of the settlor. The only relevant consideration is whether there was an outright disposition in favour of charity. Where this is so, funds which cannot be applied to the original purpose, whether because that purpose is impossible, or because there is a surplus left over after the purposes have been achieved, may be applied cy près.

Re Slevin
[1891] 2 Ch 236
Court of Appeal

Facts: A legacy had been left to the Orphanage of St Dominics, Newcastle-upon-Tyne. The orphanage ceased to exist after the date of the donor's death, but before the legacy could be paid over.

Held: Since the orphanage had survived its benefactor, by however short a time, the gift was effective in favour of charity and could be applied cy près.

KAY LJ: Properly speaking, a lapse can only occur by failure of the object in the lifetime of the testator; but it is possible that a will might be so framed as that a subsequent failure of the object of the charitable gift might occasion a resulting trust for the benefit of the testator's estate. We have not been referred to any such case, nor have we found any. . . . [but see the discussion in *Re North Devon and West Somerset Relief Fund Trusts* in chapter 8]

 . . . If [the legacy] had been received, the whole might have been expended at once; and, even if not received, the amount might have been anticipated by borrowing from a banker, or otherwise, and charging this legacy with the amount so borrowed . . .

The orphanage did come to an end before the legacy was paid over. In the case of a legacy to an individual, if he survived the testator it could not be argued that the legacy would fall into the residue. Even if the legatee died intestate and without next of kin, still the money was his, and the residuary legatee would have no right whatever against the Crown. So, if the legatee were a corporation which was dissolved after the testator's death, the residuary legatee would have no claim.

Obviously it can make no difference that the legatee ceased to exist immediately after the death of the testator. The same law must be applicable whether it was a day, or month, or year, or, as might well happen, ten years after; the legacy not having been paid either from delay occasioned by the administration of the estate or owing to part of the estate not having been got in. The legacy became the property of the legatee upon the death of the testator, though he might not, for some reason, obtain the receipt of it till long after. When once it became the absolute property of the legatee, that is equivalent to saying that it must be provided for; and the residue is only what remains after making such provision. It does not for all purposes cease to be part of the testator's estate until the executors admit assets and appropriate and pay it over; but that is merely for their convenience and that of the estate. The rights as between the particular legatee and the residue are fixed at the testator's death. . . .

In the present case we think that the Attorney-General must succeed, not on the ground that there is such a general charitable intention that the fund should be administered cy près even if the charity had failed in the testator's lifetime, but because, as the charity existed at the testator's death, this legacy became the property of that charity, and on its ceasing to the Crown, who will apply it, according to custom, for some analogous purpose of charity.

Notes

1.   In *Re King* [1923] 1 Ch 243, a surplus was left after the purpose (the setting of a stained glass window in a church) was carried out. Finding that the whole fund, and not just the sum sufficient for the window, had been dedicated to charity, Romer J applied the surplus cy près (to the setting of a second window).

2.   Nor will it matter that the gift to charity was intended to be postponed until some future date under the terms of the will or gift. In other words, the relevant date is that of the original donation, even though the charity may only at that time obtain a future interest in the property. If A dies leaving property to B for his life, thereafter to C (a charity), and C ceases to exist after A's death but before B's, this is regarded as a subsequent, not an initial, failure.

Re Moon's WT, Foale v Gillians
[1948] 1 All ER 300, [1948] WN 55
Chancery Division

Facts: The testator directed that a legacy should be paid to the trustees of a Methodist church for the purposes of missionary work after the death of his widow. The purposes were no longer practicable by the time of the widow's death, because the church had been destroyed by bombing during the Second World War.

Held: Roxburgh J held that the question of whether the gift had lapsed must be resolved in relation to the time when the gift was made, that is, at the death of the testator. Since the purposes would have been practical then, there was an effective gift to charity at that time, and the failure was subsequent and not initial.

ROXBURGH J: In approaching the question of impracticability, I have, first, to consider at what date I have to regard that matter, because circumstances have changed, as the evidence shows, very greatly since the date of the death of the testator.

There was no difficulty in carrying out the charitable trust when the testator died. On the other hand, this legacy was a future legacy, and this case differs in that respect from *Re Slevin* [1891] 2 Ch 236, where there was an immediate legacy, although it had not been paid over immediately and probably, as a matter of business, could not have been paid over immediately. Nobody has been able to find any case in which this point has arisen for decision. I do not regard *Re Slevin* as deciding it, because, as I have said, that was not a case of a future legacy, but, while it is always dangerous to use passages extracted from a judgment which was directed to a somewhat different state of affairs, I cannot help feeling that Kay LJ, who delivered the judgment of the court in *Re Slevin*, expounded the principle applicable in an authoritative manner which indicates clearly the solution of the problem with which I am concerned. In *Re Slevin* the testator gave a legacy to an orphanage, voluntarily maintained by a lady at her own expense, which was in existence at the testator's death, but was discontinued shortly afterwards and before his assets were administered, and it was held (reversing Stirling J), that, on the death of the testator, the legacy became the property of the orphanage, and that, on the orphanage ceasing to exist, the property in the legacy became applicable by the Crown for charitable purposes. Kay LJ said [Roxburgh J quoted Kay LJ and continued:]

Though I admit fully that that was a case in which the legacy had not been paid, not because it ought not to have been paid according to the terms of the disposition, but for some reason connected with the administration of the estate, yet I think that case is a decision that the question whether or not the charity or the charitable purpose lapses has to be ascertained at the moment when the charity trustees become absolutely entitled to the legacy, that is to say, at the moment of the testator's death and not at the moment when it becomes payable to them, which, of course, in the case of a future legacy is a future time. Even if I am wrong on this point and if the proper time to test the question of impracticability is the date of the death of the tenant for life, which was the point of time at which the legacy became payable according to the true construction of the will, namely, 7 November 1944, I am by no means satisfied that the charitable disposition has become impracticable. That is, of course, a question of evidence. I need not go through it all because, as I have already indicated, my view is that the future of this area is still undecided, and it is not possible to say at present how far the trust is practicable and how far impracticable. Therefore even if, as a matter of law, I ought to test the matter as it stood on 7 November 1944, I should not be prepared as a matter of fact to hold that this trust was then impracticable.

Accordingly, in my judgment, this is a valid and effective charitable disposition. I am absolved from the necessity of pursuing the case any further because counsel for one of the trustees of the church, representing all of them, and the Attorney-General are in agreement that I should direct a scheme. In so doing I am not expressing any opinion on the question whether, if the trustees of the church had chosen to resist the Attorney-General, they could or could not successfully have done so on the facts disclosed in this case.

Re Wright (decd), Blizzard v Lockhart
[1954] Ch 347, [1954] 2 All ER 98, [1954] 2 WLR 972
Court of Appeal

Decision: Where a testamentary gift for the founding of a convalescent home was to take effect after a life interest, at the end of which time the property was insufficient for this purpose, the date of the testatrix's death was taken to be crucial in determining the question of whether the gift was practicable.

ROMER LJ (having considered a *res judicata* issue): The next question to be considered, then, is whether the learned judge was right in holding that the proper date for ascertaining whether the establishment of the convalescent home was practicable was the date of the testatrix's death.

The argument of counsel for the testatrix's next of kin was to the effect that the gift in the will was for a special charitable purpose, namely, for the establishment and maintenance of the convalescent home which the testatrix had in mind and which she described with such particularity; and that the gift was dependent and conditional on it being practicable to carry the purpose, as so described, into effect when the death of the life tenant, Mrs Webb, made the fund available for the home. It is not so much a question of lapse, he said, as a condition of practicability being attached to the gift, so that, if the condition could not be satisfied, the bequest would fail. Counsel for the Attorney-General, on the other hand, contended that no such condition or contingency as suggested attached to the bequest. He argued that in the case of any charitable gift by will, whether immediate or future, no question of impracticability supervening after the testator's death is of any materiality, provided that the object or purpose to which the gift is to be applied is practicable when the testator died. That is the time, he argued, when the rights of the parties – charity, on the one hand, and the next of kin or other persons taking in default, on the other – are to be ascertained and they are to be ascertained at that time once and for all.

In the present case Roxburgh J followed, on the point now under consideration, his earlier decision in *Re Moon's WT* [1948] 1 All ER 300. In that case a testator directed that after the death of his wife his trustees should pay a legacy of

£3,000 to the trustees of the Gloucester Street Wesleyan Methodist Church at Devonport on trust to invest the same in some government security and to apply the income thereof to mission work in the district served by the said Gloucester Street Wesleyan Methodist Church including particularly John Street and Moon Street.

By the time when the testator's widow died it had become impracticable to carry out the mission work which the testator envisaged. Roxburgh J held that the gift was charitable, and held further that, although the legacy was a future legacy, the question whether or not the charitable purpose lapsed for impracticability had to be ascertained at the moment when the charity trustees became absolutely entitled to the legacy, i.e., at the moment of the testator's death and not at the moment when it became payable. The learned judge was guided to this conclusion by the reasoning of the judgment of this court in *Re Slevin* [1891] 2 Ch 236, which was delivered by Kay LJ. The testator in that case bequeathed, amongst other 'charitable legacies', a legacy to an orphanage which was in existence at the time of his death, but was discontinued before his assets had been administered, and, therefore, before the legacy was or properly could be paid. The question was whether, in those circumstances, the legacy failed and fell into residue. In the course of the argument Kay LJ, rhetorically asked ([1891] 2 Ch 237):

. . . where the charity, the legatee, is in existence at the death of the testator, and has received, or might have received the legacy, does not the legacy by that very fact become impressed with charity which the residuary legatee cannot get rid of?

The judgment of the court gave an affirmative answer to that question. The following passages from that judgment (*ibid.*, 239–241) were relevant to *Re Moon* and are, I think, equally relevant to the present case.

[Romer LJ quoted Kay LJ and continued:]

As counsel for the Attorney-General pointed out, if the argument of counsel for the next of kin on the present appeal be right, the decision in *Re Slevin* would have been that the gift had failed by reason of the fact that, by the time the executors were administratively able to pay the legacy, the orphanage to which the testator had given it had been discontinued and, therefore, the purpose of the gift had become impracticable. The court did not, however, take that view, but held that, as the orphanage existed and was capable of taking when the testator died, the gift took effect just as it would have done if the legatee had been an individual who survived the testator but died before payment. The reasoning in *Re Slevin* appears to me to have been almost conclusive of the question in *Re Moon*, and, in my opinion, the decision of Roxburgh J in that case was perfectly right. It, accordingly, follows that, unless there is any distinction in principle between *Re Moon* and the present case, the appeal must necessarily fail. Counsel for the next of kin contended that a future gift, as here, to a particular charitable purpose is in a different position from a gift to a particular charitable institution, and that, although a condition of survival, as it were, may not attach to the latter, it does attach to the former. Counsel for the Attorney-General, on the other hand, says that a particular charitable purpose is, in effect, an entity just as charity generally is regarded as being, and that it could only be defeated by the next of kin in the present case if they could sufficiently show (and the onus would lie on them) that the purpose which the testatrix had in mind was doomed to inevitable failure from the moment when the testatrix died, and that they could not have discharged this onus, for the life tenant under the compromise might have died at any time, and, in particular, might have died while the purpose which the testatrix desired to achieve was still capable of fulfilment.

In my opinion, the distinction which counsel for the next of kin sought to draw between a particular charitable purpose, on the one hand, and an individual or an existing and specified charity, on the other hand, is not a sound distinction. Once money is effectually dedicated to charity, whether in pursuance of a general or a particular charitable intent, the testator's next of kin or residuary legatees are for ever excluded and no question of subsequent lapse, or of anything analogous to lapse, between the date of the testator's death and the time when the money becomes available for actual application to the testator's purpose can affect the matter so far as they are concerned. This conclusion necessarily follows, I think, on the reasoning in *Re Slevin*. In *Re Soley* (1900) 17 TLR 118 a testator bequeathed money on trust to pay the income thereof to a person for life and after his death the fund was given to the Drapers' Company to be applied by them for the benefit of their college at Tottenham either by founding a scholarship or scholarships for the encouragement of the scholars in various branches of learning, or in such other manner as the masters, wardens and court of assistants in their absolute discretion should think most suited to promote the interests of the college. The gift, accordingly, was for the promotion of a particular charitable purpose. After the testator's death, but during the lifetime of the tenant, the college ceased to exist. Byrne J, following *Re Slevin*, held that there had been no lapse of the bequest and directed that it should be applied for charitable purposes cy-près. A similar decision was that of Neville J in *Re Geikie* (1911) 27 TLR 484, and, indeed, the decision of Roxburgh J in *Re Moon* itself proceeded on the same footing. It is true that in all these cases the funds which were in question were to be paid over to other persons or bodies to be applied by them to the designated charitable purposes whereas in the present case it is the trustees themselves who were so to apply the residuary trust fund, but, in my opinion, no difference of principle arises from this. The testatrix's trustees hold the fund impressed with a charitable trust just as did the third parties to whom the gifts were directed to be paid in the other cases. I am, accordingly, of opinion that no legitimate distinction exists, either on principle or on authority, between the present case and *Re Moon* and that the learned judge's decision on this question was right and should be affirmed.

I would only add that, although the question before us is not one of construction, nevertheless a contrary conclusion in the present case would, in fact, quite clearly defeat the intention of the testatrix. The life interest in residue of Mrs Webb, which deferred for years the fulfilment of the testatrix's wishes as expressed in her will, arose from the settlement of the probate proceedings and not from any bounty of the testatrix herself. She wanted the charity to be founded immediately on her death, and, but for the change in her testamentary dispositions effected by the compromise, her next of kin could have had no possible claim to the fund. It is, therefore, without reluctance that I have reached the conclusion that the appeal should be dismissed.

Note
At the beginning of chapter 8 cases were set out (e.g., *Re Welsh Hospital (Netley) Fund* [1921] 1 Ch 655) which suggested that where funds were collected from a number of donors for a charitable purpose which later failed, there was no automatic application cy près but the intention of the donor was still relevant (although in all such cases the actual result was application cy près). It is difficult to reconcile the reasoning in these cases with *Re Slevin*, but the *dicta* in the following case suggest that they may be wrong.

Re Ulverston & District New Hospital Building Trusts, Birkett v Barrow and Furness Hospital Management Committee
[1956] Ch 622, [1956] 3 WLR 559, [1956] 3 All ER 164
Court of Appeal

Decision: The decision was that money which had been collected to build a new hospital which was never built would not be applied cy près, since there was an initial failure and no evidence of general charitable intention. Some of the money had been collected from anonymous donations, and the importance of the case for present purposes is in the views of Jenkins LJ on *Re Welsh Hospital (Netley) Fund*.

JENKINS LJ (on *Re Welsh Hospital (Netley) Fund*): With regard to this case, I would observe that it concerned the disposal of a surplus after the immediate purposes for which the fund was raised had been fully fulfilled, and was not a case of total failure *ab initio* like the case with which we now have to deal. It seems to me that this makes a material difference. The intention of a subscriber might well be that his contribution should be returned in the event of a total failure *ab initio* of the purpose for which he made it, but that, in the event of a surplus being left over after that purpose had been duly fulfilled, any share in such surplus which might be regarded as representing his subscription or some part thereof should be permanently devoted to charity. In forming his intention as to the fate of his contribution in the latter event (if, indeed, he formed one at all), he might well be influenced by the fact that the inclusion of contributions from anonymous sources, and the indiscriminate spending of a mixture of anonymous contributions and contributions from named subscribers, would make it impossible to ascertain whether the whole or any and, if so, what part of any particular contribution had been spent. In the case of initial failure different considerations apply, for the whole of the fund is ex hypothesi intact and there has been no effective application of it for the purpose for which it was raised. Moreover, I think that *Re Welsh Hospital (Netley) Fund* might well have been decided the same way simply on the strength of the language of the appeals; and, quite apart from that, I think it might well have been held that, once the charity for which the fund was raised had been effectively brought into action, the fund was to be regarded as permanently devoted to charity to the exclusion of any resulting trust. In this connection I would refer to the following passage from the judgment of Sargant LJ in *Re Monk, Giffen v Wedd* [1927] 2 Ch 197 at p. 211:

> The case is quite different from that of *Re Wilson* [1913] 1 Ch 314, so much relied on by the appellants, where the application of any part of the fund was dependent on the constitution of the whole scheme. If there should be any failure here it would be in the nature of a partial failure by matter subsequent, not as there, a total failure through failure of a condition precedent. Counsel for the respondents were not able to cite any case in which, a charity having actually been put into operation and having afterwards proved incapable of exhausting the whole charitable fund, it had then been held that there was a resulting trust for the donor, or in the case of a will for his next of kin.

Reference may also be made to the decision of Danckwerts J in *Re Wokingham Fire Brigade Trusts, Martin v Hawkins* [1951] 1 All ER 454, where the surplus funds of a disbanded local fire brigade were held to be subject to public charitable trusts and applicable cy-près. Danckwerts J said (at p. 456):

> It seems, therefore, that the funds were subject to public charitable trusts which have been in operation for a number of years. That rules out any other application of the fund. I think that the subscribers intended to part with all interest in the subscriptions when they made them for the benefit of this public purpose . . . I do not believe that when the subscriptions were made there was any thought of the future disposition of the money in such circumstances as have arisen. The only thing which I think was taken into account was the provision of the brigade or its equipment, and, that being so, the funds were devoted out and out for a charitable purpose. That purpose being no longer practicable by reason of the sale of the assets to a different body charged with the duties previously performed by the brigade, the charitable trusts do not fail. It is not necessary to consider whether there was any general charitable intention and the trusts must be modified by means of a cy près application. The declaration is that the funds were held on charitable trusts for the benefit of Wokingham and adjoining districts and should be applied cy près by means of a scheme.

It will be seen that Danckwerts J said that it was not necessary to consider whether there was any general charitable intention. I think that observation was right in the circumstances of *Re Wokingham Fire Brigade Trusts*, and would have been equally appropriate in *Re Welsh Hospital (Netley) Fund*.

For these reasons I cannot regard *Re Welsh Hospital (Netley) Fund* as providing any real authority for the Attorney-General's argument in a case of total failure *ab initio* such as the present case.

SECTION 4:   ALTERING CHARITABLE OBJECTS

A: At Common Law

Whereas no difficulties have ever arisen in the case of a clear failure, such as a charitable body ceasing to exist, when the cy près doctrine could operate on the subsequent failure, there could be problems before 1960 where charitable purposes simply became outdated and obsolete, although the original charitable body continued in existence. There was no effective system whereby moribund charities could be modernised, and of course the cy près doctrine could not apply if there was no failure.

Until the reforms introduced by the Charities Act 1960, the courts' only jurisdiction was their inherent jurisdiction to apply funds cy près, but that jurisdiction is confined to rather narrow limits, being available only where it is 'impossible' or 'impracticable' to carry out the terms of the trust. The courts' main concern was not to depart too far from the original wishes of settlors, rather than to promote the efficient administration of charities.

For example, in *Re Weir Hospital* [1910] 2 Ch 124, a testator left two houses to be used as a hospital. The premises were not suitable, and the Charity Commissioners approved a scheme to use them as a nurses' home instead, perpetuating the testator's name by renaming a hospital in his honour. The Court of Appeal held that the scheme was *ultra vires*, since the original purpose was not impossible to fulfil, merely difficult. Sir Herbert Cozens-Hardy MR's view (at p. 131) was that the court's primary duty was to give effect to the charitable intentions of the donor, rather than to seek the most beneficial application of the property:

The first duty of the Court is to construe the will, and to give effect to the charitable directions of the founder, assuming them not to be open to objection on the ground of public policy. The Court does not consider whether those directions are wise or whether a more generally beneficial application of the testator's property might not be founded.

Similar sentiments were echoed by Kennedy LJ, at pp. 140–41:

But neither the Court of Chancery, nor the Board of Charity Commissioners, which has been entrusted by statute, in regard to the application of charitable fund, with similar jurisdiction, is entitled to substitute a different scheme for the scheme which the donor has prescribed in the instrument which creates the charity, merely because a coldly wise intelligence, impervious to the special predilections which inspired his liberality, and untrammelled by his directions, would have dictated a different use of his money . . . If the charity can be administered according to the directions of founder or testator, the law requires that it should be so administered.

It is permissible under the courts' inherent jurisdiction, however, to eradicate a condition of the trust which, with the passage of time, has become inimical to its main purpose.

Re Robinson, Wright v Tugwell
[1921] 2 Ch 332
Chancery Division

Decision: A condition in a gift of an endowment for an evangelical church requiring a preacher to wear a black gown in the pulpit was cut out, since it was thought likely to offend the congregation and reduce attendance: with the passage of time, the condition had become inimical to the main purpose of the gift.

P. O. LAWRENCE J: The contention on behalf of the petitioner is that the condition as to the wearing of a black gown in the pulpit is impracticable, but that it is subsidiary to the main purpose of the bequest, and that the present case falls within that class of cases when the main charitable purpose is practicable, but a subsidiary purpose is impracticable. If that contention be correct, I am satisfied that the court, on assuming the execution of the charitable trusts declared by the testatrix, has ample jurisdiction to execute those trusts cy près and to sanction a scheme, modifying the trusts by dispensing with the subsidiary purpose, so as to carry out, as nearly as possible, the main charitable intentions of the testatrix.

In my judgment, the contention that the condition as to the black gown is subsidiary to the main purpose of the bequest is sound. The dominant charitable intention of the testatrix, as expressed in her will, was to provide a fund towards the endowment of a proposed evangelical church at Bournemouth, the right of patronage and presentation to the living of which should be vested in the trustees of a deed of November 24, 1877. This main purpose can be fully carried into effect apart altogether from the condition as to wearing a black gown in the pulpit. In these circumstances the wearing of the black gown in the pulpit, although expressly insisted upon by the testatrix as a condition of her bequest, is a purpose which is subsidiary to the main purpose of the bequest. Consequently, the court, if satisfied that the condition is impracticable, can properly sanction a scheme dispensing with it.

There remains to be considered the question whether the condition is impracticable. . . .

The evidence in support of the petition in the present case shows (1) that, although in the year 1889 (the date of the will and death of the testatrix) clergymen of the evangelistic school of the Church of England not infrequently preached in a black gown, yet since that date and especially in recent years the use of a black gown in the pulpit has become more and more unusual; (2) that in none of the churches, the advowsens of which are vested in the trustees of the deed of 1877, is a black gown worn; (3) that the wearing of a black gown in the pulpit at the present day would be detrimental to the teaching and practice of evangelical doctrines and services in the parish and in the church in question; and (4) that the use of a black gown in the pulpit would disturb the devotional feelings of the congregation, would be looked upon as an act of eccentricity, would be contrary to the wishes of the persons attending the services and therefore would have an injurious effect upon the evangelical teaching which the testatrix desired to promote and upon the carrying out of the services in the way she desired. This evidence is, in my opinion, corroborated by the fact that no incumbent has attempted to comply with the condition during the long period which has elapsed since the fund was paid into Court. Judging from the past, it seems to me that, unless the Court dispenses with the condition, the fund is likely to remain in Court for all time, thus rendering the bequest useless and defeating the main intention of the testatrix.

In these circumstances, I think that I am justified in holding that the condition is impracticable and ought to be dispensed with, and I so hold.

Re Dominion Students' Hall Trust, Dominion Students' Hall Trust v *Attorney-General*
[1947] Ch 183
Chancery Division

Decision: A colour bar was removed from a trust for the maintenance of a hostel for male students of the overseas dominions of the British Empire, since the main purpose of the trust was to promote community of citizenship among members of the Commonwealth.

EVERSHED J: The purpose of both the petition and the summons is that a restriction which has hitherto been characteristic of the charity, limiting its objects so as to exclude coloured students of the British Empire, should be removed and that the benefits of the charity should be open to all citizens from the Empire without what is commonly known as the 'colour bar'. Having regard to the interest of the Inns of Court in Imperial students, I have thought it right to be particularly careful to see that I have jurisdiction to authorize the scheme and to sanction the petition. The proposed removal of the 'colour bar' restriction has been put to a substantial number of the subscribers. Owing to the necessities of the case, it has not been possible to put it to all, but those to whom it has been put represent over 75 per cent in value of the subscription and none dissents from what is now proposed.

It is plain that I have to bear in mind the general proposition contained in the headnote to *Re Weir Hospital* [1910] 2 Ch 124, which is to the effect that funds given by a testator for a particular charitable purpose cannot be applied cy près by the court unless it has been shown to be impossible to carry out the testator's intention. True, the present is not a case of a testator and the court is, perhaps, not quite so strictly limited as in the case of a will. It is true, also, that the word 'impossible' should be given a wide significance: see *Re Campden Charities* (1881) 18 ChD 310; *Re Robinson* [1921] 2 Ch 332. It is not necessary to go to the length of saying that the original scheme is absolutely impracticable. Were that so, it would not be possible to establish in the present case that the charity could not be carried on at all if it continued to be so limited as to exclude coloured members of the Empire.

I have, however, to consider the primary intention of the charity. At the time when it came into being, the objects of promoting community of citizenship, culture and tradition among all members of the British Commonwealth of Nations might best have been attained by confining the Hall to members of the Empire of European origin. But times have changed, particularly as a result of the war; and it is said that to retain the condition, so far from furthering the charity's main object, might defeat it and would be liable to antagonize those students, both white and coloured, whose support and goodwill it is the purpose of the charity to sustain. The case, therefore, can be said to fall within the broad description of impossibility illustrated by *Re Campden Charities* and *Re Robinson*.

There is also this further point. On the facts of the case, as proved in evidence, including particularly the substantial promises received of further financial support if the 'colour bar' is removed, it seems clear that the original class of beneficiaries, so far from being adversely affected by the proposed change, should gain as a consequence. Notionally, there might be two complementary charities, one for white and one for coloured students, both of which the trust could administer and, in practice, should administer, together. In the circumstances, I am happy to think that I can make the order which I have been asked to make. I am also assisted by the circumstance that Mr Danckwerts, for the Attorney-General, who has considered the matter from all points of view both of charity generally and of the original subscribers, did not feel that the case was one in which he could offer opposition, either on merits or on jurisdiction.

Re J.W. Laing Trust
[1984] Ch 143
Chancery Division

Decision: Peter Gibson J was prepared to strike out a term requiring trustees to distribute, within 10 years of the settlor's death, a fund which by then had risen significantly in value (from some £15,000 in 1922 when the trust was set up, to over £24 million in 1982). The increase in value had been quite unforeseen when the trust was set up, partly because the settlor had lived much longer than expected (to the age of 98). The recipients of the income from the charity (Christian evangelical bodies) had come to depend upon it, whereas it would have been impossible to distribute such a large amount of capital in such a way as to ensure continuance of the causes which the settlor wished to support.

PETER GIBSON J (on the inherent jurisdiction of the court): On this question Mr Picarda and Mr McCall submit, and I accept, that the court is not fettered by the particular conditions imposed by section 13(1)(e)(iii), but can, and should, take into account all the circumstances of the charity, including how the charity has been distributing its money, in considering whether it is expedient to regulate the administration of the charity by removing the requirement as to distribution within ten years of the settlor's death.

The evidence before me shows that the settlor throughout his life was a man of strong religious convictions and particularly interested, and personally involved, in the activities of the religious group known as the Christian (or Open) Brethren. That group has never had any central organisation of the group's churches or their missionaries. There are approximately 450 such missionaries. The plaintiff company is now a charity. Although in 1922 it did not hold its property for exclusively charitable purposes, nevertheless it was founded to hold property for missionary purposes and for the transmission of funds for the missionary and other work of the Christian Brethren, and there can be no doubt that it was chosen by the settlor to act as trustee because of its connections with the Christian Brethren.

When the charity was founded in 1922 the 15,000 shares in John Laing & Sons Ltd were worth little more than their par value, £15,000. No doubt because of a prudent failure to diversify the charity's investments, the assets of the charity, which largely consist of shares and loan stock in Laing companies (which are now public companies), had increased by June 30, 1982, to no less than £24 million. In August 1922 no one would have foreseen either that the settlor would live for more than half a century longer and attain the age of 98 before he died on January 11, 1978, or that the assets of the charity would increase so astonishingly. The income of the charity in the year to June 30, 1982, exceeded £1.2 million.

The settlor acted as agent of the plaintiff in effecting distribution until the end of 1964. He followed an income distribution policy which fostered Christian evangelical activities, and since then the plaintiff has, in the exercise of its discretion, continued an active distribution policy, financing home and overseas evangelism and the relief of poverty. Various Christian causes have come to depend on the charity for their continued support and, in the view of the plaintiff, they are in need of continued support from the charity in the manner adopted hitherto. By far the greater part of the distributions have been to individuals or bodies not well suited to receive large sums of capital to finance their future activities. There is a particular difficulty in relation to providing for the future work of the Christian Brethren because they do not accept any organisation as a governing or controlling body but operate on an individual basis. There would be severe practical inconveniences and difficulties in distributing the very large sums of capital now held by the plaintiff in a way that would ensure continuance of the causes which the settlor wished to support by the charity. The court should always be slow to thwart a donor's wishes, but in this case the settlor himself, as early as October 5, 1932, indicated to the plaintiff by letter that he wished the plaintiff to be at liberty to disregard the requirement as to distribution. On January 26, 1939, the settlor wrote again to the plaintiff, referring to the capital value of his gift as then worth £30,000, and saying:

> considering that the capital value is more, and in view of many Christian activities, I wish to withdraw the stipulation that the capital should be distributed within 10 years of my death.

It is clear that even then, after that comparatively modest increase in capital value in that comparatively short period of the charity's existence, the settlor appreciated that the requirement as to distribution was inexpedient.

The chairman of the directors of the plaintiff, Mr Andrew Gray, in his affidavit, says of the plaintiff:

> The plaintiff, itself a registered charity in its own right, has broad experience in the field of Christian ministry and (so far as not already covered by that concept) the relief of the poor. It considers that this experience makes it sensitive to the ever-changing needs of the modern world, and enables it to adapt to such changes by shifts in the emphasis of its giving. The plaintiff would not presume to claim that no other body has this capability, but having regard to its long association with the settlor, who remained a director of the plaintiff until his death, it considers that it may reasonably suggest that it may be better able than most to fulfil his wishes for the distribution of the funds he so generously provided.

The plaintiff has considered causing another charitable body to be set up to carry on permanently the work now conducted by the charity, but it took the view that it would be unacceptable for it to adopt such a device to circumvent the restriction as to distribution. For my part, I would have thought that the plaintiff could distribute the capital to any other charitable body or bodies if it thought fit, but that merely serves to emphasise the unimportance of the requirement as to distribution.

In my judgment, the plaintiff has made out a very powerful case for the removal of the requirement as to distribution, which seems to me to be inexpedient in the very altered circumstances of the charity since that requirement was laid down 60 years ago. I take particular account of the fact that this application is one that has the support of the Attorney-General. Although the plaintiff is not fettered by the express terms of the gift as to the charitable purposes for which the charity's funds are to be applied, it is, in my view, proper for the plaintiff to wish to continue to support the causes which the settlor himself wished the charity to support from its inception, and which would suffer if that support was withdrawn as a consequence of the distribution of the charity's assets. I have no hesitation in reaching the conclusion that the court should, in the exercise of its inherent jurisdiction, approve a scheme under which the trustees for the time being of the charity will be discharged from the obligation to distribute the capital within 10 years of the death of the settlor. I shall discuss with counsel the precise form of order that is appropriate.

Note

An alternative application based on s. 13 of the 1960 Act (s. 13(1)(e)(ii)), considered below, failed because the section does not apply to provisions which are purely administrative in nature, only where there are difficulties in carrying out the donor's original purpose. See further below.

Question

This provision was held to be 'inexpedient'. Is that the same as 'impractical' in the previous two cases? If not, does the *J. W. Laing* test apply only to certain types of term, and if so, which terms?

Oldham Borough Council v *Attorney-General*
[1993] 2 All ER 432
Court of Appeal

Facts: The Clayton Playing Fields in Oldham had been conveyed to the Council (or more accurately, the bodies which preceded it prior to the local government reorganisation in 1974) in 1962, for recreational purposes. The Borough Council proposed to sell the land for development, but also to provide a new site which (it was assumed) would be used for exactly the same charitable purposes. The Attorney-General opposed the sale.

Held: The sale would be approved. Although the council expressly disclaimed reliance on the Charities Act 1960, since clearly none of the heads (enumerated below) could apply in this case, the Court of Appeal took the view that the sale of the land would have been approved prior to the Charities Act.

DILLON LJ: By an originating summons dated 16th May 1991, the Oldham Borough Council, as trustee of a charity founded by a deed of gift of 16th April 1962, sought, by way of relief under para 1 of the summons, that it might be determined whether the court has power to authorise the council to sell or exchange all or any part of the freehold land, referred to as 'the blue land', vested in the council as a trustee of the charity, being the existing site of the Clayton Playing Fields.

The summons further asked by para 2 that if the answer to the question in para 1 was Yes, the council might be authorised to sell or exchange the blue land on such terms as the court may think fit. What lies behind this is a proposal, which has been the subject of much local debate and controversy, that the existing site of the Clayton Playing Fields should be sold to developers for a very large price, and that with that price the council should acquire a new site for playing fields which – because the price will be so high – will have much better facilities, in the way of changing rooms and car parking and so forth, than the existing site.

The originating summons came before Chadwick J, and by his order of 7th April 1992 he declared on para. 1 of the originating summons that the court does not have power to authorise the council to sell or exchange the blue land referred to in the originating summons. The council now appeals against that declaration. In the meantime, para. 2 of the originating summons stands adjourned generally under the judge's order.

The sole defendant to the originating summons, and sole respondent to the appeal, is Her Majesty's Attorney-General, as representing the interests of charities generally. He, through Mr Unwin of counsel, supports the appeal, as he supported the council in the court below in relation to para. 1; but he reserves his position in relation to the proposal, outlined above, and para. 2 of the originating summons.

It follows that we in this court are in no way concerned with the details of the proposal or with whether it is a good idea, and we express no opinion at all on that. We have merely to decide question 1 in the originating summons as a question of law, and to that end we assume that the proposal, if approved and carried through, would result in the council holding a new site on precisely the same charitable trusts as are declared, with regard to the existing site, by the deed of gift of 6th April 1962 already mentioned.

Question 1 of the originating summons has been referred to as a question of jurisdiction, but that is a bit of an over-simplification of the question.

It is not in doubt as a general proposition that charitable trustees who hold land as part of the permanent endowment of a charity or land which has been occupied for the purposes of the charity have power to sell that land with the consent of the court (or of the Charity Commissioners). That power may be classified as (i) a power conferred by section 29 of the Charities Act 1960, which replaced similar provisions in section 24 of the Charitable Trusts Act 1853, as qualified by section 29 of the Charitable Trusts Amendment Act 1855 or (ii) a general power at common law curtailed by section 29 of the 1960 Act and previously by the 1853 and 1855 Acts which made the consent of the court or the Charity Commissioners necessary or (iii) a power conferred by section 29 of the Settled Land Act 1925, which gives charitable trustees all the powers conferred by that Act on a tenant for life and on the trustees of a settlement; but for present purposes its precise classification is immaterial. In so far as the answer to question 1 depends on any of these Acts, the answer must be Yes.

[Dillon LJ then considered the Charities Act 1960 (see further below), and continued:]

But there is nothing to suggest any legislative intention in enacting section 13 to extend the cases, where a cy près scheme is necessary if anything is to be done, to cases where before the 1960 Act no scheme was required.

The cases seem to be consistent, before the 1960 Act, that mere sale of charitable property and reinvestment of the proceeds in the acquisition of other property to be held on precisely the same charitable trusts, or for precisely the same charitable purposes, did not require a scheme. See especially *Re Ashton Charity* 22 Beav 288 where, in a case decided in relation to the law in force before the passing of the Charitable Trusts Act 1853 and the 1855 Act, Sir John Romilly MR, rejecting a submission of Mr Dart of counsel that it does not form part of the administration of a charitable purpose to sell the very estate which the founder intended to uphold it, held that the Court of Chancery had a general jurisdiction, as incidental to the administration of a charity estate, to alien charity property where the court clearly sees that the alienation is for the charity's benefit and advantage. Other cases where the court decreed a sale of charity lands, otherwise than by way of cy près scheme, because the court was satisfied that the sale of those lands would be beneficial to the charity are *Re Parke's Charity*12 Sim 329, a decision of Shadwell V-C under Sir Samuel Romilly's Act (52 Geo 3 C 101) and *Re The North Shields Old Meeting House* 7 WR 541, a decision of Kindersley V-C under the Charitable Trusts Act 1853 as amended by the 1855 Act. This seems to have been the standard practice in the last century and I see no reason why Parliament should have intended to alter it by section 13 of the 1960 Act. That section is concerned with the cy près application of charitable funds, but sales of charitable lands have, in so far as they have been dealt with by Parliament, always been dealt with by other sections not concerned with the cy près doctrine.

There are of course some cases where the qualities of the property which is the subject-matter of the gift are themselves the factors which make the purposes of the gift charitable – e.g., where there is a trust to retain for the public benefit a particular house once owned by a particular historical figure or a particular building for its architectural merit or a particular area of land of outstanding natural beauty. In such cases sale of the house, building or land would necessitate an alteration of the original charitable purposes and therefore a cy près scheme because after a sale the proceeds or any property acquired with the proceeds could not possibly be applied for the original charitable purpose. But that is far away from cases such as the present, where the charitable purpose – playing fields for the benefit and enjoyment of the inhabitants of the districts of the original Donees, or it might equally be a museum, school or clinic in a particular town – can be carried on on other land.

Accordingly, I would allow this appeal, set aside the declaration made by the learned judge and substitute a declaration to the opposite effect.

Whether there should be a sale, or whether the existing site should continue to be used as the Clayton Playing Fields as now, is one of the matters for the court to consider under para. 2 of the originating summons with which we are not concerned. Accordingly, we should remit the proceedings to the Chancery Division for consideration of para. 2.

I should add finally that we were referred by counsel to the provisions of the Charities Act 1992 [subsequently replaced by the Charities Act 1993], which have not yet come into force. That Act changes the law in various respects; therefore its provisions cannot help us in deciding the questions with which we have been concerned on this appeal. Equally, however, we have not had to consider whether our decision would have been different if all the provisions of the 1992 Act had already come into force.

Question

Was it impracticable to continue to use the existing land for charitable purposes? Was it inexpedient? If not, does the *Oldham* decision apply to anything apart from sales of land?

B: Charities Act 1960 (Replaced by 1993 Act)

Following a recommendation of the Nathan Committee on the Law and Practice Relating to Charitable Trusts (1952, Cmd 8710), para. 365, s. 13 extends, presumably in the interests of more efficient administration of charities, the circumstances in which property may be applied cy près.

The purpose of this section is to modernise outmoded trusts; as we have seen this was difficult using only the inherent jurisdiction of the courts. Section 13(5) places a duty upon trustees to seek the application of property cy près if and when appropriate circumstances arise. Much of the work of the Commissioners consists in settling and approving schemes of this kind.

The precise circumstances are set out in s. 13(1). No longer is it necessary to show that it is 'impossible' or 'impracticable' to carry out the terms of the trust. It is enough that the original purpose has been fulfilled as far as possible, or cannot be carried out according to the directions given and the spirit of the gift, or if there is a surplus left over, or if the purposes have been adequately provided for by other means, or become useless or harmful to the community. Cy près may also apply where the original purposes relate to an area, or class of persons, which has ceased to have any relevance, having regard to the spirit of the gift. There are also provisions for the amalgamation of small charities if that is more efficient.

Charities Act 1993

(Replacing equivalent provisions from the 1960 Act.)

13. Occasions for applying property cy près

(1) Subject to subsection (2) below, the circumstances in which the original purposes of a charitable gift can be altered to allow the property given or part of it to be applied cy près shall be as follows —

(a) where the original purposes, in whole or in part —

(i) have been as far as may be fulfilled; or

(ii) cannot be carried out, or not according to the directions given and to the spirit of the gift; or

(b) where the original purposes provide a use for part only of the property available by virtue of the gift; or

(c) where the property available by virtue of the gift and other property applicable for similar purposes can be more effectively used in conjunction, and to that end can suitably, regard being had to the spirit of the gift, be made applicable to common purposes; or

(d) where the original purposes were laid down by reference to an area which then was but has since ceased to be a unit for some other purpose, or by reference to a class of persons or to an area which has for any reason since ceased to be suitable, regard being had to the spirit of the gift, or to be practical in administering the gift; or

(e) where the original purposes, in whole or in part, have, since they were laid down —

(i) been adequately provided for by other means; or

(ii) ceased, as being useless or harmful to the community or for other reasons, to be in law charitable; or

(iii) ceased in any other way to provide a suitable and effective method of using the property available by virtue of the gift, regard being had to the spirit of the gift.

(2) Subsection (1) above shall not affect the conditions which must be satisfied in order that property given for charitable purposes may be applied cy près except in so far as those conditions require a failure of the original purposes.

(3) References in the foregoing subsections to the original purposes of a gift shall be construed, where the application of the property given has been altered or regulated by a scheme or otherwise, as referring to the purposes for which the property is for the time being applicable.

(4) Without prejudice to the power to make schemes in circumstances falling within subsection (1) above, the court may by scheme made under the court's jurisdiction with respect to charities, in any case where the purposes for which the property is held are laid down by reference to any such area as is mentioned in the first column in Schedule 3 to this Act, provide for enlarging the area to any such area as is mentioned in the second column in the same entry in that Schedule.

(5) It is hereby declared that a trust for charitable purposes places a trustee under a duty, where the case permits and requires the property or some part of it to be applied cy près, to secure its effective use for charity by taking steps to enable it to be so applied.

Re Lepton's Charity, Ambler v Thomas
[1972] 1 Ch 276
Chancery Division

Decision: Under a will of 1715 the testator left land, whose profits amounted to £5 a year, with a direction to trustees to pay £3 a year to the minister, and the residue to the poor of Pudsey. In 1967 the income from the investments representing the land was £791 14s 6d. Pennycuick V-C approved an application under s.13 of the Charities Act 1960 to increase the income of the minister to £100 a year, the residue going, as before, to the poor of Pudsey.

PENNYCUICK V-C: One must next consider whether in relation to a trust for payment of a fixed annual sum out of the income of a fund to charity A and payment of the residue of that income to charity B the expression 'the original purposes of a charitable gift' in s. 13(1) should be construed as referring to the trusts as a whole or must be related severally to the trust for payment of the fixed annual sum and the trust for payment of residuary income. Mr Browne-Wilkinson [for the Attorney-General, arguing for the scheme] contends that the former is the correct view. Mr Griffith [for the Official Solicitor] contends that the latter is the correct view.

It seems to me that the words 'the original purposes of a charitable gift' are apt to apply to the trusts as a whole in such a case. Where a testator or settlor disposes of the entire income of a fund for charitable purposes, it is natural to speak of the disposition as a single charitable gift, albeit the gift is for more than one charitable purpose. Conversely, it would be rather unnatural to speak of the disposition as constituting two or more several charitable gifts each for a single purpose. Nor, I think, is there any reason why one should put this rather artificial construction on the words. The point can, so far as I can see, only arise as a practical issue in regard to a trust of the present character. A trust for division of income between charities in aliquot shares would give rise to different considerations, inasmuch as even if one treats it as a single gift the possibility or otherwise of carrying out the trusts of one share according to the spirit of the gift could hardly react upon the possibility or otherwise of carrying out the trusts of the other share according to the spirit of the gift. The same is true, *mutatis mutandis*, of trusts for charities in succession. But in a trust of the present character there is an obvious interrelation between the two trusts in that changes in the amount of the income and the value of money may completely distort the relative benefits taken under the respective trusts. The point is familiar in other instances of fixed annuity and residual income.

Once it is accepted that the words 'the original purposes of a charitable gift' bear the meaning which I have put upon them it is to my mind clear that in the circumstances of the present case the original purposes of the gift of Dickroyd [the land devised under the original will] cannot be carried out according to the spirit of the gift, or to use the words of [Charities Act 1960, s. 13] paragraph (e)(iii) 'have ceased . . . to provide a suitable and effective method of using the property . . . regard being had to the spirit of the gift'. The intention underlying the gift was to divide a sum which, according to the values of 1715, was modest but not negligible, in such a manner that the minister took what was then a clear three fifths of it. This intention is plainly defeated when in the conditions of today the minister takes a derisory £3 out of a total of £791.

It is not suggested that [Charities Act 1960, s. 13] subsection (2) has any significant bearing upon the present question, for it is precisely the condition requiring the failure of the original purposes that subsection (1)(a)(ii) and subsection (1)(e)(iii) are concerned to modify.

If, contrary to my view, the words 'the original purposes of a charitable gift' must be read severally in relation to the trust for payment of the fixed annual sum and to the trust for payment of residuary income, I think it is no less clear that [Charities Act 1960, s. 13(1)] paragraphs (a)(ii) and (e)(iii) would have no application. On this footing it would be impossible to maintain in respect of either trust that the original purposes cannot be carried out in the spirit of the gift. The minister is available to receive £3 a year, for what it is worth, and it is conceded by Mr Browne-Wilkinson that there are sufficient poor, aged and necessitous people in Pudsey to absorb £788 a year.

Notes

1.   Before the Charities Act 1960 there could have been no possibility of a cy près scheme in a case like this, since there was no subsequent failure.
2.   The court felt that after the change the relative distribution between the minister and the poor of Pudsey remained as in the spirit of the gift.
3.   The main argument in the case was whether s. 13 applied to the trusts in the will as a whole, or to each of the two trusts separately (a trust to pay the £3 a year to the minister, and a separate trust to pay the residue to the poor of Pudsey). Only if (as Pennycuick V-C held) the spirit of the gift related to the will as a whole could the court alter the relative proportions of each part.
4.   Section 13 does allow the courts to alter any term which is not part of 'the original purposes of a charitable gift'.

Re J. W. Laing Trust
[1984] Ch 143
Chancery Division

Decision: The facts and decision have been set out at p. 434 above. The term was struck out using the inherent jurisdiction of the court, but was not one of the 'purposes' within s. 13.

PETER GIBSON J (on the application of the 1960 Act): It is common ground between Mr Picarda for the plaintiff and Mr McCall for the Attorney-General that the purpose of subsection (2) is to preserve the requirement under the law prior to the Act of 1960 that the donor must show a general charitable intent by his gift. This requirement is manifestly satisfied by the gift in this case, expressly devoted, as it is, to charitable purposes. The duty imposed by subsection (5) is new. The plaintiff considers itself to be under that duty and submits that the present case is a case falling within section 13(1)(e)(iii).

For the court to have jurisdiction to make the order sought by the plaintiff under section 13 two questions must be answered affirmatively. (1) Is the requirement to distribute before the expiration of 10 years from the settlor's death included in 'the original purposes' of the charitable gift? (2) If so, have the original purposes, in whole or in part, since they were laid down, ceased to provide a suitable and effective method of using the property available by virtue of the gift?

Mr Picarda and Mr McCall unite in submitting that both questions should be answered in the affirmative, though on the first question Mr Picarda did not disguise his own predilection for the view that the requirement as to distribution was an administrative direction rather than a purpose of the gift.

To answer the first question it is necessary to identify the original purposes of the gift. I venture to suggest that, as a matter of ordinary language, those purposes in the present case should be identified as general charitable purposes and nothing further. I would regard it as an abuse of language to describe the requirement as to distribution as a purpose of the gift. Of course, that requirement was one of the provisions which the settlor intended to apply to the gift, but it would, on any natural use of language, be wrong to equate all the express provisions of a gift, which *ex hypothesi* the settlor intended to apply to the gift, with the purposes of a gift. To my mind the purposes of a charitable gift would ordinarily be understood as meaning those charitable objects on which the property given is to be applied. It is not meaningful to talk of the requirement as to distribution being either charitable or non-charitable. The purposes of a charitable gift correspond to the beneficiaries in the case of a gift by way of a private trust.

However, as Mr McCall rightly submits, the meaning of 'purposes' in section 13 must be construed in its statutory context. He submits that in the Charities Act 1960 a distinction is recognised between the purposes of a gift and its administration. Thus in section 46 the word 'trusts' in relation to a charity is defined as meaning the provisions establishing it as a charity and regulating its purposes and administration. He also drew my attention to section 18(1)(a) under which the Charity Commissioners have power to establish a scheme for the administration of a charity, and submitted that such a scheme is to be contrasted with section 13 under which the original purposes of a charitable gift can be altered to allow a cy près application of property the subject of that gift. I accept, therefore, that the question I must answer is whether the requirement as to distribution is part of the original purposes or a provision relating to administration.

The other guidance that I can obtain from the Act as to the meaning of 'purposes' is from the references to purposes in section 13. From them it is apparent that the relevant purposes are those for which the property given is applicable, and that the relevant purposes include those which provide a use for part only of the property available by virtue of the gift, those which were laid down by reference to an area or class of person, those which have been provided for by other means, those which have ceased to be in law charitable, and (in section 13(1)(e)(iii)) those which have ceased in some other way to provide a suitable or effective method of using the property. Save possibly for the last reference, none of those references seems to me to support a meaning for the word 'purposes' wide enough to cover the direction as to distribution; rather, they support the view that the purposes in question are the particular charitable purposes for which the property is to be applied and nothing further. Section 13(1)(e)(iii) does, however, contemplate that the purposes may provide a method of using the property and, in one sense, a requirement to use capital by the particular date might be said to provide a method of using the property. But, to my mind, that is an unnatural way of construing section 13(1)(e)(iii) as the requirement as to distribution is not so much a method of using the property as a direction as to the date by which the property is to be used. This tells one nothing of that on which the capital is to be applied. If the words of that sub-paragraph are given their natural meaning in their cy près context, to my mind they refer to a specific mode of application of the property in respect of which the donor has indicated a general charitable intention. The internal evidence of section 13 itself does not, therefore, encourage an interpretation of 'purposes' extending beyond what I have ventured to suggest was that word's natural meaning.

Mr McCall submitted that the distinction between 'purposes' and 'administration' is akin to that recognised elsewhere in the law between dispositive and administrative provisions. He drew my attention to *Pearson v IRC* [1981] AC 753, 774 where Viscount Dilhorne, after referring to section 8(1) of the Perpetuities and Accumulations Act 1964 (which itself distinguished between the administration and the distribution of property), recognised a distinction in the context of the capital transfer tax legislation between dispositive and administrative powers of trustees. I was also referred to what was said in *Lord Inglewood v IRC* [1983] 1 WLR 366, 373, where, again in a capital transfer tax context, Fox LJ, giving the judgment of the Court of Appeal, referred to a similar distinction. But while I do not question that the distinction between administrative and dispositive provisions exists and is relevant in other contexts, it does not seem to me to follow that it is precisely the same distinction that is being drawn in the Charities Act 1960 when Parliament has simply referred, in the context of charitable gifts, to purposes on the one hand and administration on the other.

Mr McCall submitted that the purposes of a gift included not only the specific charitable purposes, but also any provision as to time affecting the gift and that 'purposes' could also include the identity of the property given, the identity of the trustee and any other provisions affecting distribution, such as, for example, in the present case, the agency of the settlor in making distributions. In effect, that is to equate every provision which may affect how the trust property is to be distributed with the purposes of the gift. That seems to me to be a very strange use of language and, in the context of section 13, an impossible construction. For example, it is clear that the property and the purposes for which the property is applicable are treated as distinct. Mr McCall posed the example of a trust to charity A for 20 years, followed by a trust to charity B and submitted that the purposes of the gift must include the fact that the interest of charity A is limited to a period of 20 years, and that it is subject to that limited interest that the property is held for charity B. Let me assume (without deciding) that in that case the identification of the purposes must include the time by which A's interest is limited. Nevertheless, the present case is readily distinguishable. The interest of charity in the present case is immediate, unlimited and absolute, extending, as it does, to both capital and income forthwith.

Both Mr McCall and Mr Picarda advanced a more subtle argument on the following lines. (1) Section 13 not merely re-enacted the circumstances in which cy près applications were allowed under the previous law but also extended those circumstances. (2) Prior to the Act of 1960 the court had allowed by way of cy près schemes the removal of impracticable conditions attached to charitable gifts. (3) Such conditions must be regarded as purposes within the meaning of section 13. (4) The requirement as to distribution is also to be treated as, or as similar to, a condition and so a purpose within section 13.

I accept the first and second of these propositions. The first is supported by the remarks of Sir John Pennycuick V-C in *Re Lepton's Charity* [1972] 1 Ch 276, 284. The second is illustrated by cases such as *Re Robinson* [1921] 2 Ch 332 and *Re Dominion Students' Hall Trust* [1947] Ch 183.

But I have difficulty with the third and fourth propositions. I baulk at the universality of the third. Take the case of *Re Robinson*. The testatrix gave money for the endowment of an evangelical church but imposed 'an abiding condition' that a black gown be worn in the pulpit, a condition held by P. O. Lawrence J to be impracticable as defeating the main evangelical intention of the gift. It is not clear from the report whether the money that was given could be used for the provision of black gowns. If it could, then I would accept that the condition might accurately be described as a subsidiary purpose, as indeed the judge, at p. 336, appears to describe the condition. But if not, to my mind this case is more accurately described as falling within the class of cases where the main charitable purpose is practicable but a subsidiary purpose or direction is impracticable. I was referred by Mr Picarda to *Tudor on Charities and Mortmain*, 4th ed. (1906), pp. 202 *et seq.*, where there is a heading 'Subordinate Purpose Impracticable.' But the text goes on to refer to 'subsidiary purpose or direction.' If a purpose is limited, as I think section 13 requires, to that for which the property comprised in the gift is to be applied and the money given could not be applied in providing a black gown, I do not think that the wearing of a black gown would be a purpose within section 13. But I do not see why the circumstances of *In re Robinson* cannot be fitted within section 13(1)(a)(ii) on the footing that the condition stipulated for is a direction and not an original purpose.

On the other hand, the relevant condition in *Re Dominion Students' Hall Trust* [1947] Ch 183 went to defining the class of persons to whom the benefits of the charity were limited, that is to say male students of the overseas dominions of the British Empire of European origin. The requirement that the students be of European origin was removed as tending to defeat the main object of the charity. There is no difficulty in treating that condition as part of the original purposes, or alternatively as a direction, and in either event the circumstances of that case would fall within section 13(1)(a)(ii).

In argument reference was also made to *Re Lysaght (decd)* [1966] 1 Ch 191 in which a gift by a testatrix to the Royal College of Surgeons to found medical studentships limited those who could qualify for such studentships by excluding persons of the Jewish and Roman Catholic faith. That excluding condition was removed by Buckley J as tending to defeat the charitable gift, because it was an essential part of the testatrix's intentions that the Royal College should be a trustee and it refused to accept the gift with that condition. Again it seems to me that the condition would in a like case be treated as part of the original purposes of the gift, alternatively as a direction, and again in either event falling within section 13(1)(a)(ii). I would add that despite the importance attached by the testatrix to the identity of the trustees as recognised by Buckley J, it does not seem to me to follow that for the purposes of section 13 the identity of the trustee in such a case is a purpose rather than a direction within section 13(1)(a)(ii). However, I would observe that though *Re Lysaght* related to the case of the will of a testatrix who died after section 13 of the Charities Act 1960 came into operation, it was not decided under the Act and it is not apparent from the report that any consideration was given to the statutory provisions.

In my judgment, therefore, it does not follow that all conditions attached to gifts must be treated as 'purposes' within section 13. Even if I am wrong on that, it still does not seem to me to follow that the requirement as to distribution should be treated as a condition of a character similar to those in the pre–1960 cases to which I have referred. Both counsel have stressed to me, with the assistance of the contemporary documents at the time of the gift, the lack of importance that the settlor attached to the requirement as to distribution, and Mr McCall in particular rightly criticised the ground on which the Charity Commissioners had refused one of the plaintiff's applications, that is to say, because the requirement as to distribution was, as they put it, 'fundamental.' It cannot be right that any provision, even if only administrative, made applicable by a donor to his gift should be treated as a condition and hence as a purpose.

I confess that from the outset I have found difficulty in accepting that it is meaningful to talk of a cy près application of property that has from the date of the gift been devoted both as to capital and income to charitable purposes generally, albeit subject to a direction as to the timing of the capital distributions. No case remotely like the present had been drawn to my attention.

In the result, despite all the arguments that have been ably advanced, I remain unpersuaded that such a gift is capable of being applied cy près and, in particular, I am not persuaded that the requirement as to distribution is a purpose within the meaning of section 13. Rather, it seems to me to fall on the administrative side of the line, going, as it does, to the mechanics of how the property devoted to charitable purposes is to be distributed. Accordingly, I must refuse the application so far as it is based on section 13.

[Peter Gibson J went on to strike out the term using the inherent jurisdiction of the court: see above.]

Oldham Borough Council v *Attorney-General*
[1993] 2 All ER 432
Court of Appeal

Decision: The facts and decision have already been set out at p. 436. Dillon LJ also considered that the requirement that the actual land given should be used as playing fields was not part of the 'original purposes' within s. 13.

DILLON LJ: The problem arises because of . . . section 13 of the Charities Act 1960, subsections (1) and (2) of which provide as follows [Dillon LJ set out the section and continued:]

Broadly the effect of that section is that an alteration of the 'original purposes' of a charitable gift can only be authorised by a scheme for the cy près application of the trust property and such a scheme can only be made in the circumstances set out in subheads (a) to (e) of subsection (1) of section 13.

It follows that if the retention of a particular property is part of the 'original purposes' of a charitable trust, sale of that property would involve an alteration of the original purposes even if the proceeds of the sale were applied in acquiring an alternative property for carrying out the same charitable activities. If so, a sale of the original property could only be ordered as part of a cy près scheme, and then only if circumstances within one or other of sub heads (a) to (e) are made out. The particular bearing of that in the present case is that the council accepts, and the Attorney-General agrees, that the circumstances of this charity do not fall within any of these subheads.

If therefore, on a true appreciation of the deed of gift and of section 13, the retention of the existing site is part of the original purposes of the charity, the court cannot authorise any sale.

It is necessary therefore to look first at the terms of the deed of gift.

[Dillon LJ concluded that retention of the existing site was part of the original purpose of the donor, and continued:]

I come then to what I regard as the crux of this case, *viz.* the true construction of the words 'original purposes of a charitable gift' in section 13 of the 1960 Act. Do the 'original purposes' include the intention and purpose of the Donor that the land given should be used for ever for the purposes of the charity, or are they limited to the purposes of the charity, in the sense in which Lord Cranworth was using these words in the passage just cited?

Certain of the authorities cited to us can be put on one side. Thus in Re *J. W. Laing Trust* [1984] Ch 143 at 153 Peter Gibson J said, plainly correctly, that 'it cannot be right that any provision, even if only administrative, made applicable by a donor to his gifts should be treated as a condition and hence as a purpose'. In that case, however, the provision, which was held to be administrative and was plainly not a 'purpose', was a provision that the capital was to be wholly distributed within the settlor's lifetime or within 10 years of his death.

Conversely there are cases where the Donor has imposed a condition as part of the terms of his gift, which limits the main purpose of the charity in a way which, with the passage of time, has come to militate against the achievement of that main purpose. The condition was there part of the purpose, but the court found itself able on the facts to cut out the condition by way of a cy près scheme under the cy près jurisdiction, on the ground that the subsistence of the condition made the main purpose impossible or impracticable of achievement. See *Re Dominion Students' Hall Trust* [1947] Ch 183 where a condition of a trust for the maintenance of a hostel for male students of the overseas dominions of the British Empire restricted the benefits to dominion students of European origin. See also *Re Robinson* [1921] 2 Ch 332 where it was a condition of the gift of an endowment for an evangelical church that the preacher should wear a black gown in the pulpit. But unlike those conditions, the intention or purpose in the present case that the actual land given should be used as playing fields is not a condition qualifying the use of that land as playing fields.

It is necessary, in my judgment, in order to answer the crucial question of the true construction of section 13 to appreciate the legislative purpose of section 13. Pennycuick V-C has said in *Re Lepton's Charity* [1972] 1 Ch 276, 284F that the section in part restates the principles applied under the existing law but also extends those principles. But the principles with which it is concerned are the principles for applying property cy près and nothing else. The stringency of those principles as stated in *Re Weir Hospital* [1910] 2 Ch 124 had been somewhat mitigated, but to nothing like the extent contended for by the unsuccessful parties in *Re Weir Hospital*.

[Dillon LJ went on to hold that the sale could be approved without the need to rely on the 1960 Act: see above.]

C: Limit to Commissioners' Scheme-making Powers

Charities: A Framework for the Future
HMSO (May 1989)

The Commissioners' Scheme-making Powers

6.14   Section 18 of the 1960 Act sets out the Commissioners' scheme-making powers but does not enable them to make a scheme of their own volition where there is no properly constituted body of trustees able to apply formally for a scheme. In such cases the Commissioners must first appoint trustees willing, subsequently, to apply for a scheme. In the case of small charities they may rely on 'interested persons' to apply for a scheme. With small local charities, applications from two or more local inhabitants suffice.

6.15   The Woodfield Report rightly noted that, where a neglected charity needed to be reconstituted, this two stage procedure was unduly cumbersome. It recommended – and the Government accept – that powers should be conferred on the Commissioners to establish a scheme where a charity does not have properly constituted trustees.

6.16   One element of legislation not touched on by Woodfield was section 18(6) of the 1960 Act under which the Commissioners can apply to the Secretary of State to refer to them cases where the trustees have unreasonably refused or neglected to make a scheme. This provision has never been invoked and, in most cases, neglect or default should be covered by the Commissioner's powers under section 20. There may, nevertheless, be occasions where there is no maladministration in a charity so as to occasion an inquiry and the application of section 20 powers. The Government intend to provide for this possibility by according the Commissioners a reserve power to establish a scheme should trustees neglect or unreasonably refuse to apply for one, without the need to refer the case to the Secretary of State.

6.17   Section 18 of the 1960 Act gives the Commissioners the powers of the court to make schemes to alter the trusts of a charity on the application of trustees where, for example, the trusts' original purposes are out of date. In accordance with the doctrine of cy-pres, however, the charity's new objects must approximate as closely as possible to the old.

6.18   Woodfield reported that the practical application of cy près often gave rise to confusion amongst trustees, and that apparent inconsistencies in the Commission's interpretation of the doctrine, together with undue reliance on precedent, were seen as stifling new initiatives and inhibiting desirable changes to the objects, especially of parochial charities. The Report therefore recommended that the Commission should consider possible ways of relaxing the cy près doctrine and whether other changes might be desirable.

6.19   Having looked at this question closely and consulted widely the Charity Commissioners take the view, and the Government accept, that legislation would not be appropriate. The problem lies not so much with the doctrine, which has an inbuilt flexibility, nor in the scope of the 1960 charities legislation, as in the doctrine's application. Moreover, the flexibility of cy près is such that, as with the definition of charity, legislation would be positively undesirable, inhibiting its evolution and narrowing its scope. Such flexibility does of course bring with it the risk of confusion and inconsistencies in practice. The Charity Commission will, therefore, be reviewing its precedent systems and the guidance which is given to staff. Its aim will be to promote, across the board, a flexible and imaginative approach, consistent with due regard for the donor's wishes.

Charities Act 1993

(This section replaces the equivalent provision in the 1960 Act, as amended by the Charities Act 1992, s. 20.)

18.   Power to act for protection of charities

(1)   Where, at any time after they have instituted an inquiry under section 8 above with respect to any charity, the Commissioners are satisfied —

(a) that there is or has been any misconduct or mismanagement in the administration of the charity; or

(b) that it is necessary or desirable to act for the purpose of protecting the property of the charity or securing a proper application for the purposes of the charity of that property or of property coming to the charity,

the Commissioners may of their own motion do one or more of the following things —

(i)   by order suspend any trustee, charity trustee, officer, agent or employee of the charity from the exercise of his office or employment pending consideration being given to his removal (whether under this section or otherwise);

(ii)   by order appoint such number of additional charity trustees as they consider necessary for the proper administration of the charity;

(iii)   by order vest any property held by or in trust for the charity in the official custodian, or require the persons in whom any such property is vested to transfer it to him, or appoint any person to transfer any such property to him;

(iv)   order any person who holds any property on behalf of the charity, or of any trustee for it, not to part with the property without the approval of the Commissioners;

(v)   order any debtor of the charity not to make any payment in or towards the discharge of his liability to the charity without the approval of the Commissioners;

(vi)   by order restrict (notwithstanding anything in the trusts of the charity) the transactions which may be entered into, or the nature or amount of the payments which may be made, in the administration of the charity without the approval of the Commissioners;

(vii)   by order appoint (in accordance with section 19 below) a receiver and manager in respect of the property and affairs of the charity.

(2)   Where, at any time after they have instituted an inquiry under section 8 above with respect to any charity, the Commissioners are satisfied —

(a) that there is or has been any misconduct or mismanagement in the administration of the charity; and

(b) that it is necessary or desirable to act for the purpose of protecting the property of the charity or securing a proper application for the purposes of the charity of that property or of property coming to the charity,

the Commissioners may of their own motion do either or both of the following things —

(i)   by order remove any trustee, charity trustee, officer, agent or employee of the charity who has been responsible for or privy to the misconduct or mismanagement or has by his conduct contributed to it or facilitated it;

(ii)   by order establish a scheme for the administration of the charity.

(3)   The references in subsection (1) or (2) above to misconduct or mismanagement shall (notwithstanding anything in the trusts of the charity) extend to the employment for the remuneration or reward of persons acting in the affairs of the charity, or for other administrative purposes, of sums which are excessive in relation to the property which is or is likely to be applied or applicable for the purposes of the charity.

(4)   The Commissioners may also remove a charity trustee by order made of their own motion —

(a) where, within the last five years, the trustee —

(i)   having previously been adjudged bankrupt or had his estate sequestrated, has been discharged, or

(ii)   having previously made a composition or arrangement with, or granted a trust deed for, his creditors, has been discharged in respect of it;

(b) where the trustee is a corporation in liquidation;

(c) where the trustee is incapable of acting by reason of mental disorder within the meaning of the Mental Health Act 1983;

(d) where the trustee has not acted, and will not declare his willingness or unwillingness to act;

(e) where the trustee is outside England and Wales or cannot be found or does not act, and his absence or failure to act impedes the proper administration of the charity.

(5) The Commissioners may by order made of their own motion appoint a person to be a charity trustee —

(a) in place of a charity trustee removed by them under this section or otherwise;

(b) where there are no charity trustees, or where by reason of vacancies in their number or the absence or incapacity of any of their number the charity cannot apply for the appointment;

(c) where there is a single charity trustee, not being a corporation aggregate, and the Commissioners are of opinion that it is necessary to increase the number for the proper administration of the charity;

(d) where the Commissioners are of opinion that it is necessary for the proper administration of the charity to have an additional charity trustee because one of the existing charity trustees who ought nevertheless to remain a charity trustee either cannot be found or does not act or is outside England and Wales.

(6) The powers of the Commissioners under this section to remove or appoint charity trustees of their own motion shall include power to make any such order with respect to the vesting in or transfer to the charity trustees of any property as the Commissioners could make on the removal or appointment of a charity trustee by them under section 16 above.

(7) Any order under this section for the removal or appointment of a charity trustee or trustee for a charity, or for the vesting or transfer of any property, shall be of the like effect as an order made under section 16 above.

(8) Subject to subsection (9) below, subsections (11) to (13) of section 16 above shall apply to orders under this section as they apply to orders under that section.

(9) The requirement to obtain any such certificate or leave as is mentioned in section 16(13) above shall not apply to—

(a) an appeal by a charity or any of the charity trustees of a charity against an order under subsection (1)(vii) above appointing a receiver and manager in respect of the charity's property and affairs, or

(b) an appeal by a person against an order under subsection (2)(i) or (4)(a) above removing him from his office or employment.

(10) Subsection (14) of section 16 above shall apply to an order under this section which establishes a scheme for the administration of a charity as it applies to such an order under that section.

(11) The power of the Commissioners to make an order under subsection (1)(i) above shall not be exercisable so as to suspend any person from the exercise of his office or employment for a period of more than twelve months; but (without prejudice to the generality of section 89(1) below), any such order made in the case of any person may make provision as respects the period of his suspension for matters arising out of it, and in particular for enabling any person to execute any instrument in his name or otherwise act for him and, in the case of a charity trustee, for adjusting any rules governing the proceedings of the charity trustees to take account of the reduction in the number capable of acting.

(12)   Before exercising any jurisdiction under this section otherwise than by virtue of subsection (1) above, the Commissioners shall give notice of their intention to do so to each of the charity trustees, except any that cannot be found or has no known address in the United Kingdom; and any such notice may be given by post and, if given by post, may be addressed to the recipient's last known address in the United Kingdom.

(13)   The Commissioners shall, at such intervals as they think fit, review any order made by them under paragraph (i), or any of paragraphs (iii) to (vii), of subsection (1) above; and, if on any such review it appears to them that it would be appropriate to discharge the order in whole or in part, they shall so discharge it (whether subject to any savings or other transitional provisions or not).

(14)   If any person contravenes an order under subsection (1)(iv), (v) or (vi) above, he shall be guilty of an offence and liable on summary conviction to a fine not exceeding level 5 on the standard scale.

(15)   Subsection (14) above shall not be taken to preclude the bringing of proceedings for breach of trust against any charity trustee or trustee for a charity in respect of a contravention of an order under subsection (1)(iv) or (vi) above (whether proceedings in respect of the contravention are brought against him under subsection (14) above or not).

(16)   This section shall not apply to an exempt charity.

SECTION 5:   CHARITIES ACT 1993, S. 14
(REPLACING SAME SECTION OF 1960 ACT)

Charities Act 1993

14. Application cy près of gifts of donors unknown or disclaiming

(1)   Property given for specific charitable purposes which fail shall be applicable cy près as if given for charitable purposes generally, where it belongs —

(a)   to a donor who after —

(i)   the prescribed advertisements and inquiries have been published and made, and

(ii)   the prescribed period beginning with the publication of those advertisements has expired,

cannot be identified or cannot be found; or

(b)   to a donor who has executed a disclaimer in the prescribed form of his right to have the property returned.

(2)   Where the prescribed advertisements and inquiries have been published and made by or on behalf of trustees with respect to any such property, the trustees shall not be liable to any person in respect of the property if no claim by him to be interested in it is received by them before the expiry of the period mentioned in subsection (1)(a)(ii) above.

(3)   For the purposes of this section property shall be conclusively presumed (without any advertisement or inquiry) to belong to donors who cannot be identified, in so far as it consists —

(a)   of the proceeds of cash collections made by means of collecting boxes or by other means not adapted for distinguishing one gift from another; or

(b)   of the proceeds of any lottery, competition, entertainment, sale or similar money-raising activity, after allowing for property given to provide prizes or articles for sale or otherwise to enable the activity to be undertaken.

(4)   The court may by order direct that property not falling within subsection (3) above shall for the purposes of this section be treated (without any advertisement or

inquiry) as belonging to donors who cannot be identified where it appears to the court
either —

(a) that it would be unreasonable, having regard to the amounts likely to be
returned to the donors, to incur expense with a view to returning the property; or

(b) that it would be unreasonable, having regard to the nature, circumstances
and amounts of the gifts, and to the lapse of time since the gifts were made, for the
donors to expect the property to be returned.

(5) Where property is applied cy près by virtue of this section, the donor shall be
deemed to have parted with all his interest at the time when the gift was made; but
where property is so applied as belonging to donors who cannot be identified or
cannot be found, and is not so applied by virtue of subsection (3) or (4) above —

(a) the scheme shall specify the total amount of that property; and

(b) the donor of any part of that amount shall be entitled, if he makes a claim
not later than six months after the date on which the scheme is made, to recover from
the charity for which the property is applied a sum equal to that part, less any expenses
properly incurred by the charity trustees after that date in connection with claims
relating to his gift; and

(c) the scheme may include directions as to the provision to be made for
meeting any such claim.

(6) Where —

(a) any sum is, in accordance with any such directions, set aside for meeting any
such claims, but

(b) the aggregate amount of any such claims actually made exceeds the relevant
amount,

then, if the Commissioners so direct, each of the donors in question shall be entitled
only to such proportion of the relevant amount as the amount of his claim bears to
the aggregate amount referred to in paragraph (b) above; and for this purpose 'the
relevant amount' means the amount of the sum so set aside after deduction of any
expenses properly incurred by the charity trustees in connection with claims relating
to the donors' gifts.

(7) For the purposes of this section, charitable purposes shall be deemed to 'fail'
where any difficulty in applying property to those purposes makes that property or the
part not applicable cy près available to be returned to the donors.

(8) In this section 'prescribed' means prescribed by regulations made by the
Commissioners; and such regulations may, as respects the advertisements which are to be
published for the purposes of subsection (1)(a) above, make provision as to the form and
content of such advertisements as well as the manner in which they are to be published.

(9) Any regulations made by the Commissioners under this section shall be
published by the Commissioners in such manner as they think fit.

(10) In this section, except in so far as the context otherwise requires, references
to a donor include persons claiming through or under the original donor, and
references to property given include the property for the time being representing the
property originally given or property derived from it.

(11) This section shall apply to property given for charitable purposes, notwithstanding that it was so given before the commencement of this Act.

Questions

1. Does s. 14 apply where funds are raised for a charitable purpose which
later fails leaving a surplus? See *Re Ulverston and District New Hospital Building
Trusts*, above.

2. Section 14(1) is triggered only where property belongs to a donor. Is it therefore triggered, on an initial failure, where the donor has contributed by means of an anonymous street collecting box? Does the property belong to the donor in that case? If not, does s. 14(3) have any effect? See further David Wilson [1983] Conv 40.

Re Henry Wood National Memorial Trusts, Armstrong v *Moiseiwitsch*
[1967] 1 All ER 238n
Chancery Division

STAMP J (on an adjourned summons to determine what were reasonable inquiries under s. 14(2) of the 1960 Act, replaced by s. 14(3) of the 1993 Act): The following notices, together with inquiries already made, would constitute reasonable advertisements and inquiries for identifying and finding donors who have not disclaimed, *viz*. – notices inviting a donor who does not wish to give a written disclaimer to notify his name and address in writing to the designated agents of the trustees, so as to be received by them before a specified date not less than two months after publication or posting of the notice, such a notice to be inserted in two issues of each of the following newspapers, namely, *The Times*, *The Daily Telegraph* and *The Scotsman*, and to be sent by ordinary post to the address, as recorded in the books and papers of the trustees, of every donor who made any such gift and has such a recorded address (not being an address of a formation or unit of Her Majesty's Forces) but who has not already given such a written disclaimer.

SECTION 6: SMALL POVERTY CHARITIES

Many old charities for the relief of poverty required trustees to distribute money or goods, but the growth of state welfare reduced the attractiveness of these, and even rendered them counter-productive in some cases, because hand-outs can lead to a reduction in state benefit. As long ago as 1967 the Annual Report of the Charity Commissioners (paras 17–20 and App. B) recognised the problem involved in cash hand-outs by commenting on the undesirability of using charity funds to relieve the burdens of the DHSS and local authorities, and instead suggested other schemes, for example outings or home decoration. Yet many old trusts to relieve poverty bound trustees to distribute money or goods.

A possible solution to this problem existed under the provisions of the Charities Act 1960, but the mechanisms for the full scheme-making powers contained therein were arguably too complicated for very small charities. Following a report of a House of Lords Select Committee in 1984, the Charities Act 1985 addressed this problem. Section 2 allowed trustees of charities more than 50 years old, by a simplified procedure, to change the objects to more suitable ones, so long as they were within the spirit of the original donor's intentions. Under s. 3, where the annual income of a charity was less than £200, the trustees could transfer its property to another charity having similar aims, or if its income was less than £5 a year, the trustees under s. 4 could wind it up, by spending the capital as if it were income.

Charities: A Framework for the Future
HMSO (May 1989)

The Charities Act 1985

6.3   In its report, published in 1984, the House of Lords Select Committee on the Parochial and Small Charities Bills found serious shortcomings in the administration and effectiveness of small charities and local charities for the relief of poverty. Trustees were not sufficiently accountable; in many cases the purposes for which charities for the relief of poverty had been set up were no longer useful or practicable; and many charities were simply too small to be effective. The Charities Act 1985 aimed to remedy these deficiencies. It established new and simpler mechanisms to enable the objects of certain local charities for the poor to be modified, and to facilitate the amalgamation of registered charities with an income of £200 or less. The Act also, for the first time, enabled the trustees of very small permanently endowed – but non-land owning – charities to spend their capital as income.

6.4   As the Woodfield Report noted, the Act has an important role to play in improving the effectiveness of small charities. The Government agree that it would be improved by simplifying certain of its provisions, and by extending its application to all small charities. Full scheme-making procedures, subject to appeal to the court, will continue to be appropriate for charities with substantial resources.

6.5   Suggested amendments to section 1 of the Act are covered in Chapter 4. The following changes are proposed to other sections.

6.6   Section 2 of the 1985 Act currently allows trustees of local charities for the relief of poverty which are at least 50 years old to modify their objects. Section 3 enables trustees of registered charities or charities which are not required to be registered, with a gross annual income of £200 or less, to transfer the whole of the charity's property, including land, to another charity. Section 5(1)(b) gives the Secretary of State power to increase this sum 'if he thinks it expedient, with a view to increasing the number of charities which may take advantage of this provision'. The Government propose to standardise the application of sections 2 and 3. In future both these sections will apply to all charities with an income of less than £1,000 a year (including ecclesiastical charities) without distinction of age, locality or purpose. The sole exception will be those holding land for the purposes of the charity.

6.7   Under the new legislation, trustees wishing to modify their object or amalgamate with another charity would need to be satisfied:

— that the original purposes had, since they were laid down, ceased to provide a suitable and effective method of using the property; and
— that the new objects specified, or the objects of the charity to which property was being transferred, were as similar as practicable to the charity's original objects having regard to the spirit of the gift.

6.8   Trustees would continue to be required to act by unanimous resolution and with the Commissioners' concurrence, and to give reasonable public notice of their intentions. They would not, however, be required to send copies of their resolutions to the appropriate local authority: in many cases this merely duplicates information provided to local authorities by the Commissioners themselves.

6.9   Transfers of property under section 3 will, of course, continue to require the consent of the trustees of receiving charities and, as now, the property transferred will remain subject to the same restrictions on expenditure as applied before the transfer. The Government do not intend, however, that it should any longer be necessary for a charity proposing to transfer its property to another charity to be registered. This requirement is unnecessary as a spur to registration, a hindrance to transfers, and causes nugatory work for trustees and Commissioners alike.

6.10   Section 4 of the 1985 Act empowers trustees of very small permanently endowed – but not land-owning – charities to spend capital as income. The present income limit of £5 a year could not be raised to £1,000 to bring this section in line with preceding sections without breaching substantially the sanctity in charity trust law of the concept of permanent endowment. It is proposed to raise the income limit by a lesser amount, however, enabling charities with an annual income of £250 a year or less to resolve to spend capital as income. As now, it will be for trustees to judge that the property of the charity is too small in relation to its objects for any useful purpose to be achieved by the expenditure of income alone. However, as a safeguard the Commissioners will in future be required to concur. Charities will also be required to give reasonable public notice of their intentions.

6.11   The Government consider that trustees who have the power to alter objects and transfer property should also be given powers to resolve to change the administrative provisions of their trusts where these have proved deficient in some way, for example in relation to the appointment of trustees, the conduct of meetings, or investment powers. In such cases the Commissioners would need to be satisfied that the proposed changes were reasonable and practicable.

Note

The following enactment brought these proposals into force, albeit with higher financial limits.

Charities Act 1993

74.   Power to transfer all property, modify objects etc

(1)   This section applies to a charity if —

(a)   its gross income in its last financial year did not exceed £5,000, and

(b)   it does not hold any land on trusts which stipulate that the land is to be used for the purposes, or any particular purposes, of the charity,

and it is neither an exempt charity nor a charitable company.

(2)   Subject to the following provisions of this section, the charity trustees of a charity to which this section applies may resolve for the purposes of this section —

(a)   that all the property of the charity should be transferred to such other charity as is specified in the resolution, being either a registered charity or a charity which is not required to be registered;

(b)   that all the property of the charity should be divided, in such manner as is specified in the resolution, between such two or more other charities as are so specified, being in each case either a registered charity or a charity which is not required to be registered;

(c)   that the trusts of the charity should be modified by replacing all or any of the purposes of the charity with such other purposes, being in law charitable, as are specified in the resolution;

(d)   that any provision of the trusts of the charity —

(i)   relating to any of the powers exercisable by the charity trustees in the administration of the charity, or

(ii)   regulating the procedure to be followed in any respect in connection with its administration,

should be modified in such manner as is specified in the resolution.

(3)   Any resolution passed under subsection (2) above must be passed by a majority of not less than two-thirds of such charity trustees as vote on the resolution.

(4)   The charity trustees of a charity to which this section applies ('the transferor charity') shall not have power to pass a resolution under subsection (2)(a) or (b) above unless they are satisfied —

(a)   that the existing purposes of the transferor charity have ceased to be conducive to a suitable and effective application of the charity's resources; and

(b)   that the purposes of the charity or charities specified in the resolution are as similar in character to the purposes of the transferor charity as is reasonably practicable;

and before passing the resolution they must have received from the charity trustees of the charity, or (as the case may be) of each of the charities, specified in the resolution written confirmation that those trustees are willing to accept a transfer of property under this section.

(5)   The charity trustees of any such charity shall not have power to pass a resolution under subsection (2)(c) above unless they are satisfied —

(a)   that the existing purposes of the charity (or, as the case may be, such of them as it is proposed to replace) have ceased to be conducive to a suitable and effective application of the charity's resources; and

(b)   that the purposes specified in the resolution are as similar in character to those existing purposes as is practical in the circumstances.

(6)   Where charity trustees have passed a resolution under subsection (2) above, they shall —

(a)   give public notice of the resolution in such manner as they think reasonable in the circumstances; and

(b)   send a copy of the resolution to the Commissioners, together with a statement of their reasons for passing it.

(7)   The Commissioners may, when considering the resolution, require the charity trustees to provide additional information or explanation —

(a)   as to the circumstances in and by reference to which they have determined to act under this section, or

(b)   relating to their compliance with this section in connection with the resolution;

and the Commissioners shall take into account any representations made to them by persons appearing to them to be interested in the charity where those representations are made within the period of six weeks beginning with the date when the Commissioners receive a copy of the resolution by virtue of subsection (6)(b) above.

(8)   Where the Commissioners have so received a copy of a resolution from any charity trustees and it appears to them that the trustees have complied with this section in connection with the resolution, the Commissioners shall, within the period of three months beginning with the date when they receive the copy of the resolution, notify the trustees in writing either —

(a)   that the Commissioners concur with the resolution; or

(b)   that they do not concur with it.

(9)   Where the Commissioners so notify their concurrence with the resolution, then —

(a)   if the resolution was passed under subsection (2)(a) or (b) above, the charity trustees shall arrange for all the property of the transferor charity to be transferred in accordance with the resolution and on terms that any property so transferred —

(i)   shall be held and applied by the charity to which it is transferred ('the transferee charity') for the purposes of that charity, but

(ii)   shall, as property of the transferee charity, nevertheless be subject to any restrictions on expenditure to which it is subject as property of the transferor charity, and those trustees shall arrange for it to be so transferred by such date as may be specified in the notification; and

(b)   if the resolution was passed under subsection (2)(c) or (d) above, the trusts of the charity shall be deemed, as from such date as may be specified in the notification, to have been modified in accordance with the terms of the resolution.

(10)   For the purpose of enabling any property to be transferred to a charity under this section, the Commissioners shall have power, at the request of the charity trustees of that charity, to make orders vesting any property of the transferor charity —

(a)   in the charity trustees of the first-mentioned charity or in any trustee for that charity, or

(b)   in any other person nominated by those charity trustees to hold the property in trust for that charity.

(11)   The Secretary of State may by order amend subsection (1) above by substituting a different sum for the sum for the time being specified there.

(12)   In this section —

(a)   'charitable company' means a charity which is a company or other body corporate; and

(b)   references to the transfer of property to a charity are references to its transfer —

(i)   to the charity trustees, or

(ii)   to any trustee for the charity, or

(iii)   to a person nominated by the charity trustees to hold it in trust for the charity, as the charity trustees may determine.

75.   Power to spend capital

(1)   This section applies to a charity if —

(a)   it has a permanent endowment which does not consist of or comprise any land, and

(b)   its gross income in its last financial year did not exceed £1,000, and it is neither an exempt charity nor a charitable company.

(2)   Where the charity trustees of a charity to which this section applies are of the opinion that the property of the charity is too small, in relation to its purposes, for any useful purpose to be achieved by the expenditure of income alone, they may resolve for the purposes of this section that the charity ought to be freed from the restrictions with respect to expenditure of capital to which its permanent endowment is subject.

(3)   Any resolution passed under subsection (2) above must be passed by a majority of not less than two-thirds of such charity trustees as vote on the resolution.

(4)   Before passing such a resolution the charity trustees must consider whether any reasonable possibility exists of effecting a transfer or division of all the charity's property under section 74 above (disregarding any such transfer or division as would, in their opinion, impose on the charity an unacceptable burden of costs).

(5)   Where charity trustees have passed a resolution under subsection (2) above, they shall —

(a)   give public notice of the resolution in such manner as they think reasonable in the circumstances; and

(b)   send a copy of the resolution to the Commissioners, together with a statement of their reasons for passing it.

(6)   The Commissioners may, when considering the resolution, require the charity trustees to provide additional information or explanation —

(a)   as to the circumstances in and by reference to which they have determined to act under this section, or

(b)   relating to their compliance with this section in connection with the resolution;

and the Commissioners shall take into account any representations made to them by persons appearing to them to be interested in the charity where those representations are made within the period of six weeks beginning with the date when the Commissioners receive a copy of the resolution by virtue of subsection (5)(b) above.

(7)   Where the Commissioners have so received a copy of a resolution from any charity trustees and it appears to them that the trustees have complied with this section in connection with the resolution, the Commissioners shall, within the period of three months beginning with of the resolution, notify the trustees in writing either —

(a)   that the Commissioners concur with the resolution; or

(b)   that they do not concur with it.

(8)   Where the Commissioners so notify their concurrence with the resolution, the charity trustees shall have, as from such date as may be specified in the notification, power by virtue of this section to expend any property of the charity without regard to any such restrictions as are mentioned in subsection (2) above.

(9)   The Secretary of State may by order amend subsection (1) above by substituting a different sum for the sum for the time being specified there.

(10)   In this section 'charitable company' means a charity which is a company or other body corporate.

14   THE OFFICE OF TRUSTEE

SECTION 1:   STANDARD REQUIRED OF TRUSTEE

In managing the affairs of the trust, the trustees must act honestly and must take (according to Lord Blackburn in *Speight* v *Gaunt* (1883) 9 App Cas 1, 19) 'all those precautions which an ordinary prudent man of business would take in managing similar affairs of his own'. The selection of investments involves additional considerations, for although ordinary business prudence may sometimes involve accepting a degree of risk or speculation, trustees must confine themselves to those securities which are authorised by the trust instrument or by statute, and avoid hazardous investments. This was further elaborated upon in *Re Whitely* (1886) 33 ChD 347, at p. 355:

> The duty of a trustee is not to take such care only as a prudent man would take if he had only himself to consider; the duty rather is to take such care as an ordinary prudent man would take if he were minded to make an investment for the benefit of people for whom he felt morally bound to provide.

This suggests that a more conservative approach is in order than might be considered appropriate for investments on the trustee's own behalf.

Bartlett v *Barclays Bank Trust Co. Ltd (No. 1)*
[1980] Ch 515, [1980] 1 All ER 139
Chancery Division

Facts: The bank, as trustee under a settlement of shares in a private company, Bartletts Trust Ltd (BTL), had a controlling interest in that company. From 1960 the board of BTL had no director representing the settlor's family or acting for the bank. The bank made no objection at the annual general meeting of BTL in 1961, when BTL altered its investment policy to go into property development. The board of BTL accordingly embarked on two hazardous development projects, without consulting the bank, and the bank did not insist on receiving a regular flow of information on the progress of these projects. Although one of these projects, at Guildford, was successful, the project at Old Bailey, London, which involved buying at a high price on the chance that planning permission for development would be granted, was unsuccessful, and BTL sustained a large loss. The beneficiaries under the settlement sued the bank.

Held:

(a) The bank was in breach of its duty as trustee.

(b) However, since the Guildford and Old Bailey projects, although separate transactions, were part of the same overall policy of BTL, the bank was entitled to set off the profit from the Guildford transaction against the loss from the Old Bailey project.

(c) The bank could not use s. 61 of the Trustee Act 1925 (see chapter 16) as a defence, since that section protected only trustees who had acted honestly and reasonably. The bank had acted honestly, but not reasonably.

(d) However, in relation to income lost outside the limitation period, the bank could rely on s. 19 of the Limitation Act 1939 (see now Limitation Act 1980, s. 21: see chapter 16). Under s. 21(1), the limitation period does not apply in respect of a fraudulent breach of trust. The bank had not acted fraudulently, however. Although fraud for limitation purposes was wider than common law fraud or deceit, it required unconscionable conduct on the part of the trustee, something in the nature of a deliberate cover up. Here, the bank was unaware that it was acting in breach of trust, so was not guilty of fraud for limitation purposes.

BRIGHTMAN J (on the duty of the bank): What, then was the duty of the bank and did the bank fail in its duty? It does not follow that because a trustee could have prevented a loss it is therefore liable for that loss. The questions which I must ask myself are: (1) what was the duty of the bank as the holder of 99.8% of the shares in BTL and BTH [Bartlett Trust Holdings Ltd, a holding company of which BTL was a wholly owned subsidiary since 1967]? (2) was the bank in breach of duty in any and if so in what respect? (3) if so, did that breach of duty cause the loss which was suffered by the trust estate? (4) if so, to what extent is the bank liable to make good that loss? In approaching these questions, I bear in mind that the attack on the bank is based, not on wrongful acts, but on wrongful omissions, that is to say, non-feasance not misfeasance.

The cases establish that it is the duty of a trustee to conduct the business of the trust with the same care as an ordinary prudent man of business would extend towards his own affairs: see *Re Speight, Speight* v *Gaunt* (1883) 22 ChD 727 at 739, 762 per Jessel MR and Bowen LJ (affirmed on appeal (1883) 9 App Cas 1 and see Lord Blackburn at 19). In applying this principle, Lindley LJ (who was the third member of the court in *Re Speight*) added in *Re Whitely* (1886) 33 ChD 347 at 355:

. . . care must be taken not to lose sight of the fact that the business of the trustee, and the business which the ordinary prudent man is supposed to be conducting for himself, is the business of investing money for the benefit of persons who are to enjoy it at some future time, and not for the sole benefit of the person entitled to the present income. The duty of a trustee is not to take such care only as a prudent man would take if he had only himself to consider; the duty rather is to take such care as an ordinary prudent man would take if he were minded to make an investment for the benefit of people for whom he felt morally bound to provide. That is the kind of business the ordinary prudent man is supposed to be engaged in; and unless this is borne in mind the standard of a trustee's duty will be fixed too low; lower than it has ever yet been fixed, and lower, certainly than the House of Lords or this court endeavoured to fix it in *Speight* v *Gaunt*.

On appeal Lord Watson added (1887) 12 App Cas 727 at 733:

Businessmen of ordinary prudence may, and frequently do, select investments which are more or less of a speculative character; but it is the duty of a trustee to confine himself to the class of investments which are permitted by the trust, and likewise to avoid all investments of that class which are attended with hazard.

That does not mean that the trustee is bound to avoid all risk and in effect act as an insurer of the trust fund: in *Re Godfrey* (1883) 23 ChD 483 at 493 Bacon V-C said:

No doubt it is the duty of a trustee, in administering the trusts of a will, to deal with property intrusted into his care exactly as any prudent man would deal with his own property. But the words in which the rule is expressed must not be strained beyond their meaning. Prudent businessmen in their dealings incur risk. That may and must happen in almost all human affairs.

The distinction is between a prudent degree of risk on the one hand, and hazard on the other. Nor must the court be astute to fix liability on a trustee who has committed no more than an error of judgment, from which no businessman, however prudent, can expect to be immune: in *Re Chapman* [1896] 2 Ch 763 at 778, Lopes LJ said:

A trustee who is honest and reasonably competent is not to be held responsible for a mere error in judgment when the question which he has to consider is whether a security of a class authorised but depreciated in value, should be retained or realised, provided he acts with reasonable care, prudence and circumspection.

[Brightman J described the hazardous nature of the Old Bailey project and continued:]
The prudent man of business will act in such manner as is necessary to safeguard his investment. He will do this in two ways. If facts come to his knowledge which tell him that the company's affairs are not being conducted as they should be, or which put him on enquiry, he will take appropriate action. Appropriate action will no doubt consist in the first instance of enquiry of and consultation with the directors, and in the last but most unlikely resort, the convening of a general meeting to replace one or more directors. What the prudent man of business will not do is to content himself with the receipt of such information on the affairs of the company as a shareholder ordinarily receives at annual general meetings. Since he has the power to do so, he will go further and see that he has sufficient information to enable him to make a responsible decision from time to time either to let matters proceed as they are proceeding, or to intervene if he is dissatisfied. This topic was considered by Cross J in *Re Lucking's WT* [1968] 1 WLR 866 [below].
[Brightman J set out the facts of *Lucking*, and quoted the judgment of Cross J on the standard of care applicable to trustees – the last paragraph in the extract in this section – and continued:]

I do not understand Cross J to have been saying that in every case where trustees have a controlling interest in a company it is their duty to ensure that one of their number is a director or that they have a nominee on the board who will report from time to time on the affairs of the company. He was merely outlining convenient methods by which a prudent man of business (as also a trustee) with a controlling interest in a private company, can place himself in a position to make an informed decision whether any action is appropriate to be taken for the protection of his asset. Other methods may be equally satisfactory and convenient, depending on the circumstances of the individual case. Alternatives which spring to mind are the receipt of the copies of the agenda and minutes of board meetings if regularly held, the receipt of monthly management accounts in the case of a trading concern, or quarterly reports. Every case will depend on its own facts. The possibilities are endless. It would be useless, indeed misleading, to seek to lay down a general rule. The purpose to be achieved is not that of monitoring every move of the directors, but of making it reasonably probable, so far as circumstances permit, that the trustee or (as in *Re Lucking's WT*) one of them will receive an adequate flow of information in time to enable the trustees to make use of their controlling interest should this be necessary for the protection of their trust asset, namely the shareholding. The obtaining of information is not an end in itself, but merely a means of enabling the trustees to safeguard the interests of their beneficiaries.

The principle enunciated in *Re Lucking's WT* appears to have been applied in *Re Miller's Deed Trusts*, decided by Oliver J. No transcript of the judgment is available but the case is briefly noted in a journal of the Law Society (1978) 75 LS Gaz 454). There are also a number of American decisions proceeding on the same lines, to which counsel has helpfully referred me.

So far, I have applied the test of the ordinary prudent man of business. Although I am not aware that the point has previously been considered, except briefly in *Re Waterman's WT* [1952] 2 All ER 1054, I am of the opinion that a higher duty of care is plainly due from someone like a trust corporation which carries on a specialised business of trust management. A trust corporation holds itself out in its advertising literature as being above ordinary mortals. With a specialist staff of trained trust officers and managers, with ready access to financial information and professional advice, dealing with and solving trust problems day after day, the trust corporation holds itself out, and rightly, as capable of providing an expertise which it would be unrealistic to expect and unjust to demand from the ordinary prudent man or woman who accepts, probably unpaid and sometimes reluctantly from a sense of family duty, the burdens of a trusteeship. Just as, under the law of contract, a professional person possessed of a particular skill is liable for breach of contract if he neglects to use the skill and experience which he professes, so I think that a professional corporate trustee is liable for breach of trust if loss is caused to the trust fund because it neglects to exercise the special care and skill which it professes to have. The advertising literature of the bank was not in evidence (other than the scale of fees) but counsel for the bank did not dispute that trust corporations, including the bank, hold themselves out as possessing a superior ability for the conduct of trust business, and in any event I would take judicial notice of that fact. Having expressed my view of the higher duty required from a trust corporation, I should add that the bank's counsel did not dispute the proposition.

In my judgment the bank wrongfully and in breach of trust neglected to ensure that it received an adequate flow of information concerning the intentions and activities of the boards of BTL and BTH. It was not proper for the bank to confine itself to the receipt of the annual balance sheet and profit and loss account, detailed annual financial statements and the chairman's report and statement, and to attendance at the annual general meetings and the luncheons that followed, which were the limits of the bank's regular sources of information. . . .

I hold that the bank failed in its duty whether it is judged by the standard of the prudent man of business or of the skilled trust corporation.

Notes
1.   Brightman J thought that a higher standard of care is required of paid trustees than of unpaid, non-professional trustees, in that the former will be held to the standards of skill and expertise which they claim to possess.
2.   In *Bartlett*, however, the bank would have been liable on the standard applied in *Speight* v *Gaunt*, and it was unnecessary to rely on the higher standard owed by professional trustees.
3.   See also *Cowan* v *Scargill* [1984] 3 WLR 501 (chapter 15).

SECTION 2:   PERSONAL NATURE OF TRUSTEESHIP

Since trustees need not be experts in finance, etc., it is obviously very important for trustees to be able to employ others to carry out the more specialised aspects of trust management.

Equity has therefore always allowed the employment of agents in effecting specialised administrative functions, for example solicitors, accountants and stockbrokers. Prior to the intervention of the Trustee Act 1925 two principles had been established by the House of Lords in *Speight* v *Gaunt* (1884) 9 App Cas 1. First, it was permissible to employ an agent where this was reasonably necessary, or in accord with normal business practices. Secondly, where such an agent was employed, trustees would not be liable for losses attributable to the agent so long as they took proper care in his selection, employed him within his proper sphere, and exercised reasonable general supervision over his work.

A: Power to Delegate

Trustee Act 1925

23.   Power to employ agents
(1)   Trustees or personal representatives may, instead of acting personally, employ and pay an agent, whether a solicitor, banker, stockbroker, or other person, to transact any business or do any act required to be transacted or done in the execution of the trust, or the administration of the testator's or intestate's estate, including the receipt and payment of money, and shall be entitled to be allowed and paid all charges and expenses so incurred, and shall not be responsible for the default of any such agent if employed in good faith.
(2)   Trustees or personal representatives may appoint any person to act as their agent or attorney for the purpose of selling, converting, collecting, getting in, and executing and perfecting insurances of, or managing or cultivating, or otherwise administering any property, real or personal, moveable or immoveable, subject to the trust or forming part of the testator's or intestate's estate, in any place outside the

United Kingdom or executing or exercising any discretion or trust or power vested in them in relation to any such property, with such ancillary powers, and with and subject to such provisions and restrictions as they may think fit, including a power to appoint substitutes, and shall not, by reason only of their having made such appointment, be responsible for any loss arising thereby.

(3) Without prejudice to such general power of appointing agents as aforesaid —

(a) A trustee may appoint a solicitor to be his agent to receive and give a discharge for any money or valuable consideration or property receivable by the trustee under the trust, by permitting the solicitor to have the custody of, and to produce, a deed having in the body thereof or endorsed thereon a receipt for such money or valuable consideration or property, the deed being executed, or the endorsed receipt being signed, by the person entitled to give a receipt for that consideration;

(b) A trustee shall not be chargeable with breach of trust by reason only of his having made or concurred in making any such appointment; and the production of any such deed by the solicitor shall have the same statutory validity and effect as if the person appointing the solicitor had not been a trustee;

(c) A trustee may appoint a banker or solicitor to be his agent to receive and give a discharge for any money payable to the trustee under or by virtue of a policy of insurance, by permitting the banker or solicitor to have the custody of and to produce the policy of insurance with a receipt signed by the trustee, and a trustee shall not be chargeable with a breach of trust by reason only of his having made or concurred in making any such appointment:

Provided that nothing in this subsection shall exempt a trustee from any liability which he would have incurred if this Act and any enactment replaced by this Act had not been passed, in case he permits any such money, valuable consideration, or property to remain in the hands or under the control of the banker or solicitor for a period longer than is reasonably necessary to enable the banker or solicitor, as the case may be, to pay or transfer the same to the trustee.

This subsection applies whether the money or valuable consideration or property was or is received before or after the commencement of this Act.

Note

Clearly, the effect of s. 23(1) is considerably to reduce the burdens of trusteeship by permitting trustees to reduce their own workload at the expense of the trust.

The section applies only to executive or administrative functions, and does not alter the fundamental principle, at least where the property is within the UK, that trustees may not delegate the powers and discretions which belong to them alone by virtue of their office. These discretions are not of a purely executive nature, but involve real choices, for example deciding how to distribute under a discretionary trust. They may, and sometimes must, take expert advice before exercising these discretions, but the decision must be theirs alone.

In respect of property outside the UK, however, s. 23(2) allows trustees to delegate not only their powers of sale, management, etc., but also their discretions. Such delegation had been accepted as justified since the middle of the nineteenth century where property had to be administered abroad.

Section 23(3) permits the delegation to a limited class of professional agents certain functions which are most conveniently performed by such

agents, but which would not otherwise be permissible. They sanction practices that have now become normal. Section 23(3)(a) meets the case where a
receipt for money is contained in the body of a deed, a common practice in
conveyances of land. The solicitor acting for the vendor will typically hold the
deed until completion, when he will hand it over to the purchaser in exchange
for the purchase price. Were it not for this section, it would probably be
improper for trustees to employ an agent to hold a receipt, in case he
absconds with the purchase money. Because of the Act trustees who engage
in this normal (and usually harmless) practice will not be liable merely
because they appointed the solicitor. Similar protection is conferred by
s. 23(3)(c) where solicitors or bankers employed to receive money under
insurance policies are granted custody of the policy and the trustees' signed
receipt.

B: Liability for Agents

Trustee Act 1925

30.   Implied indemnity of trustees

(1)   A trustee shall be chargeable only for money and securities actually received
by him notwithstanding his signing any receipt for the sake of conformity, and shall
be answerable and accountable only for his own acts, receipts, neglects, or defaults,
and not for those of any other trustee, nor for any banker, broker, or other person
with whom any trust money or securities may be deposited, nor for the insufficiency
or deficiency of any securities, nor for any other loss, unless the same happens through
his own wilful default.

(2)   A trustee may reimburse himself or pay or discharge out of the trust premises
all expenses incurred in or about the execution of the trusts or powers.

Notes

1.   Section 30 replaced with amendments the Trustee Act 1893, s. 24, which
itself re-enacted the Law of Property Amendment Act 1859, s. 31; and under
those provisions, 'wilful default' was treated as a failure to do what was
reasonable, so that failure to supervise an agent might render a trustee liable.
Section 23(1), however (which replaced with amendments the Trustee Act
1893, s. 17), states that trustees 'shall not be responsible for the default of
any such agent if employed in good faith', which suggests that so long as the
appointment was made in good faith, liability will not arise where loss is due
to inadequate supervision.

2.   In *Re Vickery* [1931] 1 Ch 572, Maugham J attempted to resolve the issue
where the executor of a will had employed a solicitor to wind up the estate,
giving the solicitor signed authority to collect money on deposit with the post
office. About six months later, a beneficiary under the will informed the
executor that the solicitor had previously been suspended from practice and
objected to his being employed in connection with the estate. The executor
pressed the solicitor for settlement, finally placing the matter with another
solicitor, but by this time the original solicitor, and the money, had

disappeared. Maugham J held the executor not liable, finding that the appointment had been made validly and in good faith. In interpreting the meaning of 'wilful default' within s. 30(1), he relied upon the construction reached by Romer J in *Re City Equitable Fire Insurance Co.* [1925] Ch 407. In that case it was said that a person guilty of wilful default 'knows that he is committing and intends to commit a breach of his duty, or is recklessly careless in the sense of not caring whether his act or omission is a breach of duty'. In other words, it is virtually necessary to show that the trustee is fraudulent, unless the original appointment was wrongful.

3.   The decision in *Re Vickery* has been much criticised on the grounds, among others, that it imported the common law meaning of 'wilful default' into equity, and that it so widens the protection of trustees under s. 23(1) as to make the rest of that section redundant. It is only a decision at first instance, of course, and so could be wrong. Nonetheless it may be suggested that, since the whole tenor of s. 23 is to allow trustees to repose confidence in their properly appointed agents, it would be a strange interpretation which required them to supervise activities which they have properly chosen to delegate as being beyond their own competence to perform.

Re Lucking's WT, Renwick v Lucking
[1968] 1 WLR 866, [1967] 3 All ER 726
Chancery Division

Facts: Nearly 70 per cent of the shares a private company (Stephen Lucking Ltd) were held by two trustees, Mr Lucking and Mr Block, as part of the estate of the deceased, Mary Lucking; about 20 per cent belonged to Mr Lucking in his own right, and 1 per cent belonged to Lucking's wife. The directors in 1954 were Mr and Mrs Lucking and Mr Dewar, who was also the manager of the business. In 1956 Block was appointed trustee to act jointly with Lucking.

The company, which was engaged in the manufacture and sale of shoe accessories, had a small factory employing about 20 people. Dewar wrongfully drew some £15,000 from the company's bank account in excess of his remuneration, and later became bankrupt. The money was lost, and a beneficiary sued the trustees for breach of trust.

Held: Lucking was in breach in failing adequately to supervise the manager, Dewar. But Block was entitled to rely on what Lucking had told him about the company's affairs, unless he had a positive reason to disbelieve him.

CROSS J (on Lucking's liability): In support of the proportion that a trustee who is carrying on an unincorporated business is only liable for negligence in his supervision of a manager employed by him if the negligence amounts to 'wilful default', counsel relied on the decision of Maugham J in *Re Vickery, Vickery v Stephens* [1931] 1 Ch 572. In that case an executor employed a solicitor to obtain payment of sums of money due to the estate and furnished him with documents of title for the purpose. The solicitor made away with the money and it was said that having regard to what the executor had learnt of the reputation of the solicitor in question he ought to have cancelled the authority given him before the money got into his hands. Maugham J held that s. 23 of the Trustee Act 1925 empowered the executor to employ the solicitor for the purpose in question in the first instance; and he held further that as s. 30 of the Act provided, *inter alia*, that a trustee should not be liable for the defaults of any person with whom any trust money or securities might be deposited unless the resulting loss happens through his own wilful default, the executor in the case before him would only be liable if he were guilty of wilful default. I see no reason whatever to think that Maugham J would have considered that a person employed by a trustee to manage a business owned by the trust was a person with whom trust money or securities were deposited within the meaning of s. 30. In support of the proposition that directors are only liable for 'wilful default' counsel referred to *Re City Equitable Fire Insurance Co. Ltd* [1925] Ch 407; but there one of the company's articles provided that directors should only be liable for 'wilful default'. Romer J made it clear in his judgment [1925] Ch at p. 500 that, but for that article, he would have held some of the directors liable in some matters for negligence falling short of 'wilful default'. In my view, 'wilful default' does not enter into the picture in this case at all. The conduct of the defendant trustees is, I think, to be judged by the standard applied in *Re Speight, Speight* v *Gaunt* (1883) 22 ChD 727, namely, that a trustee is only bound to conduct the business of the trust in such a way as an ordinary prudent man would conduct a business of his own.

Now, what steps, if any, does a reasonably prudent man who finds himself a majority shareholder in a private company take with regard to the management of the company's affairs? He does not, I think, content himself with such information as to the management of the company's affairs as he is entitled to as shareholder, but ensures that he is represented on the board. He may be prepared to run the business himself as managing director or, at least, to become a non-executive director while having the business managed by someone else. Alternatively, he may find someone who will act as his nominee on the board and report to him from time to time as to the company's affairs. In the same way, as it seems to me, trustees holding a controlling interest ought to ensure so far as they can that they have such information as to the progress of the company's affairs as directors would have. If they sit back and allow the company to be run by the minority shareholders and receive no more information than shareholders are entitled to, they do so at their risk if things go wrong.

Note

This case is not covered by s. 30, because Dewar was a manager of the business, rather than an agent. If a trustee validly appoints an agent, then on the authority of Maugham J in *Re Vickery* the trustee is only liable for the default of the agent in the event of his own 'wilful default' in lack of supervision.

The distinction between *Lucking* and *Vickery* is probably justified: a higher standard ought in principle to be applied to supervision of an employee than of a professional agent, such as a solicitor or an accountant.

Trustee Act 1925

25. Power to delegate trusts during absence abroad

[The main part of the section allows trustees, by power of attorney, to delegate all or any of their powers and discretions for a period not exceeding 12 months, and the section continues:]

(5)   A donor of a power of attorney given under this section shall be liable for the acts or defaults of the donee in the same manner as if they were the acts or defaults of the donor.

Note

There is no equivalent to s. 30 protection where a trustee delegates under s. 25, as opposed to appointing an agent under s. 23: trustees are vicariously liable for the defaults of those to whom the power has been delegated under s. 25.

SECTION 3: FIDUCIARY NATURE OF TRUSTEESHIP

A: Payment of Trustees

There are a number of ways in which trustees and other fiduciaries may be entitled to payment, but these should be regarded as exhaustive. If a trustee does not come within one of the following heads, he is not entitled to any money for the performance of his duties:

(a)   The right to remuneration may be fixed by contract between settlor and trustee at the outset; banks' charging clauses are an example of this. Similarly, a director of a company who owes a fiduciary duty to the company may enter into a contract with the company for remuneration. The contract must be one that the company is empowered to make. In *Guiness* v *Saunders* [1990] 1 All ER 652, two Guiness directors, Thomas Ward and Ernest Saunders, claimed that they were contractually entitled to fees of £5.2 million for advice and services rendered to Guiness in connection with a take-over bid for Distillers Co. plc. The purported contract was made by a committee of three of Guiness's directors (two of whom were Ward and Saunders), but under Guiness's articles of association the committee had no power to authorise reimbursement, and the House of Lords held that the directors were not entitled to keep the £5.2 million that they had received.

(b)   Section 30(2) of the Trustee Act 1925 entitles a trustee to reimbursement for expenses, from trust funds.

(c)   The courts have a jurisdiction to authorise payment. In one of the cases involving a breach of fiduciary duty considered below, *Boardman* v *Phipps* [1967] 2 AC 46, although a solicitor as fiduciary to a family trust was not entitled to keep profits received as a result of his position, he was held to be entitled to liberal remuneration on a *quantum meruit* basis, which is to say, on a reasonable basis for work done for the benefit of the trust, including work that had been performed gratuitously. The Court of Appeal took a similar view in *O'Sullivan* v *Management Agency and Music Ltd* [1985] QB 428, another case involving a breach of fiduciary duty. The remuneration included even a reasonable profit element, but was not related to the *actual* profits obtained in breach of fiduciary duty, which had to be accounted.

In *Re Duke of Norfolk's ST* [1982] Ch 61, the Court of Appeal was prepared to exercise this jurisdiction to increase the remuneration of a trustee over the amount agreed in the original settlement. The quantity of work had increased because new property had been added to the settlement, and the tax position had been substantially altered by the introduction of Capital Transfer Tax in 1975. The trustee was held entitled to extra remuneration for the increase in work.

A claim for *quantum meruit* is essentially an implied contract claim, however, and cannot be awarded to a director where the company has no power to authorise payment. The directors in *Guiness* v *Saunders* (above) claimed an alternative *quantum meruit* entitlement, and failed, for precisely the same reasons that their claim in contract failed: Guiness were no more empowered to enter into an implied contract to pay for the services of the two directors than they were to enter into an express contract for the same.

In none of the above cases, however, is the amount of remuneration dependent on the manner in which the discretion (if any) of the trustee is exercised. Thus there can be no conflict between the interests of the trust and the personal interests of the trustee. Otherwise, trustees must not benefit in any way from their position as trustees. The courts refuse to allow *any possibility* that a conflict of interest may occur. Whether any conflict occurs in fact is not relevant. In other words, it is immaterial that the trust does not suffer, or even that it gains, from the activities of the trustee. The trustee has to show that there is no possible causal connection between his position and any profit made by him (outside the categories outlined above).

Re Duke of Norfolk's ST
[1982] Ch 61, [1981] 3 All ER 220
Court of Appeal

Decision: The court has an inherent jurisdiction to authorise the payment of trustees, or increasing the remuneration authorised under the trust instrument, if to do so would be beneficial to the administration of the trust.

FOX LJ: *Chapman* v *Chapman* [1954] AC 429 [see chapter 7], it seems to me, was concerned with the power of the court to authorise variations in the beneficial interests as such. The present problem is different. It is concerned not with beneficial interests as such, but with the administration of the trust fund. When the court authorises payment of remuneration to a trustee under its inherent jurisdiction it is, I think, exercising its ancient jurisdiction to secure the competent administration of the trust property just as it has done when it appoints or removes a trustee under its inherent jurisdiction. The result, in my view, is that there is nothing in the principle stated in *Chapman* v *Chapman* [1954] AC 429 which is inconsistent with the existence of an inherent jurisdiction in the court to increase the remuneration payable to trustees under the trust instrument. In my view, therefore, neither of the two objections which have been raised as to existence of such a jurisdiction is well founded.

There remains the question whether, on principle and authority, we can properly infer that the jurisdiction does exist. As to principle, it seems to me that, if the court has jurisdiction, as it has, on the appointment of a trustee to authorise remuneration though no such power exists in the trust instrument, there is no logical reason why the court should not have power to increase the remuneration given by the instrument. In many cases the latter may involve a smaller interference with the provisions of the trust instrument than the former. Further, the law has not stopped short at authorising remuneration to a trustee only if he seeks the authority at the time when he accepts the trusts. . . .

I conclude that the court has an inherent jurisdiction to authorise the payment of remuneration of trustees and that that jurisdiction extends to increasing the remuneration authorised by the trust instrument. In exercising that jurisdiction the court has to balance two influences which are to some extent in conflict. The first is that the office of trustee is, as such, gratuitous; the court will accordingly be careful to protect the interests of the beneficiaries against claims by the trustees. The second is that it is of great importance to the beneficiaries that the trust should be well administered. If therefore the court concludes, having regard to the nature of the trust, to the experience and skill of a particular trustee and to the amounts which he seeks to charge when compared with what other trustees might require to be paid for their services and to all the other circumstances of the case, that it would be in the interests of the beneficiaries to increase the remuneration, then the court may properly do so.

B: Purchase and Sale of Trust Property

The principle here is that if a trustee purchases trust property, he can abuse his position and buy at less than the best price obtainable. Similarly if he sells to the trust, he may be able to demand too high a price.

The self-dealing rule is very strict where trustees are concerned, so that there must be no possibility of the trustee taking advantage of his position, whether he does so in fact or not. The lengths to which the law goes is shown by *Wright* v *Morgan* [1926] AC 788, where a trustee who had resigned his trusteeship purchased trust property at a price that had been fixed by independent valuers. One may have thought that not even a possibility of conflict arose here. The arrangements had been made while he was still trustee, however, and the Privy Council held that this sale must be set aside.

It is possible for purchases by trustees to be valid, but only in very exceptional circumstances. It is essential not only that the trustee paid a fair price, as he had in *Wright* v *Morgan*, but also that he took no advantage of his position, and made full disclosure of his interest.

Holder v *Holder*
[1968] Ch 353
Court of Appeal

Facts: The defendant, Victor Holder, was appointed one of the executors of his father's will. He was also tenant of two farms which were part of the estate. After the death of his father Victor purported to renounce his office as executor, but the renunciation was technically ineffective. Nevertheless, probate was granted to two of the other executors named in the will. They put the two farms of which he was tenant up for sale by auction, where Victor, through an agent, bid successfully for them. The plaintiff, another member of the family, started an action to set aside the conveyance to Victor.

Held: The sale would not be set aside.

HARMAN LJ: The judge [Cross J] decided in favour of the plaintiff on this point because . . . (Victor) at the time of the sale was himself still in a fiduciary position and, like any other trustee, could not purchase the trust property. I feel the force of this argument, but doubt its validity in the very special circumstances of this case. The reason for the rule is that a man may not both be vendor and purchaser; but [Victor] was never in that position here. He took no part in instructing the valuer who fixed the reserves or in the preparations for the auction. Everyone in the family knew that he was not a seller but a buyer. In this case [Victor] never assumed the duties of an executor. It is true that he concurred in signing a few cheques for trivial sums and endorsing a few insurance policies, but he never so far as appears interfered in any way with the administration of the estate. It is true he managed the farms, but he did that as tenant and not as executor. He acquired no special knowledge as executor. What he knew he knew as tenant of the farms. Another reason lying behind the rule is that there must never be a conflict of duty and interest, but in fact there was none here in the case of the third defendant, who made no secret throughout that he intended to buy. . . .

Of course, I feel the force of the judge's reasoning that if . . . [Victor] remained an executor he is within the rule, but in a case where the reasons behind the rule do not exist I do not feel bound to apply it. My reasons are that the beneficiaries never looked to the third defendant to protect their interests. They all knew he was in the market as purchaser; that the price paid was a good one and probably higher than anyone not a sitting tenant would give. Further, the first two defendants alone acted as executors and sellers: they alone could convey: they were not influenced by the third defendant in connexion with the sales.

Notes

1. Danckwerts LJ expressed doubt whether today the self-dealing rule should apply where trust property is sold at public auctions, at least in a case where the sale is arranged by trustees other than the purchasing trustee. He also held that the plaintiff had acquiesced in or confirmed the sale and could not claim to have it set aside. Sachs LJ expressed the same doubt whether the self-dealing rule should apply now to a sale by auction.

2. However, *Holder* v *Holder* was limited almost to its own unusual facts by Vinelott J in *Re Thompson's Settlement* [1986] Ch 99. Vinelott J explained the decision on the narrow ground that the defendant had never acted as executor in a way which could be taken to amount to acceptance of a duty to act in the interests of the beneficiaries under his father's will. He said that the self-dealing rule (see *Wright* v *Morgan* [1926] AC 788) is an application of the wider principle that a man must not put himself in a position where duty and interest conflict or where his duty to one conflicts with his duty to another.

C: Profiting from the Position

In *Keech* v *Sandford* (1726) Sel Cas Ch 61, the trustee took over the benefit of a lease which had been devised to the trust, when that lease expired. Presumably he would not have been in a position to do so, had he not been trustee. The lessor had refused to renew the lease for the trust, on the ground that the beneficiary was an infant, against whom it would be difficult to recover rent. The trustee thereupon took the lease for his personal benefit, and profited from it. King LC held that the trustee had to assign the benefit of the lease to the infant, and account for profits received. The trustee was the one person in the world who could not take the lease for his own benefit, because by so doing he would be profiting from his position.

The principle extends to any profits made by virtue of a fiduciary position, and if the profits are to be retained, the fiduciary must show that there is no causal connection between the position and the profit. The remedy against the fiduciary is an account of profits; in effect, the profits received are held by him as constructive trustee. It is of no moment that the trust has suffered no loss; the remedy is not compensatory in nature. It is necessary that the fiduciary accounts for all profits received in order to ensure that his duty and interest can never conflict.

For example, in *Re Macadam* [1946] Ch 73 trustees who used their position to appoint themselves to directorships of a company were held liable to account to the trust for all the fees they received as directors. The causal connection between position and profit must be established, however. In *Re Gee* [1948] Ch 284, a trustee became a director after refraining from using his vote, which he had by virtue of holding trust shares. He would have been elected anyway, though, due to the votes of the other shareholders, however he had voted himself; he would even have been elected if he had voted against himself. Harman J held that the remuneration received as director was not accountable to the trust. It could not be said that the trustees had made any profit by virtue of their position.

D: Bribes and Backhanders

In *Reading* v *A-G* [1951] AC 507, Reading had been a sergeant in the British army, and had made at least £19,000 illegally by helping smugglers to transport smuggled goods, by riding in the lorries in his uniform. Unfortunately for Reading, the £19,000 was confiscated and he was forced into the role of plaintiff, petitioning for its return. He failed because as a fiduciary he was liable to account for his profits to the Crown. An army sergeant would probably not normally be regarded as a fiduciary, but the use in the case of the uniform to deceive the authorities may have been the decisive factor.

Attorney-General for Hong Kong v *Reid*
[1994] 1 All ER 1
House of Lords

Decision: The recipient of a bribe held it on trust for the person whose interests had been betrayed.

LORD TEMPLEMAN: Bribery is an evil practice which threatens the foundations of any civilised society. In particular, bribery of policemen and prosecutors brings the administration of justice into disrepute. Where bribes are accepted by a trustee, servant, agent or other fiduciary, loss and damage are caused to the beneficiaries, master or principal whose interests have been betrayed. The amount of loss or damage resulting from the acceptance of a bribe may or may not be quantifiable. In the present case the amount of harm caused to the administration of justice in Hong Kong by Mr Reid in return for bribes cannot be quantified.

When a bribe is offered and accepted in money or in kind, the money or property constituting the bribe belongs in law to the recipient. Money paid to the false fiduciary belongs to him. The legal estate in freehold property conveyed to the false fiduciary by way of bribe vests in him. Equity however which acts *in personam* insists that it is unconscionable for a fiduciary to obtain and retain a benefit in breach of duty. The provider of a bribe cannot recover it because he committed a criminal offence when he paid the bribe. The false fiduciary who received the bribe in breach of duty must pay and account for the bribe to the person to whom that duty was owed. In the present case, as soon as Mr Reid received a bribe in breach of the duties he owed to the Government of Hong Kong, he became a debtor in equity to the Crown for the amount of that bribe. So much is admitted. But if the bribe consists of property which increases in value or if a cash bribe is invested advantageously, the false fiduciary will receive a benefit from his breach of duty unless he is accountable not only for the original amount or value of the bribe but also for the increased value of the property representing the bribe. As soon as the bribe was received it should have been paid or transferred instanter to the person who suffered from the breach of duty. Equity considers as done that which ought to have been done. As soon as the bribe was received, whether in cash or in kind, the false fiduciary held the bribe on a constructive trust for the person injured. Two objections have been raised to this analysis. First it is said that if the fiduciary is in equity a debtor to the person injured, he cannot also be a trustee of the bribe. But there is no reason why equity should not provide two remedies, so long as they do not result in double recovery. If the property representing the bribe exceeds the original bribe in value, the fiduciary cannot retain the benefit of the increase in value which he obtained solely as a result of his breach of duty. Secondly, it is said that if the false fiduciary holds property representing the bribe in trust for the person injured, and if the false fiduciary is or becomes insolvent, the unsecured creditors of the false fiduciary will be deprived of their right to share in the proceeds of that property. But the unsecured creditors cannot be in a better position than their debtor. The authorities show that property acquired by a trustee innocently but in breach of trust and the property from time to time representing the same belong in equity to the cestui que trust and not to the trustee personally whether he is solvent or insolvent. Property acquired by a trustee as a result of a criminal breach of trust and the property from time to time representing the same must also belong in equity to his cestui que trust and not to the trustee whether he is solvent or insolvent.

When a bribe is accepted by a fiduciary in breach of his duty then he holds that bribe in trust for the person to whom the duty was owed. If the property representing the bribe decreases in value the fiduciary must pay the difference between that value and the initial amount of the bribe because he should not have accepted the bribe or incurred the risk of loss. If the property increases in value, the fiduciary is not entitled to any surplus in excess of the initial value of the bribe because he is not allowed by any means to make a profit out of a breach of duty. . . .

It has always been assumed and asserted that the law on the subject of bribes was definitively settled by the decision of the Court of Appeal in *Lister & Co.* v *Stubbs* (1890) 45 ChD 1.

In that case the plaintiffs, Lister & Co., employed the defendant, Stubbs, as their servant to purchase goods for the firm. Stubbs, on behalf of the firm, bought goods from Varley & Co. and received from Varley & Co. bribes amounting to £5,541. The bribes were invested by Stubbs in freehold properties and investments. His masters, the firm

Lister & Co., sought and failed to obtain an interlocutory injunction restraining Stubbs from disposing of these assets pending the trial of the action in which they sought inter alia £5,541 and damages. In the Court of Appeal the first judgment was given by Cotton LJ who had been party to the decision in *Metropolitan Bank* v *Heiron* (1880) 15 ChD 139. He was powerfully supported by the judgment of Lindley LJ and by the equally powerful concurrence of Bowen LJ. Cotton LJ said that the bribe could not be said to be the money of the plaintiffs (see 45 ChD 1 at 12). He seemed to be reluctant to grant an interlocutory judgment which would provide security for a debt before that debt had been established. Lindley LJ said that the relationship between the plaintiffs, Lister & Co., as masters and the defendant, Stubbs, as servant who had betrayed his trust and received a bribe:

> . . . is that of debtor and creditor; it is not that of trustee and cestui que trust. We are asked to hold that it is which would involve consequences which, I confess, startle me. One consequence, of course, would be that, if Stubbs were to become bankrupt, this property acquired by him with the money paid to him by Messrs Varley would be withdrawn from the mass of his creditors and be handed over bodily to Lister & Co. Can that be right? Another consequence would be that, if the appellants are right, Lister & Co. could compel Stubbs to account to them, not only for the money with interest, but for all the profit which he might have made by embarking in trade with it. Can that be right? (See 45 ChD 1 at 15.)

For the reasons which have already been advanced their Lordships would respectfully answer both these questions in the affirmative. If a trustee mistakenly invests moneys which he ought to pay over to his cestui que trust and then becomes bankrupt, the monies together with any profit which has accrued from the investment are withdrawn from the unsecured creditors as soon as the mistake is discovered. *A fortiori*, if a trustee commits a crime by accepting a bribe which he ought to pay over to his cestui que trust, the bribe and any profit made therefrom should be withdrawn from the unsecured creditors as soon as the crime is discovered.

The decision in *Lister & Co.* v *Stubbs* is not consistent with the principles that a fiduciary must not be allowed to benefit from his own breach of duty, that the fiduciary should account for the bribe as soon as he receives it and that equity regards as done that which ought to be done. From these principles it would appear to follow that the bribe and the property from time to time representing the bribe are held on a constructive trust for the person injured. A fiduciary remains personally liable for the amount of the bribe if, in the event, the value of the property then recovered by the injured person proved to be less than that amount.

The decisions of the Court of Appeal in *Metropolitan Bank* v *Heiron* (1880) 5 ChD 319 and *Lister & Co.* v *Stubbs* are inconsistent with earlier authorities which were not cited. Although over 100 years has passed since *Lister* v *Stubbs*, no one can be allowed to say that he has ordered his affairs in reliance on the two decisions of the Court of Appeal now in question. Thus no harm can result if those decisions are not followed.

E: Receiving Information as a Fiduciary

Boardman v *Phipps*
[1967] 2 AC 46
House of Lords

Facts: Boardman was solicitor to a trust, whose property included a large (but not majority) holding in a public company. He became worried about the competence of the management of the company, and tried to persuade the managing trustee of the trust to acquire a majority holding in the company. His attempts at persuasion were unsuccessful, so Boardman decided to make the acquisition himself. He did so and then, by selling off some of the assets of the newly acquired company, Boardman made a large profit for himself. Additionally, however, because the trust still had a large share in the same company, his activities resulted in a large profit for the trust as well.

It appeared that in negotiating for the majority shareholding he had, in good faith, obtained information in his capacity as solicitor to the trust, which he would not otherwise have obtained. Phipps, a beneficiary under the trust, sued for an account of profits.

Held (Viscount Dilhorne and Lord Upjohn dissenting): Boardman held the shares acquired as constructive trustee for the trust, and he must account for any profits made. He was, however, entitled to remuneration on a *quantum meruit* basis.

LORD COHEN: Wilberforce J and, in the Court of Appeal, both Lord Denning MR and Pearson LJ based their decision in favour of the respondent on the decision of your lordships' House in *Regal (Hastings) Ltd* v *Gulliver*, reported at [1967] 2 AC 134. I turn, therefore, to consider that case. Mr Walton [for the trust] relied upon a number of passages in the judgments of the learned Lords who heard the appeal: in particular on (1) a passage in the speech of Lord Russell of Killowen where he says:

> The rule of equity which insists on those, who by use of a fiduciary position make a profit, being liable to account for that profit, in no way depends on fraud, or absence of bona fides; or upon such questions or considerations as whether the profit would or should otherwise have gone to the plaintiff, or whether the profiteer was under a duty to obtain the source of the profit for the plaintiff, or whether he took a risk or acted as he did for the benefit of the plaintiff, or whether the plaintiff has in fact been damaged or benefited by his action. The liability arises from the mere fact of a profit having, in the stated circumstances, been made.

(2) a passage in the speech of Lord Wright, where he says:

> That question can be briefly stated to be whether an agent, a director, a trustee or other person in an analogous fiduciary position, when a demand is made upon him by the person to whom he stands in the fiduciary relationship to account for profits acquired by him by reason of his fiduciary position, and by reason of the opportunity and the knowledge, or either, resulting from it, is entitled to defeat the claim upon any ground save that he made profits with the knowledge and assent of the other person. The most natural and typical case of this nature is that of principal and agent. The rule in such cases is compendiously expressed to be that an agent must account for net profits secretly (that is, without the knowledge of his principal) acquired by him in the course of his agency. The authorities show how manifold and various are the applications of the rule. It does not depend on fraud or corruption.

These paragraphs undoubtedly help the respondent but they must be considered in relation to the facts of that case. In that case the profit arose through the application by four of the directors of Regal for shares in a subsidiary company which it had been the original intention of the board should be subscribed for by Regal. Regal had not the requisite money available but there was no question of it being *ultra vires* Regal to subscribe for the shares. In the circumstances Lord Russell of Killowen said:

I have no hesitation in coming to the conclusion, upon the facts of this case, that these shares, when acquired by the directors, were acquired by reason, and only by reason of the fact that they were directors of Regal, and in the course of their execution of that office.

He goes on to consider whether the four directors were in a fiduciary relationship to Regal and concludes that they were. Accordingly, they were held accountable. Mr Bagnall [for Boardman] argued that the present case is distinguishable. He puts his argument thus. The question you ask is whether the information could have been used by the principal for the purpose for which it was used by his agents? If the answer to that question is no, the information was not used in the course of their duty as agents. In the present case the information could never have been used by the trustees for the purpose of purchasing shares in the company; therefore purchase of shares was outside the scope of the appellant's agency and they are not accountable.

This is an attractive argument, but it does not seem to me to give due weight to the fact that the appellants obtained both the information which satisfied them that the purchase of the shares would be a good investment and the opportunity of acquiring them as a result of acting for certain purposes on behalf of the trustees. Information is, of course, not property in the strict sense of that word and, as I have already stated, it does not necessarily follow that because an agent acquired information and opportunity while acting in a fiduciary capacity he is accountable to his principals for any profit that comes his way as the result of the use he makes of that information and opportunity. His liability to account must depend on the facts of the case. In the present case much of the information came the appellants' way when Mr Boardman was acting on behalf of the trustees on the instructions of Mr Fox and the opportunity of bidding for the shares came because he purported for all purposes except for making the bid to be acting on behalf of the owners of the 8,000 shares in the company. In these circumstances it seems to me that the principle of the *Regal* case applies and that the courts below came to the right conclusion.

LORD HODSON: It cannot, in my opinion, be said that the purchase of shares in Lester & Harris was outside the scope of the fiduciary relationship in which Mr Boardman stood to the trust.

The confidential information which the appellants obtained at a time when Mr Boardman was admittedly holding himself out as solicitor for the trustees was obtained by him as representing the trustees, the holders of 8,000 shares of Lester & Harris. As Russell LJ put it [1965] Ch 992, 1031:

The substantial trust shareholding was an asset of which one aspect was its potential use as a means of acquiring knowledge of the company's affairs, or of negotiating allocations of the company's assets, or of inducing other shareholders to part with their shares.

Whether this aspect is properly to be regarded as part of the trust assets is, in my judgment, immaterial. The appellants obtained knowledge by reason of their fiduciary position and they cannot escape liability by saying that they were acting for themselves and not as agents of the trustees. Whether or not the trust or the beneficiaries in their stead could have taken advantage of the information is immaterial, as the authorities clearly show. No doubt it was but a remote possibility that Mr Boardman would ever be asked by the trustees to advise on the desirability of an application to the court in order that the trustees might avail themselves of the information obtained. Nevertheless, even if the possibility of conflict is present between personal interests and the fiduciary position the rule of equity must be applied. This appears from the observations of Lord Cranworth LC in *Aberdeen Railway Co.* v *Blaikie Brothers* (1854) 1 Macq 461, 471.

Note
For Lord Cohen it may have been material that the information obtained was trust property, whereas Lord Hodson's view (and also that of Lord Guest) was based simply on the fact that Boardman had benefited from his fiduciary position (i.e. the question for him was simply one of causation).

SECTION 4:   COMMENCEMENT AND TERMINATION OF TRUSTEESHIP

A: Appointment of New Trustees

Trustee Act 1925

36.   Power of appointing new or additional trustees

(1)   Where a trustee, either original or substituted, and whether appointed by a court or otherwise, is dead, or remains out of the United Kingdom for more than twelve months, or desires to be discharged from all or any of the trusts or powers reposed in or conferred on him, or refuses or is unfit to act therein, or is incapable of acting therein, or is an infant, then, subject to the restrictions imposed by this Act on the number of trustees, —

(a)   any person or persons nominated for the purpose of appointing new trustees by the instrument, if any, creating the trust; or

(b)   if there is no such person, or no such person able and willing to act, then the surviving or continuing trustee or trustees for the time being, or the personal representative of the last surviving or continuing trustee;

may, by writing, appoint one or more other person (whether or not being the persons exercising the power) to be a trustee or trustees in the place of the trustee so deceased remaining out of the United Kingdom, desiring to be discharged, or being unfit or incapable, or being an infant, as aforesaid.

(2)   Where a trustee has been removed under a power contained in the instrument creating the trust, a new trustee or new trustees may be appointed in the place of the trustee who is removed, as if he were dead, or, in the case of a corporation, as if the corporation desired to be discharged from the trust, and the provisions of this section shall apply accordingly, but subject to the restrictions imposed by this Act on the number of trustees.

(3)   Where a corporation being a trustee is or has been dissolved, either before or after the commencement of this Act, then, for the purposes of this section and of any enactment replaced thereby, the corporation shall be deemed to be and to have been from the date of the dissolution incapable of acting in the trusts or powers reposed in or conferred on the corporation.

(4)   The power of appointment given by subsection (1) of this section or any similar previous enactment to the personal representatives of a last surviving or

continuing trustee shall be and shall be deemed always to have been exercisable by the executors for the time being (whether original or by representation) of such surviving or continuing trustee who have proved the will of their testator or by the administrators for the time being of such trustee without the concurrence of any executor who has renounced or has not proved.

(5) But a sole or last surviving executor intending to renounce, or all the executors where they all intend to renounce, shall have and shall be deemed always to have had power, at any time before renouncing probate, to exercise the power of appointment given by this section, or by any similar previous enactment, if willing to act for that purpose and without thereby accepting the office of executor.

(6) Where a sole trustee, other than a trust corporation, is or has been originally appointed to act in a trust, or where, in the case of any trust, there are not more than three trustees (none of them being a trust corporation) either original or substituted and whether appointed by the court or otherwise, then in any such case —

(a) the person or persons nominated for the purpose of appointing new trustees by the instrument, if any, creating the trust; or

(b) if there is no such person, or no such person able and willing to act, then the trustee or trustees for the time being;

may, by writing, appoint another person to other persons to be an additional trustee or additional trustees, but it shall not be obligatory to appoint any additional trustee, unless the instrument, if any, creating the trust, or any statutory enactment provides to the contrary, nor shall the number of trustees be increased beyond four by virtue of any such appointment.

(7) Every new trustee appointed under this section as well before as after all the trust property becomes by law, or by assurance, or otherwise, vested in him, shall have the same powers, authorities, and discretions, and may in all respects act as if he had been originally appointed a trustee by the instrument, if any, creating the trust.

(8) The provisions of this section relating to a trustee who is dead include the case of a person nominated trustee in a will but dying before the testator, and those relative to a continuing trustee include a refusing or retiring trustee, if willing to act in the execution of the provisions of this section.

(9) Where a trustee is incapable, by reason of mental disorder within the meaning of the Mental Health Act 1983, of exercising his functions as trustee and is also entitled in possession to some beneficial interest in the trust property, no appointment of a new trustee in his place shall be made by virtue of paragraph (b) of subsection (1) of this section unless leave to make the appointment has been given by the authority having jurisdiction under Part VII of the Mental Health Act 1983.

Note
This is s. 36 as subsequently amended.

41. Power of court to appoint new trustees

(1) The court may, whenever it is expedient to appoint a new trustee or new trustees, and it is found inexpedient, difficult or impracticable to do so without the assistance of the court, make an order appointing a new trustee or new trustees either in substitution for or in addition to any existing trustee or trustees, or although there is no existing trustee.

In particular and without prejudice to the generality of the foregoing provision, the court may make an order appointing a new trustee in substitution for a trustee who is incapable, by reason of mental disorder within the meaning of the Mental Health

Act 1983, of exercising his functions as a trustee or is a bankrupt, or is a corporation which is in liquidation or has been dissolved.

(2) The power conferred by this section may, in the case of a deed of arrangement within the meaning of the Deeds of Arrangement Act 1914, be exercised either by the High Court or by the court having jurisdiction in bankruptcy in the district in which the debtor resided or carried on business at the date of the execution of the deed.

(3) An order under this section, and any consequential vesting order or convey-ance, shall not operate further or otherwise as a discharge to any former or continuing trustee than an appointment of new trustees under any power for that purpose contained in any instrument would have operated.

(4) Nothing in this section gives power to appoint an executor or administrator.

40. Vesting of trust property in new or continuing trustees

(1) Where by a deed a new trustee is appointed to perform any trust, then —

(a) if the deed contains a declaration by the appointor to the effect that any estate or interest in any land subject to the trust, or in any chattel so subject, or the right to recover or receive any debt or other thing in action so subject, shall vest in the persons who by virtue of the deed become or are the trustees for performing the trust, the deed shall operate, without any conveyance or assignment, to vest in those persons as joint tenants and for the purposes of the trust the estate interest or rights to which the declaration relates; and

(b) [Applied by the Incumbents and Churchwardens (Trust) Measure 1964 (No. 2), s. 3(3).] if the deed is made after the commencement of this Act and does not contain such a declaration, the deed shall, subject to any express provision to the contrary therein contained, operate as if it had contained such a declaration by the appointor extending to all the estates interests and rights with respect to which a declaration could have been made.

(2) Where by deed a retiring trustee is discharged under the statutory power without a new trustee being appointed, then—

(a) if the deed contains such a declaration as aforesaid by the retiring and continuing trustees, the deed shall, without any conveyance or assignment, operate to vest in the continuing trustees alone, as joint tenants, and for the purposes of the trust, the estate, interest, or right to which the declaration relates; and

(b) if the deed is made after the commencement of this Act and does not contain such a declaration, the deed shall, subject to any express provision to the contrary therein contained, operate as if it had contained such a declaration by such persons as aforesaid extending to all the estates, interests and rights with respect to which a declaration could have been made.

(3) An express vesting declaration, whether made before or after the commence-ment of this Act, shall, notwithstanding that the estate, interest or right to be vested is not expressly referred to, and provided that the other statutory requirements were or are complied with, operate and be deemed always to have operated (but without prejudice to any express provision to the contrary contained in the deed of appoint-ment or discharge) to vest in the persons respectively referred to in subsections (1) and (2) of this section, as the case may require, such estates, interests and rights as are capable of being and ought to be vested in those persons.

(4) This section does not extend —

(a) to land conveyed by way of mortgage for securing money subject to the trust, except land conveyed on trust for securing debentures or debenture stock;

(b) to land held under a lease which contains any covenant, condition or agreement against assignment or disposing of the land without licence or consent, unless, prior to the execution of the deed containing expressly or impliedly the vesting declaration, the requisite licence or consent has been obtained, or unless, by virtue of any statute or rule of law, the vesting declaration, express or implied, would not operate as a breach of covenant or give rise to a forfeiture;

(c) to any share, stock, annuity or property which is only transferable in books kept by a company or other body, or in manner directed by or under an Act of Parliament.

In this subsection 'lease' includes an underlease and an agreement for a lease or underlease.

(5) For purposes of registration of the deed in any registry, the person or persons making the declaration expressly or impliedly, shall be deemed the conveying party or parties, and the conveyance shall be deemed to be made by him or them under a power conferred by this Act.

(6) This section applies to deeds of appointment or discharge executed on or after the first day of January, eighteen hundred and eighty-two.

B: Termination of Trusteeship

Trustee Act 1925

39. Retirement of trustee without a new appointment

(1) Where a trustee is desirous of being discharged from the trust, and after his discharge there will be either a trust corporation or at least two individuals to act as trustees to perform the trust, then, if such trustee as aforesaid by deed declares that he is desirous of being discharged from the trust, and if his co-trustees and such other person, if any, as is empowered to appoint trustees, by deed consent to the discharge of the trustee, and to the vesting in the co-trustees alone of the trust property, the trustee desirous of being discharged shall be deemed to have retired from the trust, and shall, by the deed, be discharged therefrom under this Act, without any new trustee being appointed in his place.

(2) Any assurance or thing requisite for vesting the trust property in the continuing trustees alone shall be executed or done.

18. Devolution of powers or trusts

(1) Where a power or trust is given to or imposed on two or more trustees jointly, the same may be exercised or performed by the survivors or survivor of them for the time being.

(2) Until the appointment of new trustees, the personal representatives or representative for the time being of a sole trustee, or, where there were two or more trustees of the last surviving or continuing trustee, shall be capable of exercising or performing any power or trust which was given to, or capable of being exercised by the sole or last surviving or continuing trustee, or other the trustees or trustee for the time being of the trust.

(3) This section takes effect subject to the restrictions imposed in regard to receipts by a sole trustee, not being a trust corporation.

(4) In this section 'personal representative' does not include an executor who has renounced or has not proved.

15 POWERS, DISCRETIONS AND DUTIES OF TRUSTEES

SECTION 1   GENERAL POWERS OF TRUSTEES

A: Relationship Between Statutory and Express Powers

Trustee Act 1925

69. Application of Act

(1) This Act, except where otherwise expressly provided, applies to trusts including, so far as this Act applies thereto, executorships and administratorships constituted or created either before or after the commencement of this Act.

(2) The powers conferred by this Act on trustees are in addition to the powers conferred by the instrument, if any, creating the trust, but those powers, unless otherwise stated, apply if and so far only as a contrary intention is not expressed in the instrument, if any, creating the trust, and have effect subject to the terms of that instrument.

[(3) repealed]

B: Powers of Sale

Trustee Act 1925

16.   Power to raise money by sale, mortgage, etc.

(1)   Where trustees are authorised by the instrument, if any, creating the trust or by law to pay or apply capital money subject to the trust for any purpose or in any manner, they shall have and shall be deemed always to have had power to raise the money required by sale, conversion, calling in, or mortgage of all or any part of the trust property for the time being in possession.

(2)   This section applies notwithstanding anything to the contrary contained in the instrument, if any, creating the trust, but does not apply to trustees of property held

for charitable purposes, or to trustees of a settlement for the purposes of the Settled Land Act, not being also the statutory owners.

Notes

1. This section, and s. 1(1) of the Trustee Investments Act 1961 (below) applies to personal property. Settled land is covered by s. 57 of the Settled Land Act 1925 (see chapter 7). Trusts for sale of land are given separate treatment.

2. In exercising their powers of sale, trustees have an overriding duty to obtain the best price they can on behalf of the beneficiaries; and while there may be circumstances in which it will be proper to reject the highest offer, if this is suspect, the trustees will be in breach of their duty if they permit ethical considerations to entice them into accepting a lower price. This may require trustees to resile from an agreement on later receiving a better offer. See in general *Fry v Fry* (1859) 28 LJ Ch 591.

C: Power to Give Receipts

Trustee Act 1925

14. Power of trustees to give receipts
(1) The receipt in writing of a trustee for any money, securities, or other personal property or effects payable, transferable, or deliverable to him under any trust or power shall be a sufficient discharge to the person paying, transferring, or delivering the same and shall effectually exonerate him from seeing to the application or being answerable for any loss or misapplication thereof.
(2) This section does not, except where the trustee is a trust corporation, enable a sole trustee to give a valid receipt for—
(a) the proceeds of sale or other capital money arising under a trust for sale of land;
(b) capital money arising under the Settled Land Act 1925.
(3) This section applies notwithstanding anything to the contrary in the instrument, if any, creating the trust.

Note
This is s. 14 as subsequently amended.

D: Power to Insure

Trustee Act 1925

19. Power to insure
(1) A trustee may insure against loss or damage by fire any building or other insurable property to any amount, including the amount of any insurance already on foot, not exceeding three fourths parts of the full value of the property, and pay the premiums for such insurance out of the income thereof or any other property subject to the same trusts without obtaining the consent of any person who may be entitled wholly or partly to such income.

(2)   This section does not apply to any building or property which a trustee is bound forthwith to convey absolutely to any beneficiary upon being requested to do so.

Note

Apart from this section, which does not apply where property is held on a bare trust, and in the absence of any express provision in the trust instrument, trustees are under no duty to insure the trust property, and will not be liable for failure to insure if subsequent loss or damage occurs. Nor in general, does the trustee have any power to insure, unless given expressly by the trust instrument.

The rationale, it seems, for the absence of any implied duty or power to insure, is to guard against the possibility that the premiums will make significant inroads into the trust income. However, the Law Reform Committee, in its 23rd Report on the Powers and Duties of Trustees (Cmnd 8733, 1982), recommended that trustees should be under a positive duty to insure whenever a prudent man of business would do so, up to the full value of the property if necessary.

All the above applies only to first-party insurance of the trust property. There is nothing to stop the trustees insuring *themselves* for third-party liability towards the trust in the event of their own breach, although they cannot reimburse themselves from the trust property for the premiums they pay on insuring themselves.

E: Power to Compound Liabilities

Trustee Act 1925

15.   Power to compound liabilities

A personal representative, or two or more trustees acting together, or, subject to the restrictions imposed in regard to receipts by a sole trustee not being a trust corporation, a sole acting trustee where the instrument, if any, creating the trust, or by statute, a sole trustee is authorised to execute the trusts and powers reposed in him, may if and as he or they think fit —

(a)   accept any property, real or personal, before the time at which it is made transferable or payable; or

(b)   sever and apportion any blended trust funds or property; or

(c)   pay or allow any debt or claim on any evidence that he or they think sufficient; or

(d)   accept any composition or any security, real or personal, for any debt or for any property, real or personal, claimed; or

(e)   allow any time of payment of any debt; or

(f)   compromise, compound, abandon, submit to arbitration, or otherwise settle any debt, account, claim, or thing whatever relating to the testator's or intestate's estate or to the trust;

and for any of these purposes may enter into, give, execute, and do such agreements, instruments of composition or arrangement, releases, and other things as to enable him or them seem expedient, without being responsible for any loss occasioned by any act or thing so done by him or them in good faith.

SECTION 2:   MAINTENANCE AND ADVANCEMENT

The powers of maintenance and advancement have the object (in theory) of providing for infant beneficiaries (under 18) who are not as yet entitled to any of the income or capital, but who require financial support during their minority. Payments by way of maintenance are payments out of income, to provide for routine necessities such as education or board and lodging, while payments by way of advancement are sums advanced from capital, to cover major costs such as setting up the infant in his profession.

In recent decades, significant use has also been made of these powers in reducing the tax liability of trusts. For example, early advancements of capital could until 1975 be effective to avoid liability to estate duty entirely (see, e.g., *Pilkington v IRC* [1964] AC 612, below), and even now can be used to reduce inheritance tax liability, while the purpose of maintenance payments is often to reduce liability for income tax.

A: Maintenance

Trustee Act 1925

31.   Power to apply income for maintenance and to accumulate surplus income during a minority

(1)   Where any property is held by trustees in trust for any person for any interest whatsoever, whether vested or contingent, then, subject to any prior interests or charges affecting that property —

(i)   during the infancy of any such person, if his interest so long continues, the trustees may, at their sole discretion, pay to his parent or guardian, if any, or otherwise apply for or towards his maintenance, education, or benefit, the whole or such part, if any, of the income of the property as may, in all the circumstances, be reasonable, whether or not there is—

(a)   any other fund applicable to the same purpose; or

(b)   any person bound by law to provide for his maintenance or education; and

(ii)   if such person on attaining the age of [eighteen years] has not a vested interest in such income, the trustees shall thenceforth pay the income of that property and of any accretion thereto under subsection (2) of this section to him, until he either attains a vested interest therein or dies, or until failure of his interest.

Provided that, in deciding whether the whole or any part of the income of the property is during a minority to be paid or applied for the purposes aforesaid, the trustees shall have regard to the age of the infant and his requirements and generally to the circumstances of the case, and in particular to what other income, if any, is applicable for those purposes; and where trustees have notice that the income of more than one fund is applicable for those purposes, then, so far as practicable, unless the entire income of the funds is paid or applied as aforesaid or the court otherwise directs, a proportionate part only of the income of each fund shall be so paid or applied.

(2)   During the infancy of any such person, if his interest so long continues, the trustees shall accumulate all the residue of that income in the way of compound interest by investing the same and the resulting income thereof from time to time in authorised investments, and shall hold those accumulations as follows:—

(i)   If any such person —

(a)   attains the age of eighteen years, or marries under that age, and his interest in such income during his infancy or until his marriage is a vested interest; or

(b)   on attaining the age of eighteen years or on marriage under that age becomes entitled to the property from which such income arose in fee simple, absolute or determinable, or absolutely, or for an entailed interest;

the trustees shall hold the accumulations in trust for such person absolutely, but without prejudice to any provision with respect thereto contained in any settlement by him made under any statutory powers during his infancy, and so that the receipt of such person after marriage, and though still an infant, shall be a good discharge; and

(ii)   in any other case the trustees shall, notwithstanding that such person had a vested interest in such income, hold the accumulations as an accretion to the capital of the property from which such accumulations arose, and as one fund with such capital for all purposes, and so that, if such property is settled land, such accumulations shall be held upon the same trusts as if the same were capital money arising therefrom;

but the trustees may, at any time during the infancy of such person if his interest so long continues, apply those accumulations, or any part thereof, as if they were income arising in the then current year.

(3)   This section applies in the case of a contingent interest only if the limitation or trust carries the intermediate income of the property, but it applies to a future or contingent legacy by the parent of, or a person standing in loco parentis to, the legatee, if and for such period as, under the general law, the legacy caries interest for the maintenance of the legatee, and in any such case as last aforesaid the rate of interest shall (if the income available is sufficient, and subject to any rules of court to the contrary) be five pounds per centum per annum.

(4)   This section applies to a vested annuity in like manner as if the annuity were the income of property held by the trustees in trust to pay the income thereof to the annuitant for the same period for which the annuity is payable, save that in any case accumulations made during the infancy of the annuitant shall be held in trust for the annuitant or his personal representatives absolutely.

(5)   This section does not apply where the instrument, if any, under which the interest arises came into operation before the commencement of this Act.

Notes

1.   The section is set out as subsequently amended.

2.   A power to maintain is not implied into the trust instrument. Therefore it must be expressly given, or advantage may be taken of the statutory power. The statutory power operates provided no contrary intention is expressed. But where the statutory power is expressly excluded it cannot be used, even if an express power turns out to be useless. In *Re Erskine's ST* [1971] 1 WLR 162, a settlement contained a provision for accumulation which was void for perpetuity. But since the statutory power to maintain was excluded by the provisions of the trust instrument, the income which the trustees had accumulated could not be applied for the beneficiary, and resulted to the settlor's estate.

3.   The court also has an inherent jurisdiction to approve the use of income or even capital for the maintenance of infant beneficiaries, but in practice this is rarely necessary.

B: Advancement

The power of advancement permits trustees to pay capital sums to or on behalf of a beneficiary some time before he is entitled to claim the fund. The power may be given by the trust instrument or, subject to contrary intention, the power contained in s. 32 of the Trustee Act 1925 may be used.

Trustee Act 1925

32.   Power of advancement

(1)   Trustees may at any time or times pay or apply any capital money subject to a trust, for the advancement or benefit, in such manner as they may, in their absolute discretion, think fit, of any person entitled to the capital of the trust property or of any share thereof, whether absolutely or contingently on his attaining any specified age or on the occurrence of any other event, or subject to a gift over on his death under any specified age or on the occurrence of any other event, and whether in possession or in remainder or reversion, and such payment or application may be made notwithstanding that the interest of such person is liable to be defeated by the exercise of a power of appointment or revocation, or to be diminished by the increase of the class to which he belongs:
   Provided that —

(a)   the money so paid or applied for the advancement or benefit of any person shall not exceed altogether in amount one-half of the presumptive or vested share or interest of that person in the trust property; and

(b)   if that person is or becomes absolutely and indefeasibly entitled to a share in the trust property the money so paid or applied shall be brought into account as part of such share; and

(c)   no such payment or application shall be made so as to prejudice any person entitled to any prior life or other interest, whether vested or contingent, in the money paid or applied unless such person is in existence, and of full age and consents in writing to such payment or application.

(2)   This section applies only where the trust property consists of money or securities or of property held upon trust for sale calling in and conversion, and such money or securities, or the proceeds of such sale calling in and conversion are not by statute or in equity considered as land, or applicable as capital money for the purposes of the Settled Land Act 1925.

(3)   This section does not apply to trusts constituted or created before the commencement of this Act.

Note

Whatever the theoretical purpose of the power of advancement, it can obviously be used to avoid taxes on capital transfers, particularly on death, by the simple expedient of bringing the capital transfer forward.

Re Pilkington's WT
[1964] AC 612
House of Lords

Facts: Under a will which contained no provision either replacing or excluding the statutory power of advancement under the Trustee Act 1925,

s. 32, Penelope (a two-year-old girl) was entitled to a share in the capital (valued at around £90,000) at 21. The trustees proposed, under the powers contained in s. 32, to advance one-half of Penelope's share to her, and resettle it.

The resettlement was theoretically disadvantageous to her. Although she was still entitled to receive the income on the resettled sum from 21 to 30, her entitlement to the capital on the advanced funds was postponed until she reached 30. Further, if Penelope died before reaching 30, the fund would be held on trust for other children, in addition to which the other income beneficiaries necessarily benefited from the postponement of her entitlement to the capital. The child was in no need of the moneys advanced, and too young for the traditional purposes of advancement to be relevant.

The reason for the advance, and the only benefit to Penelope, was the saving of estate duty which would otherwise have been payable on the death of her father, the life tenant under the trust. The usual way to avoid estate duty was to advance as much money as possible as long as possible before the death of the father (this principle also applies to inheritance tax, introduced in 1986).

The IRC challenged the lawfulness of the advancement, and one of the issues was whether there was a sufficient benefit to Penelope.

Held:

(a)   There was no need to show that the advancement was to meet some personal need of the beneficiary, and the saving of estate duty was itself a sufficient benefit. Nor was it relevant that other persons might benefit, if the provision as a whole would benefit Penelope.

(b)   But, the resettlement infringed the rule against perpetuities as it then stood. Thus, although the advancement was valid, the resettlement was not.

VISCOUNT RADCLIFFE (on the question of benefit): I think, with all respect to the Commissioners, a good deal of their argument is infected with some of this confusion. To say, for instance, that there cannot be a valid exercise of a power of advancement that results in a deferment of the vesting of the beneficiary's absolute title (Miss Penelope, it will be remembered, is to take at 30 under the proposed settlement instead of at 21 under the will) is in my opinion to play upon words. The element of anticipation consists in the raising of money for her now before she has any right to receive anything under the existing trusts: the advancement consists in the application of that money to form a trust fund, the provisions of which are thought to be for her benefit. I have not forgotten, of course, the references to powers of advancement which are found in such cases as *Re Joicey* [1915] 2 Ch 115, CA, *Re May's Settlement* [1926] Ch 136 and *Re Mewburn's Settlement* [1934] Ch 112, to which our attention was called, or the answere supplied by Cotton LJ in *Re Aldridge* (1886) 55 LT 554, 556 to his own question 'What is advancement?'

> It is a payment to persons who are presumably entitled to, or have a vested or contingent interest in, an estate or a legacy, before the time fixed by the will for their obtaining the absolute interest in a portion or the whole of that to which they would be entitled;

but I think that it will be apparent from what I have already said that the description that he gave (it cannot be a definition) is confined entirely to the aspect of anticipation or acceleration which renders the money available and not to any description or limitation of the purposes for which it can then be applied.

I have not been able to find in the words of s. 32, to which I have now referred, anything which in terms or by implication restricts the width of the manner or purpose of advancement. It is true that, if this settlement is made, Miss Penelope's children, who are not objects of the power, are given a possible interest in the event of her dying under 30 leaving surviving issue. But if the disposition itself, by which I mean the whole provision made, is for her benefit, it is no objection to the exercise of the power that other persons benefit incidentally as a result of the exercise. Thus a man's creditors may in certain cases get the most immediate advantage from an advancement made for the purpose of paying them off, as in *Lowther* v *Bentinck* (1874) LR 19 Eq 166; and a power to raise money for the advancement of a wife may cover a payment made direct to her husband in order to set him up in business (*Re Kershaw's Trusts* (1868) LR 6 EQ 322). The exercise will not be bad therefore on this ground.

Notes
1. The House of Lords struck down the advancement, however, on the ground that it infringed against the common law perpetuity rule.
2. However widely expressed is the power of advancement, the Court of Appeal held in *Re Pauling's ST* [1964] Ch 303 that the trustees must be satisfied that the advance will be for the benefit of the advancee. Further, if the trustees decide to make him an advance for a particular purpose, they must ask themselves whether he will carry it out: they should not make a payment for a purpose and then leave him free to do with it as he pleases. The question was left open as to whether trustees can recover money which the beneficiary requests but then applies for some quite different purpose.

In that case, the life tenant and her husband habitually spent well in excess of their income, and consequently their account at the defendant bank was considerably overdrawn. The defendant bank was also trustee under the settlement, under which the plaintiffs were remaindermen. As the plaintiffs reached their majority, the life tenant and her husband persuaded them to consent to various advances, which were ostensibly made for a specific purpose, for example the purchase of a house or furniture, or house improvements, but which were in fact given to the life tenant and her husband, and used to reduce their overdraft. The bank was held to have acted in breach of trust in making the advances.

SECTION 3: INVESTMENT

A: The Statutory Power

Trustee Investments Act 1961

1. New powers of investment of trustees
(1) A trustee may invest any property in his hands, whether at the time in a state of investment or not, in any manner specified in Part I or II of the First Schedule to

this Act or, subject to the next following section, in any manner specified in Part III of that Schedule, and may also from time to time vary any such investments.

(2)   The supplemental provisions contained in Part IV of that Schedule shall have effect for the interpretation and for restricting the operation of the said Parts I to III.

(3)   No provision relating to the powers of the trustee contained in any instrument (not being an enactment or an instrument made under an enactment) made before the passing of this Act shall limit the powers conferred by this section, but those powers are exercisable only in so far as a contrary intention is not expressed in any Act or instrument made under an enactment, whenever passed or made, and so relating or in any other instrument so relating which is made after the passing of this Act.

For the purposes of this subsection any rule of the law of Scotland whereby a testamentary writing may be deemed to be made on a date other than that on which it was actually executed shall be disregarded.

(4)   In this Act 'narrower-range investment' means an investment falling within Part I or II of the First Schedule to this Act and 'wider-range investment' means an investment falling within Part III of that Schedule.

2.   Restrictions on wider-range investment

(1)   A trustee shall not have power by virtue of the foregoing section to make or retain any wider-range investment unless the trust fund has been divided into two parts (hereinafter referred to as the narrower-range part and the wider-range part), the parts being, subject to the provisions of this Act, equal in value at the time of the division; and where such a division has been made no subsequent division of the same fund shall be made for the purposes of this section, and no property shall be transferred from one part of the fund to the other unless either —

(a)   the transfer is authorised or required by the following provisions of this Act, or

(b)   a compensating transfer is made at the same time.

In this section 'compensating transfer', in relation to any transferred property, means a transfer in the opposite direction of property of equal value.

(2)   Property belonging to the narrower-range part of a trust fund shall not by virtue of the foregoing section be invested except in narrower-range investments, and any property invested in any other manner which is or becomes comprised in that part of the trust fund shall either be transferred to the wider-range part of the fund, with a compensating transfer, or be reinvested in narrower-range investments as soon as may be.

(3)   Where any property accrues to a trust fund after the fund has been divided in pursuance of subsection (1) of this section, then—

(a)   if the property accrues to the trustee as owner or former owner of property comprised in either part of the fund, it shall be treated as belonging to that part of the fund;

(b)   in any other case, the trustee shall secure, by apportionment of the accruing property or the transfer of property from one part of the fund to the other, or both, that the value of each part of the fund is increased by the same amount.

Where a trustee acquires property in consideration of a money payment the acquisition of the property shall be treated for the purposes of this section as investment and not as the accrual of property to the trust fund, notwithstanding that the amount of the consideration is less than the value of the property acquired; and paragraph (a) of this subsection shall not include the case of a dividend or interest becoming part of a trust fund.

(4)   Where in the exercise of any power or duty of a trustee property falls to be taken out of the trust fund, nothing in this section shall restrict his discretion as to the choice of property to be taken out.

3.   Relationship between Act and other powers of investment

(1)   The powers conferred by section one of this Act are in addition to and not in derogation from any power conferred otherwise than by this Act of investment or postponing conversion exercisable by a trustee (hereinafter referred to as a 'special power').

(2)   Any special power (however expressed) to invest property in any investment for the time being authorised by law for the investment of trust property, being a power conferred on a trustee before the passing of this Act or conferred on him under any enactment passed before the passing of this Act, shall have effect as a power to invest property in like manner and subject to the like provisions as under the foregoing provisions of this Act.

[Subsections (3) and (4) are detailed provisions which are not reproduced.]

6.   Duty of trustees in choosing investments

(1)   In the exercise of his powers of investment a trustee shall have regard —

(a)   to the need for diversification of investments of the trust, in so far as is appropriate to the circumstances of the trust;

(b)   to the suitability to the trust of investments of the description of investment proposed and of the investment proposed as an investment of that description.

(2)   Before exercising any power conferred by section one of this Act to invest in a manner specified in Part II or III of the First Schedule to this Act, or before investing in any such manner in the exercise of a power falling within subsection (2) of section 3 of this Act, a trustee shall obtain and consider proper advice on the question whether the investment is satisfactory having regard to the matters mentioned in paragraphs (a) and (b) of the foregoing subsection.

(3)   A trustee retaining any investment made in the exercise of such a power and in such a manner as aforesaid shall determine at what intervals the circumstances, and in particular the nature of the investment, make it desirable to obtain such advice as aforesaid, and shall obtain and consider such advice accordingly.

(4)   For the purposes of the two foregoing subsections, proper advice is the advice of a person who is reasonably believed by the trustee to be qualified by his ability in and practical experience of financial matters; and such advice may be given by a person notwithstanding that he gives it in the course of his employment as an officer or servant.

(5)   A trustee shall not be treated as having complied with subsection (2) or (3) of this section unless the advice was given or has been subsequently confirmed in writing.

(6)   Subsections (2) and (3) of this section shall not apply to one of two or more trustees where he is the person giving the advice required by this section to his co-trustee or co-trustees, and shall not apply where powers of a trustee are lawfully exercised by an officer or servant competent under subsection (4) of this section to give proper advice.

(7)   Without prejudice to section 8 of the Trustee Act, 1925, or section 30 of the Trusts (Scotland) Act, 1921 (which relate to valuation, and the proportion of the value to be lent, where a trustee lends on the security of property) the advice required by this section shall not include, in the case of a loan on the security of freehold or leasehold property in England and Wales or Northern Ireland or on heritable security in Scotland, advice on the suitability of the particular loan.

Note
Part I investments include National Savings, Government bonds and the like.
Part II investments include securities issued by or guaranteed by Her
Majesty's Government, public authority securities, mortgages, rentcharges
and some debentures. Equities come within Part III.

B: Criteria for Investment

Cowan v Scargill
[1985] Ch 270, [1984] 2 All ER 750
Chancery Division

Facts: Mr Scargill, President of the National Union of Mineworkers, was
one of the trustees of a pension fund with wide powers of investment. He
and five other trustees (the defendants) appointed by the union refused to
approve an annual investment plan unless it was amended to prohibit any
increase in overseas investment, to provide for withdrawal from existing
overseas investments, and to prohibit investments in industries which were
in direct competition with coal. Their action was in line with the policy of
the National Union of Mineworkers. The plaintiffs (five trustees appointed
by the National Coal Board) applied to the court for directions that the
defendants were in breach of their fiduciary duties as trustees.

Held: The trusts of a pension fund were governed by the ordinary law of
trusts, and the defendants were in breach of their fiduciary duties in
refusing to approve the investment plan.

SIR ROBERT MEGARRY V-C: I turn to the law. The starting point is the duty of
trustees to exercise their powers in the best interests of the present and future beneficiaries
of the trust, holding the scales impartially between different classes of beneficiaries. This
duty of the trustees towards their beneficiaries is paramount. They must, of course, obey
the law; but subject to that, they must put the interests of their beneficiaries first. When the
purpose of the trust is to provide financial benefits for the beneficiaries, as is usually the
case, the best interests of the beneficiaries are normally their best financial interests. In the
case of a power of investment, as in the present case, the power must be exercised so as to
yield the best return for the beneficiaries, judged in relation to the risks of the investments
in question; and the prospects of the yield of income and capital appreciation both have to
be considered in judging the return from the investment.
   The legal memorandum that the union obtained from their solicitors is generally in
accord with these views. In considering the possibility of investment for 'socially
beneficial reasons which may result in lower returns to the fund', the memorandum
states that 'the trustees' only concern is to ensure that the return is the maximum
possible consistent with security'; and then it refers to the need for diversification.
However, it continues by saying that:

> Trustees cannot be criticised for failing to make a particular investment for social
> or political reasons, such as in South African stock for example, but may be held
> liable for investing in assets which yield a poor return or for disinvesting in stock at
> inappropriate times for non-financial criteria.

This last sentence must be considered in the light of subsequent passages in the memorandum which indicate that the sale of South African securities by trustees might be justified on the grounds of doubts about political stability in South Africa and the long-term financial soundness of its economy, whereas trustees could not properly support motions at a company meeting dealing with pay levels in South Africa, work accidents, pollution control, employment conditions for minorities, military contracting and consumer protection. The assertion that the trustees could not be criticised for failing to make a particular investment for social or political reasons is one that I would not accept in its full width. If the investment in fact made is equally beneficial to the beneficiaries, then criticism would be difficult to sustain in practice, whatever the position in theory. But if the investment in fact made is less beneficial, then both in theory and in practice the trustees would normally be open to criticism.

This leads me to the second point, which is a corollary of the first. In considering what investments to make trustees must put on one side their own personal interests and views. Trustees may have strongly held social or political views. They may be firmly opposed to any investment in South Africa or other countries, or they may object to any form of investment in companies concerned with alcohol, tobacco, armaments or many other things. In the conduct of their own affairs, of course, they are free to abstain from making any such investments. Yet under a trust, if investments of this type would be more beneficial to the beneficiaries than other investments, the trustees must not refrain from making the investments by reasons of the views that they hold.

Trustees may even have to act dishonestly (though not illegally) if the interests of their beneficiaries require it. Thus where trustees for sale had struck a bargain for the sale of trust property but had not bound themselves by a legally enforceable contract, they were held to be under a duty to consider and explore a better offer that they received, and not to carry through the bargain to which they felt in honour bound: see *Buttle* v *Saunders* [1950] 2 All ER 193. In other words, the duty of trustees to their beneficiaries may include a duty to 'gazump', however honourable the trustees. As Wynn-Parry J said (at 195), trustees 'have an overriding duty to obtain the best price which they can for their beneficiaries'. In applying this to an Official Receiver, Templeman J said in *Re Wyvern Developments Ltd* [1974] 1 WLR 1097 at 1106 that he —

must do his best by his creditors and contributories. He is in a fiduciary capacity and cannot make moral gestures, nor can the court authorise him to do so.

In the words of Wigram V-C in *Balls* v *Strutt* (1841) 1 Hare 146 at 149:

It is a principle in this court that a trustee shall not be permitted to use the powers which the trust may confer upon him at law, except for the legitimate purposes of the trust.

Powers must be exercised fairly and honestly for the purposes for which they are given and not so as to accomplish any ulterior purpose, whether for the benefit of the trustees or otherwise: see *Duke of Portland* v *Topham* (1864) 11 HL Cas 32, a case on a power of appointment that must apply *a fortiori* to a power given to trustees as such.

Third, by way of caveat I should say that I am not asserting that the benefit of the beneficiaries which a trustee must make his paramount concern inevitably and solely means their financial benefit, even if the only object of the trust is to provide financial benefits. Thus, if the only actual or potential beneficiaries of a trust are all adults with very strict views on moral and social matters, condemning all forms of alcohol, tobacco and popular entertainment, as well as armaments, I can well understand that it might not be for the 'benefit' of such beneficiaries to know that they are obtaining rather larger financial returns under the trust by reason of investments in those activities than they would have received if the trustees had invested the trust funds in other investments. The beneficiaries might well consider that it was far better to receive less than to receive more money from what they consider to be evil and tainted sources. 'Benefit' is a word with a very wide meaning, and there are circumstances in which arrangements which work to the financial disadvantage of a beneficiary may yet be for his benefit: see, for example, *Re Towler's ST* [1964] Ch 158; *Re CL* [1969] 1 Ch 587 [see chapter 7]. But I would emphasise that such cases are likely to be very rare, and in any case I think that under a trust for the provision of financial benefits that burden would rest, and rest heavy, on him who asserts that it is for the benefit of the beneficiaries as a whole to receive less by reason of the exclusion of some of the possibly more profitable forms of investment. Plainly the present case is not one of this rare type of case. Subject to such matters, under a trust for the provision of financial benefits, the paramount duty of the trustees is to provide the greatest financial benefits for the present and future beneficiaries.

Fourth, the standard required of a trustee in exercising his powers of investment is that he must —

> take such care as an ordinary prudent man would take if he were minded to make an investment for the benefit of other people for whom he felt morally bound to provide.

See *Re Whitely, Whitely* v *Learoyd* (1886) 33 ChD at 355 per Lindley LJ, and see also at 350, 358; *Learoyd* v *Whitely* (1887) 12 App Cas 727. That duty includes the duty to seek advice on matters which the trustee does not understand, such as the making of investments, and on receiving that advice to act with the same degree of prudence. This requirement is not discharged merely by showing that the trustee has acted in good faith and with sincerity. Honesty and sincerity are not the same as prudence and reasonableness. Some of the most sincere people are the most unreasonable; and Mr Scargill told me that he had met quite a few of them. Accordingly, although a trustee who takes advice on investments is not bound to accept and act on that advice, he is not entitled to reject it merely because he sincerely disagrees with it, unless in addition to being sincere he is acting as an ordinary prudent man would act.

Fifth, trustees have a duty to consider the need for diversification of investments. By s. 6(1) of the Trustee Investments Act 1961:

> In the exercise of his powers of investment a trustee shall have regard – (a) to the need for diversification of investments of the trust, insofar as is appropriate to the circumstances of the trust; (b) to the suitability to the trust of investments of the description of investment proposed and of the investment proposed as an investment of that description.

The reference to the 'circumstances of the trust' plainly includes matters such as the size of the trust funds: the degree of diversification that is practicable and desirable for a large fund may plainly be impracticable or undesirable (or both) in the case of a small fund.

Notes

1.   It might come as a surprise that trustees may be under a duty to act dishonestly, and to 'gazump' should the interests of the beneficiaries so require.

2. On the question of protection of the investment, the general standard laid down in *Bartlett* v *Barclays Bank* applies: see chapter 14.

3. The trustees will not be liable if, although they applied the wrong criteria in their choice of investments, their decision is nonetheless justifiable on objective grounds, since then there will be no loss to the trust. In *Nestle* v *National Westminster Bank plc* [1994] 1 All ER 118, Staughton LJ observed (at p. 128):

> Winterbourne and its contents were sold in 1959, when the testator's widow, being elderly, went to live in a home. The proceeds were around £5,000.
>
> The bank's stockbrokers suggested on 9 July 1959 that to make the portfolio rather more balanced, half the proceeds should be invested in Shell Transport and Trading Co. and the other half in an electrical company, either A. Reyrolle Ltd or Electrical and Musical Industries Ltd. The bank preferred, however, to invest the entire proceeds in conversion stock. The only reason, apparent from the papers, for not accepting the brokers' recommendations was that the bank's investment section was doubtful whether the brokers' recommendations were authorised by the investment clause; but no attempt was made to obtain legal advice.
>
> The investment decision was therefore prima facie made for an untenable reason, but that is not the end of the matter since, as Sir Robert Megarry V-C pointed out in *Cowan* v *Scargill* [1985] Ch 270, 294:
>
>> If trustees make a decision upon wholly wrong grounds, and yet it subsequently appears, from matters which they did not express or refer to, that there are in fact good and sufficient reasons for supporting their decision, then I do not think that they would incur any liability for having decided the matter upon erroneous grounds; for the decision itself was right.
>
> The court has to look objectively at the circumstances, to see if there are in fact good and sufficient reasons for supporting the decision. Plainly there is such a reason in relation to the Winterbourne proceeds at that time, since more than 75 per cent of the annuity fund was already invested in equities. There was therefore a finely balanced decision for the bank, on a correct appreciation of the facts, between increasing the equity share yet further in the interests of having a somewhat more balanced portfolio, and leaving the equity percentage where it was and acquiring the conversion stock. In these circumstances a decision either way can be regarded as objectively right, and the bank cannot be held liable for not having followed the brokers' advice.

SECTION 4: APPORTIONMENT

The general duty of trustees to act even-handedly as between the beneficiaries entails the necessity, where there are successive interests under a trust, to take certain steps to ensure that a fair balance is maintained between the capital and income of the trust, so that the former is preserved for those entitled in the future while at the same time allowing a reasonable income to those currently entitled. This is the explanation for old equitable principles, such as that in *Howe* v *Earl of Dartmouth* (1802) 7 Ves Jr 137, which compels trustees in certain circumstances to sell trust property which is a wasting asset, in order to protect the remaindermen, and *Re Earl of Chesterfield's Trusts* (1883) 24 ChD 643, which assumes that where property produces no income, the capital value, to which the remaindermen are in principle entitled, depreciates by 4 per cent a year.

It is clear, however, that more complex factors also need to be taken into account. In *Nestle* v *National Westminster Bank plc* [1994] 1 All ER 118, Staughton LJ observed (at pp. 136–7):

The obligation of a trustee is to administer the trust fund impartially, or fairly (I can see no significant difference), having regard to the different interests of beneficiaries. Wilberforce J said in *Re Pauling's Settlement Trusts (No. 2)* [1963] Ch 576, 586:

The new trustees would be under the normal duty of preserving an equitable balance, and if at any time it was shown they were inclining one way or the other, it would not be a difficult matter to bring them to account.

At times it will not be easy to decide what is an equitable balance. A life tenant may be anxious to receive the highest possible income, whilst the remainderman will wish the real value of the trust fund to be preserved. If the life tenant is living in penury and the remainderman already has ample wealth, common sense suggests that a trustee should be able to take that into account, not necessarily by seeking the highest possible income at the expense of capital but by inclining in that direction. However, before adopting that course a trustee should, I think, require some verification of the facts. . . .

Similarly I would not regard it as a breach of trust for the trustees to pay some regard to the relationship between Mr George Nestle and [the plaintiff]. He was merely her uncle, and she would have received nothing from his share of the fund if he had fathered a child who survived him. The trustees would be entitled, in my view, to incline towards income during his life tenancy and that of his widow, on that ground. Again common sense suggests to me that such a course might be appropriate, and I do not think that it would be a breach of the duty to act fairly, or impartially.

The dominant consideration for the trustees, however, was that George's fund from 1960, and John's from 1969, would not be subject to United Kingdom income tax in so far as it was invested in exempt gilts. That was a factor which the trustees were entitled – and I would say bound – to take into account. A beneficiary who has been left a life interest in a trust fund has an arguable case for saying that he should not be compelled to bear tax on the income if he is not lawfully obliged to do so.

It was no more than a factor for the trustees to bear in mind, and would rarely justify more than a modest degree of preference for income paid gross over capital growth.

The 4 per cent depreciation from *Re Earl of Chesterfield's Trusts* (1883) 24 ChD 643 should not be taken as set in stone. In *Jaffray* v *Marshall* [1994] 1 All ER 143, Nicholas Stewart QC held that the defendants were in breach of trust in failing to allow the plaintiffs the opportunity of realising capital assets. Commenting on the apportionment of interest since the date of the writ, he observed (at p. 154):

In my judgment the principles and authorities do support the plaintiff's case on this point and the defendants must make compensation on the basis of the agreed value at the date of the writ.

That conclusion leaves the question of interest since the date of the writ. It is agreed that there should be interest from that date until judgment at what is now known as the special account rate. The only remaining issue is apportionment of that interest as between the life and remainder interests. The parties, who do not include Lady Jaffray, ask me to make that apportionment, which will not affect Lady Jaffray in practice as her interest will be impounded.

It is accepted that the high rates of interest in modern times contain a large element which merely preserves capital values. In principle that element should belong to the capital or remainder beneficiaries. Mr Vos says that the bulk of any interest would have been used for the income beneficiary and I should allow at least half to her. Mr Nugee argues, by reference to *Wright v British Railways Board* [1983] 2 AC 773, that I should apportion to the income beneficiary the same figure of 2 per cent which has been adopted as what might be called the real rate of the interest in cases of damages for personal injuries. However, though the analysis of what constitutes a 'real' rate of interest is equally applicable to the present case, the actual figure of two per cent is a rather broad guideline adopted some years ago in a different context. An alternative suggested by Mr Nugee, if I thought 2 per cent was too low, was the rate of 4 per cent generally adopted by equity in pre-inflationary days. Both figures seem low to me. Though there are distinct limits to judicial notice, in the very broadest terms I take account of the fact that the period since 1989 has not been a period of the very high level of inflation that has been seen at times in fairly recent years. Accordingly, the rate of return needed to preserve capital is not as high as it has been in the past, which is only another way of saying the same thing. I stress the broadness of that view and no expert evidence has been adduced on these matters. In my view a fair apportionment of the interest in this case is that half should go to income and half to capital.

16 DEFENCES TO A BREACH OF TRUST ACTION

SECTION 1: STATUTORY DEFENCE

Trustee Act 1925

61. Power to relieve trustee from personal liability
If it appears to the court that a trustee, whether appointed by the court or otherwise, is or may be personally liable for any breach of trust, whether the transaction alleged to be a breach of trust occurred before or after the commencement of this Act, but has acted honestly and reasonably, and ought fairly to be excused for the breach of trust and for omitting to obtain the directions of the court in the matter in which he committed such breach, then the court may relieve him either wholly or partly from personal liability for the same.

Notes
1. The trustees were protected by this section in *Re Wightwick* [1950] 1 Ch 260, considered in more detail in chapter 5. They had paid income from dividends to the National Anti-Vivisection Society, believing this to be a valid donation to charity. The House of Lords held the society non-charitable in 1947 (see further chapter 12). Wynn-Parry J observed:

> In paying the income, as they have done, to the association and then to the National Anti-Vivisection Society up till now, the plaintiffs have acted throughout *bona fide* and in accordance with the generally held view that the primary gift was a good charitable trust: see *Re Foveaux* [1895] 2 Ch 501. It will, therefore, be proper to declare under the Trustee Act 1925, s. 61, that they acted honestly and reasonably and ought fairly to be excused for any breach of trust which they may have committed and for omitting to obtain the directions of the court in the matter, and that they should be wholly relieved from personal liability.

2. In *Bartlett* v *Barclays Bank Trust Co. Ltd (No. 1)* [1980] Ch 515 (see chapter 14), the bank could not use this section as a defence, since it protects only trustees who had acted honestly and reasonably. The bank had acted honestly, but not reasonably.

SECTION 2: CONSENT, PARTICIPATION, RELEASE OR ACQUIESCENCE BY BENEFICIARIES

Re Pauling's ST
[1964] Ch 303
Court of Appeal

Facts: The four plaintiffs were remaindermen under a marriage settlement, of funds amounting to about £70,000, of which the defendant bank (Coutts & Co.) was trustee. Their mother (Mrs Younghusband, née Miss Pauling) was a life tenant under the settlement, and was also a customer at the bank. The marriage settlement contained a power of advancement, upon the written consent of Mrs Younghusband, of up to half the share of each remainderman, in such manner as the trustees should think fit.

Over a period from 1948 to 1954, Commander and Mrs Younghusband spent considerably in excess of their income (nearly all of which was derived from the marriage settlement itself), and Mrs Younghusband had a current account at the defendant bank which was continually overdrawn by a large amount. She and the Commander persuaded the plaintiffs (all of who had by the time of the advance obtained their majority) to consent to various advances, amounting to over £29,000. In most cases the advance was made for a specific purpose, for example the purchase of a house or furniture, or house improvements, but was given by the advancee to Commander and Mrs Younghusband, who used it to reduce their overdraft with the bank. In 1958, the plaintiffs commenced proceedings against the bank.

Held: On the facts the bank had acted in breach of trust, and with the exception of some £5,300 where they could show that the advancees had clearly assented to the advance, and a further £2,600 where they had a valid defence under s. 61 of the Trustee Act 1925, they were liable to reimburse the trust.

(a)   However widely expressed, a power of advancement must be exercised in a fiduciary manner, and the trustees must be satisfied that it was for the benefit of the advancee. *Re Pilkington's WT* [1964] AC 612 (chapter 15) applied.

(b)   If the advance was made for a particular purpose, the trustees were under a duty to ensure that it was used for that purpose, and not simply spent in any manner which the advancee chose.

(c)   Consent to an advance by an adult beneficiary was a defence to an advance which was made in breach of trust. On the question of consent, Wilberforce J had said at first instance [1962] 1 WLR 86, 108:

. . . the court has to consider all the circumstances in which the concurrence of the *cestui que trust* was given with a view to seeing whether it is fair and equitable that, having given his concurrence, he should afterwards turn round and sue the trustees: that, subject to this, it is not necessary that he should know that what he is concurring in is a breach of trust, provided that he fully understands what he is concurring in, and that it is not necessary that he should have himself directly benefited from the breach of trust.

The Court of Appeal expressed no opinion on this passage: [1964] Ch 303, 339.

(d) Where a presumption of undue influence existed, as between a parent and child who was still subject to parental influence (albeit a child who had reached his or her majority), an advance to the child which was given to his or her parent, could not be retained by the parent unless it was clear that:

(i) the gift was the spontaneous act of the child, and

(ii) the child knew what his or her rights were. It was also desirable that the child had obtained independent and, if possible, professional advice.

The courts treated with suspicion gifts from children to their parents, whereas the reverse was true of gifts the other way round (see, e.g. the presumption of advancement, in chapter 9).

(e) The court would be slow to relieve a banker under s. 61 of the Trustee Act 1925 (above), where the banker by undertaking to act as a paid trustee on behalf of a customer, had deliberately put himself into a position where his interest as banker (reduction of the life tenant's overdraft) conflicted with his duty as trustee. However, the defendants would be relieved under this section in one case where they had received a letter from the advancees' solicitors purporting to consent to an advance which was clearly made in breach of trust, although in fact the advancees were ignorant of the transaction.

(f) Where a beneficiary sues for breach of trust he must give credit for any property he has received as a result, but not for other benefits incidentally received.

(g) The plaintiffs' interests, as future interests which had not fallen into possession as a result of the invalid advances of capital made, were not time barred, by virtue of the proviso to s. 19(2) of the Limitation Act 1939 (see now s. 21(3) of the Limitation Act 1980, set out below). The consent of the life tenant did not amount to a release of her life interest.

(h) The bank could not rely on the defence of acquiescence, since until 1954 they neither knew nor ought to have known what their rights were.

SECTION 3: IMPOUNDING THE BENEFICIARY'S INTEREST

The court has an inherent power to impound the interest of a beneficiary, thus providing the trustee with an indemnity to the extent that the beneficiary's interest will suffice to replace the loss to the trust.

The power can arise where a beneficiary has merely consented to the breach, but only if some benefit to him can be proved, and then only to the extent of that benefit. If the beneficiary has gone further, and actually requested or instigated a breach, the power can be exercised whether or not he has received a personal benefit from the breach.

Needless to say, the trustee has to show that the beneficiary acted in full knowledge of the facts, but it is not necessary to show that he knew that the acts he was instigating or consenting to amounted to a breach.

There is also a statutory discretion to impound.

Trustee Act 1925

62. Power to make beneficiary indemnify for breach of trust

(1) Where a trustee commits a breach of trust at the instigation or request or with the consent in writing of a beneficiary, the court may, if it thinks fit, [and notwithstanding that the beneficiary may be a married woman restrained from anticipation,] make such order as to the court seems just, for impounding all or any part of the interest of the beneficiary in the trust estate by way of indemnity to the trustee or persons claiming through him.

(2) This section applies to breaches of trust committed as well before as after the commencement of this Act.

Note

The words in square brackets were repealed by the Married Women (Restraint upon Anticipation) Act 1949, but are set out here to explain Wilberforce J's view of the purpose of this section, set out in *Re Pauling's ST (No. 2)* [1963] Ch 576 (see below).

This section replaced an earlier enactment, and has been treated as a consolidating section.

Re Pauling's ST (No. 2)
[1963] Ch 576
Chancery Division

Facts: In *Re Pauling's ST*, above, the Court of Appeal largely upheld a decision of Wilberforce J [1962] 1 WLR 86. Pursuant to that decision, the plaintiffs took out a summons for the appointment of new trustees. The defendants resisted the appointment on the grounds that they were entitled to impound the interests of the tenant for life, Mrs Younghusband, both under equitable jurisdiction apart from statute, and under s. 62 of the Trustee Act 1925, and their removal as trustees would imperil their right to impound Mrs Younghusband's interest.

Note that Mrs Younghusband's interest as life tenant would have been in the form of continuing income (interest on the fund invested), so that it would have been impossible, for example, for the bank simply to have impounded a single capital sum.

Held: The trustees had no right to continue in office merely in order to impound Mrs Younghusband's interest. In any case, neither the equitable nor the statutory right to impound was limited to the case where the trustee continued in office, so that the appointment of new trustees would not imperil the right. However, in the light of various undertakings entered into by the bank, and the appeal on liability (eventually heard in *Re Pauling's ST*, above), the new appointments should not be made in the circumstances.

WILBERFORCE J: [Wilberforce J considered the general equitable jurisdiction, and continued:]

As regards the statutory right, that depends on the language of s. 62 of the Trustee Act 1925, and at first sight it might look as if that right only exists in favour of a person who is actually a trustee. But, on consideration, that seems to me to be a misconstruction of the section. In the first place, the same objection against limiting the right in this way applies to the statutory jurisdiction. It seems to me an absurdity that it is required as a condition of exercising the right to obtain an impounding order, that the trustee who, *ex hypothesi*, is in breach of trust, must remain as trustee in order to acquire a right of indemnity. Further, it seems to me on the authorities, and, indeed, on the very terms of the section, that the section is giving an additional right, among other things, to deal with the case of a married woman beneficiary; that the statutory right is extending the equitable right and not limiting it, and that it is not right to read the section so as to apply only to a person who was formerly a trustee. The section begins with the words: 'Where a trustee commits a breach of trust', thereby indicating that at the time the breach of trust is committed the person in question must be a trustee. Then further down in the section there is a reference to a trustee and that appears to me to be merely a reference back to the same person as the person who committed the breach of trust and not as an indication that the person in question must be a trustee at the date of the order.

Notes

1. Wilberforce J treats the right under s. 62 as extending the equitable jurisdiction. There are probably no circumstances where the equitable jurisdiction is wider than the jurisdiction under the statute.

2. The courts seem to have treated this largely as a consolidating section, rather than extending their powers, except that Wilberforce J in *Re Pauling's ST (No. 2)* [1963] Ch 576 thought that it gave an additional right, among other things, to deal with a married woman beneficiary. This additional right is no longer necessary, because of changes in legislation on family property, and that part of the section was repealed in 1949.

3. The effect of the court making such an order is that the beneficiary is not only debarred from pursuing his own claim against the trustee, but is also liable to replace the losses suffered by the other beneficiaries, to the extent ordered by the court, and perhaps up to the full value of his own interest. To this extent, the trustee is protected t the beneficiary's expense.

4. The discretion is a judicial discretion, and though the section appears to extend the inherent power of the court by giving a discretion to impound a beneficiary's interest regardless of whether he obtained a benefit, it has received a restrictive interpretation. It seems that the court will make an impounding order in any case where it would have done so before the Act;

generally speaking, in any case where the beneficiary has actively induced the breach (for which it has never been necessary to show benefit).

5. It must, of course, be shown that the beneficiary was fully aware of what was being done. In *Re Somerset* [1894] 1 Ch 231, a beneficiary had urged the trustees to invest in a mortgage of a particular property, but had left them to decide how much money they were prepared to invest. Lindley MR said (at p. 265):

> In order to bring a case within this section the cestui que trust must instigate, or request, or consent in writing to some act or omission which in itself is a breach of trust, and not to some act or omission which only becomes a breach of trust by reason of want of care on the part of the trustees.

The words 'in writing' have been held to apply only to consent, and not to instigation or request: *Griffith* v *Hughes* [1892] 3 Ch 105. So it is necessary only for a request or instigation to be oral.

6. The power to impound will not be lost upon an assignment of the beneficial interest. Nor is it lost when the court replaces the trustees in consequence of the breach. In *Re Pauling's ST* [1962] 1 WLR 86, the trustees resisted removal because they were claiming an indemnity out of the interests of the parents. Wilberforce J held that they were entitled to such indemnity and that this would be unaffected by their replacement. They were therefore unable to use this as a ground for continuing in office: see *Re Pauling's ST (No. 2)* [1963] Ch 576.

7. Apart from statute, it is the practice, where trustees have under an honest mistake overpaid a beneficiary, for the court to make allowance for the mistake in order to allow the trustee to recoup as far as possible: *Re Musgrave* [1916] 2 Ch 417. An overpaid beneficiary is not compelled to return the excess, but further payment may be withheld until the accounts are adjusted.

If a payment is made by mistake to someone who is not entitled, the trustee may recover on an action for money had and received if the mistake was one of fact, but not if it was a mistake of law: *Re Diplock* [1947] Ch 716. It is also certain that the error must be corrected where trustee-beneficiaries overpay themselves.

SECTION 4: LAPSE OF TIME AND LIMITATION

Limitation Act 1980

21. Time limit for actions in respect of trust property

(1) No period of limitation prescribed by this Act shall apply to an action by a beneficiary under a trust, being an action —

(a) in respect of any fraud or fraudulent breach of trust to which the trustee was a party or privy; or

(b) to recover from the trustee trust property or the proceeds of trust property in the possession of the trustee, or previously received by the trustee and converted to his use.

(2)   Where a trustee who is also a beneficiary under a trust receives or retains trust property or its proceeds as his share on a distribution of trust property under the trust, his liability in any action brought by virtue of subsection (1)(b) above to recover that property or its proceeds after the expiration of the period of limitation prescribed by this Act for bringing an action to recover trust property shall be limited to the excess over his proper share.

This subsection only applies if the trustee acted honestly and reasonably in making the distribution.

(3)   Subject to the preceding provisions of this section, an action by a beneficiary to recover trust property or in respect of any breach of trust, not being an action for which a period of limitation is prescribed by any other provision of this Act, shall not be brought after the expiration of six years from the date on which the right of action accrued.

For the purposes of this subsection, the right of action shall not be treated as having accrued to any beneficiary entitled to a future interest in the trust property until the interest fell into possession.

(4)   No beneficiary as against whom there would be a good defence under this Act shall derive any greater or any other benefit from a judgment or order obtained by any other beneficiary than he could have obtained if he had brought the action and this Act had been pleaded in defence.

Notes

1.   By s. 21(3), any action by a beneficiary to recover trust property or in respect of any breach of trust (other that situations covered by self-dealing and fair dealing rules) must be brought within six years from the date on which the right of action accrued.

A right of action in respect of future interests is not treated as having accrued until the interest falls into possession: this was also part of the *ratio* in *Re Pauling's ST* [1964] Ch 303.

2.   Under s. 21(1), no period of limitation applies where the action is in respect of any fraud to which the trustee was a party, or privy, or where (in summary) it is sought to recover from the trustee trust property still in his possession, or the proceeds of sale of such property. Protection is also lost where the trustee converts trust property to his own use. Conversion to the trustee's own use, however, implies application in his own favour, so that if the funds have been used to maintain an infant beneficiary, or dissipated by a fellow trustee, the protection of limitation remains available.

3.   Where fraud is the issue, this must be fraud by the trustee himself. In *Thorne v Heard* [1894] 1 Ch 599, a trustee was protected by a section in similar terms of an earlier Act, where he had left trust funds with a solicitor who had embezzled them, the trustee himself being no more than negligent. Where the trustee is in possession of trust property or its proceeds, however, no dishonesty need be shown. Fraud for these purposes is wider than common law fraud or deceit, but nevertheless requires unconscionable conduct on the part of the trustee, something in the nature of a deliberate cover up: in *Bartlett v Barclays Bank Trust Co. Ltd (No. 1)* [1980] Ch 515 (see chapter 14), the bank was held able to rely on what is now s. 21(1) of the 1980 Act, in respect of income lost outside the limitation period since, being unaware that it was acting in breach of trust, it could not be guilty of fraud for these purposes.

4. Section 22 prescribes a limitation period of 12 years for actions in respect of any claim to the personal estate of a deceased person. It is often hard to determine at what point executors have completed the administration of an estate and become trustees, but it is thought that the 12-year period will apply although for all other purposes the executors would be regarded as trustees.

5. Plaintiffs under disability are permitted an extended period in which to bring an action by s. 28; and by s. 32, where fraud, concealment or mistake is alleged, time runs only from the point when the plaintiff discovers the fraud or mistake, or could with reasonable diligence have discovered it.

6. It should be noted that a person other than a *bona fide* purchaser for value without notice who receives property from a trustee also falls within these rules.

7. Where no statutory limitation period applies, the defendant may rely on the equitable doctrine of laches, that is, he may show that it would be unjust to allow the plaintiff to pursue his claim in view of the time that has elapsed since it accrued. The court has a discretion to allow or refuse the defence, and mere delay may suffice, but where possible, the courts have preferred to regard delay as furnishing evidence of acquiescence by the plaintiff.

17 TRACING AND THIRD PARTY LIABILITY

SECTION 1: TRACING AT COMMON LAW

A: Substitution of Other Identifiable Property for Original Identifiable Property

The common law developed an action for the recovery of a specific piece of land, but never extended this 'real' remedy to allow a plaintiff to recover a specific chattel. Although the common law acknowledged the plaintiff's ownership of the chattel, his action was a personal action in detinue, the remedy for which was damages. The defendant could therefore choose whether to return the plaintiff's chattel or pay him its full value as damages.

The Common Law Procedure Act 1854, s. 78, gave the court a discretion to order specific delivery of the chattel, and this power is retained by s. 3 of the Torts (Interference with Goods) Act 1977. But there is no absolute right to the return of the chattel. The importance of the proprietary claim lies rather in the fact that it entitles the plaintiff to the full value of the chattel, in preference to the claims of the defendant's other creditors.

The common law also concluded that the plaintiff's right should continue even if the defendant has exchanged the plaintiff's property for some other property, or sold it and purchased other property with the proceeds. So long as it was possible to 'trace' his original property – that is, to show that what the defendant now holds can be regarded as simply a substitute – his claim is unaffected.

An illustration is the old case of *Taylor* v *Plumer* (1815) 3 M & S 562. Sir Thomas Plumer had handed over money to a stockbroker with instructions to purchase exchequer bonds, but the stockbroker instead purchased American investments and bullion, and attempted to abscond with these. He was caught before he could leave England, and the investments and bullion were seized by Plumer. The assignees of the stockbroker then brought an action to recover them from Sir Thomas, but failed. The investments and bullion were held to be Sir Thomas's own property. In effect, Plumer's money was traced into the investments and bullion for, according to Lord Ellenborough at p. 575, 'the product of or substitute for the original thing still follows the nature of the thing itself, as long as it can be ascertained as such'.

The right of a plaintiff to claim the substitute is commonly called the 'remedy' of tracing, but the process of tracing the original property into its new form is not strictly a remedy at all, but rather a method by which the plaintiff establishes his claim to the actual remedy of restoration of the property or its value.

B: Money Had and Received

In the case of chattels the plaintiff's action depends upon being able to trace his actual property, or in *Taylor* v *Plumer* its product or substitute, into the defendant's hands. In the case of currency title will pass to the recipient, but the law imposes upon the recipient of (e.g.) money stolen from the plaintiff an obligation to reimburse the plaintiff with an equivalent sum. This action, for money had and received, depends on the recipient having been unjustly enriched at the expense of the true owner. The action depends only on the receipt of the money, and it is not defeated by the recipient later parting with the money, or mixing it with his own money. It is defeated, however, if the recipient has not been unjustly enriched. Innocently to receive stolen money in return for full consideration is not to be unjustly enriched at all, so that for example, a shop which has innocently taken stolen money to pay for its goods is not liable to the victim of the theft. Consideration must be provided, however.

Lipkin Gorman v *Karpnale Ltd*
[1991] AC 548
House of Lords

Facts: Cass, a partner in the appellant firm of solicitors, stole a large sum of money from their clients' account and gambled it away in the Playboy Club, which was owned by the respondents. The appellants claimed the club's winnings from Cass.

Held:
(a) The club was liable in an action for money had and received. It was unable to claim that it had provided consideration for the money, since contracts by way of gaming and wagering were rendered null and void by the Gaming Act 1845, s. 18. Gambling contracts were not therefore contracts for consideration.

(b) There is a change of position defence to the restitutionary common law claim, which limited the appellants' right to recovery of the winnings taken by the casino, rather than all the money gambled by Cass. Paying out money as winnings constituted a change in position by the club.

LORD TEMPLEMAN: My Lords, Cass was a partner in the appellant firm of solicitors, Lipkin Gorman (the solicitors). Cass withdrew £323,222.14 from the solicitors' bank account. The sum of £100,313.16 was replaced, recovered or accounted for, but the balance of £222,908.98 was money which Cass stole from the solicitors and proved to be irrecoverable from him. Cass staked £561,014.06 at the gaming tables of the Playboy Club, a licensed casino owned and operated by the respondents, Karpnale Ltd (the club). Cass won £378,294.06. After making adjustments for certain cheques, the club agreed that the club won and Cass lost overall, in a matter of months, the sum of £174,745. The parties also agreed that the maximum gross personal resources of Cass amounted to £20,050 and that at least the sum of £154,695 won by the club and lost by Cass was derived from money stolen from the solicitors. The club acted innocently throughout and was not aware that it had received £154,695 derived from the solicitors until the solicitors claimed restitution. Conversion does not lie for money, taken and received as currency: see *Orton* v *Butler* (1822) 5 B & Ald 652, 106 ER 1329 and *Foster* v *Green* (1862) 7 H & N 881, 158 ER 726. But the law imposes an obligation on the recipient of stolen money to pay an equivalent sum to the victim if the recipient has been 'unjustly enriched' at the expense of the true owner. In *Fibrosa Spolka Akcyjna* v *Fairbairn Lawson Combe Barbour Ltd* [1942] 2 All ER 122 at 135, [1943] AC 32 at 61 Lord Wright said:

> It is clear that any civilised system of law is bound to provide remedies for cases of what has been called unjust enrichment or unjust benefit, that is, to prevent a man from retaining the money of, or some benefit derived from, another which it is against conscience that he should keep.

The club was enriched as and when Cass staked and lost to the club money stolen from the solicitors amounting in the aggregate to £300,000 or more. But the club paid Cass when he won and in the final reckoning the club only retained £154,695, which was admittedly derived from the solicitors' money. The solicitors can recover the sum of £154,695 which was retained by the club if they show that in the circumstances the club was unjustly enriched at the expense of the solicitors.

In the course of argument there was a good deal of discussion concerning tracing in law and in equity. In my opinion, in a claim for money had and received by a thief, the plaintiff victim must show that money belonging to him was paid by the thief to the defendant and that the defendant was unjustly enriched and remained unjustly enriched. An innocent recipient of stolen money may not be enriched at all; if Cass had paid £20,000 derived from the solicitors to a car dealer for a motor car priced at £20,000, the car dealer would not have been enriched. The car dealer would have received £20,000 for a car worth £20,000. But an innocent recipient of stolen money will be enriched if the recipient has not given full consideration. If Cass had given £20,000 of the solicitors' money to a friend as a gift, the friend would have been enriched and unjustly enriched because a donee of stolen money cannot in good conscience rely on the bounty of the thief to deny restitution to the victim of the theft. Complications arise if the donee innocently expends the stolen money in reliance on the validity of the gift before the donee receives notice of the victim's claim for restitution. Thus, if the donee spent £20,000 in the purchase of a motor car which he would not have purchased but for the gift, it seems to me that the donee has altered his position on the faith of the gift and has only been unjustly enriched to the extent of the secondhand value of the motor car at the date when the victim of the theft seeks restitution. If the donee spends the £20,000 in a trip round the world, which he would not have undertaken without the gift, it seems to me that the donee has altered his position on the faith of the gift and that he is not unjustly enriched when the victim of the theft seeks restitution. In the present case Cass stole and the club received £229,908.48 of the solicitors' money. If the club was in the same position as a donee, the club nevertheless in good faith allowed Cass to gamble with the solicitors' money and paid his winnings from time to time so that, when the solicitors sought restitution, the club only retained £154,695 derived from the solicitors. The question is whether the club which was enriched by £154,695 at the date when the solicitors sought restitution was unjustly enriched.

[Lord Templeman went on to consider whether the club had provided consideration for the money.]

LORD GOFF OF CHIEVELY (on the change of position defence): I turn then to the last point on which the club relied to defeat the solicitors' claim for the money. This was that the claim advanced by the solicitors was in the form of an action for money had and received, and that such a claim should only succeed where the defendant was unjustly enriched at the expense of the plaintiff. If it would be unjust or unfair to order restitution, the claim should fail. It was for the court to consider the question of injustice or unfairness, on broad grounds. If the court thought that it would be unjust or unfair to hold the club liable to the solicitors, it should deny the solicitors recovery. Mr Lightman QC, for the club, listed a number of reasons why, in his submission, it would be unfair to hold the club liable. These were: (1) the club acted throughout in good faith, ignorant of the fact that the money had been stolen by Cass; (2) although the gaming contracts entered into by the club with Cass were all void, nevertheless the club honoured all those contracts; (3) Cass was allowed to keep his winnings (to the extent that he did not gamble them away); (4) the gaming contracts were merely void not illegal; and (5) the solicitors' claim was no different in principle from a claim to recover against an innocent third party to whom the money was given and who no longer retained it.

I accept that the solicitors' claim in the present case is founded upon the unjust enrichment of the club, and can only succeed if, in accordance with the principles of the law of restitution, the club were indeed unjustly enriched at the expense of the solicitors. The claim for money had and received is not, as I have previously mentioned, founded upon any wrong committed by the club against the solicitors. But it does not, in my opinion, follow that the court has carte blanche to reject the solicitors' claim simply because it thinks it unfair or unjust in the circumstances to grant recovery. The recovery of money in restitution is not, as a general rule, a matter of discretion for the court. A claim to recover money at common law is made as a matter of right; and, even though the underlying principle of recovery is the principle of unjust enrichment, nevertheless, where recovery is denied, it is denied on the basis of legal principle.

It is therefore necessary to consider whether Mr Lightman's submission [for the club] can be upheld on the basis of legal principle. In my opinion it is plain, from the nature of his submission, that he is in fact seeking to invoke a principle of change of position, asserting that recovery should be denied because of the change in position of the club, who acted in good faith throughout.

Whether change of position is, or should be, recognised as a defence to claims in restitution is a subject which has been much debated in the books. It is, however, a matter on which there is a remarkable unanimity of view, the consensus being to the effect that such a defence should be recognised in English law. I myself am under no doubt that this is right.

. . .

In these circumstances, it is right that we should ask ourselves: why do we feel that it would be unjust to allow restitution in cases such as these? The answer must be that, where an innocent defendant's position is so changed that he will suffer an injustice if called upon to repay or to repay in full, the injustice of requiring him so to repay outweighs the injustice of denying the plaintiff restitution. If the plaintiff pays money to the defendant under a mistake of fact, and the defendant then, acting in good faith, pays the money or part of it to charity, it is unjust to require the defendant to make restitution to the extent that he has so changed his position. Likewise, on facts such as those in the present case, if a thief steals my money and pays it to a third party who gives it away to charity, that third party should have a good defence to an action for money had and received. In other words, bona fide change of position should of itself be a good defence in such cases as these. The principle is widely recognised throughout the common law world. . . . The time for its recognition in this country is, in my opinion, long overdue.

. . .

I wish to add two further footnotes. The defence of change of position is akin to the defence of bona fide purchase; but we cannot simply say that bona fide purchase is a species of change of position. This is because change of position will only avail a defendant to the extent that his position has been changed; whereas, where bona fide purchase is invoked, no inquiry is made (in most cases) into the adequacy of the consideration. Even so, the recognition of change of position as a defence should be doubly beneficial. It will enable a more generous approach to be taken to the recognition of the right to restitution, in the knowledge that the defence is, in appropriate cases, available; and, while recognising the different functions of property at law and in equity, there may also in due course develop a more consistent approach to tracing claims, in which common defences are recognised as available to such claims, whether advanced at law or in equity.

[Lord Goff then turned to the application of this principle to the present case.]

C: Identification of Property as Belonging to the Plaintiff

The main constraint on common law tracing is establishing that what the defendant received was in fact the plaintiff's property. While *Taylor* v *Plumer* shows that tracing is available where a straightforward exchange of the property has occurred, the position is more complicated where the property or its proceeds have been placed into a bank account, and it is in this area where equitable rules appear to be more generous. The leading authority is *Banque Belge pour L'Etranger* v *Hambrouck* [1921] 1 KB 321.

Banque Belge pour L'Etranger v *Hambrouck*
[1921] 1 KB 321
Court of Appeal

Facts: Hambrouck, who was a cashier, stole cheques from his employer, altered them so as to make it appear that they were drawn by his employer on the plaintiff bank to Hambrouck's order, and used them to pay money into a new account (at Farrow's Bank) which he opened specifically for the purpose. Farrow's Bank collected the proceeds from the plaintiff bank and credited them to Hambrouck's account. Hambrouck then paid various sums from this account to Mlle Spanoghe, with whom he was living, and she paid these sums (and no other sums) into a deposit account of her own at a different bank. Mlle Spanoghe later spent most of the money in this account, but £315 remained.

Held: The Court of Appeal held that the plaintiff bank was entitled to trace this money.

ATKIN LJ: . . . I notice that in *Sinclair* v *Brougham* [1914] AC 398, 419 Lord Haldane LC in dealing with [*Taylor* v *Plumer*] says: 'Lord Ellenborough laid down, as a limit to this proposition, that if the money had become incapable of being traced, as, for instance, when it had been paid into the broker's general account with his banker, the principal had no remedy excepting to prove as a creditor for money had and received,' and proceeds to say 'you can, even at law, follow, but only so long as the relation of debtor and creditor has not superseded the right *in rem*.' The words above 'as for instance' *et seq.* do not represent and doubtless do not purport to represent Lord Ellenborough's actual words; and I venture to doubt whether the common law ever so restricted the right as to hold that the money became incapable of being traced, merely because paid into the broker's general account with his banker. The question always was, Had the means of ascertainment failed? But if in 1815 the common law halted outside the bankers' door, by 1879 equity had had the courage to lift the latch, walk in and examine the books: *Re Hallett's Estate* (1880) 13 ChD 696. I see no reason why the means of ascertainment so provided should not now be available both for common law and equity proceedings. If, following the principles laid down in *Re Hallett's Estate*, it can be ascertained either that the money in the bank, or the commodity which it has bought, is 'the product of, or substitute for, the original thing,' then it still follows 'the nature of the thing itself.' On these principles it would follow that as the money paid into the bank can be identified as the product of the original money, the plaintiffs have the common law right to claim it, and can sue for money had and received. In the present case less difficulty than usual is experienced in tracing the descent of the money, for substantially no other money has ever been mixed with the proceeds of the fraud. . . .

Notes

1.   Atkin LJ's views were not shared by the other two judges, and it is difficult precisely to ascertain the *ratio* of *Banque Belge*. Scrutton LJ apparently took the view that the money could not be traced at common law, since it changed its identity when paid into the account at Farrow's Bank, but could be traced in equity (as is undoubtedly the case: see below). Bankes LJ felt that tracing at common law was permissible, but only because the proceeds of Hambrouck's fraud had never been mixed with any other money, either at Farrow's or Mlle Spanoghe's bank. In the passage quoted above, Atkin LJ appeared to take the view that the question of the property's identification was the same in common law and equity, in which case common law tracing would be possible even into mixed funds (on the same basis as in equitable tracing).

The orthodox view is probably that of Bankes LJ, that if the property has been converted into money, and this money mixed with other funds belonging to the defendant, it is no longer possible at common law to identify the subject matter of the plaintiff's claim, and he is thereafter limited to his personal remedy in damages. Since this will often occur in the case where funds are misappropriated, the usefulness of tracing at common law is rather limited in breach of trust situations.

2. It is also necessary to be able to follow the property at every stage from its original form into its current form. Tracing will not be possible if there is a break in the chain at any stage.

Agip (Africa) Ltd v *Jackson*
[1991] Ch 547, [1991] 3 WLR 116, [1992] 4 All ER 451
Court of Appeal

Facts: The plaintiff company's chief accountant (Mr Zdiri) fraudulently altered payment orders which had been signed by an authorised signatory of the plaintiff, altering the name of the payee to that of a company (Baker Oil), of which the defendants were directors and shareholders. The forged payment order (for over $US half a million) was taken to the Banque du Sud in Tunis, which debited the plaintiff's account and sent telexed instructions to a London bank (Lloyds) to credit the account which Baker Oil had there. The Banque du Sud also instructed its correspondent bank (Citibank) in New York to reimburse Lloyds with an equivalent sum. However, Lloyds credited Baker Oil before themselves being reimbursed by Citibank.

Baker Oil subsequently disposed of all but about $US 45,000, but the plaintiff attempted to trace the entire amount received by Baker Oil at common law.

Held: The money could not be traced at common law. The plaintiff succeeded, however, in an equitable tracing claim, and in a claim for knowing assistance, which are considered further below.

MILLETT J (whose decision was upheld by the Court of Appeal): The common law has always been able to follow a physical asset from one recipient to another. Its ability to follow an asset in the same hands into a changed form was established in *Taylor* v *Plumer*. In following the plaintiff's money into an asset purchased exclusively with it, no distinction is drawn between a chose in action such as the debt of a bank to its customer and any other asset: *Re Diplock's Estate* [1948] 2 All ER 318 at 346, [1948] Ch 465 at 519. But it can only follow a physical asset, such as a cheque or its proceeds, from one person to another. It can follow money but not a chose in action. Money can be followed at common law into and out of a bank account and into the hands of a subsequent transferee, provided that it does not cease to be identifiable by being mixed with other money in the bank account derived from some other source: *Banque Belge pour L'Etranger* v *Hambrouck* [1921] 1 KB 321. Applying these principles, the plaintiffs claim to follow their money through Baker Oil's account, where it was not mixed with any other money, and into Jackson & Co.'s account at Lloyds Bank.

The defendants deny this. They contend that tracing is not possible at common law because the money was mixed, first when it was handled in New York and secondly in Jackson Co.'s own account at Lloyds Bank.

The latter objection is easily disposed of. The cause of action for money had and received is complete when the plaintiff's money is received by the defendant. It does not depend on the continued retention of the money by the defendant. Save in strictly limited circumstances it is no defence that he has parted with it. A fortiori it can be no defence for him to show that he has so mixed it with his own money that he cannot tell whether he still has it or not. Mixing by the defendant himself must, therefore, be distinguished from mixing by a prior recipient. The former is irrelevant, but the latter will destroy the claim for it will prevent proof that the money received by the defendant was the money paid by the plaintiff.

In my judgment, however, the former objection is insuperable. The money cannot be followed by treating it as the proceeds of a cheque presented by the collecting bank in exchange for payment by the paying bank. The money was transmitted by telegraphic transfer. There was no cheque or any equivalent. The payment order was not a cheque or its equivalent. It remained throughout in the possession of the Banque du Sud. No copy was sent to Lloyds Bank or Baker Oil or presented to the Banque du Sud in exchange for the money. It was normally the plaintiffs' practice to forward a copy of the payment order to the supplier when paying an invoice but this was for information only. It did not authorise or enable the supplier to obtain payment. There is no evidence that this practice was followed in the case of forged payment orders and it is exceedingly unlikely that it was.

Nothing passed between Tunisia and London but a stream of electrons. It is not possible to treat the money received by Lloyds Bank in London or its correspondent bank in New York as representing the proceeds of the payment order or of any other physical asset previously in its hands and delivered by it in exchange for the money. The Banque du Sud merely telexed a request to Lloyds Bank to make a payment to Baker Oil against its own undertaking to reimburse Lloyds Bank in New York. Lloyds Bank complied with the request by paying Baker Oil with its own money. It thereby took a delivery risk. In due course it was no doubt reimbursed, but it is not possible to identify the source of the money with which it was reimbursed without attempting to follow the money through the New York clearing system. Unless Lloyds Bank's correspondent bank in New York was also Citibank, this involves tracing the money through the accounts of Citibank and Lloyds Bank's correspondent bank with the Federal Reserve Bank, where it must have been mixed with other money. The money with which Lloyds Bank was reimbursed cannot therefore, without recourse to equity, be identified as being that of the Banque du Sud. There is no evidence that Lloyds Bank's correspondent bank in New York was Citibank, and accordingly the plaintiffs' attempt to trace the money at common law must fail.

FOX LJ: Now in the present case the course of events was as follows. (1) The original payment order was in December signed by an authorised signatory. (2) The name of the payee was then altered to Baker Oil. (3) The altered order was then taken to BdS [Banque du Sud], who complied with it by debiting the account of Agip with $US 518,822.92 and then instructing Lloyds Bank to pay Baker Oil. BdS also instructed Citibank in New York to debit its account with Citibank and credit Lloyds with the amount of the order. (4) Lloyds credited the money to Baker Oil's account on the morning of 7 January. (5) On 8 January Lloyds in pursuance of instructions from Baker Oil transferred the $US 518,822.92 which was the only sum standing to the credit of Baker Oil's account to an account in the name of Jackson & Co. (6) Immediately before the transfer from Baker Oil, Jackson & Co.'s account was $US 7,911.80 in credit. In consequence of the transfer it became $US 526,734.72 in credit.

The inquiry which has to be made is whether the money paid to Jackson & Co.'s account 'was the product of, or substitute for, the original thing'. In answering that question I do not think that it matters that the order was not a cheque. It was a direction by the account holder to the bank.

When Atkin LJ refers in *Banque Belge Pour l'Etranger* v *Hambrouck* [1921] 1 KB 321 to the 'original money' he is, I assume, referring to the money credited by Banque Belge (the plaintiff) to Hambrouck's account. Money from that account was the only money in Mlle Spanoghe's deposit account. It was not, therefore, difficult to say that the money in issue (i.e. the residue of Mlle Spanoghe's account) could be identified as the product of the original money. There were no complexities of tracing at all. Everything in Mlle Spanoghe's account came from Hambrouck's account and everything in Hambrouck's account came from the credit in respect of the fraudulent cheque.

The position in the present case is much more difficult. BdS can be regarded as having paid with Agip's money but Lloyds (acting as directed by BdS) paid Baker Oil with its own money. It had no other (and accordingly took a delivery risk). It was, in the end, put in funds, but it is difficult to see how the origin of those funds can be identified without tracing the money through the New York clearing system.

The money in the present case did get mixed on two occasions. The first was in the New York clearing system and the second was in Jackson & Co.'s own account. The judge held that the latter was of no consequence. I agree. The common law remedy attached to the recipient and its subsequent transposition does not alter his liability. The problem arises at an earlier stage. What did Jackson & Co. receive which was the product of Agip's asset?

Baker Oil was controlled for present purposes by Jackson & Co. but Baker Oil was paid by Lloyds, which had not been put in funds from New York. It was subsequently recouped. But it is not possible to show the source from which it was recouped without tracing the money through the New York clearing system. The judge said ([1992] 4 All ER 385 at 399, [1990] Ch 265 at 286):

> Unless Lloyds Bank's correspondent bank in New York was also Citibank, this involves tracing the money through the accounts of Citibank and Lloyd's Bank's correspondent bank with the Federal Reserve Bank, where it must have been mixed with other money. The money with which Lloyds Bank was reimbursed cannot therefore, without recourse to equity, be identified as being that of the Banque du Sud.

I respectfully agree with that view. Accordingly, it seems to me that the common law remedy is not available.

I should add this. Atkin LJ's approach in the *Banque Belge* case amounts virtually to saying that there is now no difference between the common law and equitable remedies. Indeed, the common law remedy might be wider because of the absence of any requirement of a fiduciary relationship. There may be a good deal to be said for that view but it goes well beyond any other case and well beyond the views of Bankes and Scrutton LJJ. And in the 70 years since the *Banque Belge* decision it has not been applied. Whether, short of the House of Lords, it is now open to the courts to adopt it I need not consider. I would in any event feel difficulty in doing so in the present case, where, as I indicate later, it seems to me that the established equitable rules provide an adequate remedy.

Notes

1.   Millett J makes clear that the claim for money had and received does not depend on the continued retention of the money by the defendant.

2.   Millett J also distinguished between a payment order and a cheque, commenting (at p. 399) that the payment order never moved from Tunisia, and that nothing passed between Tunisia and London but a stream of electrons, so that it was not possible to treat the money received by Lloyds as representing the proceeds of the payment order or of any other physical asset (e.g., a cheque) previously in its hands and delivered by it in exchange for the money. Given the likely increase in the use of electronic banking, it would surely be a retrograde step to demand transfer of a physical piece of paper, especially as a cheque no more represents the money itself than does the stream of electrons; its possession merely confers contractual rights against the issuing bank, but there is no doubt that Lloyds had a contractual claim against the Banque du Sud at the latest when it had received and acted upon the telexed payment order. Fortunately, Fox LJ did not (at p. 465h) adopt that distinction, relying instead upon the fact that Lloyds had credited the money to Baker Oil before it was reimbursed with the plaintiff's money. It is therefore possible to trace at common law, even where electronically transmitted transfers have occurred, with a different order of transactions, and indeed it is more usual for the second bank to wait until payment has been received before crediting its customer's account: see, e.g., the description of Automated Clearing House payments in the United States in *EDI technology*, edited by Mike Griffiths, Blenheim Online (1989), pp. 172ff.

3.   Fox LJ's views of the passage from Atkin LJ in *Banque Belge* set out above are at best neutral, and at worst disapproving.

SECTION 2:   TRACING IN EQUITY

The courts of equity have themselves developed a method of tracing property which acknowledges and protects equitable interests. Equitable tracing also has the advantage that it applies where the defendant has mixed the trust money with his own. There are respects, however, in which tracing in equity is less extensive than at common law.

In accord with ordinary equitable principles the right is lost if the property comes into the hands of a *bona fide* purchaser for value who has no notice of the plaintiff's right, whereas the common law recognises no such limitation.

A: Identification of Property as Belonging to the Plaintiff

When tracing in equity it is easier to establish that what the defendant has is the plaintiff's property. Thus, the equitable right is available not only in the common law situations where the plaintiff can identify his property *in specie*, or point to a fund representing its proceeds, but also where the defendant has created a mixed fund, and possibly even when this fund has itself been converted into other property. The courts are also less concerned in equity to be able to follow the property at every stage.

Agip (Africa) Ltd v *Jackson*
[1991] Ch 547, [1991] 3 WLR 116, [1992] 4 All ER 451
Court of Appeal

Facts: The facts have already been stated at p. 510. In addition to their claim at common law (which failed), the plaintiffs also claimed that they were entitled to trace in equity.

Held: The plaintiffs were entitled to claim the money in equity.

MILLETT J (whose decision was upheld by the Court of Appeal): There is no difficulty in tracing the plaintiffs' property in equity, which can follow the money as it passed through the accounts of the correspondent banks in New York or, more realistically, follow the chose in action through its transmutation as a direct result of forged instructions from a debt owed by the Banque du Sud to the plaintiffs in Tunis into a debt owed by Lloyds Bank to Baker Oil in London.

The only restriction on the ability of equity to follow assets is the requirement that there must be some fiduciary relationship which permits the assistance of equity to be invoked. The requirement has been widely condemned and depends on authority rather than principle, but the law was settled by *Re Diplock's Estate* [1948] Ch 465. It may need to be reconsidered but not, I venture to think, at first instance. The requirement is easily circumvented since it is not necessary that there should be an initial fiduciary reltionship in order to start the tracing process. It is sufficient that the payment to the defendant itself gives rise to a fiduciary relationship: *Chase Manhattan Bank N.A.* v *Israel-British Bank (London) Ltd* [1981] Ch 105 [below].

The requirement is also readily satisfied in most cases of commercial fraud, since the embezzlement of a company's funds almost inevitably involves a breach of fiduciary duty on the part of one of the company's employees or agents. That was so in the present case. There was clearly a fiduciary relationship between Mr Zdiri and the plaintiffs. Mr Zdiri [the chief accountant] was not a director or a signatory on the plaintiffs' bank account, but he was a senior and responsible officer. As such he was entrusted with possession of the signed payment orders to have them taken to the bank and implemented. He took advantage of his possession of them to divert the money and cause the separation between its legal ownership which passed to the payees and its beneficial ownership which remained in the plaintiffs. There is clear authority that there is a receipt of trust property when a company's funds are misapplied by a director and, in my judgment, this is equally the case when a company's funds are misapplied by any person whose fiduciary position gave him control of them or enabled him to misapply them.

. . .

The tracing claim in equity gives rise to a proprietary remedy which depends on the continued existence of the trust property in the hands of the defendant. Unless he is a *bona fide* purchaser for value without notice, he must restore the trust property to its rightful owner if he still has it. But even a volunteer who has received trust property cannot be made subject to a personal liability to account for it as a constructive trustee if he has parted with it without having previously acquired some knowledge of the existence of the trust: *Re Montagu's Settlement Trusts* [1987] Ch 264.

The plaintiffs are entitled to the money in court which rightfully belongs to them. To recover the money which the defendants have paid away the plaintiffs must subject them to a personal liability to account as constructive trustees and prove the requisite degree of knowledge to establish the liability.

FOX LJ: Both common law and equity accepted the right of the true owner to trace his property into the hands of others while it was in an identifiable form. The common law treated property as identified if it had not been mixed with other property. Equity, on the other hand, will follow money into a mixed fund and charge the fund. There is, in the present case, no difficulty about the mechanics of tracing in equity. The money can be traced through the various bank accounts to Baker Oil and onwards. It is, however, a prerequisite to the operation of the remedy in equity that there must be a fiduciary relationship which calls the equitable jurisdiction into being. There is no difficulty about that in the present case since Zdiri must have been in a fiduciary relationship with Agip. He was the chief accountant of Agip and was entrusted with the signed drafts or orders upon Banque du Sud.

Notes

1.   The case clearly suggests that it is easier to establish that the defendant has received the plaintiff's property in equity than it is at common law.
2.   Because (unlike the action for money had and received) tracing in equity is a proprietary claim, it depends on retention of the money by the defendant. Baker Oil had retained only about $US 45,000, and only this amount could be traced in equity, but the plaintiffs also succeeded in respect of the amount dissipated by Baker Oil, on the basis of knowing assistance (see below).

Questions

1.   X steals a car from Y and gives it to his friend Z. Who has property in the car?
2.   X steals £500 cash from Y and gives it to his friend Z. Who has property in the cash? What, if any, is the nature of Z's liability to Y.
3.   X steals £500 cash from Y and gives it to his friend Z. Z spends £300 and has £200 of it left. Y sues Z for money had and received. For how much is Z liable? Would your answer be different if Z had paid any or all of the money into his general bank account?
4.   Would your answer to question 3 be different if X had used the £500 to purchase a car from Z, or a holiday, or the right to gamble at Z's casino, or the services of a prostitute?
5.   X is trustee for Y and in breach of trust gives £500, from the trust fund, to his friend Z (who is unaware of the source of the money). Z spends £300 and has £200 of it left. For how much, if any, if Z liable to Y? Would your answer be different if Z had paid any or all of the money into his general bank account (see also the following section)?

B: Mixing of Trust Money with Defendant's Own Money

It has long been established that where trust money is mixed with the defendant's own money, say in a bank account, the onus is on the trustee to distinguish the separate assets; and to the extent that he fails to do so they belong to the trust.

Re Hallett's Estate, Knatchbull v *Hallett*
(1880) 13 ChD 696
Court of Appeal

Facts: Hallett, a solicitor, was a trustee of his own marriage settlement. He had paid some of the money from that trust into his own bank account, into which he also paid money which had been entrusted to him for investment by a client. He made various payments in and out of the account, which at his death contained sufficient funds to meet the claims of the trust and his client, but not those of his personal creditors as well.

Held: The Court of Appeal held that both the trust and the client were entitled to a charge in priority to the general creditors, and that the various payments out of the account must be treated as payments of Hallett's own money.

SIR GEORGE JESSEL MR: . . . There is no doubt . . . that Mr Hallett stood in a fiduciary position towards Mrs Cotterill. Mr Hallett, before his death, . . . improperly sold the bonds and put the money to his general account at his bankers. It is not disputed that the money remained at his bankers mixed with his own money at the time of his death; that is, he had not drawn out that money from his bankers. In that position of matters Mrs Cotterill claimed to be entitled to receive the proceeds, or the amount of the proceeds, of the bonds out of the money in the hands of Mr Hallett's bankers at the time of his death, and that claim was allowed by the learned judge of the court below, and I think was properly so allowed. . . . The modern doctrine of Equity as regards property disposed of by persons in a fiduciary position is a very clear and well-established doctrine. You can, if the sale was rightful, take the proceeds of the sale, if you can identify them. If the sale was wrongful, you can still take the proceeds of the sale, in a sense adopting the sale for the purpose of taking the proceeds, if you can identify them. There is no distinction, therefore, between a rightful and a wrongful disposition of the property, so far as regards the right of the beneficial owner to follow the proceeds. But it very often happens that you cannot identify the proceeds. The proceeds may have been invested together with money belonging to the person in a fiduciary position, in a purchase. He may have bought land with it, for instance, or he may have bought chattels with it. Now, what is the position of the beneficial owner as regards such purchases? I will, first of all, take his position when the purchase is clearly made with what I will call, for shortness, the trust money, although it is not confined, as I will show presently, to express trusts. In that case, according to the now well-established doctrine of Equity, the beneficial owner has a right to elect either to take the property purchased, or to hold it as a security for the amount of the trust money laid out in the purchase; or, as we generally express it, he is entitled at his election either to take the property, or to have a charge on the property for the amount of the trust money. But . . . where a trustee has mixed the money with his own, there is this distinction, that the *cestui que trust*, or beneficial owner, can no longer elect to take the property, because it is no longer bought with the trust money simply and purely, but with a mixed fund. He is, however, still entitled to a charge on the property purchased, for the amount of the trust money laid out in the purchase; and that charge is quite independent of the fact of the amount laid out by the trustee. The moment you get a substantial portion of it furnished by the trustee, using the word 'trustee' in the sense I have mentioned, as including all persons in a fiduciary relation, the right to the charge follows. . . .

When we come to apply that principle to the case of a trustee who has blended trust moneys with his own, it seems to me perfectly plain that he cannot be heard to say that he took away the trust money when he had a right to take away his own money . . . What difference does it make if, instead of putting the trust money into a bag, he deposits it with his banker, then pays in other money of his own, and then draws out some money for his own purposes? Could he say that he had actually drawn out anything but his own money? His money was there, and he had a right to draw it out, and why should the natural act of simply drawing out the money be attributed to anything except to his ownership of money which was at his bankers?

Note

The principle is that where an act can be done rightly, the trustee is not allowed to say that he did it wrongfully. Hallett was not entitled to use the trust money for his personal benefit, so it was assumed that he had spent his own money, rather than the trust funds. The principle does not restrict the beneficiaries to a claim on money in the bank account, however: they have first claim on any identifiable property that can be traced back to the trust.

Re Oatway
[1903] 2 Ch 356
Chancery Division

Facts: The trustee had withdrawn money from the mixed account and invested it in shares, leaving a balance in the account which at that time was ample to meet the claims of the beneficiaries. Subsequently, however, he exhausted the account, so that it was useless to proceed against the account.

Held: The argument that he must be treated as withdrawing his own money first (so that his shares would be treated as his own property) was rejected. The beneficiaries' claim must be satisfied out of any identifiable part of the fund before the trustee could set up his own claim. They were entitled to the proceeds from the sale of the shares in priority to the general creditors.

JOYCE J: . . . Trust money may be followed into land or any other property in which it has been invested; and when a trustee has, in making any purchase or investment, applied trust money together with his own, the cestuis que trust are entitled to a charge on the property purchased for the amount of the trust money laid out in the purchase or investment. Similarly, if money held by any person in a fiduciary capacity be paid into his own banking account, it may be followed by the equitable owner, who, as against the trustee, will have a charge for what belongs to him upon the balance to the credit of the account. If, then, the trustee pays in further sums, and from time to time draws out money by cheques, but leaves a balance to the credit of the account, it is settled that he is not entitled to have the rule in *Clayton's Case* (1816) 1 Mer 572 applied so as to maintain that the sums which have been drawn out and paid away so as to be incapable of being recovered represented pro tanto the trust money, and that the balance remaining is not trust money, but represents only his own moneys paid into the account. *Brown v Adams* (1869) 4 Ch App 764 to the contrary ought not to be followed since the decision in *In re Hallett's Estate* (1880) 13 ChD 696. It is, in my opinion, equally clear that when any of the money drawn out has been invested, and the investment remains in the name or under the control of the trustee, the rest of the balance having been afterwards dissipated by him, he cannot maintain that the investment which remains represents his own money alone, and that what has been spent and can no longer be traced and recovered was the money belonging to the trust. In other words, when the private money of the trustee and that which he held in a fiduciary capacity have been mixed in the same banking account, from which various payments have from time to time been made, then, in order to determine to whom any remaining balance or any investment that may have been paid for out of the account ought to be deemed to belong, the trustee must be debited with all the sums that have been withdrawn and applied to his own use so as to be no longer recoverable, and the trust money in like manner be debited with any sums taken out and duly invested in the names of the proper trustees. The order of priority in which the various withdrawals and investments may have been respectively made is wholly immaterial. I have been referring, of course, to cases where there is only one fiduciary owner or set of cestuis que trust claiming whatever may be left as against the trustee. In the present case there is no balance left. The only investment or property remaining which represents any part of the mixed moneys paid into the banking account is the Oceana shares purchased for £2137. Upon these, therefore, the trust had a charge for the £3000 trust money paid into the account. That is to say, those shares and the proceeds thereof belong to the trust.

It was objected that the investment in the Oceana shares was made at a time when Oatway's own share of the balance to the credit of the account (if the whole had been then justly distributed) would have exceeded £2137, the price of the shares; that he was therefore entitled to withdraw that sum, and might rightly apply it for his own purposes; and that consequently the shares should be held to belong to his estate. To this I answer that he never was entitled to withdraw the £2137 from the account, or, at all events, that he could not be entitled to take that sum from the account and hold it or the investment made therewith, freed from the charge in favour of the trust, unless or until the trust money paid into the account had been first restored, and the trust fund reinstated by due investment of the money in the joint names of the proper trustees, which never was done.

The investment by Oatway, in his own name, of the £2137 in Oceana shares no more got rid of the claim or charge of the trust upon the money so invested, than would have been the case if he had drawn a cheque for £2137 and simply placed and retained the amount in a drawer without further disposing of the money in any way. The proceeds of the Oceana shares must be held to belong to the trust funds under the will of which Oatway and Maxwell Skipper were the trustees.

Notes
1. The assumption made here is that the trustee was not entitled to draw out for his personal benefit the money used to buy the shares, so it was assumed that this money, and hence the shares, belonged to the trust.
2. The cases depend on the trust moneys remaining always identifiable. Once it is clear that all money belonging to the trustee has been withdrawn, so that any further withdrawals must have been from trust money, they

cannot claim that any subsequent payments in must be taken as intended to replace the trust money, unless the trustee shows an intention to make such repayment. In such a case, the right to trace will apply up to the lowest balance of the account in the period between the trust fund being paid into the account and the time when the remedy is sought. For example, if the trustee mixes £1,000 of his own money with £3,000 of trust money and later withdraws £2,000, the right to trace will not extend beyond the £2,000 which is thereby left in the account, even if the trustee later pays in further sums of his own. (In such a case, of course, the beneficiaries will have a personal claim against the trustee for any outstanding sum.)

3. In *Re Oatway* the shares had increased in value, but were still worth less than the trust moneys paid into the account. If they are regarded as trust property, then in principle, the beneficiary ought also to be entitled to any profit made on the sale of the shares, even if they had ended up being worth more than the trust moneys paid into the account. This depends on it being established that trust money was used to purchase the shares. In the following case, it could not be established that the trustee had done more than mix trust money with her own, and the beneficiaries were not entitled to any of the profit later made by her on her investments.

Re Tilley's WT
[1967] Ch 1179
Chancery Division

Facts: A sole trustee who was also the life tenant had mixed a small amount of trust money (£2,237) in her own bank account before embarking on a series of property speculations which were so successful that upon her death her estate was worth £94,000. The beneficiaries entitled in remainder claimed a share of this wealth in the proportion which the trust money in the account bore to the balance of the account at that time.

Held: Ungoed-Thomas J held them entitled only to the return of the trust money with interest.

UNGOED-THOMAS J: For the defendants it has been rightly admitted that, if a trustee wrongly uses trust money to pay the whole of the purchase price in respect of the purchase of an asset, a beneficiary can elect either to treat the purchased asset as trust property or to treat the purchased asset as security for the recouping of the trust money. It was further conceded that this right of election by a beneficiary also applies where the asset is purchased by a trustee in part out of his own money and in part out of the trust moneys, so that he may, if he wishes, require the asset to be treated as trust property with regard to that proportion of it which the trust moneys contributed to its purchase. . . .

[Ungoed-Thomas J reviewed the facts and continued: . . .] If, of course, a trustee deliberately uses trust money to contribute with his own money to buy property in his own name, then I would see no difficulty in enabling a beneficiary to adopt the purchase and claim a share of any resulting profits; but the subjective test does not appear to me to be exclusive, or indeed adequate, if it is the only test.

It seems to me that if, having regard to all the circumstances of the case objectively considered, it appears that if the trustee has in fact, whatever his intention, laid out trust moneys in or towards a purchase then the beneficiaries are entitled to the property purchased and any profits which it produces to the extent to which it has been paid for out of the trust moneys. Even by this objective test, it appears to me, however, that the trust moneys were not in this case so laid out. On a proper appraisal of the facts of this particular case, the trustee's breach halted at the mixing of the funds in her bank account. Although properties bought out of those funds would, like the bank account itself, at any rate if the moneys in the bank account were inadequate, be charged with repayment of the trust moneys which then would stand in the same position as the bank account, yet the trust moneys were not invested in properties at all but merely went in reduction of the trustee's overdraft which was in reality the source of the purchase moneys.

Notes

1. It is clear from the above passage that the decision was based on a finding of fact that Mrs Tilley had not invested the trust money in property but merely used it to reduce her overdraft. If a trustee has in fact laid out trust money towards a purchase, the beneficiaries would then be entitled to the property and any profit to the extent that it had been paid for with trust money.

The reasoning is that if the trustee draws on a mixed fund to purchase property but leaves enough in the account to cover the trust funds, the rule in *Re Hallett's Estate* requires that the purchase be treated as made entirely with his own money, in which case, should no further dissipations to the mixed fund occur, the property, and any profit, belong to him. But should he then go further and dissipate the remaining balance, the beneficiaries will have a charge on the property (*Re Oatway*), and this may be for the proportionate part of the increased value, and not merely for the original amount of the trust fund. This solution allows the beneficiaries the choice of a charge for an amount of the trust money, which will be to their advantage where the funds are depleted, or a share in the property where its value has risen.

2. None of the above applies where the rival claims to the mixed fund arise between two or more trusts, or between the beneficiaries under a trust and an innocent volunteer, where the rule developed in *Clayton's Case* (1816) 1 Mer 572 is applied. This rule, which only appears in the context of a current bank account, enshrines the principle of 'first in, first out'. The first payment in is appropriated to satisfy the earliest debt. The basis of the rule is said to be the presumed intention of the person operating the account. A preferable solution, in the opinion of the authors of the Report of the Review Committee on Insolvency Law and Practice (Cook Report 1982, Cmnd 8558), paras 1076–1080, would be to divide the mixed fund rateably (i.e., *in pari passu*). However, in *Barlow Clowes International Ltd* v *Vaughan* [1992] 4 All ER 22, noted [1993] Conv 370, the Court of Appeal held that *Clayton's case* normally applied, Dillon LJ observing that (at pp. 32 and 33):

If the application of *Clayton's Case* is unfair to early investors *pari passu* distribution among all seems unfair to late investors. . . .

It is indeed correct that the precise situation in the present case did not arise in the reported cases. In *Re Hallett's Estate* there were indeed two separate beneficiaries claiming, but both were paid in full when it was ruled that the account holder must be deemed to have exhausted his own moneys first. . . .

None the less the decisions of this court, in my judgment, establish and recognise a general rule of practice that *Clayton's Case* is to be applied when several beneficiaries' moneys have been blended in one bank account and there is a deficiency. It is not, in my judgment, for this court to reject that long-established general practice.

The rule in *Clayton's Case* is only the starting point, however, and applies only where it provides a convenient method of determining competing claims. In the particular case, the presumed intention (from the application of the rule) was rebutted as being impractical and unjust, because a small number of investors would get most of the funds, and the fund was divided *in pari passu*.

C: Third Party Liability

The right to trace is available not only where the mixing was done by a trustee, but also where it has been done by an innocent volunteer.

In *Re Diplock* [1948] Ch 465 the testator, Caleb Diplock, gave the residue of his property 'for such charitable institutions or other charitable or benevolent object or objects in England' as his executors should, in their absolute discretion, select. In the belief that this created a valid charitable trust, the executors distributed some £203,000 among 139 different charities. Then the next of kin challenged its validity, and as we saw in chapter 12, in *Chichester Diocesan Fund* v *Simpson* [1944] AC 341 the House of Lords held the bequest void as not being exclusively for charitable purposes. The next of kin, having exhausted their remedy against the executors, claimed to recover money from the various charities. They succeeded both in a claim *in personam* (i.e., personal claim), which is not relevant to this section, and in a claim *in rem* (i.e., proprietary claim), which is. The personal claim was later confirmed, incidentally, on appeal to the House of Lords in *Ministry of Health* v *Simpson* [1951] AC 251.

On the proprietary claim, the Court of Appeal held that the right to trace into a mixed fund is not limited to cases where the defendant is the person who had mixed the funds. Nor does there need to be a fiduciary relationship as between the parties to the action (the relevance of this point will become clear in the next sub-section). The right to trace is available against an innocent volunteer. This is an application of the *bona fide* purchaser rule: a volunteer is not a purchaser, and provides no value.

On the question of volunteer liability, see also the passage set out from Millett J's judgment in *Agip Africa* v *Jackson*, above.

D: Requirement for Fiduciary Relationship

Unlike tracing at common law, tracing in equity requires that at some stage, there must have existed a fiduciary relationship of some sort which was sufficient to give rise to an equitable proprietary right in the plaintiff. The clearest case is that of the relationship of trustee and beneficiary, so that in breach of trust cases there is no problem. As we saw in chapter 14, agents and bailees (and others) may also occupy a fiduciary position. See further on this requirement the passages from *Agip Africa* v *Jackson*, quoted above.

Chase Manhatten Bank v Israel-British Bank
[1981] Ch 105, [1979] 3 All ER 1025
Chancery Division

Facts: The plaintiff, a bank in New York, was instructed to pay a substantial sum of money to another bank for the account of the defendant. The defendant was not a customer of the plaintiff bank. By mistake the money was paid twice. The defendant was later wound up in proceedings in the English High Court. The plaintiff bank claimed to trace the sum mistakenly paid into the hands of the liquidators (had it merely proved as a general creditor in the winding-up, it could not have hoped to recover the whole of the sum paid).

It was accepted that whereas the legal effects of the mistaken payment were determined in accordance with the law of the State of New York, the procedural rights and remedies were governed by English law.

Held: Under both systems of law the plaintiff had the right to trace the sum paid into the hands of the liquidators. It was not fatal that there was no fiduciary relationship between plaintiff and defendant before the money got into the wrong hands, but was sufficient that a fiduciary relationship came into being as a result of the mistaken payment being made. The existence of a fiduciary relationship at some stage is essential to the right to trace in equity in English law, however, whatever may be the position in the United States.

GOULDING J: The plaintiff's claim, viewed in the first place without reference to any system of positive law, raises problems to which the answers, if not always difficult, are at any rate not obvious. If one party P pays money to another party D by reason of a factual mistake, either common to both parties or made by P alone, few conscientious persons would doubt that D ought to return it. But suppose that D is, or becomes, insolvent before repayment is made, so that P comes into competition with D's general creditors, what then? If the money can still be traced, either in its original form or through successive conversions, and is found among D's remaining assets, ought not P to be able to claim it, or what represents it, as his own? If he ought, and if in a particular case the money has been blended with other assets and is represented by a mixed fund, no longer as valuable as the sum total of its original constituents, what priorities or equalities should govern the distribution of the mixed fund? If the money can no longer be traced, either separate or in mixture, should P have any priority over ordinary creditors of D? In any of these cases, does it make any difference whether the mistake was inevitable, or was caused by P's carelessness, or was contributed to by some fault, short of dishonesty, on the part of D?

At this stage I am asked to take only one step forward, and to answer the initial question of principle, whether the plaintiff is entitled in equity to trace the mistaken payment and to recover what now properly represents the money.

[There being no English authorities, Goulding J cited a number of American cases, and a passage from Professor A.W. Scott's *The Law of Trusts*, 27th ed. (1973), at p. 289. He continued:]

Counsel for the defendant says that . . . there is no equitable right to trace property unless some initial fiduciary relationship exists, the right being founded on the existence of a beneficial owner with an equitable proprietary interest in property in the hands of a trustee or other fiduciary agent. Counsel says further that the essential fiduciary relationship must initially arise from some consensual arrangement.

The facts and decisions in *Sinclair v Brougham* [1914] AC 398, and in *Re Diplock's Estate* [1948] Ch 465 are well known and I shall not take time to recite them. I summarise my view of the *Diplock* judgment as follows. 1. The Court of Appeal's interpretation of *Sinclair v Brougham* was an essential part of their decision and is binding on me. 2. The court thought that the majority of the House of Lords in *Sinclair v Brougham* had not accepted Lord Dunedin's opinion in that case, and themselves rejected it. 3. The court . . . held that an initial fiduciary relationship is a necessary foundation of the equitable right of tracing. 4. They also held that the relationship between the building society directors and depositors in *Sinclair v Brougham* was a sufficient fiduciary relationship for the purpose. The latter passage reads ([1948] Ch 465 at 540–1):

> . . . a sufficient fiduciary relationship was found to exist between the depositors and the directors by reason of the fact that the purposes for which the depositors had handed their money to the directors were by law incapable of fulfilment.

It is founded, I think, on the observations of Lord Parker in *Sinclair v Brougham*.

This fourth point shows that the fund to be traced need not (as was the case in *Re Diplock's Estate* itself) have been the subject of fiduciary obligations before it got into the wrong hands. It is enough that, as in *Sinclair v Brougham*, the payment into wrong hands itself gave rise to a fiduciary relationship. The same point also throws considerable doubt on counsel's submission for the defendants that the necessary fiduciary relationship must originate in a consensual transaction. It was not the intention of the depositors or of the directors in *Sinclair v Brougham* to create any relationship at all between the depositors and the directors as principals. Their object, which unfortunately disregarded the statutory limitations of the building society's powers, was to establish contractual relationships between the depositors and the society. In the circumstances, however, the depositors retained an equitable property in the funds they parted with, and fiduciary relationships arose between them and the directors. In the same way, I would suppose, a person who pays money to another under a factual mistake retains an equitable property in it and the conscience of that other is subjected to a fiduciary duty to respect his proprietary right.

I am fortified in my opinion by the speech in *Sinclair v Brougham* of Lord Haldane LC, who, unlike Lord Dunedin, was not suspected of heresy in *Re Diplock's Estate*. Lord Haldane LC (who spoke for Lord Atkinson as well as himself) includes money paid under mistake of fact among the cases where money could be followed at common law, and he proceeds to the auxiliary tracing remedy, available (as he said) wherever money was held to belong in equity to the plaintiff, without making any relevant exception. . . .

Thus, in the belief that the point is not expressly covered by English authority and that *Re Diplock's Estate* does not conclude it by necessary implication, I hold that the equitable remedy of tracing is in principle available, on the ground of continuing proprietary interest, to a party who has paid money under a mistake of fact. On that prime question, I see no relevant difference between the law of England and the law of New York and there is no conflict of laws to be resolved.

SECTION 3: STRANGERS AS CONSTRUCTIVE TRUSTEES

For an equitable tracing action to operate the trust property must still be identifiable in some form, albeit that at least in equity it need not be *physically* identifiable, so that if, for example, the trust property has been sold, it may still be possible to trace the *proceeds* of sale. There are also rules in equity for the tracing of trust money which has become mixed with other money (see above).

Suppose, however, that the property no longer exists in any identifiable form. Trust money may have been spent, for example, with nothing identifiable to show for it. If the trust property no longer exists, then clearly it is not traceable. Alternatively, it may be that it has been mixed with other funds in such a way as no longer to be traceable on the principles elaborated above. We saw above that the common law 'money had and received' action depends only on receipt of the money by the defendant and that liability is unaffected by anything that later happens to the property, but that is not the case with tracing in equity. That is not necessarily the end of the matter, however, even in equity, as there is still the possibility that a stranger could be liable as a constructive trustee.

A: Knowledge Requirements: Comparison Between Knowing Receipt and Knowing Assistance

It has long been clear that the test for knowing assistance is more stringent than that for knowing receipt. Indeed, in *Belmont Finance Corporation* v *Williams Furniture ((No. 1)* [1979] Ch 250, and *(No. 2)* [1980] 1 All ER 393), the Court of Appeal was able, on the same (unfortunately rather complicated) facts, to consider both knowing assistance and knowing receipt principles, so that a direct comparison can be drawn.

Belmont Finance Corporation v *Williams Furniture Ltd*
[1979] Ch 250
Court of Appeal

Facts: The litigation arose, in essence, from an arrangement to finance and acquire a company (Belmont Finance Corporation). Williams Furniture owned all the shares in City Industrial Finance Co., which in turn owned all the shares in Belmont. All three companies had the same secretary (Mr Foley). Belmont and City shared the same chairman (Mr James, who during the negotiations also became chairman of Williams), and most of the same directors.

Williams wanted to sell Belmont, because the company was making insufficient profit. Grosscurth and two other individuals, who between them owned all the shares in another (entirely independent) company, Maximum Finance Ltd, wished to acquire Belmont, but needed finance. Grosscurth therefore proposed to finance the deal by selling Maximum to Belmont.

The acquisition of Belmont by Grosscurth was made under a single agreement, whereby Belmont agreed to purchase all the shares of Maximum from Grosscurth and his fellow shareholders, at a price of £500,000. Under the same agreement Grosscurth, having thus received £500,000 for his Maximum shares, agreed to purchase all Belmont's shares from City (which owned all the shares in Belmont, remember) for £489,000, retaining for himself £11,000 of the £500,000.

Of course, because Maximum was, as a result of the agreement, now a wholly-owned subsidiary of Belmont, Grosscurth in purchasing Belmont from City was able to retain his interest in Maximum as well. Thus, the end result of the acquisition agreement was simply that Grosscurth had acquired Belmont. He still had Maximum, since that was now a Belmont subsidiary. He was also £11,000 richer as a result of this transaction, than he had been at the start.

In order to explain this curious state of affairs, it is necessary to consider the finance arrangement. Some form of finance was clearly necessary, since Belmont had to find the £500,000 required for its purchase of Maximum.

The finance was achieved in three ways. First, under the same agreement, City agreed to subscribe for 230,000 redeemable £1 Belmont preference shares. This was effectively a way of making a secured loan to Belmont, the money being repayable on the redemption of the shares. City therefore presented a cheque to Belmont for £230,000. Obviously there was no difficulty in their doing this, since under the acquisition arrangement they had obtained £489,000 from Grosscurth. It was also agreed that Grosscurth would purchase the redeemable preference shares over a (lengthy) period, so that the redeemable preference shares (in effect) provided security for a cash advance from City to Grosscurth.

Secondly, Grosscurth agreed to subscribe for 70,000 £1 Belmont shares, presumably out of his own money. Thirdly, City and Williams agreed to lend Belmont £200,000 for 12 months on the security of Maximum, various undertakings being given by Grosscurth about Maximum's profitability. There was no particular problem finding this amount, since City were still ahead by £259,000, £489,000 having been received from Grosscurth, and only £230,000 having been used on the redeemable preference shares.

The net effect of the various aspects of what was a single agreement was that Belmont had secured the £500,000 necessary for the acquisition of Maximum (£230,000 by subscription from City, £70,000 by subscription from Grosscurth, £200,000 by loan from City and Williams). Grosscurth had obtained Belmont for £489,000, but he had only had to provide immediately £70,000 by subscription, and since Belmont had paid £500,000 for Maximum, he had made £11,000 on the cash transactions.

Thus his immediate outlay was £59,000, the remaining £430,000 to be paid as follows: £200,000 to be paid by Belmont to City under the 12-month loan agreement, and £230,000 to be paid by Grosscurth in the long term by repurchasing the redeemable preference shares.

There was nothing wrong with this transaction in principle, except for the fact that no independent valuation of Maximum was obtained. Although the directors of Belmont and City thought that Maximum was worth £500,000, and indeed Belmont paid £500,000 for Maximum, in reality the company was worth only around £60,000. This had two legal consequences. First, because the purchase of Maximum was at a greatly inflated price, and not in Belmont's best commercial interests, the transaction was held unlawful under what was then the Companies Act 1948, s. 54. Secondly, and more importantly for the purposes of the present discussion, the transaction involved a breach of fiduciary duty by Belmont's directors.

Belmont, having in consequence lost a great deal of money on the deal, went into liquidation, and they embarked upon litigation against City and Williams. Two causes of action were alleged: first, that they were liable in common law (tortious) conspiracy, and secondly that they were liable as constructive trustees.

Held: The first case ([1979] Ch 250) was heard on the pleadings only, the full hearing being on the second case ([1980] 1 All ER 393). In the first hearing, the Court of Appeal held that on the pleadings, Belmont could pursue the claim against City and Williams for conspiracy, since James's knowledge could be imputed to City and Williams, and therefore Williams and City were aware of the facts. Given this decision, statements made on the constructive trust issue were technically *obiter dicta*. At this stage the case was pleaded as a knowing assistance case (in relation to the payment of the £500,000), and on the pleadings, fraud or dishonesty on the part of the directors of Belmont (and hence also the defendants) could not be established.

The Court of Appeal took the view that City and its directors were not liable (on the pleadings) for knowingly assisting in a fraudulent design. In particular, the court felt that constructive knowledge was not a sufficient basis for liability under that heading.

BUCKLEY LJ: The knowledge of that design on the part of the parties sought to be made liable may be actual knowledge. If he wilfully shuts his eyes to dishonesty, or wilfully or recklessly fails to make such inquiries as an honest and reasonable man would make, he may be found to have involved himself in the fraudulent character of the design, or at any rate to be disentitled to rely on lack of actual knowledge of the design as a defence. But otherwise, as it seems to me, he should not be affected by constructive notice.

GOFF LJ: Whilst wilfully shutting one's eyes to the obvious, or wilfully refraining from inquiry because it may be embarrassing is, I have no doubt, sufficient to make a person who participates in a fraudulent breach of trust without actually receiving the trust moneys, or moneys representing the same, liable as a constructive trustee, there remains the question whether constructive notice . . . will suffice.

[Goff J went on to say that in his opinion, it would not. The case clearly suggests, therefore, that at any rate in a knowing assistance case, constructive knowledge without dishonesty will not suffice.]

Belmont Finance Corporation v Williams Furniture Ltd (No. 2)
[1980] 1 All ER 393
Court of Appeal

Decision: The facts were as above. The case then came back to the Court of Appeal on the second hearing, and the conspiracy claim was heard in full, where it succeeded. More important for present purposes is the constructive trust claim. The pleadings were amended, the receiver now suing City and its directors to recover the money *received* on its sale of Belmont shares. This could relate only to the £489,000 received by them, not to the full £500,000 paid for Maximum. In other words, the second case was pleaded as knowing receipt, whereas the first had been pleaded (in respect of a slightly larger sum) as knowing assistance. The first case having failed, in the second the Court of Appeal held City *liable* as constructive trustees.

The reasoning in the second case was that payment of the £500,000 for Maximum amounted to a breach of fiduciary duty by the directors of Belmont, because it was not in Belmont's commercial interests. Of that £500,000, £489,000 found its way into the hands of City. Since the knowledge of its directors could be imputed to City, City received the money knowing all the circumstances of the transaction (including the breach of trust by Belmont's directors). As in the first case, however, dishonesty could not be shown on the pleadings.

BUCKLEY LJ (quoting *Barnes v Addy* (1874) 9 Ch App 244): If a stranger to a trust (a) receives and becomes chargeable with some part of the trust fund or (b) assists the trustees of a trust with knowledge of the facts in a dishonest design on the part of the trustees to misapply some part of a trust fund, he is liable as a constructive trustee.

Note
Since the facts of the two cases, and the knowledge of the defendants, were (to all intents and purposes) identical, the case strongly suggests that the knowledge requirements for knowing assistance and knowing receipt are not the same.

Whereas dishonesty appears to be a requirement under part (b), above, there is nothing in the above quote suggesting a need to show fraud or dishonesty under part (a). Indeed, no fraud or dishonesty was shown in *Belmont*. It appears, then, that whereas in the case of knowing assistance dishonesty is required, it is not for knowing receipt.

B: Knowing Assistance

Lipkin Gorman v *Karpnale Ltd*
[1989] 1 WLR 1340
Court of Appeal

Decision: The facts have already been stated at p. 505. In the Court of Appeal (but not in the later proceedings in the House of Lords), the bank where the solicitors' client account was based was also sued for knowing assistance. As in *Belmont (No. 1)*, it was not open on the pleadings to claim dishonesty or lack of probity against the manager, so the case had to proceed on the basis that the bank should not have honoured the cheques drawn upon it. Claims based both on contract and on constructive trusteeship failed. The contractual claim failed because the cheques were drawn within the bank's mandate, signed by a person whose signature it was authorised and required to honour (Cass). The bank could only become liable if negligence were shown and no negligence was proved.

So far as the knowing assistance claim was concerned, it was clear that there could not be any circumstances where an equitable claim would succeed where the contractual claim would not.

PARKER LJ: It is in my view clear that the bank could not have rendered itself liable as constructive trustee unless it was also liable for breach of contract and that if it was not liable for breach of contract it could not be liable as a constructive trustee. This is because, stated in broad terms, the bank's duty to pay cheques signed in accordance with its mandate is subject to the qualification that it must be performed without negligence and that (i) negligence may exist where there is no question of the circumstances giving rise to a finding of constructive trusteeship; (ii) if there is no negligence I cannot envisage, at least in this case, any facts which would found liability of the ground of constructive trusteeship.

MAY LJ (after approving statements from *Belmont (No. 1)*): In my opinion, therefore, there is at least strong persuasive authority for the proposition that nothing less than knowledge, as defined in one of the first three categories stated by Peter Gibson J in *Baden, Delvaux and Lecuit* v *Société General pour Favoriser le Développement du Commerce et de l'Industrie en France SA* [1983] BCLC 325, of an underlying dishonest design is sufficient to make a stranger a constructive trustee of the consequences of that design.

Note
It is not clear from Parker LJ's judgment (with which on this issue Nicholls LJ agreed) exactly what are the requirements for a knowing assistance claim, since elsewhere he seemed almost to equate the requirements for breach of contract with those for breach of trust. However, the passage quoted above suggests that more than mere negligence may be required to found constructive trusteeship (although the exact requirements are not laid down). May LJ's view was much clearer.

Agip (Africa) Ltd v Jackson
[1992] 4 All ER 451
Court of Appeal

Decision: The facts have already been stated at p. 510. In addition to the tracing claims, knowing assistance claims were successfully made against various defendants.

MILLETT J (whose judgment was upheld in the Court of Appeal): A stranger to the trust will also be liable to account as a constructive trustee if he knowingly assists in the furtherance of a fraudulent and dishonest breach of trust. It is not necessary that the party sought to be made liable as a constructive trustee should have received any part of the trust property, but the breach of trust must have been fraudulent. The basis of the stranger's liability is not receipt of trust property but participation in a fraud: *Barnes* v *Addy* (1874) 9 Ch App 244, and see the explanation of the distinction between the two categories of the case given by Jacobs P in *DPC Estates Pty Ltd* v *Grey* [1974] 1 NSWLR 443 at 457–459.

The authorities at first instance are in some disarray on the question whether constructive notice is sufficient to sustain liability under this head. In *Baden's* case (1982) [1992] 4 All ER 161 Peter Gibson J accepted a concession by counsel that constructive notice is sufficient and that on this point there is no distinction between cases of 'knowing receipt' and 'knowing assistance'. This question was not argued before me but I am unable to agree. In my view the concession was wrong and should not have been made. The basis of liability in the two types of cases is quite different; there is no reason why the degree of knowledge required should be the same, and good reason why it should not. Tracing claims and cases of 'knowing receipt' are both concerned with rights of priority in relation to property taken by a legal owner for his own benefit; cases of 'knowing assistance' are concerned with the furtherance of fraud. In *Belmont Finance Corp* v *Williams Furniture* [1979] 1 All ER 118, [1979] Ch 250 the Court of Appeal insisted that to hold a stranger liable for 'knowing assistance' the breach of trust in question must be a fraudulent and dishonest one. In my judgment it necessarily follows that constructive notice of the fraud is not enough to make him liable. There is no sense in requiring dishonesty on the part of the principal while accepting negligence as sufficient for his assistant. Dishonest furtherance of the dishonest scheme of another is an understandable basis for liability; negligent but honest failure to appreciate that someone else's scheme is dishonest is not.

In *Re Montagu's Settlement Trusts* (1985) [1992] 4 All ER 308 at 330, [1987] Ch 264 at 285 Megarry V-C doubted whether constructive notice is sufficient even in cases of 'knowing receipt'. Whether the doubt is well founded or not, 'knowing assistance' is an a fortiori case.

Knowledge may be proved affirmatively or inferred from circumstances. The various mental states which may be involved were analysed by Peter Gibson J in *Baden's* case [1992] 4 All ER 161 at 235 as comprising:

(i) actual knowledge; (ii) wilfully shutting one's eyes to the obvious; (iii) wilfully and recklessly failing to make such inquiries as an honest and reasonable man would make; (iv) knowledge of circumstances which would indicate the facts to an honest and reasonable man; (v) knowledge of circumstances which would put an honest and reasonable man on inquiry.

According to Peter Gibson J, a person in category (ii) or (iii) will be taken to have actual knowledge, while a person in categories (iv) or (v) has constructive notice only.

I gratefully adopt the classification but would warn against over refinement or a too ready assumption that categories (iv) or (v) are necessarily cases of constructive notice only. The true distinction is between honesty and dishonesty. It is essentially a jury question. If a man does not draw the obvious inferences or make the obvious inquiries, the question is: why not? If it is because, however foolishly, he did not suspect wrongdoing or, having suspected it, had his suspicions allayed, however unreasonably, that is one thing. But if he did suspect wrongdoing yet failed to make inquiries because 'he did not want to know' (category (ii)) or because he regarded it as 'none of his business' (category (iii)), that is quite another. Such conduct is dishonest, and those who are guilty of it cannot complain if, for the purpose of civil liability, they are treated as if they had actual knowledge.

In the present case, Mr Bowers did not participate in the furtherance of the fraud and he cannot be held directly liable on this ground. Mr Jackson and Mr Griffin, however, clearly did. Mr Jackson set up the arrangements and employed Mr Griffin to carry them out. The money was under their control from the time it was paid into Baker Oil's account until the time it left Jackson & Co.'s clients' account in the Isle of Man Bank. One or other of them gave the actual instructions to the banks which disposed of the money. They plainly assisted in the fraud. The sole remaining question is: did they do so with the requisite degree of knowledge?

Note

It seems that whereas any of the five *Baden* heads will probably suffice for liability, dishonesty or 'lack of probity' (a term used by May LJ in *Lipkin Gorman* v *Karpnale Ltd*, which requires more than mere negligence) is also required to found a constructive trusteeship claim based on knowing assistance. This has been reiterated by Vinelott J in *Eagle Trust plc* v *SBC Securities Ltd* [1992] 4 All ER 488 and by the Court of Appeal in *Polly Peck International plc* v *Nadir (No. 2)* [1992] 4 All ER 769. In *Eagle Trust* Vinelott J thought that knowledge of the fraudulent design had to be able to be imputed to the defendant, and that constructive notice of the fraudulent design would not be enough, although knowledge may be inferred in the absence of evidence if such knowledge would have been imputed to an honest and reasonable man.

C: Knowing Receipt

By contrast, *Belmont (No. 2)* suggests that there is no dishonesty requirement for knowing receipt. The extent to which the *Baden* heads are relevant to knowing receipt is unclear, but it can be argued that, in principle, the requirement should be more onerous than constructive notice for a tracing claim, since this is a personal liability which (unlike tracing) does not depend on the continued retention of the trust property.

Agip (Africa) Ltd v *Jackson*
[1992] 4 All ER 451
Court of Appeal

Decision: The facts have already been stated at p. 510. In addition to the tracing claims, knowing receipt claims were made against various defendants, unsuccessfully since none of the money was received by any of the defendants for their own use and benefit.

MILLETT J (whose judgment was upheld in the Court of Appeal): In *Baden, Delvaux and Lecuit* v *Société Géneral pour Favoriser le Développement du Commerce et de l'Industrie en France SA* [1983] BCLC 325, 403, Peter Gibson J said:

> It is clear that a stranger to a trust may make himself accountable to the beneficiaries under the trust in certain circumstances. The two main categories of circumstances have been given the convenient labels in *Snell's Principles of Equity* (28th ed.) pp. 194, 195, 'knowing receipt or dealing' and 'knowing assistance'. The first category of 'knowing receipt or dealing' is described in Snell, *op. cit.* at p. 194 as follows: 'A person receiving property which is subject to a trust . . . becomes a constructive trustee if he falls within either of two heads, namely: (i) that he received trust property with actual or constructive notice that it was trust property and that the transfer to him was a breach of trust; or (ii) that although he received it without notice of the trust, he was not a bona fide purchaser for value without notice of the trust, and yet, after he had subsequently acquired notice of the trust, he dealt with the property in a manner inconsistent with the trust.' I admit to doubt as to whether the bounds of this category might not be drawn too narrowly in Snell. For example, why should a person who, having received trust property knowing it to be such but without notice of a breach of trust because there was none, subsequently deals with the property in a manner inconsistent with the trust not be a constructive trustee within the 'knowing receipt or dealing' category?

I respectfully agree. In my judgment, much confusion has been caused by treating this as a single category and by failing to differentiate between a number of different situations. Without attempting an exhaustive classification, it is necessary to distinguish between two main classes of case under this heading.

The first is concerned with the person who receives for his own benefit trust property transferred to him in breach of trust. He is liable as a constructive trustee if he received it with notice, actual or constructive, that it was trust property and that the transfer to him was breach of trust; or if he received it without such notice but subsequently discovered the facts. In either case he is liable to account for the property, in the first case as from the time he received the property, and in the second as from the time he acquired notice.

The second and, in my judgment, distinct class of case is that of the person, usually an agent of the trustees, who receives the trust property lawfully and not for his own benefit but who then either misappropriates it or otherwise deals with it in a manner which is inconsistent with the trust. He is liable to account as a constructive trustee if he received the property knowing it to be such, though he will not necessarily be required in all circumstances to have known the exact terms of the trust. This class of case need not be considered further since the transfer to Baker Oil was not lawful.

In either class of case it is immaterial whether the breach of trust was fraudulent or not. The essential feature of the first class is that the recipient must have received the property for his own use and benefit. This is why neither the paying nor the collecting bank can normally be brought within it. In paying or collecting money for a customer the bank acts only as his agent. It is otherwise, however, if the collecting bank uses the money to reduce or discharge the customer's overdraft. In doing so it receives the money for its own benefit.

This is not a technical or fanciful requirement. It is essential if receipt-based liability is to be properly confined to those cases where the receipt is relevant to the loss.

Re Montagu's ST
[1987] Ch 264
Chancery Division

Facts: Chattels which were the subject of a family resettlement were transferred to the 10th Duke of Manchester in breach of trust. The 10th Duke sold a number of them. In the action the 11th Duke claimed against the 10th Duke's personal representatives an inquiry and account of the proceeds of the chattels that had been sold. The 10th Duke was a party to the resettlement and so at some time he had had actual notice of the precise terms of the trust. So had his solicitor, but the 10th Duke's solicitor had assured him that he was free to sell the chattels. Although the 10th Duke and his solicitor had had actual notice of the trust, at the relevant time he did not know that the chattels he was receiving or dealing with were chattels that were subject to any trust and he believed that they had been lawfully and properly released to him.

Held: No liability for knowing receipt arose.

MEGARRY V-C: . . .   (1)   The equitable doctrine of tracing and the imposition of a constructive trust by reason of the knowing receipt of trust property are governed by different rules and must be kept distinct. Tracing is primarily a means of determining the rights of property, whereas the imposition of a constructive trust creates personal obligations that go beyond mere property rights.

(2)   In considering whether a constructive trust has arisen in a case of the knowing receipt of trust property, the basic question is whether the conscience of the recipient is sufficiently affected to justify the imposition of such a trust.

(3)   Whether a constructive trust arises in such a case primarily depends on the knowledge of the recipient, and not on notice to him; and for clarity it is desirable to use the word 'knowledge' and avoid the word 'notice' in such cases.

(4)   For this purpose, knowledge is not confined to actual knowledge, but includes at least types (ii) and (iii) of *Baden* knowledge, i.e. actual knowledge that would have been acquired but for shutting one's eyes to the obvious, or wilfully and recklessly failing to make such inquiries as a reasonable and honest man would make; for in such cases there is a want of probity which justifies imposing a constructive trust.

(5)   Whether knowledge of the *Baden* types (iv) and (v) suffices for this purpose is at best doubtful; in my view, it does not, for I cannot see that the carelessness involved would normally amount to a want of probity.

(6)   For these purposes, a person is not to be taken to have knowledge of a fact that he once knew but has genuinely forgotten: the test (or a test) is whether the knowledge continues to operate on that person's mind at the time in question.

(7)(a)   It is at least doubtful whether there is a general doctrine of 'imputed knowledge' that corresponds to 'imputed notice'. (b) Even if there is such a doctrine, for the purposes of creating a constructive trust of the 'knowing receipt' type the doctrine will not apply so as to fix a donee or beneficiary with all the knowledge that his solicitor has, at all events if the donee or beneficiary has not employed the solicitor to investigate his right to the bounty, and has done nothing else that can be treated as accepting that the solicitor's knowledge should be treated as his own. (c) Any such doctrine should be distinguished from the process whereby, under the name 'imputed knowledge', a company is treated as having the knowledge that its directors and secretary have.

(8) Where an alleged constructive trust is based not on 'knowing receipt' but on 'knowing assistance', some at least of these considerations probably apply; but I need not decide anything on that, and I do not do so.

Notes

1. Megarry V-C's view was unnecessary to the actual decision in the case, since he did not think that the Duke had the requisite knowledge under any of the five *Baden* heads. At p. 286B he said that 'even if, contrary to my opinion, all of the five *Baden* types of knowledge are in point, instead of only the first three, I do not think that he had any such knowledge'.

2. The most important point about this case is the distinction drawn between knowing receipt and tracing. The distinction between constructive notice and the requisite knowledge for knowing receipt has been criticised as being wrong in principle, for example by Harpum (1987) 50 MLR 217.

3. Although it is not yet clear how far, if at all, the courts will treat *Re Montagu's ST* as good law, it is now becoming clear that the courts indeed distinguish between tracing and knowing receipt. As observed above, property can be traced in equity into the hands of anyone in possession of it who is not a *bona fide* purchaser for value without notice. The notice doctrine developed in the field of property transactions on the assumption that there would be a full and careful investigation of title, and the courts appear unwilling to impose constructive trusteeship in commercial transactions without something more akin to constructive knowledge, as opposed to notice. In *Eagle Trust plc v SBC Securities Ltd* [1992] 4 All ER 488 and *Cowan de Groot Properties Ltd v Eagle Trust plc* [1992] 4 All ER 700 this was treated as being similar to the first three *Baden* heads, but it may be an oversimplification to assume that that will always be so.

INDEX